Lucy Hutchinson and the English Revolution
Gender, Genre, and History Writing

Lucy Hutchinson and the English Revolution

Gender, Genre, and History Writing

CLAIRE GHEERAERT-GRAFFEUILLE

Great Clarendon Street, Oxford, OX2 6DP,
United Kingdom

Oxford University Press is a department of the University of Oxford.
It furthers the University's objective of excellence in research, scholarship,
and education by publishing worldwide. Oxford is a registered trade mark of
Oxford University Press in the UK and in certain other countries

© Claire Gheeraert-Graffeuille 2022

The moral rights of the author have been asserted

First Edition published in 2022

Impression: 1

All rights reserved. No part of this publication may be reproduced, stored in
a retrieval system, or transmitted, in any form or by any means, without the
prior permission in writing of Oxford University Press, or as expressly permitted
by law, by licence or under terms agreed with the appropriate reprographics
rights organization. Enquiries concerning reproduction outside the scope of the
above should be sent to the Rights Department, Oxford University Press, at the
address above

You must not circulate this work in any other form
and you must impose this same condition on any acquirer

Published in the United States of America by Oxford University Press
198 Madison Avenue, New York, NY 10016, United States of America

British Library Cataloguing in Publication Data

Data available

Library of Congress Control Number: 2022940845

ISBN 978–0–19–285753–8

DOI: 10.1093/oso/9780192857538.001.0001

Printed and bound by
CPI Group (UK) Ltd, Croydon, CR0 4YY

Links to third party websites are provided by Oxford in good faith and
for information only. Oxford disclaims any responsibility for the materials
contained in any third party website referenced in this work.

For Tony, Clémentine, and Émilie

Acknowledgments

When I set out to write a book on Lucy Hutchinson's *Memoirs*, I could not have imagined that ten years later it would be published with Oxford University Press. I wish to express my deepest gratitude towards the people and institutions which helped me carry out this project.

The completion of the book would not have been possible without the assistance of my research team, ERIAC (Équipe de Recherches Interdisciplinaires sur les Aires Culturelles, Université de Rouen Normandie), and the support of its directors, Miguel Olmos, Marc Martinez, Luc Benoit à la Guillaume, and Karine Winkelvoss. I also wish to thank my colleagues and students at the Department of Anglophone Studies for their support and patient listening to the stories of John and Lucy Hutchinson. I am grateful to the staff both at the British Library's Manuscripts Reading Room and at Nottinghamshire Archives for giving me access to Lucy Hutchinson's manuscripts. I wish to thank Karen Raith at Oxford University Press for her help, kind advice, and patience during the process of submission and publication.

This book is based on my Habilitation à Diriger des Recherches (Accreditation to Supervise Research). I wish to express my warmest thanks to my HDR examiners, Luc Borot, Anne Dunan-Page, Ann Hughes, Christine Sukic, and Susan Wiseman, for their most insightful readings, their thought-provoking remarks, and their encouragement to publish this monograph. It gives me great pleasure to express my gratitude to Line Cottegnies who supervised my HDR and who first encouraged me to write about Lucy Hutchinson's *Memoirs*. Her friendship, intellectual rigour, and meticulous readings were essential in the writing and finalization of this book. This book owes much to early modern literary critics and historians whose works on Lucy Hutchinson, women's writing, and the Civil Wars have inspired my research for over twenty-five years. I am greatly indebted to David Norbrook's immense scholarship which has constantly nourished my work. I sincerely thank him for his enthusiasm for my project, his most generous reading of an earlier version of this book, and for his invaluable advice to revise it. I am most grateful for his sharing with me his transcription of the 'Notebook' manuscript which I could not access during the pandemic. I would like to extend my thanks to Ann Hughes for her perspicacious reading of the manuscript, her bibliographical suggestions, and her very helpful remarks as regards the structure of the book. My thanks also go to Anna Wall for her generous reading of the manuscript and her most perceptive comments. I owe special thanks to Neil Keeble for kindly sharing his ideas and his most recent work on the *Memoirs*. It is through his edition of the *Memoirs* that I first encountered Lucy Hutchinson: she soon became one of the many protagonists of 'La Cuisine et le forum', my PhD dissertation on women and the Civil Wars. I wish to extend my gratitude to my PhD supervisor, Gisèle Venet, for giving me the taste for research and introducing me to the epistemological crises of the baroque age. I am greatly indebted to her Épistémè seminar, where I met so many friends and colleagues, and where the journey of the early modern journal *Études Épistémè* started.

My heartfelt thanks go to my colleagues whose encouragements and friendship helped me to complete this book: Sylvaine Bataille, Gilles Bertheau, Anne Besnault, Claire Boulard-Jouslin, Florence Cabaret, Armel Dubois-Nayt, Stéphane Jettot, Gérard Milhe-Poutingon, Lynn S. Meskill, Marc Martinez, Aude de Mézerac-Zanetti, Anne-Marie Miller-Blaise, Clotilde Prunier, and Christine Sukic. I wish to warmly thank Sandrine Parageau for her constant interest in my work, her fruitful suggestions, and her reading of the manuscript. I also want to express my whole-hearted gratitude to my friend and first reader Géraldine Vaughan for giving me the confidence to write this monograph and turn it into a book. Her friendship, enthusiasm, and generous reading dissipated many doubts and obstacles during the long gestation of this opus.

Finally, may my most affectionate thanks be extended to my daughters, Émilie and Clémentine, for their patience and encouragements and to my husband, Tony Gheeraert, for his unfailing support and friendship over the years, as well as for his enthusiasm and stimulating everyday conversations on the seventeenth century.

Table of contents

Notes on conventions — xi
List of tables and illustrations — xiii

Introduction — 1
1 *History and memory* — 11
2 *Gender* — 22
3 *Lucy Hutchinson's discursive horizon* — 28
4 *Forms of history* — 32

1. Life-writing and exemplarity — 39
1 *The art of exemplarity* — 40
2 *A life of virtue* — 47
   a) The portrait of a Christian gentleman — 47
   b) The life of a saint — 62
3 *Idealization and the limits of exemplarity* — 72
   a) Difficulties of representation — 72
   b) Risks of idolatry — 78

2. The *Memoirs* and historiography — 85
1 *Historiographical debates before the Civil War* — 86
2 *Historical truth in the turmoil of the Civil Wars* — 94
   a) Civil War historiography — 94
   b) Memoir-writing and the truth of history — 99
3 *Testifying to the truth* — 106
   a) Historiographical assumptions — 107
   b) Writing the defence of John Hutchinson — 113

3. The experience of the Civil War in Nottingham — 117
1 *Writing the English Civil War: from experience to words* — 118
   a) Lucy Hutchinson, witness and confidant — 119
   b) Nottingham Castle and the experience of the Civil War — 128
   c) Eye-witnessing the Civil War — 138
2 *Behind the scenes of national history: an anatomy of the Civil War* — 147
   a) Intelligence and negotiations — 148
   b) The Committee of Nottingham: a civil war in miniature — 154

4. Writing oneself into history: the paradoxes of Lucy
   Hutchinson's agency   166
   1 *Gender paradoxes: Lucy Hutchinson taking part in history*   168
     a) The patriarchal framework   169
     b) Lobbying at the Restoration   172
   2 *Autobiographical memoirs: Coming to grips with one's past*   180
   3 *Tinkering with history and memory*   190
     a) The affair of the forged letter   191
     b) Between forgery and truth   194
     c) The art of equivocation   199

5. The historian's craft (1): Lucy Hutchinson's art of narration   203
   1 *The attraction of romance*   206
     a) Romance and history   206
     b) Love at first sight   208
   2 *The Civil War through the prism of romance*   215
     a) Tempests   215
     b) A Civil War adventure: Nottingham's magazine of powder   218
     c) Confused identities   221
     d) Warfare and romance   224
   3 *The ubiquity of treachery: a darker vein of history*   229
     a) Turncoats   229
     b) Traitors and spies   235
     c) Oliver Cromwell as the great dissembler   243

6. The historian's craft (2): Lucy Hutchinson's art of digression   253
   1 *Historical flashbacks: 'the long-conceived flame of civill warre'* 256
   2 *Narrative digressions: a polemical history of the English Civil Wars* 263
     a) Lucy Hutchinson's art of disposition   264
     b) A synoptic view of the war   268
     c) A defence of tyrannicide   274
   3 *Politico-moral digressions: a defence of Colonel Hutchinson*   282
     a) Lucy Hutchinson's anti-Puritanism   282
     b) A gallery of portraits   287

   Conclusion   297
   1 *A tragic vision of the English Revolution*   297
   2 *From persecution to martyrdom*   301
   3 *Commemoration and resistance*   305

Bibliography   309
  Manuscripts   309
  Primary sources   309
  Secondary sources   316
Index   335

Notes on conventions

The phrase 'English Civil War'—sometimes abbreviated as 'Civil War'—refers here to the period going from 1642 (the King raising the Royal Standard at Nottingham on 22 August) to 1649 (the execution of Charles I on 30 January). It encompasses the First Civil War (1642–1646) and the Second Civil War (1648). The phrase 'Civil Wars' conveniently covers the period of political and military conflicts of the 1640s and 1650s.

Unless otherwise stated, quotations from Lucy Hutchinson's *Memoirs of the Life of Colonel Hutchinson* are drawn from James Sutherland's edition (London: Oxford UP, 1973). Sutherland's edition is based on the autograph manuscript kept at Nottinghamshire Archives (DD/HU4). Page references, given in the text, are first to Sutherland's edition and then to N. H. Keeble's edition of *Memoirs of the Life of Colonel Hutchinson* (London: Phoenix Press, 1995).

I have kept the complete name of Lucy Hutchinson throughout the book to avoid confusion with other members of her family.

OED is used to refer to *Oxford English Dictionary* (Oxford UP, 2020).

When quoting Lucy Hutchinson's manuscripts, I have kept her original spelling as much as possible, but expanded contractions for clarity's sake.

List of tables and illustrations

1.1. Colonel Hutchinson by Robert Walker (engraving) from Lucy Hutchinson's *Memoirs of the Life of Colonel Hutchinson*, ed. Julius Hutchinson (London, 1806). 71
3.1. Nottingham Castle in the fifteenth century. From Harry Gill, *A Short History of Nottingham Castle* (1904). Courtesy of Nottinghamshire History (http://www.nottshistory.org.uk/). 131
4.1. Lucy Hutchinson by Robert Walker (engraving) from Lucy Hutchinson's *Memoirs of the Life of Colonel Hutchinson*, ed. Julius Hutchinson (London, 1806). 167
6.1. Civil War Digressions—An Overview. 270

Introduction

Lucy Hutchinson is best remembered as the author of the *Memoirs of the Life of Colonel Hutchinson*, a best-seller in the nineteenth century, first published in 1806 by the Reverend Julius Hutchinson, a descendant of Colonel Hutchinson's half-brother, Charles Hutchinson, who had inherited her manuscripts.[1] As Governor of the town and castle of Nottingham, the Colonel had fought on the side of Parliament during the Civil War. In 1649, as a member of the High Court of Justice, he decided in conscience to vote for the execution of Charles I. Although at the Restoration his name figured in the Act of Indemnity and Oblivion (1660), he was soon suspected of plotting against the restored regime and was imprisoned without trial.[2] He died in captivity at Sandown Castle in Kent in 1664. It was presumably between 1664 and 1667 that Lucy Hutchinson wrote the *Memoirs of the Life of Colonel Hutchinson*.[3] This was a period when the 'composition and possession' of a republican manuscript was liable to a charge of treason, and it was therefore unthinkable for her to publish the life of a man—her husband—who had signed the King's death warrant.[4] Unlike some memoirs, including the republican *Memoirs* of the regicide Edmund Ludlow, which were published at the turn of the eighteenth century, Lucy Hutchinson's *Memoirs* remained in manuscript until

---

[1] Lucy Hutchinson, *Memoirs of the Life of Colonel Hutchinson*, ed. Julius Hutchinson (London, 1806). By 1868, there had been ten editions of the *Memoirs* based on Julius Hutchinson's edition. Unless otherwise stated, quotations from Hutchinson's *Memoirs* are drawn from James Sutherland's edition of *Memoirs of the Life of Colonel Hutchinson* (London: Oxford UP, 1973). Page references, given in the text, are first to Sutherland's edition and then to N. H. Keeble's edition of *Memoirs of the Life of Colonel Hutchinson* (London: Phoenix Press, 1995). On the various existing editions of the *Memoirs*, see David Norbrook, '"But a Copie": Textual Authority and Gender in Editions of "The Life of John Hutchinson"', *New Ways of Looking at Old Texts III*, ed. W. Speed Hill (Tempe, AZ: Center for Medieval and Renaissance Studies, 2004) 109–30, here 126–128 (on Sutherland and Keeble's editions).

[2] On the absence of trial, see P. R. Seddon, 'The Dating of the Completion of the Composition of the *Memoirs of Colonel John Hutchinson*: The Evidence of the Imprisonments of Captain John Wright and Lieutenant Richard Franck', *Transactions of the Thoroton Society* 120 (2016): 114–17.

[3] Seddon, 'The Dating of the Completion of the Composition of the *Memoirs*'. Until Seddon's article, the *Memoirs* were assumed to have been composed between 1664 and 1671.

[4] See N. H. Keeble, '"The Colonel's Shadow": Lucy Hutchinson, Women's Writing and the Civil War', *Literature and the English Civil War*, ed. Thomas Healey and Jonathan Sawday (Cambridge: Cambridge UP, 1990) 236.

1806.[5] The chief reason for this was that the *Memoirs* were held by the royalist branch of the Hutchinson family who did not wish to publicize their links with their republican and Puritan ancestor, John Hutchinson, whose name was mentioned in all the accounts of the regicide.[6] The refusal to circulate the manuscript was noted by the biographer and antiquarian Mark Noble in his *Lives of the English Regicides* who had heard of 'a MS. written by the widow of the guilty Mr Hutchinson, relative to the important times in which she lived: it was hoped that it would have been lent, to copy what must have been highly gratifying to both the public, and the writer of these volumes; but he was not fortunate enough to obtain the perusal of it.'[7] According to Julius Hutchinson, the first editor of the *Memoirs*, some people may even have had the opportunity to glance through it, especially when it was in the possession of Sir Thomas Hutchinson, the uncle of the first editor of the *Memoirs*, but its publication was never authorized:[8]

> The *Memoirs of the Life of Col. Hutchinson* had been seen by many persons, as well as the editor, in the possession of the late Thomas Hutchinson, Esq. of Nottinghamshire, and of Hatfield Woodhall, in Hartfordshire; and he had been frequently solicited to permit them to be published, particularly by the late Mrs. Catharine Maccaulay, but had uniformly refused.[9]

Even though it cannot be ascertained to what extent the manuscript circulated, Mark Noble and Catharine Macaulay's interest in the text is evidence of the value that was attached to the *Memoirs* as a historical testimony in the late years of the eighteenth century.[10] Given the fact that in her *History of England*, Macaulay makes frequent references to the writings of Restoration historians

---

[5] See Edmund Ludlow, *Memoirs of Edmund Ludlow Esq.* (Vevey, 1698). The editor was probably John Toland. See Edmund Ludlow, *A Voyce from the Watch Tower*, ed. Blair Worden, Camden Fourth Series 21 (London, 1978) 1–17, and Blair Worden, *Roundhead Reputations. The English Civil Wars and the Passions of Posterity* (London: Penguin, 2001) 10–11.

[6] See Mark Burden, 'Editing Shadows: The Changing Text of Lucy Hutchinson's *Memoirs of the Life of Colonel Hutchinson*', *Textual Transformations: Purposing and Repurposing Books from Richard Baxter to Samuel Taylor Coleridge*, ed. Tessa Whitehouse and N. H. Keeble (Oxford: Oxford UP, 2019) 176. For 'incriminating references', see for instance Heneage Finch, *An Exact and Most Impartial Account of the Indictment [...] of Twenty-Nine Regicides* (London, 1660).

[7] Mark Noble, *The Lives of the English Regicides and other Commissioners of the Pretended High Court of Justice* (London, 1798), vol. 1, 367.

[8] For a clear presentation of family links in the Hutchinson family, see Sutherland, 'Note on the Text', *Memoirs* xxi.

[9] Julius Hutchinson, 'Preface', *Memoirs* i.

[10] Devoney Looser believes that Lucy Hutchinson may have circulated the manuscript of the *Memoirs* in her own lifetime. See Looser, *British Women Writers and the Writing of History 1670–1820* (Baltimore and London: Johns Hopkins UP, 2000) 32. On the circulation of the manuscript in the eighteenth century, see Burden, 'Editing Shadows', 177.

such as Edmund Ludlow, John Rushworth, Edward Hyde, and Gilbert Burnet, it is probable that she considered Lucy Hutchinson's republican *Memoirs* as another potential historical source for her own work.[11] Similarly, the first editors of the *Memoirs* understood their historical importance. In his preface to his 1806 edition, Julius Hutchinson eloquently called them a 'history of a period the most remarkable in the British annals, written one hundred and fifty years ago'.[12] The title he chose for the volume foregrounds the historical dimension of the work:

> Memoirs of the Life of Colonel Hutchinson, Governor of Nottingham Castle and Town, Representative of the County of Nottingham in the Long Parliament, and of the Town of Nottingham in the First Parliament of Charles II, etc. with Original Anecdotes of Many of the Most Distinguished of his contemporaries and a Summary Review of Public affairs [...] to which is prefixed the Life of Mrs. Hutchinson, Written by Herself, a Fragment.

Meanwhile, in France, the nineteenth-century French historian François Guizot included the translation of Lucy Hutchinson's *Memoirs* in his collection of English historical memoirs which served as a basis for his *Histoire de la Révolution d'Angleterre de Charles I à Charles II*, the first volume of which was published in 1826–1827.[13] At the beginning of the preface, he writes meaningfully: 'I have published the original memoirs of the English revolution; I now publish its history.'[14] In England, the historiographical quality of Julius Hutchinson's edition did not go unnoticed: the *Monthly Review* concluded that the *Memoirs* '[form] a valuable addition to our records, and is justly intitled to stand by the side of those of Rushworth, Clarendon, and Ludlow'.[15] According to *The Eclectic Review*, '[h]ad this volume been published in its own day, its merits would have raised it to a high rank among contemporary histories.'[16]

---

[11] On Catharine Macaulay's use of sources, see Bridget Hill and Christopher Hill, 'Catharine Macaulay's *History* and her Catalogue of Tracts', *The Seventeenth Century* 8.2 (1993): 269–85. For Macaulay's mention of Civil War historians, see the fifth volume of Macaulay, *The History of England, from the Accession of James I. to that of the Brunswick Line* [1763–1783], vol. 4 (London, 1770).
[12] Julius Hutchinson, 'Preface', *Memoirs* x.
[13] See Lucy Hutchinson, *Mémoires de Mistriss Hutchinson* in François Guizot, ed., *Collection des Mémoires relatifs à la Révolution d'Angleterre*, vol. 10 and 11 (Paris, 1823–1825).
[14] François Guizot, *Histoire de la Révolution d'Angleterre depuis l'avènement de Charles Ier jusqu'à la restauration de Charles II. 1re partie* (Paris, 1826–1827), translated by William Hazlitt as *The History of the English Revolution of 1640, Commonly Called the Great Rebellion* (London: D. Bogue, 1846) vii.
[15] Rev. of *Memoirs of the Life of Colonel Hutchinson*, by Lucy Hutchinson, *The Monthly Review* 53 (1807): 273.
[16] Rev. of *Memoirs of the Life of Colonel Hutchinson*, by Lucy Hutchinson, *Eclectic Review* 3.1 (1807): 16.

Similarly, in an 1847 review from *The Christian Examiner*, an American Unitarian periodical, the *Memoirs* were read alongside other books about the history of the English Revolution.[17] In the twentieth century the popularity of the *Memoirs* declined, but they were still studied at school, especially at the turn of the century. In *A Source Book of English History* (1912), out of the thirteen texts anthologized in Chapter 2 ('Civil War and Commonwealth. 1641-1660'), four are excerpts from the *Memoirs* and the name of Lucy Hutchinson appears in the list of 'authorities cited', next to the names of Cromwell, Clarendon, and Marvell.[18] In the same way, the *Notes on the Memoirs of Colonel Hutchinson*, published in 1904 in the 'Normal Tutorial Series', offer a decidedly historical approach to Lucy Hutchinson's text. They provide a map, a chronological summary of the period as well as 'Explanatory, Historical and Etymological Notes'.[19] Alfred Wood, in *Nottinghamshire in the Civil War*, considers Lucy Hutchinson's *Memoirs* as a key source for local history.[20] More recently, Royce MacGillivray and Robert Mayer confirmed that Lucy Hutchinson must be considered as a major historian of the Restoration in her own right. The present study owes much to their pioneering work.[21]

However, this historiographical dimension was often downplayed, or even overlooked, by many reviewers who preferred to emphasize the literary qualities of the *Memoirs* and the portrait of Lucy Hutchinson as the ideal Puritan wife. Devoney Looser has decisively demonstrated how Lucy Hutchinson's historical *Memoirs* were often de-historicized in the nineteenth and even in the twentieth century.[22] Today's scholarship, she argues, continues to minimize their historiographical relevance, privileging their autobiographical and domestic

---

[17] The books reviewed were John Forster, *The Statesmen of the Commonwealth of England* (New York, 1846); J. H. Merle d'Aubigné, *The Protector: a Vindication* (New York, 1847); Lucy Hutchinson, *Memoirs of the Life of Colonel Hutchinson*, 5th edition, ed. Henry G. Bohn (London, 1846); Armand Carrel, *History of the Reign of James II* (London, 1847); C. J. Fox, *History of the Reign of James II* (London, 1846). The review was published in *The Christian Examiner and Religious Miscellany* 44, Fourth Series, 9 (1847): 205–23.

[18] Arthur D. Innes, *A Source-Book of English History for the Use of Schools* (Cambridge: Cambridge UP, 1914), vol. 2, 58–111. Hutchinson's texts illustrate the following points: 'After Strafford's Death' (58–62); 'The Presbyterian Turn on the Army' (70–2); 'The Army Asserts Itself' (73–6); 'Regicide' (80–6).

[19] George Mansell Handley, *Notes on the Memoirs of Colonel Hutchinson [by Mrs. L. Hutchinson]* (London: The Normal Press, [1905]).

[20] Alfred C. Wood, *Nottinghamshire in the Civil War* [1937] (Wakefield: S. R. Publishers Limited, 1971) 33–4.

[21] Royce MacGillivray, *Restoration Historians and the English Civil War* (The Hague: Martinus Nijhoff, 1974) 170–84 and Robert Mayer, 'Life-writing and Historiography, Fiction and Fact: Baxter, Clarendon, and Hutchinson on the English Revolution', *History and the English Novel. Matters of Fact from Bacon to Defoe* (Cambridge: Cambridge UP, 1992) 75–93. See Mayer, 'Lucy Hutchinson: A Life of Writing', *The Seventeenth Century* 22.2 (2007): 305–35. For a historicized approach to Hutchinson's *Memoirs*, see David Norbrook's numerous articles (cf. bibliography).

[22] Looser, *British Women Writers* 47–8.

dimensions.[23] For her own part, she contends that Lucy Hutchinson's text should be 'understood as a historiographical contribution – one that used selected mainstream historical forms and rejected others'.[24] There is much textual evidence for this in the *Memoirs*. First, Lucy Hutchinson describes her own manuscript as 'history' (S36/K55) while she discusses the analyses of other historians, in particular Thomas May, with great authority (S53/K75).[25] Second, although she dedicates 'The Life of John Hutchinson' to her children and describes it as a consolatory narrative meant to 'moderate her woe' (S1/K16), she also specifies that it was composed for 'the benefitt of all' (S2/K17) and in order to 'instruct the erring children of this generation' (S1/K16). There is no doubt, therefore, that she imagined the possibility of her manuscript being read by a broader audience, the historical and political contents of her work reaching out beyond a restricted family readership.[26] Calling the Restoration age 'wicked' (S1/K16), and 'darke' (S3/K18), she unequivocally positioned herself as an opponent of Charles II's monarchy. Her main goal was to provide her readers with an apology of her husband, as well as to refute official royalist historiography and dispel suspicions about the Colonel's loyalties at the Restoration. Like many memorialists of her age, she wished her narrative to reach a wide audience, and some scholars have suggested that, were it not for the circumstances of the Restoration, she may well have had publication in mind.[27] During her lifetime, the manuscript of the *Memoirs* probably did not circulate beyond a close circle, which included her brother, Sir Allen Apsley, her cousin, Anne Wilmot, Countess of Rochester, and Arthur Annesley, Earl of Anglesey, her patron, who, on 8 October 1682, made the following observation in his diary: 'The morning was much

---

[23] Looser, *British Women Writers* 29–31. In his analysis of the *Memoirs*, Derek Hirst goes into the detail of history, but he nevertheless privileges romance (Hirst, 'Remembering a Hero: Lucy Hutchinson's Memoirs of her Husband', *The English Historical Review* 119.482 (2004): 682–91, here 689). Sharon Cadman Seelig also highlights romance elements in Seelig, 'Pygmalion's Image: The Lives of Lucy Hutchinson', *Autobiography and Gender in Early Modern Literature* (Cambridge: Cambridge UP, 2006) 73–89.
[24] Looser, *British Women Writers* 31.
[25] Thomas May, *The History of the Parliament of England* (London, 1647).
[26] See Mayer, 'Lucy Hutchinson: A Life of Writing', 323–4.
[27] James Sutherland challenges Sydney Race's assumption that Lucy Hutchinson may have had publication in mind ('Note on the Text', xix). See Sydney Race, 'The British Museum MS. of the Life of Colonel Hutchinson and its Relation to the Published Memoirs', *Transactions of the Thoroton Society* 18 (1914): 35–66.
See http://www.nottshistory.org.uk/articles/tts/tts1914/hutchinson1.htm (accessed 29/08/2018). See Norbrook, 'But a Copie', 129. On memoir-writing and publication, see Emmanuèle Lesne, *La Poétique des mémoires (1650–1685)* (Paris: Honoré-Champion, 1996) 323.

delighted in reading pious Mrs Hutchesons diary and put thereby in mind of close walking wth God as she did.'[28]

Lucy Hutchinson's use of manuscript-writing to commemorate her husband's life in history was not only a means of disseminating her republican ideas; it was also a mode of writing with which, as a woman of the aristocracy, she had been familiar for more than twenty years.[29] In the *Memoirs*, for example, she reports how John Hutchinson felt compelled to meet her when he heard someone reading one of her sonnets which circulated among the members of the court gathered at Richmond. The exchange of letters and papers is materialized in the 'Notebook', another manuscript in Lucy Hutchinson's hand, in which she copied several official letters and documents.[30] Her *Literary Commonplace Book*, written by different hands, is a collection of translations, anthologized poems, and letters; it is typical of coterie writing, as it was practised at the Stuart court in the 1630s as well as in the 1650s and at the Restoration.[31] It includes, among other poems, Edmund Waller's *A Panegyrick to My Lord Protector* (1655), to which Lucy Hutchinson gave a satirical response, now kept in the Hyde Papers in the British Library.[32] Furthermore, the fact that her literary activities were known in royalist networks in the 1650s is evidenced in

---

[28] The Earl of Anglesey's diary is quoted in David Norbrook, 'Introduction', *The Works of Lucy Hutchinson*, vol. 1, *The Translation of Lucretius, part 1*, ed. Ashley Reid Barbour, David Norbrook, and Maria Cristina Zerbino (Oxford: Oxford UP, 2012) cxix. For these assumptions, see Norbrook, 'Order and Disorder: The Poem and its Contexts', *Order and Disorder*, ed. Norbrook (Oxford: Blackwell, 2001) xix–xxi. On manuscript-writing and polemics, see Noah Millstone, *Manuscript Circulation and the Invention of Politics in Early Stuart England* (Cambridge: Cambridge UP, 2016). On Lucy Hutchinson's manuscripts, see David Norbrook, 'The Fortunes of the Manuscripts: Publication and Dispersal', *The Works of Lucy Hutchinson*, vol. 2, *Theological Writings and Translations*, ed. Elizabeth Clarke, David Norbrook, and Jane Stevenson (Oxford: Oxford UP, 2018) xxiii–xxviii. See also https://web.warwick.ac.uk/english/perdita/html/ (accessed 13/07/2021).

[29] See David Norbrook, 'Lucy Hutchinson's "Elegies" and the Situation of the Republican Woman Writer [with Text]', *English Literary Renaissance* 27.3 [1997]: 484. On manuscript-writing, see Arthur F. Marotti's ground-breaking *Manuscript, Print, and the English Renaissance Lyric* (Ithaca, NY: Cornell UP, 1995); Harold Love and Marotti, 'Manuscript Transmission and Circulation', *The Cambridge History of Early Modern English Literature*, ed. David Loewenstein and Janel Mueller (Cambridge: Cambridge UP, 2002) 55–80. On women, print, and manuscript, see Margaret J. M. Ezell, *Writing Women's Literary History* (Baltimore and London: Johns Hopkins UP, 1996) 37–8 and 53–8. See also her 'Women and Writing', *A Companion to Early Modern Women's Writing*, ed. Anita Pacheco (Oxford: Blackwell, 2009) 77–94.

[30] The British Library, Add. MS 25901, 90–96^v. On the Notebook, see Chapter 5. See also Anna Wall, '"Not so much open professed enemies as close hypocritical false-hearted people": Lucy Hutchinson's Manuscript Account of the Services of John Hutchinson and Mid-Seventeenth-Century Factionalism', *The Seventeenth Century* 36.4 (2021): 623–51. On the early modern practice of letter-writing, see James Daybell, *The Material Letter in Early Modern England. Manuscript Letters and the Culture and Practices of Letter-Writing* (Basingstoke: Palgrave Macmillan, 2012).

[31] Nottinghamshire Archives, *Literary Commonplace Book*, DD/HU1. On this manuscript, see Jerome de Groot, 'John Denham and Lucy Hutchinson's Commonplace Book', *Studies in English Literature* 48.1 (2008): 147–63.

[32] See David Norbrook, 'Lucy Hutchinson versus Edmund Waller: An Unpublished Reply to Waller's A Panegyrick to My Lord Protector', *The Seventeenth Century* 11.1 (1996): 61–3.

a poem by Sir Aston Cockayne, who urges his friend Alexander Brome to continue her translation of Lucretius's *De Rerum Natura*, which she, as a woman, 'must needes give out'.[33] In 1675, Lucy Hutchinson finally offered her full translation of Lucretius to her patron, the Earl of Anglesey, in whom she saw a protection 'against all the censures a booke might expose me to'—a claim which is here to remind us that manuscript-writing was a form of publication in its own right.[34]

However, despite her expertise in manuscript-writing and transmission, Lucy Hutchinson was not averse to print. Admittedly, she distrusted the books and pamphlets which poured off the press in the 1640s, but she, like her husband, was aware of the advantages of print publication, and it is significant that she did not object to the publicity of the Colonel's defence of Nottingham in pamphlets and newsbooks during the Civil War.[35] When writing the *Memoirs*, she drew on the Colonel's narrative of imprisonment that had been published in 1664.[36] Also in the *Memoirs*, it is eloquent that she should advise her readers 'to informe [themselves] better of by [Parliament's] printed papers and Mr. Maye's History' (S53/K75), thereby claiming a place for her own account amidst the published histories of the times. This attitude to print publication brings her close to her royalist neighbour, Margaret Cavendish, who, by the time Lucy Hutchinson was writing the *Memoirs*, had already published several works in her own name in the 1650s, in particular her Epicurean *Poems and Fancies*.[37] To a large degree, Lucy Hutchinson's attitude to print also connects her with some Civil War historians and memorialists whose works, both republican and royalist, were published either during the Exclusion Crisis or at the turn of the seventeenth century.[38] If Lucy Hutchinson's *Memoirs* had not been kept secret by her husband's family, it is conceivable that they could have been published at the end of the seventeenth century, like the memoirs of another regicide, Edmund Ludlow, to whom she has often been compared.[39] Finally, two years before her death in 1681, the

---

[33] Aston Cockayne, *Small Poems of Divers sort* (London, 1658) and Norbrook, 'Introduction', *The Works of Lucy Hutchinson*, vol. 1, xxiii.

[34] Norbrook, 'Introduction', *The Works of Lucy Hutchinson*, vol. 1, cvii–cxxiv; 15 (quotation).

[35] *A Discovery of the Treacherous Attempts of the Cavaliers, to have Procured the Betraying of Nottingham Castle into their Hands* (London, 1643).

[36] See John Hutchinson, *A Narrative of the Imprisonment and Usage of Colonel John Hutchinson* [1664], *Harleian Miscellany*, vol. 3 (London, 1745) 284–90; David Norbrook, 'Memoirs and Oblivion: Lucy Hutchinson and the Restoration', *Huntington Library Quarterly* 75.2 (2012): 233–83, here 268–9.

[37] Norbrook, 'Introduction', *The Works of Lucy Hutchinson*, vol. 1, xxxiii. See Margaret Cavendish, *Poems and Fancies* (London, 1653); *Philosophical Fancies* (London, 1653); *The Worlds Olio* (London, 1655); *The Philosophical and Physical Opinions* (London, 1655); *Natures Pictures Drawn by Fancies Pencil to the Life* (London, 1656).

[38] For more examples, see Chapter 2, 2, b ('Memoir-writing and the truth of history').

[39] On the proximity between Ludlow and Hutchinson, see MacGillivray, 'Edmund Ludlow and Mrs. Hutchinson', *Restoration Historians* 170–84, and Norbrook, 'But a Copie', 129–30.

first five cantos of her biblical epic, *Order and Disorder*, were published anonymously, which confirms that she was not hostile to print publication, even though, unlike Margaret Cavendish, she concealed her authorship.[40]

The autograph manuscript of the *Memoirs*, on which Julius Hutchinson's first edition was based, was bought by Nottingham Castle Museum in 1921.[41] It contains various pieces which all relate to Lucy Hutchinson's experience of the Revolution: a dedication, 'To my Children' (twenty-nine pages), 'The Life of John Hutchinson of Owthorpe in the County of Nottingham Esquire' (319 pages), a one-page meditation (only reproduced in Keeble's edition under the title of 'Final Meditation'), and sixty-nine pages of biblical verses and references, which were published neither by Julius Hutchinson nor by subsequent editors.[42] 'The Life of John Hutchinson' is far longer than the other sections, and critics and historians have often found it convenient to refer to this life narrative as the *Memoirs*, an appellation that has been kept here. Besides these items, Julius Hutchinson's 1806 edition also reproduces a short autobiographical fragment, the manuscript of which was lost after the dispersal of Lucy Hutchinson's manuscripts at the death of the editor.[43] Its writing method recalls the 'Life of John Hutchinson' as it brings together the author's story of her own early life with England's national history. It is, however, very short and stops abruptly, which makes it difficult to decide whether it was censored by some member of the Hutchinson family or interrupted by Lucy Hutchinson herself.[44]

Until the publication of Sutherland's edition in 1973, the reliability of Julius Hutchinson's edition was not challenged, all the more so as he claimed to have been faithful to the original manuscript: 'The only deviation we have made from the MS. is in putting the U and V in their proper places; they being

---

[40] *Order and Disorder: Or, the World Made and Undone Being Meditations upon the Creation and the Fall* (London, 1679). On its publication see Norbrook, 'Order and Disorder: The Poem and its Contexts', xii–xiii.

[41] For new evidence about the fortunes of Lucy Hutchinson's manuscripts, in particular that of the *Memoirs*, see Norbrook, 'General Introduction', *The Works of Lucy Hutchinson*, vol. 2, xxiii–xxviii. Information on the lost and found manuscripts of the *Memoirs* can be found in Sidney Race, 'Notes on Mrs. Hutchinson's Manuscripts', *Notes and Queries* 145 (1923): 3–4; Race, 'Colonel Hutchinson: Manuscript and Printed Memoirs', *Notes and Queries* 199 (1954): 161. A fresh look at the manuscript is taken by Wall in 'Not so much open professed enemies', 623–4.

[42] Nottinghamshire Archives, *Memoirs*, DD/HU4. On the manuscript, see Sutherland, 'Note on the Text', *Memoirs* xx–xxi and Keeble, 'Note on the Text', *Memoirs* xxx–xxxi. For a detailed description of the manuscript, see https://web.warwick.ac.uk/english/perdita/html/ms_NADDHU4.htm (accessed 06/12/2019).

[43] Julius Hutchinson describes it as '[a] Fragment, giving an account of the early part of her own life' (i).

[44] See Norbrook, 'Hutchinson [née Apsley], Lucy (1620–1681), Poet and Biographer' (2016), *Oxford Dictionary of National Biography*, DOI: 10.1093/ref:odnb/14285; https://doi-org.janus.bis-sorbonne.fr/10.1093/ref:odnb/14285.

written promiscuously.'[45] Still, this statement is misleading for at least two reasons. First, as David Norbrook has shown, Julius Hutchinson was 'an interventionist editor, frequently revising Hutchinson's wording to shorten sentences and clarify meaning'. Second, as James Sutherland highlighted in the preface to his 1973 edition, the first editor 'omitted passages amounting to about 9,000 words'.[46] Many of the cancelled passages dealt with religion, which Julius Hutchinson deemed to be 'so little in fashion' when he was preparing the edition of the *Memoirs*.[47] In the dedication, 'To My Children', he chose to cut references to Calvin, whether they be direct or indirect,[48] as well as the passages in which John Hutchinson is characterized as a saint and martyr.[49] Julius Hutchinson also cancelled an eight-page portrait of Colonel Hutchinson, which Lucy Hutchinson describes as 'another assay' after a first description which she 'much dislike[s]'.[50] Even if Lucy Hutchinson does not say which portrait she favours, it has been the decision of the first editor and of his successors to leave out this second portrait, which underscores—even more overtly than the first—the Colonel's status as a saint and martyr. The editor seems to have been guided by the same principles when he passes in silence the three last pages of 'The Life of John Hutchinson', in which the Colonel's death is viewed in a providential light.[51] In a similar way, the removal of both the dark Calvinistic 'Final Meditation'[52] and the compilation of biblical verses[53] tend to deconfessionalize the original manuscript. All these editorial choices, which aim at erasing the revolutionary violence of the regicide, and at downplaying the Puritanism and the republicanism of the *Memoirs*, are consonant with Julius Hutchinson's preface to the *Memoirs*, in which he argues that the Revolution of 1688—the triumph of constitutional monarchy—is to be read in

---

[45] See *Memoirs*, ed. Julius Hutchinson, 18 and Norbrook, 'But a Copie', 115–19.
[46] See Sutherland, 'Note on the Text', *Memoirs*, xxiv.
[47] See 'The Life of Mrs. Hutchinson, written by herself. A fragment', *Memoirs*, ed. Julius Hutchinson, note a, 1: 'That noble turn of thought which led Mrs. Hutchinson to open her work with thanks to her Maker, instead of apologies to the readers, [...] will probably, by its originality, recommend itself, and prevent the distaste which the air of religion, it wears, might give to many, in times when it is so little in fashion.' In the preface (vi–vii), the editor declares that 'Divinity as a science was a study then in vogue, and seems to have tinctured the conversation and writings of the greater part of society.'
[48] See for instance 'To My Children', *Memoirs*, ed. Sutherland, 5–7 and ed. Keeble, 21–3. The reference to Calvin is removed from Julius Hutchinson's edition. See also the longer passage about the Colonel's calling (S35–6/K54–6).
[49] See for instance 'To My Children': 'When God aflicted him, he fell downe at his feete [...] God called him to something elce' (S13/K29).
[50] *Memoirs*, ed. Julius Hutchinson, 17. The passage cancelled is in *Memoirs*, DD/HU4, 22–9.
[51] For other cancelled passages that are not religious, see Sutherland, 'Note on the Text', xxiv, and Norbrook, 'But a Copie', 118–19.
[52] This is the title which Keeble gives to it in his edition (337). It has no title in the original manuscript (DD/HU4, [421]).
[53] *Memoirs*, DD/HU4, [423–79].

continuity with the demands of the supporters of Parliament in the early years of the First Civil War. In Julius Hutchinson's view, the Colonel did nothing but assert the 'claims of the people to command, through their representatives, the public purse, the freedom of debate in parliament, and the responsibility of ministers'.[54] These claims, Julius Hutchinson maintains, were widely accepted even among the Tories of his day: 'Upon a fair review of the contest it will be seen that what the Tory and the Courtier of the present day, the friend or even the flatterer of kingly power, admits as axioms, were the grand desiderata of the Whig and the Patriot of those times, and that what were then cried out upon as daring encroachments now pass as the most moderate and unquestioned claims.'[55]

In the present monograph, I shall mostly focus on the *Memoirs* as edited by Sutherland (1973) and Keeble (1996). I have also used the Nottingham Manuscript (DD/HU4) to quote unpublished sections of the *Memoirs* and to locate revisions and deletions. In the course of the book, I also pay special attention to an autograph manuscript covering the years 1642–1645, which is held at the British Library.[56] In his 1806 edition of the *Memoirs*, Julius Hutchinson calls it 'a book without a title, but which appears to have been a kind of diary made use of when she came to write the Life of John Hutchinson'.[57] In his 1885 edition, the historian C. H. Firth did not view this manuscript as a diary, but as a sketch or a draft which Lucy Hutchinson used to write 'The Life of John Hutchinson'. He chose to call it the 'Note-book', a term that shall be kept here as a convenient shorthand.[58]

I will also occasionally refer to Lucy Hutchinson's Commonplace Books,[59] as well as to the 'Elegies' which in their own ways constitute a singular historiographical enterprise.[60] The manuscript of these Elegies is now kept in the Nottinghamshire Archives; it has been edited by David Norbrook, who assumes that the twenty-three poems were composed around the time when

---

[54] Julius Hutchinson, ed., *Memoirs* v.   [55] Julius Hutchinson, ed., *Memoirs* vi.
[56] Race, 'The British Museum MS. Of the Life'. On the history of those fragments, see Norbrook, 'General Introduction', *The Works of Lucy Hutchinson*, vol. 2, xxvii. Some extracts are reproduced in C. H. Firth's 1906 edition of the *Memoirs of the Life of Colonel Hutchinson* (London: Routledge, 1906) 406–7; 408; 415–16; 423–4; 431–2. The *Memoirs* were first edited by Firth in two volumes in 1885. Further references are to Firth's more compact 1906 edition.
[57] Julius Hutchinson, Preface, *Memoirs* i.
[58] *Memoirs*, ed. Firth, x–xi. On the *genre* of the Notebook, see Chapter 5 and a forthcoming chapter, 'From Local to National History: Lucy Hutchinson as a Historian of the English Revolution'.
[59] Nottinghamshire Archives, *Religious Commonplace Book*, DD/HU3; Nottinghamshire Archives, *Literary Commonplace Book*, DD/HU1. Selections from the *Religious Commonplace Book* are published in *The Works of Lucy Hutchinson*, vol. 2, *Theological Writings and Translations*, ed. Elizabeth Clarke, David Norbrook, and Jane Stevenson (Oxford: Oxford UP, 2018) 1–154.
[60] Norbrook, 'Lucy Hutchinson's Elegies', 469.

Lucy Hutchinson was writing the *Memoirs*, that is to say between 1664 and 1667, which may explain why there are 'innumerable verbal echoes between the two texts'.[61] The new Oxford edition of the *Memoirs*, edited by David Norbrook, will, in all likelihood, highlight their intertextuality and their links with other Hutchinson's texts, and provide an edition of the unpublished parts—the sixty-nine pages of biblical verses and meditation to be found at the end of the Nottingham manuscript.[62]

1. History and memory

The Civil Wars stimulated the writing of many lives which were then understood as histories rather than as biographical explorations of an individual's personality or character.[63] 'Charles II's return to England in 1662,' Ian Donaldson remarks, 'initiated a period of intense interest in the chronicling of lives, especially of those who had played a major part in the great political and religious events of the preceding decades.'[64] Lives, as a genre of writing, were indeed a major way of history writing until the beginning of the eighteenth century.[65] A very useful definition, quoted by some Restoration life-writers, was provided by Francis Bacon's historiographical typology in *The Advancement of Learning*.[66] Lives, according to Bacon, were 'perfect history'

---

[61] Norbrook, 'Lucy Hutchinson's Elegies', 470.

[62] See *Memoirs*, DD/HU4 and Norbrook, 'But a Copie', 113.

[63] For an excellent presentation of 'life-writing', see Thomas F. Mayer and Daniel R. Woolf, 'Introduction', *The Rhetorics of Life-Writing in Early Modern England. Forms of Biography from Cassandra Fedele to Louis XIV* (Ann Arbor: U of Michigan P, 1995) 1–38. The term 'biography' appeared for the first time in John Fell, *The Life of that reverend divine, and learned historian, Dr. Thomas Fuller* (1661) 105. See also Judith H. Anderson, *Biographical Truth: The Representation of Historical Persons in Tudor-Stuart Writing* (New Haven: Yale UP, 1984) 13; Allan Pritchard, 'The Growth of Biographical Writing', *English Biography in the Seventeenth Century* (Toronto: Toronto UP, 2009) 9–29; Mayer, *History and the Early English Novel* 80: 'before 1660 the author of a life was denominated not a biographer but a historiographer.'

[64] Ian Donaldson, 'National Biography and the Arts of Memory', *Mapping Lives: The Uses of Biography*, ed. Peter France and William St Clair (Oxford: Oxford UP, 2002) 67.

[65] See Kevin Sharpe and Steven N. Zwicker, 'Introducing Lives', *Writing Lives: Biography and Textuality, Identity and Representation in Early Modern England*, ed. Sharpe and Zwicker (Oxford: Oxford UP, 2008) 1–26, here 4; Mayer, 'Lifewriting and Historiography', 75–93. On the relationships between history and biography, see Pritchard, *English Biography* 94–5.

[66] Francis Bacon, *The Two Bookes of Francis Bacon. Of the Proficience and Advancement of Learning, Divine and Humane. The Second Book* (London, 1605). David Lloyd quotes Bacon's *Of the Proficience and Advancement of Learning* in Lloyd, 'The Epistle Dedicatory', *Memoires of the Lives, Actions, Sufferings & Deaths of those Noble, Reverend, and Excellent Personages, that Suffered by Death, Sequestration, Decimation* (London, 1668) [sig. B^v]. Margaret Cavendish refers to the same passage, though not quoting it exhaustively, in Cavendish, *The Life of the Thrice Noble, High, Puissant Prince William Cavendishe* (London, 1667) 103: 'to render the History of his Life more perfect and compleat.' On Bacon's typology, see Nicolas Dubos, *Thomas Hobbes et l'histoire: Système et récits à l'âge classique* (Paris: Publication de la Sorbonne, 2014) 53–5.

that 'excelle[d] in profit and use'. 'Lives,' he continued, 'if they be well written, propounding to themselues a person to represent, in whom actions both greater and smaller, publique & priuate haue a commixture; must of necessitie containe a more true, natiue, and liuely representation.'[67] Lucy Hutchinson does not mention Bacon, but his definition of a life reflects her own project. 'The Life of John Hutchinson' is indeed 'well written' and displays the 'commixture' that Bacon advocates, the private being never split from the public, the personal from the historical. In this regard, the Colonel's public career can only be understood if one considers his own motivations and the bonds that tied him to his wife and to God. Moreover, Lucy Hutchinson's *tour de force* lies in her ability to link her husband's life to what Bacon calls 'Chronicle', that is, to national history.[68] Combining the history of someone's 'life' with the history of their 'times' was a frequent practice after the Civil Wars. Two well-known examples are Baxter's *Reliquiæ Baxterianæ*, subtitled *Mr Richard Baxter's Narrative of the Most Memorable Passages of his Life and Times*,[69] and Clarendon's *History of the Rebellion*, which was in fact the conflation of a history of England (started in the 1640s) with his own life (composed during his exile in 1668 and 1669).[70] Such a combination was close to the genre of 'memoirs', which were histories written 'by such persons who have had a hand in the management, or else have been eye-witnesses of the transacting of affairs, containing a plain narration, either of the actions of their prince or statesmen, or of themselves'.[71] Matthew Sylvester, the editor of Baxter's *Reliquiæ Baxterianæ* (1696), speaks of 'the Author's ordering and digesting of his own *Memoirs*',[72] while Baxter himself claims that he 'must bear this

---

[67] Bacon, *The Second Booke* 10.
[68] Bacon, *The Second Booke* 11: 'HISTORY which may be called IVST and PARFITE Historie, is of three kinds, according to the obiect which it propoundeth, or pretendeth to represent; for it either representeth a TIME, or a PERSON, or an ACTION. The first we call CHRONICLES, the second LIVES, and the third NARRATIONS, or RELATIONS.'
[69] Richard Baxter, *Reliquiæ Baxterianæ, Or Mr Richard Baxter's Narrative of the Most Memorable Passages of his Life and Times*, ed. Matthew Sylvester (London, 1696); ed. N. H. Keeble, John Coffey, Tim Cooper, and Tom Charlton (Oxford: Oxford UP, 2020). On Baxter's narrative see Keeble, 'The Autobiographer as Apologist: *Reliquiæ Baxterianæ* (1696)', *The Literature of Controversy*, ed. Thomas N. Corns (London: Frank Cass, 1987) 105–19. See also Keeble, '*Reliquiæ Baxterianæ* and the Shaping of the Seventeenth Century', *A Concise Companion to the Study of Manuscripts, Printed Books, and the Production of Early Modern Texts*, ed. Edward Jones (Chichester: Wiley, 2015) 229–48.
[70] Edward Hyde, Earl of Clarendon, *The History of the Rebellion and Civil Wars in England* [1888], ed. W. Dunn Macray, 6 vols. (Oxford: Clarendon, 1969) vol. 1. On the combination of life-writing and historiography see Mayer, *History and the English Novel* 76. On Clarendon writing separately the *History* and his *Life*, see Paul Seaward, 'Clarendon, Tacitism and Europe's Civil Wars', *Huntington Library Quarterly* 68.1–2 (2005): 305; Martine Watson Brownley, *Clarendon and the Rhetoric of Historical Form* (Philadelphia: U of Pennsylvania P, 1985) 30–1.
[71] See Nathan Bailey, *The Universal Etymological English Dictionary*, vol. 2 [1727] (London, 1731).
[72] Sylvester, 'The Preface to the Reader', Baxter, *Reliquiæ Baxterianæ* sig. [b4ᵛ]; ed. Keeble et al, vol. 4: *Documents and Appendices* 424.

faithful Witness to those times, *that as far as [he] was acquainted*'.[73] Hyde does not use the term 'memoirs' in his *History of the Rebellion*, but he too insists that he was a witness to many political transactions and debates:

> And as I may not be thought altogether an incompetent person for this communication, having been present as a member of parliament in those councils before and till the breaking out of the Rebellion, and having since had the honour to be near two great kings in some trust, so I shall perform the same with all faithfulness and ingenuity.[74]

For that matter, the first editor, Julius Hutchinson, highlights the proximity of the approaches taken by Edward Hyde and Lucy Hutchinson, even signalling the superiority of the latter's 'representation of affairs':

> although there are many histories of the same period, there is not one that is generally considered satisfactory; most of them carry evident marks of prejudice or partiality; nor were any of those which are now read written at or near the time, or by persons who had an opportunity of being well acquainted with what was passing, except that of Clarendon. But any one who should take the pains, which the Editor has done, to examine Clarendon's State Papers, would find therein documents much better calculated to support Mrs. Hutchinson's representation of affairs than that which he himself has given.[75]

Unsurprisingly, Guizot also includes the *Mémoires de Lord Clarendon, grand-chancelier d'Angleterre sous le règne de Charles I*, in his *Collection des Mémoires relatifs à la Révolution d'Angleterre*, which gathered a wide range of historical texts from Thomas May's *Histoire du Long Parlement* to the *Mémoires de Mistriss Hutchinson*.[76]

From this perspective, and contrary to what has sometimes been argued, the term 'memoirs', chosen by Julius Hutchinson for his 1806 edition, is a fitting term for Lucy Hutchinson's autograph manuscript, which does not bear an overall title.[77] There is no reason to believe that the first editor betrayed his

---

[73] Baxter, *Reliquiæ Baxterianæ*, Part I, §139, 96; ed. Keeble et al, and vol. 1, *Introduction and Part I* 429. See Keeble, *Richard Baxter: Puritan Man of Letters* (Oxford: Oxford UP, 1982) 145-6.
[74] Hyde, *The History of the Rebellion*, vol. 1, 3.   [75] Julius Hutchinson, ed., *Memoirs* x.
[76] François Guizot, *Collection des Mémoires relatifs à la Révolution d'Angleterre, accompagnés de notices et d'éclaircissements historiques*, 25 vols. (Paris: Béchet, 1823-1825).
[77] Looser's contention that the term 'memoirs' was anachronistic (*British Women Writers* 36) and Norbrook's view that the term 'memoir' corresponds to a 'certain softening of the text's political edge'

ancestor's intentions when he published her manuscript under the title *Memoirs of the Life of Colonel Hutchinson*.[78] Admittedly, he may have been influenced by the publication in 1698 of another republican testimony, the *Memoirs of Edmund Ludlow*.[79] He may also have wanted to capitalize on the nineteenth-century fashion for the memoir genre. According to David Norbrook, his 'decision to publish the *Memoirs*, by subscription, was in part an attempt to recoup his fortunes. The book did well, going through three editions in four years.'[80] But Julius Hutchinson's choice to call Lucy Hutchinson's life of her husband 'Memoirs' was not only guided by a nineteenth-century vogue. It testifies to his good grasp of her historiographical and literary enterprise and matched the definition of the 'memoir' (in the plural or singular), which refers, according to the *OED*, to '[r]ecords of events or history written from the personal knowledge or experience of the writer, or based on special sources of information [2a]'. This choice was endorsed by Firth in his 1885 edition of Lucy Hutchinson's *Memoirs of the Life of Colonel Hutchinson*, as well as in the *Memoirs of the Duke and Duchess of Newcastle; the Life of William Cavendish, Duke of Newcastle*, which he published in 1886.[81]

In Restoration England, the term 'memoirs' (which comes from the French *mémoires*) was less often used in this sense than in the nineteenth century, and before 1660 the use of 'memoir(s)' for this kind of writing was rare.[82] Nevertheless, some 'memoirs' were published in the wake of the English Civil Wars, which indicates that late seventeenth-century historians were acquainted with the genre.[83] The term 'memoir' was frequently paired with the term 'life', the two words being near in meaning, the former merely adding

('But a Copie', 20), come from a partial reading of what *historical* memoirs were. In 1990, in 'The Colonel's Shadow' (237–8), Keeble originally deemed Lucy Hutchinson's 'Life of John Hutchinson' too impersonal to be called 'Memoirs'. His views have shifted as he now considers her 'Life of John Hutchinson' as a memoir sharing many features with other Restoration memoirs. See his '*Reliquiæ Baxterianæ* and the Shaping of the Seventeenth Century', §17.1–§17.4, and his 'Lucy Hutchinson and the Business of Memoirs', *The Review of English Studies* 2022, https://doi.org/10.1093/res/hgac007.

[78] On such practices, see Frédéric Charbonneau, *Les Silences de l'histoire. Les Mémoires français du XVIIe siècle* (Sainte-Foy: Presses de l'Université de Laval, 2000) 9–10.

[79] For this interpretation, see Norbrook, 'Memoirs and Oblivion', 236. See Edmund Ludlow, *Memoirs of Edmund Ludlow* (London, 1698).

[80] Norbrook, 'General Introduction', *The Works of Lucy Hutchinson*, vol. 2, xxiii. The 1806 edition opens with the list of subscribers.

[81] Margaret Cavendish, *Memoirs of the Duke and Duchess of Newcastle; The Life of William Cavendish, Duke of Newcastle*, ed. C. H. Firth (London, 1886).

[82] Even in France, the term 'Mémoires' was rarely used by memorialists who called their works 'Relation', 'Vie' or 'Journal'. Before 1660, 'mémoires' often designated collections of documents. See Christian Jouhaud, 'Écritures de la Fronde: Le collectif et le singulier', *La Fronde des Mémoires (1648–1750)*, ed. Marc Hersant and Éric Tourrette (Paris: Classiques Garnier, 2019) 139–40.

[83] On the fashion for memoirs in late seventeenth-century England and for examples, see Chapter 2, 2, b ('Memoir-writing and the truth of history').

the idea that the account of one's 'life' was based on a first-hand experience of history or, at least, a reliable testimony. In France, the *Memoirs of the Cardinal de Retz*, written between 1675 and 1677 (and only published in 1717), were originally entitled the *Vie du Cardinal de Rais*; Madame de la Guette's *Memoirs*, published in 1681 (but written in the 1670s), present themselves explicitly as the story of 'her life'.[84] In England too, the two genres were often connected. This was the case of David Lloyd's *Memoires of the Lives, Actions, Sufferings & Deaths of those Noble, Reverend, and Excellent Personages* (1668), or Gilbert Burnet's *The Memoires of the Lives and Actions of James and William Dukes of Hamilton and Castleherald* (London, 1677).

The memoir genre as practised in England and France in the seventeenth century was not strictly codified. It belonged to a European historiographical tradition that went back to Caesar's *Commentaries* and Philippe de Commynes's *Memoirs* and became prominent from the beginning of the sixteenth century.[85] Frédéric Charbonneau has shown that the genre covered a great variety of texts, at the intersection of several traditions, among which the lives of Plutarch and Suetonius, the *Confessions* of Augustine, and the chronicles of Froissard.[86] The Whig historian Gilbert Burnet, himself a memorialist, thus recognized that 'Of all Nations in the world the *French* have delighted most in these Writings [...] every year we get over new *Memoires* of some one Great Person or another. [...] this way of Writing takes now more in the World than any sort of History ever did.'[87] Burnet's

---

[84] Quoted in Frédéric Briot, *Usage du monde, usage de soi. Enquête sur les mémorialistes d'Ancien Régime* (Paris: Le Seuil, 1994) 28–9. On the under-estimated proximity between memoirs and lives, see Charbonneau, *Les Silences de l'histoire* 4 and 8. *La Vie du Cardinal de Rais* only became the *Mémoires de Monsieur le Cardinal de Retz* in 1717.

[85] Pierre Nora refers to Commynes 'whose memoirs served as a breviary for statesmen and as the model for the genre'. See his 'Memoirs of Men of State', *Rethinking France. Les Lieux de mémoire, vol. 1: The State* [1984], ed. David P. Jordan, trans. Mary Trouille (Chicago: U of Chicago P, 2001) 403. Commynes's *Memoirs* were originally published in French in 1524 under the title *Cronique et hystoire faicte et composee par feu messire Phelippe de Commines [...] contenant les choses advenues durant le regne du roy Loys XIe, tant en France, Bourgongne, Flandres, Arthois, Angleterre que Espaigne et lieux circonvoisins* (Paris, 1524). The term 'memoirs' appears in the 1552 edition (*Les Memoires de messire Philippe de Commines* [Paris, 1552]). They were translated into Latin by Jean Sleidan as 'Commentaries'/*Commentarii: De rebus gestis Ludovici, ejus nominis undecimi* (1545). The first English translation is *The historie of Philip de Commines Knight, Lord of Argenton* (1596). The English term 'memoirs' only appears in the 1674 edition (*The Memoirs of Philip de Comines Lord of Argenton containing the history of Lewis XI & Charles VIII Kings of France* [London, 1674]).

[86] Charbonneau, *Les Silences de l'histoire* 8–10. Fumaroli highlights the impact of the French translation of Augustine's *Confessions* on memoir-writing. See Fumaroli, 'Les Mémoires au carrefour des genres en prose', *La Diplomatie de l'esprit: De Montaigne à la Fontaine* (Paris: Hermann, 1994) 183–215, here 203–4.

[87] Burnet, 'Preface', *The Memoires of the Lives and Actions of James and William Dukes of Hamilton and Castleherald* (London, 1677) sig. [a^v]. Quoted in Susan Wiseman, *Conspiracy and Virtue: Women, Writing, and Politics in Seventeenth-Century England* (Oxford: Oxford UP, 2006) 315–16.

sense of a French literary superiority was corroborated a century later by Madame de Staël's observation: 'There are no memoirs, confessions, or autobiographies in England; the pride of the English character refuses such details and avowals.'[88] Staël's statement was predicated on a slightly later meaning of the term 'memoirs' as 'autobiographical observations; reminiscences'.[89] She was not aware of the historical significance of the word that prevailed in the sixteenth and seventeenth century, when it was almost exclusively used to designate writings in the style of Caesar's *Commentaries* or Commynes's *Memoirs*, that is, based on the historical experience of the author. It was eloquently used in this latter sense for instance by Pierre Le Moyne in *Of the Art both of Writing & Judging of History* to designate the writings of '*Beleagnangis, Montluc,* the Duke *de Nevers,* the Sieurs *Castelneau, de Tavannes,* or *Suille*'.[90]

As a matter of fact, although Restoration England may not have had a Cardinal de Retz or a Duc de Saint Simon, many historians opted for particular history when it came to relating the Civil War and Interregnum. 'The history of the Revolution and Restoration,' Zwicker and Sharpe claimed, was written by 'biographical narratives' telling the lives of heroes, martyrs, politicians, or less famous actors, at a time when there was 'an appetite and market for lives'.[91] Many of these lives fall in within the broad category of 'memoir(s)', a most important historical genre according to Susan Wiseman:

> As memoir, taken broadly, was one of the dominant genres in which history of the Civil War was made in the period from 1660 to the publication of Catherine Macaulay's pioneering *History* in the late eighteenth century, the test to which such writing was subjected by its readers was that of political commitment. Was it true? Whose side was it on?[92]

---

[88] Germaine de Staël, *De la littérature, considérée dans ses rapports avec les institutions sociales* (Paris, 1829) 262 (my translation). On the French specificity of 'Mémoires' as a genre, see Fumaroli, 'Les Mémoires au carrefour des genres en prose', 189–90. On memoirs considered as literature, see Lesne, *La Poétique des mémoires*, Briot, *Usage du monde, usage de soi*, and Charbonneau, *Les Silences de l'Histoire*.

[89] See 'Memoirs', *OED*, 2b.

[90] Pierre Le Moyne, *Of the Art Both of Writing & Judging of History* (London, 1695) 12–13 and, in French, *De l'Histoire* (Paris, 1670) 18–20. On Le Moyne, see Béatrice Guion, '"Une narration continue des choses vraies, grandes, et publiques": l'histoire selon le Père Le Moyne', *Œuvres et Critiques* 35.2 (2010): 91–102.

[91] Sharpe and Zwicker, 'Introducing Lives', 19. See also Alice Hunt, 'Les mémoires républicaines des guerres civiles anglaises dans les années 1650', *Dix-septième siècle* 275.2 (2017): 253–8.

[92] Wiseman, *Conspiracy and Virtue* 316. Donaldson, 'National Biography', 67–8. On memoirs, see also Matthew A. Fitzsimmons, Alfred G. Pundt, and Charles E. Nowell, 'Political Histories and Memoirs in the Seventeenth Century', *The Development of Historiography* (Harrisburg, PA: Stockpole Company, 1954) 133–45.

What is implied here is that truth and impartiality, the qualities one has come to expect from historical writing, were not met in most histories of the Civil Wars, whose authors turned polemicists, as they felt called to defend a party, a man, or a church. For the Church historian, Thomas Fuller, this plurality of views amounted to a return to Babel:

> Such as lived *after* the *Flood*, and *before* the *Confusion* of *Tongues*, were happy in *this particular*, that they did *Hear* to *Understand*, and *Speak* to be *Understood* with all persons in their *Generation*. [...] Happy those *English Historians* who wrote some *sixty years* since before our *Civil Distempers* were born or conceived [...]. But alas! Such *as wrote in or since our Civil Wars*, are seldom apprehended *truly* and *candidly* save of such of their own perswasion, whilest others *doe not* (or what is worse *will not*) understand them aright.[93]

When the nation was divided against itself, it could no longer be identified with the King. Pro-monarchical national chronicles, which some historians had found insufficient for at least fifty years, became obsolete. 'By the mid-seventeenth century,' Daniel R. Woolf remarks, 'the twilight of the chronicle as a published genre was turning to night.'[94] The traditional definition of history as a narration, in which 'were laid up and deposited the Actions and glorious Exploits of preceding Worthies' was no longer relevant.[95] Parliament's official historian, Thomas May, was aware of this when he wished in the preface to *The History of the Parliament of England* that his 'Theame could rather have been the prosperity of these Nations, the Honour and happinesse of this King, and such a blessed condition of both [...] [t]hen the description of Shipwracks, Ruines, and Desolations'.[96] Furthermore, as Martine Watson

---

[93] Thomas Fuller, *The Appeal of Iniured Innocence* (London, 1659) 1. On partisan readings of the English Civil War, see David Cressy, 'Remembrancers of the Revolution: Histories and Historiographies of the 1640s', *Huntington Library Quarterly* 68.1-2 (2005): 257-68 and Paulina Kewes, 'History and Its Uses: Introduction', *Huntington Library Quarterly* 68.1-2 (2005): 1-31. On Fuller see W. B. Patterson, *Thomas Fuller: Discovering England's Religious Past* (Oxford: Oxford UP, 2018).

[94] Daniel R. Woolf, 'The Death of the Chronicle', *Reading History in Early Modern England* (Cambridge: Cambridge UP, 2000) 29-78, here 76. See also Woolf, *The Idea of History in Early Stuart England* (Toronto: U of Toronto P, 1990) 192-3; Claire Gheeraert-Graffeuille, 'Entre polémique et histoire: comment écrire les guerres civiles anglaises', *La Guerre civile: représentations, idéalisations, identifications*, ed. Emmanuel Dupraz and Gheeraert-Graffeuille (Mont-Saint-Aignan: Presses universitaires de Rouen et du Havre, 2014) 51-69, here 59-60.

[95] Richard Brathwaite, *A Survey of History: Or, A Nursery for Gentry* (London, 1638) 2. For a similar definition, see Jacques Amyot, 'Amiot to the Readers', Plutarch, *The Lives of the Noble Grecians and Romanes*, trans. Thomas North (London, 1579) 4: 'the greatest & highest things that are done in the world'.

[96] May, *The History of the Parliament of England* [sig. A4ᵛ]. See J. G. A. Pocock, 'Thomas May and the Narrative of the Civil War', *Writing and Political Engagement in Seventeenth-Century England*, ed.

Brownley remarks in her monograph, *Clarendon and the Rhetorical Form*, 'in the peculiar merging of public and private concerns that was characteristic of the English civil wars, history became reduced not only to personal polemical views, but also to individual experiences'.[97] For Woolf, this means there was no longer any 'broadly unified ideological perspective' from which history could be written: 'The collapse of stable government, the virtual disappearance, for a time, of effective censorship, and the emergence of competing religious and political ideologies swept forever away the univocal narrative historical writing of the earlier period.'[98] In that deeply divisive period, particular histories—especially lives and memoirs—although they were partisan and incomplete, were deemed to be more reliable and truthful than general histories because they were narrower in focus and based on first-hand knowledge.[99] As Firth remarks: 'More trustworthy materials were supplied by the early biographers: though they vindicated or glorified their personages they often wrote from personal knowledge and sometimes based their lives on manuscript materials.'[100] This is a late nineteenth-century point of view, but it could have been shared by many Restoration authors of lives and memoirs who were also aware of the advantages of the genre. It was, for instance, what Margaret Cavendish argued in *The Life of William Cavendish*: contrary to a 'general history' or a 'national history', 'the History of the life and actions of some particular Person [...] goes not out of its own Circle, but turns on its own Axis, and for the most part keeps within the Circumference of Truth'.[101]

Given the high status assigned both to the witnesses of history and to particular history, it is not surprising that what was most valued in Civil

---

Derek Hirst and Richard Strier (Cambridge: Cambridge UP, 2009) 112–44, here 114. On May, see David Norbrook, 'May, Thomas (c.1596–1650), Writer and Historian' (2008), *Oxford Dictionary of National Biography*, DOI: 10.1093/ref:odnb/18423.

[97] Brownley, *Clarendon and the Rhetoric of Historical Form* 7.

[98] Daniel R. Woolf, 'Narrative Historical Writing in Restoration England: A Preliminary Survey', *The Restoration Mind*, ed. W. Gerald Marshall (Newark: University of Delaware Press, 1997) 210. The existence of a 'broadly unified ideological perspective' is qualified by Patrick Collinson in 'Truth, Lies, and Fiction in Sixteenth-Century Protestant Historiography', *The Historical Imagination in Early Modern Britain. History, Rhetoric, and Fiction, 1500–1800*, ed. Donald R. Kelley and David Harris Sacks (Cambridge: Cambridge UP, 1997) 45–7.

[99] See Bacon, *The Second Booke* 10: 'Narrations, and Relations of actions as the War of *Peloponnesus*, the Expedition of *Cyrus Minor*, the Conspiracie of *Catiline*, cannot but be more purely and exactly true, then HISTORIES of TIMES, because they may choose an argument comprehensible within the notice and instructions of the Writer: whereas he that undertaketh the story of a time, specially of any length, cannot but meet with many blankes, and spaces, which hee must be forced to fill vp, out of his own wit and coniecture.' See Sharpe and Zwicker, 'Introducing Lives', 9. Brownley, *Clarendon and the Rhetoric of Historical Form* 7.

[100] See C. H. Firth, 'The Development of the Study of Seventeenth-Century History', *Transactions of the Royal Historical Society. Third Series* 7 (1913): 25–48, here 27.

[101] Cavendish, *Life of William Cavendish*, sig. (c^v). On Margaret Cavendish and history, see Sandrine Parageau, 'Catching "the Genius of the Age": Margaret Cavendish, Historian and Witness', *Études Épistémè* 17 (2010), https://doi.org/10.4000/episteme.662.

War memoirs was that they were based on autopsy, understood as 'the action or process of seeing with one's own eyes; personal observation, inspection, or experience'.[102] As will be apparent, Lucy Hutchinson, like Thucydides and Polybius before her, and many of her humanist predecessors and contemporaries, made much of her position of eye-witness or ear-witness.[103] She was present in the castle of Nottingham throughout the Civil War, not only dressing the wounds of the injured soldiers but also sharing her husband's political and military experience, and sometimes making important decisions. This unique experience of the war—what she saw, heard, and said—gives her narration a historical authority she could not have claimed in other circumstances.

Finally, memoirs were often also conceived as acts of remembrance and almost invariably displayed a double temporality, merging the recorded past with the time of writing.[104] In this sense, Lucy Hutchinson's *Memoirs*, written in the 1660s, are not only a record of the Civil War in Nottinghamshire; they are also about the way she remembers the Civil War at the Restoration, when silence was the only option for republicans and dissenters like herself. The political stakes of memory were indeed high when the 1660 Act of Indemnity and Oblivion stipulated the necessity to erase the Rebellion from public memory:[105]

> That if any person or persons within the space of three yeares next ensueing shall presume malitiously to call or alledge of, or object against any other person or persons any name or names, or other words of reproach any way tending to revive the memory of the late Differences or the occasions thereof, [...] shall forfeit and pay unto the party grieved in case such party offending shall be of the degree of a Gentleman or above ten pounds, and if under that degree the summe of forty.[106]

---

[102] See 'Autopsy', *OED* 1. On autopsy, see Adriana Zangara, 'Voir l'histoire. Théories anciennes du récit historique. Présentation', *Anabases* 7 (2008), https://doi.org/10.4000/anabases.2540.

[103] See "Civil War historiography" (Chapter 2, 2, a) and "Lucy Hutchinson, witness and confidant" (Chapter 3, 1, a).

[104] On Hutchinson and memory, see Kate Chedgzoy, *Women's Writing in the British Atlantic World. Memory, Place and History, 1550-1700* (Cambridge: Cambridge UP, 2007) 153-64. On the Restoration politics of memory and continuity between the 1650s and 1660s, see Janet Clare, ed., *From Republic to Restoration: Legacies and Departures* (Manchester: Manchester UP, 2018) 1-22. See also Erin Peters, '"L'objet de moquerie le plus colossal et le plus honteux du monde" : récits de la honte nationale en 1660', *Dix-septième siècle* 275.2 (2017): 269-84.

[105] Jonathan Scott, *England's Troubles. Seventeenth-Century English Political Instability in European Context* (Cambridge: Cambridge UP, 2000) 163. See David Norbrook, 'Introduction: Acts of Oblivion and Republican Speech-Acts', *Writing the English Republic: Poetry, Rhetoric and Politics* (Cambridge: Cambridge UP, 1999) 1-22, especially 3.

[106] 'Charles II, 1660: An Act of Free and Generall Pardon Indemnity and Oblivion', *Statutes of the Realm*, vol. 5, 1628-80 (s. l.: Great Britain Commission, 1819), clause xxiv, https://www.british-history.ac.uk/statutes-realm/vol5/pp226-234#h3-0024 (accessed 13/11/2018). On 'Acts of Oblivion', see Judith Pollmann, *Memory in Early Modern Europe 1500-1800* (Oxford: Oxford UP, 2017) 140-58.

Another symbolic instance of the determination to cancel out the memory of the Civil Wars was the decision to exhume the bodies of parliamentary supporters, most notoriously those of the regicides Oliver Cromwell, Henry Ireton, John Bradshaw, and Thomas Pride. Even more significant for the present study is the removal from Westminster Abbey of the remains of Thomas May, the Parliament's historian and secretary, on whose work Lucy Hutchinson copiously drew in the *Memoirs*.[107] Logically enough, in 1660, Charles II gave the title of 'historiographer royal' to James Howell, who had served his father in the 1630s, which indicates a desire to restore a sense of continuity with pre-revolutionary England.[108] Ultimately, the Restoration politics of memory extended to language.[109] As Mark Stoyle observes,

> euphemistic language became commonplace. Most people avoided speaking about the war in public, and when forced to do so, resorted to carefully neutral formulations. They did not speak of the conflict as "the rebellion," for example – a term which would have implied criticism of the former rebels – but referred delicately instead to "the late warres," "the late unhappy times," "the troublesome times," or just "the troubles."[110]

Yet, despite the hopes of Charles II's supporters, the 1662 settlement failed to restore the monarchy as it was before the Civil Wars or to create a new era of political stability. On the contrary, the unresolved conflicts of the English Revolution, the fears of a new civil war, and the impossibility to obliterate the past could well explain the uncertainty of the Restoration period and the crisis of 1688-1689.[111]

The complexity of the politics of memory has been recently explored by two historians working in the field of memory studies.[112] Matthew Neufeld, in

---

[107] Mark Stoyle, 'Remembering the English Civil War', *The Memory of Catastrophe*, ed. Peter Gray and Kendrick Oliver (Manchester: Manchester UP, 2004) 19-30, 22. On the symbolic memory of the English Revolution, see Jonathan Sawday's important article, 'Re-Writing a Revolution: History, Symbol and Text in the Restoration', *The Seventeenth Century* 7.2 (1992): 185-8.

[108] Matthew Neufeld, 'The Restoration Regime and Historical Reconstructions', *The Civil Wars after 1660. Public Remembering in Late Stuart England* (Woodbridge: Boydell Press, 2013) 24.

[109] Woolf, 'Narrative Historical Writing', 226-7.

[110] Stoyle, 'Remembering the English Civil War', 22. See Donaldson, 'National Biography', 68: Hyde himself insisted on the necessity of forgetfulness.

[111] Scott, *England's Troubles* 161-2. See Tim Harris's seminal study, *Restoration: Charles II and his Kingdoms 1660-1685* [2005] (London: Penguin, 2006).

[112] See Royce MacGillivray's pioneering *Restoration Historians*; Mayer and Woolf, *The Rhetorics of Life-Writing*; David Norbrook, 'The English Revolution and English Historiography', *The Cambridge Companion to Writing of the English Revolution*, ed. N. H. Keeble (Cambridge: Cambridge UP, 2001) 233-50. On memory and the Restoration, see Paulina Kewes, 'Acts of Remembrance, Acts of Oblivion: Rhetoric, Law and National Memory in Early Restoration England', *Ritual, Routine, and Regime*, ed. Lorna Clymer (Toronto: Toronto UP, 2006) 103-31.

The Civil Wars after 1660, has researched the different ways in which the monarchy of Charles II 'attempted to shape the public remembering of the Civil War and Interregnum', looking in particular at the official anti-Puritan reconstruction of past events in published histories.[113] Meanwhile, Edward Legon takes a different standpoint by investigating the 'seditious memories' of the Revolution, that is, the unauthorized recollections of those who remained loyal to the 'good old cause'—the republic.[114] These memories, which challenged royalist views of the Revolution, constitute a counter-memory which has been relatively less explored than the royalist memory of the wars. This alternative vision of history is present in various 'seditious' speeches to be found in state papers and court records as well as in diaries, memoirs or letters, which either have remained unpublished or were published after 1688.[115]

It is clear that Lucy Hutchinson's *Memoirs* furnish a very good instance of these 'seditious memories'.[116] In his wake, I suggest that Lucy Hutchinson's reconstruction of the past can be interpreted as a republican response to Restoration politics and contribute to enriching our appreciation of the Restoration counter-memory of the Civil Wars.[117] For instance, she sees the death of John Hutchinson as a direct consequence of the politics of Charles II's monarchy. Nowhere does she entertain any hope in the new régime; she deplores instead that the 'glorious Parliament' (i.e. the Long Parliament) 'gave place to the fowlest mists that ever overspread a miserable people' (S224/K274). But the *Memoirs* are a complex testimony that evades easy ideological categorization. The first official reason she gives for the 'preservation of [her husband's] memory' is ostensibly her love for him—politics only come second:

> I that am under a command not to grieve att the common rate of desolate woemen, while I am studying which way to moderate my woe, and, if it were possible, to augment my love, can for the present find out none more just to your deare father no consolatory to myselfe than the preservation of his memory. (S1/K16)

---

[113] Neufeld, *The Civil Wars after 1660*, back cover. George Southcombe and Grand Tapsell, *Restoration Politics, Religion and Culture* (Basingstoke: Palgrave Macmillan, 2010): 'Remembering was figured as rebellion' (9).

[114] See Edward Legon's recently published book, *Revolution Remembered. Seditious Memories after the British Civil Wars* (Manchester: Manchester UP, 2019).

[115] Legon, *Revolution Remembered* 17–18. See Stoyle, 'Remembering the English Civil War', 27 on 'the pro-Cromwellian counter-tradition' which 'survived beneath the surface'.

[116] Legon, *Revolution Remembered*, 7.

[117] MacGillivray, *Restoration Historians* 2–3: almost all histories published in the 1660s were royalist. A greater variety of histories (parliamentarian, royalist, Whig) were published between 1688 and 1702.

This is why, while emphasizing the importance of Lucy Hutchinson's historiographical and polemical contribution, I will not lose sight of her broader project to commemorate her husband's memory.[118] The second reason why the *Memoirs* cannot be reduced to polemical counter-history is Lucy Hutchinson's moral outlook. By retrospectively imposing a moral agenda onto past events, she offers a disenchanted vision of the English Revolution from which no-one seems to come out unscathed. Instead of being driven by ideals, all the actors in history, royalists and parliamentarians alike, are shown to be moved by base passions, and figures of national importance make no exception. From Lucy Hutchinson's retrospective point of view, Charles I himself appears to be morally responsible for the tragedy of the Civil War, while Cromwell, driven by ambitious tyranny, is described as having annihilated all hopes of a republican alternative to monarchy.

2. Gender

Another reason why Lucy Hutchinson's 'Life of John Hutchinson' has not always been read as a historical narrative in its own right comes from the fact that early modern women were usually excluded from the field of history as *historia rerum gestarum*, a field that was traditionally gendered as masculine. This tendency to masculinize history is perceptible in the editions of the *Memoirs* which, until 1968, 'overruled or simplified [Lucy Hutchinson's] own preferences, and subtly contributed to the impression of a specifically "masculine" woman writer'.[119] It is true that before Catharine Macaulay's *History of England*, women's histories were quite rare, but there were some exceptions such as Anne Dowriche's verse account of the French wars of religion or Elizabeth Cary's *The History of the Life, Reign, and Death of Edward II*.[120] As Natalie Zemon Davis has argued in a landmark article, women's practice of history was much limited by their own condition, as

---

[118] On the working of memory in relation to history, see Geoffrey Cubitt, 'History and Memory: An Imagined Relationship', *History and Memory* (Manchester: Manchester UP, 2007) 26–65; Paul Ricœur, *Memory, History, Forgetting*, trans. Kathleen Blamey and David Pellauer (Chicago: U of Chicago P, 2004).
[119] Norbrook, 'But a Copie', 110.
[120] See Armel Dubois-Nayt, 'Anne Dowriche et l'histoire de France ou d'Angleterre?' *Études Épistémè* 17 (2010), https://doi.org/10.4000/episteme.659 and Karen Britland, '"Kings are but Men": Elizabeth Cary's Histories of Edward II', *Études Épistémè* 17 (2010), https://doi.org/10.4000/episteme.660.

well as their lack of experience and education.[121] A great majority of early modern women writers were barred from politics and the battlefields; they travelled less than men, and were not as well read in classical authors. According to Daniel R. Woolf, the gender division was even stronger at the Restoration, a period which coincided with 'the emergent understanding of historical knowledge as in itself masculine, taken either as classroom for political action or, alternatively [...], as a field of knowledge to be invaded, conquered, and "mastered"'.[122]

In the 1970s and the 1980s, the scarcity of histories written by women and the absence of women from history led some feminist scholars to investigate women's *own history*—sometimes labelled *herstory*—a history for women, told by women about women, which was meant to fill in the gaps of male history. Such scholarship started by focusing on the nineteenth and twentieth centuries before looking at earlier centuries. Since the late 1980s it has unquestionably contributed to the re-discovery and dissemination of many early modern women authors and their texts.[123] Elaine Hobby's pioneering *Virtue of Necessity*, originally published by Virago Press in 1988, shed light on many previously overlooked texts by women, ranging from religious prophecies to cookery books and memoirs.[124] For students working on early modern women in the early 1990s, Hobby's work, along with Hilda Smith's bibliography of women's writings, was the starting-point of any further research in the field.[125]

From these feminist studies has emerged the notion that there were specifically female historiographical practices and forms to be discovered in the margins of 'male' history. In *Women Writing History*, Megan Matchinske has shown how early modern women engaged with history in their own ways, in 'less explicit forms as advice, counsel and memory', as in 'mother's legacy,

---

[121] Natalie Zemon Davis, 'Gender and Genre: Women as Historical Writers, 1400–1820', *Beyond their Sex: Learned Women of the European Past*, ed. Patricia H. Labalme (New York: New York UP, 1980) 153–82. See for more nuanced views, Daniel R. Woolf, 'A Feminine Past? Gender, Genre and Historical Knowledge in England, 1500–1800', *American Historical Review* 102.3 (1997): 645–579, here 645–6 and Joanne Wright, 'Questioning Gender, War, and the "Old Lie": The Military Expertise of Margaret Cavendish', *The History of British Women's Writing*, vol. 3, ed. Mihoko Suzuki (Basingstoke: Palgrave Macmillan, 2011) 254–69, here 254–5.

[122] Woolf, 'A Feminine Past', 658–9. According to Woolf, 'Clio's femininity aside, true history acquired in the violent seventeenth century a male rigor, an authoritative forcefulness that contrasted with the unreliability of tales and traditions associated with old wives' (659).

[123] Elaine Hobby, *Virtue of Necessity: English Women's Writing, 1646–1688* (London: Virago Press, 1988; Ann Arbor: U of Michigan P, 1989).

[124] Hobby, *Virtue of Necessity* 23–4.

[125] See Hilda L. Smith and Susan Cardinale, *Women and the Literature of the Seventeenth-Century: An Annotated Bibliography Based on Wing's Short-Title-Catalogue* (New York: Greenwood Press, 1990).

religious verse history, diary writing, closet drama and tabloid news'.[126] Yet she denies early modern women the possibility of participating in mainstream historiography, alleging that '[their] voices were not inscribed in narratives of kings and counsellors'.[127] In another collection of essays, Matchinske qualifies the idea that women did not write in the same genres as men. Looking at the *Memoirs of the Life of Colonel Hutchinson*, she portrays Lucy Hutchinson as a 'competent and factual historian' who was 'no doubt fully aware of what history "ought" to look like'.[128] Her perspective, however, is not to show how Lucy Hutchinson used a mainstream male historiographical tradition, but rather to demonstrate how the 'affect-driven' life of John Hutchinson differs from a more formal 'masculine' history.[129] Although her equation between emotions and femininity is questionable, her point is still of interest as it brings out Lucy Hutchinson's concern with passions and emotions, an important aspect of her history writing, which is not to be exclusively understood in gendered terms.

Such approaches, which tend to draw a clear line between male and female writing, have been interrogated by Erica Longfellow in her own study of Lucy Hutchinson. In Longfellow's view, gender-specific categories should not be restricted to women's writing but applied to texts both by male and female authors: 'Hutchinson's writing demonstrates that women as well as men could use gendered metaphors to discuss ungendered subjects, whether the true form of the English Church or the future of the English Republic, and should remind us not to reconfine women to the ghetto of gender through our critical attention to the subject.'[130] In *British Women Writers and the Writing of History*, Devoney Looser shares Erica Longfellow's methodological standpoint and rejects the idea that early modern women had a special way of writing history—and therefore their own historiography—because of their sex.[131] She argues accordingly that women used the same historical forms as men, and maintains that 'herstory's myths—particularly about the lack of women who have recorded history—require revision'.[132] Logically therefore she rejects the

---

[126] Megan Matchinske, *Women Writing History in Early Modern Europe* (Cambridge: Cambridge UP, 2009) 1, 2, and 6: 'Because women operated at some remove from traditional historical discussions even before history's entry into disciplinary circles and because the written record documenting that past did not address their lives or their dreams, their need to look to other forms and different historical experiences was both highly fraught and highly sought.'
[127] Matchinske, *Women Writing History* 3.
[128] Megan Matchinske, 'History's "Silent Whispers": Representing the Past through Feeling and Form', *Attending to Early Modern Women: Conflict and Concord*, ed. Karen Nelson (Newark: U of Delaware P, 2013) 59, 60.
[129] Matchinske, 'History's "Silent Whispers"', 60, 65.
[130] Erica Longfellow, *Women and Religious Writing in England* (Cambridge: Cambridge UP, 2004) 48.
[131] Looser, *British Women Writers* 2.   [132] Looser, *British Women Writers* 1.

notion that Lucy Hutchinson, Margaret Cavendish, and Catharine Macaulay should be regarded as 'eccentric rarities'.[133] Although early modern women's engagement with historical discourse was unquestionably gendered—as predicated on the 'conditions and norms of its production'—their writings should be submitted to the same kind of reading as history written by men.[134]

An approach which does not exclude women from historiography is also supported by the fact that early modern women among the elite were in contact with historical discourse. Histories had started to proliferate under the reign of Elizabeth and the historical was present everywhere: not only in chronicles or general histories but also in plays, romances, lives, memoirs, letters, and so on.[135] In this context, as Woolf explains, women 'were very much interested in the past and contributed in several ways to what may be called the "social circulation" of historical knowledge by reading history, by acquiring familiarity with its details and certain documentary sources, and by discussing this knowledge conversationally or in private writings'.[136] Was not Elizabeth I herself reported to have translated Sallust? According to Worden, drawing on a comment by Sir Henry Savile, she probably wrote some 'historical reflections'.[137] In *A Survey of History*, a book destined for the gentry, the polygraph Richard Brathwaite extols the ladies of antiquity who were 'much addicted both to perusing and compiling Histories', specifying that 'neither were these Tasks onely for masculine *Spirits*'.[138] Zenobia, he claims, read 'both Romane and Greeke Histories' and 'abridged the *Alexandrian*, and all the *Orientall* Histories', while 'the daughter of *Pythagorias*' 'excell[ed] in all Historical discourses'.[139] It is likely that Brathwaite's admiration for ancient female readers and compilers of history was meant as a commentary on early modern practices, and an invitation to include, rather than exclude, women from historiographical practices.[140] Mihoko Suzuki has also shown that Anne Clifford, who was taught by Samuel Daniel, was an avid reader of history.

---

[133] Looser, *British Women Writers* 6.   [134] Looser, *British Women Writers* 6.
[135] Daniel R. Woolf, 'From Hystories to the Historical: Five Transitions in Thinking about the Past, 1500–1700', *Huntington Library Quarterly* 69.1–2 (2005): 33–70, here 37; 60–2. See F. Smith Fussner, 'The Varieties of History', *The Historical Revolution. English Historical Writing and Thought 1580–1640* (London: Routledge and Kegan Paul, 1962) 150–90.
[136] Woolf, 'A Feminine Past', 647.
[137] Blair Worden, 'Historians and Poets', *Huntington Library Quarterly* 68.1–2 (2005): 71–93, here 80. See also John-Mark Philo, 'Elizabeth I's Translation of Tacitus: Lambeth Palace Library, MS 683', *Review of English Studies* 71 (2020): 44–73.
[138] Brathwaite, *A Survey of History* 16.   [139] Brathwaite, *A Survey of History* 16–19.
[140] On the inclusion of women in the 'republic of letters', see David Norbrook, 'Women, the Republic of Letters, and the Public Sphere in the Mid-Seventeenth Century', *Criticism* 46.2 (2004): 223–40, here 224: 'Some women in the seventeenth century did indeed assume that certain spheres of discourse were universal, rather than specifically masculine.'

In *The Great Picture*, a large portrait recording her family history, she is portrayed with books of her own private library including William Camden's *Britannia* (1610), Samuel Daniel's *Chronicles of England* (1612), Plutarch's *Lives*, Commynes's *History* (1596)—all books that Lucy Hutchinson was also likely to have read.[141]

In a context where gentlewomen were encouraged to read and study history, it is no wonder that some of them felt as capable and entitled as men to relate their own experience of the traumatic events that they had gone through during the Civil War and Interregnum.[142] Such was the case of Ann Fanshawe, Anne Halkett, or Brilliana Harley, but also of Margaret Cavendish and of her neighbour in the 1660s, Lucy Hutchinson.[143] There is no evidence that Cavendish and Hutchinson ever met, but there is every reason to believe, according to Norbrook, that '[t]here was [...] an important dialectic between these writers. Hutchinson was arguably very powerfully influenced by Cavendish.'[144] In fact, the Duke of Cavendish is often mentioned in the *Memoirs*—but not his wife, in spite of her being quite a celebrity. Although William Cavendish was the leader of the royalists in the 1640s, Lucy Hutchinson does not describe him in hostile terms, introducing him as 'a Lord so much once beloved in his Country' (S61/K84), and still depicting him as a benevolent man, 'treat[ing] [the Colonel] very honorably' (S246/K300), when he was imprisoned at the Restoration.[145]

---

[141] Mihoko Suzuki, 'Anne Clifford and the Gendering of History', *Clio* 30.2 (2001): 195–219, here 211–13.

[142] Claire Gheeraert-Graffeuille, 'Mémoires de guerre au féminin : "Histoire singulière" et histoire nationale', *La Cuisine et le forum. L'émergence des femmes sur la scène publique pendant la Révolution anglaise* (Paris: L'Harmattan, 2005) 241–67. For an anthology of female memoir-writing of the Civil Wars, see Roger Hudson, *The Grand Quarrel: From the Civil War Memoirs of Mrs Lucy Hutchinson; Mrs Alice Thornton; Ann, Lady Fanshawe; Margaret Duchess of Newcastle; Anne, Lady Halkett, & the Letters of Brilliana, Lady Harley* (London: The Folio Society, 1993).

[143] See MacGillivray, *Restoration Historians* 5: 'The *feeling* of what it was like to live in the times of the war, a feeling that later historians have had to recapture by laborious study, by legitimate efforts of the imagination, and by uncertain conjecture, was a part of the experience of these historians.'

[144] David Norbrook, 'Margaret Cavendish and Lucy Hutchinson: Identity, Ideology and Politics', *In-Between* 9.1–2 (2000): 179–203, here 182. See also Norbrook, 'Introduction', *The Works of Lucy Hutchinson*, vol. 1, xxxiii–xxxiv. For other early comparisons between Lucy Hutchinson and Margaret Cavendish, see A. H. Upham, 'Lucy Hutchinson and the Duchess of Newcastle', *Anglia* 36 (1912): 200–20; Royce MacGillivray, 'The Upham Thesis and the Literary Debts of Mrs. Lucy Hutchinson', *Revue de l'université d'Ottawa* 40 (1970): 618–30; Gloria Italiano, 'Two Parallel Biographers of the Seventeenth Century: Margaret Cavendish and Lucy Hutchinson', *Critical Dimensions: English, German and Comparative Literature Essays in Honour of Aurelio Zanco*, ed. Mario Curreli and Alberto Martino (Cuneo: Saste, 1978) 241–51.

[145] Race, 'The British Museum MS. of the Life of Colonel Hutchinson', http://www.nottshistory.org.uk/articles/tts/tts1914/hutchinson1.htm (accessed 16/06/2019). See also Martyn Bennett, '"Every county had the civill warre, more or lesse within itselfe": The Realities of War in Lucy Hutchinson's Midland Shires', *The Seventeenth Century* 30.2 (2015): 191–206, here 195–7.

But the urge to write history was not felt by women alone; it was widely shared among people, men and women alike, who were not professional historians.[146] A similar desire manifested itself after the Fronde (1648–1653) in France: '[w]hen the fury of fighting subsided, when the guns fell silent, when people resigned themselves to defeat, then the memoir genre became self-evident, it imposed itself collectively as a necessity to recount experiences perceived as extraordinary.'[147] This was not a new phenomenon, if we believe Lucian:

> ever since the present situation arose – the war against the barbarians, the disaster in Armenia and the run of victories – every single person is writing history; nay more, they are all Thucydideses, Herodotuses and Xenophons to us, and very true, it seems, is the saying that "War is the father of all things" [note: Heraclitus] since at one stroke it has begotten so many historians.[148]

Most men and women who wrote memoirs and lives in the wake of the Civil Wars did not publish them.[149] There was nonetheless the notable exception of Margaret Cavendish, who, in 1667, published the *Life of William Cavendish* and boldly claimed her right as a woman to 'write of wars', justifying her putting pen to paper on the grounds of her acquaintance with the protagonists of the war and her belonging to the same country as those who fought in the Civil War:

> Nor is it inconsistent with my being a Woman, to write of Wars, that was neither between *Medes* and *Persians*, *Greeks* and *Trojans*, *Christians* and *Turks*; but among my own Countreymen, whose Customs and Inclinations, and most of the Persons that held any considerable Place in the Armies, was well known to me; and besides all that (which is above all) my Noble and Loyal Lord did act a chief Part in that fatal Tragedy, to have defended

---

[146] In 1622, Camden founded a lectureship in history at Oxford, which still exists. See Wyman H. Herendeen, 'William Camden (1551–1623), Historian and Herald' (2008), *Oxford Dictionary of National Biography*, DOI: 10.1093/ref:odnb/4431.

[147] Hersant and Tourrette, 'Introduction', *Le Front des Mémoires* 15–16 (my translation).

[148] Lucian, *How to Write History*, trans. K. Kilburn, Loeb Classical Library 430 (Cambridge, MA: Harvard UP, 1959) §2, 5. Edmund Bolton refers to Lucian with precision in *Hypercritica: Or, A Rule of Judgment, for Writing or Reading our History's* in *Ancient Critical Essays upon English Poets and Poësy*, vol. 2, ed. Joseph Haslewood (London: Robert Triphook, 1815) 225, 238. *Hypercritica* was written between 1618 and 1621. On Lucian in England, see Neil Rhodes, 'Pure and Common Greek in Early Tudor England', *The Culture of Translation in Early Modern England*, ed. Tania Demetriou and Rowan Tomlinson (Basingstoke: Palgrave Macmillan, 2015) 54.

[149] See Ann Fanshawe, *The Memoirs of Lady Fanshawe*, ed. Nicholas Harris Nicolas (London, 1829); Anne Halkett, *The Autobiography of Anne Lady Halkett*, ed. John Gough Nichols (London: Camden Society, 1875); Brilliana Harley, *Letters of the Lady Brilliana Harley*, ed. Thomas Taylor Lewis (London, Camden Society, 1854).

(if humane power could have done it) his most Gracious Soveraign, from the fury of his Rebellious Subjects.[150]

Cavendish's self-authorization to write of wars draws a significant link between history writing and early modern women's political commitment, suggesting more gender fluidity than is often assumed.[151] Contrary to Margaret Cavendish, Lucy Hutchinson does not defend women's right to write history in the *Memoirs*, but she nonetheless intervenes in her narration, asserting in various ways her authority as a historian. It is therefore my intention to confront the *Memoirs of the Life of Colonel Hutchinson* with other Restoration histories, written both by men and women, in order to show why and how the *Memoirs* may qualify as an important piece of Restoration historiography.[152]

3. Lucy Hutchinson's discursive horizon

The comparison of Lucy Hutchinson's works with Restoration histories is made possible by what Susan Wiseman calls 'her deep and rigorous engagement with the materials of elite masculine culture'.[153] In the 1817 preface to her theological works, Julius Hutchinson, who assumed that she was the author, not just the translator of *Of Theologie*, was already sensitive to her extensive learning:

> And it will be found, that there are displayed throughout the Work great scriptural learning, argumentative acuteness, classical genius, and extensive research, conjoined with an ample knowledge of the leading works of the Jewish, Heathen, and Christian writers on Theology, Ethics, Philosophy, Logic, and other branches of literature connected with the subjects brought under discussion.[154]

---

[150] Cavendish, *Life of William Cavendish* [sig. c^v].

[151] On the notion of gender fluidity in the context of the 'Fronde' (sometimes called the French Civil War), see Sophie Vergnes, 'Des discours de la discorde: Les femmes, la Fronde et l'écriture de l'histoire', *Études Épistémè* 19 (2011), https://doi.org/10.4000/episteme.627.

[152] See for instance: Edmund Ludlow, *Memoirs of Edmund Ludlow* (London, 1698); Denzil Holles, *Memoirs of Denzil Lord Holles, Baron of Ifield in Sussex, from the year 1641 to 1648* (London, 1699); Richard Baxter, *Reliquiæ Baxterianæ* (London, 1696); Edward Hyde, *The Life of Edward Earl of Clarendon* (Oxford, 1759); Thomas Fairfax, *Short Memorials of Thomas Lord Fairfax Written by Himself* (London, 1699). For a confrontation of Hutchinson, Clarendon, and Baxter, see Mayer, 'Lifewriting and Historiography', 75–93.

[153] Wiseman, *Conspiracy and Virtue* 209, 231.

[154] Lucy Hutchinson, *On the Principles of The Christian Religion, Addressed to her Daughter; and on Theology*, ed. Julius Hutchinson (London, 1817) iv. See the new edition in *The Works of Lucy Hutchinson*, vol. 2 and Norbrook's 'General Introduction', xv–xli.

Lucy Hutchinson's immense scholarship first stems from her humanist education. In the story of her own 'Life', she insists that she was educated in languages, as her father 'spar'd not any cost for the education of both his sons and daughters in languages, sciences, musick, dancing, and all other quallities befitting their father's house' (S207/K255). She only mentions French and Latin, but according to Norbrook she read and wrote Greek as well.[155] She was indeed an excellent Latinist, and reminds the reader that she 'was so apt that [she] outstript [her] brothers who were at schoole' (S288/K14). This ambition to 'outstrip' her brothers has led to the assumption that she may have undertaken the daunting translation of Lucretius's *De Rerum Natura* in order to compete with other translators of her time.[156] It is also highly probable that she had read most of the authors of the curriculum studied by the male educated gentry and aristocracy, in particular Sallust, Tacitus, Livy, Polybius, and Caesar.[157] Given her intellectual curiosity and her interest in books, she must have been aware of the contemporary publication of important historical translations, such as Lucan's *Pharsalia* by Thomas May, Thucydides' *Wars of the Peloponnese* by Thomas Hobbes, and Polybius's *History* by Edward Grimestone, all published in the first half of the seventeenth century.[158] It should also be noted that histories of the Wars of the Roses and of the French wars of religion—both considered as 'civil wars'—as well as of the Roman Civil Wars were also published in English in the 1640s.[159]

Unsurprisingly, Lucy Hutchinson's discursive horizon, defined by Kate Narveson as the 'full range of texts [she] read in print and manuscript and the oral discourses [she] participated in', was very broad, and not

---

[155] See David Norbrook, 'Lucy Hutchinson: Theology, Gender and Translation', *The Seventeenth Century* 30.3 (2015): 139–62, here 152.

[156] For an introduction to Hutchinson's interest in Lucretius, see Norbrook, 'Introduction', *The Works of Lucy Hutchinson*, vol. 1, xv–xlii. For other explanations, see Norbrook, 'Lucy Hutchinson: Theology, Gender and Translation', 140. He mentions the possible rivalry between Owthorpe and the 'Cavendish estates' as 'intellectual centres'.

[157] Elizabeth Scott-Baumann, *Forms of Engagement. Women, Poetry and Culture 1640-1680* (Oxford: Oxford UP, 2013) 24: 'The range of Hutchinson's writings reflects the range of her reading.' For an idea of the classical education received by Lucy Hutchinson, see Woolf, *The Idea of History* 186–7. See also Peter Burke, 'A Survey of the Popularity of Ancient Historians, 1450–1700', *History and Theory* 5.2 (1966) 135–52.

[158] Thucydides, *Eight Bookes of the Peloponnesian Warre*, trans. Thomas Hobbes; Lucan, *Lucans Pharsalia [...] Translated into English by T. M.* (London, 1626); Polybius, *The History of Polybius the Megalopolitan*, trans. Edward Grimeston (London, 1633).

[159] See Giovanni Francesco Biondi, *History of the Civill Wares of England* (London, 1641); Enrico Davila, *Historie of the Civill Warres of France* (London, 1647); Richard Fanshawe, 'A Short Discourse of the Long Civill Warres of Rome', in his translation of *Il Pastor Fido* (1648). See David Armitage, *Civil Wars: A History in Ideas* (New York: Penguin/Alfred A. Knopf, 2017) 101–3.

particularly 'feminine'.[160] It included ancient authors, such as Cicero, Plutarch, and Seneca, whom she quotes in the dedication, 'To my Children', and who reflected her fascination for books of all sorts, a fascination perceptible in her description of the library belonging to her husband's father, Sir Thomas Hutchinson. It was, she writes, the 'choycest library in that part of England' (S16/K33) which probably contained around one thousand books and was 'vallued at a thousand pounds' (S34/K53).[161] Unfortunately, no inventory of this library is extant, but we know that it held many theological works, as Thomas Hutchinson is reported to have 'entertain'd his melancholly among the old fathers and schoolemen' (S16/K33).[162] As for John Hutchinson, who benefited from his father's library at Owthorpe, he is said to have spent much time studying theology, especially the works of Calvin. It was an interest he must have shared with his wife, whose familiarity with the works of the Protestant Reformers and lay devotional culture is manifest in several of her writings.[163] Her religious Commonplace Book, filled after the Civil Wars and typical of female reading practices, contains excerpts from *The Institutes*, notes taken at sermons, some verses, and various religious reflections.[164] She was also the author of *On the Principles of the Christian Religion*, an educational treatise in the Calvinist faith dedicated to her daughter, and *On Theology*, the translation into English of the first two parts of John Owen's Latin treatise *Theologoumena Pantodapa*, a complex work that included passages in Greek and Hebrew and discussed many theological and philosophical sources. Both texts, published together in 1817, display Lucy Hutchinson's deep knowledge of theology.[165] Her exceptional theological discursive horizon was finally

---

[160] See Kate Narveson, *Bible Readers and Lay Writers in Early Modern England. Gender and Self-Definition in an Emergent Writing Culture* (Farnham: Ashgate, 2012) 15, 143. On Hutchinson's broad discursive horizon, see Scott-Baumann, *Forms of Engagement* 17–18.

[161] On this library and Lucy Hutchinson's writing and reading practices, see Norbrook, 'Lucy Hutchinson: Theology, Gender and Translation', 144–5.

[162] On this library and the theological culture of the Hutchinsons, see Norbrook, 'The Hutchinsons and Theology', *The Works of Lucy Hutchinson*, vol. 2, 3–12.

[163] On lay devotional culture, see Narveson, *Bible Readers* 4–5. In the *Memoirs* (S21/K38), Hutchinson mentions Lewis Bayly, *The Practise of Piety* (London, 1613). See Mark Burden, 'Lucy Hutchinson and Puritan Education', *The Seventeenth Century* 30.2 (2015): 163–78. Burden (167) gives evidence for her use of William Perkins, *The Whole Treatise of Cases of Conscience* (Cambridge, 1606) and William Ames, *The Marrow of Christian Divinity* (London, 1642). On Lucy Hutchinson's knowledge of theology, see all the introductory material to *The Works of Lucy Hutchinson* vol. 2, and Burden 166–9.

[164] Nottinghamshire Archives, *Religious Commonplace Book*, DD/HU3.

[165] Lucy Hutchinson, *The Principles of Christian Religion, Addressed to her Daughter, and on Theology*. Both treatises have been republished in *The Works of Lucy Hutchinson*, vol. 2, 155–432. See Elizabeth Clarke and Jane Stevenson's introductory materials to these works (155–80; 275–326). On *On Theology*, see Burden, 'Lucy Hutchinson and Puritan Education', 169–72. See Kate Narveson, 'The Source for Lucy Hutchinson's *On Theology*', *Notes and Queries* 36 (1989): 40–1. On Hutchinson's religious discursive horizon, see Elizabeth Clarke, 'Contextualizing the Woman Writer: Editing Lucy

completed by the conversations and disputations that took place within the Hutchinson household, the most famous example being a debate about paedobaptism she herself initiated.[166] Despite the radical ideas they discussed and tolerated, the Hutchinsons do not seem to have been members of an Independent church. Dealing with Lucy Hutchinson's religious ideas, Norbrook concludes that she 'had been consistently attached to what she would have considered to have been the mainstream of Reformed Protestantism'.[167] In the Restoration period, she could be called a Nonconformist in the original sense of the term: she did not agree with certain rituals of the Church of England. She did not officially separate from it, although there is evidence that after her husband's death, she attended John Owen's congregationalist conventicle in London.[168]

Another more secular commonplace book, probably filled 'around 1634–36 and the late 1640s until 1655 or so', reveals another important aspect of Lucy Hutchinson's discursive horizon: her familiarity with pre-Civil War Cavalier culture.[169] This notebook is a collection of various items written by several hands, among which can be found a transcription of John Denham's translation of *The Aeneid*, pieces of Cavalier poetry, ballads, pamphlets, and so on.[170] In the *Memoirs*, this Cavalier milieu is described in the pre-Civil War section, when Lucy Hutchinson was staying at Richmond where the 'Prince's court was' and where she met her future husband.[171]

Finally, Lucy Hutchinson's highly politicized *Memoirs* reveal her interest in contemporary politics, both at local and national levels. The Hutchinsons were regular readers of the many pamphlets and newsbooks which poured off from the presses in the middle years of the seventeenth century. When they arrived

---

Hutchinson's Religious Prose', *Editing Early Modern Women*, ed. Sarah C. E. Ross and Paul Salzman (Cambridge: Cambridge UP, 2016) 77–95. Norbrook thinks that Owen may have been more arduous to translate than Lucretius ('Lucy Hutchinson: Theology, Gender and Translation', 148).

[166] Norbrook, 'Lucy Hutchinson: Theology, Gender and Translation', 143. See *Memoirs*, ed. Sutherland, 34, 168–9, and ed. Keeble, 53, 210–11.

[167] Norbrook, 'The Hutchinsons and Theology', *The Works of Lucy Hutchinson*, vol. 2, 8, 17–18.

[168] N. H. Keeble, *The Literature of Nonconformity in Later Seventeenth-Century England* (Leicester: Leicester UP, 1987) 7: 'the term [nonconformity], in its original sense, referred to beneficed members of the established church whose Puritan convictions led them to omit some parts of the liturgy and to refuse to conform to some of the ceremonies laid down in the *Book of Common Prayer* and the canons of the church.' On Lucy Hutchinson attending John Owen's conventicle, see Norbrook, '*Order and Disorder*: The Poem and its Contexts', *Order and Disorder* xv–xvi.

[169] De Groot, 'John Denham and Lucy Hutchinson's Commonplace Book', 152; Norbrook, 'Lucy Hutchinson: Theology, Gender and Translation', 143. Ann Moss, *Printed Commonplace Books and the Structuring of Renaissance Thought* (Oxford: Oxford UP, 1996) 215–54.

[170] De Groot, 'John Denham', 149–50 for a list of the items to be found in Lucy Hutchinson's Commonplace Book. Nottinghamshire Archives, *Literary Commonplace Book*, MS DD/HU1.

[171] See *Memoirs*, ed. Sutherland, 45–61, and ed. Keeble, 27–32. De Groot, 'John Denham', 152. On Richmond see http://www.luminarium.org/encyclopedia/richmondpalace.htm (accessed 26/01/2019). See Scott-Baumann, *Forms of Engagement* 24–5.

at Owthorpe in 1641, 'Mr. Hutchinson [...] applied himselfe to understand the things then in dispute, and read all the publick papers that came forth betweene the King and Parliament, besides many other private treatises' (S53/K75). Lucy Hutchinson advises her readers to do the same and to consult the Parliament's 'printed papers' to understand 'the righteousnesse of the Parliament's cause in poynt of civill right' (S53/K75). Throughout the *Memoirs* she displays her ability to discuss all the theological and political issues of her troubled age. What is particularly remarkable is that in her posthumous debate with Thomas May about the origins of the Civil War, she is not afraid to challenge his views, de facto putting herself on the same footing as other Civil War historians.

4. Forms of history

Lucy Hutchinson did not only have an exceptional knowledge of the classics and of theology; she was also an incomparable mistress of literary form, surpassing many historians of the Restoration. This aspect of her work has rarely been studied although her stylistic and formal qualities have been recognized in passing. According to Norbrook, 'in casting her relationship within aesthetic terms [...] she reminds us that she and not her husband was the real artist'.[172] MacGillivray praises Lucy Hutchinson's 'style of exceptional clarity, expressiveness and rhetorical force'.[173] He considers her ability to interweave the narrative of her husband's life with national history unequalled among her contemporaries, and argues that her art was superior to that of Margaret Cavendish and Edmund Ludlow.[174] As a reader of literature and ancient history, Lucy Hutchinson was effectively aware of the formal work which the writing of history required. This was underscored by Lucian in his treatise on *How to Write History*—a treatise that inspired most *artes historicae* of the Renaissance:[175]

> they think it is perfectly simple and easy to write history and that anyone can do it if only he can put what comes to him into words. As to that, I'm sure you know as well as I do, my dear friend, that history is not one of those

---

[172] David Norbrook, 'Lucy Hutchinson, *Memoirs*', *A Companion to Literature from Milton to Blake*, ed. David Womersley (Oxford: Blackwell, 2001) 182–8, here 183.

[173] MacGillivray, *Restoration Historians* 175. Looser calls Hutchinson's *Memoirs* 'a narratively skilled text' (*British Women Writers* 38).

[174] See MacGillivray, 'Edmund Ludlow and Mrs. Lucy Hutchinson', 170–85; Mayer, 'A Life of Writing', 319. On the art of composition see Susan Cook, '"The story I most particularly intend": The Narrative Style of Lucy Hutchinson', *Critical Survey* 5.3 (1993): 271–7.

[175] J. H. M. Salmon, 'Precept, Example, and Truth: Degory Wheare and the *Ars Historica*', *The Historical Imagination*, ed. Kelley and Sacks, 13.

things that can be put in hand without effort and can be put together lazily, but is something which needs, if anything does in literature, a great deal of thought if it is to be what Thucydides calls "a possession for evermore."[176]

Thomas Hobbes, who translated Thucydides' *Peloponnesian Warres*, similarly underlined the importance of form, asserting that 'in *Truth* consisteth the *Soule*, and in *Eloquution* the *Body* of History. The latter without the former, is but a picture of History; and the former without the latter, unapt to instruct.'[177] It seems that Hobbes and Thucydides's concern with form, which was widespread among early modern historians and commentators, has sometimes been overlooked by literary critics and historians today, who tend to dwell on the documentary contents and neglect the eloquence of memoirs and lives.[178] Yet, '[w]e need,' as Sharpe and Zwicker signalled, 'a deeper sense of the rhetoric of the early modern life'.[179] The practice of history, Roger Chartier reminds us, is not only about facts but also about form(s) which always produce meaning. Therefore, when studying Lucy Hutchinson's *Memoirs*, we should—in Chartier's words—look at 'their discursive and material organization, their conditions of production, and their strategic utilization'.[180]

The main obstacle to a formal approach to the *Memoirs* lies in the fact that critics and readers have often privileged the gendered and political issues of the text over its rhetorical and formal aspects, which were yet fundamental in a late seventeenth-century context of writing. Critics, since the middle of the nineteenth century, have focused on the tensions between Lucy Hutchinson's

---

[176] Lucian, *How to Write History*, §5, 6–7.
[177] Hobbes, 'On the Life and History of Thucydides', *Eight Bookes of the Peloponnesian Warre*, np.
[178] For scholarship drawing on memoirs as sources of history, see Charles Carlton, *Going to the Wars. The Experience of the British Civil Wars 1638-1651* (London and New York: Routledge, 1992); Mark Kishlansky, 'Mission Impossible: Charles I, Oliver Cromwell and the Regicide', *The English Historical Review* 125.515 (2010): 844–74; Roger B. Manning 'Styles of Command in Seventeenth-Century English Armies', *The Journal of Military History* 71.3 (2007): 671–99; Micheál Ó Siochrú, 'Atrocity, Codes of Conduct and the Irish in the British Civil Wars 1641–1653', *Past and Present* 195.1 (2007): 55–86.
[179] Sharpe and Zwicker, *Writing Lives* 6. See Mayer and Woolf, *The Rhetorics of Life-Writing* 1–37 and Lesne, *La Poétique des mémoires*. For a special attention to language, see Isabel Rivers, *Reason, Grace, and Sentiment. A Study of the Language of Religion and Ethics in England 1660-1780* (Cambridge: Cambridge UP, 1991), vol. 1, 2–3. Charbonneau (*Les Silences de l'histoire* 5) also insists on the form of history and on its overall neglect by critics. Such an approach is also forcefully advocated by Lucia Bergamasco, 'Hagiographie et sainteté en Angleterre aux XVIe-XVIIIe siècles', *Annales, Économies, Sociétés, Civilisations* 5 (1993): 1053–85, here 1056. Bergamasco chooses to employ the methodologies of literary scholars to approach religious lives to show their complexity and their proximity with hagiography.
[180] Roger Chartier, *On the Edge of the Cliff: History, Language, and Practices*, trans. Lydia G. Cochrane (Baltimore: Johns Hopkins UP, 1997) 5 and *The Order of Books: Readers, Authors, and Libraries in Europe Between the Fourteenth and Eighteenth Centuries*, trans. Lydia G. Cochrane (Stanford: Stanford UP, 1994) 2–3.

patriarchal representation of herself as good Puritan wife and the radical politics of the *Memoirs*, more rarely with Lucy Hutchinson's craft as a historian. The formal approach to women's poetry advocated by Elizabeth Scott-Baumann in *Forms of Engagement* seems particularly apposite to examine the work of Lucy Hutchinson whom she ranks, with Margaret Cavendish and Katherine Philips, among the 'formal pioneers'. What Scott-Baumann writes about Lucy Hutchinson's poetry can be applied to her prose *Memoirs* in which the use of form is also crucial: '[Poetic] form,' she argues, 'is a site for experimentation and engagement, and [...] women poets' choices and uses of form reveal their close engagement with their literary and intellectual culture.'[181] Like Looser and Longfellow before her, Scott-Baumann rejects the assumption that women's writing practices were *in essence* different from those of men. On the contrary, without denying the specificities of women's writing—women did not write in the same circumstances as men—she believes they drew on the same literary traditions and codes, and calls therefore for further work on the appropriation of these conventions by women. As Sasha Roberts puts it:

> We need further to grasp that the formal conventions, experiments and innovations of early modern women's writing were made in the context of a literary and critical culture that placed high value on form; hence the emphasis in so much Renaissance literary criticism on rhetorical forms, imitation (that is, understanding formal models), and decorum (adapting form and style to subject matter). Or more succinctly, early modern women's writing is *predicated* on their engagement with literary form.[182]

It will therefore be necessary, in order to assess the significance of Lucy Hutchinson's *Memoirs*, to take into account their formal and discursive features as well as their composition.

Such a study appears all the more necessary as English Restoration memoirs, despite a few notable exceptions, have mainly been used for their historical contents.[183] Contrary to French memoirs, which have been the object of several important literary studies in recent years, little attention has been paid

---

[181] Scott-Baumann, *Forms of Engagement* 3.
[182] Sasha Roberts, 'Feminist Criticism and the New Formalism: Early Modern Women and Literary Engagement', *The Impact of Feminism in English Renaissance Studies*, ed. Dympna Callaghan (Basingstoke: Palgrave, 2007) 76, quoted in Scott-Baumann, *Forms of Engagement* 15.
[183] Some studies favour a more formal approach. See Keeble, *Richard Baxter: Puritan Man of Letters*; Brownley, *Clarendon and the Rhetoric of Historical Form*; Wiseman, *Conspiracy and Virtue*.

so far to the poetic and rhetorical qualities of English Restoration memoirs and they would therefore greatly benefit from being studied as literary works.[184] This is particularly the case with Lucy Hutchinson's *Memoirs* which Julius Hutchinson, in his 1806 preface, described as a 'literary curiosity of no mean sort'.[185] To start with, as I will show in the following chapters, they stem from the same literary traditions and models as their French counterparts—mostly ancient and humanist historical writings—and are based on comparable experiences of history, their authors being either spectators or actors of the events they record. Next, another striking poetic feature that they have in common with French memoirs is their generic hybridity, noted by Julius Hutchinson who maintains that Lucy Hutchinson's writing 'carries with it all the interest of a novel'.[186] The poetic genres on which she draws, sometimes mentioned in passing, have never been explored in detail.[187] This is the case with historical genres—chiefly lives and memoirs—but also with other genres which she occasionally taps—anecdotes, historical summaries, short biographies, portraits, and satirical and polemical pieces—which all deserve further attention. The result of such hybridity is a protean text, difficult to categorize, unless we recognize that Lucy Hutchinson's handling of genres offers a unique insight into the history of the English Revolution.

Therefore, following Scott-Baumann's advice to concentrate on form, I will contend that Lucy Hutchinson's contribution to Restoration historiography can only be fully apprehended if one takes into consideration her meticulous craft as well as her appropriation of different forms and genres. In other words, my approach to the *Memoirs* will be both contextualizing and formalistic, for the two aspects are inseparable like the two sides of the same coin.[188] The historiographical angle chosen here aims at contributing to the exploration of a rich and complex work which has never been to this day the object of a monograph. Despite sustained interest in the *Memoirs* for more than twenty years now, there is still room for further research. As David Norbrook has

---

[184] Lesne calls 'poetics' the features shared by the French memoirs (1650–1685) she studies (23). For studies of French memoirs, see Kuperty-Tsur, Lesne, Charbonneau, Briot, Fumaroli mentioned above.
[185] Julius Hutchinson, 'Preface', *Memoirs* x.   [186] Julius Hutchinson, 'Preface', *Memoirs* xiv.
[187] Looser looks at the *Memoirs* as history, but she does not study in detail Lucy Hutchinson's use of genres.
[188] See Nora, 'Memoirs of Men of State', 402. Nora deplores the split between history and literature: 'This ever-changing, multiform and omnipresent genre [memoirs] appears torn between the view of the historian, who searches for hidden truths in memoirs that are presumed suspect, and that of the literary critic, who is more concerned with the aesthetic evolution of the genre than with the historical conditions in which the texts were produced' (402).

argued: '[f]rom having been the only work of Hutchinson's to receive attention, the *Memoirs* have fallen into eclipse.'[189]

*

The present monograph starts by exploring the several historical genres brought together in 'The Life of John Hutchinson', in order to show how Lucy Hutchinson builds her authority as a historian of the Civil Wars. Chapter 1, 'Life-writing and exemplarity', aims to highlight the different modes of life-writing which Lucy Hutchinson drew upon in order to construct the exemplarity of her husband. After an overview of early modern exemplarity, it examines her twofold indebtedness to humanist life-writing inherited from Plutarch and to the Protestant tradition of godly lives. By extolling the Colonel as a Renaissance gentleman and a saint, Lucy Hutchinson seeks to persuade the reader to follow his example by emulating his commitment to the public cause. However, such extreme idealization of the Colonel's virtues, especially in her dedication to her children, borders on idolatry, a sinful attitude that is vigorously condemned by Calvinists. The chapter will study Lucy Hutchinson's ambivalent treatment of her husband's virtues and aura, as well as the strategies she adopts to describe him as a true Protestant saint.

Chapter 2, 'The *Memoirs* and historiography', surveys early modern historiographical debates before and after the Civil Wars. It brings to the fore a growing 'culture of facts', the distrust of rhetoric, and the obsession with historical truth, before turning to the impact of the mid-seventeenth-century crisis on historiographical debates. In those times of conflict, the sense that all truth was divided—and even lost—gave more credit to first-hand testimonies than to more general histories. As shall be argued in this chapter, Lucy Hutchinson's experience-based *Memoirs* reflect—and respond to—contemporary historiographical debates, thus deserving pride of place among the many testimonies that were written in the wake of the Civil Wars.

Chapter 3, 'The experience of the Civil War in Nottingham', demonstrates that Lucy Hutchinson's historiographical undertaking cannot be understood outside the epistemology of experience on which the memoir genre is based. It starts by examining her paradoxical position as a witness of the Civil War in Nottingham. Even though she was kept at a distance from military operations, living in the castle of Nottingham and being the Colonel's confidant put her in a unique position to record the events experienced by her husband and, occasionally, by herself. This privileged position also enabled her to disclose

---

[189] See Norbrook, 'Lucy Hutchinson: Theology, Gender and Translation', 141.

to the reader what was taking place behind the scenes of history, in particular the negotiations conducted between the Colonel and his royalist enemies, as well as the machinations that tore apart the Nottingham Committee of War. The chapter ends with the paradox that Lucy Hutchinson's local account also serves as a commentary on national politics and provides an exceptional insight into the anthropological realities of the Civil War.

Chapter 4, 'Writing oneself into history: the paradoxes of Lucy Hutchinson's agency', concentrates on the final quarter of the *Memoirs* covering the years 1660–1664 when, as she was stepping out of her own sphere to intervene in Restoration politics, Lucy Hutchinson's role changed from witness to actor—a highly prized role among early modern memoir-writers. By exploring the links between Lucy Hutchinson, an agent in history, and Lucy Hutchinson, the author of the *Memoirs*, this chapter looks at the ways in which, despite patriarchal prohibitions, she writes herself into history to come to grips with her past. In this autobiographical portion of the *Memoirs*, Lucy Hutchinson's search for personal intelligibility proves to be inseparable from her vindication of the Colonel. Simultaneously, her profession of truth becomes more problematic as she ostensibly tinkers with history and memory.

Chapter 5 and Chapter 6 delve into the historian's workshop. Chapter 5, 'The historian's craft (1): Lucy Hutchinson's art of narration', confronts Lucy Hutchinson's earlier relation of her husband's role during the Civil War between 1642 and 1645—'the Notebook'—with the corresponding account in the *Memoirs*. In the Notebook, Lucy Hutchinson was offering the defence of her husband as a governor of the town and castle of Nottingham; she had not conceived the full project of the *Memoirs* as a monument to his memory yet. But this does not mean she lacked historiographical and literary ambition. This chapter first charts how, in both narratives, Lucy Hutchinson exploits romance tropes so as to give shape and meaning to the confused realities of the Civil War. Second, it shows how she unremittingly fathoms the treacherous motives of the Colonel's adversaries, showing her art as a moralist, a story-teller, and a polemicist. Chapter 6, 'The historian's craft (2): Lucy Hutchinson's art of digression', seeks to articulate Lucy Hutchinson's use of digressions with her apologetic purpose, namely the rehabilitation of the Colonel's actions during the Civil War and Interregnum. For the sake of clarity, a typology of digressions is presented. First, the polemical digressions, which explore the long- and short-term causes of the Civil Wars, provide an apt discursive strategy to write about national history. Second, the politico-narrative digressions offer both a synoptic vision of the English Civil War and a defence of tyrannicide. Third, the moral digressions shed light on the persecution of the Colonel in the 1640s and foreshadow his final sufferings and death. The chapter finally argues that providence plays a crucial part in the economy of the *Memoirs* by allowing the convergence of several narrative lines and the integration of the life of Colonel Hutchinson into a larger eschatological framework.

Chapter 1
Life-writing and exemplarity

In 1645, when he was still a very young man of eighteen, John Hall completed a historiographical treatise, *A Method in History*, about the reading and the use of histories, which owed much to other *artes historicae*, composed both in England and on the Continent.[1] In the final pages of his work, he deplores the shortcomings of histories 'fraught wth impertinent & lying Legend', as well as of epitomes that were 'bodyes sine succo & sanguine'.[2] By contrast, he praises lives as being a 'profitable kind of writing'. Unlike other accounts, he argues, lives give access to the true self of historical figures:

> I had forgot to speake of the Writers of Liues [. . .]. They are a profitable kind of writing, they pull of the disguises of great men & paint them in their natiue colours, a man's interiour actions being the best Indices of his mind. It was a wise scrutiny & not so curious as honest in Mountague [Montaigne] to know rather what Brutus did in his Tent the night before the battayle, then in the battayle it selfe, men in their publick actions being almost meer Mimicks, in their priuate they put off their assumed habits & become themselues again.[3]

When Hall refers to the profitability of lives, he points to the 'morall instruction' that is dispensed in this type of history.[4] His treatise significantly ends with an interesting reading list of 'lives' that goes from William Martyn's *The Historie, and Lives, of Twentie Kings of England* (1615) to William Camden's *Annales: The True and Royall History of the Famous Empresse Elizabeth* (1630).[5] The centrality of exemplarity in early modern lives—the chief genre in which the history of the Revolution was written—is well underlined by

---

[1] See Joad Raymond, 'Hall, John (bap. 1627, d. 1656), poet and writer' (2004), *Oxford Dictionary of National Biography*, DOI: 10.1093/ref:odnb/11969. On that treatise, see Raymond, 'John Hall's *A Method of History*: A Book Lost and Found (with transcription)', *English Literary Renaissance* 28.2 (1988): 267–98, here 270–2. Hall's treatise shares similarities with Wheare's *De ratione et methodi legendi historias*; it is also much indebted to Bacon's *Advancement of Learning*.
[2] Hall, *A Method of History* [15]–[15^v], ed. Raymond, 296.
[3] Hall, *A Method of History* [17]–[17^v], ed. Raymond, 297.
[4] Hall, *A Method of History* [17^v], ed. Raymond, 297.
[5] Hall, *A Method of History* [18]–[18^v], ed. Raymond, 297–8.

Sharpe and Zwicker, who point out that behind the variety of lives and their diversity of purpose lie their authors' concern with exemplarity:

> exemplarity is at the heart of early modern lives and early modern life writing. From classical antiquity and medieval hagiography, Renaissance writers inherited, edited and re-presented exemplary lives of scholarship, sanctity, and civic virtue. [...] And the exemplary life was more often than not a polemical as much as pedagogic text, an ethical example, an ideological formation, but also a political argument. Early modern lives were above all lives written for use.[6]

This chapter argues that exemplarity in its various aspects—ethical, political, and religious—was central to the 'Life of John Hutchinson'. From the outset the Colonel is indeed set as an example that is neither questioned nor tarnished in the entire narrative.[7] Nevertheless, Lucy Hutchinson was not an indiscriminate flatterer: she was acutely aware of the difficulties attending the task of representing exemplary virtue and did not ignore the inherent risks of idolatry.

1. The art of exemplarity

Since the time of Plutarch, 'that true Moral Historian' and 'the Father of *Histories*',[8] lives had been regarded as particular history and often preferred to general history.[9] Amyot, in his preface to the translation of Plutarch's *Lives* (1579), insisted on the diversity of history and made a distinction between 'two chiefe kinds' of history, the better to show the advantages of 'lives' over 'historie'—here understood as general history—

---

[6] Sharpe and Zwicker, 'Introducing Lives', 4. On life-writing and history, see Pritchard, *English Biography*; Albert Buford, 'History and Biography', *A Tribute to George Coffin Taylor. Studies and Essays*, ed. Arnold Williams (Richmond: U of North California P, 1952) 100–12; Debora Shuger, 'Life-Writing in Seventeenth-Century England', *Representations of the Self from the Renaissance to Romanticism*, ed. Patrick Coleman, Jayne Lewis, and Jill Kowalik (Cambridge: Cambridge UP, 2000) 63–78. Shuger notes that life-writing includes 'memoirs, diaries, epistolary collections, hagiographies, character sketches and royal lives' (63).

[7] On life-writing and the issue of representation, see Sharpe and Zwicker, 'Introducing Lives', 9–10.

[8] Brathwaite, *A Survey of History* 113. On the front page of Amyot's 1579 edition, Plutarch is called 'that graue learned Philosopher and Historiographer'.

[9] On the origins of life-writing before Plutarch, see Mayer and Woolf, *The Rhetorics of Life-Writing* 10–11. On Plutarch, as a moral philosopher, see François Hartog, *Anciens, modernes, sauvages* (Paris: Galaade, 2005) 101–10.

The one which setteth downe mens doings and adventures at length, is called by the common name of an historie: the other which declareth their natures, sayings, and maners, is properly named their liues. [...] the one is more common, and the other more priuate: the one concerneth more the things that are without the man, and the other the things that proceede from within: the one the euents, the other the consultacions.[10]

Such distinctions were made by most subsequent commentators. Bodin, in his *Methodus* (1566), established a tripartite distinction between the history of nations (*maximae respublicae*), the history of cities (*minimae respublicae)* and lives (*res gestae virorum*).[11] Bacon, in *The Advancement of Learning* (1605), argued that lives should be privileged over more general history: 'I doe finde strange,' he wrote, 'that these times haue so little esteemed the vertues of the times, as the Writing of liues should be no more frequent.'[12] The reason why Bacon preferred lives to history of times comes from the fact that the latter '[pass] ouer in silence the smaller passages and Motions of men and Matters',[13] which were nevertheless essential for a historian intent on uncovering the 'true and inward resorts' of men's actions. In highlighting particulars and the individual's character, Bacon was still indebted to Plutarch who wrote that lives, in their attention to detail, were indeed more likely to reveal men's vices then epics and chronicles:

my intent is not to write histories, but only liues. For the noblest deedes doe not always shew mens vertues and vices, but oftentimes a light occasion, a word, or some sporte makes mens naturall dispositions and maners appeare more plaine, then the famous battells wonne, wherein a slaine tenne thowsand men, or the great armies, or cities wonne by siege or assault.[14]

This unanimously praised ethical utility of lives was closely associated with their use in the education of princes and statesmen, who were the target readers of exemplary history.[15] In the words of Richard Brathwaite, history

---

[10] Plutarch, 'Amiot to the Readers', np. Thomas North's English edition of Plutarch's *Lives* (1579) was based on the French translation by Amyot of Plutarch's work (1559). North also translated the French preface.

[11] On this distinction see Donald R. Kelley, 'The Development and Context of Bodin's Method', *Jean Bodin* [1973, 2006], ed. Julian H. Franklin (London: Routledge, 2016) 142.

[12] Bacon, *The Second Booke* 14. On the distinction between *life* and *history* in Bacon and Plutarch, see Buford, 'History and Biography, the Renaissance Distinction', 105–7.

[13] Bacon, *The Second Booke* 12.   [14] Plutarch, *The Lives*, 'The Life of Alexander the Great', 722.

[15] The translator, Thomas North, writes: 'there is no prophane studye better then Plutarke'; 'he hath written the profitablest story of all Authors' ('To the Reader', np). See Donald R. Kelley, 'Philosophy

was seen as a store 'of Eminent Types and Copies'.[16] This conception of history, directly inherited from Cicero's conception of history as *historia magistra vitae*,[17] was echoed by Amyot, in his preface to Plutarch's *Lives*, who recommended the reading of Plutarch's opus to the 'great Princes and Kings'.[18] Lives, Amyot continued, were most valued because they were thought to teach future rulers 'how to judge of things present, & to foresee things to come: so as we may knowe what to like of, & what to follow, what to mislike, and what to eschew'.[19] As for the English humanist and historiographer Thomas Blundeville, he argued, in a preface dedicated 'to the most Noble Erle of Leycester', that the 'reading of Hystories, the true Image and portrature of Mans lyfe' was an invaluable help for a statesman 'to direct [his] priuate actions, as to giue Counsell lyke a most prudent Counseller in publyke causes, be it matters of warre, or peace'.[20] Also following Plutarch, he believed exemplarity was central in preparing men to action. The example of the wise should teach us, he wrote, to 'behaue our selues in all our actions, as well priuate as publique, both in time of peace and warre'.[21] What mattered for Blundeville was the moral profit which individuals and commonwealths could draw from history. Meanwhile, he considered that a history only seeking 'the discents, genealoges, and petygrees, of noble men', that is, the sort of history practised by antiquarians, was vain because devoid of any clear moral purpose.[22] Bacon followed suit, when he pointed out how lives 'excelled [history of times] in profit and in use'.[23] In his *Essayes* he claimed accordingly that 'men in great place' should conform to the best examples of the past in order to become in their turns good examples worthy to be imitated: 'In the discharge of thy place set before thee the best examples; for imitation is a globe of precepts. [...] Neglect not also the examples of those that have carried themselves ill in the same place; not to set off thyself by taxing their memory, but to direct thyself what to avoid.'[24]

---

and Humanistic Disciplines: The Theory of History', *Cambridge History of Renaissance Philosophy*, ed. C. B. Schmitt, Jill Kraye, Eckhard Kessler, and Quentin Skinner (Cambridge: Cambridge UP, 1988) 750. See also Hartog, *Anciens, modernes, sauvages* 103–5.
[16] Brathwaite, *A Survey of History* 3. Worden speaks of 'a storehouse of example, a database of knowledge and wisdom' ('Historians and Poets', 77).
[17] Cicero, *De oratore* II, 9, 36: '*historia vero testis temporum, lux veritatis, vita memoriae, magistra vitae*. In English: 'history, the witness of the times, the light of truth, the life of memory, the teacher of life' (my translation).
[18] Plutarch, 'Amiot to the Reader', np.   [19] Plutarch, 'Amiot to the Reader', np.
[20] Thomas Blundeville, *The True Order and Methode of Wryting and Reading of Hystories* (1574) [sig. Aij].
[21] Blundeville, 'What order and methode is to be obserued in reading hystories' (Fij^v).
[22] Blundeville, *The True Order and Methode* [sig. Hiv].   [23] Bacon, *The Second Booke* 11.
[24] Francis Bacon, '11. Of Great Place', *Essays or Counsels, Civil and Moral* [1625], in *The Major Works*, ed. Brian Vickers (Oxford: Oxford UP, 1996) 360. A similar idea was put forward by

For all these early modern commentators, examples, whether good or bad, had more persuasive force than other precepts taught by general history. As Puttenham put it, 'no kinde of argument in all the Oratorie craft doth better perswade and more uniuersally satisfie then example, which is but the representation of old memories, and like successes happened in times past.'[25] Because they were more cogent than precepts and demonstrations, exemplary lives were more likely to spur people into action than general histories and chronicles. In other words, according to Amyot, their singular force lay in their eloquence:

> examples are of more force to move and instruct, than are the arguments and proofes of reason or their precise precepts, bicause examples be the very formes of our deedes, & accompanied with all circumstances. Whereas reasons and demonstrations are generall, and tend to the proofe of things, and to the beating of them into understanding: and examples tende to the showing of them in practise and execution, bicause they doe not only declare what is to be done, but also worke a desire to do it.[26]

Lucy Hutchinson's 'Life of John Hutchinson' falls within this humanist tradition of life-writing inherited from Plutarch and makes ample use of exemplarity, as when the Colonel is described as 'a notable [example] of living' that should be 'registered in perpetual memory'.[27] Giving examples of the Colonel's excellence is the best way for Lucy Hutchinson to persuade 'succeeding generations' of his integrity, which both royalists and republicans questioned at the Restoration.[28] The former blamed him for signing the King's death warrant while the latter considered the presence of his name in the Act of Oblivion as betrayal. The demonstration of Colonel Hutchinson's exemplariness was not only a way for his wife to clear his name but also a means to turn him into a historical figure to be emulated by future generations. She wanted to give a lesson in history and, to this end, it had to be, to quote Amyot again,

---

Machiavelli in *The Prince*: 'For men almost always follow in the footsteps of others, imitation, being a leading principle of human behaviour,' but 'a shrewd man,' he adds, 'will always follow the methods of a remarkable man, and imitate those who have been outstanding.' See Niccolò Machiavelli, *The Prince*, ed. Quentin Skinner and Russel Price (Cambridge: Cambridge UP, 1988), Chapter 6, §968 (Kindle edition). See John D. Lyons, *Exemplum: The Rhetoric of Example in Early Modern France and Italy* (Princeton: Princeton UP, 1989) 35–71.

[25] George Puttenham, 'Of Historicall Poesie', *The Arte of English Poesie* (London, 1589), 31.
[26] Plutarch, 'Amiot to the Reader', np. On the rhetorical force of exemplarity in history, see Salmon, 'Precept, Example, and Truth', 12–13.
[27] This quote is drawn from what N. H. Keeble calls 'Final Meditation' (337) in his edition of the *Memoirs*. These two pages are not reproduced in Sutherland's edition. See *Memoirs*, DD/HU4, [421].
[28] Lucy Hutchinson, 'Final Meditation', *Memoirs*, ed. Keeble, 337; see *Memoirs*, DD/HU4, [421].

'an eloquent history'.[29] This programme is clearly announced in the dedication, 'To my Children', placed before the 'Life of John Hutchinson', which gives a synthetic picture of the Colonel's exemplarity.

Lucy Hutchinson was acutely aware that the force of exemplarity depended on the rhetorical quality of her narrative; in other words, her own success in persuading her readers was predicated on her mastery of the 'oratorie craft'. This is what she implies in the following hyperbolic statement in the Dedication: 'had I but the power of *rightly disposing* and *relating* these [virtues], his [the Colonel's] single example would be more instructive than all the rules of the best moralists' (S5/K20–1, my emphasis). The opening pages of the 'Life' (S15–23/K30–41) also reveal that she was familiar with the formal conventions of life-writing as they were for instance formulated by Thomas Blundeville.[30] Drawing on Francesco Patrizi's *Della Historia*, the historian explains 'what order and disposition in writing hystories [hystoriographers] ought to use'.[31] Among the most important ingredients to write a life, he lists the man's pedigree and background, his physical appearance, his education, his actions, his speeches—all the things which may help understand his destiny as well as the motions of his mind:

> To bring therefore into a briefe summe those things which are chiefly to bee considered by the wryter, who hath to chronicle any mans life: I saye that they be these. The name of the man, his familie, his parentes, and his Countrye, and also his destinie, fortune, and force or necessitie, (if they seeme manifestly to appertayne to the action) his nature, affections, and election, proceeding eyther of wisedome, passion, or custome, his education, exercises, deedes, and speaches, and also the age, and time, wherein every notable acte was done, and the qualities of his bodye, whither they were signes and tokens of his mynde, or else helps to the actions. And as the writer is bounde to shew the education of the person chronicled, and those exercises, and studyes, whereby hee hath formed hys maners: so also he is bounde to tell euery deede, worde, signe, or token, that maye signifie eyther his maners, his nature, his affections, thoughts, or any maner of motion of the mynde.[32]

---

[29] Plutarch, 'Amiot to the Reader', np.
[30] On Blundeville, see the commentary and edition of the treatise in Hugh G. Dick, 'Thomas Blundeville's *The True Order and Methode of Wryting and Reading Hystories*', *Huntington Library Quarterly* 3 (1940): 149–70.
[31] Blundeville, *The True Order and Methode* [sig. E[iv]].
[32] Blundeville, *The True Order and Methode* [sig. D j[v]].

To a large extent, Lucy Hutchinson follows these instructions. At the beginning of the life *per se* she starts by presenting 'his familie, his parentes, and his Countrye' in accordance with Blundeville's method. She establishes a genealogy of virtue, honour, and piety, and grounds it in Nottinghamshire, in order to legitimize the long narrative that follows. Her 'act of genealogical inscription' is here essential:[33]

> He was the eldest surviving sonne of Sir Thomas Hutchinson and the Lady Margarett, his first wife, one of the daughters of Sir John Biron, of Newsted, in the same county, two persons so eminently vertuous and pious in their generations that to descend from them was to sett up in the world upon a good stock of honor, which oblieg'd their posterity to emproove it, as much as it was their privilledge to inheritt their parents' glories. (S15/K31)[34]

The virtue of John Hutchinson's family is next guaranteed by the stories of his ancestors, which Lucy Hutchinson collected from people of her acquaintance:

> I spoke with one old man who had knowne five successions of them in these parts, where their hospitallity, their love to their country, their plaine and honest conversation with all men, their generous and unambitious inclinations, had made the famely continue as belov'd and reputed as any of the prouder houses in the country. (S15/K31–2)

When she tackles the story of John Hutchinson's mother, Lucy Hutchinson represents herself as the depositary of family stories and the 'recorder' of a 'chronicle'. Once again, she uses the first-person narrative—a relatively isolated practice within the *Memoirs* where she mostly refers to herself as 'Mrs. Hutchinson', that is, the wife of John Hutchinson:

> [John Hutchinson's mother] was a wise and bountifull mistresse in her famely, a blessing to her tenants and neighbourhood, and had an indulgent tendernesse to her infants; but death veiled all her mortall glories in the 26th yeare of her age, and the stories I receiv'd of her have bene but scanty epitaphs of those things which were worthy of a large chronicle and a better Recorder than I can be. (S18/K34)

---

[33] See Burden, 'Editing Shadows', 174.
[34] See Norbrook, 'Memoirs and Oblivion', 253. Norbrook mentions a full study on the Hutchinsons and Birons. Violet M. Walker, *The House of Byron: A History of the Family from the Norman Conquest 1066–1988*, revised and completed by Margaret J. Howell (London: Quiller Press, 1988).

By taking the role of family historian, Lucy Hutchinson engages in historical practices with which women were often associated, as they collected evidence and anecdotes for the benefit of antiquarians.[35] What is interesting about this page of family history is that it reads like a digression which is considered as an indispensable record for the understanding of John Hutchinson's life:[36]

> There is a story of her father and mother so memorable that, though it be not alltogether pertinent to their grandchild's affaires, which I only intend, yet I shall here putt it in, since the third generation, for whom I make this collection, is not alltogether unconcern'd in the greate grandfather, who was not the eldest sonne of his father, Sir John Byron, but had an elder brother that had married a private gentleman's daughter in the country, and so displeas'd his father in that match, that he intended an equall part of his estate to this Sir John Biron, his younger sonne, and thereupon married him to a young lady who was one of the daughters of my lord [Fitzwilliam], that had bene Deputy of Ireland in the reigne of Queene Elizabeth, and liv'd as a prince in that country.   (S18/K35)

The way the various elements of family history are concatenated and condensed in one single sentence in the above quotation leaves the reader in no doubt that Lucy Hutchinson has a plan, which is to introduce all the protagonists of her story, as if she had to write the exposition of a play, which would soon turn into a 'greate Tragedie' (S53/K75).[37] Among the major protagonists are the seven brothers of John Hutchinson's mother, who all took the royalist side during the Civil Wars—'Sir John Biron, afterwards Lord Biron, and all his brothers, bred up in Arms and gallant men in their owne persons, were all passionately the King's' (S61/K85).[38] Sir John Biron is characterized as a most generous man who, after the death of his sister, took into his own home his brother-in-law, Thomas Hutchinson, and his two sons, John and George. On the other hand, Sir Richard Biron, who is not depicted in this expository section, is later portrayed with some severity as one of the fiercest enemies of the Colonel during the Civil Wars.[39] In the rest of the narrative, Lucy Hutchinson follows the chronological order of events, in accordance with

---

[35] Woolf, 'A Feminine Past', 651.   [36] On the use of digressions, see Chapter 6.
[37] It is also used by Margaret Cavendish, a royalist, who speaks of her husband's 'chief Part in that fatal Tragedy' (*Life of William Cavendish* [sig. (c)ᵛ]).
[38] See Norbrook, 'Memoirs and Oblivion', Appendix 3, for the pedigree of the Biron family.
[39] See *Memoirs*, ed. Sutherland, 90, and ed. Keeble, 118. See also *Memoirs*, ed. Keeble, 346, note 54.

the Plutarchan tradition summed up by Blundeville.[40] Chronology, however, is not followed for its own sake; it is meant to bring out the Colonel's progress in the path of virtue—which is the very purpose of the *Memoirs*, from the Dedication to the collection of biblical verses at the end: 'To number his vertues is to give the epitome of his life, which was nothing elce but a *progresse* from one degree of vertue to another, till in a short time he arriv'd to that *height* which many longer lives could never reach' (S5/K20, my emphasis).

2. A life of virtue

To understand Lucy Hutchinson's analysis of her husband's virtues throughout the *Memoirs*, it is necessary to take into account her broad discursive horizon which includes classical works of antiquity, medieval and reformed theology, and Jesuit texts, as well as contemporary literature.[41] An awareness of this background is necessary to appreciate her twofold portrait of Colonel Hutchinson as a saint and as a gentleman, both figures being at the same time distinct and inseparable. My point here is not so much to trace the sources of this double portrait, but rather to point to a few significant convergences between Lucy Hutchinson's *Memoirs* and earlier or contemporary texts theorizing virtue.[42] I will chiefly focus on the dedication, 'To my Children', which offers an epitome of the Colonel's virtues both as a gentleman and as a Protestant saint. This dedication falls into two parts. Only the first one is reproduced in the existing editions of the *Memoirs*. Lucy Hutchinson's 'another assay' will be quoted from the manuscript of the *Memoirs*.[43]

a) The portrait of a Christian gentleman

Any reader of the *Memoirs* is bound to be struck by the characterization of John Hutchinson as a perfect gentleman, a characterization which echoes similar descriptions in Baldassare Castiglione's *Courtyer* and Sir Thomas

---

[40] Blundeville, *The True Order and Methode* [sig. F1ʳ]: 'bycause tyme doth accompany all maner of actions, and euery action hath his proper and peculiar tyme, the writer must giue to euery action his dewe time accordingly.'
[41] See Narveson, *Bible Readers and Lay Writers in Early Modern England* and Introduction, 3 ('Lucy Hutchinson's discursive horizon').
[42] On virtues, see Shawn R. Tucker's useful work, *The Virtues and Vices in the Arts: A Sourcebook* (Eugene, OR: Cascade Books, 2015).
[43] *Memoirs*, DD/HU4, 22–9.

Elyot's *Governour*, two books that Lucy Hutchinson was likely to have had in hand at some point, given her humanist culture and education.[44] From the outset, the title of the main portion of the *Memoirs* specifies the rank of the Colonel—'The Life of John Hutchinson *of Owthorpe* in the County of Nottingham, Esquire' (S15/K31)—a social status that he had to live up to if he wanted to maintain his reputation:

> He ever preserv'd himselfe in his owne rank, neither being proud of it so as to despise any inferior, nor letting fall that just decorum which his honor oblieg'd him to keepe up. [...]he was farre from vaine affectation of popularity, so he never neglected that just care that an honest man ought to have of his reputation. (S11/K27–8)

Likewise, it was important for Lucy Hutchinson, at the beginning of the *Memoirs*, to mark the Colonel off from the vulgar, and to associate his station in life with his practice of honour and virtue:

> It is further observable in their descent that though none of them before Sir Thomas Hutchinson advanc'd beyond an Esquire, yet they successively matcht into all the most eminent and noble famelies in the country; which shewes that it was the unambitious genius of the famely rather than their want of meritt which made them keepe upon so even a ground after their first atchievements had sett them upon a stage elevated enough from the vulgar to performe any honorable and vertuous actions. (S15/K31)

John Hutchinson's virtue and his status in the local gentry are reminiscent of Castiglione's ideal gentleman at the beginning of the *Courtyer*:

> I wyll haue this our Courtyer therfore to be a Gentleman borne & of a good house. For it is a great deale lesse dyspraise for him that is not born a gentleman to faile in the actes of vertue then for a gentleman. If he swarne

---

[44] Baldassare Castiglione, *The Courtyer of Count Baldessar Castilio Diuided Into Foure Bookes*, trans. Thomas Hoby (London, 1561) and Sir Thomas Elyot, *The Boke Named the Governour* (London, 1531). Quotes from Elyot's *The Governour* are drawn from the Luminarium edition, http://www.luminarium.org/renascence-editions/gov/gov1.htm (accessed 15/01/2019). On the reception of the *Courtyer* in England, see Peter Burke, *The Fortunes of the Courtier* (Cambridge: Polity Press, 1995). Some pages of Burke's book are devoted to Elyot's *Governour* (86–7). Burke also makes connections between the *Courtyer* and 'exemplary lives' (95–8); Gabriele Rippl, '"Merit, Justice, Gratitude, Duty, Fidelity": Images of Masculinity in Autobiographies of Early Modern English Gentlewomen and Aristocrats', *Constructions of Masculinity in British Literature from the Middle Ages to the Present* (Basingstoke: Palgrave Macmillan, 2012) 69–87.

from the steppes of his auncestours, he stayneth the name of his familie, and doeth not onely not get, but loseth that is already gotten.⁴⁵

In addition, Lucy Hutchinson starts her presentation of her husband by enhancing his physical appearance and his manners, which, within a Neoplatonic framework, is another way of confirming both his moral superiority and his gentility. In 'His Description', she places him above the common run of mankind and insists on his well-proportioned body, his 'gracefull' lips, his 'gracefull' motions, and his 'sweetnesse' (S3/K19). Even when he is angry, the Colonel has 'such a grace as made him to be fear'd' (S4/K20). The terms 'sweetness', 'grace', and 'graceful' echo Castiglione's depiction of the ideal courtier endowed with 'suche graces, that they seeme not to haue bene borne, but rather facioned with the verye hande of some God'. The Courtier, Castiglione continues, 'hath in hym a certayne sweetenesse, & so comely demeanours, that whoso speaketh with hym or yet beholdeth hym, muste nedes beare him an affeccion for euer'.⁴⁶

Furthermore, the physical exercises practised by John Hutchinson matched the activities recommended by Castiglione for his Courtier and by Elyot for his Governour. Like the Governour, John Hutchinson 'was apt for any bodily exercise, and any that he did became him; he could dance admirably well [. . .]. He had skill in fencing such as became a gentleman' (S3–4/K19).⁴⁷ Like the Courtier, he had been taught the art of hawking.⁴⁸ Like him, he was a very good soldier capable of leading men. Not only did he shoot 'excellently in bowes and gunns' (S4/K19), but he 'understood well, and as well perform'd when he undertooke it, the millitary Art in all parts of it, and naturally lov'd the employment as it suited with his active temper more than any, receiving a mutuall delight in leading those men that lov'd his conduct' (S11/K27).⁴⁹ Regarding his manners and his conduct in society at large, John Hutchinson also behaved like Renaissance gentlemen. Lucy Hutchinson mentions his 'generall affabillity' (S12/K29), his 'curtesy' (S12/K29) and 'a naturall civillity and complaisance to all people as made his converse very delightfull' (S4/K20).

---

⁴⁵ Castiglione, 'The fyrst boke', [sig. C2ᵛ].   ⁴⁶ Castiglione, 'The fyrst boke', [sig. C2ᵛ], sig. C3.
⁴⁷ See Elyot, 'XVI. Of sondry fourmes of exercise necessary for euery gentilman'; 'XVII. Exercises wherby shulde growe both recreation and profite'; 'XIX. That all daunsinge is nat to be reproued'.
⁴⁸ See *Memoirs*, ed. Sutherland, 4, and ed. Keeble, 19. See Elyot, 'XVIII. The auncient huntyng of Greekes and romanes'.
⁴⁹ Castiglione, 'The fyrst boke', [sig. C4ᵛ]: 'I iudge the principall and true profession of a Courtyer ought to be in feates of armes, the which aboue all I will haue hym to practise liuely, and to bee knowen among other for his hardinesse.' Elyot, 'XXVII. That shotyng in a longe bowe is Principall of all other exercises'.

These dispositions were made possible by the education he successively received in Nottingham, Lincoln and Cambridge.[50] In this respect, the comparison of Lucy Hutchinson's portrait of the Colonel with the two humanist works is illuminating: like the Governour and the Courtier, John Hutchinson was taught oratory and 'had a very good facultie in perswading, and would speake very well, pertinently and effectually without premeditation upon the greatest occasions that could be offer'd' (S4/K20).[51] He was a man of letters—a 'farre greater schollar than is absolutely requisite for a gentleman' (S8/K24)— and also a musician, since 'for his diversion he chose musick, and gott a very good hand, which afterwards he improov'd to a greate mastery, on the Violl' (S25/K42).[52] More generally, he was an amateur of the arts, and bought several 'workes in payntings, sculptures, gravings, and all other such curiosities' during the Protectorate (S207/K254). Like the Courtier, he 'had greate judgment in paintings, graving, sculpture, and all excellent arts' (S4/K19).[53]

Thus, John Hutchinson was endowed with all the virtues of a gentleman, but what made him truly exceptional and exemplary in the eyes of his wife is his 'heroique glorie' (S12/K29), both as Governor of Nottingham and as a Christian martyr. This heroism is conceived as the expression of the Colonel's high-mindedness or of his magnanimity, both terms being used in English to translate the Greek word μεγαλοψυχία. For Aristotle, in the *Nicomachean Ethics*, the reward which the high-minded man receives for his 'noble deeds' is honour:

> The high-minded man, then, in respect of the greatness of his deserts, occupies an extreme position [...]. For desert has reference to external good things. Now, the greatest of external good things we may assume to be that which we render to the Gods as their due, and that which people in high stations most desire, and which is the prize appointed for the noblest

---

[50] See *Memoirs*, ed. Sutherland, 22, 24, and ed. Keeble, 39, 42.

[51] Castiglione, 'The fyrst boke', sig. C4: 'Therfore shall our Courtyer be esteemed excellent, and in euerye thyng he shall haue a good grace, and especially in speaking.' Elyot also insists on the necessity to teach oratory to the Christian Prince (X): 'The utilitie that a noble man shall haue by redyng these oratours, is, that, when he shall happe to reason in counsaile, or shall speke in a great audience, or to strange ambassadours of great princes, he shall nat be constrayned to speake wordes sodayne and disordred, but shal bestowe them aptly and in their places.'

[52] Castiglione, 'The fyrst boke', sig. A3: 'I beleue for the reasons you alledge and for many other, that musicke is not onelye an ornament, but also necessarie for a Courtyer.' Cf. Elyot, 'VII. In what wise musike may be to a noble man necessarie'.

[53] See, for instance, Castiglione, 'The fyrst boke', [sig. I3ᵛ]: 'the knowledge in the very arte of peincting'. On John Hutchinson as an art-collector, see Linda Levy Peck, *Consuming Splendor: Society and Culture in Seventeenth-Century England* (Cambridge: Cambridge UP, 2005) 268–9.

deeds. But the thing that answers to this description is honour, which, we may safely say, is the greatest of all external goods. Honours and dishonours, therefore, are the field in which the high-minded man behaves as he ought.[54]

The term 'magnanimity' as well as its variants and synonyms—'great spirit', 'noble spirit(s)', 'generous spirits', 'generosity', 'the greatness of his mind', 'natural greatness'—are all used in the *Memoirs* to designate the exceptional nature of John Hutchinson and his capacity for 'heroic glory'. So are the term 'honour', defined by Aristotle as 'the prize appointed for the noblest deed', and its cognates: the Colonel's soul is 'shining in honor' (S10/K27) and his life is 'holy, vertuous, honorable' (S3/K18).

The centrality of magnanimity in the construction of the Colonel's exemplarity reflects the aristocratic ethos which, in Deborah Shuger's view, 'shapes the Hutchinsons' republicanism, their demand for religious and political liberty, their lofty integrity amid the Interregnum's frenzied power struggles and the vengeful persecutions of the Restoration'.[55] This aristocratic ethos manifests itself in such virtues as liberality and hospitality, but these are in no way as determining as high-mindedness, which is, to quote Aristotle's *Nicomachean Ethics* again, 'the crowning grace, as it were, of the virtues; it makes them greater, and cannot exist without them. And on this account it is a hard thing to be truly high-minded; for it is impossible without the union of all the virtues.'[56] To advance that magnanimity is the '*crowning* grace [...] of the virtues' would be nevertheless problematic, for it comes into contradiction with Lucy Hutchinson's statements in the *Memoirs* about the centrality of Christianity. Besides, in the unpublished part of the Dedication ('another assay'), in which she tries to draw a more satisfactory delineation of her husband's virtues, she starts by stating that 'Christianity was the *crowne* of all his vertues'.[57] In the published section, she is equally straightforward about the importance of religion in the life of the Colonel: 'in the head of all his vertues I shall sett that which was the head and spring of them all, his Christianity, for this alone is the true royall blood that runs through the whole body of vertues' (S5/K21). Later, in her translation of John Owen's treatise, the superiority of Christian virtues over Aristotle's secular ones is

---

[54] Aristotle, *The Nichomachean Ethics of Aristotle*, trans. F. H. Peters, 5th edition (London: Kegan Paul, Trench, Truebner & Co., 1893) IV, 3, 11, https://oll.libertyfund.org/titles/aristotle-the-nicomachean-ethics/simple (accessed 15/01/2019).
[55] For such a reading see Shuger, 'Life-Writing in Seventeenth-Century England', 71–4.
[56] Aristotle, *The Nichomachean Ethics of Aristotle*, IV, 3, 16.
[57] *Memoirs*, DD/HU4, 22 (my emphasis).

underscored: 'Not one true virtue is truly taught in all Aristotles bookes to Nichomachus; nor ever did any one, by the learning of them arrive to be just, good, or really excellent, or aniething but a masquerading hipocrite.'[58]

A possible way of reconciling the Christian framework of the *Memoirs* and the Colonel's aristocratic ethos would be to consider, like the author, that the pagan virtues of wisdom, justice, valour, and temperance, codified by ancient philosophers, such as Cicero, Plutarch, and Seneca—all three mentioned by Lucy Hutchinson—were regenerated and consecrated in and by Christianity:[59]

> This is that sacred fountaine [Christianity] which baptizeth all the Gentile vertues that so immortalize the names of Cicero, Plutarch, Seneca, and all the old Philosophers; herein they are regenerated and take a new name and nature. Dig'd up out of the willdernesse of nature, and dipt in this living spring, they are planted and flourish in the Paradice of God.   (S5/K21)

In the unpublished section of the Dedication ('another assay'), more importance is granted to virtues being 'baptized in the flood of gods grace'. This regeneration makes John Hutchinson superior to 'greate men' whose virtues are not grounded in grace. In his wife's hyperbolic praise, he becomes a truly *Christian* gentleman and a 'more instructive example'. From the outset, we also understand that Christianity is the cornerstone of the 'Life''s apologetic programme:

> Whatever strait rule of wisedome iustice vallour temperance can be drawne out from the precepts of the best morall philosophers to furnish a compleate vertuous person his practise heightned it and made a more instructive example because his vertues were all baptized in the flood of gods grace and from thence tooke a new name and nature [...] There are many greate men who haue attaind to be soe by being eminent in some one eminent vertue but he was arriud to such an admirable degree of perfection in all that twas as hard to say which was [...] the morall vertue he most excelld in as

---

[58] Hutchinson, *Of Theologie* in *The Works of Lucy Hutchinson*, vol. 2, 376–7; *On the Principles of the Christian Religion, addressed to her daughter; and on Theology*, ed. Julius Hutchinson (London, 1817) 240.

[59] For references to the four cardinal virtues, see Marcus Tullius Cicero, *De Officiis*, trans. Andrew P. Peabody (Boston: Little, Brown, and Co., 1887) Book 1, V–VIII, https://oll.libertyfund.org/titles/542 (accessed 25/11/2018); Seneca, *Moral Letters to Lucilius*, Letter 120, 'More about Virtue', https://en.wikisource.org/wiki/Moral_letters_to_Lucilius/Letter_120 (accessed 25/11/2018); Plutarch, 'The First Oration of Plutarch Concerning the Fortune or Virtue of Alexander the Great', *Plutarch's Morals. Translated from the Greek by Several Hands. Corrected and Revised by William W. Goodwin, with an Introduction by Ralph Waldo Emerson* (Boston: Little, Brown, and Co., 1878), vol. 1. https://oll.libertyfund.org/titles/plutarch-the-morals-vol-1 (accessed 16/01/2019).

which is in it selfe most excellent His virtues regenerated and converted into graces bore an image of their fathers glory and were not to be considerd distinct but all one and one in all[60]

As a matter of fact, Lucy Hutchinson's view of secular virtues—wisdom, justice, valour, and temperance—as baptized by Christianity is typical of humanism, whose influence on seventeenth-century Protestantism was considerable as Margo Todd's pioneering work has shown.[61] But the Christianization of moral virtues is also an inheritance of medieval theology, in particular that of Aquinas.[62] For the school-man, there was indeed no opposition between Aristotelian ethics and Christianity as long as secular virtues could lead the Christian towards God:

Again, since man by his nature is a social animal, these virtues, in so far as they are in him according to the condition of his nature, are called "social" virtues; since it is by reason of them that man behaves himself well in the conduct of human affairs. It is in this sense that we have been speaking of these virtues until now.

But since it behooves a man to do his utmost to strive onward even to Divine things, as even the Philosopher declares in Ethic. x, 7, and as Scripture often admonishes us—for instance: "Be ye [...] perfect, as your heavenly Father is perfect" (Matthew 5:48), we must needs place some virtues between the social or human virtues, and the exemplar virtues which are Divine.[63]

Medieval scholasticism was often opposed by the Reformers and there is, therefore, an undeniable paradox in applying a scholastic grid onto Lucy Hutchinson's Protestant *Memoirs*. Lucy Hutchinson's own Calvinist perplexity towards school divinity surfaces in her translation of John Owen's Latin treatise *Theologoumena Pantodapa*:[64]

---

[60] *Memoirs*, DD/HU4, 22-3.

[61] Margo Todd, 'The Transmission of Christian Humanist Ideas', *Christian Humanism and the Puritan Social Order* (Cambridge: Cambridge UP, 1987) 75. Brendan Bradshaw, 'Transalpine Humanism', *The Cambridge History of Political Thought*, ed. J. H. Burns (Cambridge: Cambridge UP, 1991) 95-131, here 103; see also Jens Zimmermann, ed. *Re-Envisioning Christian Humanism: Education and the Restoration of Humanity* (Oxford: Oxford UP, 2017), especially part II, 'Christian Humanism in the Renaissance Reformation'.

[62] Thomas Aquinas, *Summa Theologiae*, II, I, question 61. http://www.newadvent.org/summa/2061.htm (accessed 26/09/2019). See Tucker, *The Virtues and Vices in the Arts*, for a rich account of the representation of the virtues from antiquity to the Renaissance.

[63] *Summa Theologiae* II, I, Question 61, Article 5.

[64] See Hutchinson, *Of Theologie*, in *The Works of Lucy Hutchinson*, vol. 2, 289-90. Owen was a 'careful reader of Aquinas' (290); he had studied Aquinas at university. On the influence of John Owen's theology on Lucy Hutchinson's works, see Norbrook, '*Order and Disorder*: The Poem and its

Hence the schoolemen, stirrd up with an itch of disputation, contend about their theologie, whither it be *science* practicall or speculative, or *prudence* or *wisedome*: which word soever they fix on, weighing it upon all philosophicall accounts, they wrack their braines to accomodate it to their theologie, and make it their businesse to fish out of humane learning all that is attributed to it.[65]

This position is also exemplified by John Hutchinson who rejected 'schoole learning' and was 'weary of all those vaine disputes and studies'.[66] But the rejection of sterile disputations does not mean that scholasticism was altogether rejected by Protestants. It was taught at university and John Owen himself had a very wide knowledge of 'the whole field of Greek and Latin theology, from the Apostolic Fathers [...] to Thomas Aquinas'.[67] Similarly, the Hutchinsons' dislike of scholasticism does not mean that, like most reformed theologians, they were not experts at it.[68] John Hutchinson and his Puritan father, Sir Thomas, are said to have been reading school-divinity in several places of the *Memoirs* which, in Norbrook's terms, amounts to 'the movement of scholastic divinity from the university to the household'.[69] As regards John Hutchinson, during his first two years at Owthorpe, he 'employ'd his time in making an entrance upon the study of Schoole Devinity' (S34/K53). Lucy Hutchinson does not mention studying scholastic theology herself, but her strong intellectual bonds with the Colonel and her later theological works lead us to believe that she had read at least some of the books in the library at Owthorpe and may have discussed them with her husband. In her own 'life', she also stresses her early interest in 'the knowledge of God': 'It pleas'd God that thro' the good instructions of my mother, and the sermons she carried me

---

Contexts', xix–xx. According to Norbrook, The *Memoirs* can indeed be seen as a transitional work between the Lucretius translation and later specifically theological writings' ('Theology, Gender and Translation', 141).

[65] Hutchinson, *Of Theologie* 332. [66] *Memoirs*, DD/HU4, 26.

[67] Stevenson, ed., *Of Theologie* 289. For the status of scholasticism among Reformers, see M. W. F. Stone, 'Aristotelianism and Scholasticism in Early Modern Philosophy', *A Companion to Early Modern Philosophy*, ed. Steven Nadler (Oxford: Blackwell, 2002) 7–24, especially 14. Stone also reminds us of 'the disparaging comments that modern philosophers such as Bacon, Hobbes, Descartes and Locke directed at their scholastic teachers' (8). See also J. H. Burns, 'Scholasticism: Survival and Revival', *The Cambridge History of Political Thought*, ed. Burns, 132–55 and Craig Martin, 'Religious Reform and the Reform of Aristotelianism', *Subverting Aristotle: Religion, History and Philosophy in Early Modern Science* (Baltimore: John Hopkins UP, 2014) 86–101.

[68] Norbrook, 'Introduction', *The Works of Lucy Hutchinson*, vol. 2, 6, and Norbrook, 'Theology, Gender and Translation', 144.

[69] On Lucy Hutchinson and scholasticism, see Burden, 'Lucy Hutchinson and Puritan Education', 169–72; Norbrook, 'Theology, Gender and Translation', 148. Sir Thomas was reported to have had 'a most choyce library' (K34/S53).

to, I was convinc'd that the knowledge of God was the most excellent study, and accordingly applied myselfe to it, and to practise as I was taught' (S288/K15). The two extant pages from a lost theological notebook, of which the 1806 edition of the *Memoirs* provides a facsimile, confirm Lucy Hutchinson's predilection for theology.[70] They contain a transcription of a sermon by Robert Sanderson (published in 1627), dealing with the distinction made by Aquinas between two sorts of grace. According to Norbrook, Lucy Hutchinson's omission of a passage from Sanderson in the transcription could indicate 'a slightly uneasy self-consciousness with which Calvinists might appropriate scholastic divinity; a phenomenon of which she was well aware'.[71] Additionally, the two commonplace books, kept at the Nottinghamshire Archives, display her acute interest in theology, regardless of confessional divides. The religious Commonplace Book, which she kept after 1667, contains notes from Calvin's *Institutes*, statements of belief, sermon notes, a personal treatise, and verses. It testifies to Lucy Hutchinson turning to theology after writing 'The Life', which Norbrook calls a 'slow process of reorientation after the blow of her husband's death'.[72] A second commonplace book, probably filled around 1634–1635 and also in the late 1640s and 1655,[73] has been called 'secular' in opposition to the 'religious' Commonplace Book, also kept in the Nottinghamshire Archives.[74] It was mostly written in the 1630s, when Lucy Hutchinson had contacts with the Catholic court of Henrietta Maria, a period in her life when she was less concerned with reformed theology and piety than in the late 1660s and 1670s.[75] Yet, this 'secular' notebook is far from being entirely profane and it includes, among other items, notes taken from the fourth tome of the *The Holy Court*, written by the Jesuit Nicolas Caussin, about passions and virtues.[76] This borrowing

---

[70] On this lost theological notebook, see Norbrook, 'Introduction', *The Works of Lucy Hutchinson*, vol. 2, 43–7.
[71] Norbrook, 'Introduction', *The Works of Lucy Hutchinson*, vol. 2, 47.
[72] Norbrook, 'Introduction', *The Works of Lucy Hutchinson*, vol. 2, 3. On the practice of note-taking at sermons, see Alec Ryrie, 'Experiencing the Sermon', *Being Protestant in Reformation Britain* (Oxford: Oxford UP, 2013) 306–64.
[73] De Groot, 'John Denham and Lucy Hutchinson', 152.
[74] De Groot, 'John Denham and Lucy Hutchinson', 152.
[75] *Literary Commonplace Book*, MS DD/HU1, Nottinghamshire Archives, 147–91 ('Love'). A useful description is to be found at https://web.warwick.ac.uk/english/perdita/html/ms_NADDHU1.htm (accessed 27/09/2019). Lucy Hutchinson's notes are not based on the 1634 edition mentioned by De Groot (149).
[76] The edition used by Lucy Hutchinson was Nicolas Caussin, *The Holy Court. The Command of Reason over the Passions [Fourth Tome]*, trans. T. H. ([Rouen], 1638). For the other tomes, see *The Holy Court in Three Tomes. The third Tome now first published in English; The first and second newly reuiewd, and much augmented according to the last Edition of the Author* ([Rouen], 1634). On the

once again betrays Lucy Hutchinson's interest in theology, including Jesuit theology.

In Lucy Hutchinson's portrait of her husband's virtues, prudence appears to be the most important moral virtue: 'Christianity in him was the fountaine of all his vertues, and diffus'd it selfe into every streame. That of his prudence falls into next mention' (S7/K23). In Aquinas's classification, 'prudence' is 'a principal virtue', which is 'rational in essence' and '[exists] in the very act of reason'.[77] He adds that 'any virtue that causes good in reason's act of consideration, may be called prudence'.[78] The definition Aquinas gives of prudence covers Lucy Hutchinson's use of the notion and corresponds to the Latin *prudentia*, which signifies 'foresight, providence, practical understanding, proficiency, wisdom, sagacity'. The Colonel had thus a precocious ability to deliver counsel and show his wisdom as well as his foresight:[79] 'He from a child was wise, and sought to by many that might have bene his fathers for *counsell*, which he could excellently give to himselfe and others; [...] he had as great a *foresight*, as strong a judgment, as cleare an apprehension of men and things as no man more' (S7/K23, my emphasis). The Colonel's prudence is repeatedly signalled by Lucy Hutchinson who, like Aquinas, almost systematically connects it to his use of rational faculties whenever he is in a position to deliberate. Prudence here appears as a rational force against the seduction of the political and religious leaders of his time:

> He was as ready to heare as to give councell, and never pertinacious in his will when his *reason* was convinc'd. [...] the greatest names in the world could never lead him without *reason*; he would deliberate where there was time, but never lost an oppertunety of aniething that was to be done by tedious dispute. (S7/K23)

In early modern England, prudence was a virtue which statesmen were expected to acquire through their reading of history, especially Tacitus.[80] As

---

influence of Caussin at the court of Henrietta Maria, see Reid Barbour, *English Epicures and Stoics: Ancient Legacie in Early Stuart Culture* (Amherst: U of Massachusetts P, 1998) 101–5. See Clarke, introduction to *On the Principles of the Christian Religion*, The Works of Lucy Hutchinson, vol. 2, 171–2. See Anthony Milton, 'A Qualified Intolerance: The Limits and Ambiguities of Early Stuart Anti-Catholicism', *Catholicism and Anti-Catholicism in Early Modern Texts*, ed. Arthur F. Marotti (Basingstoke: Palgrave Macmillan, 1999) 91.

[77] *Summa Theologiae* II, I, question 61, article 2.
[78] *Summa Theologiae* II, I, question 61, article 3.
[79] In the *OED*, prudence is defined as the 'ability to recognize and follow the most suitable or sensible course of action; good sense in practical or financial affairs; discretion, circumspection, caution'.
[80] See Brian Vickers's Introduction in Francis Bacon, *The History of the Reign of King Henry VII*, ed. Vickers (Cambridge: Cambridge UP, 1998) xviii; Burke, 'Tacitism, Scepticism, and Reason of State', *The*

far as John Hutchinson's political decisions were concerned, prudence proved crucial when, for instance, he had to ponder his choice to commit himself publicly for the cause of Parliament. In 1645, in his dealings with the Nottingham Committee, at a time when machinations were hatched against him, he was again reported to have acted out of 'prudence', ascertaining that the soldiers were paid and the provisions and ammunitions were gathered.[81] In August 1648, at the moment of parting with Colonel Thornhagh, a friend whom he was seeing for the last time, the Colonel was equally praised for his 'prudence' (S180/K223), which is interpreted as a form of political prescience regarding the fatal events to come. Finally, in a passage which serves as a reflexive digression over the years of the Cromwellian Protectorate, Lucy Hutchinson retrospectively justifies her husband's retirement from political life, arguing that this decision was made not only out of prudence but also out of conscience, which Giuseppina Iacono Lobo interestingly defines as 'a mediating agent between his understanding of God's providence and his actions in the world'.[82] After Cromwell's dissolution of the Rump Parliament on 21 April 1653, Colonel Hutchinson considered that he was no longer answerable to any authority: 'he seeing that Authoritie to which he was in duty bound so seemingly taken quite away, thought he was free to fall in or oppose all things, as prudence should guide him, upon generall rules of conscience' (S216/K265).[83] This conscience, founded in the Colonel's strong faith, is carefully opposed to the worldly prudence of some of his contemporaries, especially those who eventually failed to sign the King's death warrant. The explanation, in the first person, is retrospective and based on an evangelical reading of events:

> I know upon certeine knowledge that many – yea, the most of them – retreated not for conscience, but for feare and worldly prudence, foreseing that the insolency of the Armie might grow to that heigth as to ruine the cause, and reduce the kingdome into the hands of the enemie [...]. And these poore men did privately animate those who appear'd most publiquely, and I knew severall of them in whom I lived to see that saying of Christ fulfill'd: *He that will save his life shall loose it, and he that for my sake will*

Cambridge History of Political Thought, ed. Burns, 479–98; Seaward, 'Clarendon, Tacitism, and the Civil Wars of Europe', 306; Salmon, 'Precept, Example, and Truth', 12: 'the Stoics saw history as a vicarious means of acquiring prudence and applying it to both private life and public life.'

[81] See *Memoirs*, ed. Sutherland, 152, and ed. Keeble, 191.

[82] Giuseppina Iacono Lobo, 'Lucy Hutchinson's Revisions of Conscience', *English Literary Renaissance* 42.2 (2012): 317–41, here 330.

[83] On the importance of this event for Republicans, see Norbrook, *Writing the English Republic* 3.

loose his life shall save it, when after it fell out that all their *prudent* declensions sav'd not the lives of some nor the estates of others.

(S190/K235)[84]

In Lucy Hutchinson's hierarchy of virtues, justice appears next, the Colonel being 'as excellent in justice as in wisdom' (S8/K24). According to Aquinas 'every virtue that causes the good of right and due in operation, be called justice'.[85] Justice, he explains, is 'a certain rectitude of the mind, whereby a man does what he ought in any matters';[86] it is an uprightness which is copiously illustrated in the *Memoirs*, as the Colonel's moral principles never waver. It implies an indefectible love of truth, which is also typical of the gentlemanly ethos:[87]

> the greatest advantage, nor the greatest danger, nor the dearest interest or friend in the world could not prevaile on him to pervert justice even to an enemie [...]. Never fearing aniething he could suffer for the truth, he never at any time would refreine a true or give a false witnesse; he lov'd truth so much that he hated even sportive lies and gulleries. (S8/K24)

As a matter of fact, John Hutchinson's actions are described as resulting from a sense of justice inspired to him by God. In the summer of 1643, at the moment of his father's death, 'Conscience to God, and truth and righteousnesse according to the best information he could gett, engag'd him in that party he tooke' (S91/K120). The Colonel's virtue of justice took an even more solemn and sacred dimension when he was appointed governor first of the town (29 June 1643), then of the castle of Nottingham (20 November 1643). It was then clear to him that he 'was call'd of God to the carrying on of the interest of truth, righteousnesse and holinesse, and to the defence of his country' (S107/K138). In addition, in the early years of the Commonwealth, when he no longer assumed any military role, the administration of justice kept him busy as the new regime was introducing important new legal reforms:

---

[84] Matthew 16:25.
[85] *Summa Theologiae* II, I, question 61, article 3. See also Nicolas Caussin, 'The Practice of Justice', *The Holy Court in Three Tomes* 176–8.
[86] *Summa Theologiae* II, I, question 61, article 4.
[87] See Steven Shapin, *A Social History of Truth: Civility and Science in Seventeenth-Century England* (Chicago: Chicago UP, 1994) xx–xxi.

he had for about a yeare's time applied himselfe, when the Parliament could dispense with his absence, to the administration of justice in the country, and to the putting in execution of those wholsome lawes and statutes of the land provided for the orderly regulation of the people. (S206/K253)

Colonel Hutchinson's steady sense of justice was tried by various circumstances during his lifetime. First, his appointment as governor of the castle and the town of Nottingham aroused many jealousies, especially among the Nottingham Committee, and from the start he 'knew that it was unpossible to keepe on a constant careere of vertue and justice and to please all men' (S107/K138).[88] In the following years, the tensions with the Nottingham Committee increased. Although they were supposed to support the cause of Parliament, most of its members hatched petty machinations against the Colonel and tried to obstruct the normal course of justice, as it was the case in November 1644 with the Committee of Both Kingdoms.[89] In December 1649, the Colonel's integrity was put to the test even more directly by another Committee, headed by Bradshaw, in charge of settling conflicts related to the sequestration of royalist estates. In 1651, the Colonel took the defence of his royalist brother-in-law, Sir Allen Apsley, because the 'articles at the rendition of Barnstaple' (S200/K247) were broken. The latter, Lucy Hutchinson explains, was indeed a victim of 'horrible lies', as he was 'put to vast expence and horrible vexation by severall persons, but especially by one wicked woman who had the worst and the smoothest tongue that ever her sex made use of to mischiefe' (S200–1/K247). Although she presented herself as a supporter of Parliament, this woman was retrospectively identified by Lucy Hutchinson as a royalist spy driven by greed and envy. In any case, faced with such a perversion of justice, the Colonel appears to act out of conscience and mercy, never confusing his own political interests with his ideal of justice and truth. His wife exploits this politically and morally complex situation to evidence her husband's desire to dissociate himself from the Commonwealth regime, at a time when 'delayes in the administration of justice and such perverting of right' (S205/K252) were common:

The Collonell prosecuting the defence of truth and justice in these and many more things, and abhorring all councells of securing the young Commonwealth by cruelty and oppression of the vanquisht [...] – the

---

[88] On these disputes within the Nottingham Committee, see Chapter 3, 2, b ('Nottingham Castle and the experience of the Civil War').
[89] See *Memoirs*, ed. Sutherland, 144–6, and ed. Keeble, 182–6.

> Colonell, I say, disdaining such thoughts, displeas'd many of his owne party, who in the maine, wee hope, might have bene honest, although through divers temptations guilty of horrible slips, which did more offend the Colonell's pure zeale, who detested these sins more in brethren than in enemies. (S201/K248)

The third cardinal virtue for which the Colonel is praised is temperance. It is described by Aquinas as an act of reason imposing order on 'the passions' which 'need a curb', a definition repeated verbatim by Lucy Hutchinson who warns that they are to be 'kept within their owne just bounds' (S8/K24).[90] In the Dedication, his anger is highlighted. '[U]pon occasion [...] he would be very angrie [...], yet he was never outrageous in passion' (S4/K20).[91] More generally, to represent the Colonel's control over his passions, Lucy Hutchinson uses the model of the psychomachia, depicting how his soul, assisted by religion and reason, reigned supreme over the senses and was fully disposed to serve the commonwealth: 'His soule ever reign'd as king in the internall throne, and never was captive to his sence; religion and reason, its two favour'd councellors, took order that all the passions kept within their owne just bounds, there did him good service, and further'd the publick weale' (S8/K24).[92] In this portrait of Hutchinson, temperance is not equated with the suppression of passions. As is frequently the case in the 'Life of John Hutchinson', we are reminded that the passions are useful and necessary. Their elimination would indeed 'damp his spiritt in any noble enterprize' (S8/K23).[93] In the unpublished section of the Dedication, anger is for instance delineated as a useful passion that should not be squashed entirely. In the Colonel, it was a 'noble passion', governed by reason, which never degenerated into malice or revenge:

> his anger was fierce for the time but of very short duration especially if not opposd and then he iustly maintaind it because reason euer was on his side

---

[90] *Summa Theologiae* II, I, question 61, article 2. On temperance, see Caussin, *Holy Court* (1634) 169–71.

[91] See also *Memoirs*, DD/HU4, 27: 'He would be very angrie but allwayes with such a good grace as advantagd him and effected his designe in it for discretion euer governd his passion.' See the Colonel's anger after being betrayed by the royalist troops from Newark as well as by some people from Nottingham (*Memoirs*, ed. Sutherland, 95, and ed. Keeble, 24).

[92] What is of interest here is the politicization of the psychomachia which, by analogy, stands for intemperate governments, presumably those of Charles I and Cromwell.

[93] See *Summa Theologiae* II, I, question 61, article 5: 'the aforesaid virtues cannot be without passions.' For other examples, see Elegy [5], 'On the Picture in Armour', where 'Temperance was leiftenant of ye Tower / Whoe Captiue kept ye passions rebell Power' (l.29–30), 'Lucy Hutchinson's Elegies', ed. Norbrook, 495.

but as soone as the offender was brought to submission whatever the cause were all his wrath ceast anger neuer turnd into mallice or revenge in him when he fell into the hands of little vnworthy people not all their base provocations could make him throw away so noble a passion on them whom he past by with a iust contempt[94]

Later, when his authority was challenged by the Nottingham Committee of War, the Colonel's anger again proved very useful against his enemies: 'But he, perceiving their drift, shew'd them that he govern'd his anger, and suffer'd it not to master him, and that he could make use of it to curb their insolency, and yet avoyd all excursions that might prejudice himselfe' (S136/K172).

Similarly, the passion of love is envisioned in a positive way. During the courtship of his wife, John Hutchinson felt no 'irregular passions', Lucy Hutchinson writes, because they were enjoyed with temperance. At first, on hearing that Lucy could well be already married, he was submerged by his emotions: he 'immediately turn'd pale as ashes, and felt a fainting to seize his spiritts, in that extraordinary manner that finding himselfe ready to sink att table, he was faine to pretend something had offended his stomach, and to retire from the table into the Garden' (S30/K48). But this state of emotional disorder was only momentary and he soon began 'to recollect his wisdome and his reason' (S30/K48). Marriage finally came to temper that 'great passion' John Hutchinson had for Lucy Apsley; it 'shew'd that an affection bounded in the just rules of duty farre exceeds every way all the irregular passions in the world' (S10/K26).[95]

Showing that passions, when they are governed by temperance, are not to be rejected, Lucy Hutchinson takes her distance from stoicism as an ideal of freedom from passion. She finds herself close to the Jesuit Caussin, whose treatise she paraphrases in her secular Commonplace Book: 'It is not expedient,' he writes, 'to be without passion, nor is it possible to humane nature; but it is much to obtayne by discretion the moderation of a thing, of which we by necessity have the experience.'[96] Moreover, and quite logically, Lucy Hutchinson's conception of temperance leaves room for moderate pleasure. In her portrayal of the Colonel, she thus unequivocally states that the practice of temperance does not mean the suppression of the delights of life, only their 'true, wise, and religious government':

---

[94] *Memoirs*, DD/HU4, 28. For a defence of anger, see Edward Reynolds, *A Treatise of the Passions and Faculties of the Soule of Man* (London, 1640).
[95] On John Hutchinson's 'passion' for Lucy Hutchinson, see Chapter 5, 1, b ('Love at first sight').
[96] Caussin, 'A Tast of Severall Dispositions of Men', *The Holy Court [Fourth Tome]* np.

> His whole life was the rule of temperance in meate, drinke, apparell, pleasure, and all those things that may be lawfully enjoy'd; and herein his temperance was more excellent than in others' in whom it is not so much a vertue which proceeds from want of appetite or gust of pleasure, as that in him which was a true, wise, and religious government of the desire and delight he tooke in the things he enjoy'd. (S13/K30)

One could even advance the idea that the Colonel's experience of pleasure delineated above—'the desire and delight [...] in the things he enjoy'd'—could be the result of Lucy Hutchinson's own Epicurean reminiscences: in the 1650s, when the Colonel enjoyed, with moderation, the pleasures of life at Owthorpe, she was indeed translating Lucretius, who in the second book of his *De rerum natura*, advocated a moderate enjoyment of pleasures: 'Learne then from hence, that humane natures are / With little pleasd, and best themselues enioy, / When payne doth not torment, nor pleasure cloy.'[97]

Finally, the cardinal virtue of fortitude, which designates the courage of the soul, is also a prominent one in the *Memoirs*. It includes the Colonel's heroic magnanimity—with which we started—but also his heroic patience at the moment of his death. Aquinas's definition of fortitude sheds an interesting light on this two-sided virtue which is primarily a form of moral and rational resistance. It is a virtue which, he explains, is exercised when the passions '[withdraw] us from following the dictate of reason, e.g. through the fear of danger or toil: and then man needs to be strengthened for that which reason dictates, lest he turn back; and to this end there is "Fortitude".'[98] Fortitude, he adds, is not only a moral virtue but a way for the soul 'to [rise] to heavenly things'.[99] In this Christian sense, one understands well how the Colonel's magnanimity, already steeped in his faith during the Civil Wars, gradually gave way to patient fortitude in the 1660s, when he accepted to become a martyr as 'his faith and patience wonderfully carried him on under all his sufferings' (S268/K326).

b) The life of a saint

On the portrayal of John Hutchinson as a Christian gentleman is grafted another one, that of a Protestant saint, written in the tradition of Protestant

---

[97] Hutchinson, *The Translation of Lucretius*, part 1, Book 2, 85.
[98] *Summa Theologiae* II, I, question 61, article 2.
[99] *Summa Theologiae* II, I, question 61, article 2.

godly lives. Lucy Hutchinson makes her borrowing from this tradition explicit when she states her intention to 'celebrate the glories of a saint' (S2/K17) and specifies, at the same time, that the word 'saint' should be taken in its Protestant sense, as a model to be imitated or as a 'guide' to show the way.[100] Already in his lifetime, the Colonel behaved like a saint. According to his wife, he was 'very desireous to communicate the grace of God given him, and to instruct others what God had taught him, and neglected not to exhort his children and famely to diligence in searching after the knowledge of God, and to prayer and to holinesse and to watchfulnesse in this evill day' (S7/K22). Once in heaven, he remained 'a comfortable *testimony* with all [those] were about him'; '[b]y the gracious precepts he left with his children to transfer to their posterity he will preach truth and holiness to succeeding generations'.[101]

To tell the story of a saint, Lucy Hutchinson had some Protestant models at her disposal. Although the Reformation rejected the Catholic cult of saints as intercessors, lives of saints continued to be written especially in England, where the established Church encouraged the writing of godly biographies as a way to promote the vision of Protestant England as an elect nation.[102] Patrick Collinson has shown how godly biographies, held in suspicion in the early years of the Reformation, became increasingly popular after Foxe's *Acts and Monuments*, especially 'for the three generations which intervened between the Elizabethan settlement and the Puritan commonwealth the Bible and Foxe between them entirely satisfied the demand for edifying biographical history. Foxe was their Plutarch.'[103] The historian of English Protestantism also highlighted the extent to which Plutarch's *Lives* as well as Erasmus's work shaped the writing of Protestant biographies especially in the middle decades of the seventeenth century and during the Restoration.[104] In one of these collections of biographies, Thomas Fuller, who was a Church of England minister, advanced that the 'maine motive of publishing the ensuing Treatise' was 'to furnish our present age with a Magazeen of religious

---

[100] This term is often used as a synonym for a godly man. See Julius Hutchinson's note repeated in *Memoirs*, ed. Firth, 22: 'Saints. An expression commonly used in that time to signify good and religious people.— J. H.'

[101] Hutchinson, 'Final Meditation', *Memoirs*, ed. Keeble, 337; see *Memoirs*, DD/HU4, [421].

[102] Pritchard, *English Biography* 10. Sharpe and Zwicker, 'Introducing Lives', 1–26, here 2. See Bergamasco, 'Hagiographie et sainteté', 1061–2 for important definitions of sainthood in the Protestant and Catholic traditions.

[103] Patrick Collinson, '"A Magazine of Religious Patterns": An Erasmian Topic Transposed in English Protestantism', *Godly People: Essays on English Protestantism and Puritanism* (London: The Hambledon Press, 1983) 498–527, here 507.

[104] Collinson, 'A Magazine of Religious Patterns', 499–501; 511–13. See Alexandra Walsham, 'History, Memory and the English Reformation', *The Historical Journal* 55.4 (2012): 899–938, here 912.

Patterns for their Imitation'.[105] Among the exemplary models he offered for imitation, he included humanists (Erasmus, John Colet, William Tyndale), forerunners of Protestantism (Berengar of Tours, John Wycliffe, Jan Hus), Protestant reformers (Martin Luther, Ulrich Zwingli, Martin Bucer, John Calvin, John Knox), Protestant martyrs (Thomas Cranmer or Hugh Latimer), and learned ministers (Robert Bolton or William Perkins). In the Protestant mind, all those lives were thought to be more persuasive than doctrines and precepts. This is what the Protestant divine, Edmund Calamy, explains in the opening preface to Samuel Clarke's collection of lives: 'The nature of man is more apt to bee guided by *examples* than by *precepts*; [...]. There is *heavenly power and efficacie* in the good examples of men eminent in *place and godlines*, to draw others to Pietie and Holiness.'[106]

Lucy Hutchinson's familiarity with the genre of godly lives is pervasive throughout the *Memoirs*. Although she does not share Fuller's Episcopalianism, she celebrates, in terms similar to his, 'Wickliffe and other faithful witnesses, whom God rais'd up after the black and horrid midnight of antichristianisme' (S281/K6). The term 'witness' is here to be taken in the Christian sense of '[o]ne who testifies for Christ or the Christian faith' (*OED*), sometimes by death.[107] This was the case of John Hutchinson, who was a witness of Christ and also a martyr, in the sense that he placed God and the cause of the godly above earthly matters, including his own family.[108] The extension of the word 'witness' to 'martyr' was justified on biblical grounds by Calamy in his preface to Clarke's collection of lives: 'The Apostle having in the eleventh chapter to the *Hebrews* given us a *little book of Martyrs,* in the beginning of the twelfth chapter hee call's them, *A cloud of witnesses.*' This verse (Hebrews 12:1) was recurrent in the Protestant literature of the age and was for instance used in Fuller's *Abel Redevivus* and reproduced in full on the title-page of the *Marrow.*[109]

---

[105] Thomas Fuller, *Abel Redivivus; Or, the Dead yet Speaking. The Lives and Deaths of Modern Divines* (London, 1651) sig. A2–A2ᵛ.

[106] Edmund Calamy, 'Preface', in Clarke, *The Marrow of Ecclesiastical Historie, Conteined in the Lives of the Fathers, and Other Learned Men, and Famous Divines* (London, 1650).

[107] On the proximity between martyrs and witnesses of history, see François Hartog, *Évidence de l'histoire. Ce que voient les historiens* (Paris: Édition de l'EHESS, 2005) 203–4.

[108] See *Memoirs*, ed. Sutherland, 6, and ed. Keeble, 22: 'being perswaded neither his estate, honor, wife, children, nor his owne life weigh'd aniething with him in the ballance against Christe and his interest, and having often cheerefully sett them att the hazard, he att last joyfully parted with them all att God's call and for God's cause. The more God chasten'd him, the more he lov'd him, kissing the rod and rejoycing in the scourge that drove him neerer to God.'

[109] 'Wherefore, seeing wee are compassed about with so great a cloud of witnesses, let us laie aside everie weight, and the sin which doth easily beset us, and let us run with patience the race which is set before us.' See Fuller, *Abel Redevivus* 306, 551.

Central to the hagiographic portrayal of John Hutchinson as a saint are the theological virtues of faith, love and hope which, Aquinas argued, 'direct us to God' and to 'Divine happiness'.[110] For Lucy Hutchinson, 'true faith and hope are neuer seperated from charitie which is alsoe a gift and grace of God', as she writes in her religious Commonplace Book.[111] Following the divine's teaching on theological virtues, she links faith and supernatural happiness in her 1667 profession of faith, stating that 'the chiefe felicity of man consists in the true knowledge and enioyment of God in communion with whom all light life and blessednesse is only to be found & without whom there is nothing but eternal darknesse woe and death'.[112] Accordingly, in the 'Final Meditation', she writes that '[h]is faith was [strong] in the last hour of trial and great was his peace and joy in believing'.[113] In the rest of the narrative, however, the Colonel's faith is described in more confessional terms as 'that universall habitt of grace which is wrought in a soule by the regenerating Spiritt of God, whereby the whole creature is resign'd up into the devine will and love, and all its actions design'd to the obedience of that for the glory of its maker' (S5/K21). In her account of her husband's faith, Lucy Hutchinson mentions her husband's adherence to Calvinism, but the passage where she refers to Calvin is crossed out in the manuscript:[114]

> the first knowledge he labour'd for was the knowledge of God, which by a dilligent examination of the scripture, and the severall doctrines of greate men pretending that ground, he at length obtein'd; *and for the doctrinall principles of religion was convinc'd and establisht much in the doctrine of Mr. Calvin, but not as his way, but the way of God.* (S6/K21)

Lucy Hutchinson does not make any more mentions of Calvin in the *Memoirs*, but in a typically Protestant way, she multiplies references to the Scripture as the basis of the Colonel's Christianity: '[i]n matters of faith his reason allwayes submitted to the Word of God, and what he could not comprehend he would believe because 'twas written' (S7/K23).[115] In her religious Commonplace

---

[110] See *Summa Theologiae* II, I, question 62, article 1.
[111] *Religious Commonplace Book*, DD/HU3, 85; *Selections from the Theological Notebook*, in *The Works of Lucy Hutchinson*, vol. 2, 112. Norbrook prefers to call that bound manuscript the 'theological notebook'.
[112] *Religious Commonplace Book*, DD/HU3, 53; *The Works of Lucy Hutchinson*, vol. 2, 95. Among theological virtues, Aquinas places faith first in the order of generation and second in order of perfection (II, I, question 62, article 4).
[113] Lucy Hutchinson, 'Final Meditation', *Memoirs*, ed. Keeble, 337; see *Memoirs*, DD/HU4, [421].
[114] *Memoirs*, DD/HU4, 8.
[115] It is a statement we also find in her religious Commonplace Book, where she describes God as 'eternall infinite incomprehensible in wisedome power iustice and goodnesse' (*Religious Commonplace Book*, DD/HU3, 116; *The Works of Lucy Hutchinson*, vol. 2, 127).

Book, she also pinpoints that 'the true saving knowledge of God is only taught by that revelation he hath made of himselfe in his word'.[116] By the same token, in the *Memoirs*, she connects the unmistakable signs of the Colonel's election with his intimate acquaintance with the Bible: 'The power he had to approach it [the Word], his delight in transcribing it, and his finall perseverance in that laudable delight were all but extracts of Christ drawne upon his spiritt by the Spiritt of God' (S2/K17).[117] The last fifty-five pages of the manuscript of the *Memoirs*, which have never been published, further confirm the centrality of the Scripture in the Colonel's faith as they reproduce, under various headings, the biblical verses which he had marked in his Bible, and upon which he meditated, presumably at the most critical moments of his life.[118]

Yet Lucy Hutchinson does not deal with the Colonel's faith for its own sake as someone recounting a spiritual journey would do.[119] She rather chooses to subordinate his spiritual progress to the overall narrative of the 'Life of John Hutchinson' in order to highlight its public and historical dimension. To this end, she engages the reader 'to take up the parallel of the greate Hebrew Prince' (S36/K55) and draws typological parallels, starting with a comparison between John Hutchinson's quiet early days at Owthorpe and 'the preparation of Moses in the wildernesse' (S35/K54), while reminding the reader that, like Moses, Colonel Hutchinson 'had a call to goe back to deliver his country, groaning under spirituall and civill bondage' (S36/K55). From that angle the Colonel's exemplary life of faith takes its full meaning: it is not only a private testimony but also that of a man who has been invested with a public mission by God.

Connected with his faith is the Colonel's charity, for, as Lucy Hutchinson remarks, 'His faith being established in the truth, he was full of love to God and all his saints' (S6/21-2). Lucy Hutchinson's definition of charity combining the love of God and the love of all his saints is a slightly adapted version of Aquinas, who asserts that it is 'the same act whereby we love God and whereby

---

[116] *Religious Commonplace Book*, DD/HU3, 53; *The Works of Lucy Hutchinson*, vol. 2, 95.

[117] On Calvinist double predestination, see DD/HU3, 63; *The Works of Lucy Hutchinson*, vol. 2, 100: 'God hath a certeine predestinated number of men and angells ordeind to life and glory' as well as creatures 'predestinated also vnto dishonor wrath condemnation and eternall death for their sinne'. See also Lucy Hutchinson's notes on *Calvin's Institutes* in DD/HU3, 7-50; *The Works of Lucy Hutchinson*, vol. 2, 59-77.

[118] See, for instance, the following examples: 'He then cast off all other studies, and wholly applied himselfe to the Scriptures, and they were sweete councellors and refreshment to him in all his adversities' (S6/K22); '"I have," said he, "discovered much more of the mystery of truth in that Epistle"' (S270/K328). On those reading practices see Narveson, 'Reading the Bible: Clerical Prescriptions and Lay Reading Practices', *Bible Readers* 19-50.

[119] On spiritual autobiography, see Kathleen Lynch, *Protestant Autobiography in the Seventeenth-Century Anglophone World* (Oxford: Oxford UP, 2012); Dean Ebner, *Autobiography in Seventeenth-Century England, Theology, and the Self* (The Hague: Mouton, 1971); Owen C. Watkins, *The Puritan Experience: Studies in Spiritual Autobiography* (London: Routledge, 1972).

we love our neighbour'.[120] The *Memoirs* give many examples of John Hutchinson's charity, always based on his love of God, 'the burnisht gold wherein all his graces shind', according to his wife.[121] In the Dedication, charity is the bond that linked the Colonel to her and to those who loved him: '[o]ur conjunction, if wee had any with him, was indissoluble; if we were knitt together by one spiritt into one Body of Christ, wee are so still; if we were mutually united in one love of God, good men, and goodness, wee are so still' (S3/K18). But in the narrative of the 'Life' itself charity extends beyond this mystical union and takes on a public dimension. In accordance with the Gospel commandment 'Love your enemies' (Matthew 5:44), John Hutchinson is reported to have loved his political enemies despite his hatred for their sins: he 'lov'd even his bitterest enemies so well that I am witnesse how his soule mourn'd for them [...]; but their wickednesse his righteous soul abhorr'd' (S9/K25). This example of 'charitable hatred', praised by Church fathers and school divines alike, is further illustrated by the conduct of the Hutchinsons in September 1643 after the occupation of Nottingham by some royalists from Newark.[122] The Presbyterian minister, Captain Palmer, reproached the Hutchinsons for their evangelical conduct towards the prisoners who, he argued, were 'the enemies of God' (S99/K129). More specifically, he upbraided Lucy Hutchinson for dressing the wounds of 'three of the prisoners sorely cutt and carried downe bleeding into the Lion's Den', to which rebuke she replied that 'she had done nothing but what she thought was her duty in humanity to them, as creatures, not as enemies' (S99/K129). The same reproach was cast upon John Hutchinson who had sent for a few prisoners to have dinner in the castle, an action 'for which Captaine Palmer bellow'd lowdly against him, as a favourer of Malignants and Cavaliers' (S99/K129).[123]

Another meaningful manifestation of the Colonel's charity is evidenced by his mercy, which is an 'act of charity', defined by Aquinas, following Augustine (*De Civitate Dei* ix, 5), as 'heartfelt sympathy for another's distress, impelling us to succor him if we can. For mercy takes its name "misericordia" from denoting a man's compassionate heart [*miserum cor*] for another's

---

[120] *Summa Theologiae* II, II, question 25, article 1. In her *Literary Commonplace Book*, Lucy Hutchinson quotes Caussin's description of charity, which is very close to that of Aquinas: 'Love towards God as a father and towards men as the lively images of his goodnesse is the foundation of all vertues' (DD/HU1, 147). Caussin's actual definition reads: 'tendrenesse towards God as a Father, towards men as the liuely Images of his Goodnesse; is, the principall foundation of all vertues' (*Holy Court* [1638] 2).
[121] *Memoirs*, DD/HU4, 22.
[122] On 'charitable hatred', see Alexandra Walsham, *Charitable Hatred: Tolerance and Intolerance in England 1500-1700* (Manchester: Manchester UP, 2005) 1-2, 39-50.
[123] For examples of the Governor's clemency, see *Memoirs*, ed. Sutherland, 141-2, and ed. Keeble, 178-9.

unhappiness.'[124] Such evangelical mercifulness (Matthew 9:36), proof of the Colonel's love for God and for his fellow-creatures, takes on a clear ideological edge in the polarized context of the Civil War: 'When he was most exalted he was most mercifull and compassionate to those that were humbled. At the same time that he vanquisht any enemie he cast away all his ill will to him, and entertain'd thoughts of love and kindnesse so long as he was not in a posture of opposition' (S12/K29). We are given several instances of the Colonel's mercy, as for instance when the 'delinquents' were judged by the Council of State, of which he was an appointed member in the early years of the Commonwealth. On that occasion he was said to have been moved 'by meere compassion and generosity' (S192/K238), and to have defended even his enemies:

> [his] excellent gentlenesse was such that he not only protected and sav'd these enemies, wherein there was some glory of passing by revenge, but was *compassionately* affected with the miseries of any poore weomen or children who had bene unfortunately, though deservedly, ruin'd in this civill warre [...]. And as it was a misery to be bewail'd in those dayes that many of the Parliament party exercis'd cruelty and oppression and injustice to their conquer'd enemies, wherever he discover'd it he violently oppos'd it, and defended even those enemies that were by might oppress'd and defrawded of the mercies of the Parliament. (S200/K246, my emphasis)

Finally, the charity of the Colonel towards his political enemies exercised itself through friendship, a social bond that is fundamental in the *Memoirs*, the sort of charity that will be perfected in heaven.[125] According to his wife, unlike many of his contemporaries, John Hutchinson was 'as faithfull a friend as the world had' (S10/K26), and a most charitable one, including in respect to his political enemies. This was the case with the royalist army officer, Sir Allen Apsley, Lucy Hutchinson's brother. After surrendering Barnstaple Castle (of which he was the Governor) in April 1646, the latter 'retir'd to the Governor's house till his composition with the Parliament was compleated' (S170/K211). Unexpectedly, despite the deep politico-religious divisions of the age, the

---

[124] *Summa Theologiae* II, II, question 30, article 1.
[125] *Summa Theologiae* II, II, question 23, article 1 and 3—'Whether charity is friendship?' On friendship in Lucy Hutchinson's works, see Penelope Anderson's important chapter, 'Honouring Friendship's Shadows: Marriage and Political Reputation in Lucy Hutchinson's Writings', *Friendship's Shadows: Women's Friendship and the Politics of Betrayal in England 1640-1705* (Edinburgh: Edinburgh UP, 2012) 189–221, here 207. On the relationship between friendship and charity, see Lucy Hutchinson's notes on Caussin (*Literary Commonplace Book*, DD/HU1, 152-5): 'those that are wise may differ in their sentiments of severall things and not breake the yoake of amity for a friend is not to be like a Chameleon changing into colours' (155; *Holy Court* 29).

friendship between the two men is said to have remained unaltered. Lucy Hutchinson relates how fourteen years later, at the Restoration, it was Sir Allen's turn to support the Colonel in front of the Convention 'with all the kindest zeale of friendship that can be imagin'd' (S230/K282), in ways that could have certainly ruined his political career.[126] She also reports how, on his death, the Colonel was grateful for his brother-in-law's charity which he calls 'his labour of love to him' (S272/K330). Yet, as Norbrook has shown, this friendship may not have been as unfailing as it appears in the *Memoirs*. An important letter from Lucy Hutchinson's brother to Secretary Bennet reveals that he put his own political ambition above his friendship for Colonel Hutchinson.[127]

The third and final Christian virtue that contributes to the Colonel's characterization as a saint is hope, the object of which is also 'eternal happiness',[128] or to quote Lucy Hutchinson's own words from her religious Commonplace Book: 'Hope is also a guift and grace God whereby faith is heightned to a certeine and ioyfull expectation of the accomplishment of our salvation and all the other free and gracious and glorious promises of God which makes vs waite patiently for them.'[129] This virtue is at first sight less conspicuous in the *Memoirs* than charity and faith, as it mostly manifests itself during the Colonel's last weeks of life at Sandown Castle, in Kent, where he is waiting for his own death, still full of hopes for the saints. For many, including his wife, his sufferings signalled his defeat and that of his community. For John Hutchinson, on the contrary, this martyrdom made sense in God's scheme of things; his sufferings were a paradoxical promise of salvation and a source of hope for her, whom he encouraged to follow his 'example':[130]

> Once when his wife was lamenting his condition, having sayd many things to comfort her, he told her he could not have bene without this affliction, for if he had flourisht while all the people of God were corrected, he should have fear'd he had not bene accounted among his children if he had not shared their lott; then would with thankfulnesse repeate the kind and gentle dealings of the Lord att all times toward him, and erect a firme and mighty hope upon it, and wonderfully encourage her to beare it patiently, not only by words, but by his owne admirable example. (S265/K323)

[126] See Paul Seaward, 'Apsley, Sir Allen (1616–1683), royalist army officer and politician' (2004), *Oxford Dictionary of National Biography*, DOI: 10.1093/ref:odnb/600.
[127] Norbrook, 'Memoirs and Oblivion', 272–3.
[128] See for instance *Summa Theologiae* II, II, question 17, article 3.
[129] *Religious Commonplace Book*, DD/HU3, 85; *The Works of Lucy Hutchinson,* vol. 2, 112.
[130] On the theological virtue of faith, see Thomas, *Summa* II, II, 17: 'Question 17. Hope, considered in itself.'

The final moments of the Colonel and especially his final words, spoken in his wife's absence, also exemplify the Colonel's virtue of hope for himself as well as for all his community. They are best understood if one remembers that for an early modern reader, last dying speeches were thought to convey prophetic truth, or, to use John of Gaunt's own speech in Shakespeare's *Richard II*: 'O, but they say the tongues of dying men / Enforce attention like deep harmony: / Where words are scarce, they are seldom spent in vain, / For they breathe truth that breathe their words in pain' (II, 1). Like John of Gaunt's words, those of the Colonel are spoken in public, the 'public' being metonymically represented by the 'doctor' who, Lucy Hutchinson insists, neither belonged to the family nor shared John Hutchinson's beliefs. He thus stood as a witness guaranteeing the veracity of the Colonel's words; he also contributed to making the portrayal of Colonel Hutchinson as a saint irrefutable:

> The Doctor, who had when religion was in fashion bene a pretender to it, came to him, and askt him if his peace was made with God; to which he replied, "I hope you do not thinke me so ill a Christian, to have bene thus long in prison, and have that to doe now!" The Doctor asked him concerning the ground of his hope; to which he answer'd, "There's none but Christ, none but Christ, in whom I have unspeakable joy, more than I can expresse; yet I should utter more but that the sorenesse of my mouth makes it difficult for me to speake. (S271/K329–30)

The words he addresses to his daughter shortly afterwards are of the same vein and serve the same exemplary function, but the message of hope, through the tears of the Colonel's daughter, affects the reader's emotions rather than his reason: 'and as his daughter sat weeping by him, "Fie, Bab," sayd he, "doe you mourne for me as for one without hope? Doe not so: there is hope"' (S272/K330). Those words, fuelling millenarian hopes, repeat in another way the typological parallel developed at the beginning of the book between Moses and the Colonel:

> To one of these he was led up to see the promis'd land, and had a soule-refreshing view of it; such a one made him forgett on what side of the river he stood, while by faith he tooke possession of future glory, and resign'd himself in the assured hope of returning with the Lord and his greate Armie of Saints (S36/K56).[131]

---

[131] On the combination of the public and intimate in Lucy Hutchinson's *Memoirs*, see Chedgzoy, *Women's Writing in the British Atlantic World* 154.

Figure 1.1 Colonel Hutchinson by Robert Walker (engraving) from Lucy Hutchinson's *Memoirs of the Life of Colonel Hutchinson*, ed. Julius Hutchinson (London, 1806).

3. Idealization and the limits of exemplarity

The idealization of the Colonel's virtues raises two sets of questions. The first one concerns the difficulties of representation Lucy Hutchinson faced when describing the Colonel's perfection. The second one revolves around the risk of idolatry inherent in such an idealized and eulogistic portrait.

a) Difficulties of representation

Lucy Hutchinson's decision to write her husband's life originally came from the fact that she did not want to 'lett loose the winds of passion to bring in a flood of sorrow, whose ebbing tides carry away the deare memory of what they have lost' (S1/K16). Commemorating her husband's 'Life' through writing was a way of resisting the temptation of forgetfulness; it was a process fraught with difficulties, both because her grief was insuperable and because her memory of him was 'treacherous' (S3/K18).[132] Her 'greate memory' (S288/K14), about which she boasts in her autobiographical fragment, left her almost helpless in her hard work of remembrance. The Colonel's absence, she writes in the unpublished portion of the Dedication, 'distracts [her] memory with iust woe that [she] cannot call things forth in their due formes & order'.[133] In other words, to the pain and difficulty of remembering the past is added a third challenge, consisting in representing the Colonel's perfection with imperfect tools—here an 'unskilful pen':

> I am almost stopt before I sett forth to trace his steps; [and] finding the number of [his virtues] by which he still outwent himselfe more than my unperfect arithmatick can count, and the exact figure of them such as my unskillfull pen cannot describe, I feare to injure that memory which I would honor, and to disgrace his name with a poore monument. (S1/K16–17)

This difficulty of coming up with an adequate representation of the Colonel's virtues is again acknowledged at the very end of the section entitled 'His vertues', where Lucy Hutchinson concludes that her first portrayal was not satisfactory: 'All this and more is true, but I so much dislike the manner of

---

[132] See Kate Chedgzoy, Elspeth Graham, and Katharine Hodgkin, 'Researching Memory in Early Modern Studies', *Memory Studies* 11.1 (2018): 14–15, Chedgzoy, *Women's Writing in the British Atlantic World* 155–6.

[133] *Memoirs*, DD/HU4, 29.

relating it that I will make another assay' (S14/K30).[134] This 'assay' is cut from all existing editions of the *Memoirs*, which does not do justice to the way Lucy Hutchinson grappled with the difficulties of representation she encountered.[135] The manuscript, however, reveals that the 'manner' of this 'assay' is not so blatantly different from the rest of the Dedication. Overall, it is more intent on bringing out the coherence of the Colonel's spiritual life than the published section, while it leaves out his physical appearance and social status.

The sense of an unbridgeable discrepancy between the perfection of the Colonel and the deficiencies of her art leads Lucy Hutchinson to disparage herself and her ability to represent her husband's virtues. This posture was not uncommon among women of her age, who did not want to be suspected of seeking their own glory in their writings. The poet Eliza thus excuses herself for her poems' 'imperfections' and 'desires onely to advance the glory of God, and not her own',[136] while the Independent pamphleteer and petitioner, Katherine Chidley, apologized for her 'ignorance' and 'unskilfulnesse'.[137] Lucy Hutchinson uses a variant of this modesty topos, when she belittles herself (and her pen) the better to celebrate her husband's virtues: 'His vertues come very much sullied out of my hands; and indeed he that would commemorate his heroique glorie should have a soule equally greate to conceive and expresse that which my dejected and inferior spiritt cannot performe' (S12/K29).[138] Nevertheless, she recognizes that the recourse to the imperfect 'medium' of words—metaphorically equated with 'a very thick cloud'—is the only way of accommodating the godliness of the Colonel to 'the world's weak eyes':[139]

> that resplendent body of light [...] will through my apprehension and expression shine as under a very thick clowd, which will obscure much of their lustre; but there is need of this *medium to the world's weake eies*, which I feare hath but few people so vertuous in it as can believe, because they find themselves so short, any other could make so large a progresse in the race of piety, honor, and vertue. (S1/K16, my emphasis)

[134] For commentaries on this unpublished section, see Sutherland, ed., xxii.
[135] See Norbrook, 'But a Copie', 115–16.
[136] Frontispiece and 'To the Reader', *Eliza's Babes; or, The Virgins-Offering. Being Divine Poems, and Meditations* (London, 1652) sig. A3^v.
[137] Katherine Chidley, 'To the Christian Reader', *The Justification of the Independent Churches of Christ Being an Answer to Mr Edwards His Booke* (London, 1641) sig. 2^{rv}. More examples in Gheeraert-Graffeuille, *La Cuisine et le forum* 112–14.
[138] See Hutchinson, *Order and Disorder* 5.
[139] See Norbrook, 'Lucy Hutchinson's Elegies', 473. On cloud imagery in devotional poetry, see Tony Gheeraert, 'Les nuées du fantasme. Vapeurs et nuages d'Augustin à Port-Royal', *Le Parcours du comparant. Pour une histoire littéraire des métaphores*, ed. Xavier Bonnier (Paris: Classiques Garnier, 2014) 361–88.

An attempt at overcoming these acknowledged limits of representation can be seen in Lucy Hutchinson's ekphrasis of her husband in the subsection entitled 'His Description'. In these pages, she tries to recreate verbally a picture of the Colonel she may have had under her eyes, possibly a painting by Robert Walker that the Hutchinsons had in their possession (see Figure 1.1).[140] From the outset, however, she confesses that words cannot compensate for the Colonel's absence. 'His Description' is only a second best, intended for the Colonel's family and friends, especially for those 'as have not *seene* him to remember his person' She places the visual representation of the painter above her verbal one:

> Desiring, if my treacherous memory have not lost the dearest treasure that ever I committed to its trust, to relate to you his holy, vertuous, honorable life, I would put his picture in the front of his booke, but my unskillfull hand will injure him. Yet to such of you as have not *seene* him to remember his person, I leave this.   (S3/K18, my emphasis)

Here, the trope of modesty is a way for Lucy Hutchinson to exhibit her rhetorical accomplishments without being suspected of vanity. It leaves her freer to follow the advice of Quintilian in his *Institutes of the Orator*—at the centre of the grammar school curriculum in the sixteenth and the seventeenth centuries—to bring 'the living truth' of facts to the 'eyes of the mind' through *enargeia*, that is, through a vivid description.[141] Human oratory is undeniably imperfect, but the use of *enargeia* can compensate for the flaws of art:

> we must place among ornaments that ἐνάργεια which I mentioned in the rules which I laid down for the statement of facts, because vivid illustration,

---

[140] Keeble, ed. (*Memoirs* 345, note 38) and Norbrook ('Lucy Hutchinson's Elegies', 474) both assume that a portrait of Colonel Hutchinson by Robert Walker may have served as the basis of Lucy Hutchinson's portrayal. On that picture, the Colonel is in full armour while his son is standing on his right-hand side, holding his father's helmet. The portraits included in the 1806 edition were in the possession of Julius Hutchinson. They are traced in Sidney Race, 'Colonel Hutchinson, the Regicide', *Notes and Queries* 197 (1952): 32 and 'Colonel Hutchinson: Manuscript and Printed Memoirs', *Notes and Queries* 199 (1954): 166. Cf. the note in Julius Hutchinson's edition (1806): 'The editor is happy to have it in his power to do this in a manner that will be gratifying to the lovers of the arts. The original pictures of Mr. and Mrs. Hutchinson, with their two children were found by him in their house at Owthorpe, and are now deposited, along with the manuscript, at Messrs. Longman's and Co' (3–4). On Walker, see also Angus Haldane, 'The Face of Civil War: Robert Walker (1599): His Life and Portraits', *The British Art Journal* 17.2 (2016): 20–9.

[141] On Quintilian being taught in grammar schools, see Foster Watson, *The English Grammar Schools to 1660: their Curriculum and Practice* (Cambridge: Cambridge UP, 1908) 4–6. On *enargeia*, see Adriana Zangara, *Voir l'histoire. Théories anciennes du récit historique IIe siècle avant J.-C.–IIe siècle après J.-C.* (Paris: Vrin, 2007) 14.

or, as some prefer to call it, representation, is something more than mere clearness, since the latter merely lets itself be seen, whereas the former thrusts itself upon our notice. It is a great gift to be able to set forth the facts on which we are speaking clearly and vividly. For oratory fails of its full effect, and does not assert itself as it should, if its appeal is merely to the hearing, and if the judge merely feels that the facts on which he has to give his decision are being narrated to him, and not displayed in their living truth to the eyes of the mind.[142]

Following the rhetorical tradition of *enargeia*, Lucy Hutchinson offers a potent visual representation of the Colonel. She literally follows Erasmus's advice in *De copia* (based on Quintilian), where the humanist suggests that one way of enriching subject-matter is to use *enargeia*, that is, vividness: 'we employ [this] whenever [...], instead of setting out the subject in bare simplicity, we fill in the colours and set it up like a picture to look at, so that we seem to have painted the scene rather than described it, and the reader seems to have seen rather than read.'[143] This is exactly what Lucy Hutchinson tries to achieve in her physical description of the Colonel, as the readers find themselves in the position of 'all that saw him':[144]

> He was of a middle stature, of a slender and exactly well-proportion'd shape in all parts, his complexion fair, his hayre of a light browne, very thick sett in his youth, softer than the finest silke, curling into loose greate rings att the ends; his eies of a lively grey, well-shaped and full of life and vigour, graced with many becoming motions; his visage thinne, his mouth well made, and his lipps very ruddy and gracefull, allthough the nether chap shut over the upper, yett it was in such a manner as was not unbecomming; his teeth were even and white as the purest ivory, his chin was something long, and the mold of his face, his forehead was not very high, his nose was rays'd and sharpe, but withall he had a most amiable countenance, which carried in it

---

[142] Quintilian, *Institutio Oratoria*, 8, 4, 63. Latin Texts & Translations, http://perseus.uchicago.edu/perseus-cgi/citequery3.pl?dbname=LatinAugust2012&getid=1&query=Quint.%208.4 (accessed 22/01/2019). On the notion of *enargeia* see Brian Vickers, *In Defence of Rhetoric* (Oxford: Clarendon, 1998) 321–2; Christine Noille-Clauzade, 'La figure de la description dans la théorie rhétorique classique', *Pratiques* 109.110 (2001): 5–14, here 5 and 11; Heinrich F. Plett, *Enargeia in Classical Antiquity and the Early Modern Age. The Aesthetics of Evidence* (Leiden: Brill, 2012) 7–22.
[143] Erasmus, *Copia: Foundations of the Abundant Style/De duplici copia verborum ac rerum commentarii duo*, trans. Betty I. Knott, *The Collected Works of Erasmus*, ed. Craig R. Thompson (Toronto: Toronto UP, 1979), vol. 24, 577.
[144] On other occasions, Lucy Hutchinson tries to create the physical presence of John Hutchinson. See *Memoirs*, ed. Sutherland, 31, and ed. Keeble, 49.

something of magnanimity and majesty mixt with sweetnesse, that at the same time bespoke love and awe in *all that saw him.*

(S3/K18–19, my emphasis)

As this ekphrasis reveals, the Colonel's outer beauty is connected with his moral qualities—'magnanimity and majesty mixt with sweetenesse' (S3/K19). Lucy Hutchinson is not only interested in the physical description of her husband, but she wants to show how the physical details reveal his character. In other words, his face is worth a description because it is the place where moral qualities—here his magnanimity—are best reflected. Such an approach is reminiscent of some remarks by Plutarch in the 'Life of Alexander', where the moralist considers that painters rightly fix their attention on the faces of their models because faces are morally more significant than other parts of the body.[145] One of Lucy Hutchinson's 'Elegies', 'On the Picture in Armour', contemporary with the *Memoirs*, offers another ekphrasis of Walker's painting, and can also be interpreted as another attempt to recreate the Colonel's presence through words.[146] As in the opening of 'His Description', Lucy Hutchinson aims at turning a physical portrait into a moral one—anger, love and wisdom being more important than the features themselves:

> This table faintly represents That face
> Where glorious ferceness dwelt wth Charming grace
> Lightning oft darted from y:^{t} angrey Eie
> Whence oftener did loues gentle arrowes flie
> [...]
> Those lipps were wisdomes gates wch neuer did
> Vnseasnably disclose nor keepe her hid.[147]

Despite the moral potentialities of ekphrasis, which she exploits both in the *Memoirs* and in the 'Elegies', Lucy Hutchinson comes to the conclusion that no 'copy' of the Colonel can ever capture the divine that was present in him when he was alive:

---

[145] Plutarch, *The Lives* 722.
[146] Other *ekphrases* are to be found in 'Upon two Pictures' (Elegy [4], ed. Norbrook, 'Lucy Hutchinson's Elegies', 494), and 'On the Picture of the Prisoner' (Elegy [6], ed. Norbrook, 'Lucy Hutchinson's Elegies', 497–8).
[147] Elegy [5], ed. Norbrook, 495. On commemorative portraits in the 'Elegies', see Wiseman, 'No Publick Funerall' 213.

> In all his naturall and ordinary inclinations and composure there was somthing extraordinary and tending to vertue, beyond what I can describe or can be gather'd from a bare dead description; there was a life of spiritt and power in him that is not to be found in any copie drawne from him. (S5/K20)

Because it only offers 'a bare dead description' and limits itself to the 'outward frame and disposition' of the Colonel, the rhetoric of ekphrasis remains too external to the taste of the portraitist; it accounts only for the body of the Colonel, understood as a mere receptacle for the soul, described as the 'prince' in charge of administering virtues:

> To summe up therefore all that can be sayd of his outward frame and disposition, wee must truly conclude that it was a very handsome and wellfurnisht lodging prepar'd for the reception of that prince who in the administration of all excellent vertues reign'd there a while, till he was called back to the pallace of the universall emperor. (S5/K20)

Such a dichotomy between body and soul is much in keeping with Lucy Hutchinson's syncretic Neoplatonism, but out of step with mainstream Christian thinking.[148] Therefore, to rule out the suspicion of heresy which the depreciation of the body could arouse, she gives us to read an unequivocally orthodox account of the Colonel's resurrection: 'What have wee then lost? His flesh? – No – that is but lay'd to sleepe that it may wake againe more vigorous and beautifull' (S2/K18). Furthermore, John Hutchinson's resurrection and reunion with God are movingly represented in the 'Final Meditation' as a transfiguration.[149] As Erica Longfellow has shown, Lucy Hutchinson assimilates the death of the Colonel to that of the prophet Elijah, whose body was carried to heaven by 'a chariot of fire and horses of fire' (2 Kings 2:11).[150] Like Elijah, John Hutchinson is 'granted the privilege of immediate union with God'. As the word 'translated' suggests, his transformation is a 'transfiguration' and 'transubstantiation' from the earthly into the heavenly:

---

[148] See Hutchinson's *Literary Commonplace Book*, DD/HU1, 147–8. In the first two pages adapted from *The Holy Court*, she integrates, into the main body of her own text, Caussin's marginal citations of Hermes Trismegistus, of William of Auvergne, of Augustine, and of Ficino. See Longfellow, *Women and Religious Writing* 190.
[149] Lucy Hutchinson, 'Final Meditation', *Memoirs*, ed. Keeble, 337–8; see *Memoirs*, DD/HU4, [421].
[150] Longfellow, *Women and Religious Writing* 192–3.

It is true the fiery chariot of a fever was sent to fetch him out [of] the double prison, that of his oppressors and that of his flesh which the [ ] soul was more oppressed with than the other while he remained in it, [and] was translated out of this world into the Father's glory.[151]

Eventually, it turns out that to build a monument for her husband, Lucy Hutchinson absolutely needs rhetorical tools. Despite their moral and aesthetic shortcomings, ekphrasis and the epideictic mode prove the best means to enhance the ethical perfection of John Hutchinson, whose exemplarity is never challenged in the *Memoirs*, his example being never, in Montaigne's phrase, an 'uncertain looking-glass, all-embracing, turning all ways'.[152]

b) Risks of idolatry

According to Alexandra Walsham, '[t]he relatively belated reappearance of biography as a mode of historical writing in post-Reformation England may itself be a measure of residual anxiety about turning the virtuous dead into objects of popish veneration, and of transgressing the newly redrawn line between idolatry and memory.'[153] Lucy Hutchinson was acutely aware of that line, and of the risk of idolatry in her memorializing Colonel Hutchinson as an epitome of all virtues: an excessive celebration of his moral perfection could easily be taken as evidence she placed him before God. She was resolute to shun such a risk, but her encomiastic description of her husband, despite her efforts to the contrary, puts her and the readers on the brink of idolatry.

The laudatory dimension of the Dedication is the object of several perspicuous remarks by Julius Hutchinson in his 1806 edition of the *Memoirs*. Naturally, the editor copiously extols the literary qualities and the beauty of Lucy Hutchinson's 'dirge', but he is also alert to her extreme idealization of the Colonel's virtues, which were 'recorded in heaven's annalls, and can never

---

[151] 'Final Meditation' *Memoirs*, ed. Keeble, 337.
[152] Michel de Montaigne, *Complete Essays*, trans. M. A. Screech (London: Penguin, 2004). We here quote Screech's translation of Montaigne's essays that is closer to the French original than Florio's translation: 'Example is a bright looking-glasse, vniversall and for all shapes to looke-into.' ('Of Experience', *Essays*, trans. John Florio [London, 1613], III, 614). See also the French text: 'L'exemple est un mirouer vague, universel à tout sens.' https://fr.wikisource.org/wiki/Essais/Livre_III/Chapitre_13 (accessed 02/10/2019). On seventeenth-century debates on exemplarity, see Wiseman, 'Theories of the Example', *Conspiracy and Virtue* 49–58.
[153] See Walsham, 'History, Memory, and the English Reformation', 912.

perish' (S2/K18).[154] Even if the editor indulgently observes that her 'ability to ornament and embellish' is restricted 'to such occasions as are most suitable' and is less frequent in the narrative of the life itself than in the Dedication, he nonetheless asks the question of Lucy Hutchinson's *excessive* use of rhetoric: 'Highly panegyrical as the character Mrs. Hutchinson here gives of her husband may appear, yet every point of it will be completely exemplified in the narrative; but if the widow's fondness for his memory should have led her into some excess, who will blame it?'[155] Despite his indulgence for the author, Julius Hutchinson deliberately cut out some passages celebrating the Colonel's faith, probably because he felt they were excessively commendatory and too religious in tone for a nineteenth-century Protestant readership.[156]

Ironically enough—but this is not surprising given her self-conscious art—Lucy Hutchinson herself was aware of the dangers of excessive eloquence. This is perceptible from the beginning of the Dedication, in which, as if to ward off the suspicion of idolatry, she promises 'a naked undrest narrative', clearly taking her distance with the high-flown oratory of the hired preachers who, in their funeral sermons, like the sophists of antiquity, were said to prefer flattery to truth:[157]

> I need not guild [the preservation of his memory] with such flattring commendations as the hired preachers doe equally to the truly and titularly honorable. *A naked undrest narrative, speaking the simple truth of him*, will deck him with more substantial glorie than all the Panegyrics the best pens could ever consecrate to the vertues of the best men. (S1/K16, my emphasis)

Lucy Hutchinson's claim to a 'naked, undressed narrative' is convenient to situate the 'Life' in early modern historiographical debates. The *vera et pura narratio* was indeed a common trope in humanist debates, which served to contrast plain historical narratives—in the style of memoirs—with more eloquent and epic histories.[158] Evidently, such a promise, however essential

---

[154] Julius Hutchinson, ed., 'To my Children', *Memoirs*, note h, 1.
[155] Julius Hutchinson, ed., *Memoirs* 6.
[156] *Memoirs*, DD/HU4, 8: on that page, pencil marks show how Julius Hutchinson proceeded when he edited the manuscript. A confrontation of Julius Hutchinson's 1806 edition with the manuscript reveals the extent of the deletions to be found in all editions of the *Memoirs* up until the publication of James Sutherland's edition in 1973.
[157] See Vickers, 'Plato's Attack on Rhetoric', *In Defence of Rhetoric* 83–146. See also, as a comparison, Keeble, 'The Puritan Style', *Richard Baxter* 49–68, here 50: Baxter takes his distance with 'metaphysical writers and Ciceronians'.
[158] See also Nadine Kuperty-Tsur, *Se dire à la Renaissance. Les Mémoires au XVIe siècle* (Paris: Vrin, 1997) 92. An interesting example is provided by Marguerite de Valois's *Mémoires*, which echo Lucy Hutchinson's statement: 'Je traceray mes memoires, a qui je ne donneray un plus glorieux nom bien qu'ils meritassent celuy d'hystoire, pour la verité qui y est contenue nuement et sans ornement.' On this

it may be to interpret the 'Life of John Hutchinson', is at variance with the Dedication's description of the Colonel's virtues, which is neither plain nor sober, but clearly eulogistic. Julius Hutchinson, for that matter, was not the only one to have some reservations about the commendatory portrait of Lucy Hutchinson. In his study of the 'Elegies' which, as we saw, also include several portraits of the Colonel, Norbrook considers that the 'extreme idealization' of John Hutchinson may turn him into 'an improbable paragon of every single virtue'.[159]

The other ambiguity of a high-flown rhetoric stems from the fact that the Colonel's 'Life' dangerously resembles the hagiography of a Catholic saint. This is true of the Dedication but also of the narrative of the 'Life' as a whole.[160] Lucy Hutchinson was aware of the perils of idolatry as she admonished readers—and herself—using the inclusive first-person plural, not to idolize the Colonel: 'let us not excesse of love and delight in the streame make us forgett the fountaine: he and all his excellencies came from God, and flow'd back into their owne spring, that is to say God' (S2/K17). Hence her resolution, in order to eschew that sin she had not been fully able to avoid during the Colonel's lifetime, to systematically refer 'the glories' of the Colonel to God alone, or, to use Norbrook's felicitous phrase, to '[effect] an inner iconoclasm':[161]

> If therefore, while I had a happie enjoyment of him and communication of his guifts and graces during his abode in the flesh, I did not looke so farre beyond the creature as I ought, delighting more than I ought to have done in the mirror that reflected the creator's excellence, which I should have allwayes admir'd in its owne fountaine, I desire not to persue that sinne, but, while I celebrate the glories of a saint, that I and any for whom I may declare them may give God the first and chiefest glory for all the goodnesse he gives to the children of men.   (S2/K17)[162]

---

humanist debate, see Marc Fumaroli, 'Mémoires et histoire: le dilemme de l'historiographie humaniste au XVIe siècle', *Les Valeurs chez les mémorialistes français du XVIIe siècle avant la Fronde*, ed. Noemi Hepp and Jacques Hennequin, Actes et Colloques 22 (Paris: Klincksieck, 1979) 21–45, here 21–3.

[159] Norbrook, 'Lucy Hutchinson's Elegies', 474.

[160] In the *Memoirs*, idolatry is associated with 'the idolatrous practises' of papists and of princes (S38/K58), and with Arminianism: 'He never mist the Chapell, where he began to take notice of their stretching superstition to idolatrie' (S25/K42).

[161] Norbrook, 'Lucy Hutchinson's Elegies', 472.

[162] For an enlightening reading of this passage that can also be read as a 'bridge into the biblical excerpts', see Norbrook, 'But a Copie', 20.

Lucy Hutchinson's desire not to deviate from Protestant orthodoxy logically leads her to stress the differences between Catholic and Protestant saints. The latter could only be models to be commemorated and imitated; they were not intercessors and objects of veneration. Therefore, the Colonel should only be represented as a guide, a model, a conduit of heavenly glory, whose holiness ultimately comes from God:

> if our teares did not putt out our eies, we should see him, even in heaven, holding forth his flaming lamp of vertuous examples and precepts to light us through the darke world. It is time that I open the shutt [eyes] and lett in to your knowledge that splendor which while it cheares and enlightens your heavy senses, let us remember to give all his and all our glorie to God alone, who is the only father and fountaine of all light and excellence. (S3/K18)

Lucy Hutchinson's precautionary phrases ('this necessary caution' S1/K17), however, do not dispel all ambiguities concerning the status of Colonel Hutchinson as a saint in her text. They do not alter the porosity existing between the 'Life of John Hutchinson' and the medieval lives of saints which, like Protestant godly lives, were supposed to arouse admiration and encourage imitation.[163] They cannot hide either the fact that the main archetypal ingredients that go into the composition of Catholic hagiographies can also be found in the 'Life of John Hutchinson': the origins of the saint (country, city, family, date of birth of the hero), the crucial moments in his life when he had to make choices (childhood and youth, education), his experience of faith and conversion, the type of life that he lived, and his sayings.[164] Finally, in spite of the fact that the veneration of relics was proscribed in Protestantism there are some disturbing references to relics in the 'Elegies'. In Elegy [1], probably composed just after the Colonel's death, Lucy Hutchinson disturbingly refers to 'That Cold Graue which his deare reliques keepes', imagining herself in the grave with the Colonel, a fantasy reminiscent of Donne's own elegy 'The Relic'.[165] In Elegy [16], the same 'deare reliques', hidden by a 'weeping Stone',

---

[163] Philippe Sellier, 'Pour une poétique de la légende: "La vie de Monsieur Pascal"', *Port-Royal et la littérature*, vol. 1 (Paris: Honoré Champion, 1999) 31–2. On this porosity, see Bergamasco, 'Hagiographie et sainteté', 1054–5. Bergamasco reminds us that medieval saints were present in the post-Reformation book market.

[164] Sellier, 'Pour une poétique de la légende', 32.

[165] See Elegy [1], ed. Norbrook, l.5, 487. See John Donne, 'The Relic', *The Complete English Poems*, ed. A. J. Smith [1971] (London: Penguin, 1996) 75–6. See Scott-Baumann, 'Katherine Philips and Lucy Hutchinson Reading John Donne', *Forms of Engagement* 113–43.

await resurrection, but, this time, John Hutchinson is no longer the lover, but the 'Patriot' and the 'Martier'.[166]

In this context, it is clear that Lucy Hutchinson is intent on showing that her hagiographic pages do not make of Colonel Hutchinson an equal or a rival of God. First, in Christianized Neoplatonic terms, she defines God as the only model and source of Glory—the 'originall of all excellencie [being] God him [selfe] and God alone' (S2/K17).[167] John Hutchinson, she obsessively insists, was only a copy of that model, a 'mirror that reflected the Creator's excellence', 'a blessed image of his owne glory', or 'an imperfect image of him' (S2/K17). It is interesting to notice, however, that in his wife's view, John Hutchinson remains an *exceptional* copy. In the 'Final Meditation', she presents him as 'one of the *fairest* copies in the exemplary book of honour and virtue'.[168] Second, in order to differentiate the Colonel from a theoretically sinless, Catholic saint, she emphasizes some of his defects. '[H]is fetters, his sins, his infirmities, his diseases' are all presented as marks of his fallen condition (S2/K18); he 'was yett but a man: a sonne of Adam, an inheritor of his corrupted nature, subject to all the sins and miseries that attend it' (S2/K17). One of the Colonel's weaknesses to which, as we have seen, Lucy Hutchinson returns several times is thus his proneness to anger. But these defects, instead of tarnishing the portrait of the Colonel, serve only to enhance his exceptional qualities, in particular, his temperance and his discretion.

Ultimately, the *Memoirs* are shot through with the tension between epideictic rhetoric and the ideal of plainness. But this tension is perhaps less problematic than it seems at first reading, as sobriety and praise, however oxymoronic the terms may be, were both commanded by Lucy Hutchinson's desire to defend her husband. On the one hand, she had recourse to laudatory oratory to defend the Colonel's 'truth' against falsehood, which, according to Augustine's recommendation in his *De Doctrina Christiana*, was perfectly legitimate:

Now, the art of rhetoric being available for the enforcing either of truth or falsehood, who will dare to say that truth in the person of its defenders is to take its stand unarmed against falsehood?

---

[166] See Elegy [16], ed. Norbrook, ll. 17–20, 516.

[167] See, for instance, her *Literary Commonplace Book*, DD/HU1, 148–9 for paraphrases of Hermes Trismegistus and Ficino. On Lucy Hutchinson's Christianized Neoplatonism, see Longfellow, *Women and Religious Writing* 185, 190; Norbrook, 'Lucy Hutchinson's Elegies', 471–2; see Katharine Gillespie, 'Lucy Hutchinson, Hermeticism, and Republicanism in the Restoration', *Women Writing the English Republic, 1625–1681* (Cambridge: Cambridge UP, 2017), 282–333, here 295–6.

[168] Lucy Hutchinson, 'Final Meditation', *Memoirs*, ed. Keeble, 337 (my emphasis); see *Memoirs*, DD/HU4, [421].

[...]
Since, then, the faculty of eloquence is available for both sides, and is of very great service in the enforcing either of wrong or right, why do not good men study to engage it on the side of truth, when bad men use it to obtain the triumph of wicked and worthless causes, and to further injustice and error?[169]

On the other hand, Lucy Hutchinson's claim to plainness was motivated by her refusal of a *false* and lying rhetoric which would damage the integrity of the Colonel and his engagement to the cause of the Parliament and Commonwealth. It was grounded in a historiographical approach, widely shared in humanist circles and among historians and memorialists of her age, according to which only a plain narrative could convey historical truth. This ideal plainness, totally absent from the Dedication, was more present in the section devoted to the Civil War in Nottingham, in which the narrative is more factual. In these pages, John Hutchinson's behaviour is vindicated, but the 'idolatrous' idealization of the Dedication is far less perceptible than in the dedication.

*

One of the historiographical consequences of the Colonel's exemplarity in the *Memoirs* is that he is given the status of a great man. By contrast, King Charles I is deprived of all virtues; he is portrayed as 'a prince that had nothing of faith or truth, justice or generosity in him' (S47/K68) and ultimately held responsible for the Civil Wars. The Colonel's exemplary deeds form the main narrative thread of the 'Life' and constitute the prism through which we are invited to read the whole text. For example, in May 1660, when the Colonel had to stand before Parliament, his 'cleare and upright carriage' was put forward by people who 'knew his principle [was] contrary to theirs' (S231/K282). Because of his exemplarity, he can first be seen, to use Timothy Hampton's terms, 'as a marked sign that bears the moral and historical authority of antiquity and engages the reader in a dialogue with the past – a dialogue to be played out [...] on the stage of public action'.[170] If we follow Plutarch, the Colonel's life of virtue should also be seen as a mirror in which the readers may look at themselves in order to fashion their own lives. This was a function of lives defined by Plutarch at the beginning of the 'Life of

---

[169] See Augustine, *De Doctrina Christiana*, Book 4, Chapter 2, 'Texts and Translations'. http://faculty.georgetown.edu/jod/augustine/ddc.html (accessed 17/11/2018).

[170] See Timothy Hampton, *Writing from History. The Rhetoric of Exemplarity in Renaissance Literature* (Ithaca and London: Cornell UP, 1990) 5.

Paulus Aemilius': 'When I first beganne to write these liues, my intent was to profit other: but since, continuing and going on, I haue muche profited my self by looking into these histories, as if I looked into a glasse, to frame and facion my life, to the mowld and patterne of these vertuous noble men.'[171]

'The Life of John Hutchinson', however, exceeds the limits of the genre of lives as it was practised by humanists. The difference lies in the fact that, unlike Thomas More and Francis Bacon who wrote the lives of Richard III and Henry VII, Lucy Hutchinson intimately knew the protagonist of her narrative; unlike them, she could draw upon her own experience and knowledge of the English Revolution. Writings of this kind, based on the experience of their authors, were highly prized in the wake of the Civil Wars among readers and writers of history because they were thought to give a more direct access to 'historical truth'.

---

[171] Plutarch, *The Lives* 263. Zangara, *Voir l'histoire* 86.

Chapter 2
The *Memoirs* and historiography

The rise of empiricism in early modern culture—what Barbara Shapiro calls the 'culture of fact'—has often been said to coincide with a 'historical revolution', which Robert Mayer synthetically describes as follows:[1]

> In the medieval period, historians were content to present what was generally accepted about the past, but from the sixteenth century certain scholars sought to establish what was known, to criticize that which was believed but seemed improbable, and to uncover new sources of historical evidence. The rejection of conjecture and of invented speeches or scenes, the concentration on secondary (human) rather than primary (providential) explanation, the commitments to impartiality and to a plain style – all these did represent a clear departure from past practice, and many of the best-known historians of the period were in this sense "revolutionaries": Leland, William Camden, Walter Ralegh, John Stow, John Selden, Francis Bacon, Henry Spelman, James Harrington, Robert Brady, William Dugdale, and Thomas Hearne, all have been discussed as "heroes" of the historical revolution by one or more of the students of this transformation.[2]

The development of English antiquarianism and philological research between 1580 and 1640 is part of the historiographical revolution, aptly summarized above by Mayer's quote and defended, among others, by Fussner, Levy, and Pocock.[3] Still, this vision of history tends to leave out major histories, especially those with a political slant, written in the humanist tradition—among which, for example, the works of Thomas More, Francis Bacon, or Edward

---

[1] On the developing culture of 'facts', see Barbara J. Shapiro, *A Culture of Fact. England, 1550–1720* (Ithaca and London: Cornell UP, 2000), and especially '"Fact" and History', 34–62.

[2] Mayer, *History and the Early English Novel* 9.

[3] See Mayer, *History and the Early English Novel* 19. The works which are discussed by Mayer are Fussner, *The Historical Revolution*; F. J. Levy, *Tudor Historical Thought* (San Marino: The Huntington Library, 1967); J. G. A. Pocock, *The Ancient Constitution. A Study of English Historical Thought* [1957] (Cambridge: Cambridge UP, 1987). On the 'historical revolution', see Stephen Davies, *Empiricism and History* (Basingstoke: Palgrave Macmillan, 2003) 1–23, and especially 11–12, and Joseph H. Preston, 'Was There an Historical Revolution?' *Journal of the History of Ideas* 38.2 (1977): 353–64.

Hyde.[4] It also contributes to marginalizing the politicized accounts of the English Revolution, among which lives and memoirs, which granted much importance to the facts of experience and were 'central', as Susan Wiseman puts it, to 'the construction of the Restoration political world's understanding of the English Civil War'.[5] Yet, these often undervalued lives and memoirs, because they draw on first-hand testimonies, should be considered—no less than antiquarian histories—as an integral part of the developing 'culture of fact', a culture that valorized experience and over which no historiographical trend had a monopoly in the seventeenth century.

1. Historiographical debates before the Civil War

Among European humanists, the German scholar Cornelius Agrippa was probably the most severe critic of history as it was still practised in Europe at the beginning of the sixteenth century.[6] In his *De incertitudine et vanitate scientiarum* (1531), he claimed that the histories of his age contradicted the Ciceronian definition of history as the 'light of truth' and considered historians in general to be liars.[7] In a chapter entitled 'Of Histories', he wrote that history 'being a thing that above all things promises Order, Fidelity, Coherence, and Truth, is yet defective in every one; For Historians are at such variance among themselves, delivering several Tales of one and the same Story, that it is impossible but that most of them must be the greatest Lyers in the World.'[8] Historians, he argued, failed in their mission which was to tell the truth, because 'they were not living at the same time, or were not present at the Actions, or conversant with the persons, taking their Relations upon trust at the second hand, mist the chief scope of Truth and Certainty.'[9] Regretting the

---

[4] Thomas More, *History of Richard III*, in *The Works of Sir Thomas More* (London, 1557); Bacon, *The History of the Reign of King Henry VII*; Hyde, *The History of the Rebellion and Civil Wars*. Mayer, *History and the Early English Novel* 10. For a similar view, see Norbrook, 'The English Revolution', 233. On Bacon, see Fritz Levy, 'The Advancement of Learning and Historical Thought', *Francis Bacon and the Refiguring of Early Modern Thought: Essays to Commemorate the Advancement of Learning (1605-2005)*, ed. Julie Robin Solomon and Catherine Gimelli Martin (Aldershot: Ashgate, 2005) 203-21, here 220-1.

[5] Wiseman, *Conspiracy and Virtue* 316. MacGillivray, *Restoration Historians*.

[6] On 'rhetorical' humanist history that was criticized by Agrippa, see Peter Burke, *The Renaissance Sense of the Past* (London: Edward Arnold, 1969) 105-30.

[7] Cicero, *De Oratore* II, 36.

[8] Heinrich Cornelius Agrippa von Nettesheim, *The Vanity of Arts and Sciences* [1531] (London, 1676) 27. On Agrippa's anthropology and his scepticism, see Charbonneau, *Les Silences de l'histoire* 48-9. See also Marc Van Der Poel, 'The Battle of *De incertitudine*: Agrippa in the World of Humanism', *The Humanist Theologian and his Declamations* (Leiden: Brill, 1997) 116-53.

[9] Agrippa, *The Vanity of Arts and Sciences* 27.

fact that writers of history were too often alien to the reality they recorded, Agrippa put forward the necessity for them to have first-hand knowledge of the events they recounted.

Agrippa's scepticism was not isolated in humanist circles.[10] In his seminal article 'Mémoires et Histoire', Marc Fumaroli gives us a detailed overview of the humanist debates which shaped much of the seventeenth-century historiography both on the Continent and in England.[11] While they were not as radical as Agrippa, it appears that Ronsard, du Bellay, Vives, Sleidan, and Montaigne were unanimous in considering many histories to be full of lies, too copious, and exceedingly rhetorical.[12] Instead they insisted on the 'pragmatic' side of history and upheld an ideal of *vera et pura narratio*—which they recurrently traced back to Caesar's *Commentaries*. Montaigne, in his essay 'Of Books', writes for instance that 'Caesar above all doth singularly deserve to be studied' and praises the historians who had 'but the care and diligence to collect whatsoever come unto their knowledge, and sincerely and faithfully to register all things, without choice or culling, by the *naked truth* leave our judgement more entire and better satisfied'.[13] In the same essay, Montaigne praises Philippe de Commynes, 'a man well-borne, and brought vp in high negotiations'—both for his role in history as well as for the simple clarity of his narratives, favouring contents over excessive rhetoric:[14]

> In my *Philip de Comines*, there is this: In him you shall find a pleasing-sweet, and gently-gliding speach, fraught with a purely-sincere simplicitie, his narration pure and vnaffected, and wherein the Authours vnspotted-good meaning doth evidently appeare, void of all maner of vanitie or ostentation speaking of himselfe, and free from all affection or envie speaking of others.[15]

---

[10] On scepticism and empiricism, see Davies, *Empiricism and History* 12–14.
[11] See Marc Fumaroli, 'Mémoires et histoire: le dilemme de l'historiographie humaniste au XVIe siècle', and Kuperty-Tsur, *Se dire à la Renaissance* 91–4. Kuperty-Tsur shows how the debate was taken up by memoir-writers in the Renaissance. Lesne also insists on the memorialists' indebtedness to, among others, Plutarch, Caesar, and Commynes (63). On Caesar, the oratory tradition, the ideal of plainness, see Charbonneau, *Les Silences de l'histoire* 35–8.
[12] On the Renaissance humanist debates, see Kelley, 'Philosophy and Humanistic Disciplines', 746–8. See also Olivier Guerrier, 'Affirmation de vérité, revendication de véracité: formes et enjeux d'une coexistence dans les récits historiques de la seconde moitié du XVIe siècle en France', *Littératures classiques* 94.3 (2017): 85–94; Ernst Breisach, 'Two Turning-points: The Renaissance and the Reformation', *Historiography: Ancient, Medieval & Modern* [1987] (Chicago: U of Chicago P, 2007) 171–98.
[13] Michel de Montaigne, 'Of Books', *Essays* [1603], trans. John Florio (London, 1613) 230, 231.
[14] Montaigne, 'Of Books', 232. On Commynes, see Charbonneau, *Les Silences de l'histoire* 52–3.
[15] Montaigne, 'Of Books', 232.

In brief, the history which Montaigne privileges is plain and written by eye-witnesses and actors of history, and not by rhetoricians.[16] This was also the kind of experience and autopsy-focused history that was practised by Thucydides and Polybius, and recommended by Lucian, whose influence was considerable in early modern Europe:[17]

> The only good histories are those that are written by such as commanded, or were imploid themselves in weighty affaires, or that were partners in the conduct of them, or that at least have had the fortune to manage others of like qualitie. Such in a maner are all the Graecians and Romans.[18]

This sceptical approach to history, which places the historian's *experience* over his *art*, was theorized by Jean Bodin, whom Montaigne calls 'a good moderne Author'.[19] Bodin's historical views were recorded in his *Methodus ad facilem historiarum cognitionem*, a voluminous treatise on the art of writing and reading history which was first published in Paris in 1566 and widely circulated in England throughout the seventeenth century.[20] Chapter 4 of Bodin's *Methodus* appeared in English as an 'Epistle to the Reader' in Thomas Heywood's 1608 translation of Sallust's *Conspiracy of Catiline* and *Jugurthine War*.[21] In his turn, like some of his contemporaries, Bodin contrasted rhetoric and history, and cautioned the reader against the temptation to confuse those two distinct disciplines: 'let not any thinke, that in an History he can discharge both the part of an Orator & Historiographer.'[22] Likewise, he condemned 'those Historiographers, who will audiouslie commit to publique beliefe the flying reports of fame and the vulgar',[23] drawing a neat line between true history and a history based on rumours. By contrast, he set much value on narrations based on a genuine experience of history and praised in

---

[16] On the historian as witness in the late Renaissance, see Guerrier, 'Affirmation de vérité', 91–4.

[17] See Lucian, *How to Write History*, §37, 52–3: a historian should not be 'a stay-at-home or one who must rely on what people tell him.' On Polybius, Thucydides, and eye-witnessing, L. V. Pitcher, 'Classical War Literature', *The Cambridge Companion to War-Writing*, ed. Kate McMcLoughlin (Cambridge: Cambridge UP, 2010) 76–7. On Lucian's influence, see Salmon, 'Precept, Example, and Truth', 13.

[18] Montaigne, 'Of Books', 232.

[19] Montaigne, 'A Defence of Seneca and Plutarke', 404; 'Of Books', 231–2. On the centrality of experience, see Charbonneau, *Les Silences de l'histoire* 42–5.

[20] See Leonard P. Dean, 'Bodin's *Methodus* in England before 1625', *Studies in Philology* 39.2 (1942): 160–6. Daniel R. Woolf, 'From Hystories to the Historical: Five Transitions in Thinking about the Past, 1500–1700', *Huntington Library Quarterly* 68.1–2 (2005): 33–70. On Bodin's scepticism, see Davies, *Empiricism and History* 17.

[21] Jean Bodin, 'Of the choice of History, by way of Preface', in Sallust, *The Two Most Worthy and Notable Histories [...] the conspiracie of Cateline, vndertaken against the gouernment of the Senate of Rome*, trans. Thomas Heywood (London, 1608). Sallust's conception of history was endorsed by many memorialists. On Sallust and memoir-writing, see Charbonneau, *Les Silences de l'histoire* 33, 38.

[22] Bodin, 'Of the choice of History', sig. ¶.   [23] Bodin, 'Of the choice of History', sig. [¶ᵛ].

Commynes 'a man that spent his whole time either in place of government, or in the wars, or in famous Embassies'.[24] However, Bodin does not blindly trust testimony: he postulates the possibility of false testimony and argues that a good history should be based on concordant reports: 'if a History haue such and so many witnesses as cannot be contested, it hath the greater apparancie of truth.'[25] Despite these precautions the access to historical truth was never considered straightforward; experience was not enough. It was better if historians '[adjoined] much reading of Law and Historie to dailie experience'.[26] Historians also needed time and hindsight to circumscribe a historical truth that was always receding and which Bodin called 'obscure': 'For such is the Nature and obscurity of truth, that [...] it will hardly appear like it selfe, but best then, when the reports, the flatteries and passions of the vulgar are buried with their bodies.'[27] Bodin's reflections here echo the historiographical dilemmas of Civil War historians, who were similarly overwhelmed by divergent reports: '[t]herefore when Authors disagree amongst themselues, I take it the safest course to beleeue the latest, at leastwise if their reasons co-here necessarily, and their Arguments are strong to proue what they say.'[28] Unsurprisingly, his list of trustworthy historians chiefly includes authors who 'were Actors in the affaires', from ancient times to his own time: 'Xenophon, Thucidides, Tranquillus, Caesar, Guicciardine and Sleydan'.[29] At the end of the 'Epistle', the French philosopher adds that some histories about the 'affaires of England' were not worth reading because they deviated from the truth. He dismisses 'Beda, Guagun, Gacus, Saxo, and such like, who handled the said Histories without method or order', and he retains Polydore Vergil, whose history of England was the only one worth reading.[30]

Bodin's work occupies a central place in English historiography in the first half of the seventeenth century. He is quoted in Degory Wheare's *De ratione et methodo legendi historias dissertatio*, first published in 1623, a compilation of *artes historicae* written in Latin, which was several times re-published, expanded, and finally translated at the Restoration.[31] According to

---

[24] Bodin sig. ¶3, 'Of the choice of History'. See Mark Greengrass, 'The Experiential World of Jean Bodin', *The Reception of Bodin*, ed. Howell A. Lloyd (Leiden: Brill, 2013) 67–96.
[25] Bodin, 'Of the choice of History', sig. [¶ᵛ].
[26] Bodin, 'Of the choice of History', sig. [opening page].
[27] Bodin, 'Of the choice of History', sig. ¶2.   [28] Bodin, 'Of the choice of History', sig. ¶2.
[29] Bodin, 'Of the choice of History', sig. [¶2ᵛ]. He also adds Sallust and Commynes who were 'Actors in the affaires' (sig. [¶3ᵛ]).
[30] Bodin, 'Of the choice of History', sig. [¶5ᵛ].
[31] Degory Wheare was appointed to the lectureship in civil history established by William Camden in 1622. His *De ratione et methodo legendi historias dissertatio* (London, 1623) was based on his inaugural lecture. It was only translated into English in 1685 as *The Method and Order of Reading Both Civil and Ecclesiastical Histories* (1685). On Bodin's influence, see Angus Vine, *In Defiance of Time:*

Daniel R. Woolf, Wheare's opus contributed to propagating in England continental historiography, especially the writings of Bodin, Bartholomew Keckermann, Justus Lipsius, and Gerrard Vossius.[32] Nevertheless, the diffusion of continental writings in England had started earlier, in particular through the publication of Thomas Blundeville's *The True Order and Methode of Wryting and Reading Histories* (1574), a synthesis of Francesco Patrizzi and Giacomo Concio's treatises on history, which contended that history should not be limited to the high deeds performed by great men in the past, but could just as well concern the world, a nation, or an individual, either in the past or in the present.[33] Through the translation of these Italian treatises, which anticipated Bodin's *Methodus*, Blundeville shared the Italian historians' distrust of fiction and rhetoric in history:[34]

> Of those that make anye thyng, some [hystoriographers] doe make much of nothing, as God dyd in creating the Worlde of naught, and as Poets in some respect also doe, whilest they faine fables and make thereof theyr poesies, and poeticall Hystories: [...] some of little doe make much, & of muche little, as the Oratours whylest sometyme they extoll small things, & sometime abase great thinges.[35]

On the other hand, Blundeville argued, 'the dutie and office of hystoriographers' was 'to tell things as they were done without either augmenting or diminishing them, or swaruing one iote from the truth. Whereby it appeareth that the hystoriographers ought [...] truely to reporte euery such speach, and deede, euen as it was spoken, or done.'[36]

Additionally, in pre-Civil War England, the issue of 'writing' and 'reading' history was taken up by the Roman Catholic historian, Edmund Bolton, the author of *Hypercritica: Or, A Rule of Judgment, for Writing or Reading our*

Antiquarian Writing in Early Modern England (Oxford: Oxford UP, 2010) 63. On Wheare (1573–1647), see J. H. M. Salmon, 'Wheare, Diagory [Degory] (1573–1647), historian' (2004), *Oxford Dictionary of National Biography*, DOI: 10.1093/ref:odnb/29180.

[32] Woolf, *The Idea of History* 186–8.

[33] Francesco Patrizi, *Della Historia Diece Dialoghi* (Venice, 1560). Giacomo Concio's work (*Delle osservazioni et avvertimenti che haver si debbono nel legger delle historie*) was not published when Blundeville translated it. On Blundeville's work, see Dick, 'Thomas Blundeville's *The True Order and Methode of Wryting and Reading Histories*', 150–1. On Patrizi, see Kelley, 'Philosophy and Humanistic Disciplines', 757.

[34] Dick, 'Thomas Blundeville's *The True Order*', 151.

[35] Blundeville, *The True Order and Methode* sig. [Eiv–Eiv^v].

[36] Blundeville, *The True Order and Methode* sig. [Eiv^v].

History's, written between 1618 and 1621, but not published until 1722.[37] Bolton's treatise, conceived as a preamble to a novel history of England, testifies to the continuities existing between the humanist Renaissance and the seventeenth century.[38] Its author, a reader of ancient history and an admirer of Polybius, unambiguously subordinates rhetoric to truth: 'For without Truth, Art and Style come into the Nature of Crimes by Imposture. It is an act of high Wisdom, and not of Eloquence only, to write the History of so great, and noble a People as the English.'[39] Quoting Lucian's *How to Write History*, Bolton addresses the question of historical truth in the following terms:

> Truth is the soveraigne praise of an History. For want whereof Lucian did condemn unto his hell, Ctesias, Herodotus, and other of his Country men. And although himself were as false a Companion as any, yet Learning and Reason told him, that Truth in Story was only to be sacrificed unto, as the Goddess of that brave Province; and that all other respects came after, with a very large distance between.[40]

Once again, historical truth is presented as dependent upon a genuine experience of history. Under Bolton's pen we find the names of two historians who played a public role, '*Philip de Comines*, and our *Sir Thomas More* (both of them great Counsellors of State to their several Princes)'.[41] Bolton did not play any public role himself (he was a Roman Catholic and thus was barred from government), but he nonetheless intended to write a history of England based on manuscript archives, coins, and inscriptions, that is, on what he considered to be reliable and accurate 'facts'. Like some antiquarians to whom he was close—he was a friend of William Camden's and Sir Robert Cotton's—he valued the material vestiges of history and contended that the past had to be purged of its supernatural mythical elements.[42] The historian, he argued, had

---

[37] Edmund Bolton, *Hypercritica: Or, A Rule of Judgement, for Writing or Reading our History's* [1722], in *Ancient Critical Essays upon English Poets and Poësy*, ed. Joseph Haslewood (London, 1815) 221–54. See Thomas H. Blackburn, 'The Date and Evolution of Edmund Bolton's *Hypercritica*', *Studies in Philology* 63.2 (1966): 196–202, here 193; Daniel R. Woolf, 'Bolton [Boulton], Edmund Mary (b. 1574/5, d. in or after 1634), antiquary and historian' (2004), *Oxford Dictionary of National Biography*, https://doi.org/10.1093/ref:odnb/2800.

[38] Bolton, *Hypercritica* 236: 'the Herculean, and truly noble Labour of composing an entire, and compleat Body of *English* affairs, a Corpus rerum Anglicarum, a general History of *England*.' See Woolf, 'Bolton', *ODNB*.

[39] Bolton, *Hypercritica* 224.

[40] Bolton, *Hypercritica* 225. See Lucian, *How to Write History*, §40, 55.

[41] Bolton, *Hypercritica* 225.

[42] On antiquarianism, see Graham Parry, *The Trophies of Time: English Antiquarians of the Seventeenth Century* (Oxford: Oxford UP, 1995). See Lydia Janssen, 'Antiquarianism and National History. The Emergence of a New Scholarly Paradigm in Early Modern Historical Studies', *History of*

'to set forth, without Prejudicies, Depravations, or sinister terms things as they are'.[43] Quoting Bodin, he insisted that History was 'as it were a Table of things done'.[44] In this context, it is logical that Bolton should in turn blame the medieval chronicles of Monmouth for their 'want of Truth, and modesty'.[45]

But Bolton's conception of history is complex: unlike the modern 'adversaries', the humanists '*Vives, Junius, Buchanan, Polidor, Bodin &c.* [...] all of them Strangers',[46] he did not fully reject Monmouth's history, because, in his view, the presence of the fictional in his work did not necessarily preclude the emergence of truth: 'it pleased me well, what once I did read in a great Divine, that *in Apocryphis non omnia esse Apocrypha*. And that very much of *Monmouths* book, or pretended Translation, *de Origine & gestis Britannorum* be granted to be fabulous, yet many Truths are mixed.'[47] As a matter of fact, Bolton was aware that historical truth was not necessarily to be conceived as the opposite of fiction. He would not have gone so far as to accept Sidney's Aristotelian assertion of the superiority of poetry over history, but Sidney's famous statement, at the beginning of the *Defence of Poetry*, sheds nonetheless an interesting light on the porosity between truth and fiction in historical writings:[48]

> And euen Historiographers, (although theyr lippes sounde of things doone, & veritie be written in theyr fore-heads,) haue been glad to borrow both fashion, and perchance weight of Poets. [...] So that truely, neyther Phylosopher nor Historiographer, coulde at the first haue entred into the gates of populer iudgements, if they had not taken a great pasport of Poetry, which in all Nations at this day wher learning florisheth not, is plaine to be seene.[49]

What the example of Bolton suggests is that there were no strict boundaries between the various ways of practising history.[50] This corroborates Shapiro's

---

European Ideas 43.8 (2017): 843–56. On the developing culture of 'facts', see Shapiro, *A Culture of Fact*, '"Fact" and History', 34–62; Burke, 'The Antiquarian Movement', *The Renaissance Sense of the Past* 21–32.

[43] Bolton, *Hypercritica* 232.   [44] Bolton, *Hypercritica* 232.

[45] He explicitly refers to *de Origine & gestis Britannorum* (226), now more often referred to as *Historia Regum Britanniae*. On Monmouth, Burke, *The Renaissance Sense of the Past* 8–9.

[46] Bolton, *Hypercritica* 225. See also the example of the humanist Polydore Vergil, quoted in Burke, *The Renaissance Sense of the Past* 71–2.

[47] Bolton, *Hypercritica* 226.

[48] On this debate between Sidney and historians, see Levy, 'The Advancement of Learning and Historical Thought', 203–6. Shapiro, *A Culture of Fact* 34–5; 41–2. Thomas More's *Richard III* and Shakespeare's historical plays are given as examples of histories mixing fact and fiction.

[49] Philip Sidney, *An Apologie for Poetry* (London, 1595) sig. B3. Collinson, 'Truth, Lies, and Fiction in Sixteenth-Century Protestant Historiography', *The Historical Imagination in Early Modern Britain* 38–40.

[50] Burke, *The Renaissance Sense of the Past* 127: A similar conclusion could be reached with the antiquarian William Camden who 'never quite rejects humanist history, while in practice moving away from it'.

conclusion that one should 'view the early modern historical enterprise as a continuum, with the "perfect" political historian being at one end and the sophisticated, erudite collector-critic of documentary evidence at the other, with a considerable number of historical practitioners falling somewhere in the middle'.[51]

An index of this fluidity is again provided by Bolton who was also conscious that historians could not dispense with '[l]anguage and style' in their narratives.[52] Under his pen, Bacon, both an antiquarian and a humanist historian himself, stood as an ultimate model in matters of form: 'Most of all Sr Francis Bacons Writings which have the freshest, and most savoury form and aptest utterances, that (as I suppose) our Tongue can bear.'[53] On the one hand, Bacon grants much importance to the facts of history, and praises the 'Commentaries', as a sort of 'imperfect history' (in the sense of unfinished), 'which set downe a continuance of the naked events & actions, without the motiues or designes, the counsells, the speeches, the pretexts, the occasions, and other passages of action'.[54] On the other hand, Bacon's stress on plain facts—his empiricism—is matched by his concern with form. When he describes 'lives'—a type of particular history which he views as far preferable to general history—he also points to the necessity of a 'lively representation', that is, the rhetorical mastery of *enargeia*: 'Lives if they be well written [...] must of necessitie containe a more true, natiue, and liuely representation.'[55] In other words, Bacon requires of lives that they be compelling and engage the reader in the way they are written—in so doing he highlights the centrality of rhetoric that cannot be reduced to the art of sophistry.[56] This rhetorical dimension of history which was so important for ancient historians, far from declining in the seventeenth century, became a major asset during the Civil Wars, Interregnum and Restoration, when historians from across the political spectrum were in quest for adequate ways of writing the history of their own times.[57] As Shapiro pointed out, '[i]f early modern historiography remained inextricably tied to rhetoric, it was a rhetoric that came to emphasize

---

[51] Shapiro, *A Culture of Fact* 60. [52] Bolton, *Hypercritica* 247.
[53] Bolton, *Hypercritica* 249. Bolton was influenced by the work of Bacon, to whom he refers several times in his treatise.
[54] Bacon, *The Second Booke* 10. See also Brathwaite, *A Survey of History* 30.
[55] Bacon, *The Second Booke* 12.
[56] It is probably Bacon's *History of the Reign of King Henry VII*, which, by requiring of lives to be 'true, native and lively', best reflects the humanist heritage. On Bacon and history, see Fussner, *The Historical Revolution*, 'Sir Francis Bacon and the Idea of History', 253–75; Brownley, *Clarendon and the Rhetoric of Historical Form* 4–5; Mayer, *History and the Early English Novel* 22; Anthony Grafton, *What Was History? The Art of History in Early Modern Europe* (Cambridge: Cambridge UP, 2007) 62–7; Vickers, 'Introduction', in Bacon, *The History of the Reign of King Henry VII*, xv–xxiii.
[57] Kelley, 'Philosophy and Humanistic Disciplines', 752.

"fact," truth, and impartiality, to be suspicious of artfulness, partiality and ornamented style, and to prefer first-hand witnesses over citations to authority.'[58]

2. Historical truth in the turmoil of the Civil Wars

During the Civil Wars and at the Restoration, the terms of the historiographical debate around 'modern history' (what we would call contemporary history) were not significantly altered.[59] The regime of historicity—understood as the way society and individuals relate to the past, present, and future—which prevailed in the sixteenth and earlier seventeenth century, did not abruptly change after 1650.[60] Historiographical controversies continued to focus chiefly on historical truth, understood as the coincidence between facts and narrative.[61] The epistemological crisis of the English Revolution, however, had a durable impact on historiography—both as history writing and as the study of history writing—and contributed a great deal to radicalizing and polarizing debates.[62]

a) Civil War historiography

During the Civil Wars, *artes historicae* continued to be published and written, although in smaller numbers than before 1640.[63] Matthias Prideaux's *An Easy and Compendious Introduction for Reading all Sorts of Histories* was thus re-issued throughout the Revolution and Restoration periods.[64] In the 1640s,

---

[58] Shapiro, *A Culture of Fact* 3. On the emerging notion of impartiality in the seventeenth century, see Kathryn Murphy and Anita Traninger, eds., *The Emergence of Impartiality* (Leiden: Brill, 2014) especially 1–29.

[59] The writing of modern history is recommended by Blundeville (Dick, 'Thomas Blundeville's *The True Order*', 150). On modern history, see Woolf, 'From Hystories to the Historical', 53. Paolo Sarpi, *The Historie of the Councel of Trent* (London, 1620) and Enrico Caterino Davila, *The Historie of the Civil Warres of France* [1630] (London, 1647) are among the most read modern histories.

[60] See François Hartog, 'Introduction: Orders of Time and Regimes of Historicity', *Regimes of Historicity: Presentism and Experiences of Time* [2003], trans. Saskia Brown (New York: Columbia UP, 2015) 1–20.

[61] Hartog, *Evidence de l'histoire* 94: 'Times of crisis, even within the same regime of historicity, are always historiographically charged with meaning, and the English Revolution was no exception' (my translation). See Gheeraert-Graffeuille, 'Entre polémique et histoire: comment écrire les guerres civiles anglaises', 51–63.

[62] On this controversy, see Mayer, *History and the Early English Novel* 18–33; MacGillivray, *Restoration Historians* 15–47.

[63] For example, it is striking that Degory Wheare's Latin treatise *De ratione et methodo legendi historias dissertatio* (1623), re-published in Latin in 1625, 1637, and 1662 and translated into English in three subsequent editions (1685, 1695, and 1698), was not published during the revolutionary years.

[64] Mathias Prideaux, *An Easy and Compendious Introduction for Reading all Sorts of Histories* (London, 1648). It was re-issued in 1650, 1654, 1655, 1664, 1672, and 1682.

John Hall, who was to become an important journalist, also contributed to these *artes historicae*, with the intention of giving 'directions in the reading of history'.[65] In his advice to the readers of history, we find a typically humanist preference for modern history written by eye-witnesses or actors of history.[66] Comparing different types of history, Hall thus praises histories written by 'Guicciardine & Comines, both being αυτοπλαι & writ what they knew & help'd to act'.[67]

Such an emphasis was to become a leitmotiv in historiographical writings in the 1650s and throughout the Restoration period. But during the profoundly divided times of the Civil Wars, the experience of history was still problematic, as it was partial, from both an epistemological and political point of view. Thucydides in his history of the Peloponnesian wars had to deal with very similar issues, and his remarks about the difficulty of finding any *certainty* in often biased testimonies could easily be transposed to Civil War England:

> But of the Acts themselues done in the Warre, I thought not fit to write all that I heard from all Authors, nor such as I my selfe did but thinke to bee true; but onely those whereat I was my selfe present; and those of which with all diligence I had made particular enquirie. And yet euen of those things, it was hard to know the certainty, because such as were present at every Action, spake not all after the same manner, but as they were affected to the Parts, or as they could remember.[68]

In this context of epistemological uncertainty, whether in ancient Greece or in seventeenth-century England, writing a comprehensive narrative of a civil war appeared to be a near impossible task.[69] The Civil War historian Thomas May was confronted with this challenge when he was commissioned to write the history of Parliament.[70] In times of divisions, a historical narrative was necessarily partisan and could only suit the readers who shared the historian's views:

---

[65] Hall, *A Method of History* [3ᵛ], ed. Raymond, 287. About Hall, see Raymond, 'John Hall's *A Method of History*', 272, 276, 279. His treatise bears the mark of the Civil War. See for instance a reference to the militia, see *A Method of History* [8ᵛ], ed. Raymond, 292.
[66] Hall, *A Method of History* [14]–[14ᵛ], ed. Raymond, 295–6.
[67] Hall, *A Method of History* [15ᵛ], ed. Raymond, 296.
[68] Thucydides, *Eight Bookes of the Peloponnesian Warre* 13.
[69] Woolf, 'Narrative Historical Writing', 210. See Malcom Wanklyn, 'Recapturing the Past', *Decisive Battles of the English Civil Wars: Myth and Reality* (Barnsley: Pen & Sword, 2006) 5–32.
[70] On May, see David Norbrook, 'May, Thomas (c.1596–1650), writer and historian' (2008), *Oxford Dictionary of National Biography*, https://doi.org/10.1093/ref:odnb/18423. See Pocock, 'Thomas May and the Narrative of the Civil War', 112–44.

The Subject of this work is a Civill War [...]; a Warre as cruell as unnaturall; that has produced as much rage of Swords, as much bitterness of Pens, both publike and private, as was ever knowne; and divided the understandings of men, as well as their affections, in so high a degree, that scarce could any vertue gaine due applause, any reason give satisfaction, or any Relation obtaine credit, unlesse amongst men of the same side.[71]

The description of battles is also necessarily biased and limited in focus, as is noted by Richard Bulstrode, who fought on the King's side during the Civil War. From the difficulties he meets when relating the indecisive battle of Edgehill, he infers the following lesson:

There is always great Difference in Relation of Battles, which is usually according to the Interest of the Relators; when it is certain, that, in a Battle, the next Man can hardly make a true Relation of the Actions of him that is next him; for, in such a Hurry and Smoke as in a set Field, a Man takes Notice of nothing but what relates to his own Safety.[72]

A further obstacle to writing the history of the Civil Wars was the strong geographical variations which made it problematic to have a satisfying overview of the conflict. The accounts varied considerably according to the place where information was collected: the 'reality' of the conflict was not the same in London and in the provinces, and also varied much from one county to the other. This variation was noted by May, whose residence in London did not give him a satisfactory view of the military events he was commissioned to narrate and made him dependent on informers:

But where Warre continues, people are inforced to make their residence in severall Quarters, and therefore severall, according to the places where they converse, must their information be concerning the condition and state of things. From whence arises not onely a variety, but a great discrepancy for the most part in the Writings of those who record the passages of such times.[73]

---

[71] Thomas May, *The History of the Parliament of England* (London, 1647) [sig. A4ᵛ]. See also Thomas Fuller, *The Appeal of Injured Innocence* (London, 1659) 1: 'it is impossible for the Pen of any Historians writing in (as our's) a divided Age, to please all Parties, and how easie it is to Cavil at any Author.'

[72] Richard Bulstrode, *Memoirs and Reflections upon the Reign and Government of King Charles the 1ˢᵗ and K. Charles the IIᵈ* (London, 1721) 84. See C. H. Firth, 'The "Memoirs" of Sir Richard Bulstrode', *English Historical Review* 10 (1895): 266–335.

[73] May, *The History of the Parliament* sig. B–[sig. Bᵛ]. The Fronde sparked off very similar debates. See Fumaroli, 'Les Mémoires au carrefour des genres', 194–5.

To the complex task of writing a unified narrative of the Civil War one should add the difficulty of telling the truth from lies, the borderline between history and fiction being then more blurred than ever. The royalist Peter Heylin, commenting on contemporary histories, thus argued 'truth was often times irrecoverably lost, the Reader led aside from the waies of Verity into the Crooked lanes of Errour.'[74] Again, as seen above, this was not a new issue, but it took on unprecedented dimensions in the middle of the seventeenth century, when the propagation of errors was massively blamed on the pamphlets and newsbooks which started to pour off the press in 1641 after the collapse of censorship. Historians were suspected of falsifying the truth like their fellow pamphleteers and journalists.[75] The falsification of truth, Thomas May insisted, was most insidious:

> Some Historians, who seeme to abhorre direct falshood, have notwithstanding dressed Truth in such improper Vestments, as if they brought her forth to act the same part that falshood would; and taught her by Rhetoricall disguises, partiall concealements, and invective expressions, instead of informing, to seduce a Reader, and carry the judgement of Posterity after that Byas which themselves have made.[76]

With a little more insight, but much in the same vein, the former supporter of Parliament, John Rushworth, deplored in the preface to his *Historical Collections*, published at the Restoration, that most historians were bent more on serving their own interests than historical truth:

> other mens Fancies were more busie then their hands, forging Relations, building and battering Castles in the Air; publishing Speeches as spoken in Parliament, which were never spoken there; Printing Declarations, which were never passed; relating Battels which were never fought, and Victories which were never obtained [...] to abet a Party or Interest.[77]

---

[74] Peter Heylin, *Examen Historicum: Or, A Discovery and Examination of the Mistakes, Falsities, and Defects in some Modern Histories* (London, 1659) sig. [A2ᵛ]–A3. For a similar analysis of the French wars of religion, see René de Lucinge, *La manière de lire l'histoire* [1614], ed. Michael J. Heath (Geneva: Droz, 1993). Lucinge targets two historians of the Ligue, Mathieu and Cayer: Mathieu 'est partial partout, et si ouvertement, pour le party des Huguenots, qu'il semble ou leur avoir vendu sa plume, ou que pour faire plaisir aux rois sous lesquels les temps de son histoire s'adressent, il y aye avantagé leur cause' (93–4).
[75] See Joad Raymond, 'Exporting Impartiality', *The Emergence of Impartiality*, ed. Murphy and Traninger, 141–67, here 141.
[76] May, *The History of the Parliament* sig. A3.
[77] See John Rushworth, *Historical Collections* (London, 1659) sig. [bᵛ]–b2.

Despite this climate of suspicion, memorialists and life-writers, whatever their views, indefatigably repeated that all histories should be committed to truth. As early as 1647, when *The History of the Parliament of England* was first published, May, who was on the Parliament's side, declared: 'I will only professe to follow that one Rule, Truth, to which all the rest [...] may be reduced, against which there are many waies, besides plain falsehood, whereby a Writer may offend.'[78] During the Interregnum, the same sense of loss permeated royalist historiography. History that swerved from truth was a mere 'romance', that is, here, fiction understood as the opposite of truth.[79] At the beginning of *The Reign of King Charles*, Hamon L'Estrange exclaimed, 'what is History without its *Idiome*, Truth, but a meer *Romance*?'[80] As for Heylin, he indefatigably insisted that historians should be guided by their concern for truth:

> it concerns all those who apply themselves to the writing of Histories, to take special care that all things be laid down exactly, faithfully, and without deviation from the truth in the least particular. For if the Witnesses be suborned, the Record falsified, or the Evidence wrested, neither Posterity can judge rightly of the actions of this present time, or this time give a certain judgement of the Ages past.[81]

Likewise, Margaret Cavendish distanced herself from contemporary historians 'who have written of the late Civil War with but few sprinklings of Truth, like as Heat-drops upon a dry barren Ground; knowing no more of the Transactions of those Times, then what they learned in the Gazets, which, for the most part [...] contain nothing but Falshoods and Chimeraes'.[82] For Burnet, the errors of many contemporary histories were to be attributed to the mercenary motives of their authors, to their neglect of truth, and to their taste for fiction:

> most Writers of History have been men that lived out of business, who took many things upon trust, and have committed many palpable Errours in matters of Fact, and either give no account at all of the secret Causes and

---

[78] May, *The History of the Parliament* sig. A3.
[79] On the different uses of the term 'romance', see Christine S. Lee, 'The Meanings of Romance: Rethinking Early Modern Fiction', *Modern Philology* 112.2 (2014): 287–311, especially 314.
[80] Hamon L'Estrange, *The Reign of King Charles: An History Faithfully and Impartially Delivered and Disposed into Annals* (London, 1655).
[81] Heylyn, *Examen Historicum* sig. A2.
[82] Cavendish, *Life of William Cavendish* [sig. c^v]–sig. (d).

Counsels of the greatest Transactions, or when they do venture upon it, it is all Romance, and the effect of their Imagination or Interest.[83]

In the face of this epistemological crisis, which coincided with the Revolution and continued after the Restoration, histories written by ocular witnesses, despite their defects, continued to be seen as the more reliable, or to use the words of the prolific historian Thomas Fuller, 'the *most Informative Histories* to *Posterity* and such as are most *highly prized* by the *judicious*, are such as were *written* by the *Eye-witnesses* thereof, as Thucydides, the *reporter* of the *Peloponnesian Warre*.'[84]

b) Memoir-writing and the truth of history

The valorization of testimony explains, at least in part, why memoirs, understood as 'histories written by such persons who have had a hand in the management, or else have been eye-witnesses of the transacting of affairs', appeared to be the most suitable genre to make the history of the Civil Wars.[85] In the *Life of William Cavendish*—which has all the features of a memoir although it was only entitled *Memoirs* in the nineteenth century—Margaret Cavendish claims that history can only be written 'by the Prime Actors, or the Spectators of those Affairs and Actions of which they write, as *Caesars Commentaries* are'.[86] Similarly, Burnet, in his preface to *The Memoires of the Lives and Actions of James and William Dukes of Hamilton and Castleherald*, holds that the best historians are the witnesses of the events they record. The list of 'authentick' histories provided by Burnet once again relates the Restoration historiographical debates to the reflections of the humanists and their followers, who also preferred the more reliable genre of the 'Commentaries'—a category Furetière uses interchangeably with 'Mémoires'—to general histories[87]:

---

[83] Burnet, 'The Preface', *The Memoires of the Lives and Actions*, sig a.2.
[84] Thomas Fuller, *The Church History of Britain* (London, 1656) Book X, sig. Ggg2v.
[85] See Bailey's definition in *The Universal Etymological English Dictionary*. On the homology between *res* and *verba* in memoirs see Charbonneau, *Les Silences de l'histoire* 27–8. See also Hartog, *Évidence de l'histoire* 78.
[86] Cavendish, *Life of William Cavendish* [sig. c^v].
[87] Antoine Furetière, ed., *Dictionnaire universel* (Paris, 1690): 'Mémoires, au pluriel, se dit des Livres d'Historiens, escrits par ceux qui ont eu part aux affaires ou qui en ont esté tesmoins oculaires, ou qui contiennent leur vie ou leurs principales actions: Ce qui répond à ce que les Latins appelloient *commentaires*.'

Of all men those who have been themselves engaged in Affairs, are the fittest to write History, as knowing best how matters were designed and carried on, and being best able to judge what things are of that Importance to be made Publick, and what were better suppressed. And therefore *Caesars Commentaries* are the most Authentick, and most generally valued pieces of History, and in the next Form to these Philip de *Comines, Guicciardine, Sleidan, Thuanus,* and *Davila,* are the best received, and most read Histories, (only the last hath failed in some particulars:) for these men wrote of things in which they were considerable Actors, and had great Interest and good Information.[88]

Under these conditions, memoir-writers, who claimed to be either actors or witnesses to history, considered that they were the best placed to guarantee the truthfulness of their narratives and, thereby, to counter fallacious histories. This necessity to restore truth was for instance stated by Hugh Cholmley in a dedication to his son: 'I would have you to understand that, in doing this, I desire to forget my relations, and so perform the duty of an historian, which is to express all things with as much truth and clearness as may be.'[89] In the narrative of his life and times, *Reliquiæ Baxterianæ*—which closely matches the definition of memoirs—the Nonconformist minister Richard Baxter similarly promised to write his relation 'only in faithfulness Historically to relate things as indeed they were'.[90] He saw his undertaking as a way of responding to all the 'most Notorious Falsehoods' that were published which 'greatly depressed [his Esteem] of most History, and of Humane Nature'.[91]

However epistemologically satisfactory these testimonies could be, they remained partial and incomplete. Montaigne argues that individual accounts by actors of history are necessary but not sufficient. The truth of battle could only come from a confrontation of witnesses as in a court of law:

---

[88] Burnet, 'The Preface', *The Memoires of the Lives and Actions*, sig. a. Burnet also wrote the memoirs of his life. In his *History of His Own Times,* he admits that he was not a 'witness' of the Civil Wars (he was born in 1643), but his father was a most reliable source of information: 'I had while I was very young a greater knowledge of affaires than is usual at that age. [...] My father, who had been engaged in great friendships with men of both sides, [...] took a sort of pleasure to relate to me the series of all publick affairs [...]. Where I was in the dark, I past over all, and only opened those transactions that I had particular occasions to know.' See Gilbert Burnet, 'The Preface', *Bishop Burnet's History of His Own Times,* vol. 1 (London, 1724–1734) 1–2.

[89] Hugh Cholmley, *The Memoirs of Sir Hugh Cholmley [...] Taken from an Original Manuscript, in his own Hand-writing* [1787] (np, 1870) 3–4.

[90] Baxter, *Reliquiæ Baxterianæ,* Part I, §49; ed. Keeble et al., vol. 1, 277.

[91] Baxter, *Reliquiæ Baxterianæ,* Part III, §51, 187; ed. Keeble et al., vol. 2, 576.

no man can put any assured confidence concerning the truth of a battel, neither in the knowledge of him, that was Generall, or commanded over it, nor in the soldiers that fought, of any thing, that hath hapned amongst them; except after the maner of a strict point of law, the severall witnesses are brought and examined face to face, and that all matters be nicely and thorowly sifted by the objects and trials of the successe of every accident.[92]

In times of civil wars, such a confrontation of testimonies was also expected of the reader of history. For Hall, who wrote his *Method of History* during the Civil War, the reader must 'get the best information he can' about the historian he intends to study. In particular, he should 'compare him wth other of ye same subject, To reconcile if [he] can the differences, or encline to him y^t brings the more colourable reasons or better Authority'.[93] In case of political division, this confrontation was crucial, and the best way of obtaining an account of the Civil War, May argues, was to read narratives from both sides—'how much Worth, Vertue, and Courage, some particular Lords, Gentlemen, and others have shewed, unlesse both sides do write, will never perfectly be known.'[94] This is in keeping with the idea put forward by Bacon that if particular histories were compiled together, they would facilitate the writing of a 'complete historie of times':

For NARRATIONS and RELATIONS of particular actions, there were also to be wished a greater diligence therein, for there is no great action but hath some good penne which attends it. And because it is an abilitie not common to Write a good History, as may well appear by the small number of them: yet if particularitie of actions memorable, were but tolerably reported as they passe, the compiling of a complete HISTORIE of TIMES mought be the better expected.[95]

Bacon's idea of 'compiling a complete historie of times' did not go unheeded. It was for example taken up by the publisher of Denzil Holles's *Memoirs* (1699), the Irish free thinker John Toland, who reflected that collecting the 'Memoirs of all parties' would allow to '[frame] a true Generall History' of the Civil War;[96]

---

[92] Montaigne, 'Of Books', 231. [93] Hall, *A Method of History* [6^v], ed. Raymond, 290.
[94] May, *The History of the Parliament* sig. B2. [95] Bacon, *The Second Booke* 14.
[96] Toland, 'The Publisher to the Reader', *Memoirs of Denzil Lord Holles* ix. On Holles and the identification of the 'Publisher' as James Toland, see Pierre Lurbe, 'Du temps vécu au temps de l'histoire: les mémoires de Denzil, Lord Holles', *Le Char ailé du temps. Temps, mémoire, histoire en Grande-Bretagne au XVIIe siècle*, ed. Louis Roux (Saint-Étienne: Publications de l'Université de Saint-Étienne, 2003) 111–28, here 112 and 118.

it was the most suitable way, he argued, to make the history of a highly conflictual and divisive period:

> Such as really desire to know the naked Truth [...] have ever exprest a desire in their Writings of seeing the Memoirs of all parties made public, as the most effectual means of framing a true General History: For in those places where nothing is licens'd to appear but what visibly tends to the advantage of one side, there can be no sincere representation of Affairs.[97]

From this defence of the memoir genre by Toland emerges a polyphonic conception of history which dominated the Restoration—a period when the writing of memoirs and lives came to constitute a corrective to general and partisan histories of the Civil Wars.[98] Nevertheless, it should not be taken for granted that memoirs—especially those of Denzil Holles—were always looked upon as 'sincere representations of affairs' and altogether escaped contemporary suspicion of partiality.[99] As we shall have occasion to demonstrate, life-writings—and Lucy Hutchinson's *Memoirs* were a case in point—did not escape 'the continuing polemical warfare' of the Restoration.[100] Two brief examples will suffice to show more concretely how the publication of Civil War memoirs contributed to fuelling the writing of competing narratives.

The first paper war that illustrates this point broke out at the time of the Popish Plot (1678), around the commercially profitable publication in 1680 of the *Memoirs* of James Touchet, Earl of Castlehaven, an English Catholic royalist, who played an active part in the Irish Confederate wars in the 1640s.[101] Addressing Charles II, Touchet presents his work as a history of the 1641 Irish rebellion related by one of its witnesses: 'I Lay at your Majesties

---

[97] Holles, *Memoirs* ix.

[98] Worden, 'Introduction', in Ludlow, *A Voyce from the Watch Tower*, ed. Worden, 1–2: 'The chief histories of the Puritan Revolution published in the Restoration period—Heath, Dugdale, Nalson, Rushworth, Whitelocke—were often animated by party zeal or adorned by commentary, but they drew principally upon official publications and newspapers.' See Norbrook, 'The English Revolution', 223–50.

[99] This has been confirmed by the authors of the *ODNB* articles who consider that Cholmley and Holles are tinkering with historical truth in their Memoirs. In his biography of Denzil Holles, John Morrill speaks of the 'composition of misleading accounts of his rise and fall'. See 'Holles, Denzil, first Baron Holles (1598–1680)' (2004), *Oxford Dictionary of National Biography*, https://doi.org/10.1093/ref:odnb/13550. Likewise, in his biography of Hugh Cholmley (1600–1657), Jack Binns writes that Cholmley 'was embarrassed by his parliamentarian record, in the house and on the battlefield, and minimized or even omitted it entirely from his autobiography'. See 'Cholmley, Sir Hugh, first baronet' (2004), *Oxford Dictionary of National Biography*, https://doi.org/10.1093/ref:odnb/5341.

[100] Sharpe and Zwicker, 'Introducing Lives', 19.

[101] James Touchet, Earl of Castlehaven, *The Memoirs of James, Lord Audley, Earl of Castlehaven, his Engagement and Carriage in the Wars of Ireland from the year 1642 to the year 1651 written by himself* (London, 1680). As a Catholic he had been excluded from the House of Lords by the 1678 Test Act.

feet these my Memoirs, with an Appendix relating Wars abroad, that I have either seen, or came within the compass of my knowledge, I being of the Armies, though not present in every occasion.'[102] But we soon understand that the author's intention was not only to 'set down truths', but also to write 'his own story', that is, his own version of the 1641 uprising, when, as a Catholic, he was not trusted by the English army to suppress the Irish rebels. Without any doubt, writing his memoirs was a way for Touchet to put the record straight and defend his reputation, after he was called a rebel in Edmund Borlase's *History of the Execrable Irish Rebellion*:[103]

> Being one day in *S. Pauls Church-yard*, amongst the *Stationers*, some Books fell into my hands lately set forth: Histories of the Rebellion begun in *Ireland*, in the year *1641* [...]; and finding my self in many places cited, acting as a confederate Catholick, which in plain English is as a Rebel; I thought fit to publish something, setting forth my own story (not to excuse the Rebellion, or those who were forced into it, as I was [...]), but what I write is chiefly to draw from the world some compassion, my case being singular, as I hope my Memoirs will make out.[104]

In *A Letter from a Person of Honour*, a response to Touchet's *Memoirs*, published anonymously in 1681, the Protestant Arthur Annesley, Earl of Anglesey, who was of Anglo-Irish origins, in turn entered the controversy, trying to distance himself from both Touchet and the Duke of Ormond.[105] He accused the Duke of having betrayed Protestant interests during the Irish insurrection and the wars that followed. Another letter was written to Annesley by the Duke of Ormond, which was circulated at court.[106] Annesley, who was also Lord Privy Seal, answered this letter in a published pamphlet

---

[102] This address is drawn from the slightly enlarged 1681 edition with an appendix and observations. James Touchet, *The Memoirs of James, Lord Audley, Earl of Castlehaven [...] with an Appendix, Relating Wars abroad that he hath either seen or known; with some Observations on the whole* (London, 1681) sig. a2.

[103] Edmund Borlase, *The History of the Execrable Irish Rebellion* (London, 1680).

[104] Touchet, *Memoirs* (1681) sig. [a3–a4ᵛ].

[105] Arthur Annesley, Earl of Anglesey, *A Letter from a Person of Honour in the Countrey Written to the Earl of Castlehaven: being observations and reflections upon His Lordships memoires concerning the wars of Ireland* (London, 1681). See M. Perceval-Maxwell, 'Annesley, Arthur, First Earl of Anglesey (1614–1686), politician' (2004), *Oxford Dictionary of National Biography*, https://doi.org/10.1093/ref: odnb/562. On Arthur Annesley's interest in historiography, see Justin Begley, 'Arthur Annesley, Margaret Cavendish, and Neo-Latin History', *Review of English Studies* 69 (2018): 855–87, here 868–70 and Eamon Darcy, 'Writing the Past in Early Modern Ireland: Anglesey, Borlase and the Craft of History', *Irish Historical Studies* 40.158 (2016): 171–91.

[106] James Butler, Duke of Ormond, *A Letter from His Grace James Duke of Ormond, Lord Lieutenant of Ireland, in answer to the Right Honourable Arthur Earl of Anglesey Lord Privy-Seal, his observations and reflections upon the Earl of Castlehaven's Memoires concerning the rebellion of Ireland* (London, 1682).

(which included Ormond's letter).[107] Castlehaven's memoirs provoked yet another reaction, that of Borlase, the author of *The History of the Execrable Irish Rebellion*, which is the text that initially prompted Touchet to write his *Memoirs*. In his *Brief Reflections on the Earl of Castlehaven's Memoirs*, Borlase promises to rectify what he calls 'that Rhapsodie of Fictions and Untruths', and to offer instead 'an Epitome of the Irish scene'.[108] Finally, and as a consequence to all this, Touchet published a revised version of his *Memoirs*, in which he tried to restore the truth: 'finding myself mentioned afresh, not without some new Aggravations [...], I find myself under a necessity to say something in my own Defence, by setting forth the truth of my story, in as brief and plain a method as possible, to obviate the false and Malicious Calumnies of these forging Scriblers.'[109]

Another enlightening controversy that sprang in the aftermath of the Civil Wars crystallized around the posthumous publication of the *Memoirs of Edmund Ludlow*, which, MacGillivray notes, have 'so much common in origin, form, and interpretation' with the *Memoirs of the Life of Colonel Hutchinson* that the two texts deserve to be 'treated together'.[110] If Lucy Hutchinson's *Memoirs* had not been kept private by her royalist family, the chances are high that they would have aroused a similar controversy to the one raised by the *Memoirs* of Ludlow, who, like John Hutchinson, had signed the King's death warrant and sat on the Council of State:

> It was [...] possibly in January, but probably in February, that the *Memoirs of Edmund Ludlow* [...] were published in two volumes. They sold unexpectedly well, and caused considerable stir. Their vivid narrative provided fresh information which could only have been available to a leading politician which had seen the events of the Puritan Revolution from the inside. Those events were presented for the first time through the eyes of a fully rounded personality.[111]

---

[107] Arthur Annesley, *A letter from the Right Honourable Arthur Earl of Anglesey Lord Privy -Seal, in answer to His Grace the Duke of Ormond's letter of November the 12th, 1681 about his Lordships observations and reflections upon the Earl of Castle-Haven's memoires, concerning the rebellion of Ireland* (London, 1682).

[108] Edmund Borlase, *Brief Reflections on the Earl of Castlehaven's Memoirs of his engagements and carriage in the wars of Ireland by which the government at that time, and the justice of the crown since, are vindicated from aspersions cast on both* (London, 1682) sig. A4–[A4v].

[109] James Touchet, *The Earl of Castlehavens Review: Or his Memoirs of his Engagement and Carriage in the Irish Wars. Enlarged and Corrected* (London, 1684) 4–5.

[110] MacGillivray, *Restoration Historians* 170. See the section 'Edmund Ludlow and Mrs Hutchinson', 170–85. For an overview of the historiographical context of the 1690s and early 1700s, see Keeble, 'Reliquiæ Baxterianæ and the Shaping of the Seventeenth Century', §17.18 and §17.19.

[111] Worden, 'Introduction', *A Voyce from the Watch Tower*, ed. Worden, 1.

Ludlow's *Memoirs*, which were presumably revised by the Irish republican John Toland, sold well and were very soon published in French in Amsterdam in 1699.[112] In their wake, and in the context of a controversy over William III's intention to keep a large standing army after the treaty of Ryswick (1697), the memoirs of Denzil Holles, Thomas Fairfax, and Sir John Berkeley were published the same year by a group of radical publishers, among whom the same John Toland.[113] These Whig publications were closely followed by Tory responses, with the memoirs of Sir Philip Warwick and Sir Thomas Herbert (1701), as well as Edward Hyde's *History of the Rebellion,* which was largely memorial in form since it incorporated the author's 'life' and his experience of the 'rebellion'.[114] According to Worden, the publication of these 'memoirs' was essential, for they '[supplied] a new genre of Civil War history', a genre, he claims, which was the most appropriate one to reflect the experience of the English Civil Wars and Interregnum.[115]

The genre, brought into fashion in England by the publication of Ludlow's *Memoirs*, was not to everyone's taste, however. This was evidenced by the response of William Baron, the chaplain to the second earl of Clarendon and the author of *Regicides, No Saints Nor Martyrs* (1700). According to Baron, Ludlow's publishers debased themselves when 'notwithstanding the *Books* [Ludlow's *Memoirs*], and their many Prejudices against *France*', they resolved to 'send it forth in that *Allamode* way of *Memoirs*'.[116] From Baron's critical standpoint, Ludlow's *Memoirs* were no better than the general histories and chronicles of the Civil Wars: they were 'such a *Farrago*, such an *Hodgpodg*, of *Calumnies*, and *Falshoods*', and the same recycling of 'superannuated Stories, and Commonwealth Fictions, which serv'd their several turns from 41. forward, as if Time, the Mother of Truth, had not yet brought forth anything of clearer discovery'.[117] In other words, by presenting Ludlow's

---

[112] See Edmund Ludlow, *Les Mémoires d'Edmond Ludlow*, 2 vols. (Amsterdam, 1699) and *A Voyce from the Watch Tower*, 1–2, note 1. On the context of publication, see Gaby Mahlberg, *The English Republican Exiles in Europe during the Restoration* (Cambridge: Cambridge UP, 2020) 13–14, 167–200.

[113] Ludlow, *A Voyce from the Watch Tower* 23–4. See Edmund Ludlow, *Memoirs of Edmund Ludlow Esq* (Vevey, 1698), Ludlow, *Memoirs of Lieutenant General Ludlow serving to confirm and illustrate many important passages of this and the preceding volumes: to which is added, a table to the whole work* (Vevey, 1699).

[114] On the Whig side, see Holles, *Memoirs*; Thomas Fairfax, *Short Memorials of Thomas Lord Fairfax written by himself* (London, 1699); John Berkeley, *Memoirs of Sir John Berkeley* (London, 1699). On the Tory side, see Philip Warwick, *Memoirs of the Reign of King Charles I* (London, 1701); Edward Hyde, *The History of the Rebellion and Civil Wars*, vol. 1 (London, 1702); Thomas Herbert, *Memoirs of the Two Last Years of the Reign of that Unparall'd Prince, of Ever Blessed Memory, King Charles I* (London, 1702). On Holles and Ludlow, see Lurbe, 'Du temps vécu au temps de l'histoire', 111–28.

[115] Ludlow, *A Voyce from the Watch Tower* 22.

[116] William Baron, *Regicides, No Saints Nor Martyrs Freely Expostulated with the publishers of Ludlow's Third Volume, as to the truth of things and characters* (London, 1700) 8, and Baron, *A Just Defence of the Royal Martyr King Charles I from [...] Ludlow's Memoirs* (London, 1699).

[117] Baron, *Regicides* 4.

work as an imposture, Baron broke the conventional equation between experience, truth, and history on which English memoir-writers had capitalized since the 1650s.

As a counterpoint, it should eventually be pointed out that very much as in England, the memoir genre flourished in France in times of ideological divisions, first, after the wars of religion (c.1552–1598), and then, after the Fronde, especially during Louis XIV's absolute rule. Despite their growing popularity among writers and readers throughout the seventeenth century, memoirs were deemed inferior to more general and eloquent histories, and often despised as mere drafts of or sources for history.[118] However, despite their detractors, among whom the Jesuits René Rapin and Pierre Le Moyne, it has now been established, notably by Marc Fumaroli, that seventeenth-century French memoirs were the pieces of a polyphonic history and, thereby, the main genre—if not the only genre—in which history could be efficiently written in the seventeenth century.[119]

3. Testifying to the truth

Unlike Heylin, Milton did not believe that truth was 'lost' but that it had been 'hewd [...] into a thousand pieces' by Roman Catholics, and that its fragments had therefore to be recovered at all costs by Protestants, even by the 'schismaticks and sectaries' among them, that is, by Christians who stood outside the Established Church.[120] In other words, a pluralistic and contradictory debate—what Milton called 'wars of truth'—was necessary for the emergence of truth.[121] The *Memoirs* are intensely anti-Catholic, but, like Milton, the Hutchinsons were tolerant of other Protestant denominations, having, for

---

[118] For Le Moyne, 'History is a continued Narration of things True, Great and Publick, writ with Spirit, Eloquence and Judgment; for instruction to Particulars and Princes, and Good of Civil Society' (*Of the Art Both of Writing & Judging of History* 53–4). He continues, 'But History requires not only they should be True, but Great and Politick; and by that in the fourth place, raises itself above *Memoirs* and *Journals*, that entertain with Private and Domestic, and sometimes with Trifles, which Posterity might very well be ignorant of without Prejudice' (55); René Rapin, *Instructions for History* (London, 1680) 94: 'The Historian has his matter given him by the Memoirs wherewith he is supply'd, but the distribution of it is his peculiar province.' In French, Rapin, *Instructions pour l'Histoire* (Paris, 1677) 149. See Fumaroli, 'Les Mémoires au carrefour des genres en prose', 184–5 and Briot, *Usage du monde* 84.

[119] Lucinge, *La manière de lire l'histoire* 132: this is essentially what René de Lucinge, claimed after the French wars of religion: 'Ceux d'entre les escrivains qui alleguent hardiment les tesmoins de leurs relations, et de qui ils tiennent les instructions de leurs rapports, sont les moins suspects, si on met en controverse la verité de leur histoire.'

[120] John Milton, *Areopagitica*, in *The Major Works*, ed. Stephen Orgel and Jonathan Goldberg (Oxford: Oxford UP, 1991) 263.

[121] Milton, *Areopagitica* 269.

instance, been tempted by Baptism.[122] Therefore, she would not have disowned the idea that dissidents could contribute to building truth, which is at the core of Milton's complex rewrite of the Isis and Osiris myth in *Areopagitica*:

> Truth indeed came once into the world with her divine master, and was a perfect shape most glorious to look on: but when he ascended, and his Apostles after Him were laid asleep, then strait arose a wicked race of deceivers, who, as that story goes of the Ægyptian Typhon with his conspirators, how they dealt with the good Osiris, took the virgin Truth, hewed her lovely form into a thousand pieces, and scattered them to the four winds. From that time ever since, the sad friends of Truth, such as durst appear, imitating the carefull search that Isis made for the mangled body of Osiris, went up and down gathering up limb by limb still as they could find them.[123]

The fact that Lucy Hutchinson advises the reader of the *Memoirs* to read pamphlets and histories, even those written by adversaries, suggests that her conception of truth was very close to that of Milton in *Areopagitica*. In the wider context of Restoration historiography, the *Memoirs*—as one 'limb' of Osiris's fragmented body—could contribute, as much as the histories and memoirs written by her contemporaries, to the emergence of the 'naked truth' and to 'framing of a true General History', wished for, as seen above, by Francis Bacon and the Irish Whig John Toland.[124] The question of truth is as important in Lucy Hutchinson's work as in many of the books and pamphlets published during and in the wake of the English Civil Wars, her aim being to establish both historical truth understood as the coincidence of *gesta* and *verba*—the adequacy between words and facts—as well as the truth of Colonel Hutchinson, which like 'the truth of God' is 'above the testimony of men' (K72/S98).

a) Historiographical assumptions

It is difficult to know with precision to what extent Lucy Hutchinson was in contact with pre-Civil War historiographical debates, but given her extended

---

[122] *Memoirs*, ed. Sutherland, 168–71, and ed. Keeble, 209–11. See Mark Burden, 'Lucy Hutchinson and Baptist Confessions of Faith', *Dissenting Experience* (2016), https://dissent.hypotheses.org/1618 (accessed 02/03/2022). On Milton and toleration, see Sharon Achinstein, *Literature and Dissent in Milton's England* (Cambridge: Cambridge UP, 2003) 126–30.

[123] Milton, *Areopagitica* 263.

[124] See Toland, 'The Publisher to the Reader', *Memoirs of Denzil Lord Holles*, ix. Lurbe, 'Du temps vécu au temps de l'histoire', 118, 121.

discursive horizon it is reasonable to think that she was familiar with Montaigne and Bacon, whose works were widely available in England throughout the seventeenth century. Bacon was mentioned by some Restoration memorialists, including Margaret Cavendish, who, as pointed out above, was a neighbour of Lucy Hutchinson's.[125] Welbeck Abbey, where the Cavendish family lived, was itself an intellectual centre, not very distant from Owthorpe; it was a place which the Hutchinsons could not ignore, even before the Civil Wars, where such people as Robert Payne, Walter Warner and Thomas Hobbes met around William Cavendish and his brother Charles.[126]

What is more, in several places of her narrative, Lucy Hutchinson refers the reader to the histories that were then being written. By the time she wrote the *Memoirs* she had at her disposal several histories of the Civil Wars, not only May's *History of the Parliament* and *Breviary*, but also, among others, the accounts of Walker, Heath, and Rushworth—which, however, she does not mention, but may have consulted.[127] Indeed, after a long digression about the causes of the Civil Wars, she urges her readers to read and consider other histories 'impartially', even if they were written by the opposite party:[128]

> if any one have a desire of more particular information, there were so many bookes then written as will sufficiently give it them; and although those of our enemies are all fraught with abominable lies, yett if all ours were supprest, even their owne writings impartially consider'd would be a sufficient chronicle of their injustice and oppression.   (S37/K57)

Then, when she tackles the history of the Commonwealth, she advises her reader to consult other historical writings—which may indicate that, at one point, she did the same:

> But how the publique businesse went on, how Cromwell finisht the Conquest of Ireland, how the angrie Presbiterians spitt fire out of their pulpitts and

---

[125] See Cavendish, *The Life* 103: 'to render the History of his Life more perfect and compleat.' See Bacon's conception of a 'IVST and PARFITE history', *The Second Booke* 11.

[126] See Timothy Raylor, 'Newcastle's Ghosts: Robert Payne, Ben Jonson, and the "Cavendish Circle"', *Literary Circles and Cultural Communities in Renaissance England*, ed. C. J. Summers and T. L. Pebworth (Columbia: U of Missouri P, 2000), 92–114.

[127] See May, *The History of the Parliament* and *A Breviary of the History of the Parliament of England* (London, 1650); Clement Walker, *The Compleat History of Independency* (London, 1661); James Heath, *A Brief Chronicle of All the chief Actions so fatally falling out in these three kingdoms, viz. England, Scotland & Ireland from the year, 1640, to this present twentieth of November, 1661* (London, 1662); Rushworth, *Historical Collections*.

[128] On 'Impartial Readers', see Raymond, 'Exporting Impartiality', 151–8.

> endeavour'd to blow up the people against Parliament, how they enter'd into a treasonable conspiracy with Scotland, who had now receiv'd and crown'd the sonne of the late king, who led them in hither in a greate Armie [...], I shall leave to the stories that were then written. (S191/K236)

In a number of other passages, she takes for granted that the reader has a good knowledge of events. When the Rump was restored on 26 December 1649, she observes: 'The manner of it and the contest and treaty in the North between Monck and Lambert, are too well-known to be repeated' (S72/K272). But when she uses historical accounts, she does not do so indiscriminately. For example, she discusses the accuracy and the truthfulness of May's account in his *History of the Parliament* and *Breviary*, thereby asserting her own authority as a historian and articulating, at the same time, a clear republican vision: 'Mr. Maye's History, which I find to be impartially true, so farre as he hath carried it on, saving some little mistakes in his owne judgement, and mis-informations which some vaine people gave of them selves, and more indulgence to the King's guilt than can justly be allow'd' (S53/K75). Such an authoritative judgment was made possible not only by her familiarity with other histories but also, naturally, by hindsight. When she wrote about the Civil Wars, between 1664 and 1667, she knew the outcome of the conflict, which was not the case with Thomas May when he was composing his own history. To take but one example, her trenchant view of the Commonwealth (1649-1653), stated in the present tense, can only have been formulated at the Restoration, when she knew the whys and wherefores of past debates: 'It is true that at that time every man allmost was fancying [a] forme of Government, and angrie, when this came forth, that his invention tooke not place' (S191/K236).

The fact that Lucy Hutchinson, despite her familiarity with Civil War histories, did not choose any specific historiographical or literary model was typical of memorialists, who tended to blend together several genres of writing.[129] In addition, her promise of a 'naked undrest narrative, speaking the simple truth of him' (S1/K16) recalls the common trope of the *narratio nuda*, advocated by humanists and their heirs, in particular Bodin, Montaigne, and Bacon, as well as many memorialists in early modern Europe.[130] In England, it can be found under the pen of Margaret Cavendish, who professed

---

[129] Lesne, *La Poétique des mémoires* 58–62; see Fumaroli, 'Les Mémoires au carrefour des genres en prose'.
[130] See Fumaroli, 'Mémoires et histoire', 31.

to write the history of her husband in '[her] own plain style', rejecting 'elegant flourishings' and considering '[r]hetorick was fitter for Falshoods then Truths.'[131] But this claim was often made in other contemporary histories. In *Anglia Rediviva*, one of the earliest accounts of the Civil War, Joshua Sprigge, an Independent minister who had been Fairfax's chaplain, explains his reasons for rejecting the 'trappings of words', adding that he 'should count [him]self unhappy, to detain the Reader in the *Artifice* of the *Style,* from the *Greatnesse* of the *Matter;* Lofty language, is but to Mount *Pigmee* actions, and to please a *lower* Sense.'[132] One must read these statements against the lies of rhetoric with a degree of caution, of course, for memorialists and historians did not actually reject but incorporated rhetoric in their writings; what they objected to were *excesses* of rhetoric.

Under these conditions, it is not surprising that like many other Civil War historians, Lucy Hutchinson distrusted the pamphlets, newsbooks, and sensational histories which poured off the presses.[133] She does not issue a blanket condemnation of cheap print, however, but repeatedly denounces the calumnies which circulated in newsbooks and pamphlets. Through the character of John Gell, the Sheriff of Derbyshire and parliamentarian general, she reveals how news and reputation were fabricated by journalists for mercenary ends. For the Sheriff, newsbooks were a means of building himself a reputation: 'This man kept the diurnall makers in pension, so that whatever was done in any of the neighbouring counties against the enemie was ascrib'd to him; and he hath indirectly purchas'd himselfe a name in story which he never merited' (S68/K92). Unlike Gell, John Hutchinson is said to have refused to bribe the diurnal-makers and to use them for his own profit. The Colonel's distrust of the developing culture of news serves here as evidence of his integrity. It is corroborated by Lucy Hutchinson's own contempt for the practices of the mercenary scribblers:

> Mr. Hutchinson, on the other side [...], never would give aniething to buy the flatteries of those scriblers, and when one of them had once, while he was

---

[131] Cavendish, *Life of William Cavendish* [sig. b4ᵛ].

[132] Joshua Sprigge, 'To all true English-men', *Anglia Rediviva. Englands recovery being the history of the motions, actions, and successes of the army under the immediate conduct of His Excellency Sr. Thomas Fairfax* (London, 1647) np.

[133] The denunciation of gazettes was also a commonplace in French memoirs. See Lesne, *La Poétique des mémoires* 48–50. On the culture of news, see Jason Peacey, *Print and Public Politics in the English Revolution* (Cambridge: Cambridge UP, 2013); Joad Raymond, *Pamphlets and Pamphleteering in Early Modern Britain* (Cambridge: Cambridge UP, 2003); Raymond, 'Irrational, Impractical and Unprofitable: Reading the News in Seventeenth-Century Britain', *Reading, Society and Politics in Early Modern England* (Cambridge: Cambridge UP, 2003) 185–212.

in Towne, made mention of something done at Nottingham with falsehood, and given Gell the glory of an action wherein he was not concern'd, Mr. Hutchinson rebuk'd him for it, whereupon the man beg'd his pardon, and told him he would write as much for him the next weeke; but Mr. Hutchinson told him he scorn'd his mercenary pen, only warn'd not to dare to lie in any of his concernments, whereupon the fellow was awed, and he had no more abuse of that kind. (S68/K93)

All pamphlets, however, are not presented as the vehicles of lies in the *Memoirs*. At least twice, John Hutchinson adroitly uses the press in order to make his case public. In December 1643, his exchanges with Colonel Dacre and Captain Poulton about the Earl of Newcastle's summons to deliver the castle were printed in a pamphlet entitled *A Discovery of the Treacherous Attempts of the Cavaliers to Have Procured the Betraying of Nottingham Castle*.[134] Similar exchanges were published in issues of *Mercurius Britannicus* (23–29 August 1643) and *Britain's Remembrancer* (26 March–2 April 1644).[135] Almost twenty years later, when the Colonel was a captive in the Tower in 1663–1664, Lucy Hutchinson threatened the lieutenant of the Tower, a certain Robinson, to publish a letter written by her husband, which recorded all the exactions and persecutions of which he had been a victim.[136] In actual facts, around the same period (the autumn of 1663 and the following winter), Colonel Hutchinson had a relation of his imprisonment in the Tower of London published, in order to publicize his cause, a narrative on which Lucy Hutchinson drew in the *Memoirs*.[137] Finally, by comparing Lucy Hutchinson's 'Defence of John Hutchinson' in the Notebook with similar texts, Anna Wall makes the hypothesis that it could have been a 'draft of what was supposed to be a printed pamphlet'.[138]

---

[134] See also *Memoirs*, ed. Firth, Appendix XIV, 409–15. See Wall, 'Not so much professed enemies', 638–9 and Andrew Hopper, 'Treachery and Conspiracy in Nottinghamshire during the English Civil War', *East Midlands History and Heritage* 22: 'the Hutchinsons sought to fashion themselves as beyond temptation in a very public manner. Resorting to print also raised their stock within Parliament's coalition by showing that the royalists thought them important enough to try to subvert.'

[135] *Memoirs*, ed. Firth, Appendix X, 405–6, and Appendix XXII, 425.

[136] *Memoirs*, ed. Sutherland, 258–60, and ed. Keeble, 314–17.

[137] See John Hutchinson, *A Narrative of the Imprisonment and Usage of Colonel John Hutchinson* [1664], *Harleian Miscellany*, vol. 3 (London, 1745) 284–90. It is mentioned in the *Memoirs*, ed. Sutherland, 256, and ed. Keeble, 312. On prison writing during the Civil Wars and Interregnum, with a focus on royalist literature, see Lois Potter, *Secret Rites and Secret Writing: Royalist Literature* (Cambridge: Cambridge UP, 1989) 134–40.

[138] Wall, 'Not so much professed enemies', 636. See for instance, John Gell, *The Several Accompts of Sir John Gell, Baronet and Colonell* (London, 1644), or Nathaniel Fiennes, *A relation made in the House of Commons by Col. Nathaniel Fiennes concerning the surrender of the city and castle of Bristoll* (London, 1643).

Finally, like many historians of her age, as seen with the examples of L'Estrange and Burnet, Lucy Hutchinson rejected romance, which she held to be synonymous with falsehood. Her understanding of 'romance' as referring to 'nearly everything that was not fact' was much in line with her times. This was not an easy stance to take, however, because romance, as a 'genre of imaginations and the passions', seems to have been a real temptation when she was writing the *Memoirs*.[139] When recounting the siege of January 1644, she identifies all the ingredients of a romance in the extraordinary victory of the Colonel's troops against the Newark royalist forces. Still, she eventually rules out the option of romance considering this miraculous success was exclusively the work of God's Providence, not of an 'excess of gallantry':

> If it were a Romance, wee should say, after the successe that the Heroes did it out of excesse of gallantry, that they might better signalize their vallour upon a foe who was not vanquisht to their hands by the inclemency of the season; but while wee are relating wonders of Providence wee must record this as such a one as is not to be conceived from a relation, in the admirable mercy that it brought forth; but to those who saw and shar'd in it, it was greate instruction that even the best and highest courages are but the beames of the Almighty. (S114–115/K147)

Lucy Hutchinson maintains this hostility to romance throughout the *Memoirs*, insisting that the truth of history could only emerge from a detailed account of God's Providence. Such distrust of fiction was paradoxical for, as David Norbrook explains,

> [w]omen were expected to fictionalize history in the mode of romance, fusing public events with private love affairs. In the *Memoirs* Lucy Hutchinson instead offers a much more analytic discourse, bringing in the minutiae of political and military history, in which her idealization of her husband can perhaps be seen as a residual romance element – the "Elegies" show that they gave each other romance names.[140]

In addition, Lucy Hutchinson's views in the *Memoirs* are consistent with her preface to *Order and Disorder*, in which she discards 'romance', as being in

---

[139] On the essential semantic shift affecting the word 'romance' in the seventeenth century, from 'the genre of male heroics' to 'one of imagination and the passions', see Lee, 'The Meanings of Romance', 299–311.

[140] Norbrook, 'Lucy Hutchinson's Elegies', 483. On romance, see also Norbrook, 'Margaret Cavendish and Lucy Hutchinson', 185.

every way contrary to her project of a Christian epic: 'Had I had a fancy, I durst not have exercised it here; for I tremble of turning Scripture into a romance.'[141] However, her rejection of this genre as the opposite of truth—a commonplace in historiographical debates—did not stop her from using romance tropes: as we shall see in Chapter 4, her emplotment of historical reality, although it theoretically rejected the idealized and fanciful world of romance, often required the craft of a romance writer.

b) Writing the defence of John Hutchinson

In her monograph on sixteenth-century French memoirs, Nadine Kuperty-Tsur argues that from its infancy the memoir genre has been characterized by its apologetic dimension.[142] She considers that Philippe de Commynes's *Mémoires*, which combine a factual historical narrative with a *pro domo* plea, constitute the first instance of the 'new' genre of memoirs that flourished in France and in Europe in the early modern period.[143] The *Memoirs of the Life of John Hutchinson* are no exception: from the dedication, 'To my Children', to the final pages of 'The Life', Lucy Hutchinson is resolved to dissipate the 'ignorance and misinformation' heaped upon the Colonel over the years (S150/K88). By embracing the role of apologist, her goal was to offer a testimony to counter all the lies circulating about him, in his lifetime and after his death, both locally and nationally, at court and in Parliament. In this light, the 'Life of John Hutchinson' can be construed as a deposition in his favour, meant to provide the legal evidence of his political, moral, and religious integrity—what Lucy Hutchinson calls the truth of him, when referring to his charge as Governor of Nottingham in the 1640s: 'this testimony is a truth of him, that in his whole actings in this cause he never prosecuted any private lust, either of revenge, ambition, avarice, or vaine glory, under a publick vizard, but was most truly publick spirited' (S91/K120).[144]

---

[141] Hutchinson, *Order and Disorder* 5. On romance, see Chapter 4, 1.
[142] See Fumaroli, 'Les *Mémoires* au carrefour des genres en prose', 194: 'Memoirs are therefore to be taken in a very concrete sense, that of a case presented before the court of posterity' (my translation).
[143] Kuperty-Tsur, *Se dire à la Renaissance* 19–23: 'The Memoirs, first of all, share the same situation of enunciation. Whatever the status of the memorialist, the narrative of his actions is motivated by the desire to repair an injustice committed against him. A memorialist has a cause to plead, an image to defend' (my translation).
[144] On the legal aspects of witness testimony, see Shapiro, '"Fact" and the Law', *A Culture of Fact* 8–33 and Guerrier, 'Affirmation de vérité, revendication de véracité', 92–3.

The rectitude of the Colonel, Lucy Hutchinson argues, was recognized by many people, including some who did not share his views. When his case was examined by the Convention in June 1660, 'there was not at that day any man that receiv'd a more generall testimony of love and good esteeme of all parties than he did, at that time [...] divers most worthy persons giving such a true and honorable testimony of him' (S231/K282). Nevertheless, writing the Colonel's defence was an audacious undertaking in the early 1660s, when the passions and polemics of the Revolution were far from extinct. Some regicides had been executed, others exiled, while some fears remained about the possibility of a new Civil War.[145] By writing a plea in favour of the Colonel who had signed the king's death warrant, Lucy Hutchinson was incurring a real danger, all the more so as several people mentioned in the *Memoirs* were still alive. Sir Walter Raleigh's warning about the perils of '[following] the truth too neer the heels', often quoted by her contemporaries—here by Thomas Fuller in 1656—must also have haunted her:[146]

> I must tread tenderly, because I goe not (as before) on mens graves, but am ready to touch the quick of some yet alive. I know how dangerous it is to follow Truth too neere to the heels; yet better it is that the teeth of an Historian be struck out of his head for writing the Truth than that they remain still and rot in his Jaws, feeding too much on the sweet-meats of flattery.[147]

Like Sir Walter Raleigh, however, Lucy Hutchinson believed there was nothing worse than 'the sweet-meats of flattery' and therefore she made it her duty to confute the rumours which were rife about her husband. Early in the narrative, she rejects the rumour that the Hutchinson brothers were disinherited by Sir Thomas because they supported the cause of Parliament. But, in the general economy of the *Memoirs*, the Colonel's father had to be presented as a Puritan gentleman devoted to the parliamentary cause. Lucy Hutchinson's financial predicament—which was mostly the result of her father-in-law's decision to favour the royalist children of his second marriage—is overshadowed here in order to give Colonel Hutchinson a truly Puritan pedigree:

---

[145] See N. H. Keeble, *The Restoration: England in the 1660s* (Oxford: Blackwell, 2002) 32–54.

[146] Walter Raleigh, 'The Preface', *History of the World* (London, 1614) [sig. E4]: 'Who-so-ever in writing a modern History, shall follow truth too neare the heels, it may happily strike out his teeth.'

[147] Fuller, *The Church History of Britain* 232.

it was given out that he was displeas'd with his sons' engagement, and for that cause dispos'd away so much of his estate from them, but that was not soe. Indeed, at the time of his death the Parliament's interest was so low that he might looke upon them as lost persons, and so what he gave away to the unengaged infant he might well look upon as all that could be preserv'd. [...] Yet all the Parliament's losses griev'd him, and all their successes pleas'd him. (S92/K120-121)

This highly political passage, in which Lucy Hutchinson asserts that the Colonel's father, the former High Sheriff for Nottinghamshire, was on the side of Parliament, was not to the taste of one anonymous reader of the manuscript, presumably Julius Hutchinson, the royalist grandson of Sir Thomas, who was the great uncle of Julius Hutchinson, the first editor of the *Memoirs*.[148] This early eighteenth-century reader crossed out Lucy Hutchinson's correction in the above quotation ('But that was not so... preserved'), and indicated instead, in a note in the margin of the next page, that 'Sr Thomas H: sat longer in y^t house than many other honest men' and that he 'heard attested' by his grandmother (Sir Thomas's wife) that Sir Thomas was 'afflicted' by the conduct of John and Lucy Hutchinson.[149] Another aspersion that Lucy Hutchinson had to deal with was that in early 1647, after the First Civil War, Colonel Hutchinson was 'call'd a Cavalier, and sayd to have chang'd his party, and a thousand more injuries' (S170/K211), because he had protected his royalist brother-in-law 'only in that which was just' (S170/K211). Paradoxically, the worst slanderers, according to Lucy Hutchinson, were the Presbyterians who 'could not keepe that secret fire from rising up in a black smoke against the most faithfull asserters of [the cause]' (S170/K212). A Scottish minister, whom John Hutchinson had recruited by order of Parliament in 1648, spread calumnies about the Hutchinsons among Nottingham Presbyterians, reviving the quarrels of the First Civil War:

this rogue, before he went out of the country, went to the Presbiters att Nottingham, and told them his conscience would not permit him to stay in

---

[148] Julius Hutchinson (1678-1738), John Hutchinson's nephew, was the son of Charles Hutchinson (c.1638-c.1695)—John Hutchinson's half-brother—and Isabella Botiler. See the family tree, appended to the 1806 edition, between 'To my Children' (17) and 'The Life of John Hutchinson' (19).

[149] See *Memoirs*, DD/HU4, 148-9; *Memoirs*, ed. Keeble, note 221, and ed. Sutherland, xxi-xxii. See other political annotations signalled by Burden, 'Editing Shadows', 175 (DD/HU4, 65, 272). Burden considers Julius Hutchinson (the elder) as a moderate Whig.

the Collonell's house, because his wife and he were such violent Sectaries that no orthodox man could live comfortably with them; and this scandall these charitable priests were ready to receive and more largely spread it abroad.

(S178-9/K221)

In this context rife with rumours, one understands why the Colonel's unconditional love of truth is so central to the economy of the *Memoirs*. Not only is it pivotal in the eulogistic Dedication—'he never at any time would refreine a true or give a false witnesse; he lov'd truth so much that he hated even sportive lies and gulleries' (S8/K24)—but it is also crucial in the rest of the *Memoirs*, the Colonel's 'zeal for truth' standing as the yardstick against which to assess the truth and falsehood of his contemporaries.

Chapter 3
The experience of the Civil War in Nottingham

Lucy Hutchinson's historiographical project cannot be understood outside the epistemology of experience which was highly valued during the Civil Wars and, even more so, at the Restoration. At that time, when the scars of the Civil Wars had not been healed, testimonies, based on a direct experience of history, were deemed more valuable and more reliable than general histories. This ethos of testimony is cogently defined by Ricœur in the following terms:

> The specificity of testimony consists in the fact that the assertion of reality is inseparable from its being paired with the self-designation of the testifying subject. The typical formulation of testimony proceeds from this pairing: I was there. What is attested to is indivisibly the reality of the past thing and the presence of the narrator at the place of its occurrence.[1]

Like her fellow-memorialists, Lucy Hutchinson consistently describes herself as a witness to the events she recounts;[2] she even sometimes reports how she took an active part in them, especially after 1660, when she managed to obtain an amnesty for her husband.[3] As seen earlier in Chapter 2, the historiographical model she chose was promoted by many humanist historians and commentators who followed Caesar's *Commentaries* and Commynes's *Memoirs*.[4] It is within this experiential framework that I propose to assess Lucy Hutchinson's authority as a historian of the English Revolution.

---

[1] See Ricœur, 'Testimony', *Memory, History, Forgetting* 163–4.
[2] According to the *OED*, a witness is '[o]ne who is or was present and is able to testify from personal observation; one present as spectator or auditor'. On the status of witness in memoirs, see Lesne, *La Poétique des mémoires* 257. See Charbonneau, *Les Silences de l'histoire* 77–86.
[3] See Chapter 4.
[4] See Julius Caesar, *Iulius Cesars Commentaryes, newly translatyd owte of laten in to englysshe* (London, 1530). Caesar's *Commentaries* were discovered by Petrarch in the fourteenth century. See also Philippe de Commynes, *Les mémoires de messire Philippe de Commines* (Paris, 1552).

Lucy Hutchinson and the English Revolution: Gender, Genre, and History Writing. Claire Gheeraert-Graffeuille, Oxford University Press. © Claire Gheeraert-Graffeuille 2022. DOI: 10.1093/oso/9780192857538.003.0004

1. Writing the English Civil War: from experience to words

Lucy Hutchinson's experience of the First Civil War in Nottingham (1642–1646) spans half of the *Memoirs*.[5] The quality of this section of the narrative comes from the fact that it is built on an earlier narrative, now kept at the British Library, which Firth, the second editor of the *Memoirs*, called the 'Note-book'.[6] It is to be edited separately by David Norbrook, in the third volume of the *Works of Lucy Hutchinson* as 'The Defence of John Hutchinson'.[7] This previous record was probably elaborated with a view to defending the Colonel in his legal proceedings before the Nottingham Committee which repeatedly challenged his authority, although no evidence has been found that it actually served as a legal defence.[8] Such a reading is made possible by the opening sentence of the manuscript which starts as a list of the things achieved by the Colonel for his county, a sort of deposition made by his wife in his favour—'The first service m^r John Hutchinson vnder tooke in this County'.[9] When the Colonel's authority was no longer challenged in April 1645, Lucy Hutchinson stopped drawing on that first narrative which she calls 'the collection': 'Thus farre was transcrib'd out of a more particular *collection*. What followes will be but a *generall summe* of those things that were done in the Garrison till the time of its reduction' (S157/K196, my emphasis).

The Notebook, however, is not Lucy Hutchinson's unique source in the *Memoirs*. She also drew on private papers and letters, as well on printed sources such as newsbooks and pamphlets.[10] A few politically important letters written by the Colonel were copied at the end of the Notebook in Lucy Hutchinson's hand.[11] Some of these and other letters were also reproduced by Firth in his edition of the *Memoirs*.[12] As suggested in the *Memoirs*, the Hutchinsons highly valued their papers and letters. When the Colonel heard that the Cavaliers were approaching Owthorpe in July 1648, 'they put Arms and writings and other things of vallue and sent them away in a Cart'

---

[5] *Memoirs*, ed. Sutherland, 59–190, and ed. Keeble, 82–235.
[6] There are four fragments of the Notebook. Three manuscripts are kept at the British Library, Add. MS 39779, Add. MS 46172, and Add. MS 25901. For more detail on the Notebook, see Chapter 5, 197.
[7] See https://earlymodern.web.ox.ac.uk/works-lucy-hutchinson-0#Volume%203 (accessed 12/06/2019).
[8] Norbrook, 'But a Copie', 111. Norbrook's choice of a 'defence' as a title for the manuscript is discussed in Wall, 'Not so much open professed enemies', 632–33.
[9] Notebook, Add. MS 39779, 42. 'The first service m^r John Hutchinson vnder tooke in this County, was to accompany a petition, which the well affected of the County had made to his M^{tie}, y^t he would be pleased to returne to his Parliament, which Petition was carried to Yorke by the some of the men of best qualltie whose hands were to it and delivered in the spring 1641.'
[10] Norbrook, 'Lucy Hutchinson: Theology, Gender and Translation', 155.
[11] Notebook, Add. MS 25901, 90–96^v. [12] Hutchinson, *Memoirs*, ed. Firth, 387–456.

(S177/K220). Here I will not seek to identify new textual sources, but rather aim to show *how* Lucy Hutchinson re-creates the experience of the Civil War which the Colonel—and occasionally she herself—went through.[13]

a) Lucy Hutchinson, witness and confidant

According to Polybius, the eye of the witness was more trustworthy than his ear: 'To see an operation with one's own eyes is not like merely hearing a description of it. It is, indeed, quite another thing; and the confidence which such vivid experience gives is always greatly advantageous.'[14] Similarly, Lucian believed a good student of history should not 'rely on what people *tell* him'.[15] In the early modern period, as in ancient times, more credibility was granted to the historians who had attended the events they reported. Even Brathwaite advised historians 'to bee personally present at those Conquests or Discomfits whereof they write'.[16] But this requirement was problematic, for historians were rarely, strictly speaking, eye-witnesses. The necessity to also rely on ear-witnesses was for instance acknowledged by Hyde in his *History of the Rebellion*. At the beginning of his opus, he claims not only to have attended Parliament in the years that preceded the Civil War but also to have had the confidence of two kings, Charles I and Charles II, both of whom he served as a councillor:

> And as I may not be thought altogether an incompetent person for this communication, having been present as a member of parliament in those councils before and till the breaking out of the Rebellion, and having since had the honour to be near two great kings in some trust, so I shall perform the same with all faithfulness and ingenuity.[17]

Hyde's statement was not isolated in the latter part of the seventeenth century. According to the royalist historian Hamon L'Estrange, who was writing in the 1650s, a modern historian, when he could not be a spectator, had to be a judicious auditor, capable of discriminating between reliable and unreliable information, between a trustworthy and an untrustworthy witness:

---

[13] Norbrook, 'Theology, Gender and Translation', 141.
[14] Polybius, *Histories*, 20. See Hartog, *Évidence de l'histoire* 61, 77–8, 98; Zangara, *Voir l'histoire* 7. The hierarchy between the eye and the ear is repeated by Cardinal de Retz, *Mémoires de monsieur le Cardinal de Retz*, vol. 3 (Amsterdam, 1717) 495.
[15] Lucian, *How to Write History* §37, 53 (my emphasis).
[16] Brathwaite, *A Survey of History* 32.   [17] Hyde, *History of the Rebellion*, vol. 1, 3.

Ocular observation of the Author is not absolutely necessary to the credibility of a story; [...] and they who wrote the memorials of their own times, as *Thucydides, Xenophon, Herodian* and others, who are the most accurate Reporters, ingenuously confesse, they as well derive some things, *upon trust from others,* as other things they deliver upon their own credit.[18]

In his preface to Baxter's *Reliquiæ Baxterianæ* (1696)—subtitled *Mr. Richard Baxter's Narrative of the Most Memorable Passages of his Life and Times*—the editor, Matthew Sylvester, quoting Virgil, also stresses the fact that eye-witnessing was not the only way of obtaining information, but that research and knowledge were equally important in memoir-writing: 'The Things here treated on were Things transacted in his day, *quaeque ipse vidit; Et quorum pars magna fuit.* Much he knew and felt, and was himself passively concerned in, and the rest he was inquisitive after, observant of, and acquainted with.'[19] In many respects, what Sylvester says about Baxter applies to Lucy Hutchinson, whose historical narrative—primarily based on her experience of the revolutionary decades—also includes investigations and reflections.

The historians' concern with the trustworthiness of their sources resonates with contemporary scientific debates on experimentalism in which direct observation is equally essential—without ocular witnesses the knowledge produced by experiments cannot be founded; facts, whether in science, law, or history, do not exist unless they are attested by eye-witnesses.[20] Robert Boyle, for instance, insists that 'the bulk of the matters of fact [he] deliver[s] should consist of things, whereof [he] was [him]self an actor or an eye-witness.'[21] However, Boyle could not attend all experiments: he had to rely on the reports of others, whose credibility had to be carefully checked.[22] In his preface to *The Sceptical Chymist* (1661), a dialogue against alchemy, he argues that only experiments reported by reliable witnesses can be trusted:

---

[18] L'Estrange, *The Reign of King Charles* [sig. A4] (my emphasis).
[19] Sylvester, 'The Preface to the Reader', sig. b, *Reliquiæ Baxterianæ*, Part III, §2; ed. Keeble et al., Vol. 4, 411. The Latin is an adaptation from Virgil's *Aeneid*, Book 2, ll. 5–6.
[20] Steven Shapin, 'Pump and Circumstance: Robert Boyle's Literary Technology', *Social Studies of Science* 14.4 (1984): 481–520. 'If knowledge was to be empirically based, as Boyle and other English experimentalists insisted it should, then its experimental foundations had to be attested by eye-witnesses' (487).
[21] Quoted by Shapiro, *A Culture of Fact* 119. Robert Boyle, *The Works of the Honourable Robert Boyle* (London, 1772), vol. 5, 569.
[22] Shapin, 'Pump and Circumstance', 493. See also Shapin, 'Epistemological Decorum: The Practical Management of Factual Testimony', *A Social History of Truth* 193–242.

For though unwillingly, Yet I must for the truths sake, and the Readers, warne him not to be forward to believe Chymical Experiments when they are set down only by way of Prescriptions, and not of Relations; that is, unless he that delivers them mentions his doing it upon his own particular knowledge, or upon the Relation of some credible person, avowing it upon his own experience.[23]

Among the criteria which define the credibility of a witness in natural philosophy, there were the 'social status, but also the experience, skill, fidelity, and impartiality of the observer and the number of supporting observers'.[24] Thus, except for the number of witnesses that is required in science and not necessarily in history, the criteria of credibility are analogous in the two disciplines. Besides, in the two fields, when direct witnessing is not sufficient, the experiments and testimonies of others become essential. Historians, like Thomas May, Hamon L'Estrange, and, as we shall have occasion to show, Lucy Hutchinson, needed to broaden their own experience by reading and borrowing from the works of others. Similarly, when Boyle reflected about the ways in which he could write natural history, he acknowledged, in the wake of Bacon in *Sylva Sylvarum*, the necessity to draw on the experiments of others: ''tis not to be expected, that, as the Silk-worm draws her whole Mansion altogether out of her own Bowels, so a single man should be able to write a Natural History out of his own Experiments and Thoughts. And he that will strictly confine himself to those, will be often reduc'd to omit things very pertinent.'[25] As a woman, Lucy Hutchinson was present neither on the battlefields nor in Parliament, and—like most historians and natural philosophers of her age—she often had to rely on the 'Relation of some credible person', that is, on second-hand testimonies and also on her own knowledge of history. I wish to show here that by foregrounding the reliability of her sources and by highlighting her own experience of the war, Lucy Hutchinson builds her authority as a historian of the Civil War. Her strategies of self-authorization undeniably bear the mark of ancient historiography, but they are also strikingly akin to the

---

[23] Robert Boyle, 'A Praeface Introductory', *The Sceptical Chymist: or Chymico-Physical Doubts & Paradoxes* (London, 1661) [sig. A3ᵛ].
[24] Shapiro, *A Culture of Fact* 118.
[25] Robert Boyle, 'Advertisements about the Disposition of the Following Treatise', *Experimenta & Observationes Physicæ: Wherein are briefly treated of several subjects relating to natural philosophy in an experimental way* (London, 1691) XI, np; Francis Bacon, *Sylva Sylvarum: Or A natural historie* (London, 1628). I wish to thank Sandrine Parageau for generously sharing these references with me. On this subject, see Parageau, 'Bacon, Boyle et l'écriture de l'histoire naturelle', *Archives de philosophie* 84.1 (2021): 73–91.

experimentalists' ways of producing knowledge: without the witnesses validating their experiments, no scientific facts could be established.[26]

At the beginning of the narrative, even before the outbreak of the Civil War, Lucy Hutchinson tentatively presents herself as an ear-witness, explaining how she gathered the early pieces of the Colonel's early life, often through hearsay. Her interventions are eloquent: 'I have heard say' (S19/K36), 'I think I have heard that' (S19/K36), 'I have heard her servants say' (S19/K36).[27] In the rest of the narrative, she is more assertive and is less hesitant about the information she conveys because she fully trusts her chief informant—namely the Colonel himself, repeatedly describing herself as his confidant.[28] In the Dedication to her children, she programmatically declares: 'I that have bene the faithfull depositary of all his secretts must witnesse for him in all times his heart was sincere and steadfast to the Lord' (S7/K22). At the end of the *Memoirs*, she confesses that 'Mrs. Hutchinson' was occasionally her husband's secretary, 'being us'd sometimes to write the letters he dictated' (S230/K281)—a role she may indeed have played on several occasions, not only to write letters but also to take down notes for him.[29] When he was a prisoner at Sandown Castle, for example, she 'set [...] downe' 'the severall observations' he made on the Epistle to the Romans (S270/K328).[30] It should be noted that throughout the Civil War, the Hutchinsons lived with George Hutchinson, John Hutchinson's brother who had married Lucy Hutchinson's sister, Barbara. He was in charge of the castle in the Governor's absence and was a source of information throughout the Civil Wars, although Lucy Hutchinson does not mention him as an informant.

Lucy Hutchinson's position as a confidant was not an isolated one among early modern memorialists. It was for example a role claimed by Madame de Motteville in her *Mémoires pour servir à l'histoire d'Anne d'Autriche*.[31] In an

---

[26] As was seen in Chapter 2, the parallel is also possible with law, the *Memoirs* being a *testimony* in the legal sense of the term. Shapiro has convincingly shown how the culture of facts crossed disciplinary boundaries. See Shapiro, '"Fact" and the Law', *A Culture of Fact* 8–33.

[27] Lucy Hutchinson used her role as an ear-witness to tell the family chronicle (S18/K34).

[28] A role briefly mentioned by Matchinske in 'History's "Silent Whispers"', 61.

[29] The Colonel, she writes, 'caus'd his wife to write a letter to Fleetwood and complaine of the affronts had bene offer'd him, and to tell him that he was thereupon retir'd till he could dwell safely att home' (S221/K271). For another instance of collaborative writing, see Chapter 4, 3, a, 'The affair of the forged letter'. See James Daybell, 'Gendered Archival Practices and the Future Lives of Letters', *Cultures of Correspondence in Early Modern Britain*, ed. Daybell and Andrew Gordon (Philadelphia: U of Pennsylvania P, 2016) 210–37.

[30] Charlotte Duplessis Mornay claims similar bonds with her husband. Kuperty-Tsur refers to the 'pleasures of a spiritual and conjugal solidarity' (*Se dire à la Renaissance* 86).

[31] On Madame de Motteville, see Lesne, *La Poétique des mémoires* 262–3 and Mélanie Aron, *Les Mémoires de Madame de Motteville: Du dévouement à la dévotion* (Nancy: Presses universitaires de Nancy, 2003) 113–31. Madame de Motteville was also the confidant of Queen Henrietta Maria (Anne of Austria's sister-in-law) during her exile in France. One can note her concern with the faithfulness to

essay about this author, Marc Fumaroli reminds us that 'the confidant in a tragedy is the *mirror* of the heroine she serves, her foil, a trustworthy interlocutor [...]. Because of her position and by definition, the confidant cannot have other feelings than her loyal attachment to the heroine who made her the depositary of her secrets' (166).[32] Much of this can be transposed to 'Mrs. Hutchinson' who, like Madame de Motteville, is portrayed as a 'mirror' of the Colonel as well as his 'shadow': 'she was a very faithfull mirror, reflecting truly, though but dimmely, his owne glories upon him, so long as he was present [...]. Soe, as his shadow she waited on him every where, till he was taken into that region of light which admits of none, and then she vanisht into nothing' (S32-3/K51). These metaphors, which have been interpreted in various ways,[33] are tellingly placed before the actual beginning of the Civil War, a period when Lucy Hutchinson was already acting not only as the Colonel's secretary but also as his confidant. In this passage, as almost in every page of the *Memoirs* (except for the Dedication), Lucy Hutchinson refers to herself in the third person as 'Mrs. Hutchinson', whom she portrays as the typical, good Protestant wife as was celebrated in the contemporary conduct books. This situation of enunciation reflects the hierarchical relationship between husband and wife, of course, but it is also particularly fitting to express the special bond between a hero and his confidant.[34]

The characterization of Lucy Hutchinson as the Colonel's confidant, however, is something of a *trompe-l'oeil* in the *Memoirs*. At first sight, as the passage of the 'faithful mirror' intimates, it entails abnegation and self-disappropriation which was expected of the good Puritan wife. But 'Mrs. Hutchinson', in conformity with the ideal of companionship, is consistently described as her husband's friend, that is, as his fellow and spiritual equal—a status which most Protestant conduct books granted to wives and which gave them autonomy.[35] According to

---

the Queen's words, as she carefully distinguishes between the things of which the Queen was a direct witness and the things of which she was indirectly informed (Françoise de Motteville, *Mémoires pour servir à l'histoire d'Anne d'Autriche* [Amsterdam, 1750], vol. 1, 238).

[32] Marc Fumaroli, 'La Confidente de la reine: Madame de Motteville et Anne d'Autriche', *Exercices de lecture: De Rabelais à Paul Valery* (Paris: Gallimard, 2006) 166.

[33] See Keeble, 'The Colonel's Shadow', 232 and Norbrook, 'Lucy Hutchinson's Elegies', 471-3. The 'mirror' refers to Lucy Hutchinson's conjugal subordination but is also part of a wider Neoplatonic scheme.

[34] On this type of third-person narration in memoir-writing, see Lesne, *La Poétique des mémoires* 343-8, more specifically her analysis of *Mémoires de Madame de Motteville* [1723] 346-7, as well as Kuperty-Tsur, 'Esthétique et poétique de l'écriture mémorialiste', *Se dire à la Renaissance* 18-44.

[35] Several instances of the ideal of companionship are to be found in the *Memoirs*, for instance: 'For conjugall affection to his wife [Lucy Hutchinson], it was such in him as whosoever would draw out a rule of honor, kindnesse, and religion to be practized in that estate, need no more but to draw out exactly his example' (S10/K26). See also Milton's panegyric on marriage in *Paradise Lost*, ed. Alastair Fowler (London: Longman, 1971), Book IV, ll. 750-762, 240-1.

the Protestant divine Edward Reyner, marriage was the most elevated form of Christian friendship:[36]

> It is the strictest bond of any relation, and therfore a fellowship of the dearest amitie, nearer then that between Parents and Children. [...] All Society must be left, that this between man and wife may be kept. [...] The wife must be an individual companion of life. The saying of the Philosopher, that perfect friend is onely between two, is most true, in this case, between man and wife, because they two are by marriage made one.[37]

Because 'Mrs. Hutchinson' was the Colonel's friend, her depiction as a good wife cannot therefore be merely viewed in terms of female passivity.[38] Her affectionate proximity with him invites us to interpret her posture of submission as a calculated strategy to claim an authoritative stance as a narrator of history, whose voice, as the expression of her soul, is freed from the social constraints weighing on wives in early modern England. Hence, as the Colonel's companion and not only his subjected wife, Lucy Hutchinson enjoyed privileged access to his political and military experience, for example during the occupation of Nottingham, the sieges in Nottinghamshire, the disputes of the Nottingham Committee, the parliamentary debates and votes, and finally the trial of the King.

Lucy Hutchinson often takes the trouble to specify her sources of information in order to give more authority to her narrative. For instance, just before the outbreak of the Civil War, at a time when he had not yet occupied an official position, it is a Lord who had decided 'not to stay with [the King]' who first 'acquainted Mr. Hutchinson with the sad sense he had, discovering that falsehood in the king' (S59/K82). Later, when he was an MP for Nottinghamshire, his cousin Ireton kept him informed about the army's negotiations with the King, then a prisoner at Hampton Court. Basing herself on what the Colonel told her, Lucy Hutchinson seems to reproduce Ireton's exchanges with Charles I verbatim, and then the conversation between Ireton and her husband. The use of direct speech serves to introduce orality in the written narrative and to produce verisimilitude. It also conveys the impression

---

[36] See Claire Cross, 'Reyner, Edward (1600–1660)' (2004), *Oxford Dictionary of National Biography*, DOI: 10.1093/ref:odnb/23402.

[37] Edward Reyner, *Considerations Concerning Marriage: The Honours, Duties, Benefits, Troubles, of It* (London, 1657) 12. On gender order and the ideal of companionship, see Gheeraert-Graffeuille, *La Cuisine et le forum* 31–4 and 41–6.

[38] Anderson, *Friendship's Shadows* 203.

that the readers are witnessing the exchanges between the protagonists of national history.[39] Strikingly enough, by making us 'virtual' witnesses of this scene, Lucy Hutchinson adopts a method that was recommended by Robert Boyle for experimental reports. It is a technique which Steven Shapin has interestingly called 'virtual witnessing'—'the production in a reader's mind of [. . .] an experimental scene':[40]

> upon some discourses with him, the King uttering these words to him, "I shall play my game as well as I can," Ireton replied, "If your Majestie have a game to play, you must give us alsoe the liberty to play ours." Colonell Hutchinson privately discoursing with his cousin about the communications he had had with the King, Ireton's expressions were these: "He gave us," sayd he, "words, and wee pay'd him in his owne coyne when wee found he had no reall intention to the people's good, but to prevaile upon our factions to regaine by art what he had lost in fight."   (S172/K214)[41]

Additionally, because of the mutual trust existing between the Hutchinsons, the readers can often get an intimate perspective on events, including controversial ones such as the regicide. Because she knew the secrets of the Colonel's soul, Lucy Hutchinson could recount how he was led in conscience to sign the King's death warrant in January 1649:[42]

> As for Mr. Hutchinson [. . .] he addresst himselfe to God by prayer; desiring the Lord that, if through humane frailty he were led into any error or false opinion in these greate transactions, that he would open his eies, and not suffer him to proceed, but that he would confirme his spiritt in the truth, and lead him by a right enlight'ned conscience.   (S190/K235)

Armed with the knowledge of what had happened in the High Court of Justice, Lucy Hutchinson gained an inside understanding of the commissioners' motives either to vote for the King's death or to backtrack: 'for I know upon certeine knowledge,' she explains, 'that many—yea, the most of them—retreated not for conscience, but for feare and worldly prudence'

---

[39] In the manuscript (*Memoirs*, DD/HU4, 261), Lucy Hutchinson also reports the scene in direct speech. The only difference between the manuscript and Keeble's and Sutherland's editions is that, in the manuscript, Hutchinson does not use any inverted commas.
[40] Shapin, 'Pump and Circumstance', 491. See also Stephen Shapin and Simon Schaffer, *Leviathan and the Air-Pump. Hobbes, Boyle, and the Experimental Life* (Princeton: Princeton UP, 1985) 60.
[41] On the reporting of conversations in memoirs, see Lesne, *La Poétique des mémoires* 211.
[42] On the centrality of conscience, see Lobo, 'Lucy Hutchinson's Revisions of Conscience', 331–3.

(S190/K235). In May 1659, when the Rump was restored, the Colonel, after a long period of retirement (from 1653 to 1659) returned to Parliament.[43] He thus became again an essential source of information for his wife, for instance enabling her, thanks to his 'observations', to speculate on what would have happened if the regicide MP, Arthur Haselrig, had behaved differently and had not refused to sit with the 'secluded members' (S223/K273).[44]

After 1660, the Colonel being estranged from public life, Lucy Hutchinson had to turn to other sources of information to cover the Restoration period. Her main informant appears to have been her royalist brother, Sir Allen Apsley, who had been the Governor of Barnstaple Castle during the First Civil War. As a loyal servant to the King, whom he visited in Newcastle in October 1646 to receive his knighthood, he probably took part in the negotiations between the King and the army in the summer of 1647.[45] Despite their political differences, Lucy Hutchinson and her brother remained close during the Civil War, Protectorate, and Restoration. As for Sir Allen and John Hutchinson's friendship, however improbable it may appear, it presumably dated back to pre-Civil War years at Richmond, where they moved in the same court circles.[46] Anyhow, these family circumstances help explain why in the years 1646–1647, 'after the surrender of [his] Garrison [Sir Allen Apsley] came and retir'd to the Governor's house till his composition with the Parliament was compleated' (S170/K211), and why, in 1660, the situation being reversed, Sir Allen was in a position to help his sister and brother-in-law. He had then become a public figure who knew many people at court, and he was notably a friend and trusted agent of the King's councillor, Edward Hyde.[47] In 1660, he became Keeper of the King's Hawks and shortly afterwards the treasurer to the Duke of York. Although he may have been a less reliable informant than John Hutchinson,[48] Sir Allen Apsley was extremely valuable to his sister, for his royalist views considerably enriched her reading of events. Nowhere does she

---

[43] See *Memoirs*, ed. Sutherland, 206, 214, and ed. Keeble, 254, 263. John Hutchinson had been a member of the Council of State until February 1651, and member of the Rump until its dissolution in April 1653. See S. R. Seddon, 'Hutchinson, John (1615–1664), parliamentarian army officer and regicide' (2004), *Oxford Dictionary of National Biography*, DOI: 10.1093/ref:odnb/14283.

[44] See Christopher Durston, 'Hesilrige [Haselrig], Sir Arthur, second baronet (1601–1661), army officer and politician' (2004), *Oxford Dictionary of National Biography*, DOI: 10.1093/ref:odnb/13123.

[45] Seaward, 'Apsley, Sir Allen (1616–1683)' (2004), *Oxford Dictionary of National Biography*, DOI: 10.1093/ref:odnb/600, and *Memoirs*, ed. Firth, 247, note 1: Allen, according to the testimonies of Berkeley and Ludlow, participated as a messenger in the negotiations—a mission which Lucy Hutchinson does not mention in the *Memoirs*. See also Guizot, ed., *Mémoires*, vol. 2, 137, note 1.

[46] This is also what Elizabeth St. John infers from the sources in her fictional account of Lucy Hutchinson's life in the *Lydiard Chronicles* (2016–2019). See in particular *By Love Divided* (2017).

[47] Sir Allen Apsley was one of the Chancellor's 'more trusted agents and friends'. See *Memoirs*, ed. Firth, 334, note 1.

[48] On the ambiguity of Sir Allen, see Norbrook, 'Memoirs and Oblivion', 272–3.

specify that her brother confided in her, but the accounts of some private exchanges which neither she nor the Colonel could have attended are evidence to the contrary. This is for example the case when we are given to overhear Hyde and Sir Allen discussing Colonel Hutchinson's predicament after he refused to identify the signatures on the King's death warrant. According to Lucy Hutchinson, this conversation marked the beginning of her husband's fall despite her brother's attempts to defend him in front of his royalist friends:

> When Sir Allen Apsley came to the Chancellor he was in a greate rage and passion, and fell upon him with much vehemence. "O Nall," sayd he, "what have you done? You have sav'd a man that would be ready, if he had operturnity, to mischiefe us as much as ever he did." Sir Allen was forc'd to stop his mouth, and tell him, that he believed his brother a less dangerous person than those he had brought into the King's Councell, meaning Maynard and Glynne. (S236/K288)

It is unlikely that such a passage could have been written from memory by Lucy Hutchinson. It is more probable that she either wrote it down just after it was reported to her by Sir Allen, or that it was part of a correspondence, now lost. In any case, the readers, as in the previous example with Ireton, are effectively placed into the position of witnessing a lively scene whose reality they have no reason to question.

In conclusion, what emerges is that, in the *Memoirs*, Lucy Hutchinson's role as a confidant (and accessorily as a secretary) is of double importance. On the one hand, by establishing her as a reliable witness and reporter of history, it reinforces the authority of her narrative as a testimony of the Civil War. On the other hand, by turning the readers into virtual witnesses of the scenes she stages, Lucy Hutchinson persuades them of the impartiality of her account. Still, her claims to truthfulness are to be taken most cautiously as the *Memoirs* are not always faithful to events as they happened.[49] They constitute a partisan narrative and the product of memory. As the local historian Anthony Wood pointed out, Lucy Hutchinson's testimony underestimated the strength of the parliamentary party in Nottingham: 'if the townsmen had in fact been "more malignant than well affected" as she asserts, the King would have received more support when he arrived to erect his standard, and Colonel Hutchinson

---

[49] On pacts of sincerity established by memorialists, see Lesne, *La Poétique des mémoires* 221–2; Charbonneau, *Les Silences de l'histoire* 32–3; Kuperty-Tsur, *Se dire à la Renaissance* 28.

could not so easily have secured the castle.'[50] In this light, and if placed in the context of Civil War historiography, Lucy Hutchinson's *Memoirs* are just as partisan as all the histories and memoirs written during the Interregnum and at the Restoration.[51]

b) Nottingham Castle and the experience of the Civil War

Lucy Hutchinson's role as her husband's confidant does not mean that she did not have a specific experience of the Civil War. The mere fact of living in Nottingham Castle almost uninterruptedly from June 1643 to June 1646 placed her in a unique position to observe what happened within and without the city walls. It should be added that the castle, surrounded by the rivers Lene and Trent, benefited from an exceptional geographical situation, standing 'at one end of the Towne upon such an eminence as commands the chiefe streetes of the towne' (S83/K110). This was a highly strategic location that was coveted both by the supporters of the King and those of Parliament. In the winter of 1642,[52]

> [t]he preservation of this Towne was a speciall service to the Parliament, being a considerable passe into the North, which, if the enemie had first possest themselves of, the Parliament had been cut off of all entercourse betweene the North and South, especially in the winter time, when the river of Trent is not foordable, and only to be pass'd over by the bridges of Nottingham and Newark, and up higher at a place call'd Wilden Ferrie, where the enemie alsoe had a garrison.   (S75/K101)

Nottingham was key to the defence of parliamentary positions; yet it was vulnerable because it was surrounded with royalist fortified strongholds, which Lucy Hutchinson identifies with precision to point out that the town

---

[50] Wood, *Nottinghamshire in the Civil War* 35.

[51] On Lucy Hutchinson's partiality, see Chapter 4. On the historiography underpinning Restoration histories and memoirs, see Chapter 2, especially section 2 ('Historical truth in the turmoil of the Civil Wars').

[52] See also Lucy Hutchinson's account: 'considering of what advantage it was to the Parliament to keepe that place, by reason of the commodious situation of it and the passe which might be there maintain'd between the North and South, and the happie retreate it might afford to their Northerne forces, he [Sir Thomas Fairfax] very much presst the Governor and the Committee to rayse all the force they could, offering arms and Commissions for them' (S104/K134–5). See Martyn Bennett, 'Holding the Centre Ground: The Strategic Importance of the North Midlands 1642–1646', *East Midlands History and Heritage* 1 (2015): 4–8, and 'Every County', 194–5.

could easily have switched to the royalist side. With this description she also introduces the royalist actors who will be further mentioned in her story of the Civil War in Nottinghamshire:

> Sir Richard Biron was come to be Governor of Newark. A house of my Lord Chaworth's in the Vale was fortified and some horse putt into it, and another house of the Earle of Chesterfield's, both of them within a few miles of Nottingham. Ashby de la Zouch, within eight miles of Nottingham on the other side, was kept by Mr. Hastings. On the forrest side of the country the Earle of Newcastle's house had a Garrison in it, and another Castle of his, within a mile, was garrison'd. Sir Roger Cooper's house at Thurgaton was alsoe kept; so that Nottingham, being thus beleaguer'd with enemies, seem'd very unlikely to be able either to resist the enemie or support themselves.
> (S80/K107)[53]

This highly politicized topographical account, which reflects the importance of geography in memoir-writing and, more generally, in history, is completed by a full description of the castle.[54] The depiction of 'a strong tower, which they called the Old Tower, built upon the top of all the rock' (S83/K110) first evokes the Norman castle that was built around the time of the Conquest on the foundations of an older construction that was destroyed.[55] In a very skilful way Lucy Hutchinson intertwines the architectural history of the building with the Governor's role in improving the fortification of the stronghold during the Civil War. The beginning of the description—a good example of Lucy Hutchinson's use of *enargeia*[56]—is strikingly written in the present tense and expresses how vivid the place remained in her mind about twenty years after

---

[53] We do not have a comparable comprehensive vision in the Notebook which only mentions Wiverton (Notebook, Add. MS 25901, 9). For a sociology of the county of Nottingham, see Wood, *Nottinghamshire in the Civil War* 33–4.

[54] On the relationships between geography, history, and memoir-writing, see Charbonneau, *Les Silences de l'histoire* 29–30. Geography was both subordinated to history and its prerequisite. This was asserted by Lucian, but also by Bodin in his *Methodus*, or by Charles Sorel in his *Bibliothèque françoise* [1667]. On the use of geography in Herodotus and Polybius's writings, see Hartog, *Évidence de l'histoire* 272, 275 and note 10.

[55] See Scott Lomax, *Nottingham: The Buried Past of a Historic City Revealed* [2013] (Havertown, PA: Pen & Sword, 2019), especially 'Where is the Castle?' 57–69. On the castle, see Harry Gill, *A Short History of Nottingham Castle* (Nottingham: Henry B. Saxton, 1904), http://www.nottshistory.org.uk/gill1904/contents.htm (accessed 09/08/2021).

[56] In his discussion of *enargeia* in his *Copia,* Erasmus devotes a full section to 'the description of places': '[a]nother method of enrichment is by inserting descriptions of places [...]. This is a very common method of introducing a narrative, used by poets and historians, and by orators too, on occasion. [...] In this the whole appearance of a place is described so that we can see it, a city for example, a hill, a region, a river, a harbor, a country estate, gardens, a sports arena, a spring, a cave, a temple, a grove' (*Copia* 587).

the actual events happened. The remainder of the description makes visible and tangible to 'the eyes of the mind' the different phases of construction of the medieval castle which was razed in 1651 on the order of Colonel Hutchinson.[57] Here again it is tempting to highlight the analogy between Lucy Hutchinson's vivid description of the castle and Boyle's attempts, in scientific reports and observations, to 'mimic [the] immediacy and simultaneity of experience afforded by pictorial representations'.[58] Almost all the details, from the dove-cote to the yard, have their importance in Lucy Hutchinson's description as they set the scenery for later episodes:

> [the] ascent to the Top is very high, and, not without some wonder, at the top of all the rock there is a spring of water; in the midway to the top of this Tower there is a little peice of the rock on which a dovecoate had bene built, but the Governor tooke down the roof of it, and made it a platforme for two or three peices of Ordinance, which commanded some streetes and all the meadowes better than the higher Tower. Under that Tower, which was the old Castle, there was a larger Castle, where there had been severall Towers and many noble roomes, but the most of them were downe; the inward yard of that was pretty large, and without the gate there was a very large yard that had bene wall'd, but the walls were all downe, only it was scituated upon an ascent of the rock, and so stood a pretty heighth above the streetes; and there were the ruines of an old paire of gates, with turretts on each side.   (S83/K111)

More anecdotally, but nonetheless very evocatively, Lucy Hutchinson's personal attachment to the place is materialized in the Notebook by a sketch, almost a graffiti—a stylized tower on a hill which looks like Nottingham Castle.[59] It is difficult to tell whether the drawing was made at the time of writing the Notebook, or later, in the 1660s, when she was using it as a basis for the *Memoirs*, but, in any case, it makes the author's experience of the war in the castle almost palpable.

Lucy Hutchinson's fascination for the castle also stems from its rich mythico-historical past with which she was familiar.[60] She does not provide a full list of sieges, battles and royal visits that occurred there, but chooses instead to concentrate on three symbolical events, which respectively turn the

---

[57] *Memoirs*, ed. Sutherland, 203, and ed. Keeble, 250.
[58] Shapin, 'Pump and Circumstance', 493.   [59] Notebook, Add. MS 25901, 2.
[60] See William Howie Wylie, *Old and New Nottingham* (London: Longman, 1853). See Figure 3.1.

Figure 3.1 Nottingham Castle in the fifteenth century. From Harry Gill, *A Short History of Nottingham Castle* (1904). Courtesy of Nottinghamshire History (http://www.nottshistory.org.uk/).

castle into a place of forbidden romance, of monarchical tyranny and of religious resistance. For two pages, she abandons the ethos of testimony and draws on legends which were physically connected to the place. First, her taste for tragic romance surfaces when she refers to 'that place where Queene Izabell, the mother of King Edward the Third, was surpriz'd with her paramour Mortimer, who by secret windings and hollows in the rock, came up into her chamber from the meadowes lying low under it [...]. At the entrance of this rock there was a spring, which was called Mortimer's Well, and the cavernes Mortimer's hole' (S83/K110). These stories serve to convey a sense of mystery and clandestinity that was, as it were, engraved in the rock. They also arouse thrill and wonder in the readers who have to imagine a dark medieval place full of winding passages. Next, Lucy Hutchinson connects the castle with a legend about 'King Richard the Third', associating memories of his monstrous tyranny with the landscape: '[b]ehind [the castle] was a place call'd the Park, that belong'd to the Castle, but then had neither deere no trees in it, except one, growing under the Castle, which was allmost a prodigie, for from the roote to the top, there was not one streight twig or branch of it: some say it was planted by King Richard the Third, and resembled him that sett it' (S84/K111). This ominous reference to Richard III echoes a later one in the *Memoirs,* when the Colonel is imprisoned in the Tower of London, the very place where the tyrant of ill memory perpetrated some of his worst murders: 'There is a tradition that in this roome the Duke of Clarence was drown'd in a but of Malmsey; from which murthers this roome, and that joyning it where Mr. Hutchinson lay, was called the bloody Tower' (S251/K306). With Richard III haunting Nottingham Castle and the Tower of London, the destiny of Colonel Hutchinson, it is suggested, was already sealed in 1643. Finally, the castle is connected to 'David, a Scotch king' who 'was kept in cruell durance, and with his nayles had scratcht the story of Christ and his twelve Apostles on the wall' (S84/K111).[61] This is yet another legend that makes of the castle a place of faith and suffering, and prefigures the Colonel's fate. This apocryphal story, based on a material vestige, was actually mentioned in Camden's chronicle, which Lucy Hutchinson seems to have read. Like the legends of Queen Isabel and King Richard III, it reveals how Lucy Hutchinson carefully inscribes the story of Colonel Hutchinson in a broader mythico-historical scheme.[62]

---

[61] David II, King of Scotland (1329–1371).

[62] See *Memoirs,* ed. Keeble, note 213, 361. Wylie, *Old and New Nottingham* 59: 'According to Camden, this was one of the state prisons occupied by David II of Scotland, during the eleven years' bondage in which the English monarch held him after his capture in 1346 on the field of Neville's Cross. In describing the castle dungeon in which the King was confined, the old chronicler says that "in

Lucy Hutchinson's evocation of the place seems to have appealed to the nineteenth-century taste for historical romances about the national past.[63] Charles Knight in *Household Words* rewrites her description of the castle, conjuring up the image of the memorialist sitting in 'one of the upper chambers of the old and ruinous castle'.[64] The romance potential was also noticed by Lina Chaworth-Musters, a descendant of the Chaworths, a powerful Nottinghamshire royalist family during the Civil War, whose seat, Wiverton Hall, was fortified in December 1642 by the second Viscount Chaworth (S80/K107).[65] In *A Romance of the Vale of Belvoir*, which draws upon the *Memoirs*, Chaworth-Musters depicts some secret passages not mentioned by Lucy Hutchinson but which she may have heard of or read about.[66] In a passage that presents 'Mrs. Hutchinson' as someone who knew all the secrets of the place, the novelist implies that the governor's wife may have intentionally played down her own role in the defence of the place:[67]

"Ah! Trust a woman to find out the way," said Mrs. Hutchinson, drawing her husband towards the north of the Castle yard [...]. "I had read somewhere," said the lady, "that King Henry the Third expressly ordered, 'a sally port to be made on the north-west side of the castle,' and when I knew it was a matter of life and death to us, I determined to try and find it. The children had talked of long passages in the rock, where they lost their balls, and so I searched till I found an old doorway blocked up, and brother George and I despatched the messengers but half-an-hour ago."[68]

The description of the castle does not only fulfil the nineteenth-century readers' appetite for romance, and in particular Gothic romance, but it also plunges them into the reality of the war. The castle was indeed a place of

---

the first court we descend with lights, down many steps, into another subterraneous vault, and arched rooms cut in the rock itself, on the walls of which are carved Christ's passion, and other things by the hand (as they say) of David King of Scots, who was there imprisoned".'

[63] Rosemary Mitchell, 'Picturing the English Past in Nineteenth-Century Britain – Historical Consciousness and National Identity', *Picturing the Past: English History in Text and Image, 1830–1870* (Oxford: Clarendon, 2000) 1–19.

[64] Charles Knight, 'Shadows. The Shadow of Lucy Hutchinson', *Household Words* 3.70 (1851): 430–2.

[65] On this family and Wiverton house, see *Memoirs* (S80/K107) and Wood, *Nottinghamshire in Civil War* passim. There is a fuller account of the role of this fortified house in the Notebook (Add. MS 25901, 9^r) than in the *Memoirs* (107). See *Memoirs*, ed. Firth, Appendix IX, 403–4.

[66] Lina Chaworth-Musters, *A Cavalier Stronghold: A Romance of the Vale of Belvoir* (London, 1890) 252. In a footnote (p. 252), she gives another reference for the discovery of the passage. See John Hicklin, *History of Nottingham Castle* (London, 1831) 201–2.

[67] See Chapter 4 for examples of Lucy Hutchinson's agency.

[68] Chaworth-Musters, *A Cavalier Stronghold* 252.

defence, a garrison, brimming with rowdy soldiers, and the mere fact that Lucy Hutchinson lived in this fort for four years can in many ways explain how a woman was able to write what constitutes a military narrative. At the centre of garrison's life, for instance, there was the question of supplies and ammunition. The lack of resources with which the Hutchinsons were confronted as soon as they arrived was chronic throughout the Civil War, as the Parliament was very slow in funding the war effort. As a consequence, the Colonel's liberality and hospitality soon became a financial burden for his family:

> Then the Committee of Nottingham, so many of them as were remaining in the Towne, and all the Ministers of the Parliament's party there, came up to the Castle, and with the Officers of the Garrison eate at the Governor's, to a very greate charge, considering that he was so farre from receiving pay at that time that all the mony he could procure of his owne creditt, or take up with others, he was forc'd to dispend for the severall necessities of the souldiers and Garrison. (S88/K116)

The tension between the Hutchinsons' generosity and the 'present poverty of their condition' (S88/K116) was exacerbated at the death of Sir Thomas, John Hutchinson's father, who, as seen above, 'gave all his personall estate and all that was unsettled at Mr. Hutchinson's marriage to his second wife and her children' (S90/K118). We also learn that, in the wake of his father's demise, John Hutchinson 'lost the most part of his rents all while the country was under the adverse power' (S91/K119). Moreover, around the same period, he 'had some small stock of his owne plunder'd, and his house, by the perpetuall haunting of the enemie, defac'd and for want of inhabitation render'd allmost unhabitable' (S91/K119).[69] As a matter of fact, in the 1640s, all the family's financial resources went to the service of the public cause, and Lucy Hutchinson obsessively harps on the debt which the Colonel's 'publick employment had runne him into' (S173/K215) and on the financial consequences of the Colonel's 'noble heart' (S90/K118). After the execution of the King, the Hutchinsons were in relatively better financial circumstances, and the Colonel employed some of his time and money to renovate and improve

---

[69] In 1647, when he was back in his house at Owthorpe, he 'found that having stood uninhabited, and bene rob'd of every thing which the neighbouring Garrisons of Shelford and Wiverton could carrie from it, [his house] was so ruinated that it could not be repair'd to make a convenient habitation' (S173/K215).

Owthorpe, showing great generosity towards his neighbours—including the royalist gentry.[70]

In the difficult times of the Civil War, the role of Lucy Hutchinson as the Governor's wife was decisive. Her great concern for lodgings and food indicates that she must have been in charge of running the household, for keeping accounts was a task often performed by gentlewomen in the seventeenth century.[71] For example, the list of the few supplies they found in the castle when they moved in in June 1643 shows how dutifully she performed this task. As she notes, there were 'but 10 barrells of pouder, 1150 pounds of butter, and as much cheese, 11 quarters of bread corne, 7 beeves, 214 flitches of Bacon, 560 fishes, and 15 hogsheads of beere' (S84/K111). By reproducing these figures from the Notebook verbatim, Lucy Hutchinson gives evidence of her role in managing the household, but five pages later she specifies that the Colonel *alone* was responsible for increasing their supplies.[72] The situation was indeed a little improved after '[t]he Governor had procured 40 barrells of pouder, and 2,000 weight of Match from London, and had encreased the store of provision as much as the present poverty of their condition would permitt him' (S88/K116).

The same vindicatory logic prevails in Lucy Hutchinson's physical description of the ill-fortified castle of Nottingham which the Colonel, as Governor of the place, managed to save from ruin. On the one hand, she insists that, although it was built 'upon a rock', it was 'very ruinous and unhabitable' (S83/K110) and that the 'many large caverns' (S84/K111) were in too bad repair to be of any use for soldiers or even the storage of ammunition. Besides, the 'Castle was not flanker'd, and there were no workes about it [...], but only a little brestworke before the outmost gate' (S84/K111). On the other hand, the

---

[70] On the issue of property in the *Memoirs*, see Pamela S. Hammons, 'Lucy Hutchinson's Polluted Palaces and Ekphrastic Empire', *Gender, Sexuality and Material Objects in English Renaissance Verse* (Farnham: Ashgate, 2010) 165–84, here 179–80.

[71] See Sara Mendelson and Patricia Crawford, *Women in Early Modern England 1550–1720* (Oxford: Clarendon, 1998) 303–13. On early modern gender roles, Anthony Fletcher, 'The Working of Patriarchy', *Gender, Sex and Subordination in England 1500–1800* (New Haven: Yale UP, 1995) 99–279, and Patrick Collinson, 'The Protestant Family', *The Birthpangs of Protestant England: Religious and Cultural Change in the Sixteenth and Seventeenth Centuries* (London: Macmillan, 1998) 60–93.

[72] See Notebook, Add. MS 25901, 11^v–12:

There was at that time in y^t Castle this provision
10 barrells of pouder
seven beeues
eleuen quarter of bread corne
one thousand a hundred & fiftie pound of butter
a thousand a hundred and 50 pound of cheese
5 hundred and 60 fish
214 flicks of bacon.
Hogsheads of beare

better to defend the Colonel, she dwells on how, only in a few months' time, he heroically managed to turn the dilapidated castle into a stronghold, where mainly soldiers were able to find protection:

> Assoone as the Governor receiv'd his charge, he made proclamation in the Towne that whatsoever honest persons desir'd to secure themselves or their goods in the Castle should have reception there, if they would repair their quarters, which divers well affected men accepting, it was presently made capable of accommodating 400 men commodiously.   (S84/K111–12)[73]

From the moment he was appointed Governor, in June 1643, until the end of the First Civil War, fortifying the castle to defend Nottingham was indeed a priority for John Hutchinson.[74] After the Earl of Newcastle's summons at the beginning of August 1643, the 'Governor immediately sett upon the fortification of his Castle, made a worke behind it, another to the Line side, turn'd the Dovecoate into a platforme, and made a Court of Guard in Mortimer's hole' (S90/K118). Once the Trent Bridges were recovered, four months later, in October 1643, major improvements were achieved again: with the help of his engineer, Captain Hooper, and much determination on his side, he had indeed 'caus'd a mount neere the Castle to be bullwarkt, and made a platforme for Ordinance, and rays'd a new worke before the Castle Gates to keepe off approaches, and made a new inworke in the fort at the Bridges' (S104/K134).

Finally, at the core of the Hutchinsons' experience of the Civil War in Nottingham, there was the political rift between the town and the castle, as the town sided with the King, while the castle was unambiguously pro-Parliament. In July 1643, a month after the pillage of Nottingham, Lucy Hutchinson notices that 'townsmen, especially those that were ill affected to the Parliament', were angry at the Colonel who, after due reflection, had ordered ordnances and guns to be drawn up to the castle (S84/K112).[75] Fearing that the Governor should desist from defending the city, they 'made a greate mutiny, threat'ning they would pull the Castle downe but they would have their Ordinance againe upon their workes, and wishing it on fire and not one stone upon another' (S84/K112).[76] This episode is meant to illuminate

---

[73] See Notebook, Add. MS 25901, 12.
[74] On the issue of fortification in Nottingham during the Civil War, see Thomas Pert's article, 'Colonel Hutchinson (1615–1664) and Nottingham in the English Civil War, 1643–1646', *East Midlands History and Heritage* 1 (2015): 24–6, here 24–5.
[75] On this episode, see P. R. Seddon, 'Colonel Hutchinson and the Disputes between the Nottinghamshire Parliamentarians, 1643–45', *Transactions of the Thoroton Society* 98 (1994): 72.
[76] See Notebook, Add. MS 25901, 15^v–16. See Wood, *Nottinghamshire in the Civil War* 53–4.

the rivalry between the castle and the town, which lasted until the final months of the Civil War. It is depicted in moral terms as the unavoidable consequence of 'hate', 'envy', and 'discontent'. In September 1643, a few days before the occupation of Nottingham by the Newark forces took place, '[the] Townsmen [...] began to envie, then to hate the Castle [...]. In this hate and discontent, all the souldiers being Townsmen except some of the Governor's owne Company, they resolv'd they would not goe into the Castle to behold the ruine of their houses' (S87/K115).[77] These moral concerns are prominent in the description of Nottingham's townspeople throughout the *Memoirs*. Thus, the appointment of John Hutchinson as Governor of the *town* of Nottingham (when he was already Governor of the castle) was said to have fuelled calumny and jealousies of all sorts: 'the Townsmen [...] were so sawcy, so negligent, and so mutinous that the most honorable person in the world could expect nothing but scandall, reproach, and ingratitude for the payment of his greatest meritt' (S106/K137).

The opposition between the town and the castle is reinforced by the fact that, in the eyes of his enemies, John Hutchinson became identified with the castle. From the beginning of the Civil War, a way of challenging his power consisted in criticizing his politics of fortification and his use of the castle in his defence of the parliamentary cause. The account of this local conflict is more developed in the Notebook than in the *Memoirs*. The disputes ranged from Colonel Francis Pierrepont refusing the appointment of John Hutchinson as Governor[78] to innumerable discussions and wrangling in the Nottingham Committee,[79] for instance the argument between Captain Pendock and Hooper, the engineer, about the town-works.[80] These quarrels reached a climax in April 1645, at a time when the Colonel was in London to be heard by the Committee of Both Kingdoms. This was the moment chosen by the Cavaliers to attack the highly strategic Fort at the Bridges. According to Lucy Hutchinson, her brother-in-law, George Hutchinson, an 'excellent person', was not to blame, and it was the soldiers, who were 'out of their quarters' when the assault took place, that 'were guilty of the losse of the place' (S157/K196). Not without irony, for they had been the Colonel's detractors all

---

[77] This vocabulary of passion was already present in the Notebook where we are told that 'the Towne being much discontented that the force was drawne out of it and their houses deserted presently began out of envie to hate the Castle as grieued that anithing was preserved when their houses could not be kept and out of that hatred they resolued they would not goe into it' (Notebook, Add. MS 25901, 13ᵛ).
[78] Notebook, Add. MS 25901, 31–2, and *Memoirs*, ed. Sutherland, 104, 121–2 and ed. Keeble, 135, 155. On this issue, see Seddon, 'Colonel Hutchinson and the Disputes between the Nottinghamshire Parliamentarians', 72–3.
[79] Notebook, Add. MS 25901, 40–2 and *Memoirs*, ed. Sutherland, 104–5, and ed. Keeble, 135–6.
[80] Notebook, Add. MS 25901, 66ᵛ and *Memoirs*, ed. Sutherland, 130, and ed. Keeble, 165. Pierrepont's opposition to the fortifications is mentioned before in the Notebook, Add. MS 25901, 11ᵛ.

along, they 'all cried out now to have the Governor sent for, as if he himself had bene their Castle' (S157/K196). The castle, as is apparent here, was not only a strategic place. It also stood metonymically for all the values and ideas that Colonel Hutchinson embodied and defended, for better and for worse, both in the eyes of his family and of his contemporaries. It is also from that very place that Lucy Hutchinson constructed her own narrative of the Civil War, exploiting her position as a witness in most ingenious ways.

c) Eye-witnessing the Civil War

The online 2012 Bartleby edition of the *Memoirs*, based on Firth's 1906 edition, is interestingly subtitled: 'The eyewitness biography of the rise and fall of a Puritan combatant during the English Civil War'.[81] Meanwhile, commenting on Lucy Hutchinson's account of the second occupation of Nottingham by the Newark forces, the editor of the *Memoirs*, James Sutherland, remarks: 'Much of this Mrs. Hutchinson must have seen with her own eyes,'[82] implying that Lucy Hutchinson's circumstantial narrative derived from a first-hand experience of the Civil War. As a matter of fact, Lucy Hutchinson's rendering of the battles and sieges was comparatively more sophisticated and detailed than many accounts written by her contemporaries. Hyde, for instance, mainly focuses on constitutional matters, and Baxter asserts that 'the recital of Military passages there and elsewhere, belongeth not to my present purpose.'[83] Roger B. Manning, for one, does not hesitate to connect Lucy Hutchinson's *Memoirs* with the tradition of *military* memoirs:

> Particularly noteworthy among the new varieties of martial literature was the memoir – both autobiographical and biographical. [...] Among the classic military memoirs written by or about swordsmen from the British Isles in the seventeenth century were those by Robert Monro, Sir James Turner, James Touchet, third earl of Castlehaven, and Lucy Hutchinson, wife of Col. John Hutchinson.[84]

---

[81] See *Memoirs of the Life of Colonel Hutchinson*, https://www.bartleby.com/362/ (accessed 09/12/2019). Lucy Hutchinson's *Memoirs* are taken as an instance of 'eyewitness account' in John Eric Adair, *By the Sword Divided. Eyewitness Accounts of the English Civil War* [1983, 1998] (Barton-under-Needwood: Wrens Park, 2001) 29–32.

[82] Hutchinson, *Memoirs*, ed. Sutherland, xiv.

[83] Baxter, *Reliquiæ Baxterianæ*, Part I, §65, 45–6; ed. Keeble et al., vol. 1, 310. On Clarendon, see Norbrook, 'The English Revolution', 242–4.

[84] Roger B. Manning, *Swordsmen: The Martial Ethos in the Three Kingdoms* (Oxford: Oxford UP, 2003) 35–6. See Peter Young and Norman Tuker, eds., *Military Memoirs of the Civil War: Richard Atkyns, John Gwyn* (London: Longman, 1967); Robert Monro, *Monro His Expedition with the Worthy*

As we have already seen, Nottingham Castle was an excellent place of observation and it is very likely that what Lucy Hutchinson saw there, and from there, between 1642 and 1646 shaped her whole account of the Civil War. It should be observed, however, that the *Memoirs* do not provide a raw testimony of the Civil War but a complex verbal representation, shaped by her political principles and her deeply moral outlook.[85] It is therefore legitimate to interrogate the status of autopsy—in the sense of ocular perception—in Lucy Hutchinson's account of the Civil War in Nottingham.

Lucy Hutchinson's descriptions of battles and sieges, the 'set-pieces' of ancient history, are explicitly based on eye-witnessing.[86] The two attacks and brief occupations of Nottingham by the Newark royalist forces, from 23 to 28 September 1643 and on 26 January 1644, provide examples of her art of war-writing. In both cases, the castle proved an excellent vantage point, although, as was often the case, the Colonel must have been her chief informant for the events she describes. Through the accumulation of verbs and descriptive notations, she manages to conjure up the scene and successfully places the reader in the position of an eye-witness:

> Though there were two musketts at the gate where they enter'd, both of them were surrender'd without one shott to give notice, and all the horse, and above two parts of the Castle souldiers, betrey'd, surpriz'd, and seiz'd on in their bedds, but there were not above fourscore of the Castle foote taken; the rest hid themselves, and privately stole away, some into the country, some by night came up to the Castle and got in in disguizes by the river side.
>
> (S95/K124)

While describing the attack, Lucy Hutchinson also investigates its causes, which makes her adopt an ethical stance again. To explain what happened she invokes the negligence and the unreliability of the city guards: 'Alderman Toplady, a greate Malignant, having the watch, the enemie was, by treacherie lett into the Towne, and no Alarum given to the Castle' (S95/K124). More predictably, she severely discredits the immoral behaviour of the enemy driven by their greed for pillage—an attitude systematically condemned throughout

---

Scots Regiment (London, 1637), https://www.exclassics.com/monro/monroint.htm (accessed 17/10/2019); Touchet, *The Memoirs of James, Lord Audley, Earl of Castlehaven*; James Turner, *The Memoirs of His Life and Times* (Edinburgh, 1829).

[85] On accounts of sieges during the Civil War, see Ronald Bedford, Lloyd Davis, and Philippa Kelly, 'Besieged Cities: The Civil War', *Early Modern English Lives: Autobiography and Self-Representation 1500–1660* (Aldershot: Ashgate, 2007) 148–59.

[86] Burke, *The Renaissance of the Past* 106–17.

the *Memoirs*:[87] '[i]n the meane time the Cavalliers that came from Newark, being about six hundred, fell to ransack and plunder all the honest men's houses in the Towne, and the Cavaliers of the Towne, who had call'd them in, helpt them in this worke' (S96/K125). Following the same logic, she advances that the ease with which the malignant invasion was carried out resulted from the lack of discipline and cohesion among the Colonel's troops, who, for the most part, disobeyed him and preferred to lodge in town with their wives rather than in the uncomfortable castle. On the other hand, by accumulating action verbs and connectors, Lucy Hutchinson emphasizes the Colonel's rapidity of action, his determination and dedication to the cause:

> it was no time to be angrie, but to applie himselfe to doe what was possible to preserve the place; wherefore he immediately dispatcht messengers, by a private sally-port, to Leicester and Derby, to desire their assistance [...]. Assoone as the Governor had dispatcht his messengers he went up to the Towers, and from thence play'd his Ordinance into the Towne, which seldome fail'd of execution upon the enemie.   (S95/K125)

The Colonel's conduct is thus systematically depicted in a positive way, the better to bring out his moral superiority not only over his enemies but also over Nottingham's townsmen, the description of his action being an integral part of his wife's defence of him.[88]

With the second attack on Nottingham by the Newark royalist forces led by Charles Lucas on 16 January 1644, Lucy Hutchinson uses a similar technique, combining a visual description of what happened in Nottingham with moral and political commentary.[89] The difference with her account of the 1643 siege, however, is that, although her relation starts rather factually, it conveys a more complex moral vision of the Civil War.[90] She starts by reporting the episode very vividly in a way that is reminiscent of her description of 1643—once again offering a potent visual description, through her use of *enargeia*. We thus learn that 'the Horse, perceiving the enemie's body to be a greate one, retreated to the Castle, and the foote seeing them gone, and none of the Townsmen came forth to their assistance, made alsoe an orderly retreate back to the Castle'

---

[87] See for example *Memoirs*: 'he chose all loss, rather than to make up himself by rapine and violence' (S91/K120).

[88] On the Colonel's moral superiority, see Chapter 6, 3 ('Politico-moral digressions: a defence of Colonel Hutchinson').

[89] On that episode, see Wood, *Nottinghamshire in the Civil War* 64.

[90] A reading of that episode is to be found in Mayer, 'A Life of Writing', 315–16.

(S112/K145); the attack was also facilitated by the fact that the fortifications were 'unperfect' and could thus be 'easily enter'd' (S113/K145). The movements of troops are of course fundamental here, but what matters even more are the emotions and passions which the attack aroused on both sides. Lucy Hutchinson thus dwells on the initial lack of courage of the horse, whose sense of discouragement did not last, as they were galvanized by the angry speech of the Colonel, who 'stirr'd them up to such a generous shame that they dismounted, and all tooke musketts to serve as foote, with which they did so very good service so that they exceeding well regain'd their reputations' (S113/K145). By highlighting the force of two passions, anger and shame, and their capacity to provoke a heroic counterattack, Lucy Hutchinson offers a moral and psychological interpretation of events, which does not feature either in the Notebook, or in the two letters written by John Hutchinson on 16 January 1644, which all relate the same episode in a more factual and less explanatory way.[91] Unlike the *Memoirs*, these texts do not mention that the Colonel's speech to his troops was decisive in reversing the balance of power: by chiding his soldiers for their apathy he did indeed succeed in inspiring 'very wonderfull and commendable actions' in them (S115/K147). What shows up in this pivotal speech—another typical set-piece of ancient history—is the moralizing voice of the Colonel, whose 'handsome reproaches' worked wonders among the soldiers (S115/K147).

The counterattack, which took place within the city walls, was probably seen by Lucy Hutchinson, who lived then in the castle. In any case she gives us a visual description of the scene, replete with affect.[92] What emerges from the fighting is death and despair, not partisanship or a warlike heroic spirit. The visual image of the blood soiling the snow, which is described in the *Memoirs*, Notebook, and in a letter of Colonel Hutchinson dated 16 January 1644,[93] is particularly effective in conjuring up the horror of the siege and in turning the reader into the spectator of a tragedy that took place both within and without Nottingham:

---

[91] See *Memoirs*, ed. Firth, Appendix XVIII, 418–20.
[92] Matchinske, 'History's "Silent Whispers"', 65.
[93] See Notebook, Add. MS 25901, 46: 'The Governor had intelligence y^t abundance of y^m were dead in ye wood & seuerall townes as they returned that abundance were runne away & wounded they left a track of blood for 2 miles spoyld many of their horses & tired out their men.' In the letter John Hutchinson's aim is to show how 'straitened' they were and how 'potent' the enemy was: 'we traced them two miles in the snow by much blood which we found spilt, and we hear that they left dead and wounded men in the towns as they passed' (*Memoirs*, ed. Firth, Appendix XVIII, 419). James Sutherland speaks of a 'sort of miniature retreat from Moscow' (xiv).

> the Governor's men chased them from streete to streete till they had clear'd the Towne of them, who runne away confusedly. [...] Betweene thirty and forty of them were kill'd in the streetes, fourscore were taken prisoners, and abundance of armes were gather'd up, which the men flung away in hast as they ran. [...] Their horse fac'd the Towne in a vally where their reserve stood, while their foote marcht away, till towards evening, and then they all drew off. Many of them died in their returne, and were found dead in the woods and in the townes they past through. Many of them, discourag'd with this service, ran away, and many of their horses were quite spoyl'd: for two miles they left a greate track of blood which froze as it fell upon the snow.
> (S113–14/K146)

To pursue her account of the Cavaliers' disarray—the parliamentary reaction came as a surprise to them—Lucy Hutchinson shifts her point of view, and offers a description of the scene from the enemy's perspective, in order to emphasize the unexpected and extraordinary character of the counterattack carried out by the Nottingham's soldiers. She recalls the easiness with which the Cavaliers entered the town as well as the lack of a fighting spirit among the Colonel's troops which, at first, made a parliamentary victory impossible to imagine. The references to the harsh weather conditions are meant to arouse compassion in the reader:

> it was such bitter weather that the foote had waded allmost to the middle on snow as they came in, and were so nummed with the cold when they came into the Towne that they were faine to be rubbed to gett life in them, and in that condition were more eager of fires and warme meate to refresh them than of plunder, which sav'd many men's goods, and their security, that did not believe an enemie who had unhandsomely, to speake truth, suffer'd them to enter the Towne without any dispute, would have durst at such greate odds to have sett upon driving them out. (S114/K146-7)

What makes this extraordinary scene believable is precisely Lucy Hutchinson's use of autopsy, namely her capacity to arouse strong emotions in the readers as if they were themselves eye-witnesses of the scene.[94] The vision of the fighting,

---

[94] Hartog, *Évidence de l'histoire* 192; Zangara, *Voir l'histoire* 8. On the complexity of eye-witnessing, and on testimony being a construct, see Andrea Frisch, 'The Testimony of History', *The Invention of the Eyewitness: Witnessing and Testimony in Early Modern France* (Chapel Hill: U of North California P, 2004) 11-19. For examples of autopsy in ancient history, see Burke, *The Renaissance Sense of the Past* 110-11.

by producing terror, invites them to pity the soldiers as human beings, and the emphasis on sight is telling: only 'those that *saw* that day' (S114/K147, my emphasis), only 'those who *saw* it and shar'd in it' (S114/K147, my emphasis) could believe what happened. Autopsy serves here to validate the description and replaces further speculations about the Colonel's motivations.[95] All the conditions are met for us to read Lucy Hutchinson's description of the siege as a *real* tragedy, in which many contradictory human passions come into play, and in which it is impossible to designate a victor:[96]

> Indeed, no one can believe, but those that saw that day what a strange ebbe and flow of courage and cowardize there was in both parties that day. The Cavaliers marcht in with such terror to the Garrison, and such gallantry, that they startled not when one of their leading files fell before them all at once, but marcht boldly over the dead bodies of their friends, under the mouth of their enemies' cannon, and carried such valliant dreadfullnesse about them, as made very couragious stout men recoyle. [...] Our horse, who ranne away frighted at the sight of their foes when they had breastworkes before them, and the advantage of freshness to beate back assaylants allready vanquisht with the sharpnesse of the cold and a killing march, within three or four howers, as men that thought nothing too greate for them, return'd fiercely upon the same men after their refreshment, when they were entered into defensible houses. (S114/K147)

The symmetry between the Cavaliers and the Roundheads, who both demonstrate heroism and cowardice, calls into question the value of war as the expression of masculine heroic virtue. It also suggests that ideology is momentarily suspended and disappears behind the cruelty of the fighting and the contradictory aspirations of the soldiers.[97] This tragic suspension of meaning does not last, however, and the miraculous preservation of Nottingham is soon given a providential interpretation:

---

[95] We have similar speculations in the Notebook, Add. MS 25901, 45ᵛ: 'the reason why the Governor did not command to follow the reare was because he intended they should fall into their quarters at night for which he gave orders but the CL 19 would not march after he had received orders from yᵉ Governor.' CL 19 was Colonel Francis Thornhagh.

[96] This tragic transcription of the siege earlier is prepared by Lucy Hutchinson describing Nottingham as one of the stages 'whereon the Tragedie of the civill warre was acted' (S78/K104–5). See also 'this greate Tragedie' (S53/K75) and Conclusion, 1 ('A tragic vision of the English Revolution').

[97] See McLoughlin, 'War and Words', *The Cambridge Companion to War-Writing* 15–16. See also Baxter's uncommitted description of the indecisive battle of Edgehill (*Reliquiæ Baxterianæ*, Part I, §61, 43; ed. Keeble et al., vol. 1, 304). On the description of the indecisive battle of Edgehill and the questioning of male identity, see Diane Purkiss, *Literature, Gender and Politics during the English Civil War* (Cambridge: Cambridge UP, 2005) 32–6.

it was a greate instruction that even the best and highest courages are but the beames of the Almighty, and when he with-holds his influence, the brave turne cowards, feare unnerves the most mighty, makes the most generous base, and greate men to doe those things they blush to thinke on. When God againe inspires, the fearefull and the feeble see no dangers, believe no difficulties, and carry on attempts whose very thoughts would at another time shiver their joynts like agues. (S114–15/K147)

The uncertainty of Lucy Hutchinson's narrative is also reflected in her hesitation about the number of victims, when Nottingham was under siege, in both 1643 and 1644. During the first occupation of Nottingham in September 1643, she points out the discrepancy between what John Hutchinson saw and his difficulty to make sense of the situation: 'Att length on Saturday, the 23rd of September, in the afternoone, the Governor *saw* a greate many goods and persons going over the Line bridge, *and not knowing what it meant,* sent some cannon bulletts after them; *when,* on the other side of the Towne, he discern'd a body of men whom he *knew not* at first whether friends or foes' (S96–7/ K126, my emphasis). When the Newark soldiers went away after the siege, it was again impossible for the Colonel to figure out the number of soldiers who were taken prisoners, wounded, or killed. Using the pronoun 'we' Lucy Hutchinson includes herself among the witnesses of the scene and presents her testimony as uncertain: '[t]here were not above five and twenty of the Newark souldiers taken. How many were slaine at their going off and during the time of their stay *wee* could not certeinely tell, because they had meanes of carrying them off by the Bridge' (S97/K127, my emphasis).[98] The account of the siege in January 1644 is just as uncertain. In a letter dated 16 January, Colonel Hutchinson reports that there were 'a great many killed, the certain number whereof I cannot relate', adding that it was difficult to know *exactly* what was happening.[99] In the corresponding passage in the Notebook (very possibly based on that same letter), Lucy Hutchinson signals that 'there were abundance wounded betweene 30 and 40 slaine and about 80 taken prisoners.'[100] In the *Memoirs*, finally, she gives other figures, writing that '[b]etweene thirty

---

[98] My emphasis. We find the equivalent passage in the Notebook, Add. MS 25901, 23^v: 'to say certeinly how many of the enemie were slaine while they stayd in towne and at their going out is more than we knew one of ye Captaines y^t came from Derby was slaine and some 5 or six of our men wounded & no more wee tooke some fiue & twenty prisoners that were souldiers besides abundance of countrie men and Townsmen y^t joined with them in their mischiefs against the honest people in the Towne.'
[99] *Memoirs*, ed. Firth, Appendix XVIII, 418.   [100] Notebook, Add. MS 25901, 45.

and forty of them were kill'd in the streetes, fourscore were taken prisoners' (S114/K146), apparently conflating different versions of the same event.

Thus, ocular perception, even when the observer found himself or herself on the battlefield, remained often uncertain, superficial and flawed; it could not give access to a full knowledge of what was going on.[101] Montaigne made the same observation about the epistemological uncertainty of historical reports, remarking that even Caesar 'could not possiblie oversee all things with his owne eyes, that hapned in his Armie, but was faine to relie on the reports of particular men, who often related untruths unto him'.[102] Therefore, he continued, 'nothing [was] so hard, or so vncertaine to be found-out, as the certaintie of a Truth.'[103] One could add that in the case of the *Memoirs*, the uncertainty was even accentuated by the fact that Lucy Hutchinson's story was, to use Puttenham's words, 'no more than a masse of memories assembled' and therefore liable to distortions, omissions, and even errors.[104] However, the memorialist was not discouraged by the limits of her own eye-witnessing. What mattered to her in these pages was to produce, through her observations, an impression of truth—what could be called verisimilitude—and thereby to persuade her reader of the validity of the Colonel's actions.[105] In so doing she drew upon historiographical practices, which went back to ancient historiography and which were revived at the Renaissance. The historian's ability to make history visible and believable was praised, after Plutarch, by Thomas Hobbes in his preface to Thucydides's *Peloponnesian Wars*:

> He filleth his narration with that choice of matter, and ordereth them with that judgment, and with such perspicuity and efficacy expresseth himself that, as Plutarch saith, maketh his auditor a spectator. For he setteth his reader in the assembly of the people and in the senate, at their debating; in the streets, at their seditions; and in the field, at their battles.[106]

By presenting a vivid picture of the Civil War in Nottinghamshire, Lucy Hutchinson thus reveals her indebtedness to the historiographical tradition

---

[101] Lesne, *La Poétique des mémoires* 47-8 on the memorialists' scepticism towards eye-witnessing. On the failure of visual perceptions to reflect ontological truth, see Line Cottegnies, *L'Éclipse du regard. La poésie anglaise du baroque au classicisme (1525-1660)* (Geneva: Droz, 1997) 316-19.
[102] Montaigne, 'Of Bookes', 231.   [103] Montaigne, 'Of Bookes', 231.
[104] Puttenham, 'Of historicall Poesie', 31.
[105] MacGillivray, *Restoration Historians* 182. See Zangara, *Voir l'histoire* 7-9 and 55-81.
[106] Hobbes, 'To the Readers', Thucydides, *Eight Bookes of the Peloponnesian Warre* np. See Plutarch, *Moralia*, vol. 4, *Were the Athenians More Famous in War or in Wisdom?* (Cambridge: Harvard UP, 1936) 501.

of an 'eloquent' history, delineated above by Hobbes. This was for instance noted in the nineteenth century by the reviewer of the *Critical Review*, who claims that Lucy Hutchinson, as a genuine witness of history, effectively conveyed through words the 'actions' of history: 'we are frequently gratified to meet with a natural and vivid representation of events which bring long passed times before us with the clearness of a present scenery, and which communicate to us all the enthusiasm of an actual spectator of the actions which are described.'[107]

Finally, both the potentialities of eye-witnessing and its limits show again strong convergence between Lucy Hutchinson's historiographical approach in the *Memoirs* and contemporary experimental practices in which visual perception was key—in both cases, Bacon's inheritance was fundamental.[108] Like experimentalists, Lucy Hutchinson knew indeed that first-hand visual observations, however epistemologically necessary, often produced an uncertain knowledge. When, for instance, she reports that her husband cannot tell foes from friends during the first siege of Nottingham, her phrasing is strikingly close to the style of Boyle who deliberately uses 'so often, *perhaps, it seems, it is not improbable*, and such other expressions' when he relates experiments.[109] As Shapin has argued, such display of modesty, which can be found in his experimental reports but also in most of Boyle's prefaces, is not to be taken literally as an admission of failure, but rather to be considered as evidence of anti-dogmatism and as a strategy to give the reader an assurance that the knowledge has been produced experimentally, by flawed faculties. In this sense, Lucy Hutchinson's own uncertainty and hesitations could be seen as a strategy to anchor her own narrative of the Civil War in an authentic experience of history and to make it more persuasive: the uncertainty of visual perceptions can be interpreted *a contrario* as proof of the veracity and genuineness of her testimony, however imperfect it may be. From this perspective, the place given to experience in Lucy Hutchinson's *Memoirs* can be taken as evidence, especially when it comes to ocular observation, of the proximity existing between a historian and an experimentalist's epistemological approaches. However, as Shapiro remarks, the epistemological models on which experimentalism drew were not new when Lucy Hutchinson was writing the *Memoirs*, but still largely indebted to empiricism, which Bacon

---

[107] See Rev. of *Memoirs of the Life of Colonel Hutchinson, Critical Review* 10 (1807): 66.
[108] On the importance of eye-witnessing for lawyers, judges, and scientists, see Shapiro, 'Eyewitnesses and "Ocular Testimony"', *A Culture of Fact* 119–21.
[109] See Boyle's letter to his nephew, quoted in Shapin, 'Pump and Circumstance', 495–6.

decisively contributed to developing in all fields of knowledge in the early years of the seventeenth century.[110]

After some decades of relative neglect, Civil War memoirs and lives have been the object of revived interest among historians, because they offer a unique insight into the experience of the Civil Wars and the way it was remembered. Among them, Bennett describes his book, *The Civil Wars Experienced*, as 'an account or series of accounts of the experiences of a range of people across the British Isles. In it are narratives of segments of lives affected by the Civil Wars. There is little here of the grand narrative in the sense that it is always in the background rather than always to the fore.'[111] In the field of memory studies, the historian Edward Legon exploits life-writing, in particular the narratives of Richard Baxter, Edmund Ludlow, Bulstrode Whitelocke, John Shawe, and Philip Henry.[112] Similarly, the literary scholar, Kate Chedgzoy, has shown the importance of life-writing—and of Lucy Hutchinson's *Memoirs* in particular—to investigate women's memories of war. This type of writing, she claims, by blurring the private and the public, frees 'history writing [...] from the hierarchization of public and private spheres'.[113] I believe that future histories of Civil War *experience* would greatly benefit from integrating into their corpus the under-exploited Interregnum and Restoration memoirs of the Civil War, all being experience-based stories that could potentially enhance our understanding of such a complex period.

2. Behind the scenes of national history: an anatomy of the Civil War

Lucy Hutchinson took full advantage of her position as a witness to write the local day-to-day chronicle of the Civil War in Nottinghamshire, to which authors of more general histories, such as May, in his *History of Parliament* and *Breviary*, did not have access. Taking full advantage of her position as the

---

[110] See Shapiro, *A Culture of Fact* 117; Shapiro, *Probability and Certainty in Seventeenth-Century England* (Princeton: Princeton UP, 1983); Richard W. Serjeantson, 'Proof and Persuasion', *The Cambridge History of Science, vol. 3, Early Modern Science*, ed. Katharine Park and Lorraine Daston (Cambridge: Cambridge UP, 2006) 132-75. On probability, see Ian Hacking, *The Emergence of Probability* (Cambridge: Cambridge UP, 2006).

[111] Martyn Bennett, *The Civil Wars Experienced. Britain and Ireland, 1638-61* (London: Routledge, 2000) x. See Erin Peters, 'Trauma Narratives of the English Civil War', *Journal for Early Modern Cultural Studies* 16.1 (2016): 79-94.

[112] Legon, *Revolution Remembered* 36-8; 96.

[113] Chedzgoy et al., 'Researching Memory', 14; Chedzgoy, '"Shedding for England's loss": Women's Writing and the Memory of War', *Women's Writing* 125-66.

Colonel's confidant, she offers a systematic presentation of the members of the local nobility and gentry, a 'list of characters' indispensable to understanding the next hundred and fifty pages, notably the diplomatic exchanges and disputes within the Nottingham Committee. My contention here is that Lucy Hutchinson's local point of view, anchored in Nottinghamshire affairs, allows her to write a history of the Civil War in which the local and national are tightly intertwined, as well as to give the reader an exceptional insight into the anthropological realities of war.

a) Intelligence and negotiations

Like many memorialists of her age, Lucy Hutchinson sought to disclose what external observers could not relate, namely the details about the negotiations that were then conducted, sometimes in secret and by spies, between Colonel Hutchinson and the royalist enemy.[114] She was neither a spy nor even a go-between, but she had a unique inside view of events. John Hutchinson, we are told, 'employ'd ingenuous persons, and was better inform'd of the true state of things [than Sir John Gell], and so oftentimes communicated those informations to the chiefe commanders' (S68/K93). On 15 January 1644, false intelligence was communicated about the royalist forces from Newark: these, it was said, were 'to march upon a design upon Sleaford in Lincolnshire', but this was a pretence as they were actually marching on Nottingham. Fortunately, the Colonel had been warned 'by two of his intelligencers' 'that the designe was against Nottingham' (S112/K145).

Lucy Hutchinson's awareness of secret negotiations is often materialized by her insistent references to the letters the Colonel sent and received, and which she may have had under her eyes when she was writing the *Memoirs* between 1664 and 1667. Some of these letters are copied in her own hand and inserted at the end of the Notebook.[115] They are used as historical evidence and add weight and authority to her narrative.[116] Additionally, several passages reveal

---

[114] On intelligence, see Barbara Donagan, *War in England 1642–1649* (Oxford: Oxford UP, 2008) 99–114.

[115] The final pages of Add. MS 25901 (90–6) are copies, in Lucy Hutchinson's hand, of letters signed by Digby, Chaworth, Sutton, Millington, Pierrepont, Biron, Meldrum, Plumtre, etc. Most of these letters are reproduced in *Memoirs*, ed. Firth, 398–425. On these letters, see Wall, 'Not so much open professed enemies', 631.

[116] On the centrality of letters, summonses, and responses in testimonies of the war, see Bedford, Davis, and Kelly, 'Besieged Cities', 151–4. See also Nadine Akkerman, *Invisible Agents: Women and Espionage in Seventeenth-Century Britain* (Oxford: Oxford UP, 2018) 12.

that she was acutely aware not only of the local gentry's ideological and private interests but also of the age-old loyalties that held her local community together.[117] It is no wonder, therefore, that she was in a position to write a unique account of the protracted negotiations which took place from October 1642 to March 1644, between John Hutchinson and the Cavaliers who wanted him to deliver the strategic fort of Nottingham. In her circumstantial relation of these diplomatic exchanges, at the intersection of local and national warfare, she unfailingly displays her excellent knowledge of the rituals of war, her acquaintance with the protagonists, whether parliamentarian or royalist, and her art of story-telling—all these qualities being combined to bring out, in all possible ways, the loyalty of the Hutchinson brothers who rejected all promises of money and favour, despite the financial difficulties they were encountering.

The *Memoirs* first focus on the traps set by John Digby, the High Sheriff of Nottinghamshire, in order to obtain the fort.[118] After the battle of Edgehill, in late October 1642, he sent a summons in which he requested to meet the local parliamentarian gentlemen at Newark—a rendezvous which John Hutchinson soon discovered was a snare. In a way typical of the Civil War section of the *Memoirs*, Lucy Hutchinson meticulously reconstructs the circulation of intelligence—essentially through letters—between the local gentry, both parliamentarian and royalist, in order to bring out the Colonel's unequalled qualities as a negotiator, which lead to his final success in thwarting Digby's plan.[119] This first summons was followed by another letter sent by Digby on 9 December 1642, 'desiring a meeting with them [Mr. Francis Pierrepont and Mr. John Hutchinson] to consult for the peace of the country, security of their estates and such like fair pretences' (S74/K100).[120] These negotiations about neutrality were conducted in a *civil* way again, but the context had changed since October—the local militia had been settled, several regiments had been raised by order of Parliament and, in Nottingham, a Committee of War had been appointed. Lucy Hutchinson gives a very precise relation of the exchanges, as if, again, providing evidence for a trial. Her talent for setting the scene, her identification of the protagonists, and her description of their every move plunge the reader into a history of the Civil War that was also

---

[117] John Adrian, 'Izaak Walton, Lucy Hutchinson, and the Experience of Civil War', *Local Negotiations of English Nationhood, 1570–1680* (Basingstoke: Palgrave Macmillan, 2011) 136.
[118] On this episode, see http://www.ournottinghamshire.org.uk/page_id__1458.aspx?path=0p31p64p (accessed 09/11/2019) and Wood, *Nottinghamshire in the Civil War* 29–30.
[119] See *Memoirs*, ed. Sutherland, 69–70, and ed. Keeble, 94–5.
[120] This proposal of treaty (December 1642) was signed by Digby and sent to all the justices of peace (Notebook, Add. MS 25901, 4^v). See 'Six Letters Relating to the Proposed Treaty of Neutrality for Notts, December 1642', *Memoirs*, ed. Firth, Appendix VII, 398–403.

fought locally in the county of Nottinghamshire. This time, however, her story of these negotiations ends with the Colonel's failure to discover the treachery:

> [Digby's] letter was civilly answer'd them againe, and the treaty kept on foote some fourteene dayes by letters sign'd by the Lord Chaworth, Sir Thomas Williamson, Mr. Sutton, Sir Gervase Eyre, Sir John Digbie, Sir Roger Cooper, Mr. Palmer, Mr. John Millington. At length a meeting was appoynted att a village in the country, on the Forrest side, where Mr. Sutton should have mett Mr. John Hutchinson. Mr. Hutchinson came to the place, but found not Mr. Sutton there, only the Lord Chaworth came in and call'd for sack, and treated Mr. Hutchinson very kindly; when Mr. Hutchinson telling my Lord he was come according to appoyntment to conclude the treaty which had bene betweene Nottingham and Newark, my Lord told him he knew nothing of it. (S74–5/K100–1)

After Digby's attempts to have Nottingham delivered failed, there were those of the Earl of Newcastle, William Cavendish, who commanded the royalist troops in the North until the royalist defeat at Marston Moor (July 1644). On 6 August 1643, the Colonel, who had been appointed Governor of the Castle of Nottingham on 29 June, received, from Newcastle, 'a summons for the delivery of the Towne and Castle' (S88/K116). In exchange for the surrender of Nottingham and in the King's name, the royalist General, who was in a position of strength after several victories in the north of England, promised him 'mercy and favour'.[121] But if the town and the castle were not delivered, he warned that 'blood [would] be shed in that quarrel.'[122] The Colonel was not intimidated, however, and the summons was answered by a 'civill defiance in writing' (S88/K117). This bellicose—although civil—exchange was published in *Mercurius Britannicus* (23–29 August 1643), which indicates that what was happening *behind the scenes* was of interest to the public at large: it was not only a local business but also a national one.[123] Lucy Hutchinson does not provide the documents—something which Margaret Cavendish did, for instance in the *Life of William Cavendish*[124]—but she chooses instead to

---

[121] 'The Earl of Newcastle's Letter to the Committee of Nottingham', *Memoirs*, ed. Firth, Appendix X, 405. On Newcastle's victories (Howley House, Adwalton Moor, Bradford, Lincoln, Gainsborough), see Lynn Hulse, 'Cavendish, William, first Duke of Newcastle upon Tyne (bap. 1593, d. 1676)' (2004), *Oxford Dictionary of National Biography*, DOI: 10.1093/ref:odnb/4946. On Newcastle's military strategies, see Bennett, 'Every County', 196–7.
[122] 'The Earl of Newcastle's Letter', 405.   [123] 'The Earl of Newcastle's Letter', 406.
[124] Cavendish, *The Life of William Cavendish*, 97–105 (description of William Cavendish's estates); 113–15 (a list of garrisons and their governors), 115–17 (a list of army officers).

focus on the exchanges. By putting the reader in the position to witness the Governor's meeting with Major Cartwright, the Earl of Newcastle's emissary, Lucy Hutchinson skilfully dramatizes the fateful shift from a war of words—in the form of summons, letters and parleys—into a war of swords, that is, an overt military crisis.[125] She also brings to the fore the ideological conflict underpinning the negotiations, portraying the Governor as a champion of anti-Popery and an adversary of the 'atheistical general', William Cavendish:

> Cartwright, having receiv'd [the answer], and being treated with wine by the Governor and the rest of the Officers, grew bold in the exercise of an abusive witt he had [...], but when my Lord should come with his armie, he should find them in other termes, humbly beseeching my Lord to spare them as misled young men, and suffer them march away with a cudgell. "And then," sayd he, "shall I stand behind my Lord's chaire and laugh." At which the Governor being angrie told him he was much mistaken, for he scorn'd ever to yeild on any terms to a Papisticall Armie led by an Atheisticall Generall. Mr. George Hutchinson told him, if my lord would have that poore Castle, he must wade to it in blood; which words they say he told his Generall.
> (S88–9/K117)

Against all expectations, Newcastle did not attack, in the end: '[a]fter this summons, my Lord Newcastle came not according to their bravadoes, but diverted his armie to Hull to besiege my Lord Fairfax there' (S90/K118). The threat, however, was real, and mobilized the Colonel's soldiers.[126]

Newcastle's attempt to have the town and castle of Nottingham delivered was not the last one—it was part of a more general strategy of the royalist army to seize parliamentary strongholds.[127] A month later, in late August 1643, a similar attempt was made by the royalist Governor of Newark, Sir Richard Biron, who happened to be John Hutchinson's cousin.[128] The summons, carried by a messenger, 'one Mr. Ascough, a Gentleman of the county', stipulated that, should John Hutchinson 'returne to his obedience to the King, he might not only preserve his estate but have what reward he pleas'd to propound for so doing' (S92–93/K121). Although the message was officially

---

[125] See Wood, *Nottinghamshire in the Civil War* 55.
[126] See Wood, *Nottinghamshire in the Civil War* 55–6.
[127] Andrew Hopper, *Turncoats and Renegadoes. Changing Sides during the English Civil Wars* (Oxford: Oxford UP, 2012) 129–31.
[128] On the genealogy of the Hutchinson and Biron families, see *Memoirs*, ed. Keeble, 346, note 54, and the family tree, appended to the 1806 edition, between 'To my Children' (17) and 'The Life of John Hutchinson' (19).

sent 'out of love and tender compassion' (S93/K122), and only a few weeks before the first occupation of Nottingham by Newark royalist forces, it was in fact a declaration of war. The appeal to the Colonel's feelings for his family and estate was nothing but a form of psychological blackmail: 'Sir Richard Biron, out of that tender naturall affection which he ever had for him and still preserv'd, desir'd him now to consider his wife and children, and the losse of his whole estate, which was so inevitable, if he persisted in the engagement he was in, that some had allready bene suing to the Earle of Newcastle for it' (S93/K121). For the writing of this episode Lucy Hutchinson heavily drew upon the Notebook, where she had meticulously transcribed the exchange in direct speech.[129] What seems probable is that the narrative was written soon after the events occurred, but whether from the Colonel's own words or from an official document, it is difficult to tell. Moreover, in her account, Lucy Hutchinson displays her keen understanding of the psychological strife going on between the two cousins.[130] Despite their blood ties and undeniable proximity, she takes pains to describe them as being 'to each other the most uncivill enemies that can be imagined' (S90/K118). The emphasis on this family quarrel was calculated. It served to ward off any suspicion of royalist collaboration, in a way consistent with Lucy Hutchinson's vindication of the Colonel as a republican. Besides, by staging Sir Richard Biron's machinations, she highlights the Colonel's commitment to God and his staunch dedication to the public cause, which comes first, even before the welfare of his own family:

> the Governor bade him returne Sir Richard answer, that "except he found his owne heart prone to such treachery, he might consider there was, if nothing elce, so much of a Biron's blood in him that he should very much scorne to betrey or quitt a trust he had undertaken; but the grounds he went on were such that he very much scorn'd so base a thought as to sell his faith for base rewards or feares, and therefore could not consider the losse of his estate, which his wife was as willing to part with as himselfe in this cause, wherein he was resolv'd to persist in the same place in which it had pleased God to call him to the defence of it." (S93/K122)[131]

---

[129] See Notebook, Add. MS 25901, 19ᵛ–20.
[130] See Bedford, Davis, and Kelly, 'Besieged Cities', 153 for other examples of 'psychological war' drawn from memoirs and diaries.
[131] Norbrook, 'Memoirs and Oblivion', 253 on John Hutchinson's relations with the Biron side of the family. His relations with Sir Richard improved under the Protectorate.

Regardless of the Colonel's refusal to 'sell his faith', new attempts to bribe the Colonel and obtain the city and castle were made in December, only three months after the brief occupation of Nottingham (18–23 September 1643), in the context of an imminent siege of Nottingham ('nothing was expected at Derby and Nottingham but a siege,' S108/K140).[132] Lucy Hutchinson this time does not emphasize family links, but explains how Newcastle exploited the strong bonds of friendship existing between George Hutchinson (Lieutenant-Colonel) and Colonel Dacre (Newcastle's emissary) who 'loved each other as well if they had bene brothers' (S108/K140). In this particular episode, Lucy Hutchinson's behind-the-scenes position allows her to disclose how the Civil War broke old loyalties. She thus exposes the hypocrisy of Dacre who made 'many endearing expressions', 'notwithstanding their contrary engagements' (S109/K140), with the intent again of buying Nottingham. Colonel Dacre told Captain Poulton that if the 'Governor would deliver up the Castle he should be receiv'd into favour, have the Castle confirm'd to him and his heires, have 10,000 in mony, and be made the best Lord in the country' (S110/K142). Despite these enticing promises of money and favour, the Governor and the Nottingham Committee of War decided to have their answers read in Parliament and further publicized in pamphlet form (printed on 30 December), in order to vindicate the Colonel's incorruptibility and loyalty to the Parliament. In so doing they wanted to ward off suspicion of treachery.[133] The pamphlet's epilogue, however significant it may be for the public image of the Hutchinsons, is left out by the memorialist who returns to the situation in Nottingham. Although she does not tell the whole story, her account is more explanatory than the pamphlet which only reproduces the letters exchanged with no specific commentaries, only stating on the title-page the 'constant Resolution never to betray the Trust the Parliament hath reposed in them'. By comparison, Whitelocke's record of the same episode in his own *Memorials* is only three lines long (instead of at least three pages in the *Memoirs*) and exclusively factual; it does not tell us anything about the pressure that Colonel Hutchinson had to undergo and about his former links of friendship with Colonel Dacre, Newcastle's emissary.[134]

---

[132] Wood, *Nottinghamshire in the Civil War* 60–1.
[133] On the episode see Andrew Hopper, 'Treachery and Conspiracy in Nottinghamshire during the English Civil War', *East Midlands History and Heritage* 19–23, here 22, and his *Turncoats and Renegadoes* 131. See also Keeble, ed. *Memoirs*, note 234. See *A Discovery of the Treacherous Attempts of the Cavaliers, to have Procured the Betraying of Nottingham Castle into their Hands* (London, 1643) unpaginated.
[134] Bulstrode Whitelocke, *Memorials of the English Affairs, or An historical Account of what passed from the beginning of the reign of Charles the First, to King Charles the Second his happy restoration*

Lucy Hutchinson mentions two more summons sent to the Colonel to obtain the surrender of Nottingham. The first one, sent by Sir Charles Lucas on 16 January 1644, on the day Nottingham was attacked by the Newark royalist forces, contained a threat to 'sack and burne the Towne' (S113/K145): it never reached the Colonel whose troops, as seen above, repelled the enemy in an unexpected manner. The second one, dated 25 March 1644, menacingly reported 'that the Prince [Rupert] intended to advance against Nottingham and to fire the Towne if [the Governor] did not immediately throw downe the workes, which if he should not doe, the world would then take notice of him as the only ruine of his native country' (S124/K158–9).[135] The Colonel's answer was essentially the same: 'though the whole kingdome were quit besides this towne, yet he would maintaine it so long as he was able, and he trusted that God would preserve it in his hands; but if he perish'd, he was resolv'd to bury himselfe in the ruines of it, being confident that God would after vindicate him to have been a defender and not a destroyer of his county' (S124–5/K159). This long sentence—the conclusion to two years of pressure on the Colonel—foreshadows his final sufferings, which can only make sense within a national context, however.

What emerges from Lucy Hutchinson's meticulous account of the negotiations which took place between October 1642 and March 1645 is her concern to prove over and over again the loyalty of the Colonel. In her apologetic relation, the description of the negotiations, with a special emphasis on the exchange of letters, is meant to prove that every single reported fact really happened.[136] Moreover, by highlighting the national political stakes of local negotiations, Lucy Hutchinson shows that the *Memoirs*, notwithstanding their parochial undertones, do have a national scope—the cause for which the Colonel was indefatigably fighting in Nottingham had supporters all over England.

b) The Committee of Nottingham: a civil war in miniature

The Committee of Nottingham was set up in January 1643 after the formation of the militia and the appointment of three colonels, Sir Francis Thornhagh,

---

(London, 1682) 75. 'Colonel *Hutchinson* Governour of *Nottingham Castle,* acquainted the Parliament with an offer of the Earl of *New Castle* to pay him 10000 *l.* and to make him a Lord, and Governour of that Castle to him and his heirs, if he would deliver it to him, for the King, which *Hutchinson* refused'.

[135] *Memoirs*, ed. Firth, Appendix XXII, 425.

[136] On letters as historical proofs in memoirs, see Myriam Tsimbidy, 'Introduction', *La Mémoire des lettres. La lettre dans les Mémoires* (Paris: Classiques Garnier, 2013) 10–13.

Sir Francis Molineux, and Mr Francis Pierrepont, 'Mr. John Hutchinson and his brother [being] perswaded to be Lieftenant Collonell and major to Collonell Pierrepont's Regiment of foote' (S732–4/K99). The setting up of the Committee in Nottingham was, in Lucy Hutchinson's view, the logical sequel to these military appointments:

> They sent alsoe to the Parliament, and receiv'd from them a Commission, with instructions whereby they were impower'd to leavie forces and to rayse contributions for the maintaining them, with all authority of seizing delinquents, sequestering, and the like. The Committee appoynted were the Parliament men that serv'd for the County, Mr. Francis Pierrepont, Mr. John Hutchinson, Mr. Francis Thornhagh, Mr. Gervase Pigott, Mr. Henry Ireton, Mr. George Hutchinson, Mr. Joseph Widmerpole, Mr. Gervas Lomax, Dr. Plumptre, the Mayor of Nottingham, Mr. James Chadwick, and Mr. Thomas Salusbury. (S74/K100)[137]

In June 1643, Lucy Hutchinson reports how, after the failure of the Newark siege in February, the Nottingham Committee of war decided 'upon deliberation' that 'Mr. Hutchinson [was] the most able to manage it and the most responsible for it, both Sir John [Meldrum] and the whole Committee order'd him to take the Castle into his charge' (S83/K110). John Hutchinson felt called to accept it although he had no previous military experience.[138] However, conflicts soon arose in this assembly of 'conspirators' (S138/K175), and the machinations of two members in particular, Chadwick and Pierrepont, as early as October 1643, obliged the Colonel to have 'the Government of the Castle confirm'd on [him] by authority of Parliament' (S105/K136). Although strife within the Committee continued at least until May 1645, when the Fort of the Trent was retaken, the Colonel's overall record as Governor has been positively assessed in recent historical scholarship: 'Colonel Hutchinson was successful in his fulfilment of the civic and military necessities facing Nottingham as a Garrison town [...] in the only Midlands county where the King's supporters were in a majority.'[139]

---

[137] See Wood, *Nottinghamshire in the Civil War* 124–33 and 124, note 4.
[138] Seddon, 'Colonel Hutchinson and the Disputes between the Nottinghamshire Parliamentarians', 71–81. According to Seddon, Lucy Hutchinson's account is biased in favour of her husband, whom she portrays as the victim of a quarrelsome and persecutory Committee.
[139] Pert, 'Colonel Hutchinson', 24. Pert concludes, '[t]he fact that there were relatively few civilian casualties between 1643–1646 is testimony to Hutchinson's success as Governor.' On the Colonel's

The episodic account of the strife within the Nottingham Committee of War is not the most appealing section of the *Memoirs*.[140] Francis Jeffrey, the reviewer of the *Edinburgh Review*, considers that Julius Hutchinson would have made 'the book infinitely more saleable [...] too, if without making the slightest variation in what is retained, he would omit about 200 pages of the siege of Nottingham, and other parish business'.[141] Largely based on the Notebook, which may have been originally conceived as a defence of the Colonel in response to the attacks of the Committee, these pages are indeed strongly apologetic and local in outlook: Lucy Hutchinson wanted to bring to full daylight all the injustices of which her husband was a victim—an essential step in her project to establish 'the truth of him'.[142] In so doing she unrelentingly exposed the opportunism, greed and jealousy that drove the predominantly Presbyterian Committee members to conspire against the Colonel.[143] Her description of their machinations is repetitive, and I shall therefore mostly concentrate on the period from October 1644 to April 1645, when the conspiracy against him reached a climax. It is my contention here that by unveiling what was hidden from the public eye—the factionalism and the moral baseness of the Nottingham Committee members—Lucy Hutchinson sheds a precious light both on Civil War politics and on the final defeat of the so-called Puritan Revolution.

With the help of several informants—her husband, his brother, George Hutchinson, the members of the Committee she could trust (notably Thornhagh, Pigott, and Lomax[144])—Lucy Hutchinson brings together various pieces of a story of treachery that was all made up to destabilize her husband. She reveals that the 'conspiracy [of some members of the Committee] was to accuse the Collonell and his brother as persons that had betrey'd the Towne

---

relationship with Nottingham Committee, see David Norbrook, '"Words more than civil": Republican Civility in Lucy Hutchinson's "The Life of Colonel Hutchinson"', *Early Modern Discourses*, ed. Jennifer Richards (Houndmills: Palgrave Macmillan, 2003) 68–84, here 71–2.

[140] MacGillivray, *Restoration Historians* 182: 'While her narrative grows tedious to most readers who are not Nottinghamshire people, it does recapture impressively the uncertainties, gambles, rivalries, and personal conflicts of a minor garrison.'

[141] Francis Jeffrey, Rev. of *Memoirs of the Life of Colonel Hutchinson by Lucy Hutchinson*, *Edinburgh Review* 13.25 (1808): 1–25, here 25. The reviewer from the *Critical Review* equally regrets that the reader 'must wade through long details of petty broils and skirmishes, hardly interesting when they actually occurred, and now of no value' (81).

[142] On the Notebook as a Defence, see Chapter 3.

[143] See more examples in *Memoirs*, ed. Sutherland, 111, 137, and ed. Keeble, 143, 173. The Presbyterian Clement Walker also associated passions, faction, and civil war. See Walker, *The Mystery of the two Iuntos Presbyterian and Independent* (London, 1647) 18: 'A long peace begat Plenty, Plenty begat Pride, and her sister Riot; Pride begot Ambition, Ambition begot Faction, Faction begot Civill War.'

[144] See *Memoirs*, ed. Sutherland, 72–3, and ed. Keeble, 98–9.

and Castle and were ready to surrender them to the enemie' (S143/K180). By reconstructing all the stages of a complicated plot that aimed at undermining the Hutchinson brothers, she discloses the machinations of the Committee members, as well as of their accomplice, John Gell, 'a man ready enough to have promoted their wickednesse' (S143/K180). She adds, not without bitterness, that 'they had devided the spoyle before they caught the Lions' between Chadwick, Mason, White, and Palmer, while Thornhagh, a friend of Colonel Hutchinson, was 'to be wrought out of his command' (S146/K183-4).

The aborted project of conspiracy and the conflicts of the Nottingham Committee were brought to the knowledge of the parliamentary Committee of Both Kingdoms in London.[145] What Lucy Hutchinson's account makes plain is that this assembly, meant to arbitrate the Nottingham conflict, was just as liable to manipulation as the Nottingham Committee and that the situation in London was hardly more favourable for the Colonel than it was in Nottingham.[146] In the absence of allies, the rumours, essentially spread by Gilbert Millington, the local MP, made his defence most uncertain.[147] She reports for instance how Millington had 'given [the Committee of Both Kingdoms] such false impressions of the Governor and so prepossess'd them against him that was a stranger to them all' (S145/K182). The rumour was also that Mr. Millington 'undertooke to have lodg'd their [the Governor and his brother's] petitions so in the Parliament that they should never have bene heard and reliev'd' (S146/K183). The description of the members of the London Committee of Both Kingdoms is equally damning, they '[being] not so ready to relieve [the Governor] as they ought to have bene, because they could not doe it without a high reflection upon one of their owne members, who encourag'd all those little men in their wicked prosecution of him' (S145/K183). Once again, it is essential to bear in mind that this disenchanted view of politics was not contemporary with the events reported; it was that of a disillusioned woman, writing twenty years after the conspiracy.[148]

In Lucy Hutchinson's version of facts, the conspiracy of the Committee members is a sheer act of 'villainy', hatched in 'the cursed forge of their own

---

[145] On the Committee of Both Kingdoms, see http://bcw-project.org/church-and-state/first-civil-war/committee-for-both-kingdoms (accessed 10/02/2020).

[146] Seddon revises Ann Hughes's interpretation, arguing that 'Parliament and its intermediaries had little success in their attempts to find solutions to the disputes' ('Colonel Hutchinson and the Disputes' 71). According to him, Hughes is wrong to assert that 'local loyalties were easier to harmonize with Parliamentarianism than with Royalism' (Ann Hughes, 'The King, the Parliament, and the Localities during the English Civil War', *Journal of British Studies* 24.2 [1985]: 246).

[147] Wood gives a different portrait of that supporter of Parliament (*Nottinghamshire in the Civil War* 131).

[148] See corresponding passage in the Notebook, Add. MS 25901, 68-71.

hearts' (S143/K180). Its protagonists were no better than 'exquisite rogues', who 'under pretence of honesty and conscience, [...] told [the Colonel] how, not so much dislike of him as covetousnesse and ambition to advance themselves upon his ruines, engag'd them thus against him, and made them contrive that Villainy to accuse him and his brother of treachery' (S145-6/K183). Their political ideas are deliberately passed under silence. They are merely depicted as base fellows, who '[had forgotten] the Publick quarrel in their private contention' (S146/K184). And, she adds, full of indignation, how 'lamentable it was to behold how these wretched men fell away under this temptation, not only from publick spiritednesse, but from sobriety and honest morall conversation; not only conniving at and permitting the wickednesse of others, but themselves conversing in Taverns and Brothells' (S146/K184). This moral discourse, however, is far from being politically neutral, for the most depraved of the Committee-men were close to the Presbyterians, who in the Colonel's view had renounced the ideal of a morally reformed society that they originally defended.[149] Their 'scandalous conversation' (S147/K185), as Pigott, a friend of the Colonel, calls it, undermines the very ideal of godliness upheld by the Governor and most of the Independents, to whom he was close even though his wife claimed he 'never was any man's Sectary, either in religious or civill matters' (S167/K208).[150] In Lucy Hutchinson's eyes, the Presbyterians' debauchery and their hatred of the Colonel's attempt to reform manners paradoxically connects them with the Cavaliers—the 'mallignant and debosht people' that 'would joyne with them to destroy the Governor, whom they hated for his unmooved fidelity in his trust, and his severe restriction of lewdnesse and vice' (S146/K184). This unnatural alliance with the royalists is taken by her as an index of their hostility to John Hutchinson, who is not only an advocate of the reformation of manners but also a supporter of liberty of conscience. It should be pointed out that in the summer of 1644, his protection of the Cannoneers—who were separatists—had already caused him much trouble, no less than 'a great mutinie in the Priests against him' (S131-2/K167);[151] 'because he favour'd and protected godly men that were sober, although they seperated from the

---

[149] On the reformation of manners, see Bernard Capp, *England's Culture Wars. Puritan Reformation and its Enemies in the Interregnum 1649-1660* (Oxford: Oxford UP, 2012), especially introduction and Chapter 2: 'Clearing the Way: Challenges and Agenda', 14-32.
[150] See David Underdown, 'Presbyterians and Independents', *Pride's Purge. Politics in the Puritan Revolution* (Oxford: Clarendon, 1971) 55 (on John Hutchinson).
[151] Lucy Hutchinson's relation of the Colonel's treatment of the cannoneers (separatists) is different in the two accounts. See Lobo, 'Lucy Hutchinson's Revisions of Conscience', 324-6 and Seddon, 'Colonel Hutchinson and the Disputes between the Nottinghamshire Parliamentarians', 75-6.

publick Assemblies, this open'd wide the mouths of all the priests and all their idolaters, and they were willing enough to lett the children of Hell crie out with them to make the lowder noyse' (S146/K184). The alliance of the Presbyterian Committee members with the 'enemies of both [God and the Parliament]' had terrible consequences, she continues (S146/K184). First, it led to the persecution of Colonel Hutchinson by the Committee of Nottingham. Second, she argues, the divisions among the supporters of Parliament which she dates back to 1643–1644—earlier than has often been assumed—were not restricted to Nottingham, and may more generally account for the final defeat of the Puritan cause—a contention to which Lucy Hutchinson recurrently returns in the *Memoirs*:

and as wee have since seene the whole cause and party ruin'd by the same practice, so at that time the zealotts for God and the Parliament turn'd all the hate they had to the enemies of both, and call'd them to assist them in executing their mallice upon the faithful servant and generous champion of the Lord's and his countrie's just cause. (S146/K184)

It should be observed that her above comment on the ruin of 'the whole cause and party' is a later addition to the earlier narrative of the Notebook, which was presumably written soon after the events. It is typical of the retrospective mode of the memoir genre and reflects Lucy Hutchinson's bitterness and disillusion at the time of writing.

In her relation of the next conspiracy against the Governor in January 1645, Lucy Hutchinson confirms the exemplary value, in her eyes, of what happens in Nottingham. In this episode, the Presbyterians are still driven by 'envy and malice', but this time the Independents distinguish themselves by their 'justice and honour'. She makes it clear that the factionalism prevailing in Nottingham was transposable to London, since many Presbyterians in the London Committee backed the Nottingham Presbyterian plotters. Once again, it is useful to remember that Lucy Hutchinson was writing in the 1660s and that she had in mind Pride's purge and the Restoration Indemnity debate. Hence her stress on divisions which ran even deeper in 1649 and 1660 than in 1645:[152]

[The Committee men] at London were as maliciously active to make more confusions, and contriv'd many false and frivolous Articles and Petitions against [the Governor] [...]. And Mr. Pierrepont and Sir H. Vane being now

[152] On factionalism, see Underdown, 'Presbyterians and Independents', 45–76.

taken notice of as Leaders of the Independent faction, when these gentlemen out of mere justice and honor discountenanc'd their envy and mallice, they applied themselves to the Presbyterian Faction, and insinuating to them that the justice of those gentlemen was partiallity to the Governor, because he was a protector of the now hated Seperatists, they prevail'd to have Sir Philip Stapleton and Sir Gilbert Garrett, two fierce Presbiterians, added to the Subcommittee to ballance the other faction.   (S153/K191-2)

A later development in this plot in February 1645 led the Committee of Both Kingdoms to transfer the Nottingham affair to the House of Commons. Refusing to be told by Mr. Millington how to proceed, the London gentlemen 'ordered [...] that the businesse should be reported to the House' (S155/K194).[153] Two months later, on 22 April 1645, while the business with the Nottingham Committee had not yet been settled, John Hutchinson appeared himself before the House of Commons to account for the recent loss of the Trent, attributing this important military setback to the 'dissensions in the garrison' and again laying the blame on one particular member of the House, Mr. Millington. The Colonel's speech was strongly political and contributed to polarizing the ensuing debates:

he told them how their Fort was lost, and for ought he knew the Garrison by that time, which was no more than what he had long expected through the countenance that was, by one of their members, given to a malignant faction who obstructed all the publick service, disturb'd all the honest soldiers and officers in their duty, and spent the publick Treasury to carrie on their private mallice. He further told them, how dishonorable as well as destructive to their cause it was that their Members should be protected in such injust prosecutions, and should make the privilledge of the House their shelter to oppress the most active and faithfull of their servants.

(S157-8/K197)

The Colonel's addresses to Parliament reminds us here of the strong link existing between local and central politics, a link which Lucy Hutchinson never fails to mention, as it was essential for Parliament to know precisely what happened in the counties.[154] The quarrels between the different factions

---

[153] See the letters in *Memoirs*, ed. Firth, Appendix XXIII, 425-9.

[154] 'To some the recital of these municipal broils may appear rather tedious, but Whitelock's Memorials shew that these, and such like, in various parts of the kingdom required the serious and frequent attention of the parliament' (*Memoirs*, ed. Julius Hutchinson, 1806, 217-18, note z).

did not completely cease in the Committee after that episode, but they subsided, the Colonel being welcomed back and voted a 'Burgess' of the town on 23 November 1645.[155] If things eventually quietened down in Nottingham, this was not the case in London, however. In the summer of 1646, when Colonel Hutchinson sat for the first time as an MP in the House of Commons, he was struck to find there the same fierce factionalism as in Nottingham. The context, however, was slightly different. In the early summer of 1646, the New Model Army (dominated by the Independent faction) had won the First Civil War. This time the bone of contention, still between the Presbyterians and Independents, was the adoption of the Directory of Worship which, according to Lucy Hutchinson, was a pure product of Presbyterian intolerance and synonymous with renewed persecution:

> when he came there, he found a very bitter spiritt of discord and envie raging among them, and the Presbyterian faction [...] endeavouring a bitter persecution, upon the account of conscience [...] And thereupon their Directory of Worship was at length sent forth for three yeares' triall, and such as could not conforme to it mark'd out with an evill eie, and hated and persecuted under the name of Seperatists. (S166/K207)

Furthermore, it went without saying that for Lucy Hutchinson, as well as for her contemporaries, similar plots and machinations happened elsewhere—in London, but also in every county dominated by Parliament.[156] '[A]llmost all the Parliament Garrisons,' she writes, 'were infested and disturb'd with like factious little people' (S158/K197). On a larger scale, as she warns her readers earlier in the *Memoirs*, 'every County had more or lesse the civill warre within it selfe' (S60/K84), a reality which is confirmed by the recent historiography of the Civil Wars that has highlighted the internal strife that divided both parties.[157] In this sense, the civil war which Lucy Hutchinson depicts is not so much to be taken in the sense of *bellum civile*, that is, as a confrontation between two armies of citizens, as in the Greek sense of *stasis*, a broader

---

[155] Wood, *Nottinghamshire in the Civil War* 90. See Seddon, 'Hutchinson, John', *ODNB*.
[156] In a very similar way, Baxter wrote in *Reliquiæ Baxterianæ* that, with the exception of the counties which were either fully for Parliament or for the King, 'almost all the rest of the Counties had Garrisons and Parties in them on both sides, which caused a War in every County' (*Reliquiæ Baxterianæ*, Part I, §62, 44; ed. Keeble et al., vol. 1, 307). On disputes in the parliamentarian committees, see John Morrill, 'The Attack on Committees', *The Revolt in the Provinces: Conservatives and Radicals in the English Civil War, 1630-1650* (London: Allen and Unwin, 1976; Longman, 1999) 155-66.
[157] Hopper, *Turncoats and Renegadoes* 5-6.

concept which refers to internal conflicts, insurrections, the disorders harming the body politic, and, by extension, the individual.[158] It was a disease which affected the town of Nottingham, for instance, which became 'so infirme within it selfe', as 'the disaffected [...] foment[ed] the ill-humors of the factious Committee men and priests' (S125/K159). In fact, in Lucy Hutchinson's description, the whole commonwealth—from the head of state to every citizen—was affected by the disease of faction:[159]

> Nor was the faction only in particular Garrisons, but the Parliament House it selfe began to fall into the two greate oppositions of Presbitery and Independency. And, as if Discord had infected the whole English ayre with an Epidemicall hart-burning and dissension in all places, even the King's Councells and Garrisons were as factiously devided. (S158/K198)

Lucy Hutchinson's outlook was not only historical but also anthropological, as her vision of Civil War factionalism was inseparable from the disease that affected the state and resulted from the disordered passions—ambition, envy, and greed—that drove her contemporaries.[160] From her perspective, the Committee squabbles offer a forceful vision of the Civil War that traditional academic research cannot fully recapture. It does so by suggesting that what happened in Nottingham is nothing but the Civil War in miniature. In other words, by providing an anatomy of local politics—with Nottingham as a microcosm—Lucy Hutchinson simultaneously gives a striking picture of the macrocosm, England, torn apart by the Civil Wars. This was cogently pointed out by Guizot, in his introduction to his edition of the *Memoirs*. Thanks to her husband's particular and local experience, he argued, Lucy Hutchinson, as a behind-the-scenes historian, managed to convey the gist of the Civil War:

> Sir John Hutchinson's *rôle* was not an important one – the trial of Charles I was the only important act in which he had taken a part; and yet he had done much, felt much; around him, in his county, within the walls of the

---

[158] Armitage, 'Inventing Civil War', *Civil Wars* 1–58. See Michael Palmer, 'Stasis in the War Narrative', *The Oxford Handbook of Thucydides*, ed. Ryan Balot, Sarah Forsdyke, and Edith Foster (Oxford: Oxford UP, 2017) 409–25; Nicolas Dubos, ed., *Le Mal extrême: La guerre civile vue par les philosophes* (Paris: CNRS, 2010) v–xii; and Nicole Loraux, *La Cité divisée* (Paris: Payot, 1997) 13–33.

[159] Jonathan Scott, 'The Peace of Silence: Thucydides and the English Civil War', *The Certainty of Doubt: Tributes to Peter Munz*, ed. Miles Fairburn and William Hosking Oliver (Wellington: Victoria UP, 1997) 90–1.

[160] See for example Francis Bacon, '15. Of Seditions and Troubles', *Essays or Counsels, Civil and Moral* [1625], in *The Major Works*, ed. Brian Vickers (Oxford: Oxford UP, 1996) 367–8: 'As for discontentments, they are in the politic body like to humours in the natural, which are apt to gather a preternatural heat and to inflame.'

town of Nottingham, all the passions, all the vicissitudes, of the struggle which was disturbing England were felt. [...] These are the scenes which Mrs. Hutchinson shows us, living pictures, which are an essential part of history, although history says almost nothing about them.[161]

Interestingly, the issue of the 'interrelationships' between Nottingham and London during the Civil Wars in the *Memoirs* echoes more recent historiographical debates about the causes and nature of the English Revolution between 1960 and 2000.[162] There were, according to Ann Hughes, 'many avenues through which local and factional struggles could become bound up with national politics', but two models of interaction can be schematically distinguished.[163] On the one hand, historians such as Alan Everitt, Ronald Hutton and John Morrill, among others, have tended, with great variations, to consider county communities as self-contained entities, with their own loyalties.[164] These historians have demonstrated that, during the Civil War, 'allegiance was determined largely by contingent military factors: the proximity of London or of the King's army or the relative effectiveness of the small number of local partisans. [...] the central and the local [were] seen as fairly distinct and usually antagonistic spheres.'[165] On the other hand, other scholars, like Hughes herself, or Clive Holmes, see the local and the national spheres as overlapping entities, impacting each other, especially from the 1630s and throughout the English Revolution.[166] The latter historians place the emphasis on 'the close and complex integration of central and local

---

[161] Guizot, 'Introduction', in Lucy Hutchinson, *Memoirs of the Life of Colonel Hutchinson Written by his Widow Lucy* (London: Dent, 1908). Translation adapted.

[162] See the significant title of Morrill's landmark book *The Nature of the English Revolution* (Harlow: Longman, 1993). On this debate, see R. C. Richardson, 'The Twentieth Century: Local and Regional Studies', *The Debate on the English Revolution*, 3rd edition (Manchester: Manchester UP, 1998) 162-83, and, more recently, Jacqueline Eales and Andrew Hopper, *The County Community* (Hatfield: University of Hertfordshire Press, 2012), especially Andrew Hopper, 'The Impact of the County Community Hypothesis', 1-15.

[163] See Hughes, 'The King, the Parliament, and the Localities during the English Civil War', 238.

[164] See among many possible examples: Alan Everitt, *The Community of Kent and the Great Rebellion* (Leicester: Leicester UP, 1966); Morrill, *The Revolt in the Provinces*; Ronald Hutton, 'The Royalist War Effort', *Reaction to the English Civil War, 1642-1649*, ed. John Morrill (London: Macmillan, 1982) 51-65. On this approach, see Richardson, *The Debate on the English Revolution* 171-2. On the specificities of Morrill's approach, see his 'Introduction' in the 1999 edition of *The Revolt in the Provinces* and 'Introduction: County Communities and the Problem of Allegiance in the English Civil War', *The Nature of the English Revolution* 179-90.

[165] Hughes, 'The King, the Parliament, and the Localities', 237.

[166] Clive Holmes, 'The County Community in Stuart Historiography', *Journal of British Studies* 19.2 (1980): 54-73; Clive Holmes, *The Eastern Association in the English Civil War* (Cambridge: Cambridge UP, 1974); Ann Hughes, *Politics, Society and Civil War in Warwickshire 1620-1660* (Cambridge: Cambridge UP, 1987).

interests within a national culture and a national administrative and political structure'.[167]

The second model of interaction between the local and the provincial spheres more closely matches the realities of the *Memoirs*. Firstly, Lucy Hutchinson was undeniably aware of the local specificities. Before launching into her narrative of the Civil War, she gives us a picture of Nottinghamshire, a county dominated by age-old loyalties where '[a]l the Nobility and Gentry and their dependants were generally for the King [. . .]. The greatest famely was the Earle of Newcastle's' (S61/K84). She also indicates that many townspeople sought to protect their goods and estates, and longed for peace, accommodation, and neutrality. Secondly, she never loses sight of national debates, even when dealing with local subjects. This is clear in her account of the negotiations with Digby, Biron and Newcastle who all wanted to have Nottingham Castle delivered in the name of the King.[168] This is also perceptible in her relation of the Committee squabbles, which were the result not only of personal rancour but also of political and religious differences: the Nottingham Independent–Presbyterian divide found resonance in national debates, in the House of Commons and the Committee for Both Kingdoms.[169] Lucy Hutchinson does not fail to mention either that MPs, as their counties' representatives, were messengers between London and the Provinces, carrying letters and dispatches, and acted de facto as links between the centre and the periphery. Thirdly, John Hutchinson, the Governor of Nottingham, the defender of the castle, is constantly depicted as a national hero, perfectly informed of national debates, through his reading of newsbooks and various printed papers.[170]

The comparison between the *Memoirs*' description of Nottinghamshire squabbles and today's local and regional approaches should stop here, however, for Lucy Hutchinson's *Memoirs* do not meet the standards of rigour expected in contemporary historiography. Her narrative is not based on statistics and archives; her outlook is geographically and sociologically limited. Her account is also personal, and often biased and polemical, so quite alien to current historiographical practices, marked by a strong culture of 'facts'.[171] But

---

[167] Hughes, 'The King, the Parliament, and the Localities', 238.
[168] See Chapter 3, 2, a ('Intelligence and negotiations').
[169] See David R. Como, *Radical Parliamentarians and the English Civil War* (Oxford: Oxford UP, 2018) 215–32 and 256–71.
[170] This is not the view of Bennett, who considers that Lucy Hutchinson is first interested in the local side: 'without the advantages of this approach which lay over three centuries in the future, the war Lucy recounted remained mostly local' ('Every County', 193).
[171] On the importance of local archives in the post-1960 'local' studies, see Morrill, *The Revolt in the Provinces* 9–10. Bennett shows that Lucy Hutchinson's account covers a rather small area: 'Lucy's war is

trends are changing in the field of historiography too, and life-writing is gradually more and more taken into consideration as a historical genre.[172] By allowing us access to the inner workings of history, Lucy Hutchinson brings out the epistemological superiority of 'The Life of John Hutchinson' over many histories of her age, which, most of the time, lacked a first-hand experience of the Civil War and failed to capture its truth in all its political and psychological complexity. Recently, historian Martyn Bennett has pointed out the superiority of Lucy Hutchinson's *Memoirs* over other contemporary local accounts, considering that her analysis of 'the motivations of individuals' made her narrative 'an essential source for exploring the driving force of local royalism and parliamentarianism'.[173] Nevertheless, although he recognizes Lucy Hutchinson's 'broad vision' and thinks her *Memoirs* more satisfactory than other accounts of the Civil War in Nottinghamshire, he denies her work a national scope, claiming that the *Memoirs* do not 'convey a sense of the regional strategies or the larger scale national strategies into which the region fitted'.[174] He adds that '[s]uch a tight focus gives the book something of the tone of the sort of geo-centricity and egocentricity of a Calvinist spiritual diary in which everything happened to heighten the relationship between the author and God.'[175] On the other hand, I think the *Memoirs* do not qualify as a spiritual autobiography. Admittedly, Lucy Hutchinson gives the reader the sense of the Colonel's assurance of being saved, but by laying bare the interplay between the local and the national, and between the personal and the collective, she brings out the fundamentally national dimension of a conflict that first took place locally, in every English county.[176]

---

focused almost entirely within the counties bordering Nottinghamshire. Indeed, for the most part, on the corridor of territory stretching from Derby to Nottingham and on to Newark; a strip of land on either side of the present A52 (Brian Clough Way) and the A612' ('Every County', 200).

[172] This also the tendency in France. In his book on the Fronde, Michel Pernot copiously draws on memoirs. See Michel Pernot, *La Fronde: 1648–1653* [1994] (Paris: Tallandier, 2012). Over the last two decades, much research has been carried out on 'life-writings' ('les écrits du for privé') by French historians. See for example http://ecritsduforprive.huma-num.fr/ (accessed 15/07/2022) and Jean-Pierre Bardet, Élisabeth Arnoul, and François-Joseph Ruggiu, *Les écrits du for privé en Europe (du Moyen Age à l'époque contemporaine)* (Bordeaux: Presses universitaires de Bordeaux, 2010).

[173] Bennett, 'Every County', 196.

[174] Bennett severely remarks that 'everything recounted by [Lucy Hutchinson] did not happen because of the seeming orbital attraction of John Hutchinson, but because of the tactical potential of the castle and river and the strategic role of the Midlands' ('Every County', 204).

[175] Bennett, 'Every County', 204.

[176] See Adrian, *Local Negotiations* 120. Chapter 6 argues that this combination of the local and national is skillfully achieved with digressions.

Chapter 4
Writing oneself into history
the paradoxes of Lucy Hutchinson's agency

In the final quarter of the *Memoirs* covering the years 1660–1664, Lucy Hutchinson's position changes from witness to actor, as she directly intervenes in Restoration politics. Her position as an agent in history—a status many memoir-writers shared—has the effect of foregrounding her own experience of history and heightening her 'epistemic agency', that is, her authority to deal with history and her ability to make sense of it through writing.[1]

In her account of the Civil Wars, Lucy Hutchinson tends to downplay her agency and confines herself to the role of witness and nurse.[2] Such a conventional distribution of roles changed in the spring of 1660, around the time when the Colonel was elected as a member of the Convention Parliament. From then on until his death in 1664, she appears 'to have had a hand in the management [...] of the transacting of affairs', which puts her in a very favourable position to write historical memoirs.[3] During those years, and especially in 1660–1661 and 1663–1664, she repeatedly stepped out of her sphere to intercede on behalf of the Colonel whose life was at stake. It is this portion of the *Memoirs* which, in many respects, is the closest to the testimonies of Lucy Hutchinson's contemporaries, Ann Fanshawe and Anne Halkett,[4] or of the French *Frondeuses* who, in their own memoirs, gave evidence of their military and diplomatic influence.[5]

---

[1] See Joanne H. Wright, 'Not Just Dutiful Wives and Besotted Ladies: Epistemic Agency in the War Writing of Brilliana Harley and Margaret Cavendish', *Early Modern Women: An Interdisciplinary Journal* 4 (2009). 1–25. See figure 4.1 and book cover.

[2] There are some exceptions as when the Colonel asks his wife to plead his case with Ireton in January 1649 (S191/K236).

[3] See Bailey's definition in *The Universal Etymological English Dictionary*.

[4] See *The Memoirs of Anne, Lady Halkett and Ann, Lady Fanshawe*, ed. John Loftis (Oxford: Clarendon, 1979).

[5] Charbonneau, *Les Silences de l'histoire* 139–40. Memoirs are an important source in Sophie Vergnes, *Les Frondeuses. Une révolte au féminin* (Seyssel: Champ Vallon, 2013). See also Wiseman's important chapter, '"The most considerable of my troubles": Anne Halkett and the Writing of Civil War Conspiracy', *Women Writing, 1550–1750*, ed. J. Wallwork and P. Salzman, Meridian 18.1 (2001): 25–45; Madeleine Bassnet, '"All the ceremonyes and civilityes": The Authorship of Diplomacy in the *Memoirs* of Ann, Lady Fanshawe', *The Seventeenth Century* 26.1 (2011): 94–118.

WRITING ONESELF INTO HISTORY 167

Figure 4.1 Lucy Hutchinson by Robert Walker (engraving) from Lucy Hutchinson's *Memoirs of the Life of Colonel Hutchinson*, ed. *Julius Hutchinson* (London, 1806).

This chapter explores further the links between Lucy Hutchinson, an agent in history, and Lucy Hutchinson, the author of the *Memoirs*. To do so, focusing on the Restoration section of the *Memoirs*, I will look at the way she writes herself into history and ultimately emerges as a fully-fledged historian, whose work must be considered on a par with the other histories of the English Revolution.[6]

1. Gender paradoxes: Lucy Hutchinson taking part in history

In early modern Europe, women were marginalized from politics and excluded from the battlefields. There were nonetheless notable exceptions when women had a direct experience of the war as civilians. This was the case in England, Scotland, and Ireland in the middle of the seventeenth century, but also in France during the wars of religion (1562–1598) or during the Fronde (1648–1653). In those times of trouble, some women played an active role and had their voices heard.[7] To be sure, Lucy Hutchinson was no activist, but, as the Governor's wife, she had a direct experience of the Civil War in Nottinghamshire. As seen in Chapter 3, she probably monitored much of what was going on in the garrison. Furthermore, like many other women of the English Revolution, she played roles she would not have played in times of peace. For example, in her account of the first occupation of Nottingham in September 1643, she mentions that she was obliged to nurse the wounds of the soldiers. Here as elsewhere, her use of the possessive 'our' is indicative of her involvement in the Civil War alongside the Colonel:

> In the encounter one of the Derby Captaines was slaine, and only five of our men hurt, who, for want of another Surgeon were brought to the Governor's wife, and she having some excellent balsoms and plaisters in her closett, with the assistance of a gentleman that had some skill, drest all their wounds (whereof some were dangerous, being all shotts) with such good successe that they were all cured in convenient time.   (S99/K129)[8]

---

[6] Norbrook, 'The English Revolution and English Historiography', 235; Lesne, *La Poétique des mémoires* 263–5; Looser, *British Women Writers* 42–4.

[7] See Cavendish's argument, in her *Life of William Cavendish* [sig. c^v], quoted 27–8. See also Vergne, *Les Frondeuses* and Gheeraert-Graffeuille, *La Cuisine et forum*.

[8] See also, for a similar example, *Memoirs*, ed. Sutherland, 95, and ed. Keeble, 125. Julius Hutchinson reminds us that 'the mother of Mrs. Hutchinson had patronized and assisted Sir Walter Ralegh, when prisoner in the Tower, in his chemical experiments, and had acquired a little knowledge of medicine; whether her daughter had obtained instructions from her mother, or the mother herself was here (for she passed the latter part of her life with her daughter, and died in her house at Owthorpe), is uncertain' (Julius Hutchinson's footnote quoted in *Memoirs*, ed. Firth, 146, note 1).

A similar nursing role was played by many women during the Civil Wars, for instance Anne Halkett who, in her *Memoirs*, reports how she had to dress the wounds of soldiers injured at the battle of Dunbar in September 1650. The circumstances, related in the first person, are close to those described by Lucy Hutchinson:

> I cannot omitt to insert here the opertunity I had of serving many poore wounded soldiers [...] And betwixt that time [Saturday] and Monday that we left that place [Kinrose], I beleeve threescore was the least that was dressed by mee and my woman and Ar. Ro., who I impoyed to such as was unfitt for me to drese; and besides the plaisters and balsom I aplied, I gave everyone of them as much with them as might drese them 3 or 4 times.[9]

As a matter of fact, in these exceptional situations, many women, whatever their stations in life, participated in their own ways in the war effort. Some of them, in their husbands' absence, were even forced to bear arms and defend their besieged properties—this was for example the case of the Puritan Brilliana Harley.[10] As regards Lucy Hutchinson, she recounts how, after the Cavaliers from Newark were beaten out of the city walls in the autumn of 1643, the 'well-affected' women of Nottingham 'were forced' to organize themselves in order 'to prevent the burning':

> Presently after the Cavaliers were gone out of Towne, some naughty people, sett on by them fir'd the Towne, but it was quenched without burning above two or three houses. Yett for a fortnight together it was perpetually attempted, fire being lay'd to haybarnes and other combustible places, insomuch that the weomen were forc'd to walke by fiftie in a night to prevent the burning. (S100/K130)

a) The patriarchal framework

These heroic female actions, because they were understood to be temporary and absolutely necessary, do not call into question the early modern

---

[9] Anne Halkett, 'The Memoirs of Anne, Lady Halkett', *The Memoirs of Anne, Lady Halkett and Ann, Lady Fanshawe* 55. See Wiseman, *Conspiracy of Virtue*, 313–33 (especially 325–7) for her inspirational reading of Anne Halkett's *Memoirs*.
[10] See Antonia Fraser, *The Weaker Vessel. Woman's Lot in Seventeenth-Century England* [1984] (London: Mandarin, 1989) 183–207 and Alison Plowden, *Women All on Fire: The Women of the English Civil War* (Stroud: Sutton Publishing, 1998) 47–60.

patriarchal order, which Lucy Hutchinson largely endorses in the *Memoirs* and in her later writings,[11] for instance, in the preface to the treatise addressed to her daughter,[12] and in her 1675 dedication to the Earl of Anglesey about her Lucretius translation.[13] Likewise, in the *Memoirs,* John Hutchinson is significantly portrayed as an exemplary head of the household, providing for his wife and children, who are sometimes represented as objects, both literally and grammatically. For example, just before the battle of Edgehill, he is said to have 'carried' his wife and children (who had been staying in Leicester) to 'his house' at Owthorpe (S67/K91), about nine miles south-east of Nottingham. In late December 1642, he eventually 'fetcht away his wife and children to Nottingham' (S75/K101) because he found they were no longer safe in Owthorpe. In the same patriarchal vein, Lucy Hutchinson describes men being busy at war while women did the cooking within the castle. There, '*his* weomen, while the men were all otherwise employ'd, had provided him as a large a supper as the time and present condition could permitt, at which he entertain'd all the strangers and his owne Officers and gentlemen' (S98–9/K128, my emphasis).

But the Colonel's authority over the members of his household was always combined with gentleness: 'As he maintain'd his authority in all relations, so he endeavour'd to make their subjection pleasant to them, and rather to convince them by reason than compell them to obedience, and would decline even to the lowest of his famely to make them enjoy their lives in sober cheerefulnesse, and not find their duties burthensome' (S208/K255).[14] As far as the education of his children was concerned, he thus did not use any 'constraint': he being 'their instructor in humillity, sobrietie, and all godlinesse and all vertue, which he rather strove to make them exercise with love and delight than by constraint' (S207/K255). There were strong bonds of affection

---

[11] See Keeble, 'The Colonel's Shadow', 233. See also *Memoirs*, ed. Keeble, xxv; Norbrook, 'Order and Disorder: The Poem and its Contexts', xiii.

[12] See Lucy Hutchinson, *On the Principles of the Christian Religion*, in *The Works of Lucy Hutchinson*, vol. 2, ed. Elizabeth Clarke, David Norbrook, and Jane Stevenson (Oxford: Oxford UP, 2018) 192: 'The Apostle reproaches the weakenesse of our sex more than the other when speaking of the prevalency of seducers he says they lead about silly weomen who are euer learning and neuer able to come to the knowledge of the truth, therefore euerie wise and holy woman ought to watch strictly ouer herselfe that she becomes not one of these.'

[13] See Hutchinson, 'To the Right Honorable Arthur Eale of Anglesey', *The Translation of Lucretius*, part 1, 5–15. She insists that her sex's 'more becomming virtue is silence' (5) and recognizes she 'did attempt things out of [her] owne Sphære' (5). The letter is reproduced in *Memoirs*, ed. Firth, Appendix XXXVII, 451–6. On the letter to the Earl of Anglesey, see Wiseman, *Conspiracy and Virtue* 228 and Shannon Miller, 'Family and Commonwealth in the Writings of Lucy Hutchinson', *The Oxford Handbook of Literature and the English Revolution*, ed. Laura Lunger Knoppers (Oxford: Oxford UP, 1992) 670; Mayer, 'A Life of Writing', 313.

[14] This is a reference to Matthew 11:30: 'For my yoke is easy and my burden is light.'

between them and him. For instance, when he was taken to prison in London on 31 October 1663, 'his wife and his eldest sonne and daughter [went] with him' (S248/K303); his children also visited him in prison, serving as messengers.[15] Finally, on his deathbed, he affectionately addressed his last words—which were words of hope—to his daughter Barbara.[16] It is his benign authority, defined as the opposite of tyranny, that is eventually underlined in respect to the Colonel's domestic government: 'he [...] manag'd the reines of government with such prudence and affection that she who would not delight in such an honourable and advantageable subjection much have wanted a reasonable soule. He govern'd by perswasion, which he never employ'd but to things honorable and profitable for her selfe' (S10/K26). As we have already seen, Lucy Hutchinson was the Colonel's confidant and his companion; in her own words to her he was a friend 'who had wisdom and vertue enough to be trusted with her councells' (S31/K50) and, she adds, 'he lov'd her at such a kind and generous rate as words cannot expresse' (S10/K26).[17]

In the *Memoirs*, the characterization of 'Mrs. Hutchinson' as a good wife and the celebration of other good Protestant women, like John Hutchinson's mother, fit into this patriarchal pattern in which 'Mrs. Hutchinson''s virtue mattered as much as John Hutchinson's integrity.[18] But Lucy Hutchinson's assertion of patriarchal values is far from gratuitous and naïve.[19] It is meant to confer respectability on the full text of the *Memoirs*, and goes hand in hand with Lucy Hutchinson's silence about some of her activities, in particular her translation of the immoral Lucretius.[20] Similarly, her emphasis on the hierarchy between husband and wife, in the Pauline tradition, was a way for her to exonerate her husband from the suspicion of uxoriousness, which her independent behaviour at the Restoration may have aroused.[21] Lucy Hutchinson's ingenious enunciative strategy—which she was not the only memorialist or historian to choose—serves the same purpose.[22] The use of the third person to

---

[15] See *Memoirs*, ed. Sutherland, 272, and ed. Keeble, 306.

[16] See *Memoirs*, ed. Sutherland, 272, and ed. Keeble, 330.

[17] See Chapter 3, 1, a ('Lucy Hutchinson, witness and confidant').

[18] For the description of John Hutchinson's mother, see *Memoirs*, ed. Sutherland, 18, and ed. Keeble, 34.

[19] The representation of Mrs. Hutchinson as a submissive wife serves as a persuasive device. See Seelig, *Autobiography and Gender* 88, and Robert Cockcroft, *Rhetorical Affect in Early Modern Writing. Renaissance Passions Reconsidered* (Basingstoke: Palgrave Macmillan, 2003) 96.

[20] Norbrook, 'Introduction', *The Works of Lucy Hutchinson*, vol. 1, xvi: '[Lucy Hutchinson's] silence about the Lucretius and other more secular writings, sometimes ascribed to an excessive wifely deference, can also be seen as part of her polemical purpose in playing down any elements in John Hutchinson's own background that might temper the image of the pure austere martyr.'

[21] See for example 1 Timothy 2:11–15 and 1 Corinthians 11:3–13.

[22] Edward Hyde, Earl of Clarendon, also makes a distinction between the narrator of history, an occasional 'I', and 'Mr Hyde' to whom he referred in the third person. See Brownley, *Clarendon and the*

designate 'Mrs. Hutchinson' creates a distance between the author—who sometimes intervenes in the first person narration—and the character of 'Mrs. Hutchinson'.[23] To a large extent, this narrative device protects Lucy Hutchinson as the author of the *Memoirs*, while it gives credence and authority to her as a historian of the English Revolution or, as Kate Chedgzoy nicely puts it, as 'an agent of memory'.[24] All in all, the rhetoric of the 'godly household' permeating the *Memoirs* may have been, to use Norbrook's expression, a strategy of 'camouflage' the better to articulate a radical vision of politics and history.[25]

b) Lobbying at the Restoration

The art of 'camouflage'—the emphasis on 'Mrs. Hutchinson''s virtue—was all the more essential as several events before and after 1660 show that she did not always act as a subservient wife.[26] A first instance of Lucy Hutchinson's self-assertion can be illustrated by an early episode, in the autumn of 1642, when John Hutchinson, after refusing to lodge a royalist general in his father's home, had to flee. In his absence, his wife, who found herself at the head of the household, proved extremely resourceful, even managing to make her brother-in-law pass for her husband.[27] For the next twenty years or so, the *Memoirs* stage no other unconventional performance on the part of 'Mrs. Hutchinson';

Rhetoric of Historical Form 51–2. See also Kuperty-Tsur, *Se dire à la Renaissance* 35: the use of the third person is a way to disguise personal discourse and to protect the author. Jean Starobinski, 'Le style de l'autobiographie', *L'Œil vivant II. La Relation critique* (Paris: Gallimard, 2001) 115, my translation: 'The third person creates a narrative that does not differ from history in its form; it is necessary to learn, through external information, that the narrator and the hero of history are one and the same person. [...] The effacing of the narrator (who takes on the impersonal role of historian) and the objective presentation of the protagonist in the third person work to the benefit of the event, and, secondarily, reflect back on the personality of the protagonist the glory of the actions in which he has been involved.'

[23] For examples of authorial interventions, see Chapter 6, 2 ('Narrative digressions: a polemical history of the English Civil Wars').

[24] Chedgzoy et al., 'Researching Memory', 14. Hobby, *Virtue of Necessity* 79; Keeble, 'The Colonel's Shadow', 232–4, 238; *Memoirs*, ed. Keeble, xxv–xxvii; Longfellow, *Women and Religious Writing* 180. Susan Staves, *A Literary History of Women's Writing in Britain, 1660–1789* (Cambridge: Cambridge UP, 2006) 40.

[25] Norbrook argues that the 'domestic setting' (her children's schoolroom), in which Lucy Hutchinson claims to have translated Lucretius, was 'camouflage' ('Lucy Hutchinson's Elegies', 483). For a similar interpretation, see Longfellow, *Women and Religious Writing* 180–1.

[26] This aspect is studied in detail in Claire Gheeraert-Graffeuille, 'Lucy Hutchinson : Bonne épouse ou femme rebelle ?', *Les Femmes et leurs représentations en Angleterre de la Renaissance aux Lumières*, ed. Marlène Bernos, Sandrine Parageau, and Laetitia Sansonetti (Paris: Nouveau Monde Editions, 2009) 81–94; Keeble, 'The Colonel's Shadow', 227–47; Seelig, *Autobiography and Gender* 88, Mayer, 'A Life of Writing', 313; Hobby, *Virtue of Necessity* 79–84.

[27] See Chapter 5, 2, c ('Confused identities').

but, after the Rump was recalled in 1659, the situations in which she played a man's role and displayed a spirit of independence multiplied.[28] She thus distinguished herself when there was a royalist conspiracy hatched against her family: 'the plott was layd that fifty men neere the Collonell's house should [...] take my Lord's Arms away, with all the rest of the Collonell's that they could find' (S217/K266). After the betrayal actually took place, and was disclosed to her by a young page, 'Mrs. Hutchinson'—who was alone at Owthorpe with her children—hid her 'plate and jewells and what she had of vallue' (S217/K267) and had her house guarded. Her settling the business alone without telling her husband was a first act of disobedience to which critics have not paid much attention; it nonetheless paved the way for the lies she would have to invent at the Restoration:

> Mrs. Hutchinson, not willing to take for all this such publick notice of [Ivie's] treason as to cast him into prison, tooke him immediately to London with her, and sayd nothing till he came there, and then told him how base and treacherous he had bene; but to save her own shame for having entertain'd so false a person, and for her mother's sake whom he had formerly serv'd, she was willing to dismisse him privately without acquainting the Collonell.
> (S218/K267)

On several occasions after 1660, political circumstances compelled Lucy Hutchinson to subvert gender roles.[29] The lives of the former regicides were then at stake: the Colonel was no exception, and she had to defend him by all means, regardless of patriarchal prohibitions.[30] The atmosphere at Court and in Parliament was one of revenge: '[t]he Presbiterians [...] fell a thirsting, then hunting after blood, and urging that God's blessing could not be upon the land till justice had cleans'd it from the late king's blood' (S227/K278). General Monk was 'as forward to sett vengeance on foote as any man' (S229/K280). Yet, the Declaration of Breda, read in Parliament on 1 May 1660, manifested the King's clemency and benevolence by allowing, for forty days, every subject to 'lay hold upon [the King's] grace and favour':

---

[28] See also Norbrook, 'Lucy Hutchinson's Elegies', 482-3.

[29] See Miller, 'Family and Commonwealth', 669-85: Miller argues that a positive vision of female agency is to be found in Lucy Hutchinson's translation of Lucretius (probably written in the 1650s) and in her Christian epic, *Order and Disorder* (probably written after the *Memoirs*).

[30] The Colonel's name figured for instance in a broadside of 8 May 1660, entitled *The Great Memorial: or, A list of the names of those pretended judges who sate, and sentenced our late sovereign King Charles the First, in the place which they called the High Court of Justice, January 27. 1648* (London, 1660). More examples in Norbrook, 'Memoirs and Oblivion', 241-2.

> We do by these Presents declare, That We do grant a free and general Pardon, which We are ready upon Demand to pass under our Great Seal of *England*, to all Our Subjects, of what Degree or Quality soever, who, within Forty Days after the Publishing hereof, shall lay Hold upon this Our Grace and Favour, and shall by any Public Act declare their doing so and that they return to the Loyalty and Obedience of good Subjects (excepting only such Persons as shall hereafter be excepted by Parliament).[31]

The declaration interestingly specifies that there would be some exception in the King's 'free and general Pardon', and that those exceptions would be decided by Parliament.[32] The difficulty of deciding who among the regicides would be excepted explains why the bill of Indemnity and Oblivion was discussed for almost four months before being enacted on 29 August 1660. It is in this context of emergency that Lucy Hutchinson's determination to have the Colonel's name included in the Bill of Indemnity and Oblivion must be understood.[33]

The paradox is that Lucy Hutchinson presents her lobbying as necessary and logical, while still supporting conservative patriarchal values. She would probably not have objected to the stipulation in the 1632 *Lawes Resolutions of Womens Rights*, a legal compilation about the rights of English women, that 'Women have no voyse in Parliament, They make no Lawes, they consent to none, they abrogate none.'[34] And she would probably have accepted the assumption that women's exclusion from politics originated in Eve's original sin: 'Eve because shee had helped to seduce her husband hath inflicted on her, an especiall bane. In sorrow shalt thou bring forth thy children, thy desires shall bee subject to thy husband, and he shall rule over thee.'[35] At any rate, Lucy Hutchinson had the utmost contempt for Henrietta Maria, the Catholic Queen, to whom King Charles 'became a most uxorious husband' (S46/K67). In the *Memoirs*, she accuses her of being the cause and origin of all the evils that befell the kingdom of England and, ultimately, of the Civil War:

---

[31] https://www.british-history.ac.uk/lords-jrnl/vol11/pp6-9#h3-0009 (accessed 09/07/2019). On the Restoration, see Tim Harris, *Restoration: Charles II and his Kingdoms* (London: Penguin, 2005) 1–84.

[32] On the Declaration of Breda, see Keeble, *The Restoration* 67–70.

[33] On the 'Act of Oblivion', see Keeble, *The Restoration* 70–6. See also *Memoirs*, ed. Keeble, 372, note 311. On John Hutchinson, see Wood, *Nottinghamshire in the Civil War* 183–4 and Norbrook, 'Memoirs and Oblivion', 240–1.

[34] Thomas Edgar, *The Lawes Resolutions of Womens Rights: Or, The Lawes Provision for Woemen* (London, 1632) 6.

[35] Edgar, *The Lawes Resolutions* sig. B3ᵛ.

the King had another instigator of his owne violent purpose, more powerfull than all the rest, and that was the Queene, who, growne out of her childhood, began to turne her mind from those vaine extravagancies she liv'd in at first to that which did lesse become her, and was more fatall to the kingdome, which never is in any place happie where the hands that are made only for distaffes affect the management of Sceptres. (S48/K70)

She also alludes to the compromising letters of the Queen seized at the battle of Naseby and to their sensational publication in pamphlet format. These did not only manifest the 'falsehood' of the King but also proved that he had 'given himselfe up to be govern'd by the Queene in all affairs both of State and religion' (S160/K200).[36] Lady Fairfax's sway over her husband was equally despicable to Lucy Hutchinson: with the help of her Presbyterian chaplains—pictured as analogous to Henrietta Maria's Catholic priests—she estranged the General from many of his friends as early as 1646 and made him resign his commission as General of the New Model Army on the eve of the war with Scotland on 25 June 1650. According to Lucy Hutchinson, this resignation was again the result of Fairfax's uxoriousness and the responsibility of an Eve-like Lady Fairfax: 'But this greate man was then as unmoovable by his friends as pertinacious in obeying his wife; whereby he then died to all his former glory, and became the monument of his owne name, which every day wore out' (S195/K241).[37] The list of dangerous women interfering in politics in the *Memoirs* also includes Mary Stuart, 'a wicked Queene' (S39/K59), and Lady Lambert, as 'proud as her husband' (S204/K251).[38] Meanwhile, and quite paradoxically, Lucy Hutchinson celebrates 'the felicity of [Queen Elizabeth's] reigne' as 'the effect of her submission to her masculine and wise Councellors' (S48/K70), thus offering an alternative view of a female sovereign who was nevertheless famous for claiming that she had 'the heart and stomach of a king'.[39]

---

[36] See *The Kings Cabinet Opened; or, Certain Packets of Secret Letters and Papers Written with the Kings Own Hand and Taken in His Cabinet at Nasby-Field* (London, 1645).

[37] For an alternative view, see Thomas Fairfax, *Short Memorials of Thomas Lord Fairfax Written by Himself* (London, 1699): 'Thus have I given you the Sum of the most considerable Things, for which the World may Censure me, during this unhappy War; and I hope in all my Weakness and Failings there shall not be found Crimes of that Magnitude to make me numbred with those who have done these Things through Ambition and Dissimulation' (128). See David Underdown, *Pride's Purge. Politics in the Puritan Revolution* (Oxford: Clarendon, 1971) 190.

[38] Interestingly Madame de Motteville writes that 'Ladies are usually the first causes of the greatest overthrows of states; and the wars which ruin kingdoms and empires almost always proceed from the effects produced by their beauty or their malice' (*Mémoires de Madame de Motteville, pour servir à l'histoire d'Anne d'Autriche* [Paris, 1822], vol. 1, 209, my translation).

[39] See Carole Levin, *The Heart and Stomach of a King: Elizabeth and the Politics of Sex and Power*, 2nd edition (Philadelphia: U of Pennsylvania P, 1993).

These references to overbearing wives echo the literature of the times, from the Civil War pamphlets to Milton's condemnation, in *Eikonoklastes*, of the 'magistrates' who are 'govern'd and oversuaid at home under a Feminine usurpation'.[40] They throw a negative light on Lucy Hutchinson's decision at the Restoration to disobey her husband: 'Mrs. Hutchinson [...] saw that he was ambitious of being a publick sacrifice, and therefore, herein only in her whole life, resolv'd to disobey him' (S229/K280).[41] In these pages, 'Mrs. Hutchinson' manipulates the Colonel's feelings and his sense of familial duty: 'to emproove all the affection he had to her for his safety, [she] prevail'd with him to retire; for she sayd she would not live to see him a prisoner' (S229/K280). Further down, Lucy Hutchinson reports how she even acted as the Colonel's mentor—and no longer his confidant—this time to prevent him from answering the 14 May proclamation which asked him to surrender.[42] By so doing, she went against his opinion and the advice of his friends. Her psychological sway— which continues to be presented as a negative influence here—is most blatant when she makes him promise not to sacrifice himself without her accord:

> Collonell Hutchinson, not being of the number of those seven [who were excluded from the Act], was advised by all his friends to surrender himselfe in order to securing his estate, and he was very earnest to doe it, when Mrs. Hutchinson would by no means heare of it; but being exceedingly urg'd by her friends that she would hereby obstinately loose all their estate, she would not yet consent that the Collonell should give himselfe into custody, and she had wrought him to a strong engagement that he would not dispose of himselfe without her.   (S229/K281)

The climax of Lucy Hutchinson's 'endeavours and labours' (S234/K286), however, consists in her decision to forge 'a letter in [the Colonel's] name to

---

[40] John Milton, *Eikonoklastes* [1649], in *Complete Prose Works*), vol. 3, ed. Merritt Y. Hughes (New Haven: Yale UP, 1962) 420–21: 'He ascribes *Rudeness and barbarity worse then Indian* to the English Parliament and *all virtue* to his Wife [...]. Examples are not farr to seek, how great mischief and dishonour hath befall'n to Nations under the Government of effeminate and Uxorious Magistrates. Who being themselves govern'd and oversuaid at home under a Feminine usurpation, cannot but be far short of spirit and authority without dores, to govern a whole Nation.' For more examples in pamphlets, see Gheeraert-Graffeuille, *La Cuisine et le forum* 366–73.

[41] According to Norbrook, Lucy Hutchinson could well have been aware of Katherine Philips's action on behalf of her husband, the regicide James Philips. See 'Memoirs and Oblivion', 257. Many wives wrote petitions to defend their husbands. This was the case of Leveller wives who indefatigably demanded the release of their imprisoned husbands between 1649 and 1653. See, for example, *To the Supream Authority of this Nation, the Commons Assembled in Parliament: The humble petition Of divers wel-affected Women* (24 April 1649).

[42] See *Memoirs*, ed. Sutherland, 230, and ed. Keeble, 281. See *Memoirs*, ed. Firth, 322, note 2.

the Speaker', in which he begged 'his liberty upon his parolle, till they should finally determine of him' (S229/K281).[43] Her course of action was discrepant with the views of the Colonel (who was hiding) and of his friends regarding the political strategy to adopt in order to save him. Her point was therefore to justify her divergence from them and to explain that her decision, however transgressive, was the only acceptable one.[44] The phrasing of the following paragraph, and notably the choice of verbs, testifies to her agency and determination of acting in her own right, as she thought best. Her goal—to save her husband—justified all means, including calculation and counterfeiting:

[she] being oppos'd both by himselfe and all his friends, and accus'd of obstinacy in not giving him up, att length devis'd a way to trie the House, and writt a letter in his name to the Speaker [...]. Which letter she conceiv'd would trie the temper of the house: if they granted this, she had her end, for he was still free; if they denied it, she might be satisfied in keeping him from surrend'ring himself. (S229–30/K281)

Nowhere does Lucy Hutchinson play down the gravity of her action which, in the end, proved fruitful: '[he] was voted to be free without any engagement, and his punishment only to be discharg'd from the present Parliament, and from all office, military or civill, in the State for ever' (S230/K281).[45] She even confesses that she did not have time to show the letter to her husband because she had a very special opportunity to send it through 'a friend', namely a political ally of hers. The verb 'contrive' and the other action verbs of the

---

[43] See 'Petition of Colonel Hutchinson to the House of Commons, June 1660', *Memoirs*, ed. Firth, Appendix XXXIV, 446–8, and *Memoirs*, ed. Sutherland, 290–2. According to Norbrook this episode 'forms a high point of the *Memoirs*' ('Memoirs and Oblivion', 234), while Derek Hirst calls it 'the turning-point of Lucy Hutchinson's life' ('Remembering a Hero', 683).

[44] Norbrook, 'Memoirs and Oblivion', 256. Norbrook argues that from a legal angle, Lucy Hutchinson acted as a *feme coverte* and, in this respect, it can be said that the responsibility for her lobbying was accepted by her husband, and was therefore not *public*.

[45] See *Memoirs*, ed. Firth, 325, note 2. 'The *Commons Journals* state, June 5, 1660: "Mr Speaker communicates a letter dated the 5th of June 1660, directed to himself and signed by Colonel Hutchinson, who was one of those who sat in judgment upon the late King's majesty when sentence of death was pronounced against him, which was read. Resolved that Colonel John Hutchinson be at liberty on his own parole to be given to Mr. Speaker. On June 9th, the House went on to vote that Colonel John Hutchinson, (1) Be discharged from being a member of this House; (2) Be incapable of bearing any office of place of public trust in his kingdom. (3) In respect of his signal repentance [the 5th of June letter], shall not be within that clause of exception in the Act of general pardon and oblivion, as to any fine, or forfeiture of any part of his estate not purchased of or belonging to the public.' See *House of Commons Journal*, vol. 8, 5 June 1660, https://www.british-history.ac.uk/commons-jrnl/vol8/p56 and vol. 8, 9 June 1660, https://www.british-history.ac.uk/commons-jrnl/vol8/pp59-61 (accessed 05/11/2019). The Act of Indemnity and Oblivion was passed on 29 August 1660.

passage show that she acted as a crafty politician, taking full responsibility for the counterfeiting with no qualms of conscience:

> Having contriv'd and written this letter, before she carried it to the Collonell a friend came to her out of the House, neere which her lodgings then were, and told her if they had had but any ground to begin, the House was that day in a most excellent temper towards her husband; whereupon she writt her husband's name to the letter, and ventur'd to send it in, being us'd sometimes to write the letters he dictated, and her character not much different from his. (S230/K281)

As evidenced above, Lucy Hutchinson did not act on her own, however: she had an efficient and supportive network of relationships, both family and friends, with, at its centre, her brother, the royalist Sir Allen Apsley, who, as we have already seen, was fully dedicated to serving his sister's interests, even at the cost of lies and make-believe. Her portrayal of this gentleman as cunning and unscrupulous bears the mark of Machiavellianism which, in the early Restoration context, appears to have been the main mode of action for all those who wanted to save their skins:

> Sir Allen Apsley too, who, with all the kindest zeale of friendship that can be imagin'd, endeavour'd to bring off the Collonell, had us'd some artifice in engaging friends for him. There was a young gentleman, a kinsman of his, who thirstily aspir'd at preferrment, and Sir Allen had given him hopes, upon his effectuall endeavours for the Collonell, to introduce him; who, being a person that had understanding enough, made no conscience of truth when an officious lie might serve his turne. (S230/K282)

It is remarkable to see how in these pages Lucy Hutchinson unashamedly praises Sir Allen, who, in order to help her, used his network—notably Chancellor Edward Hyde and an MP, Allen Brodrick—with great dexterity and efficiency, but with no regard for the ethical dimension of his actions.[46] He 'sollicited all his friends, as it had bene for his own life, and divers honorable persons drew up a certificate, with all the advantage they could, to procure him favour' (S232/K284).[47]

---

[46] On Sir Allen's connections, especially Sir Allen Brodrick and Sir Edward Hyde, see Norbrook, 'Memoirs and Oblivion', 246–7, 252–3 and 'Appendix 2: John Hutchinson's supporters', 280.

[47] For the 'certificate', see *Memoirs,* ed. Firth, Appendix XXXXV, 449–50. Norbrook comments on all the signatories of the 'certificate' and establishes their links with the Hutchinsons. See 'Memoirs and Oblivion', 253–4.

According to his sister, his role, which implied lying, was precious: 'Sir Allen Apsley's interest and most fervent endeavours for him was that which only weigh'd the scales' (S233/K285). This was, however, only a temporary victory. Soon, Lord Lexington got the upper hand and, 'the very last day in a huddle gott the bill past the Lords' House' (S233/K285), which meant that special provisoes could still be voted and added to the Act of Oblivion. For the Hutchinsons, it signified that their property and estate were once again jeopardized. As a result of this new development, in the autumn of 1660, 'Mrs. Hutchinson' was 'sent up' by the Colonel 'to sollicit his businesse in the house, that the Lord Lexington's Bill might not passe the lower house' (S236/K289). She proved extremely resolute, resorting to the same unscrupulous methods as her brother, addressing directly an ally of the Chancellor who was not favourable at all to her husband. Writing several years after it occurred, she did not fail to mention that she was behaving in accordance with God's will:

> at her first coming to Towne a Parliament man, a creature of Worcester House [the London residence of Edward Hyde], being in his coach, she out of hers call'd to him, who was her kinsman, and desir'd his vigilancy to prevent her injury. "I could wish," sayd he, "it had bene finisht last time, for your husband hath lately so ill behav'd himselfe that it will passe against him." To whom she answer'd, "I pray," said she, "lett my friends but doe their endeavours for me, and then lett it be as God will." He, smiling att her, replied, "It is not now as God will, but as wee will." However she, notwithstanding many other discouragements, waited upon the businesse every day, when her adversaries as diligently sollicited against her. (S236/K289)

Three years later, after the Colonel was arrested, the context was very different as Lucy Hutchinson now accepted her husband's desire for martyrdom, but her commitment to defending him remained steadfast throughout his eleven months' imprisonment, first at Newark, then in the Tower, and finally at Sandown Castle. Again, she solicited the authorities to defend her husband and estate—in particular she was a suitor to the Privy Council[48]—but, as months went by, she appeared to be more and more resigned to the Colonel's self-sacrifice.

---

[48] See *Memoirs*, ed. Sutherland, 253, and ed. Keeble, 308.

2. Autobiographical memoirs: Coming to grips with one's past

The final section of the *Memoirs* (1660–1664) is still historical—it is the history of the Restoration directly seen through Lucy Hutchinson's eyes. However, by interweaving history and the author's experience, they take on an autobiographical edge and, in many ways, the 'Life of John Hutchinson' can be read as a 'Life of Lucy Hutchinson' too.[49] As a matter of fact, it often happens that authors of historical memoirs, even though they are not the main protagonists of their own narratives, are still writing about themselves.[50] For example, the *Memoirs*, written by Charlotte Duplessis-Mornay about her husband, a Huguenot apologist and the architect of the Edict of Nantes, are also about her own life.[51] Likewise, in the latter half of the seventeenth century, the *Mémoires pour servir à l'histoire d'Anne d'Autriche* by Madame de Motteville offer not only a portrait of the Queen but also that of her confidant.[52] A similar duality can be found in *The Memoirs of the Life of Colonel Hutchinson*, as the intelligibility sought by Lucy Hutchinson is not only historical but also personal.[53] This autobiographical dimension has fascinated generations of scholars and readers since the publication of the text in 1806. Nineteenth-century British readers, who were enthralled by the character of Lucy Hutchinson, the good wife of the Puritan Revolution, have drawn biographies of Lucy Hutchinson from

---

[49] Norbrook, 'Memoirs and Oblivion', 236. The *Memoirs* is a text 'deliberately shaped and phrased and reflecting a particular authorial identity'.

[50] This is not so surprising since '[t]he seventeenth century recognized no clear general distinction between the writing of a life and the writing of one's life' (Mayer, *History and the English Novel* 78). On the connections between biography and autobiography, see Mayer and Woolf, *Rhetorics of Life-Writing*, 8 and note 37; Briot, 'L'égotropisme des Mémoires', *Usage du monde, usage de soi*, 115–46, especially 117. See also Kathleen Lynch, 'Inscribing the Early Modern Self. The Materiality of Autobiography', *A History of English Biography*, ed. Adam Smyth (Cambridge: Cambridge UP, 2016), 56–69, here 65–7.

[51] See Kuperty-Tsur, *Se dire à la Renaissance* 86 and Charlotte Duplessis-Mornay, *Les Mémoires de Madame de Mornay*, ed. Nadine Kuperty-Tsur (Paris : Honoré Champion, 2010). On Charlotte Duplessis-Mornay, see Susan Broomhall and Colette H. Winn, 'Femmes, écriture, foi : les Mémoires de Madame Duplessis-Mornay', *Albineana. Cahiers d'Aubigné* 18 (2006) : 587–604. On Duplessis-Mornay writing a defence of her husband, see Nadine Kuperty-Tsur, 'Le portrait de Philippe Duplessis-Mornay dans les mémoires de son épouse : entre hagiographie et apologie', *Albineana. Cahiers d'Aubigné* 18 (2006) 565–85.

[52] Fumaroli, 'La Confidente de la reine', 165.

[53] See Seelig, *Autobiography and Gender* 82; Line Cottegnies, 'The Garden and the Tower: Pastoral Retreat and Configuration of the Self in Auto/Biography', *Mapping the Self: Space, Identity, Discourse in British Auto/Biography*, ed. Frédéric Regard and Geoffrey Wall (Saint-Étienne: Publications de l'Université de Saint-Étienne, 2003) 125–44. Cottegnies considers that Hutchinson and Cavendish's 'Lives' of their husbands are 'modes of self-expression' (141). See Lesne, *La Poétique des mémoires* 394: 'The distinction between historical Memoirs and pre-autobiographical Memoirs is not based on fundamentally different subject matter, but on the type of intelligibility that was sought, either historical or personal' (my translation).

the 'Life' of her husband.[54] In France, the autobiographical dimension of the *Memoirs* was pointed out by Guizot's daughter, Henriette Guizot de Witt, in her book *Les femmes dans l'histoire*: 'Lady Fanshawe and Mistriss Hutchinson both wrote their husbands' lives; as a consequence of which they also wrote—almost unintentionally and unknowingly—their own lives.'[55]

Obviously Philippe Lejeune's definition of autobiography as a '[r]etrospective prose narration written by a real person concerning his [or her] own existence, where the focus is his [or her] individual life, in particular the story of his [or her] personality' does not fully apply to the *Memoirs*, and would be anachronistic.[56] But, as Kathleen Lynch has pointed out in her study of *Protestant Autobiography in the Seventeenth-Century Anglophone World*, the term 'autobiography' is nevertheless suitable to analyse early modern texts because 'as a controlling generic term [it] best keeps in focus the hermeneutic challenges of grappling with the relations among auto (self), bio (life), and graphe (writing).'[57] In the seventeenth century the analysis of an individual's psychology and personality came only second to the investigation of the relation of the self with others, with history and with God.[58] This enquiry was very much the focus of Lucy Hutchinson in the Restoration section of the *Memoirs*: by re-enacting her husband's life and her role in his life, she was trying, within a providential framework, to come to terms with both history and her own grief. To put it in a more scholarly way, writing the life of her husband was a self-fashioning strategy, that is, a way of giving shape and meaning to her identity through the narration. In other words, the art of narrative emplotment was crucial in the construction of what we may call, after *Ricœur*, Lucy Hutchinson's 'narrative identity'.[59]

---

[54] See, for instance, Camilla Newton Crosland, *Memorable Women: The Story of Their Lives* (Boston, 1854); Lydia Maria Francis Child, *Good Wives*, Lady's Family Library, vol. 3 (New York: C. S. Francis, 1855); William Russell, *Extraordinary Women: Their Girlhood and Early Life* (London, 1857); Charles Bruce, ed., *The Book of Noble English Women: Lives Made Illustrious by Heroism* (Edinburgh: William P. Nimmo, 1875); Samuel Burder, Thomas Gibbons, and George Jerment, eds., *Memoirs of Eminently Pious Women*, revised edition, 2 vols. (London, 1827), vol. 2.

[55] See Henriette Guizot de Witt, *Les femmes dans l'histoire*, 2nd edition (Paris, 1889) 187 (my translation).

[56] Philippe Lejeune, *On Autobiography [Le Pacte autobiographique, 1971]*, trans. Katherine Leary (Minneapolis: U of Mineapolis P, 1989) 5, quoted in Lloyd Davis, 'Critical Debates and Early Modern Autobiography', *Early Modern Autobiography: Theories, Genres, Practices*, ed. Ronald Bedford, Lloyd Davis, and Philippa Kelly (Ann Arbor: U of Michigan P, 2006) 22–3. See also Bedford, Davis, and Kelly, *Early Modern English Lives* 6–7.

[57] Lynch, *Protestant Autobiography* 12.

[58] Norbrook, '*Order and Disorder*: The Poem and its Contexts', xiii: 'Hutchinson's writings are in a fundamental sense passionately personal, but the passion was informed by a complex and coherent set of political and religious ideas.'

[59] Paul Ricœur, *Time and Narrative*, vol. 3, trans. Kathleen Blamey and David Pallauer (Chicago: U of Chicago P, 1988) 246–9, here 246: 'As the literary analysis of autobiography confirms, the story of

From this perspective, the *Memoirs* can be construed as a prequel to Lucy Hutchinson's autobiographical fragment, which had probably been written around 1671, and not earlier as has long been thought.[60] While the *Memoirs* intertwine the Colonel's life with England's national history, the autobiographical fragment weaves together Lucy Hutchinson's life with a mythical version of England's history.[61] In a very similar way, Lucy Hutchinson's elegies do not discard history, as her grief appears to be inseparable from the Puritan defeat and her husband's ensuing martyrdom.[62] In these lyrical texts as in the *Memoirs*, she tries to make sense of her decision to act against her husband's advice and desire at the Restoration, a course of action which haunts her works.[63] Was she right to disobey her husband and go against his calling to be a martyr? The text does not provide any simple answer. Did Lucy Hutchinson have any regrets when she wrote the *Memoirs*? Should she have supported her husband's desire for public sacrifice and kept silent? The fact that, within the same paragraph, she returns four times to the Colonel's 'preservation' or 'deliverance', seems to point to her own uneasiness about the providential interpretation she offers. She is showing no real enthusiasm, as if this interpretation was a rational choice, guided by resignation:

> notwithstanding that he himselfe, by a wonderfull over-ruling providence of God, in that day was preserved, yett he look'd upon himselfe as judg'd in their judgement, and executed in their execution; and although he was most thankfull to God, yett he was not very well satisfied in himselfe for accepting the deliverance. And his wife, who thought she had never deserv'd so well of

---

a life continues to be refigured by all the truthful or fictive stories a subject tells about himself or herself. This refiguration makes this life itself a cloth woven of stories told.' See also Dosia Reichardt, 'The Constitution of Narrative Identity in Seventeenth-Century Prison Writing', Bedford, Davis, and Kelly, *Early Modern Autobiographies* 115–30, and Johann Michel, 'Narrativité, narration, narratologie: du concept ricœurien d'identité narrative aux sciences sociales', *Revue européenne des sciences sociales* 41.125 (2003): 125–42.

[60] 'The Life of Mrs. Lucy Hutchinson, Written by Herself. *A Fragment*', *Memoirs*, ed. Sutherland, 278–89, and ed. Keeble, 3–15. The manuscript of this fragment is lost. See Introduction, 19. For the dating, Norbrook, 'Lucy Hutchinson: Theology, Gender and Translation', 141, and 'Memoirs and Oblivion', 257. The dating is based on Lucy Hutchinson referring to 'my house at Owthorpe' in her autobiography, the possessive 'my' indicating that, when she wrote that text, she was the sole owner of Owthorpe (which was sold in 1672 to John Hutchinson's half-brother, Charles Hutchinson).

[61] On the interaction between autobiographical narratives and histories, see Maryline Crivello and Jean-Noël Pelen, 'Avant-propos', *Individu, récit, histoire* (Aix-en-Provence : Presses universitaires de Provence, 2008) 5–10.

[62] Norbrook, 'Lucy Hutchinson's Elegies', 470–2. On the continuity between the *Memoirs* and the 'Elegies', see Miller, 'Family and Commonwealth', 681.

[63] Norbrook, 'Margaret Cavendish and Lucy Hutchinson', 192–3. According to Norbrook, '[Lucy Hutchinson's] betrayal in miniature was the betrayal of the whole nation which abandoned its chance of republican liberty to welcome back the King. Her guilt left a deep emotional scar which informed and perhaps provoked all Hutchinson's later writings.'

him as in the endeavours and labours she exercis'd to bring him off, never displeas'd him more in her life, and had much adoe to perswade him to be contented with his deliverance; which, as it was eminently wrought by God, he acknowledg'd it with thankfulnesse, but while he saw others suffer, he suffer'd with them in his mind, and, had not his wife perswaded him, had offer'd himselfe a voluntary sacrifice. But being by her convinc'd that God's eminent appearance seem'd to have singled him out for preservation, he with thankes acquiesced in that thing. (S234/K286)

Lucy Hutchinson's ambivalent account of her lobbying—which Lobo calls 'anxious'—does not answer any questions, but causes more perplexity in the reader.[64] Was she right to behave like Henrietta Maria or Lady Fairfax and go against her husband's wishes to the point of provoking his anger?[65] Was she not, like these overbearing women, re-enacting Eve's sin? The 'Elegies', probably composed around the same time as the *Memoirs*, are permeated with a strong sense of guilt and represent the poet's disobedience as a sin.[66] In Elegy [2A], she confesses her 'sad remorce & ugly guilt', considering that by trying to save her husband, she had betrayed him and failed in her role as a good wife, in a way very similar to Eve. In a tragic rephrasing of Petrarchan commonplaces, and in the first person, Lucy Hutchinson accuses herself of the sin of pride and sees herself as wholly responsible for killing the Colonel, which she never does in the *Memoirs*:

>if on my sinn defiled self I gaze
>my nakednesse & spots do me amaze
>if on thee a private glance reflect
>confusion does my shamefull eyes deject
>Seeing ye man I Love by me betrayd,
>By me who for his mutual help was made.
>Who to preserve thy life ought to haue dyed,
>& I haue killd' thee by my foolish pride.[67]

These lines from Elegy [2A], which describe Eve's 'woeful state' after the Fall, were presumably copied from the manuscript of Lucy Hutchinson's Christian

---

[64] Lobo, 'Lucy Hutchinson's Revisions of Conscience', 318.
[65] Cf. Chronology in Norbrook, '*Order and Disorder*: The Poem and its Contexts', x.
[66] On Lucy Hutchinson's 'Elegies' and their interpretation in the Restoration context, see Wiseman, *Conspiracy and Virtue* 209–29.
[67] Elegy [2A], ed. Norbrook, ll. 33–8, 491. The same lines are to be found in *Order and Disorder*, Canto 5, v. 431–8, 79.

epic, *Order and Disorder*, which is a rewriting of the Book of Genesis.[68] In the 'Elegies" manuscript, a note, also presumably written by Julius Hutchinson (the grandfather of the first editor), specifies that the context of these lines was the Colonel's imprisonment.[69] Besides, the conflation between the characters of Eve and Lucy Hutchinson is echoed in an earlier passage from the fifth Canto of *Order and Disorder*, where the Devil's 'forgery'—which is a transparent reference to Lucy Hutchinson's own forgery—is confused with truth:[70]

> His lies could never have prevailed on Eve
> But that she wished them truth, and did believe
> *A forgery* that suited her desire,
> Whose haughty heart was prone enough to aspire.[71]

What Lucy Hutchinson's identification with Eve suggests is that, by the time she was writing these lines, she was bitterly regretting her decision to have signed a letter in the name of the Colonel and somehow considered herself a traitor entirely responsible for his Fall.[72]

The *Memoirs*, however, allow for a more positive interpretation of Lucy Hutchinson's lobbying than transpires in the 'Elegies' and *Order and Disorder*. Her activism can indeed be construed as an extension of her duties as a wife, namely as the only possible way for her to preserve the integrity of her household and the many interests—political, religious, economic—she shared with the Colonel. Moreover, the argument of the imminent ruin of their families was commonly put forward by Civil War women as justifications for political action. It was for example used by Leveller wives who petitioned Parliament to obtain the release of their husbands from prison. In their petitions, the defence and protection of their households were pivotal.[73] Of

---

[68] Elegy [2A], ed. Norbrook, ll. 30, 490. See Sarah C. E. Ross, '"I see our nerer, to be reenterd paradice": Lucy Hutchinson's "Elegies" and *Order and Disorder*', *Women, Poetry, and Politics in Seventeenth-Century Britain* (Oxford: Oxford UP, 2015) 174–210, here 188–9.

[69] Elegy [2A], ed. Norbrook, 491. 'Mem^{dm} these verses were writ by Mrs Hutchinson on the occasion of ye Coll: her Husbands being then a prisoner in ye Tower: 1664.'

[70] See Norbrook, '*Order and Disorder*: The Poem and its Contexts', xvi: 'The date on the only surviving manuscript of the poem is 1664.' For hypotheses concerning the date of composition see xvi–xvii. The first five Cantos were published in 1679. The manuscript, now kept at Yale University Library, originally belonged to Anne Wilmot, Countess of Rochester (liii).

[71] Hutchinson, *Order and Disorder*, Canto 5, v. 44–7, 66. On the representation of original sin as forgery, see Norbrook, 'Memoirs and Oblivion', 270.

[72] See Miller, 'Women Writers and the Narrative of the Fall', *The History of British Women's Writing*, vol. 3, ed. Suzuki, 64–79, here 71–4.

[73] Ann Hughes, 'Gender and Politics in Leveller Literature', *Political Culture and Cultural Politics in Early Modern England*, ed. Susan Dwyer Amussen and Mark A. Kishlansky (Manchester: Manchester UP, 1995) 162–89.

course, considering Lucy Hutchinson's lobbying from this contemporary perspective does not dispel all the contradictions in the text, but allows us to see some logic in her intervention. Thus, in June 1660, in order not to have the Colonel's name included in the Act of Indemnity and Oblivion, the author of the forged letter—who was either Lucy Hutchinson impersonating her husband or, more probably, both she and he collaborating[74]—tried to arouse the compassion of the House by using this rhetoric: 'though I acknowledge myself involved in so horrid a crime as merits no indulgence, yet having a miserable family that must, though innocent, share all my ruin, I cannot but beg the honourable House would not exclude me from the refuge of the King's most gracious pardon.'[75] In 1664, after the Colonel had spent three months in prison ('from November till Candlemasse terme' [S253/K308]), following his advice, she went to see Secretary Bennet 'to urge to [him] the mischiefe and ruine her husband's imprisonment brought upon his famely and estate' (S254/K309-10), again using the same rhetoric.

Seen from this angle, lobbying was not synonymous with transgression and did not contradict the norms of wifely duty;[76] it was legitimate and sensible, a manifestation of dutifulness to her family, at a time when the Hutchinson household was in dire straits, especially after 'certeine pictures and other things the Collonell had bought out of the late king's Collection [...] were all taken from him' (S239/K292).[77] In addition, Lucy Hutchinson's decision was in line with the advice of Protestant ministers who listed a number of situations in which women, who were in charge of the well-being of their families, were allowed to act without their husbands' consents. According to the Puritan minister Daniel Rogers, there were some cases—'hazarde of estate, children, yea liberty it self'—in which a wife was allowed to disobey for the sake of conscience and expediency. These were indeed the very situations with which Lucy Hutchinson was confronted:

---

[74] Norbrook considers the writing the letter to Parliament was a 'shared responsibility' ('Memoirs and Oblivion', 270).

[75] *Memoirs*, ed. Firth, Appendix XXXIV, 448.

[76] Hirst opposes 'the pious acknowledgement of the norms of gender and marriage' and the 'guilt born of concealment and untruth, and real resentments' ('Remembering a Hero', 690). For him Lucy Hutchinson's actions and fabrications 'call into question her obtrusive self-characterization as the epitome of wifely duty and dependence' (691).

[77] After the Colonel's death, Lucy Hutchinson had to sell the Colonel's property at Lowesby (Leicestershire), where she may have composed the *Memoirs*. See Norbrook, 'Hutchinson [née Apsley], Lucy (1620–1681), poet and biographer' (2016), *Oxford Dictionary of National Biography*, DOI: 10.1093/ref:odnb/14285.

Shee is not so to be subject as if in all cases, she ought alike to stand or fall at the barre and prerogative of her husbands will: Some cases fall out betweene them of greater difficulty, doubt and danger, then ordinary: such as extend to the hazarde of estate, children, yea liberty it selfe. In such cases, (if they be but arbitrary) as removall from present dwelling, upon great charge and losse, or, to places of ill health, ill neighbors, with losse of Gospell; long voyages by sea, to remote Plantations, or in the sudden change of Trades, or venturing of a stocke upon some new project, lending out, or borrowing of great sums, avoyding of debts, setling of estate, providing for children, costly buildings, great enterteynments beyond ability, or such like instances, wherin the woman is like to share as deep in the sorrow, if not more, then the husband.[78]

In this light, Lucy Hutchinson's influence over the Colonel should be understood as a way of protecting her own family. Her lobbying did not go against the ideal of the good wife but paradoxically fulfilled it, and can therefore be interpreted as the ultimate manifestation of her dedication to her family.[79]

Lucy Hutchinson's autobiographical agenda is also perceptible in her desire to assuage her own grief. As she explains in the Dedication, writing her husband's *Memoirs* is a response to his command on his deathbed that she should not 'grieve att the common rate of desolate woemen' (S1/K16). Memorializing the Colonel was meant to prevent her 'flood of sorrow' from '[carrying] away the memory' of the man she loved (S1/K16).[80] As a matter of fact, Lucy Hutchinson's grief crops up whenever she evokes the love bond that united her to her husband, from the moment of their meeting to his death and even beyond.[81] The text's lyricism reaches a climax with the account of the Colonel's arrest in October 1663, after he was suspected of being an accomplice in the Northern Plot.[82] Despite her husband's injunction not to show her

---

[78] Daniel Rogers, *Matrimoniall Honour, or, The Mutuall Crowne and Comfort of Godly, Loyall, and Chaste Marriage* (London, 1642) 264.

[79] Burden speaks of the 'topos of family cohesion' in the *Memoirs*. See Burden, 'Editing Shadows', 174.

[80] See Mary Beth Rose, 'Gender, Genre, and History: Seventeenth-Century English Women and the Art of Autobiography', *Women in the Middle Ages and the Renaissance*, ed. Rose (Syracuse: Syracuse UP, 1986) 245–78, here 248.

[81] See *Memoirs*, ed. Sutherland, 3, and ed. Keeble, 18. Matchinske, 'History's "Silent Whispers"', 61–2.

[82] Ronald Hutton, *The Restoration* (Oxford: Oxford UP, 1986) 204–6. See also Alan Marshall, '"Plots and Dissent": The Abortive Northern Rebellion of 1663', *From Republic to Restoration. Legacies and Departure*, ed. Janet Clare (Manchester: Manchester UP, 2018) 85–101. On John Hutchinson's involvement in the Northern Plot, see Seddon, 'The Dating of the Completion of the Composition of the *Memoirs*', 113–15.

sadness, the description of the moment of parting is full of pathos and grief. The narration, carefully orchestrating the comforting words of the Colonel with the woeful thoughts of his wife, lays bare the difficulty for Lucy Hutchinson to contain her sorrow and accept her husband's longing for martyrdom:

> Mrs. Hutchinson was exceedingly sad, but he encourag'd and kindly chid her out of it, and told her it would blemish his innocence for her to appeare afflicted, and told her if she had but patience to waite the event, she would see it all for the best, and bade her be thankfull for the mercy that she was permitted this comfort to accompany him in the journey, and with divers excellent exhortations chear'd her, who was not wholly abandon'd to sorrow while he was with her; who, to divert her, made himselfe sport with his guards, and deceiv'd the way, till upon the 3rd of November he was brought to the Crowne in Holborne. [...] His wife, by his command, restrain'd herselfe as much as she could from shewing her sadnesse, whom he bad to remember how often he had told her that God never preserv'd him so exterordinarily at first but for some greate worke he had further for him to doe or to suffer in this cause, and bad her be thankfull for the mercy by which they had so long in peace enjoy'd one another since this eminent change, and bade her trust God with him; whose faith and chearefullnesse were so encouraging that it a little upheld her, but, alas! her devining heart was not to be comforted: she rememb'red what had bene told her of the cruell resolutions taken against him, and saw now the execution of them.
>
> (S249/K303–4)

The interjection—'but alas!'—that directly follows the exchange betrays her retrospective awareness of the fatal ending of the story and constitutes an unmistakable index of how painful the process of remembering their separation was. Here, Lucy Hutchinson does not stand as a 'disembodied historian [recording] the public activities which comprised the *Life* of John Hutchinson',[83] but shows herself to be an emotionally committed memorialist intent on serving her husband's cause to the last.

The autobiographical quality of the narrative can finally be traced in the metaphorical description of 'Mrs. Hutchinson' as a mirror or shadow reflecting her husband's virtues. This complex imagery, already studied above, resonates throughout the *Memoirs* and the 'Elegies'. It has been

---

[83] Keeble, 'The Colonel's Shadow', 238.

principally interpreted in two, non-exclusive, ways, either as an index of her subordination and self-effacement, or as a manifestation of the Neoplatonic framework of the *Memoirs* in which mirrors and shades can be understood as conduits to the divine.[84] These two readings are not incompatible with a third one, as these images could also be seen as tropes to express the author's inconsolable grief over her husband's death. It is in this context of mourning and melancholy that I wish to interpret Lucy Hutchinson's spiritual rewriting of the stereotype of the good, submissive wife into an ideal of 'mutual care':[85] 'If he esteem'd her att a higher rate than she in her selfe could have deserv'd, he was the author of that vertue he doted on, while she only reflected his owne glories upon him: all that she was, was him, while he was here, and all that she is now at best is his pale shade' (S10/K26). The metaphors of shades and reflections are carried on in a passage that comes after the relation of John Hutchinson's courtship, this time expressing the author's desire for annihilation and death, very much as in Elegy [1]:[86]

> she was a very faithfull mirror, reflecting truly, though but dimmely, his owne glories upon him, so long as he was present; but she, that was nothing before his inspection gave her a faire figure, when he was remoov'd, was only filled with a darke mist, and never could againe take in any delightfull object, nor returne any shining representation [. . .]. Soe, as his shaddow, she waited on him every where, till he was taken into that region of light which admitts of none, and then she vanisht into nothing.   (S32–3/K51)

Two more occurrences of this shadow imagery are to be found at either ends of the *Memoirs* manuscript. In the unpublished part of the Dedication to her children Lucy Hutchinson describes herself as 'a pale and liueless shade wandering about his sepulchre',[87] while in an untitled piece, published by

---

[84] For the first line of interpretation, see Keeble, 'The Colonel's Shadow' and Norbrook, 'Lucy Hutchinson's Elegies', 471–2.

[85] See Sharon Achinstein, 'Saints or Citizens? Ideas of Marriage in Seventeenth-Century English Republicanism', *The Seventeenth Century* 25.2 (2010): 240–64, here 255–6. Achinstein shows how Lucy Hutchinson 'forwards a model of mutual care' in *Order and Disorder* and throughout the *Memoirs*. See *Order and Disorder*, Canto 3, 477–88: 'From heaven I did descend to fetch up thee, / Rose from the grave that thou mightst reign with me. / Henceforth no longer two but one we are. / Thou dost my merit, life, grace, glory share.'

[86] See Elegy [1], ed. Norbrook, ll. 3–7, 487: 'For, 'twas not he, twas only I That died / In That Cold Graue which his deare reliques keeps / My substance into ye darke vault was laide / And now I am my own pale Empty Shade.' In 'No Publick Funeral', Wiseman considers the 'Shade' as 'our ghostly guide to the nocturnal, enchanted labyrinth of grief' (207).

[87] *Memoirs*, DD/HU4, 25. See Erin Murphy, '"I remain, an airy phantasm": Lucy Hutchinson's Civil War Ghost Writing', *English Literary History* 82.1 (2015) 87–113, especially 87–90.

Keeble as the 'Final Meditation' and inserted in the manuscript of the *Memoirs* between the 'Life' and the Biblical verses, she movingly figures herself, in the first person, as a ghost haunting her husband's 'sepulchre'. Here, Lucy Hutchinson, haunting an in-between place of suffering, does no longer belong to the world of the living: 'Yet after all this he is gone hence and I remain, an airy phantasm walking about his sepulchre and waiting for the harbinger of day to summon me out of these midnight shades to my desired rest.'[88] In the preceding page, the final page of the 'Life of John Hutchinson', we are told that Sandown Castle, 'a lamentable old ruin'd place', 'unwholsome', 'damp', and 'mouldie' (S262–3/K319–20), is intermittently 'disturb'd with evill spiritts before the Collonell came' (S277/K336). After the Colonel's death, it continues to be haunted, not by a 'phantasm' or 'a shade', but by a ghost which very much resembles 'Mrs. Hutchinson' herself:

> But the spring after, there came an apparition of a gentlewoman in mourning, in such a habitt as Mrs. Hutchinson us'd to weare there, and affrighted the guards mightily at the first, but after a while grew familliar to them, and was often seene walking in the Collonell's chamber and on the platforme, and came sometimes into the guard among them. *Which is certeinely true*, but *we* knew not how to interprett it; neither can believe that he was poyson'd, although we know his enemies had mallice and wickednesse enough to doe it. (S277/K336, my emphasis)

The author's intriguing intervention—in the first-person plural—disturbingly points to the fact that the apparition may not be as subservient and as vulnerable as it looks, but that it could be a revengeful creature reminiscent of the ghost of Hamlet's father. In this sense, the apparition can be said to epitomize the conflicting emotions that continued to prey upon Lucy Hutchinson well after the death of her husband, as she was torn between the necessity of accepting his death and an unavowable desire for revenge that had been whetted by the rumour that the Colonel could well have been poisoned.[89] In any case, the spectral tropes, like the shadow metaphors, point to her insatiable quest for meaning and to the text's inherent autobiographical quality—the 'airy phantasm' being for Line Cottegnies no less than a

---

[88] Lucy Hutchinson, 'Final Meditation', *Memoirs*, ed. Keeble, 337; *Memoirs*, DD/HU4, [421]. See similar imagery and atmosphere in Elegy [9], ed. Norbrook, ll. 53–6, 504: 'The shades of death hath hemd me round / My late Crowne lyes in ye Cold ground / And my glories are become / Only the trickments of a tombe.'

[89] See *Memoirs*, ed. Sutherland, 277, and ed. Keeble, 336.

figuration, within the *Memoirs*, of the author who 'stages her own fading away from the text in an ostentatious way'.[90]

In conclusion, it appears that for Lucy Hutchinson, writing a narrative about how she lobbied in favour of her husband amounts to a quest for self-intelligibility—a way of reconstructing what had happened in 1660 the better to understand why she had been so reluctant to let her husband become a martyr of the republican cause. In her enterprise, she did not try so much to scrutinize her soul—which is what authors of spiritual autobiographies did[91]— as to capture her *historical* self in the tumultuous years of the Restoration. Bringing together the paradoxes of the self and history, the *Memoirs* should thus be apprehended as a shifting and reversible object that can be read either as a public record of history or as a form of autobiography, as both are intrinsically mingled at a time when life-writing and history writing had still so much in common.[92]

3. Tinkering with history and memory

Lucy Hutchinson's political interventions at the Restoration period reveal that she was not only a witness to history but also an agent, a position that early modern commentators and historians themselves (as seen above) considered as a guarantee of historical truth. Yet, the paradox is that, despite the role she played in most of the events she recounts, Lucy Hutchinson's treatment of history in the final quarter of the *Memoirs* is far from rigorous and accurate. Some facts are kept silent, while others are distorted, which challenges her own historiographical assumptions and her earlier claims that she is writing the 'truth' of the Colonel. Drawing on Norbrook's article, 'Memoirs and Oblivion', which examines 'the evidence about the letter and its contexts more closely', this section looks in some detail at the ways in which Lucy Hutchinson relates this period dominated by the Indemnity debate, and assesses the impact of her own political interventions on her historiographical choices.[93] As we shall see, she does not eschew the perils of partiality, forgery, lying and omission—the very accusations all the historians of the English Revolution had to face to a

---

[90] See Cottegnies, 'The Garden and the Tower', 142, and Wiseman, 'No Publick Funerall', 208.
[91] On that tradition, see Ebner, *Autobiography in Seventeenth-Century England*; Watkins, *Puritan Experience: Studies in Spiritual Autobiography*; Lynch, *Protestant Autobiography*; Anne Dunan-Page, *L'Expérience puritaine. Vies et récits de dissidents (XVIIe–XVIIIe siècles)* (Paris : Éditions du Cerf, 2017).
[92] Suzuki, 'Anne Clifford and the Gendering of History', 197.
[93] Norbrook, 'Memoirs and Oblivion', 237.

certain extent. The result is that her art of history writing is finally more opaque and more complex than she claims it is elsewhere in the *Memoirs*.

a) The affair of the forged letter

In May 1660, in the middle of the Indemnity debate, Lucy Hutchinson did not want her husband to comply with the order emanating from Parliament to surrender and come under custody. As a consequence, she 'writ a letter in his name to the Speaker [...] to lett him know that [...] he desir'd not to come into custody, and yett should be as ready to appeare att their call' (S229/K281). This letter, dated 5 June and signed by John Hutchinson, which Lucy Hutchinson claims to have 'contriv'd and written' (S230/K281), resurfaced later in 1663, when the Secretary of State, Henry Bennet, presented to 'Mrs. Hutchinson' 'the copie of the letter that was sent to the House of Parliament in her husband's name, written in her hand, which when she saw she was a little confounded' (S254/K309). Surprisingly, she does not seem to have had any hesitations in dealing with the affair of the forgery in the *Memoirs*: there are no deletions or corrections in the corresponding pages of the manuscript.[94]

When Julius Hutchinson published the *Memoirs* in 1806, he did not have the letter in his possession and, like most nineteenth-century reviewers, he did not make any specific comment on the episode.[95] It was only in 1860 that a copy of the letter was discovered by the historian Ann Everett Green while editing the Calendar State Papers.[96] It was published in *The Athenaeum* in the same year, and transcribed in Firth's and Sutherland's editions.[97] Firth, who knew about Green's discovery, includes a quote in his edition of the *Memoirs* from *The Commons Journals*, which, on 5 June 1660, gave the following statement:

> Mr Speaker communicates a letter, dated the 5th of June 1660, directed to himself and signed by Colonel John Hutchinson, who was one of those who

---

[94] *Memoirs*, DD/HU4, 348–9; 385–6.
[95] Jeffrey, Rev. of *Memoirs*, 23–4 and *Memoirs*, ed. Julius Hutchinson, 369–70. In 1882, the Scottish novelist Margaret Oliphant fully quotes the episode of the forged letter which she reads as a manifestation of Lucy Hutchinson's heroism. See Margaret Oliphant, 'Autobiographies. N° VI. In the Time of the Commonwealth: Lucy Hutchinson, Alice Thornton', *Blackwood's Edinburgh Magazine* 132 (1882): 90–1.
[96] According to Norbrook, the original letter was 'destroyed in a fire' in 1834 (237).
[97] M. A. E. Green, *The Athenaeum* 168 (3 March 1860). For a thorough presentation of the letter, see Norbrook, 'Memoirs and Oblivion', 233–4 and Appendix 1, 278–9; *Memoirs*, ed. Firth, Appendix XXXIV, 446–8; and ed. Sutherland, 290–2.

sat in judgment upon the late king's majesty when sentence of death was pronounced against him, which was read. Resolved that Colonel John Hutchinson be at liberty, on his own parole to be given to Mr Speaker.[98]

The comparison of the actual letter with the account of it in the *Memoirs* shows that much of its contents and even its real purpose were not revealed by Lucy Hutchinson, who does not specify for instance that the petition sent to the Speaker was in fact a letter of recantation and repentance, meant to serve as a corrective to the equivocal speech the Colonel gave in the Convention Parliament on 12 May 1660.[99] The reason for the ambiguity and vagueness of the speech was, at least according to his wife, that her husband had not anticipated the request of the House to justify his role during the King's trial, '[h]e being surpriz'd with a thing he expected not' (S227/K279). Julius Hutchinson, in a footnote, seems hesitant about the Colonel's 'surprise' and pleads in favour of premeditation as far as his speech was concerned:

> This speech will probably be considered as a specimen of art carried as far as a man of honour would permit himself to go, and managed with as much refinement and dexterity as the longest premeditation could have produced; accordingly it furnished his friends with a topic for his defence, without giving his adversaries grounds for reproaching him with tergiversation.[100]

So Lucy Hutchinson's mention of the Colonel's 'inexperience' and 'defect of his judgement' is a strategic move on her part in order to contrast her husband's reserved attitude with that of his fellow regicides, for instance Ingoldsby who, 'with many teares, professt his repentance for that murther' (S228/K279). Instead, the Colonel ambiguously declared that he was ready to sacrifice himself, without specifying for which cause exactly he was ready to do so—'if the sacrifice of him might conduce to the publick peace and settlement, he should freely submit his life and fortunes to their dispose' (S228/K279). The closing sentence of the speech was equally, if not more, ambivalent for its patriotism could be interpreted both in a republican and a royalist sense: 'as to that particular action of the King [his execution], he desir'd them to believe he had that sence of it that befitted an Englishman, a christian, and a Gentleman'

---

[98] *Memoirs*, ed. Firth, 325, note 2.
[99] See Lobo, 'Lucy Hutchinson's Revisions of Conscience', 318: 'This petition, it seems, is an absent presence in the text: Lucy Hutchinson, after all, calls attention to it by trying to make it disappear.'
[100] *Memoirs*, ed. Julius Hutchinson, 368, note e. Norbrook agrees with Julius Hutchinson that the speech was premeditated. See 'Memoirs and Oblivion', 248.

(S228/K280). The ambiguity of the Colonel's speech was attested by witnesses whose reactions and scepticism Lucy Hutchinson does not fail to mention:

> What he expresst was to this effect, but so very handsomly deliver'd that it generally tooke the whole house: only one Gentleman stood up and sayd he had expresst himselfe as one that was much more sorrie for the events and consequences than the actions; but another replied that when a man's words might admitt of two interpretations, it befitted gentlemen allwayes to receive that which might be most favourable. (S228/K280)

However, according to the diary of William Bankes, a member of the Convention Parliament, who was present then, the speech was not really perceived as ambiguous but as in favour of the monarchy: 'John Hutchinson saith wt was donne by him was out of noe ill intent that hee hath seene ye ill effects of it, & hath since endea[vored] to bring ye k[ing] back.'[101]

In the *Memoirs*, Lucy Hutchinson is as elusive about the forged letter as she is about the speech—once again her elusiveness is tactical. The purpose of the letter was indeed very straightforward: it was meant to clear all the ambiguities of the 12 May speech which, it stated, 'was not a sufficient expression of that deep & sorrowfull sense which so heavily presses [John Hutchinson's] soule, for the vnfortunate guilt that lies vpon it'.[102] Moreover, in the letter, the Colonel unambiguously stated that he had ceased to support Cromwell before the actual dissolution of the Rump in 1653: 'euen before Cromwell broke vp the remaining part of the ~~Parliament~~ ᴴᵒᵘˢᵉ, when his ambition began to vnvaile itself, iealous of those sins I did not sooner discerne, I stopt, and left of acting wᵗʰ them.'[103] Deploying a hyperbolic rhetoric of repentance, and invoking his conscience, he exposed 'a thorough conviction of his former misled iudgement and conscience'.[104] Ironically enough, his letter resembles the fulsome recantations of former regicides, which Lucy Hutchinson despised, denouncing the inauthenticity of these theatrical speeches of contrition, like that of Colonel Ingoldsby: 'When it came to Inglesbie's turne to speak, he [. . .] told a false tale how Cromwell held his hand and forc'd him to subscribe the sentence'

---

[101] Quoted by Lobo, 'Lucy Hutchinson's Revisions of Conscience', 322. See Hirst, 'Remembering a Hero', 687–8.
[102] 'The Letter of June 5, 1660: The National Archives, Public Record Office SP29/3/39', reproduced in Norbrook, 'Memoirs and Oblivion', Appendix 1, 278.
[103] 'The Letter of June 5, 1660', 278. For a perspicuous reading of the Colonel's letter, see Lobo, 'Lucy Hutchinson's Revisions of Conscience', 318–19.
[104] 'The Letter of June 5, 1660', 279. Norbrook, 'Memoirs and Oblivion', 270: 'adopting a high-flying royalist style was certainly not beyond her skills.'

(S228/K279).[105] Some pages down, turning again a blind eye to the royalist content of the forged letter, she categorically writes that the Colonel did not abase himself by such compromising speeches, even when he was asked to make one.[106] Of course, mentioning the Colonel's repentance too openly would have imperilled the memorialist's apologetic project and stained her husband's reputation as a virtuous Commonwealthman. It would also have fuelled the arguments of his former friends who suspected him of having recanted his republicanism. But what lay beneath the surface of the letter? How can we account for such a discrepancy between the royalist recantation letter of 5 May, and the unrepentant republican account presented in the *Memoirs*?[107]

b) Between forgery and truth

In his edition of the *Memoirs*—which reproduces John Hutchinson's letter to the Speaker discovered by Green—Firth, as a positivist historian, questions Lucy Hutchinson's version of the forged letter episode. He confronts it with what people thought about the allegiances of the Colonel in 1660 and in 1663, in particular Ludlow who reproached the Colonel for his apostasy of the republican cause, and for his attitude towards the secluded members and the former Commonwealthman Henry Vane.[108] He also offers the testimony of another republican, Algernon Sidney who, in a letter dated August 1660, deplored John Hutchinson's conversion to the restored monarchy: 'If I could write and talk like Col. Hutchinson or Sir Gilbert Pickering, [...] I believe I might be quiet. Contempt might procure my safety, but I had rather be a vagabond all my life, than buy my being in my own country at so dear a rate.'[109] According to Firth, John Hutchinson's republicanism, at least in the late 1650s and at the Restoration, had wavered. The historian, who does not hesitate to refer to the 'cowardice of his conduct',[110] considers that the forged

---

[105] Keeble, *The Restoration* 74–6. [106] See *Memoirs*, ed. Sutherland, 232, and ed. Keeble, 284.
[107] Lobo speaks of the 'insurmountable tension between the *Memoirs* and the historical record regarding her husband's loyalties' ('Lucy Hutchinson's Revisions of Conscience', 324).
[108] Ludlow refused to sit with the secluded members; he also considered Colonel Hutchinson too severe with Vane (*Memoirs*, ed. Firth, 317, note 1; 318, note 1). In his introduction (xv), Firth quotes Ludlow's *Memoirs*: 'Ludlow, however, who states that Col. Hutchinson "having joined in Monk's treacherous design, had obtained a pardon from the king whilst he was beyond sea," makes far too much of the slight services Hutchinson could have rendered Monk, and his statement about the pardon is certainly erroneous.' In 1894, Firth produced a scholarly edition of *The Memoirs of Edmund Ludlow* (originally published in 1698).
[109] Quoted in *Memoirs*, ed. Firth, xvi. [110] *Memoirs*, ed. Firth, xvii.

letter read in the House of Commons—'endorsed' by Colonel Hutchinson—was 'abject' and 'dishonouring'.[111] In his eyes, the whole affair was nothing but an imposture made necessary by Lucy Hutchinson's republican agenda. The value Firth places in historical veracity leads him to voice a strong moral condemnation of Lucy Hutchinson's version of Restoration history:

> When she comes to speak of her husband's escape at the Restoration, Mrs. Hutchinson conceals much of the truth, and misrepresents many of the facts. Col. Hutchinson owed his escape at the Restoration to what the Journals of the House of Commons term his "signal repentance," and to the exertions of his friends on his behalf. They were able to plead with truth his recent exertions against Lambert's party, to which they added a number of good-natured fictions about earlier actions in favour of the Royalist cause during the Protectorate.[112]

In other words, if we follow Firth, Lucy Hutchinson is not to be taken as a reliable historian and the *Memoirs* are more fiction than history—a conclusion that I wish to qualify, as it significantly weakens my starting assumption that Lucy Hutchinson was indeed a historian of the English Revolution in her own right. This is made possible by the recent studies of Derek Hirst and David Norbrook who have both scrutinized the episode of the forged letter. Their divergent readings of the episode have the merit of highlighting Lucy Hutchinson's sophisticated rendering of controversial facts. They reveal how her role as a committed witness and actor in history had a major impact on her historiographical practices, which do not belong to a positivist era, but to seventeenth-century England, a period when, as we saw in Chapter 2, historiographical issues were fiercely debated. In 'Remembering a Hero', Hirst elaborates on Firth's evidence in order to demonstrate that by 1660 John Hutchinson had recanted his republican views and that Lucy Hutchinson did not have any responsibility in having her husband excepted in the Act of Indemnity and Oblivion. But Hirst, unlike Firth, does not trust Lucy Hutchinson's 'overall representation of her husband as a staunch republican, who had momentarily and all too understandably wavered but wavered only once'.[113] For Hirst, the story of the forged letter is mere fiction, John Hutchinson being indeed the real author of the recantation and Lucy only 'the

---

[111] *Memoirs*, ed. Firth, xv.   [112] *Memoirs*, ed. Firth, xv.
[113] Hirst, 'Remembering a Hero', 685–6. Underdown makes no doubt about the Colonel's recantation either. See Underdown, *Pride's Purge* 360. On this episode, see also Clare, 'Introduction', *From Republic to Restoration* 8–9.

amanuensis'. Like some of his fellow regicides, John Hutchinson thus 'journeyed into royalism' and his conversion was no mere 'wavering', but irreversible.[114] As a consequence, Hirst looks upon Lucy Hutchinson's story of the forged letter as a mere artifice; her portrayal of John Hutchinson as a republican is, in his eyes, a fictional construct, and the full *Memoirs* a fraud, even, perhaps, an 'early case of false memory'—Lucy Hutchinson's single intention in all this being to 'rescue Colonel Hutchinson's memory' and make her republican apologetics more credible.[115] Hirst considers that all the former readings of the episode by Keeble, Sutherland, Hutton and Norbrook are unsatisfactory, because they take Lucy Hutchinson's 'story of forgery' at face value.[116] In his revisionist perspective, which offers hardly any new evidence, the *Memoirs* have neither epistemological value nor historical relevance.[117] They are relegated to the realm of fiction and romance, Lucy Hutchinson being at best an 'imaginative writer as well as [a] reporter'.[118] What Hirst does not realize is that the other Restoration histories of the English Revolution—from Ludlow to Clarendon—are all biased, and that all, to some degree, offered 'misrepresentations' of historical reality. I believe Lucy Hutchinson's *Memoirs* are not different from those histories, and that none of these texts—not even those written by women—can be categorized as mere romances.[119]

In a major article, based on a thorough investigation of Restoration 'micropolitics', Norbrook revises Hirst's hypothesis that Lucy Hutchinson's 'account of the forgery was [...] itself a deception'.[120] Norbrook disagrees with Hirst's interpretation because it goes too far in challenging 'the larger veracity of her narrative', which, according to Norbrook, cannot be done in such a radical way.[121] It appears that Lucy Hutchinson's use of forgery can only be explained if one takes into account the extremely confused context of the late 1650s—when the opposition to the Protectorate was both republican and royalist—and the early months of the Restoration, when John Hutchinson's position on the political chessboard was 'somewhere between a royalist

---

[114] Hirst, 'Remembering a Hero', 684; 685.   [115] Hirst, 'Remembering a Hero', 689.
[116] Hirst, 'Remembering a Hero', 685, note 11. Hirst refers to Sutherland's edition of the *Memoirs* (xviii); Keeble's edition (xxvii); Norbrook's 'Elegies' (481) and Hutton, *The Restoration* 133–4.
[117] Hirst's main addition is his work on the Bankes family manuscripts ('Remembering a Hero', 687–8).
[118] Hirst, 'Remembering a Hero', 689–91.
[119] Hirst, at one point, draws an interesting parallel with Toland remodelling Ludlow's *Memoirs* in a republican direction. He does not seem to realize that both Lucy Hutchinson and Toland's rewrites were not necessarily different from other histories at the Restoration (686).
[120] Norbrook, 'Memoirs and Oblivion', abstract, 238, 233.
[121] Norbrook, 'Memoirs and Oblivion', 235.

conversion and a bowing to the inevitable'.[122] Although it is undeniable that in her account of the Restoration Lucy Hutchinson tinkers with the facts of a very uncertain history, her purpose—to bring out the truth of history—remains highly political, and alien to the genre of romance which, in the latter part of the seventeenth century, designates *imaginative* fiction in which love was an essential ingredient.[123] Lucy Hutchinson, Norbrook adds, often pictures her husband 'as a kind of anti-hero, waiting on events, subject to others' agendas', but her narrative, which 'runs counter to the courtly and generalizing style of seventeenth-century romance', is no mere fiction as it 'can be corroborated from other sources'.[124]

Norbrook's main reason for refusing Hirst's reading is that the ambiguities of the letter cannot be fully resolved: 'the question of whether she wrote the letter – either copied it out or composed it herself – remains a controversial one.'[125] Despite its rhetoric of atonement, Norbrook argues, the letter is not a straightforward answer to the proclamation to 'appear in person'. In the Colonel's alleged written statement, 'the repentance remains liminal, semi-private, and only potentially public.'[126] Drawing on internal and external evidence, notably exploiting the correspondence between Hyde and his friend, Sir Allen Brodrick, a member of the Convention Parliament, Norbrook claims that in royalist circles of the 1650s and at the Restoration, John Hutchinson was never considered to be a loyal supporter of the King.[127] Even though, like many royalists, he opposed the Protectorate, he was still viewed as a potential rebel by many of his contemporaries—his cousin Biron, his brother-in-law Apsley, the Chancellor Hyde or the Secretary of State Bennet—and was never brought to court.[128] Lucy Hutchinson thus reports that 'a Kinsman of hers, fallen into the wicked Councells of the Court' had told her that the King thought her husband 'would doe the same thing for him he did to his father, for he was still unchang'd in his principles, and readier to protect than accuse any of his associates' (S237/K289). Finally, when one looks at the early reception of the *Memoirs*, John Hutchinson was always regarded as a republican. The fact that neither the antiquarian and biographer Mark Noble nor the historian Catharine Macaulay could access

---

[122] Norbrook, 'Memoirs and Oblivion', 238–9; 259.
[123] Lee, 'The Meaning of Romance', 299–300. [124] Norbrook, 'Memoirs and Oblivion', 245.
[125] Norbrook, 'Memoirs and Oblivion', 234. [126] Norbrook, 'Memoirs and Oblivion', 249.
[127] Norbrook, 'Memoirs and Oblivion', 247; 272–3; 275.
[128] See for instance Hyde's reaction after John Hutchinson was pardoned: 'When Sir Allen Apsley came to the Chancellor he was in a greate rage and passion, and fell upon him with vehemence. "O Nall," sayd he, "what have you done? You have sav'd a man that would be ready, if he had opertunity, to mischiefe us as much as ever he did"' (S236/K288).

the manuscript in the eighteenth century further indicates that, in the eyes of most members of the Hutchinson family, the Colonel's allegiances remained dangerously republican.

Norbrook's second objection to Hirst's reading is that there is no clear evidence either that Lucy Hutchinson was only an amanuensis for her husband. On the contrary, by offering a close study of the letter manuscript and confronting it with other letters written in the Colonel's defence, he shows that Lucy Hutchinson possessed all the necessary skills to be the author of the letter.[129] It makes no doubt for him that she was capable of adopting a 'literary idiom that could appeal to royalists and republicans alike'.[130] A material and stylistic study of the 'forged' letter shows that it was indeed 'unusually tightly structured' and more elaborate than 'surviving petitions and communications from other regicides'—in short, it was very close to the kind of writing which Lucy Hutchinson adopts in the *Memoirs*.[131] Although the other letters written in the Colonel's defence in 1660 are admittedly 'more formulaic and less stylistically elaborate', Norbrook assumes that they could also have been the result of a collaboration between husband and wife, which may go back to the Civil War, possibly in 1643–1644, when the Colonel had to answer many summons of surrender in writing.[132] Furthermore, Lucy Hutchinson's rewriting of the 1663 imprisonment narrative in the *Memoirs* reveals how she may have been used to revising his texts and makes the idea of a collaboration technically plausible.[133] In the episode of the forged letter, however, collaboration was not only a question of style but a question of life and death, and in these very special circumstances, Norbrook claims, 'some compound of pressure, opportunism, and pragmatic acceptance of the inevitable may have worked together, with both husband and wife compromising to a point that left them ultimately unsatisfied.'[134]

---

[129] Norbrook, 'Memoirs and Oblivion', 271; 262–3. This assumption is reinforced by the fact that some documents, in particular the petition of 18 August 1660, could well have been written in Lucy Hutchinson's hand.

[130] Norbrook, 'Memoirs and Oblivion', 260.   [131] Norbrook, 'Memoirs and Oblivion', 261.

[132] See, for instance, John Hutchinson's letters included in *A Discovery of the Trecherous Attempts of the Cavaliers to have procured the betraying of Nottingham Castle* (London, 1643) sig. [A1ᵛ]–A2: 'I would maintaine my faithfulnesse to the Parliament, so long as I have one drop of blood left in me; [...] I am confident God wil give me strength to maintaine this Christian resolution, that I have by Covenant both with God and man bound my selfe unto; which is, that I will rather chuse to die ten thousand deaths with a clear conscience to God, and an honest heart to my Country, then to fell my soule for the purchase of my life, and all the wealth and honours this world can bestow upon me.'

[133] Norbrook, 'Memoirs and Oblivion', 268–9. See John Hutchinson, *A Narrative of the Imprisonment and Usage of Col. John Hutchinson*, in *The Harleian Miscellany*, vol. 3 (London, 1745).

[134] Norbrook, 'Memoirs and Oblivion', 246.

c) The art of equivocation

With the Indemnity debate and the episode of the forged letter, the trial and the execution of the King resurface in the *Memoirs*. In the summer and the autumn of 1660, when the Hutchinsons were interrogated about the regicide and about more recent events, they remained silent or used equivocation to preserve the Colonel's and his friends' lives. In those tense moments, the difficulty of remembering and writing the English Revolution comes to the fore. In some places, Lucy Hutchinson's text proves elusive and equivocal, far more complex than a mere historical document to which it has been sometimes wrongfully reduced.[135]

Unlike the other Commonwealthmen's wives who were interrogated at the Restoration, Lucy Hutchinson claims to have refused to satisfy the curiosity of those who questioned her, including that of a royalist relative of hers who tried to blackmail her into revealing some secret information. It is striking to see how in the name of conscience and honour, she boldly stood up to her arrogant relative who questioned her just after John Hutchinson was pardoned by Parliament (29 August 1660):[136]

> having thus affrighted her, then to draw her in by examples, [he] told her how the late Statemen's wives came and offer'd them all the informations they had gather'd from their husbands, and how she could not but know more than any of them, and if yett she would impart aniething that might shew her gratitude, she might redeeme her famely from ruine; and then particularly told her how her husband had been intimate with Vane, Pierrepont, and St. Johns [...]. But she told him she perceiv'd any safety one could buy of them was not worth the price of honor and conscience; that she knew nothing of State managements, or if she did, she would not establish her selfe upon any man's blood and ruine.   (S237/K289-90)

In this episode, the balance of power decidedly leans in favour of 'Mrs. Hutchinson'. Her silence, which probably had to do with the short Protectorate of Richard Cromwell, reflects Lucy Hutchinson's authority as a historian carefully choosing the information she wants to leave to posterity.[137] Stepping into the narrative, she retrospectively reminds the reader that

---

[135] Norbrook, 'Memoirs and Oblivion', 237.   [136] Norbrook, 'Memoirs and Oblivion', 249.
[137] See *Memoirs*, ed. Firth, 336, note 1.

'Mrs. Hutchinson' did not yield to intimidation and kept to herself the state secrets which she had been told in confidence:

> Then [her kinsman] employ'd all his witt to circumvert her in discources, to have gotten something out of her concerning some persons they aym'd at, which if he could, I believe it would have bene beneficiall to him; but she discern'd his drift, and scorn'd to become an informer, and made him believe she was ignorant, though she could have enlight'ned him in the thing he sought for; which they are now never likely to know much of, it being lockt up in the grave, and they that survive not knowing that their secretts are remoov'd into another cabinett. (S237/K290)

Lucy Hutchinson's use of secrecy is strikingly exemplified in a later episode, situated at the time of John Hutchinson's imprisonment in 1663 and in which she played an even more dangerous game. When she was interrogated by the Secretary of State Bennet about the letter her husband had sent to Parliament and which she claimed to have 'contrived'—'she told him that she could not absolutely say that was her writing, though it had some resemblance' (S254/K309).[138] Once again, neither Bennet nor the reader is given the key to the full story—which has been read by Norbrook as an example of Lucy Hutchinson's ambiguous art of equivocation.[139]

Like his wife, the Colonel was in fact a master in the art of ambiguity—he refused to answer questions about his past as a regicide and a republican, and systematically withheld any piece of information that could have endangered his republican friends. In the summer of 1660, although he had been pardoned by Parliament, he was once more 'sifted very thoroughly' (S235/K287) by the Attorney-General, who wanted to obtain information from him about the former commissioners of the King's trial. The Colonel claimed that his memory was so erratic that he could not pronounce himself about events that had occurred more than ten years before, namely whether Cromwell had really forced Colonel Ingoldsby to sign the King's death warrant (S235/K287). When he was shown the signatures on the King's death warrant, the Colonel shrewdly refused to give any clear answer to the Attorney-General, only

---

[138] Norbrook, 'Memoirs and Oblivion', 273: 'He presumably had many samples of her writing available, but he chose to send this particular letter. He could thus clear his sister of being the suspected Mrs. Hutchinson while simultaneously compromising her husband [...]. The key point is that this document, while it may have saved John Hutchinson's life in 1660, could ruin his reputation now that he is acquiring the luster of a republican martyr.'

[139] See 'Memoirs and Oblivion', 276.

providing him with the names of the men who were dead. His difficulty of remembering the regicide finds an equivalent in his wife's art of ellipsis when she tackles the same issue:

> Then being shew'd the Gentlemen's hands, he told him he was not well acquainted with them, as having never had commerce with the most of them by letters; and those he could owne, he could only say they resembled the writings which he was acquainted with; and among these he pickt out Cromwell's, Ireton's, and my Lord Grey's. (S235/K287-8)

The Colonel's exemplary silence is meant to contrast with the blatant lies of some of his fellow commissioners, who did not hesitate to falsify the past to save their own skins. After he 'was cleared both for life and estate in the House of Commons', his wife reports, he refused to answer 'the Court expectations in publick recantations and dissembled repentance and applause of their cruelty to his fellows' (S232/K284). The Colonel's reluctance for fabricated depositions is nonetheless very ambiguous, as we know through his wife that he was discharged precisely because he himself—at least temporarily—had recanted and participated in his defence in the spring and summer of 1660.

The moral integrity of the Colonel, which had been damaged by his compromising with the royalists, was nevertheless reaffirmed after he was cleared by both Houses, and further confirmed by the relation of his martyrdom which starts right afterwards. The staging of the Colonel's desire for sacrifice can be seen as a strategy on Lucy Hutchinson's part to restore his Republican reputation:

> When the Colonell saw how the other poore gentlemen were trapan'd that were brought in by proclamation, and how the whole cause it selfe, from the beginning to the ending, was betrey'd and condemn'd [...]; and although he was most thankfull to God, yett he was not very well satisfied in himselfe for accepting the deliverance. (S234/K286)

This abrupt shift to martyrdom after the Colonel was pardoned by Parliament can also be accounted for by Lucy Hutchinson's overall desire to bring out the 'truth of him', a truth which is situated beyond historical contingencies and matters to her more than veracity, understood as the adequation between facts and discourse. From this perspective, misrepresenting the Colonel's role and hers in the Indemnity debate was not a lie, but only meant to serve the rightful cause of her husband. The essential paradox which emerges from all this is that the much-celebrated exemplarity of John Hutchinson ultimately appears to be built, if not on treachery, at least on his compromising with his conscience and on his wife's lies. Lucy Hutchinson's historical narrative is thus not more transparent than that of the historians and memorialists of her age,[140] the 'cataclysmic rupture of the execution of the king'[141] obliging her, like them, to tinker with history, in order to advance her own truth about the Colonel.

*

Being an actor in history was an advantage for a historian, according to Montaigne, Bodin, Cavendish, or Burnet, who all held Caesar, the author of the *Commentaries*, as a model to be emulated.[142] But this desirable position, which enabled historians to write a narrative based on their direct experience of the events they recount, could be perilous. The hazards of such a vantage point paradoxically materialize in the last quarter of the *Memoirs*, where Lucy Hutchinson plays an active role in the story of her husband's life. In these pages, her commitment to the cause—namely her desire to save the Colonel and the republican ideal he embodied—accentuates the autobiographical bent of her narrative. The result is that the original apologetic project of the *Memoirs* is partly reoriented. Lucy Hutchinson not only seeks to vindicate her husband as a martyr of the republic but equally endeavours to justify her own agency—not just her role in the John Hutchinson's life, but also, paradoxically, her role as a historian of his life and times.

---

[140] See Philip West, 'Early Modern War Writing and the British Civil Wars', *Cambridge Companion to War-Writing* 98: 'Early modern war writing was neither transparent nor impartial, but in many ways a continuation off the field of the battles begun on it.'

[141] Chedgzoy et al., 'Researching Memory', 9.

[142] See Chapter 2, 2, a, 'Civil War historiography'.

Chapter 5
The historian's craft (1)
Lucy Hutchinson's art of narration

Lucy Hutchinson's account of the First Civil War, which starts with Charles I raising his standard in Nottingham (22 August 1642) and ends with the surrender of Oxford (24 June 1646), takes up more than a third of the *Memoirs* (S57–166/K80–206). It is based on the aforementioned Notebook, her earlier account of John Hutchinson's role during the Civil War, between 1642 and 1645, described in the *Memoirs* as a 'particular collection' (S157/K196). Although the Notebook and the *Memoirs* have much in common—both texts are strongly apologetic and grounded in local history—they do not share the same purpose. While the *Memoirs* vindicate the Colonel as a Christian republican martyr, the goal of the Notebook is more limited, as it is essentially a defence of John Hutchinson possibly before the Nottingham Committee. Hence, David Norbrook's choice, in the forthcoming edition of this text, to call it a 'Defence of John Hutchinson'.[1]

The Notebook is made up of four contiguous fragments which were originally bound together.[2] These pages, written in the same hand as the manuscript of the *Memoirs*, were in all likelihood written soon after the events reported happened, probably during the Hutchinsons' stay at Nottingham Fort between 1642 and 1645, or shortly aftwards in 1646.[3] In some places, the ink colour and the size of the handwriting vary, which may indicate distinct moments of writing.[4] There is evidence that the Notebook is not a 'diary', with regular entries, but a retrospective narrative, with its own historiographical focus.[5]

---

[1] Norbrook, 'But a Copie', 111. For a description of the third volume of *The Works of Lucy Hutchinson*, see https://earlymodern.web.ox.ac.uk/works-lucy-hutchinson-0 (accessed 07/06/2020).

[2] British Library, Add. MS 39779, Add. MS 46172, Add. MS 25901. For a material description of the Notebook and its reconstruction, see Wall, 'Not so much open professed enemies', 626–30. See also Norbrook, 'But a Copie', 111, note 3. The fragmentation of the manuscript, Wall argues convincingly, 'is the result of nineteenth-century intervention' (630).

[3] See Wall, 'Not so much open professed enemies', 624.

[4] See, for instance, Notebook, Add. MS 25901, 18. At the bottom of this page, where Lucy Hutchinson summarizes the 'conditions ye G: propounded to y^m y^t came into ye Castle', the ink is different from the previous paragraph and her handwriting is smaller.

[5] On the Notebook being called a 'diary', see Julius Hutchinson, 'Preface', *Memoirs* i.

Some omissions of dates and the repetition of imprecise phrases such as 'about this time' seem to indicate that some time elapsed between the time of writing and the events reported.[6] Still, some shifts to the present tense suggest a more contemporaneous account, as the following remark about Dr Plumtre implies: '[Plumtre] continued all the weeke [with the Cavaliers] but when they went out of Towne he alsoe went out with them [...] after he parted from the Cavalliers he went to Derby where he *yett remains*.'[7] There are no section divisions in the Notebook, but some titles are nevertheless drafted in the margins in a hand that could well be Lucy Hutchinson's. These titles materialize the strongly episodic structure of her narrative, as shown in the following sample, corresponding to the beginning of 1643:

My Lady Kingstons woman taken with letter to m^{rs} Pierpont (20^v)
Cap^n Palmers Troope raised (21^v)
Coll: Thornhagh returned (21^v)
The Towne betreyd (21^v)
The Trent Bridges fortified (22^v)
The Cavalliers beaten out (23)
Plumtre released by ye Cavalliers (23^v)

The first fragment (Add. MS 39779) deals with the Colonel's early commitment for the cause of Parliament in the spring of 1642, when he refused to obey the sheriff of the county, Sir John Digby, who had received the order to seize the powder kept in Nottingham's town-hall.[8] The second one (Add. MS 46172) relates a dramatic episode of the summer of 1642: the flight of John Hutchinson, pursued by the Cavalier troops, after he rebuffed a royalist quartermaster who wanted his men to be lodged in his father's house in Nottingham.[9] The third and longest section of the Notebook (Add. MS 25901)—the only manuscript pages Firth had in his hands when he edited the *Memoirs*—begins after the battle of Edgehill in October 1642 and ends

---

[6] See, for instance, Notebook, Add. MS 25901, 12: 'Vpon the 29th of June 1643 Mr Hutchinson received his Comission and y^e [blank] of July received it from Captain Lommax.' See the recurrence of 'about this time' in Add. MS 25901, 10^v, 16, 20^v, 41, 55, 62^v, 66^v, 68^v. For more evidence of the manuscript being planned by Lucy Hutchinson, see Wall, 'Not so much open professed enemies', 631–3.

[7] Notebook, Add. MS 25901, 24.

[8] Notebook, Add. MS 39779; *Memoirs*, ed. Sutherland, 53–56, and ed. Keeble, 75–9; MS DD/HU4, 88–93.

[9] Notebook, Add. MS 46172; *Memoirs*, ed. Sutherland, 63–67, and ed. Keeble, 87–91; MS DD/HU4, 104–9.

with the capture of the Fort at the Trent Bridges in February 1645.[10] It focuses on the Civil War in Nottinghamshire and the strife within Nottingham's Committee of War.[11] A final fragment of two more pages which seems to have been torn from the Notebook's third fragment (Add. MS. 25901) is now held in Nottingham Castle.[12]

Lucy Hutchinson directly refers to the Notebook as the main source of her Civil War account when, after an ultimate quarrel within the Nottingham Committee, she writes: 'Thus farre was transcrib'd out of a *more particular collection*' (S157/K196). This reference to the process of composition was omitted by Julius Hutchinson in his edited text of the *Memoirs*, perhaps because this authorial intervention broke the narrative flow of the *Memoirs*.[13] It is, however, a crucial observation to understand Lucy Hutchinson's historiographical method. On the one hand, it connects the Notebook with 'particular history', a dominant form of history which was often preferred to 'general' history in the early modern period.[14] On the other hand, it manifests how much Lucy Hutchinson relied on the experience-based Notebook to write the *Memoirs*. In some places, she reproduces her first record verbatim so much so that Norbrook writes that she 'cannibalize[s]' her text, although 'innumerable differences, from minutiae of phrasing to the inclusion of different episodes' can be identified.[15]

Because of these many resemblances, the Notebook was not considered as a narrative of its own by its earlier readers, but merely as a preparatory text to the *Memoirs*.[16] Charles Hutchinson, the son of Julius Hutchinson—himself a nephew of Colonel Hutchinson—in a pencil note on the manuscript, called it 'Mrs Hutchinson's earlier sketch, or journal'.[17] Firth retained the idea of a sketch, but rejected the idea of a 'journal of events' written on a regular basis

---

[10] Notebook, Add. MS 25901; *Memoirs*, ed. Sutherland 67–155, and ed. Keeble, 91–194; MS DD/HU4, 109–230.

[11] See Chapter 3, 2, b ('The Committee of Nottingham: a civil war in miniature').

[12] Those two manuscript pages are kept in Nottingham Castle. They are reproduced in Race, 'The British Museum MS of the Life'. I wish to thank David Norbrook for sending me a copy of these two pages.

[13] Norbrook, 'But a Copie', 110–11.

[14] On 'particular history', see Chapter 2, 1, 'Historiographical debates before the Civil War'. Firth also considers the Notebook as 'particular history': 'But the Note-Book gives the names of persons and places when the Memoirs do not, and particularizes when the Memoirs generalize' ('Introduction', *Memoirs*, ed. Firth, xi).

[15] David Norbrook, 'But a Copie', 111. 'Cannibalized' is taken from the description of the forthcoming new edition of the *Memoirs*: https://earlymodern.web.ox.ac.uk/works-lucy-hutchinson-0 (accessed 11/03/2020).

[16] For a similar understanding of the Notebook as a text in its own right, see Wall, 'Not so much open professed enemies', 625.

[17] Notebook, Add. MS 25901, 3.

that had been suggested by Charles Hutchinson.[18] However, as David Norbrook argues, considering the Notebook as a draft for the *Memoirs* implies 'a misleading teleology'.[19] Obviously, when she was writing the Notebook in the 1640s, Lucy Hutchinson was first and foremost writing the defence of her husband as a governor of the town and castle of Nottingham; she had not conceived the full project of the *Memoirs* as a monument to his memory yet. But this does not mean she lacked historiographical ambition. As I shall argue here, the Notebook is not a mere factual account, but offers instead a complex representation of the political and military situation in Nottingham. It goes beyond what Bacon calls 'Commentary', a form of 'imperfect' (i.e. unfinished) history, which 'set[s] downe a continuance of the naked events & actions, without the motiues or designes, the counsells, the speeches, the pretexts, the occasions, and other passages of action'.[20] On the contrary, it appears to have been carefully written to serve a specific purpose: several of its protagonists are fully characterized, while 'motives', 'pretexts', and occasions are often specified. There is, therefore, every reason to believe that Lucy Hutchinson was the author of the Notebook, even though some parts of it may have been 'written as a brief for John Hutchinson and [were] probably based on his own notes'.[21] The aim of this chapter is thus to show that in both the *Memoirs* and Notebook, Lucy Hutchinson uses her art of storytelling both to give meaning and shape to the complex reality of the Civil War, and to uncover the real motivations of the Colonel's would-be friends and adversaries.

1. The attraction of romance

a) Romance and history

In the middle of the seventeenth century, many royalists thought that romance was a genre in which to write the history of the recent past. They underlined the epistemological and generic proximity between the two genres and saw romance as 'a means of mediating historical fact'.[22] For example, Margaret Cavendish, who was herself the author of lives and romances, defined *romance*

---

[18] *Memoirs*, ed. Firth, xi.   [19] Norbrook, 'But a Copie', 111.
[20] Bacon, *The Second Booke* 10. See also Brathwaite about Caesar's *Commentaries* in *A Survey of History* 32: 'To goe on in a free and unaffected *Style*; beseemes his person: proposing things done, as if they were ocularly presented.' 'Commentaries' are one branch of 'Memorials, or Preparatory history'.
[21] Notebook, 'But a Copie', 111–12.
[22] Annabel Patterson, *Censorship and Interpretation. The Conditions of Writing and Reading in Early Modern England* (Madison: U of Wisconsin P 1984) 168. See also Salzman, 'Royalist Epic and

as 'an adulterate Issue, begot betwixt History and Poetry'.[23] It should be added that, in the royalist circles of the 1650s and 1660s, romance was not understood as a frivolous or futile genre, but more often than not as a serious response 'to a perceived crisis in historical writing'.[24] In his preface to the translation of Madeleine de Scudéry's *Artamenes*, the royalist publisher, Humphrey Moseley, pointed to the superiority of romance over history: 'Designs of War and Peace are better hinted and cut open by a *Romance* than downright Histories.'[25] For Charles Cotterell, who was the translator of La Calprenède's *Cassandra*, only romance—not history—could convey the extraordinariness of the 'Revolutions' that had taken place in England—the term 'revolution' here is not to be taken in the sense of a 'transformation', but in its astronomical and cyclical sense:

> Yet neither can the strange success of the Graecian Conqueror, the fatall destruction of the Persian Monarchy, the deplorable end of unfortunate *Darius*, the afflicted estate of his Royal Family in Exile and Captivity, the easie compliance of his Subjects with the prevailing Party, nor any other passage in it seem improbable to us, whose eyes have in as short a space been witnesses of such Revolutions as hardly any *Romance*, but sure no *History* can parallel.[26]

Unlike the royalist Cotterell, Lucy Hutchinson did not see romance as a suitable response to the historiographical dilemmas of the period: like most historians of her age, she saw fiction as the opposite of historical truth.[27] However, her narrative of the Civil War, which consistently keeps its distance from fiction, is evidence of her ability to exploit romance tropes in order to render the complexity of the political and military realities of the war. Even though she would not have acknowledged it, the *Memoirs* and the Notebook

---

Romance', *Cambridge Companion to Writing of the English Revolution*, ed. Keeble, 223–8; Woolf, 'Gender and Historical Knowledge', 661–2; Amelia Zurcher, 'The Political Ideologies of Revolutionary Prose Romance', *The Oxford Handbook of Literature and the English Revolution* 559.

[23] Cavendish, *The Worlds Olio* 9. On generic hybridity, see Michael McKeon, *The Origins of the English Novel 1600–1740* (Baltimore: Johns Hopkins UP, 1987) 26–8.

[24] Zurcher, 'The Political Ideologies of Revolutionary Prose Romance', 559 and 552–3.

[25] Humphrey Moseley, 'The Stationer to the Reader', *Artamenes or, The Grand Cyrus* (London, 1653) np. On translations of French romances in the 1650s, see Laurence Plazenet, *L'Ébahissement et la délectation. Réception comparée et poétiques du roman grec en France et en Angleterre aux XVIe et XVIIe siècles* (Paris: Champion, 1997) 705–7.

[26] Charles Cotterell, 'To the Reader', in Seigneur de Gauthier de Costes La Calprenède, *Cassandra the Fam'd Romance*, trans. Cotterell (London, 1661) sig. A4^v. On Cotterell's translation, see Philip Major, '"A Credible Omen of a More Glorious Event": Sir Charles Cotterell's *Cassandra*', *The Review of English Studies* 60.245 (2009): 406–30.

[27] On Lucy Hutchinson and fiction, see Chapter 2, 3, a ('Historiographical assumptions').

do not fully escape the lot of most mid-century histories which were, according to Roger Boyle, 'for the most Part mixt Romances'.[28]

Significantly enough, the word 'story', in either the singular or the plural, recurs in the *Memoirs*. In Firth's edition of the *Memoirs* available on line, it appears at least twenty-eight times.[29] It alternately designates the story of John Hutchinson's life—'the story I most particularly intend' (S60/K84)—or independent episodes and anecdotes, which are more or less loosely connected to the central narrative. We have seen, for instance, how, at the beginning of the *Memoirs*, Lucy Hutchinson records her ancestors' stories and claims the title of family chronicler (S18/K34). But when she writes about the Civil War and about the Colonel's role in it, she also proves to be a skilful storyteller, and despite her distrust of romance as deceitful, frivolous and too secular, she does not refrain from incorporating romance tropes into her narrative.[30] Like many writers of her age, she has the 'habit of seeing events in literary terms'—a habit which, Lois Potter writes, was 'common to both sides of the Civil War'.[31]

b) Love at first sight

In her short autobiographical fragment, Lucy Hutchinson narrates how much amorous intrigues fascinated her as a child: 'I thought it no sin,' she writes, 'to learne or heare wittie songs and amorous sonnets or poems, and twenty things of that kind, wherein I was so apt that I became the confident in all the loves that were managed among my mother's young weomen' (S288–9/K15).[32] She also confesses her youthful fondness for books, and how she 'would steale into some hole or other to read' (S288/K14). As an avid reader, she was very likely to have read Sidney's *Arcadia* and other romances in the same vein, which were much in vogue in the 1630s, especially

---

[28] Roger Boyle, 'The Preface', *Parthenissa. A Romance in Four Parts* (London, 1655), sig. B–[B ᵛ].
[29] The wordcount is based on the Bartleby edition: https://www.bartleby.com/362/ (accessed 12/03/2020).
[30] See Looser, *British Women Writers* 35, 44–5: 'if Hutchinson rejects romance, it is primarily its label and not its features that she leaves behind. The *Memoirs* does not steer away from romance elements (including stories of heroism, love and honor, stylistic elegance, and elaborate descriptions), whether in Lucy and John's courtship or in battle' (45).
[31] Potter, *Secret Rites and Secret Writing* 72–3.
[32] See 'The Life of Mrs. Hutchinson', 14: 'every moment I could steal from my play I would employ in any book I could find [...]. After dinner and supper [...] I would steal into some hole or other to read.' On Lucy Hutchinson's taste for romance, see Robert Wilcher, 'Lucy Hutchinson and *Genesis*: Paraphrase, Epic, Romance', *English: Journal of the English Association* 59.224 (2010): 25–42, here 32–3. See also Anderson, *Friendship's Shadows* 203. Anderson shows that some sentimental passages are crossed out in the manuscript of the *Memoirs* (*Memoirs*, DD/HU4, 51, 56).

in court circles, with which she was in contact when she was staying at Richmond before her marriage in 1638.[33]

In the *Memoirs*, Lucy Hutchinson's acquaintance with romance is first reflected in her description of the Colonel's virtues in the unpublished section of her Dedication: '[n]ot all that Romance can fancy,' she writes, 'can sett forth such a patterne of perfect loue and friendship to mankind as his reall example giues.'[34] Her familiarity with romance is also conspicuous in her account of John Hutchinson's past courtships, which are all meant to bring out the uniqueness of his love for Lucy Hutchinson. His first courtship (presumably in the early 1630s) was soon interrupted, as "death ravisht the young lady from him in the sweete blooming of her youth' (S23/K41). Shortly after he graduated from Peterhouse, Cambridge, in 1634, a young lady 'had conceiv'd a kindnesse for him' (S26/K44), but besides the fact that there was not 'much love of either side', 'his greate heart could never stoope to thinke of marrying into so meane a stock' (S26/K44). Around the same period, he is also said to have remained insensitive to the charms of a woman 'of such admirable tempting beauty, and such excellent good nature, as would have thaw'd a rock of ice, yet even she could never gett acquaintance with him' (S26/K44). By contrast, his encounter with Lucy Apsley in the summer of 1637 in Richmond, dramatically changed his life. This meeting is prepared by the prophecy of a gentleman who 'bid him take heed of the place, for it was so fatall for love that never any young disengag'd person went thither who return'd againe free' (S27/K45). This 'very true' story is about a gentleman who, hearing about 'the death of a gentlewoman that had lived there [Richmond]',

> grew so in love with the description that no other discourse could at first please him, nor could he at last endure any other; he grew desperately melancholly, and would goe to a mount where the print of her foote was cutt, and lie there pining and kissing of it all the day long, till att length death in some months space concluded his languishment. (S27/K45)

---

[33] See *Memoirs*, ed. Sutherland, 27, and ed. Keeble, 45. On *Arcadia*'s 'renaissance' at the court of Henrietta-Maria, see Patterson, *Censorship and Interpretation* 179. On the influence of Sidney's *Arcadia* in the 'Elegies', see Norbrook, 'Lucy Hutchinson's Elegies', 473. See Helen Hackett, 'The Readership of Renaissance Romance', *Women and Romance Fiction in the English Renaissance* (Cambridge: Cambridge UP, 2000) 4–20 and Lori Humphrey Newcomb, 'Prose Fiction', *The Cambridge Companion to Early Modern Women's Writing*, ed. Laura Lunger Knoppers (Cambridge: Cambridge UP, 2009) 272–86.
[34] *Memoirs*, DD/HU4, 24.

This encounter between Lucy Apsley and John Hutchinson so much pleased Stendhal that he quotes the scene in *De l'amour* as evidence of what he calls 'crystallysation'.[35] In his *Souvenirs d'égotisme*, he remembers reading the *Memoirs* during a stay in London in the 1820s and declares that it was 'one of [his] passions'.[36] Stendhal's reactions are not surprising, as this encounter obeys the conventions of the *scène de première vue* (or 'first sight scene'), which, according to Jean Rousset, is a recurrent component of romance, from Heliodorus to Julien Green.[37] Rousset's distinction of the key moments of 'mise en place' [placement] (time, place, characterization, situation of the characters), of 'mise en scène' [the staging of the scene] (the characters' reaction), and, finally, of mutual recognition (with the elimination of the distance separating the characters), is indeed relevant to analyse John Hutchinson's encounter with Lucy Apsley.[38] Accordingly, after recounting the circumstances of their first meeting, Lucy Hutchinson depicts each character's reaction after their eyes actually met:[39]

> yet spite of all her indifference, she was surpriz'd with unusuall liking in her soule when she *saw* this gentleman, who had haire, *eies*, shape, and countenance enough to begett love in any one at the first, and these set off with a gracefull and generous mine which promis'd an extraordinary person [...]. Although he had but an evening *sight* of her he had so long desir'd, and that at disadvantage enough for her, yett the prevailing sympathie of his soule made him thinke all his paynes well payd, and this first did whett his desire to a second *sight*, which he had by accident the next day.
>
> (S31/K49–50, my emphasis)

---

[35] Stendhal, *De l'amour* [1822] (Paris: Garnier Frères, 1906) 304. https://gallica.bnf.fr/ark:/12148/bpt6k5550781f (accessed 13/07/2020).

[36] Stendhal's *Souvenirs d'égotisme* was written in 1832 and first published in English in 1892: '[o]ne evening I was sitting on the bridge which is at the bottom of Richmond terrace, reading Mrs. Hutchinson's *Memoirs*—one of my passions' (Stendhal, *Memoirs of an Egotist*, trans. David Ellis [New York: Horizon Press, 1975] 96). See Richard Bolster, 'Stendhal et les Mémoires de Lucy Hutchinson', *Proceedings of the London Colloquium*, French Institute, 13–16 September 1983, ed. K. G. McWatters and C. W. Thompson (Liverpool: Liverpool UP, 1987) 149. According to Bolster, John and Lucy Hutchinson may have been models for Fabrice and Gina in *La Chartreuse de Parme* (52).

[37] Jean Rousset, *Leurs yeux se rencontrèrent. La scène de première vue dans le roman* (Paris: José Corti, 1981) 7–8.

[38] Rousset, *Leurs yeux se rencontrèrent* 40–6.

[39] See John Hutchinson's obsessional 'desire' to *see* Lucy Hutchinson: 'he began first to be sorrie she was gone before he had *seene* her, and gone upon such an account that he was not likely to *see* her' (S28/K47); 'it so much enflam'd Mr. Hutchinson's desire of *seeing* her that he began to wonder at himselfe that his heart [...] should have so strong impulses towards a stranger he never *saw*' (S29/K47); 'there scarcely past any day but some accident or some discourse still kept awake his desire of *seeing* this gentlewoman' (S29/K47); 'this first [sight] did whett his desire to a second sight' (S31/K50).

The 'distance' between the lovers is soon eliminated: John Hutchinson 'prosecuted his love with so much discretion, duty, and honour, that at the length, through many difficulties, he accomplisht his design' (S32/K51).[40] Another convention of romance that is prominent here is the description of love as a powerful enchantment: '[w]hen Mr. Hutchinson, being alone, began to recollect his wisdom and his reason [...], he [...] began to believe there was some magick in the place which enchanted men out of their right sences' (S30/K48-9). But a few lines down, this enchantment is re-interpreted, and becomes, from John Hutchinson's point of view, the 'miraculous power of providence' (S30/K49). Two pages later, Lucy Hutchinson goes further in her distrust of sentimental romance as she considers it inappropriate to tell the Colonel's life: 'I shall passe by all the little amorous relations, which if I would take the paynes to relate, would make a true history of more handsome management of love than the best romances describe; for these are to be forgotten as the vanities of youth, not worthy mention among the greater transactions of his life' (S32/K51). For her, just as for Calvinists, romance was synonymous with fiction and falsehood and it was too profane a genre to depict the Colonel's 'life of virtue'.[41] The genre was also despicable because it was associated with the Stuart monarchy, and more specifically with the 'royal romance' of Charles I and Henrietta Maria, which she, like John Milton, forcefully condemned.[42]

Nevertheless, when she deals with the love of Mr. and Mrs. Hutchinson, Lucy Hutchinson is not averse to a Christianized counterpart of romance, very close to the Protestant ideal of companionship. In the Dedication, she thus reminds her children that '[n]ever man had a greater passion for a woman,' but that he 'loved her in the Lord as his fellow-creature, not his idoll' (S10/K26). Similarly, she evokes her ancestors' love stories as both accidental and part of God's plan. Like her own marriage, her parents' union is treated

---

[40] See Seelig's list of romance motifs in *Autobiography and Gender* 83, 85: 'the prophetic warning, the parallel situation; the refusal to apply that warning to herself; the ironic reversal'; 'the unconcerned maiden, the rival admirers' (85).

[41] On the condemnation of romance, see William Prynne, *Histro-Mastix: The Players Scourge* (London, 1633). Prynne lumps together plays and fiction, referring to 'the obscenity, ribaldry, amorousnesse, heathenishnesse, and prophanesse of most Play-bookes, Arcadiaes, and fained Histories that are now so much in admiration' (913-14). See Patterson, *Censorship and Interpretation* 179-80. Under Milton's pen, *Arcadia* becomes 'a Book in that kind full of worth and witt, but among religious thoughts, and duties not worthy to be nam'd; nor to be read at any time without good caution' (*Eikonoklastes* in *Complete Prose Works* 3: 362).

[42] Milton, *Eikonoklastes* in *Complete Prose Works* 3: 422. On royal romance, see Potter, *Secret Rites* 76-7; Patterson, *Censorship and Interpretation* 174-90; Zurcher, 'The Political Ideologies of Revolutionary Prose Romance', 550-4. Victoria Kahn, *Wayward Contracts: The Crisis of Political Obligation in England 1640-1674* (Princeton, NJ: Princeton UP, 2004) 139.

both as an act of providence and a product of chance. After they 'accidentally' met, it was 'certainly' the Lord, she writes, 'who had ordein'd him, through so many various providences, to be yoak'd with her in whom he found so much satisfaction' (S29/K47).[43] Likewise, at the beginning of the 'Life of John Hutchinson', she pauses in the genealogy of her husband's family in order to insert 'a story [...] so memorable' (S18/K35), which is nothing else but the story of his grandparents' mutual love on his mother's side. Although John Hutchinson's grandmother had lost her mind 'in a difficult childbirth' (S19/K36), her husband, Sir John Biron, 'retein'd the same fondnesse and respect for her after she was distemper'd as when she was the glory of her age' (S20/K36). But the more 'extraordinary' part of the 'story' is that they died on the same day—'whether some strange sympathy in love or nature tied up their lives in one, or whether God was pleas'd to exercise an unusuall providence towards them [...], it can be but conjectur'd' (S20/K37). Here again, profane romance and God's plan converge to celebrate the mutual love of the memorialist's beloved ancestors. From that angle, the genre of romance appears not to be the exclusive preserve of royalist writings, but also the fabric of Lucy Hutchinson's so-called Puritan *Memoirs*.

Nineteenth-century readers of the *Memoirs* were particularly sensitive to these borrowings from the romance tradition. This was the case of the first editor, Julius Hutchinson, who expected the *Memoirs* to be read as a historical romance: '[t]he ladies will feel that it carries with it all the interest of a novel, strengthened with the authority of real history.'[44] His statement was recurrently quoted or re-written by reviewers of the *Memoirs* and biographers of Lucy Hutchinson.[45] After citing the passage where romances are rejected as the 'vanities of youth', Rev. James Anderson, in his *Memorable Women of the Puritan Times*, thus encouraged readers to imagine the missing sentimental scenes: 'The reader is therefore left to imagine those scenes of endearing interchange of thought and affection which she has not chosen to relate.'[46]

---

[43] Before being described as providential, the encounter of Lucy Hutchinson's mother, Lucy St John, with her husband, Sir Allen Apsley, is also described as 'accidental'. See *Memoirs*, ed. Sutherland, 285, and ed. Keeble, 11. See Patricia Patrick, '"All that appears most casuall to us": Fortune, Compassion, and Reason in Lucy Hutchinson's Providentialism', *Studies in Philology* 112.2 (2015): 327–52, here 336–7.

[44] Julius Hutchinson, 'Preface', *Memoirs* xiv.

[45] Julius Hutchinson's advice is taken up in Benjamin Flower's review of the *Memoirs*, *Political Review and Monthly Register* 3 (1808): 241. See also *The Monthly Review* 53 (1807): 261–4; *The Oxford Review; or, Literary Censor* 39 (1807): 44–5, and Jeffrey, Rev. of *Memoirs*, *Edinburgh Review* 9–11.

[46] James Anderson, *Memorable Women of the Puritan Times* (London, 1862), vol. 2, 62.

Emily Owen, in *The Heroines of Domestic Life*, considered that 'the umbrageous solitudes of Richmond were made the theatre of a little romance, the record of which resembles in character the creations of fiction, rather than reality; yet is, in effect, strictly true.'[47] Jeffrey, in *The Edinburgh Review*, described Lucy Hutchinson as a perfect romance heroine, in the style of Madame de Staël and Rousseau's 'Corinnes' and 'Heloises': '[T]here is something in the domestic virtue and calm commanding this English matron, that makes the Corinnes and Heloises appear insignificant.'[48] In William Russell's words, she was 'a child of a remarkable idiosyncrasy, and clearly prefigurative of the firm-minded, high-principled woman, who, though tender, loving, feminine as the pattern-lady of conventional romance, stood unflinchingly by her gallant husband alike in the shock of mortal strife'.[49] The characterization of John Hutchinson as a hero of romance did not escape nineteenth-century readers either.[50] For Julius Hutchinson, the Colonel was superior to heroes of fiction, and in particular 'to the Grandison of Richardson'.[51] Margaret Oliphant, in *Blackwood's Edinburgh Magazine*, compares him to Samuel Richardson's Grandison, and praises Lucy Hutchinson's 'chronicle of his deeds, his wisdom, his fine Grandison presence, his magnanimity'.[52] A few pages later, she concludes by celebrating her craft in portraying her husband: 'Altogether this fine Quixote Grandison stands out from the troubled background of petty plot and squabble, like a great Titian portrait full of colour and life.'[53] Some late Victorian writers even decided to elaborate on the Hutchinsons' love story.[54] In 1882, an Anglican clergyman, Joseph Antisell Allen, decided to write a play entitled *The True and Romantic Love-Story of Colonel and Mrs. Hutchinson*, which was meant 'to bridge over this very gap in their history [...] by narrating the strange, romantic, and beautiful story of his

---

[47] Emily Owen, *The Heroines of Domestic Life* (London, 1861) 153.
[48] Jeffrey, Rev. of *Memoirs*, Edinburgh Review 5. 'Corinne' is a character from Madame de Staël's *Corinne ou l'Italie* and Julie appears in the *Nouvelle Héloïse*—both novels are often labelled 'pre-romantic'.
[49] William Russell, *Extraordinary Women: Their Girlhood and Early Life* (London, 1857) 75.
[50] See *Memoirs*, ed. Sutherland, 31, and ed. Keeble, 49.
[51] Julius Hutchinson, 'Preface', *Memoirs* xiii. See Samuel Richardson, *The History of Sir Grandison* (1753).
[52] Margaret Oliphant, 'Autobiographies. N° VI — In the Time of the Commonwealth: Lucy Hutchinson — Alice Thornton', *Blackwood's Edinburgh Magazine* 132 (1882) 79–101, here 79.
[53] Oliphant, 'Autobiographies. N° VI', 88.
[54] The fictions which the *Memoirs* inspired in the nineteenth century are listed by Race, 'Further Notes on the Hutchinson Memoirs', *Notes and Queries* 145 (13th Series 1) (1923): 166. See Looser, *British Women Writers* 52–3.

love and of their courtship, attended, as they were, by great hazard and many obstacles'.[55] In his romance, *Reginald Hastings*, Warburton occasionally refers to Lucy Hutchinson's *Memoirs* and goes as far as denying them, in a footnote, the status of history, de facto associating them with romance: 'the good lady was not writing history and therefore, perhaps, did not feel obliged to tell the whole truth.'[56]

Admittedly, such nineteenth-century sentimental readings often overshadow the historical dimension of the *Memoirs*. However, they cannot be dismissed too quickly, for they illuminate Lucy Hutchinson's familiarity with the poetics and idiom of 'romance'.[57] It should be added that, by the middle of the seventeenth century, this term did not only designate love stories but also a great variety of writings, from political allegories to pastoral narratives and heroic drama, which abounded in supernatural storms, shipwrecks, scenes of plunder, heroic action, treasons, machinations, rivalries, imprisonments, stolen letters, spies, and more generally in heroic adventures of all kinds.[58] Some of these motifs are woven into the fabric of the *Memoirs* and the Notebook, and suggest that the tropes and story-telling techniques of romance are not necessarily opposed to history, but help give history its shape and meaning. In mid-seventeenth-century England, these ingredients were to be found not only in Sidney and Wroth's pre-war romances but also in contemporaneous prose fiction, for instance in Percy Herbert's *The Princess Cloria* (1652–1661) and Roger Boyle's *Parthenissa* (1651–1669), 'probably the best known of all the mid-century romances'.[59]

---

[55] Joseph Antisell Allen, *The True and Romantic Love-Story of Colonel and Mrs. Hutchinson: A Drama in Verse* (London, 1882) 7.

[56] Eliot Warburton, *Reginald Hastings: Or, A Tale of the Troubles in 164-* (London, 1850).

[57] For readings of the *Memoirs* as romance, see Seelig, *Autobiography and Gender* 5, 73–89. In her study of Halkett's *Memoirs*, Suzanne Trill demonstrates the limits of this type of sentimental reading. Most of her arguments about Halkett apply to Lucy Hutchinson's *Memoirs*. See Trill, 'Beyond Romance? Re-Reading the "Lives" of Anne Lady Halkett (1621/2?–1699)', *Literature Compass* 6.2 (2009): 446–7 and 455, note 12.

[58] See Hackett, *Women and Renaissance Fiction* 2: 'These fictions usually also involve supernatural interventions, amazing coincidences and twists of fate, amidst a general ambience of the marvellous and wondrous.' On the definition of romance see Lee, 'The Meanings of Romance'. On Lucy Hutchinson's engagement with different sorts of romance, see Emily Griffiths Jones, '"My Victorious Triumphs Are All Thine": Romance and Elect Community in Lucy Hutchinson's *Order and Disorder*', *Studies in Philology* 112.1 (2015): 166. Jones shows that 'Hutchinson effects no clear separation between romance that is amorous, psychological, or pastoral (or feminine) and romance that is martial, heroic, or political (masculine).'

[59] Zurcher, 'The Political Ideologies of Revolutionary Prose Romance', 554. On *The Princess Cloria*, see Salzman, 'Royalist Epic and Romance', 224–6 and Zurcher, *Seventeenth-Century English Romance. Allegory, Ethics and Politics* (New York: Palgrave Macmillan, 2007) 153–62. On Boyle's *Parthenissa*, see Zurcher, *Seventeenth-Century English Romance* 131–5. See also Salzman, *An Anthology of Seventeenth-Century Fiction* (Oxford: Oxford UP, 1991) which provides an extensive extract from *The Princess Cloria*.

2. The Civil War through the prism of romance

The Notebook, because it has often been considered as a draft of the *Memoirs*, has never been studied separately from the latter. It should be added that it constitutes a much less attractive narrative—it does not include the romantic encounter between John Hutchinson and Lucy Apsley and only covers the First Civil War in Nottingham.[60] My aim here is to show how, in the first two fragments of the Notebook,[61] and the corresponding passages in the *Memoirs*, some narrative tropes—and more particularly romance tropes—are essential ingredients in the relation of the Colonel's Civil War 'adventures'.[62]

a) Tempests

Tempests are recurrent tropes in ancient and early modern romances, but they also appear as metaphors in non-fictional narratives to represent the disorders of the state.[63] In his essay, 'Of Seditions and Troubles', Bacon, drawing on Virgil's *Georgics*, uses the metaphor of the tempest to describe the disorders of the state:

SHEPHERDS of people had need know the calendars of tempests in state [...]. And as there are certain hollow blasts of wind and secret swellings of seas before a tempest, so are there in states:
——*Ille etiam cæcos instare tumultus*
Sæpe monet, fraudesque et operta tumescere bella.
[Of troubles imminent and treasons dark
Thence warning comes, and wars in secret gathering. Virgil][64]

The tempest is also the metaphor chosen by Lucy Hutchinson to describe the Colonel's tribulations both in the first fragment of the Notebook (Add. MS 39779) and in the *Memoirs*. In the Notebook, she dwells heavily on his hesitations to face the brewing storm of the Civil War. To be sure, John

---

[60] See Emily Jones, 'Romance and Elect Community', 163. On generic hybridity and Lucy Hutchinson's use of romance elements, see Looser, *British Women Writers* 44–5.
[61] Notebook, Add. MS 39779, Add. MS 46172.
[62] On Bunyan, Milton, and Lucy Hutchinson's use of romance, see Keeble, *The Literary Culture of Nonconformity* 154–5.
[63] See Eva Riveline, *Tempêtes en mer. Permanence et évolution d'un topos littéraire (XVIe–XVIIIe siècle)* (Paris: Garnier, 2015).
[64] See Bacon, 'Of Seditions and Troubles', 366, and Virgil, *Georgics*, Book I, 465–6.

Hutchinson was dedicated to the cause of the 'well-affected' and he was ready to make a public commitment, but he was also sharply aware of the tumults to come as well as of the risks of 'shipwreck':

> the tempest of the state then beginning to swell very high, he forbore to take his oath, as being very vnwilling at that time if he could have avoyded it, to embarke himselfe into the troubled sea of publike employments, till the storme were past, least his want of experience should mak[e] his discretion suffer shipwrack.[65]

To a large extent, the references to the 'troubled sea', to the 'storm', and to the 'shipwreck'—all of them romance tropes—set the tone for the Notebook. They also imply that Lucy Hutchinson began writing her defence of the Colonel some time after the actual outbreak of the Civil War (August 1642), when the conflict was becoming most alarming, possibly in the spring or summer of 1643, a period when the Colonel's authority was already challenged by the Committee of War and when, therefore, his wife may have decided to write his defence. Anna Wall has recently argued that Lucy Hutchinson may have started writing the Notebook at a later date, towards 1645–1646.[66]

Interestingly, a similar tempest metaphor is used at the beginning of the *Memoirs*, in the spring of 1642, to describe the Colonel's hesitations to take his oath. However, Lucy Hutchinson does not mention any *shipwreck* in this narrative, and the Colonel, who is said to be 'convinc'd in conscience of the righteousnesse of the Parliament's cause in poynt of civill right' (S53/K75), appears here far less reluctant to get involved in public action than he was at the beginning of the Notebook:

> But he then forbore to take his oath, as not willing to lanch out rashly into publick employments while such a storme hung threat'ning overhead; yet his good affections to godlinesse and the interest of his country being a glory that could not be conceal'd, many of his honest neighbours made applications to him, and endeavoured to gaine his conduct, which he at first in modesty and prudence would not too hastily rush into. (S53–4/K76)

The comparison of the two passages reveals that the sense of doom, which is prominent at the beginning of the Notebook, is absent from the beginning of the *Memoirs* which rather stresses the Colonel's civic commitment and his

[65] Notebook, Add. MS 39779, 42.   [66] See Wall, 'Not so much open professed enemies', 624.

fervent faith. As a matter of fact, the same references to a 'troubled sea', to a 'shipwreck', and to John Hutchinson's 'publick employments' are to be found at the other end of the *Memoirs* to describe the Colonel's predicament in 1660, when he was asked by the Convention to justify his past allegiance to the cause of Parliament.[67] The tempest imagery here confirms that the Colonel's public commitment was retrospectively felt to be highly hazardous and potentially tragic. To be sure, Lucy Hutchinson claims that he eventually succeeded in saving his 'conscience' and his 'discretion' (i.e. his discernment, his ability to judge), but there is still much bitterness and irony in the following excerpt which can be read as a near admission of failure: 'the vaine expence of his age and the greate debts his publick employments had runne him into [...] yeilded him just cause to repent that ever he forsooke his own blessed quiett to embarque in such a troubled sea, where he had made a shipwrack of all things but a good conscience' (S228/K279–80). This sense of doom is confirmed by the Colonel's persisting doubts at the moment of his death: 'Sometimes he would say that if ever he should live to see the Parliament power up againe, that he would never meddle any more either in Councells or Armies' (S265/K322).

Thus, whereas, in the Notebook, the tempest metaphor reflects the tumultuous experience which the Colonel went through at the beginning of the Civil War, it serves, in the *Memoirs*, to generalize the Colonel's experience, pointing to all the 'distempers' affecting the body politic at large, what we earlier called *stasis*. In the *Memoirs*' account of the premises of the war in 1639, the tempest metaphor is used to refer to the oncoming disaster: 'the thunder was heard afarre of ratling in the troubled ayre, and even the most obscured woods were penetrated with some flashes, the forerunners of the dreadfull storme which the next yeare was more apparent' (S36/K56). In Lucy Hutchinson's autobiographical fragment, the tempest trope is first used to represent the Civil War to come. It is strikingly connected with a sexualized image of monstrous birth. Around 1620, that is, at the time of her birth, England, she writes, was 'att peace (it being towards the latter end of the reigne of king James), if that quietnesse may be call'd a peace which was rather like the calme and smooth surface of the sea, whose darke womb is allready impregnated of a horrid tempest' (S279/K4).[68] But three pages down, the extended metaphor of the

---

[67] See Chapter 4, 3 ('Tinkering with history and memory').

[68] On this kind of imagery, the links with Milton and contemporary imagery of monstrous birth, see Purkiss, 'Milton and monsters', *Literature, Gender, and Politics during the English Civil War* 201–2 and Shannon Miller, *Engendering the Fall: John Milton and Seventeenth-Century Women Writers* (Philadelphia: U of Pennsylvania P, 2008) 97–106.

tempest allows Lucy Hutchinson to articulate her own traumatic experience of the Civil Wars with the national tragedy—'that tempest wherein I have shar'd many perills, many feares, and many sorrows, and many more mercies, consolations and preservations, which I shall have occasion to mention in other places' (S281/K7). This passage from the autobiographical fragment is evidence enough of its proximity with both the *Memoirs* and Notebook, which display similar meteorological imagery.

b) A Civil War adventure: Nottingham's magazine of powder

In the first fragment (Add. MS 39779), the Colonel's hesitations to commit himself to the cause of Parliament are directly followed by an episode which shows how, in the spring of 1642, a local quarrel about a magazine of powder eventually 'enforced [John Hutchinson] to engage him selfe'.[69] This is a quasi-independent story, which falls into an exposition, a crisis and a denouement, and serves as a prologue to Lucy Hutchinson's account of her husband's public commitment. It takes the form of a lively dialogue between Lord Newark, the Lord Lieutenant of the county, who, in the King's name, wanted to dispose of the county's powder magazine, and John Hutchinson, who argues that the powder 'belong'd to the trained bands of the county' (S54/K77), that is, to the local militia. The context is that of an impending war, with the passing of 'rude people', namely royalist soldiers.[70] In the Notebook, John Hutchinson's words to Lord Newark offer a vivid picture of royalist 'greate outrages and insolencies':

> Danger yes, my Lord, greate danger there is a troope of horse now in the towne and it hath often hapned so that they haue committed greate outrages and insolencies calling diuers honest men puritanes and roagues with diuers other provoking termes and carriages I my selfe was abused by some of them as I passed on ye roade and n I chanced to meete some gentlemen who assoone as I was past enquired my name and being told it gave me another saying among themselves that I was a puritane and a traitor as or such base terms as 2 or 3 honest men y^t came behind me told me besides your Lordship may be farre of and we ruined before you can come to vs being unarmed and not able to defend our selves from any body and this country being a roade through which vnder the name of Souldiers rude people dayly passe from

---

[69] Notebook, Add. MS 39779, 42^v.   [70] Notebook, Add. MS 39779, 44.

north to South and terrifie the country which if they knew to be naked and vnarmed they would thereby be incouraged to greater insolencies and mischiefes.[71]

In the *Memoirs*, the corresponding episode is not in dialogue form and is considerably shorter. The Colonel warns Lord Newark of the danger, but the latter mentions neither John Hutchinson's reputation as a 'puritan and traitor', nor even his meeting with royalist soldiers. In addition, with the shift from direct to reported speech, the liveliness of the Notebook is lost in the *Memoirs*:

> Mr. Hutchinson told him of some grounds to apprehend danger by reason of the dayly passing of armed men through the Country, whereof there was now one Troope in the towne, and that before they could repayre to my Lord they might be destroy'd in his absence, and with all urg'd to him examples of their insolence. (S55/K77)

It was very probably to keep the vivacity of the scene that Julius Hutchinson decided to incorporate the Notebook's lively dialogue into his first edition of the *Memoirs*, arguing that 'this passage [was] more fully treated in that particular account' and that it 'might amuse some readers'.[72] What is more, in the earlier narrative; a few parenthetical observations, analogous to stage directions, help the reader visualize the scene, with Nottingham people standing at the foot of the town-hall, and Cavaliers being busy weighing the powder at the top. This hierarchy is symbolically inverted by the inhabitants of Nottingham ('the countrie'), who go upstairs and threaten the royalist officers: 'With that the countrie came very fast vp which when the Cavalier captaines which were there saw they slunk downe.'[73] This sense of upcoming conflict is accentuated by the sharp exchange between Newark and John Hutchinson, which serves as proof that the people in Nottingham are ready to draw their swords against the King's soldiers in order to defend their town—the local conflict is also a national one:

> H. My Lord I doe not know what assurance his M^{tie} hath of it but if you please but to looke out of this window [poynting to ye country men below

---

[71] Notebook, Add. MS 39779, 43^v–44.
[72] Julius Hutchinson, ed., *Memoirs* (1806), 82, note y. In the 1808 edition, the exchange is reproduced in a footnote.
[73] Notebook, Add. MS 39779, 45^v.

in ye streets]^74 you will see no inconsiderable ~~men~~ number gathered together who I feare will not be willing to part with it

N. Those are but some few factious men not to be considered

H. My Lord we haue bene happy yet in these vnhappy differences to have had no blood shed and I am confident your Lordship is soe noble to and tender of y^r country, that it would very much trouble you to haue a hand in ye first mans blod y^t should be spent in this quarrell.[75]

The political meaning of the episode slightly differs in the two accounts which were written at distinct moments in time. In the Notebook, in the closing lines of the dialogue, Lucy Hutchinson minimizes the Colonel's differences with Lord Newark and stresses his 'innocencie'. The quarrel over the magazine of powder is presented as an event which made him committed to the cause of Parliament; it is his first significant action in the Civil War, and provides some grounds for his future appointment as Governor of Nottingham. It also constitutes evidence for the integrity of his intentions from the very beginning of the conflict:

N. Cousin if you can answer it I shall be glad of it but Ile assure you I must let his M^tie know it

H. If his M^tie must know it I am very happy I spoke to none but y^r Lordship who I am confident is so noble that you will neither adde nor diminish anithing to my preiudice and then I am confident the iustnesse and reasonableness of what I haue sayd with my owne inocencie in speaking it will beare me out

N. I Cousin but your name is vp allreadie

H. Itt may be soe my Lord and I belieue those that sett it vp had no good wishes to me and as it rise in the name of god let it fall for I know my owne clearenesse and innocencie in anything that can be obiected against me[76]

In the *Memoirs*, Lucy Hutchinson does not mention the Colonel's defence of his 'clearcnesse' and 'innocencie'. The reason for it is that the two narratives do

---

[74] This is added in the margin with an 'x' as a missing element in the sentence. The handwriting is Lucy Hutchinson's.
[75] Notebook, Add. MS 39779, 45. The *Memoirs* give a very similar account of the exchange in reported speech (S56/K78).
[76] Notebook, Add. MS 39779, 45 and *Memoirs* (1806) 88.

not share the same perspective on the exchange. In the Notebook, the episode is expected to vindicate John Hutchinson, as future Governor of Nottingham, not as a regicide. In the *Memoirs*, written after the Colonel's death after the Restoration, Lucy Hutchinson stresses the sense of resignation in the Colonel, whose martyrdom is, as it were, anticipated:

> My Lord replied, he must informe the King, and told him his name was allreddy up. To which Mr. Hutchinson answer'd, that he was glad, if the King must receive an information of him, it must be from so honorable a person; and for his name, as it rise, so in the name of God lett it fall; and so tooke his leave and went home. (S56/K79)

Altogether, the confrontation of the two versions of the Colonel's first 'adventure' shows how each of them is shaped by its specific perspective on the event and its context of composition. Here, as in the affair of the 'forged letter', one realizes that historical truth is deeply unstable, and that each narrative constructs its 'own' truth, disclosing, in so doing, the high stakes of a historian's narrative skills.

c) Confused identities

Lucy Hutchinson's art of telling the Colonel's adventures is also remarkable in the second fragment of the Notebook (Add. MS 46172), which focuses on an incident, both amusing and politically instructive, that has direct consequences on the Colonel's commitment to the public cause of Parliament. In the *Memoirs*, Lucy Hutchinson repeats almost verbatim the Notebook's account of the unexpected visit, at Sir Thomas Hutchinson's Nottingham house, of an armed quartermaster who requested lodgings for a royalist general, Lord Lindsey. John Hutchinson, who was then staying at his father's, received the quartermaster, but out of exasperation at the latter's incivility, threw him out. However, as there were no other free houses in Nottingham, the royalist General ended up settling in Sir Thomas's house. In the meantime, the quartermaster, who fiercely resented John Hutchinson's affront, 'had procur'd a warrant to seize his person' (S64/K88), hence the Colonel's flight from Nottingham, and all the twists and turns that ensued. From a strictly factual point of view, the *Memoirs*' and the Notebook's versions of this incident are close: they focus on a quick succession of actions with no digression or commentary in between. The only notable difference is that the *Memoirs* clarify the action by adding several adverbs and conjunctions, as well as by removing some details in order to bring out the relentless logic of the Colonel's actions:

my Lord hauing seene ye roomes was angrie that they had quarterd him there & would have gone to another house but y^t some who were with him perswaded him to the contrary telling him y^t the towne was so full full that it was vnpossible for him to get any roome vpon which he very ciuilly told m^r Hutchinson y^t he would only desire one chamber for himselfe and one man and that he would not trouble the house with any elce Mr Hutchinson told him y^t his ~~made~~ Lordship now he had seene the house might as he pleased dispose of it after my Lord was gone one came to Mr Hutchinson and told him y^t his best way was to be gone for ~~elce~~ ye man that spoke to him at doore who was the quartermaster generall ~~would~~ had procured vpon his complaint a warrant to seize his person vpon wch Mr Hutchinson returned home with his brother to outhorp where at y^t time Sr Thomas was[77]	*Whereupon* my Lord, having seene the roomes, was very angrie they had made no better provision for him, and would not have layne in the house, but they told him the towne was so full that it was impossible to gett him roome any where elce. *Whereupon* he told Mr. Hutchinson, if they would only allow him one roome, he would have no more; and when he came upon termes of civillity, Mr. Hutchinson was as civill to him, and my Lord only employ'd one roome, staying there with all civillity to those who were in the house. *Assoone* as my Lord was gone, Mr. Hutchinson was inform'd by a friend, that the man he had turn'd out of doores was the Quartermaster Generall, who, upon his complaint, had procur'd a warrant to seize his person; *whereupon* Mr. Hutchinson, with his brother, went immediately home to his owne house at Owthorpe. (S64/K88, my emphasis)

The final twist of this episode is based on a combination of romance tropes—an intercepted letter and confused identities. The letter, in which the Colonel announced his return to Leicester to his wife, 'was intercepted at Prince Rupert's Quarters, and opened and sent her' (S65/K89).[78] This was soon followed by the machinations of a certain Captain Welch, an acquaintance of Lucy Hutchinson's family, who took advantage of her being apparently alone in the house to set a trap for her. At this point in the narrative, 'Mrs. Hutchinson' is turned into a romance heroine as she decides to deceive the man who wants to arrest her husband. Her role is a little more fleshed-out in the *Memoirs* than in the Notebook, as, in the later narrative, the reader is given her thoughts and intentions. However, her actions are more meticulously described—if slightly less neatly—in the Notebook. In both narratives, Lucy

---

[77] Notebook, Add. MS 46172, 93–93^v.
[78] On the interception of letters during the Civil Wars, see Donagan, *War in England* 110–13.

Hutchinson's taste for romance surfaces in her depiction of her cocky attempts at deceiving the scheming Captain:

vpon this Captaine Welch taking occasion to complement told M^rs H: that he admired any man y^t had such a wife as she should be so factious as to doe those things which should force him to flee from her and not dare to shew his face she told him y^t her husband durst shew his face where ever any [hon]est man durst appeare and ~~soe y^t~~ would [n]ever hide it from him he asked then how he came to be absent she told him he was mistaken he was in the house and therevpon thinking all the souldiers had bene quite gone calld downe her brother by the name of her husband Welch very civilly saluted him and told him he [w]ould haue bene glad to haue made him a prisoner had he mett him in any [oth]er place but there he would not for the world offer y^t vncivillitie and after some discourse tooke his leave and went away⁷⁹	Captain Welch [...] taking occasion to tell her of her husband's letter, by way of complement sayd it was pittie she should have a husband so unworthy of her as to enter into any faction which should make him not dare to be seene with her. Whereupon, she being peeck'd, and thinking they were all marcht away, told him he was mistaken, she had not a husband that would at any time hide himselfe from him, or that durst not shew his face wherever any honest man durst appeare. 'And to confirme you,' sayd she, 'he shall now come to you.' With that [she] call'd down her brother, who, upon a private hint, own'd the name of husband which she gave him, and receiv'd a complement from Welch that in anie other place he had bene oblieg'd to make him a prisoner, but there he was in sanctuary; and so, after some little discourse, went away. (S65/K89–90)

The nineteenth-century novelist Lina Chaworth-Musters, herself a descendant of the Chaworths who fought on the royalist side during the Civil War, did not care much about the historical aspects of the *Memoirs*, but she manifestly found them entertaining.⁸⁰ She actually liked so much Lucy Hutchinson's 'naive' description of her own 'duplicity' that she quoted the full episode of the *Memoirs* in her own novel, with only a few adjustments and rephrasings.⁸¹ Yet, the *Memoirs*' original episode was neither intended as fiction nor meant to be entertaining. On the contrary, Lucy Hutchinson aimed at making sense of the confused beginnings of the Colonel's commitment as well as of her own traumatic experience—a long separation from her husband, the fright caused

---

⁷⁹ Notebook, Add. MS 46172, 95–95^v.
⁸⁰ See 'The Chaworth-Musters Family: A Brief History', https://www.nottingham.ac.uk/manuscriptsandspecialcollections/collectionsindepth/family/chaworth-mustersofannesley/chaworth-mustersfamilyhistory.aspx (accessed 11/07/2020).
⁸¹ Chaworth-Musters, *A Cavalier Stronghold* 90–1. Unlike Lucy Hutchinson, Chaworth-Musters imagines the thoughts of Captain Welch: 'He found the quiet, demure girl he had known, changed into a lady of strong Puritanical opinions, and a violent partisan' (90).

by Captain Welch who had 'carried away Mr. Hutchinson' (S60/K90), and a premature delivery:[82] 'Mrs. Hutchinson, within few dayes after her brother was taken, was brought to bed of her eldest daughter, which, by reason of the mother's and the nurse's griefes and frights in those troublesome times, was so weake a child that it liv'd not for foure yeares, dying afterwards in Nottingham Castle' (S67/K91). Such a psychosomatic reading of the episode is absent from the Notebook. In the *Memoirs*, it corresponds to Lucy Hutchinson's attempt to retrospectively motivate events that she only sketched in the Notebook. It is also consistent with the autobiographical dimension of the *Memoirs*, in which, under the traits of 'Mrs. Hutchinson', she gives herself far more importance than in the Notebook.

Finally, this episode of confused identities does not serve the same purpose in the Notebook and in the *Memoirs*. In the Notebook, it reads, above all, as a key moment in the Colonel's political calling and directly follows the powder affair. In the *Memoirs*, there is a stronger focus on Lucy Hutchinson's agency and on her 'imprudence', which echoes not only her own wifely disobedience during the Restoration but also to the extraordinary experiences of other women of the age. I am thinking here of the adventures of two royalist ladies, Anne Halkett and Ann Fanshawe, who, in their own memoirs, bore witness to the extraordinary roles they played in the troubled years of the Civil Wars and Protectorate.[83] In their writings, they picture themselves as romance heroines in exceptional times. As in Lucy Hutchinson's *Memoirs*, one is struck by the porosity between romance and history writing, a form of hybridity which, in fact, affects most of the lives and *Memoirs* written in the wake of the English Revolution.[84]

d) Warfare and romance

Lucy Hutchinson's realistic accounts of warfare also contain romance tropes, such as flights, exchanges, spying and interceptions of letters. Some of these

---

[82] The episode starts in the summer of 1642, after the 'King [...] had now sett up his standard at Nottingham' (S65–K89). It ends when the Hutchinsons go back to Nottingham 'about that time that the battle was fought at Edge Hill' (S67/K91), i.e. 23 October 1643.

[83] See *Memoirs of Anne, Lady Halkett and Ann, Lady Fanshawe*, ed. Loftis, and Gheeraert-Graffeuille, 'Les aventures héroïques d'Ann Fanshawe et d'Anne Halkett', *La Cuisine et le forum* 252-67.

[84] On the conflicting relations between romance and memoirs, see Lesne, *La Poétique des mémoires* 407–8. On history and romance, see Mayer, *History and the Early English Novel*; Marie-Thérèse Hipp, *Mythes et réalités: Enquêtes sur le roman et les mémoires* (Paris: Klincksieck, 1976).

motifs, coupled with relatively sophisticated characterization and motivated action, are present both in the *Memoirs* and Notebook, for example in their accounts of the Colonel's attempt to retake the Fort at the Bridges after the first occupation of Nottingham (18–23 September 1643).[85] The *Memoirs*' relation of the 'very bold adventures' (S103/K133) of the Nottingham soldiers is, overall, faithful to the eventful Notebook, but it shows greater concern for the psycho-political motivations of the protagonists than the earlier record does: John Hutchinson is thus characterized as an ingenious military strategist, who is ready to use any means, including deception, in order to reach his end, namely recovering the fort—deception, a typical ingredient of seventeenth-century fiction, contaminates Lucy Hutchinson's war narrative which reads like romance:[86]

> *whereupon*, on the Lord's Day, *under colour* of hearing a sermon att the greate Church in the Towne, he went thither, and after sermon, from the steeple tooke a view of the Fort at the Bridges, *no one perceiving his designe* but his Engeneer who was with him, and had taken a full survey of Hacker's workes. *Then*, after Supper, he call'd the Committee together [...], and *so* all that time he spent in preparations against the next morning. He sent away orders to the Horse and foote that lay at Broxtow to come to him in the morning by eight of the clock, with all the pioners they could gather up in the country; he sent into the Towne, and caused all the Pioneers there to be brought up, *under pretence* of making a brestwork before the Castle gates, and *pretending to* sett them upon the Platformes, caused all the Cannon Basketts to be fill'd, which he intended for rolling Trenches.
>
> (S100/K130, my emphasis)

Additionally, and quite consistently so, Lucy Hutchinson equates the Governor's warcraft to illusory stagecraft. The enemy was thus made to believe that the assailants were more numerous than they actually were: 'Athough they [the Governor's soldiers] planted so many coulors, the Governor had but eight-score foote and a hundred horse in all that went with him out of the Castle, but he sett the pioneers fairely among them to *make the better shew*' (S101/K131, my emphasis). By contrast, the Notebook hardly signals the

---

[85] This happened on 11–13 October 1643. On the Trent Bridges, see http://www.nottshistory.org.uk/articles/potterbriscoe/trentbridges1.htm (accessed 27/02/2020).

[86] On the use of deception in seventeenth-century prose fiction and for examples of deception, see Edwina Louise Christie's dissertation, 'Dissimulating Romance. The Ethics of Deception in Seventeenth-Century Prose Romance', DPhil thesis, University of Oxford, 2016, passim.

Governor's strategic use of deception.[87] It gives instead a profusion of particulars and only mentions in passing John Hutchinson's use of pretence, merely concluding that the 'Bridge had no notice' of his scheme.[88]

Similar differences can be traced in the two versions of the siege's final phase. In the *Memoirs*, Lucy Hutchinson again probes the motivations of the Nottingham men and dwells on the Governor's ingenious scheme; there is, on her part, an obvious thrill in exposing how her husband trapped the Cavaliers by a cunning ploy and how amused he was at their predicament:

> There was in the Trent a little peice of ground which, by damming up the water, the Cavaliers had made an Island; while some of the souldiers held them in talke, others on Wednesday night cut the sluce, and by breake of day on Thursday morning had pitcht two colours in the Island within Carabineshott of the Fort, and the Governor's Companie had as much advanct their approach on the other side. When they of the Fort saw in the morning how the assailants had advanct while they were kept secure in talke all the night, they were extreamely madde, and swore like devills, which made the Governor and his men greate sport to behold their rage. (S102/K132-3)

Similarly, Lucy Hutchinson is more emphatic about the Governor's self-satisfaction in the *Memoirs*. Still, she takes an equal delight in describing the Cavaliers trapped by the Roundheads in the Notebook: 'when the Cavalliers saw what was done while they were kept in talke on the other side they were very madd & swore like divills.'[89]

It would be unwise, however, to make any hasty generalization about the differences between the *Memoirs* and the Notebook, for in some places, against all odds, the Notebook goes further in the interpretation of events than the *Memoirs*. For instance, the Notebook construes the improvement of weather conditions during the attack as a sign of providence in favour of the parliamentary army: 'though the day they went out was a most foule raynie wett morning [the Commanders and souldiers] were not at all discouraged at the

---

[87] Notebook, Add. MS 25901, 25^v–26: 'and vpon sunday in the afternoone he tooke occasion to goe to St Maries church to heare the sermon in the afternoone and after sermon went vp to ye steeple with some of ye Committee and Mr Hooper and from thence vieued the Bridges and Hackers workes after Supper the Committee being calld together they concluded vpon the designe and the Governor spent all that night in preparing things in a readinesse against the next morning and sent warrants to the Horse y^t were at Broxtow house and a foote Companie y^t lay in Wollorton House to be at Nottingham Castle by eight of the Clock in the morneing and to bring in all the pioners they could gett out of all the neighbour Townes.'

[88] Notebook, Add. MS 25901, 26.   [89] Notebook, Add. MS 25901, 27^v.

weather but persisted and it pleased god y^t after they had endured that weather 3 or 4 houres the day att length grew faire and they had and they had [sic] good weather all the time.'[90] A few lines further down, in an uncharacteristic way, it seeks explanations for the unexpected success of the Nottingham soldiers, invoking both God's mercy and the cowardice of the Governor of the Fort, Hacker:

> Maior Hutchinson & his companie were appointed to possesse the Bridges and keepe them which they did and found the fort so strong that if Hacker had not bene the basest Coward in the World and if god had not bene exceeding merciefull to vs they might haue kept it against many more thousands then we were hundreds.[91]

At this point in the *Memoirs*, Lucy Hutchinson also refers to God's providence, mentioning a day of 'solemne thanksgiving to God for this successe and the mercy in it' (S103/K133), but she leaves out the lack of courage of Hacker. On the other hand, the Notebook, while mentioning 'a solemne thanksgiving',[92] tells, in a romance mode, how a hidden letter revealed that Hacker had not obeyed Biron and Newcastle's command to break the Bridges: 'There was a letter found in Hackers chamber windore from Sr Richard Biron to Hacker wherein he writt Hacker word that he had receiued order from my Lord Newcastle to breake vp the Trent Bridges but for some reasons he did not yett intend to doe it.'[93]

The romance trope of disguise is also present in some episodes of the Civil War in both the Notebook and *Memoirs*, where it is used to describe royalist infiltration stratagems.[94] A first occurrence is to be found in the Notebook's account of the occupation of Nottingham in September 1643, when 'many of those men y^t lay hid came in ye night by the Line side in weomens apparell & other disguises vp to the Castle so y^t by Saturday there were about eight score come vp.'[95] Interestingly, the carnivalesque element of cross-dressing is downplayed in this place of the *Memoirs*, which only specify that 'some by night

---

[90] Notebook, Add. MS 25901, 28.
[91] Notebook, Add. MS 25901, 28^v. See the corresponding passage in *Memoirs* 133.
[92] Also mentioned in the Notebook: 'The next weeke there was a Solemne thanksgiving for gods mercie in delivering these Bridges out of the enemies hands Captaine Palmer and m^r Cotes preached One mercy more I must not forgett there was not a souldier of our side lost in this service nor wounded except foure and they so slightly that two of them went into the field againe next day' (28^v).
[93] Notebook, Add. MS 25901, 28^v.
[94] See David Cressy, 'Gender Trouble and Cross-Dressing in Early Modern England', *Journal of British Studies* 35.4 (1996): 438–65, here 452 for interesting examples in Elizabethan fiction.
[95] Notebook, Add. MS 25901, 23.

came up to the Castle and got in in disguizes by the river side' (S95/K124).[96] But it is conspicuous in a later episode: in February 1644, when the royalists wanted to retake the Fort at the Bridges, Lucy Hutchinson takes an obvious delight in ridiculing the appearance of the Cavaliers—some of them cross-dressed as women and carrying strange paraphernalia: 'About eleven of the clock on Saturday, the 17th of February, they [the Governor's soldiers] tooke 12 of them upon the Bridges disguiz'd like markett men and weomen, with pistolls, long knives, hatchetts, daggers, and greate pieces of iron about them' (S119/K152).[97] Among the disguised royalists, 'five were drown'd' after leaping into the Trent to save themselves, while only four were 'pluckt […] out of the water' (S119/K152).[98] The four prisoners were 'afterwards releas'd […] upon exchange, except one Slater, a souldier of his owne that had runne away to the enemie, and was this day was taken coming into the Towne, with a Mountero pull'd close about his face, but he denied that he was of the designe' (S119/K153).[99] A final use of disguise by the royalists is mentioned in the *Memoirs*' story of a certain Captain-Lieutenant Jammot who was made a prisoner in Nottingham and managed to run away incognito: 'he corrupted a souldier, who disguiz'd him and led him out, and went away with him' (S112/K144). In the Notebook, we learn that he was wearing 'a mountero cap a coate and a musket on his shoulder'.[100] Lucy Hutchinson does not make any comment on the use of disguise, but the fact that she associates it with royalist corrupted soldiers and, later, with the King suggests her Puritan contempt for this romantic practice.[101] This also echoes the contemporary Calvinist condemnations of cross-dressing, which was interpreted as effeminate and decadent. It is here significantly politicized.[102]

As appears from these examples, neither the Notebook nor the *Memoirs* have a monopoly on romance tropes when it comes to recording the Civil War. It should be noted that in some places, however, the Notebook surprisingly gives more importance to circumstances and romance details than the

---

[96] This is repeated two pages later: 'fourscore were come in by stealth' (S97/K126).
[97] *Memoirs*, ed. Keeble, 152 and Notebook 53: 'about eleuen of ye clock on Saturday ye 17th of febru: they tooke twelue of the rogues vpon the Bridge in ye disguise of markett men & weomen with a pistoll long kniues daggers hatchetts & greate peices of iron.'
[98] This episode is also echoed in Chaworth-Musters' *A Cavalier Stronghold* (288). The romance ingredient of disguise is kept, but the Bridges are not mentioned and the attack takes place in the 'spring of 1644', not in February as in the *Memoirs*.
[99] A montero was the type of cap worn by Civil War soldiers. It had flaps that could be folded down in case of bad weather. See https://deborahloughcostumes.com/17gengal1.html (accessed 10/07/2020).
[100] Notebook, Add. MS 2590, 47^v.
[101] See Lucy Hutchinson's account of the King's flight from Oxford in 1646. During the siege of Oxford 'the King was stollen out of that Towne and gone in a disguize' (S165/K206).
[102] See Cressy, 'Gender Trouble and Cross-Dressing', 441–5.

Memoirs, which, generally speaking, go further in exploring the motivations of the actors of the Civil War in Nottinghamshire.

3. The ubiquity of treachery: a darker vein of history

In the *Memoirs*, Lucy Hutchinson is obsessed with treachery not only when she describes the strife within Nottingham's Committee of War but also when she looks at the shifting alliances of the local gentry and aristocracy in time of war, or when she deals with the Commonwealth and Protectorate. Her narrative skills—those of a moralist and a story-teller—are all directed at uncovering the motives behind the masks, an ambition she shares with ancient historians, like Thucydides and Tacitus, as well as with her near contemporary, Edward Hyde, Earl of Clarendon.[103]

a) Turncoats

The *Memoirs* abound in characters whose political allegiances are not stable, and one of Lucy Hutchinson's first concerns is to try and identify the allegiances of the gentlemen revolving around the Colonel, especially those whose loyalties were not clear.[104] At the beginning of the Civil War, she makes the treacherous Colonel Thomas Ballard—the commander for Parliament of Lincolnshire—responsible for the Parliament's defeat at the siege of Newark in February 1643.[105] During the attack, Ballard, she argues, was more eager to protect 'his former royalist benefactors', than to defend Parliament with the help of troops from the neighbouring counties (Derbyshire, Lincolnshire, and Nottinghamshire).[106] Her criticism of the Captain is more concise and effective in the *Memoirs*, where she condemns his 'sloth and untoward carriage'—a moral dimension absent from the Notebook which, in this particular instance, is more descriptive than critical:

---

[103] See Burke, *The Renaissance Sense of the Past* 134–6.
[104] On the important issue of allegiances, see Rachel Weil, 'Thinking about Allegiances in the English Civil War', *History Workshop Journal* 61 (2006): 183–91. On side-changing during the Civil Wars, see Hopper, *Turncoats and Renegadoes*. Collins, *Martial Law and English Laws* 183. On this issue, see also Donagan, *War in England* 243–4; 276–8.
[105] Notebook, Add. MS 25901, 7–8ᵛ; Mayer, 'Life of Writing', 315.
[106] On Ballard, see Hopper, *Turncoats and Renegadoes* 65–66, and *Memoirs* (S76/K102–103): 'one Ballard, a gentleman who, decay'd in his famely and owing his education to many of them, had bene bred up in the warres abroad.'

wherevpon the Lincolneshire Commanders came to them & told them that they were wonderfull sorrie to see this carriage but desired them not to be discouraged at it but to goe on now they had begun and withal told them how much they had bene troubld for them least they should have come according to y\ appppointment & haue bene cut of & how Ballard had y\ day playd his ordinance a mile of from y\ towne & when Newark horse appeard vpon y\ Beacon hill y\ Lincolneshire troopes being many more in number y\ they and very disirous to haue charged them being assured of Successe if they would haue stood the fight or if they fled to fall in with them into y\ Towne Ballard would not suffer a man of them to stirre.[107]	the Lincolneshire Commanders inform'd ours of the slowth and untoward carriage of Ballard, and told them how he had that day play'd his Ordinance at a mile's distance from the Towne, and how, when the Newark Horse came out to face them, upon the Beacon Hill, he would not suffer a man of the Lincolneshire Troopes to fall upon them, though the Lincolne horse were many more in number than they, and in all probabillity might have beaten them. (S77/K103)

Similar differences in phrasing are to be found in the epilogue to the siege of Newark, in which Lucy Hutchinson's denunciation of Ballard is scathing: 'The next day all the Captaines importun'd Ballard they might fall on againe, but he neither would consent nor give any reason of his deniall; so that the Nottingham Forces return'd with greate dissatisfaction, though Ballard, to stop their mouths, gave them two pieces of Ordinance' (S77–8/K104). Significantly, Lucy Hutchinson's suspicions about Ballard, expressed both in the *Memoirs* and Notebook, were widely shared by supporters of Parliament,[108] and publicized in the press, notably in the royalist newsbook *Mercurius Aulicus*.[109]

In Lucy Hutchinson's gallery of suspected traitors, there is also Francis Pierrepont (the third son of the first Earl of Kingston, Robert Pierrepont), who stood on the Parliament's side and was appointed colonel in command of the parliamentary troops for Nottinghamshire in December 1642.[110] Although

---

[107] Notebook, Add. MS 25901, 7   [108] See Wood, *Nottinghamshire in the Civil War* 42.

[109] See Hopper, *Turncoats and Renegadoes* 66 and *Mercurius Aulicus*, 14th week, 2–9 April (Oxford, 1643) 175.

[110] On Francis Pierrepont, see David Scott, 'Pierrepont, Francis (b. after 1607–1658), politician' (2015), *Oxford Dictionary of National Biography*, DOI: 10.1093/ref:odnb/94585. The Earl of Kingston is said to have 'devided his sonns between both Parties' (S61/K84). The allegiances of the members of the Pierrepont family are best described in a crossed-out passage in the manuscript (Nottinghamshire Archives, DD/HU4, 89): 'My Lord Newarks eldest sonne to the Earle of Kingston was Lord Liefetenant and wholly of the royall Party M\ William Pierreponts next brother was of the Parliament though he [sat] not for his owne country to which notwithstanding he was a greate glory being one of the wisest Councellors and excellent speakers in the house [...] he had a younger brother living in Nottingham who coldly [ownd] the Parliament the Earle their father stood Neuter some time but at last declared unhappily for the king and was shott.'

Lucy Hutchinson portrays him as 'a man of good naturall parts [...] who was in the maine well affected to honest men and to righteous liberty' (S72/K98), she has serious reservations about his courage and genuine commitment to the cause:[111] '[a]lthough his Collonell might seeme to be in the same hazard, yet he was wise enough to content himselfe with the name, and leave Mr. Hutchinson to act all things, the glory of which, if they succeeded, he hoped to assume; if they fail'd he thought he had a retreate' (S76/K102). Lucy Hutchinson also critically refers to his 'coldnesse' (S76/K102), or 'cold behaviour' (S80/K106), which, she argues, explains why 'the affaires of the warre at Nottingham went more tardily on than elce they would have done' (S76/K102). She also underscores the contradictions between Pierrepont's public commitment and his private interests, pointing to his decision, after John Hutchinson was appointed Governor of Nottingham, to move his children and wife in safe royalist households: 'Two or three days after this he went to his mother's, and carried his children with part of his goods, and sent his wife to Sir Gervas Clifton's house' (S87/K115–16).[112] At this stage, both the *Memoirs* and Notebook denounce Pierrepont's double-talk in equivalent terms:

> But such was the double heart of the man that though in the Publick Hall he had soe declared his opinion to his companie yet to diverse people in the Towne he cast out speeches against it and some he told that for his owne part he would so long as he had life spend it for the good of the Towne that no extremitie should force him into the Castle y^t he would either die vpon the works or when he had stood out so long as he was able to defend them if he were forced to it he would flie to some other Garrison.[113]

Another more serious reason why Lucy Hutchinson is so cautious about Francis Pierrepont lies in the equivocal relationship he entertained with his mother, the wife of the first Earl of Kingston, whom she suspected to have plotted against the town of Nottingham, possibly with her son's complicity. Lucy Hutchinson circumstantially describes the exchange of letters between

---

[111] Lucy Hutchinson retrospectively rehabilitates Pierrepont (S83/K110). See also Pierrepont's defence of Colonel Hutchinson before the Committee of Both Kingdoms (S145/K183).

[112] The Cliftons were a very wealthy and influential royalist family in Nottinghamshire. See *Memoirs*, ed. Keeble, 356, note 165.

[113] See Notebook, Add. MS 25910, 14^v. See the corresponding passage in *Memoirs*, ed. Sutherland, 87–88, and ed. Keeble, 116.

mother and son, and stresses the role as go-between of an unidentified woman spy, thereby revealing how family links and political allegiances dangerously intersected in times of Civil War:[114]

> An intelligence was brought to the Committee by a friend then with the Earle of Newcastle that Mr. Francis Pierrepont kept intelligence with his mother, the Countesse of Kingston, carrying on a designe for the betraying of the Towne to the Earle, and that letters were carried betweene them by a woman who often came to Towne to the Colonell [Pierrepont], and that two men Aldermen and a chiefe officer employ'd about the Ordinance were confederates in the plot; whereupon a suspected Canoneer was secur'd, who, assoone as he obtein'd his liberty, ranne away to Newark. (S85/K112)

A second plot woven by the Countess, in which her son, Colonel Pierrepont, may well have been involved again, is exposed by Lucy Hutchinson as she reports how the same unidentified woman spy was caught carrying a highly compromising packet of letters, 'from the old Countesse to her daughter in law, the Collonell's wife, who was then at Clifton, at Sir Gervas Clifton's house' (S93/K122). The episode—especially the contents of the epistolary exchanges—is told in slightly more detail in the *Memoirs* than in the Notebook, but the two narratives are very close in their description of the Committee's reactions:[115]

> The Committee hauing read these letters sealed them vp againe in another which they sent to Coll: Pierrepont then at Derbie wherein they aquainted him y^t having mett with such letters and not knowing whether his wife might follow her mothers advice the which if she should might prooue very dishonorable to him they had sent the letters to him rather than to her: The Coll: was much discontented that they had opened his letters but sayd not much at y^t time of it[116]

These stories of intercepted letters, which were frequent in times of war, but also common motifs in romance, come as a confirmation of Lucy

---

[114] Akkerman, *Invisible Agents* 4–7.
[115] Notebook, Add. MS 25901, 20^v–21. The episode is entitled: 'My Lady Kingstons woman taken with letter to m^{rs} Pierpont'.
[116] Notebook, Add. MS 25901, 21–21^v. See *Memoirs*, ed. Sutherland, 93–94, and ed. Keeble, 122–3.

Hutchinson's suspicion of Colonel Pierrepont's duplicity.[117] They resonate with similar stories in the *Memoirs*, for instance the interception 'at Prince Rupert's Quarters' (S65/K89) of John Hutchinson's letter to his wife in the spring of 1642,[118] or Secretary Bennet's possession of compromising letters in Lucy Hutchinson's hand (S254/K309). In all cases, there is no confusion between historical reality and romance, but the sense again that it is through her ingenious use of narrative skills that Lucy Hutchinson manages to make sense of the often confused reality of Civil War allegiances.

With the story of Francis Pierrepont's father, Robert Pierrepont, the first Earl of Kingston, the memorialist goes one step further in her depiction of treachery. First described as an ambiguous character, the Earl of Kingston soon falls into the category of traitor, who deserves death. He is in fact the protagonist of an edifying self-contained tale about the perils of neutrality and political indecisiveness.[119] Strictly speaking, this story has no direct impact on the life of John Hutchinson; however, it speaks volumes for Lucy Hutchinson's rejection of all forms of compromise, which is a central tenet in the *Memoirs*. The story starts with the Earl of Kingston's prophetic imprecation by which he brings doom upon himself and ends with the fulfilment of the Earl's ominous prophecy:[120]

> My Lord professing himselfe to him rather desirous of peace, and fully resolv'd not to act on either side, made a serious imprecation on himselfe in these words: "When," said he, "I take arms with the King against the Parliament, or with the Parliament against the King, let a CannonBullett devide me betweene them"; which God was pleas'd to bring to passe a few months after; for he, going in to Gainsborough and there taking armes for the King, was surpriz'd by my Lord Willoughby, and, after a handsome defence of himselfe, yielded, and was put prisoner into a pinnace and sent downe the river to Hull; when my Lord Newcastle's Armie marching along

---

[117] The interception of the royal correspondence at the battle of Naseby was notoriously disclosed in the *Kings Cabinet Opened. Or, Certain Packets of Secret Letters & Papers*. See Potter, *Secret Rites and Secret Writing* 58–65 and Michael J. Braddick, 'Naseby and the End of the War', *God's Fury, England's Fire: A New History of the English Civil Wars* [2008], (London: Penguin, 2009) 380–3. Exchanges of letters, conveyed and intercepted letters, etc. abound in Boyle's *Parthenissa*. On the presence of epistolary culture in romance, see Andrew Zurcher, 'Allegory and Epistolarity: Cipher and Faction in Sidney and Spenser', *Cultures of Correspondence* 110–27.

[118] See Chapter 5, 2, c ('Confused identities').

[119] We also learn that 'The Earle of Kingston a few months stood neuter and would not declare himself for either party' (S79/K106). See also the case of the Hothams, whose story is only briefly told by Lucy Hutchinson. See *Memoirs* (S79–81/K106–9); Hopper, *Turncoats and Renegadoes* 8–9.

[120] On the relationship between side-changing and neutrality, see Hopper, *Turncoats and Renegadoes* 10–11, 23 (on the Earl of Kingston, Robert Pierrepont).

the shore, shot at the pinnace, and being in danger the Earle of Kingston went up upon the decks to shew himselfe and to prevaile with them to forbeare shooting, but assoone as he appear'd a Cannon bullett flew from the King's Armie and devided him in the middle, being then in the Parliament's pinnace, who perished according to his owne unhappy imprecation.

(S80/K107)

The Earl of Kingston's death is all the more ironical as he was killed by the Cavaliers with whom he had eventually sided. Lucy Hutchinson writes that his death occurred a few months after his imprecation in July 1643, but the resultative clause in the above quotation ('which God was pleased') effectively conveys the impression that divine punishment immediately followed the self-fulfilling prophecy. The crude description of the Earl of Kingston's divided body stands as a warning against side-changing and neutrality, as well as an eloquent emblem for the confusion and uncertainty of divided times.[121] In the Notebook, the same events are reported as they allegedly 'hapned'; they are more loosely connected and less meticulously dramatized than in the *Memoirs*. There is no explicit reference to a divine punishment falling on the Earl either, but the sense of immanent justice is nonetheless present. His imprecation, also reported in direct speech, is only the subject of a brief flashback situated at the precise moment of his death:

> It hapned about this time y^t my Lord Willoughbies forces surprised Gainsbourough & tooke their Generall ye Earle of Kingston who being sent in a pinnace to Hull the Cavalliers took ye pinnace but it hapned that the Earle was devided in ye middle by a Cannon bullett & so perished according to his owne imprecation on himselfe for when Capt Lommax being sent to mooue him in some things concerning this businesse vpon occasion of discourse My Lord sayd to him when euer I take armes with the King against ye Parliament let me be devided with a Cannon Bullett soe perished he betweene both being shot with a Cannon bullett by the Cavalliers and being prisoner to the Parliament.[122]

In the *Memoirs*, this edifying event, which occurred during the siege of Gainsborough, is briefly reported again, with the logic of the Earl's death

---

[121] See Murphy, 'Lucy Hutchinson's Civil War Ghost Writing', 95–6.
[122] Notebook, Add. MS 25901, 10^v.

emphasized—'the Earl of Kingston [...] was immediately sent prisoner to Hull, where he was shot according to his owne imprecation' (S82/K109–10).

In between the two accounts of the Earl of Kingston's death, Lucy Hutchinson has placed another edifying story the better to warn the reader against side-changing. The protagonists, the 'two Hothams', two parliamentary officers, the father and the son, betrayed the cause of Parliament by intriguing with the royalists, '[w]hen they marcht away, a Troope of my lord Greye's, having the charge of guarding Hotham [the younger] towards London, suffer'd him to escape, and thereby putt the Towne of Hull into greate hazard, but that the father and sonne were there unexpectedly surpriz'd, sent up prisoners to London, and after some time executed' (S82/K109).[123] Just before reaching this conclusion, Lucy Hutchinson deplores the ill conduct of Hotham (the son) and Gell's pro-Parliament troops. Her emotion is conveyed by the personification of Nottingham as a grieving woman, as it were betrayed by those who should have protected her: 'Then was Nottingham more sadly distressed by their friends than by their enemies; for Hotham's and Gell's men did not only lay upon free quarter, as all the rest did, but made such a havoc and plunder of friend and foe that 'twas a sad thing for any one that had a generous heart to *behold* it' (S81/K108, my emphasis). To substantiate her description, she brings forward her husband's similar distress at *seeing* his county betrayed by those who should have defended it: 'Mr. Hutchinson was much vext to *see* the county wasted, and that little part of it which they could only hope to have contribution from eaten up by a company of men who, instead of relieving them, devour'd them' (S81/K108, my emphasis). Lucy Hutchinson was no relativist—she stood on the side of Parliament—but she was obsessively intent on unveiling human depravity and sin beneath the 'surface' of historical reality, to the point of identifying an evil streak among her countrymen, even those who belonged to her own party.

b) Traitors and spies

In an even darker vein of moral history, the Notebook recounts how, on several occasions, Colonel Hutchinson, as head of Nottingham's Committee

---

[123] On these two men, see David Scott, 'Hotham, Sir John, first baronet (1589–1645), parliamentarian army officer' (2004), *Oxford Dictionary of National Biography*, DOI: 10.1093/ref:odnb/13852 and Scott, 'Hotham, John (1610–1645), parliamentarian army officer' (2004), *Oxford Dictionary of National Biography*, DOI: 10.1093/ref:odnb/13853. On Sir John Hotham (the younger), see Donagan, *War in England* 158. On the Hothams, see Hopper, *Turncoats and Renegadoes* 170–4 and passim.

of War, had to preside over courts-martial in order to judge men suspected of entertaining intelligence with the enemy. In parliamentary garrisons, the laws of war were regularly read to the soldiers, who were thus warned that '[a]ll such as shall practise and entertain Intelligence with the Enemy, by any manner or means or slights, or have any communication with them, without direction from my Lord Generall, shall be punished as Traitors and Rebells,' that is to say, most of the time, by death.[124] Significantly, Lucy Hutchinson hardly mentions the Colonel's administration of martial law in the *Memoirs*, while in the Notebook, she shows her intimate acquaintance with the codes and practices of war, and reveals John Hutchinson's use of torture.[125]

This difference is first conspicuous in her account of the royalists' failure to recapture the Trent Bridges in February 1644, when five soldiers from Newark were taken prisoners. Four of them, disguised as market-people, were considered to be standard prisoners of war and were exchanged with Nottingham soldiers, according to the codes of war (S120/K153–4). However, the fifth one, a certain Matthew Slater, a former soldier from the Colonel's regiment, was not exchanged, but charged with treason and sentenced to death.[126] In the *Memoirs*, Lucy Hutchinson specifies that Slater's execution was not decided by the Governor alone, but by a court-martial, that is, a jurisdiction which directly emanated from Parliament:[127]

> The Governor was in doubt whether these men taken in disguizes were to be releas'd as prisoners of warre, or executed by martiall law as spies or assassines; but though he had not car'd if the bridge souldiers had turn'd them into the Trent when they tooke them, he afterwards releas'd them all upon exchange, except one Slater, a souldier of his owne that had runne away to the enemie, and was this day taken coming into the Towne with a Mountero pull'd close about his face, but denied that he was of the designe; yet after, upon triall at a Court martiall, he was condemn'd and executed.
>
> (S119/K152–3)

---

[124] *Laws and Ordinances of Warre, Established for the Better Conduct of the Army, by His Excellency the Earl of Essex* (London, 1643) sig. A3. On articles of war, see Donagan, 'The Evolution of English Articles of War', *War in England* 141–156, and John M. Collins, *Martial Law and English Laws, 1500–c.1700* (Cambridge: Cambridge UP, 2016) 16–17; 105–9; 119–20. On treason and martial law, Collins 179–80.

[125] On the 'popular acquaintance with the ways of war', see Donagan, *War in England* 139–40.

[126] On the treatment of prisoners, see Matthew Sutcliffe, '*CHAP. XXI. Part. 8.* Comprising orders concerning booties, spoyles, and prisoners taken in warres', *Practice, Proceedings, and Lawes of Armes* (London, 1593) 338. See also Donagan, *War in England* 157–8 and Collins, *Martial Law and English Laws* 175.

[127] See Collins, *Martial Law and English Laws* 1–3, 10.

Matthew Slater's story is told twice in the Notebook.[128] First, in the same place as in the *Memoirs*, when he was caught after the royalists' failed attempt to reclaim the Trent Bridges. The emphasis is laid on the Governor scrupulously following judicial procedures: after informing Mr. Millington, the MP for Nottingham, he asked from the 'Lord Generall' (i.e. Essex) a commission in order to implement martial law, which was a way of making clear that the decision to execute Slater was not left to his own discretion:

> This day one Slater y^t was formerly the Governors souldier & ranne away to the enemie was taken but he denied that he was of ye designe The Governor immediately writt to Mr Millington the relation of the Businesse and desired a Commission for ye executing of the martiall Law & to know of my Lord Generall whether these men y^t were taken in disguize should be executed as spies or released as souldiers.[129]

Ten pages down, still in the Notebook, Lucy Hutchinson returns to the case of Slater and provides more details about his shady past. She painstakingly reconstructs the story of his successive treacheries, false repentance and promise to amend, which culminates in his breaking the Solemn League and Covenant:

> one matthew slater was condemned to be hanged [blank] by ~~was~~ a councell of warre he was formerly a souldier of ye Governors when he came first into ye castle & left his coulours when vpon ye Governor taking him he made greate expressions of sorrow & contrition for his faults and promised amendment & desired to take ye Couenant & beare armes still in ye Governors company the Governor told him if he did it not with a right heart he had much better lay downe armes & worke of his trade then to engage himselfe in such a solemne Couenant & then ~~bre~~ prooue false in it but he was very desirous to take it wherevpon Cap^n Pallmer gave it him & within two or three dayes after he had taken it he went away into ye enemies quarters and there remained till y^t day ye bridges were to haue bene surprised by shellford men & then came to Towne where he was taken comming over the Bridge mufled close in a mountero cap & kept prisoner till this councell of warre where in regard of his willfull breach of Couenant he was condemned to death & after hanged.[130]

---

[128] On martial law procedures, see Collins, *Martial Law and English Laws* 40–1, 113, 170, 180ff.
[129] Notebook, Add. MS 25901, 53^v.   [130] Notebook, Add. MS 25901, 61^v–62.

The jurisdiction which judges Slater is called 'a councell of warre' in the Notebook, while in the *Memoirs* Lucy Hutchinson calls it a 'court-martial'. The two terms are interchangeable, but Lucy Hutchinson's lexical hesitation testifies to a shift in the organization of military justice from the sixteenth to the seventeenth century, described by John M. Collins in his thorough study of early modern martial law.[131] It also indicates that Slater's condemnation to be hanged (repeated at each end of the passage) was a concerted decision between army officers, not the product of the Governor's discretionary power. All in all, the three different versions of Slater's story (one in the *Memoirs* and two in the Notebook) reveal how, in each case, Lucy Hutchinson privileges a different element to suit her narrative purpose. In her Notebook accounts, written before the execution of Charles I, her depiction of the Colonel's administration of martial law merely serves as a defence of his authority before the quarrelsome and vindictive Nottingham Committee. In the *Memoirs*, she stresses the *exemplarity* of the Colonel as Governor of the castle, but she remains vague about Slater's trial and the Governor's role in it. This difference is likely to come from Lucy Hutchinson's retrospective reluctance in the *Memoirs* to deal with an event that could be easily associated with her husband's later involvement in the trial of the King as well as his own death—he died in captivity in Sandown Castle in Kent, but he was not properly tried and the allegations against him were never proved.[132]

The case of a certain Captain Dean, a turncoat from Parliament, only mentioned in the Notebook, resembles that of Slater.[133] In a similar way, Lucy Hutchinson recounts the circumstances that brought him to his execution, despite his request for mercy. She insists once again on the fact that the Governor diligently followed the procedures. At a time when her husband's authority was challenged by the Committee, it was important for her to point out that the decision to execute Dean was not made by the Governor alone, but by a council that had once again been properly called:

---

[131] Collins shows how courts-martial changed from the beginning of the sixteenth century. Commanders, who were given the power to administrate martial law, were then expected to take the advice of other officers gathered in a 'council of war'. On courts-martial, see Collins, *Martial Law and English Laws* 107–17 and Donagan, *War in England* 134–96.

[132] See Seddon, 'Hutchinson, John (1615–1664), *ODNB*.

[133] The story of Dean is told before that of Slater in the Notebook: 'When ye Nottingham forces Horse were in ye vale of Belvoir captaine pallmers troope tooke on Captaine Deane who had formerly bene receiued a Commission from ye Earle of Essex to rayse a troope of horse in Nottinghamshire & endeavoured to doe it but before he had gotten any men went away with six case of pistolls to ye enemie & there continued about Belvoir and Wiverton till at length Captaine Pallmers men mett with him & brought him prisoner to Wiver Nottingham'. (Add. MS 25901, 61)

this & some other trialls upon life being to be determined the Governor would not call a councell of warre vpon them till he had a speciall commission from my Lord Generall wch he writt to him for & my Lord sent it to him & after it was come a Councell was called where he being brought before them & examined confessed his fault & desired ye mercie of the councell & was condemned to be shott to death 4 months after this respite of time being all ye favour they could afford him.[134]

Finally, another spy story, situated in July 1644 during the siege of York, is far more developed in the Notebook than in the *Memoirs* which only briefly evokes the capture and escape of a 'spy':

There was againe a new designe against the Garrison by the enemie discover'd, and a spie taken, who own'd a souldier in the Major's Companie that had listed himselfe there on purpose to effect his mischiefe; but through carelesse custody the spie escap'd that day that the Garrison were celebrating their joy for the greate victory at Yorke. (S134/K170)

By contrast, the Notebook goes beyond the *Memoirs*' factual account and brings to light the Governor's recourse to torture to exact confession from the spy who happens to be a young boy. This use of torture, which was not recognized as legal by the English Common Law, was frequent, however, under martial law, as is attested in Matthew Sutcliffe's treatise, *The Practice, Proceedings and Lawes of Armes* (1593).[135] It was indeed established that if there were no eyewitnesses, or if there was only circumstantial evidence, the suspect's confession was required as proof of guilt—hence the recourse to torture (the 'racke or other paine') to extort confessions from suspects.[136] In this respect, the behaviour of the Governor towards the boy spy, however

---

[134] Notebook, Add. MS 25901, 61^v.

[135] Collins, *Martial Law and English Laws* 169–70. Collins points out that '[o]ver the course of the Civil Wars and Interregnum [...] [c]ourts-martial had been authorized to punish soldiers, sailors, conspirators, and spies' (169). He adds: 'Further, parliamentary garrison courts-martial, which sat periodically throughout the war, tried civilians and soldiers for treason by martial law' (169). See George Ryley Scott, *History of Torture Throughout the Ages* [1940] (London: Luxor Press, 1959) 86–94, especially Chapter XI, 'Torture in Great Britain and Ireland', which addresses the issue of judicial torture in England; Edward Peters, *Torture*, expanded edition (Philadelphia: U of Pennsylvania P, 1996) 40–72.

[136] Sutcliffe, *The Practice, Proceedings and Lawes of Armes* 340. On Sutcliffe's treatise on martial law, see Collins, *Martial Law and English Laws* 93–6. On the use of torture in order to obtain evidence of guilt, see Collins 38, and John H. Langbein, *Torture and the Law of Proof* [1976] (Chicago: U of Chicago P, 2006) 4–5.

appalling it may have been, can be interpreted as legitimate, rational, and in keeping with the customs of the time.[137]

Lucy Hutchinson's account is doubly instructive. First, it documents the types of torture inflicted on spies who could have their fingers burned with match or have a rope tightened round their heads. Then, it reveals the identities of the spy's accomplices and their motivations, which, at the time when the narrative was written, was probably of capital importance for John Hutchinson. However, torture was only partly successful here. Despite the rope and the match, Brinsley, a turncoat and a vile traitor, refused to confess anything:

> Saturday [blank] a boy was taken gazing in the towne & brought vp vpon suspition of being a spie & being burnt with match confessed y^t he came from Newark & brought two letters to the Towne & deliuerd them to a man in ye Towne who formerly had bene a corporall at Wiverton & was sent hither to list himselfe as a souldier y^t he might haue the more oppertunitie to doe mischiefe here he sayd he knew the man & ye place where he lived but knew not his name & y^t at 4 of the clock in ye afternoone he should haue had an answer of the letters he owned the man among 40 others but ye fellow who was one Griffin a souldier in the Maiors company vtterly denied y^t he knew or had euer seene ye boy or receiued any letters from him which yet ye boy with so many circumstances soe constantly affirmed y^t ye man was first tortured with match betweene his fingers & y^n with a rope about his head y^n he confessed that had had letters twice from ye boy & had deliuered them to one Brinsley who was a butcher of this towne of a leud life & conversation & most mallignant to this cause & had from ye beginning bene a trooper vnder Sr Richard Biron at Newark but came in before ye first of march & tooke ye Couenant & soe was receiued into the Towne but ye Governor had euer held him in such distrust y^t when there was any danger he clapt him in close prison. he was vpon this tortured but would confesse nothing & though many other circumstances were prooued against him yet would he not be perswaded to confesse anithing.[138]

In *A Cavalier Stronghold*, Lina Chaworth-Musters offers a rewriting of this scene of torture. She mentions the *Memoirs* which, in her view, abounded in

---
[137] See Collins, *Martial Law and English Laws* 37.
[138] Notebook, Add. MS 25901, 70–70^v. On extracting information from prisoners, see Donagan, *War in England* 106–7.

such scenes: '[t]he cruel operation of tying burning match between the fingers of prisoners to torture them into giving information, was resorted to by Colonel Hutchinson, as his wife tells us, more than once during his governorship of Nottingham.'[139] As a matter of fact, neither this scene, nor any other scenes of this kind, can be found in the *Memoirs*. It is likely therefore that the novelist had Firth's edition of the *Memoirs* at hand, as this editor included the Notebook's scene of torture in an appendix.[140] It is also possible, as suggested in the preface of her novel, that she drew on 'local traditions'[141] as well as on family papers, since she was herself a descendant of the royalist Chaworths of Wiverton, who played an important part during the Civil Wars in Nottinghamshire. In any case, adopting a point of view opposed to Lucy Hutchinson's, Chaworth-Musters brings out the cruelty of the Governor and makes him responsible for several acts of barbarity. Although (to be fair) she depicts him in some places as 'brave and pious', she also adds that he was 'stern', 'despotick', and, she implies, barbaric. In her own narrative of the war, unlike Lucy Hutchinson, she appears less concerned with the strictly military dimension of the episode than with the melodramatic effect it could produce on the reader:

"We have burnt all his right fingers with match, sir," said the soldier named Thomas, gravely saluting, "and he still says he doesn't know; shall we go on with the left hand?"

"By all means," said the Colonel, without raising his eyes from the map, "and if that does not do, try a string round his head. We brought that Nottingham ruffian to his senses that way, I remember, and you can fetch the boy here again, Thomas, if he doesn't find his tongue after that, and just hitch a rope over that elder tree by the gate."[142]

There is undoubtedly some self-indulgence in the dramatization of this torture scene, but Chaworth-Musters's representation is not unfounded. It is confirmed by other sources which indicate that the Colonel's recourse to torture was not exceptional. According to the Presbyterian journalist, John Vicars, the

---

[139] Chaworth-Musters, *A Cavalier Stronghold* 341.
[140] See 'On the treatment of prisoners, &c.', *Memoirs*, ed. Firth, 1885, vol. 2, Appendix III, 369–71 and *Memoirs*, ed. Firth, 1906, 431–8.
[141] See the Preface (unpaginated) where the author mentions 'local traditions': '[t]he only excuse that can be made, is, that a number of local traditions, collected with some care, appeared worthy of preservation, and it was difficult to offer them in a readable form, without weaving them into a sort of narrative.'
[142] Chaworth-Musters, *A Cavalier Stronghold* 293; 340–1.

'prudent' Colonel used torture for instance to extort a confession from the disguised royalists in February 1644, an episode that is conspicuously absent from both the Notebook and *Memoirs*:

> Hereupon these *couzening Cormorants* were further examined, but were very unwilling to confess the Plot for all this, onely they said they were sent as Spies from *Newark*, but the prudent Governour (before whom they were now brought) seriously examining the businesse, and being too old a bird to be caught or couzend with such chaffe, took match and caused their fingers to be tyed therewith, and told them what they must trust to, except they would speedily discover the Plot.[143]

Although the crimes committed during the English Civil War are assumed to be less atrocious than those perpetrated during the Thirty Years' War in Germany, the Governor's repeated recourse to torture reminds us that the culture of violence was also much present in England during these years. It puts into perspective, as Barbara Donagan has argued, the cynical assumption that the Civil War was 'a kinder, gentler war' than the continental wars.[144]

The main reason—apart from literary propriety—why the Colonel's use of torture, explicitly recorded in the Notebook, is not mentioned in the *Memoirs* is that the two texts do not share the same purpose. As has been established above, the Notebook is first and foremost a defence of the Colonel in his military role as Governor. The administration of martial justice was part of his commission and this could imply condoning many evils, including torture. As Donagan argues, '[t]he codes of war forbade many evils, but they also sanctioned many.'[145] But the mention of this breach of natural law, which could be tolerated in the Notebook's military context, would have been problematic in the *Memoirs*. First, in civil society, torture was severely condemned, especially after the recent wars waged on the Continent. Sutcliffe's remark is eloquent: 'The *Spaniards* in the beginning of their warres in the Low countreys killed cruelly as many as they tooke: but when they saw them selues to be dealt withall in like sort, they repented, and perceiued that such sauage cruelty is contrary to the nature of faire warres.'[146] Second, the mention of the Colonel's

---

[143] John Vicars's chronicle *Gods Arke Overtopping the Worlds Waves, or The Third Part of the Parliamentary Chronicle* (London, 1645) 164. See also Wood, *Nottinghamshire in the Civil War* 66.
[144] Donagan, 'Atrocity, War Crime, and Treason', 1146-7 and *War in England* 135-8.
[145] Donagan, *War in England* 135.
[146] Sutcliffe, *Practices, Proceedings, and Lawes of Armes* 338. On this issue, see Donagan, *War in England* 15 and Langbein, *Torture and the Law of Proof* 8-10.

inhumanity in the *Memoirs* would have considerably weakened his status as a Christian martyr, republican leader, and defender of ancient liberties.[147] Lucy Hutchinson could not possibly denounce the illegal barbarity of her husband's gaolers at the Restoration and at the same time describe him as a torturer.[148] It would have tarnished his reputation as a 'man of conscience',[149] and contradicted his practice of the virtues of justice, charity and mercy, which are highlighted in her programmatic Dedication, as well as in other places of the *Memoirs*, as when she dwells on the Colonel forgiving his enemies in the early days of the republic.[150]

The comparison of the *Memoirs* and the Notebook helps highlight the fact that Lucy Hutchinson's narrative technique does not greatly differ in the *Memoirs* and the Notebook. Both narratives display similar literary skills, the use of similar tropes and an acute attention paid to the moral motivations of the protagonists of history, which, according to Norbrook, connects Lucy Hutchinson to humanist historians such as Sir Thomas More and George Buchanan.[151] This confirms that the Notebook should not be seen as a draft, but as a carefully-contrived narrative, focusing on the local realities of the war and the military responsibilities of Colonel Hutchinson during the First Civil War. It is also obvious that Lucy Hutchinson's later choice in the *Memoirs* to leave out entire passages from the Notebook comes from her desire to offer a defence of her husband that was not restricted to his role as Governor of Nottingham. This more ambitious project implied specific narrative choices, especially the articulation of the life of John Hutchinson with more than twenty-five years of national history. Indeed, unlike the Notebook, the *Memoirs* do not merely offer a linear narrative, but a far more complex one, based on a systematic use of digressions.[152]

c) Oliver Cromwell as the great dissembler

Lucy Hutchinson's narrative skills as a moralist and story-teller are again combined in her polemical characterization of Cromwell. In some passages

---

[147] Donagan, *War in England* 137. The *Petition of Right* limited the use of martial law to times of war. See Collins, *Martial Law and English Laws* 169–71.
[148] See *Memoirs*, ed. Sutherland, 251, and ed. Keeble, 306. The Colonel and the other prisoners of the Tower 'were barbarously used by them', namely the 'Lieftenant and his Cerberus, Cresset'.
[149] See Lobo, 'Lucy Hutchinson's Revisions of Conscience', 329.
[150] See *Memoirs*, ed. Sutherland, 200, and ed. Keeble, 246.
[151] Norbrook, 'The English Revolution and English Historiography', 233.
[152] On digressions, see Chapter 6, 'The historian's craft (2): Lucy Hutchinson's art of digression'.

of the *Memoirs*, Cromwell is described as the victor of Marston Moor (S127/K161) and as 'uncorruptably faithfull both to his trust and the people's interest' (S172/K214); in one place, he is even called 'gallant and great' (S209/K257). But he is mostly characterized as a great dissembler, that is, as a Machiavellian betrayer of the Good Old Cause, an accusation that appeared in the many books and pamphlets published during the Interregnum and after the Restoration.[153] For instance, despite their divergent political views, Ludlow, Baxter and Hyde, like Lucy Hutchinson, maintained that in the 1650s—if not before—Cromwell had betrayed the cause he had served during the two Civil Wars.[154] Cromwell was also said to have deceived all his former friends. As John Morrill points out: 'His career from 1649 is therefore littered with his betrayals of those he had previously embraced and called his friends— the Levellers, above all his old friend John Lilburne in 1647–49, the civil republicans in 1651–53, Harrison and the Fifth Monarchists in 1653, veteran army colleagues in 1654, Lambert and the paper constitutionalists in 1657.'[155]

Lucy Hutchinson repeatedly blames Cromwell for his dissimulation and his ambition, which spoiled his qualities as a political and military leader. Her perspective matches up with Bacon's ambivalent view of dissimulation, which can be considered a political accomplishment as long it coincides with 'penetration and judgement'.[156] But when dissimulation becomes 'a habit', it grows into 'a hindrance and a poorness'.[157] As for ambition, like dissimulation, it is double-edged. In Bacon's words again, '[a]mbition is like choler; which is an humour that maketh men active, earnest, full of alacrity, and stirring, if it be not stopped. But if it be stopped, and cannot have his way, it becometh adust,

---

[153] See Hyde, *History of the Rebellion*, vol. 6, 335: 'the greatest dissembler living'. MacGillivray calls him 'an arch-betrayer' (*Restoration Historians* 184). See also John Morrill, *Oliver Cromwell and the English Revolution* (London: Longman, 1990): 'What gives the charge against Cromwell – that he was the great dissembler – residual credibility is the quite remarkable number of instances in which he got what he wanted in controversial circumstances and in which denials of foreknowledge and responsibility strain credibility' (13). According to Morrill, 'Oliver Cromwell was the subject of well over two hundred tracts and broadsheets in his own lifetime' (*Oliver Cromwell* 260). On Cromwell as a Machiavellian figure, see Laura Lunger Knoppers, *Constructing Cromwell: Ceremony, Portrait, and Print 1645–1661* (Cambridge: Cambridge UP, 2000) 15–19.

[154] John Morrill invites us not to trust memorialists whose views were too 'black-and-white' and 'stereotyped': 'Without accusing Edmund Ludlow, Richard Baxter, Bulstrode Whitelocke and Edward, Earl of Clarendon of deliberate distortion, it is unsafe to depend upon their memoirs as the best guide to how Cromwell was viewed in his own lifetime' (*Oliver Cromwell* 259–60). The present study wishes to show why Lucy Hutchinson's view of Cromwell, however distorted it may be, is valuable even to the historians. On other views on Cromwell, see *Reliquiæ Baxterianæ*, Part I, 99–100; ed. Keeble et al., vol. 1, 434–5; Hyde, *History of the Rebellion*, vol. 6, 91–5; Ludlow, *Memoirs*, vol. 2, 447–50.

[155] Morrill, 'Introduction', *Oliver Cromwell*, 17.

[156] Bacon, '6. Of Simulation and Dissimulation', *Essays*, 349.

[157] Bacon, '6. Of Simulation and Dissimulation', *Essays*, 349.

and thereby malign and venomous.'[158] In her portrayal of Cromwell, Lucy Hutchinson does not mention Bacon, but she seems to share his twofold view of ambition and dissimulation and maintains that they can be used in a positive way.[159] In her portrayal of Cromwell's case, however, she sees ambition as a 'poyson' which, in the early years of the Commonwealth, 'so ulcerated [his] heart that the effects of it became more apparent than before' (S193/K239). Cromwell, she adds, was 'molding the Army to his mind, weeding out the godly and upright-hearted men [...] and filling up their roomes with rascally turnecoate Cavaliers, and pittifull sottish beasts of his own alliances, and others such as would swallow all things and make no question for conscience' sake' (S194/K239). The 'godly religious Armie', which had won the Civil War, was 'almost chang'd', Lucy Hutchinson argues in another attack on Cromwell, 'into the dissolute Armie they had beaten, bearing yett a better name' (S208/K256). In other words, Cromwell's 'private ambition' (S202/K249) eventually turned him and his 'slaves' into 'greater usurpers on the people's liberties then the former Kings' (S216/K265).[160]

This emphasis on Cromwell's tyranny was typical of Restoration historiography.[161] But what makes Lucy Hutchinson's vitriolic portrait of Cromwell a significant landmark is that her charge against him is grounded in her personal knowledge of his conduct towards Colonel Hutchinson in the 1640s and 1650s.[162] She probably did not attend their encounters herself, but there is no doubt that, here as elsewhere, the Colonel gave her circumstantial accounts of them. The relations of these occurrences may sound tedious and repetitive, but they were meant to open the eyes of 'superficiall beholders' (S194/K240)— that is, the readers—who could not see that Cromwell's 'friendship' and 'generosity' were deceptive. With scathing irony and very 'penetrating eies' (S194/K239), Lucy Hutchinson thus sketches an alternative portrait of Cromwell, using her accounts of his exchanges with the Colonel as evidence to negate the widely-held idea that he was England's new Moses.[163] This behind-the-scenes approach is typical of the memoir genre in which private

---

[158] See Bacon, '36. Of Ambition', *Essays*, 414.

[159] Baxter makes explicit references to Bacon's essay 'Of Simulation and Dissimulation' in his description of Cromwell. See *Reliquiæ Baxterianæ*, Part I, 99–100; ed. Keeble et al., vol. 1, 435.

[160] See Claire Gheeraert-Graffeuille, 'Formes et figures de la tyrannie dans les *Memoirs of the Life of Colonel Hutchinson* de Lucy Hutchinson', *Le Prince, le despote, le tyran: figures du souverain en Europe de la Renaissance aux Lumières*, ed. Myriam-Isabelle Ducrocq and Laïla Ghermani (Paris: Honoré Champion, 2019) 211–26.

[161] See Morrill, *Oliver Cromwell* 12–13, 268–70. In *Behemoth, or, An Epitome of the Civil Wars of England* (London, 1679), Hobbes associates the dissolution of the Rump with Cromwell's ambition (253).

[162] This is pointed out by MacGillivray in *Restoration Historians* 184–5.

[163] See Morrill, 'Cromwell and his Contemporaries', 271–3.

details and anecdotes serve to substantiate a moral portrait which may be in contradiction with other versions of history.[164] It is also very close to what Peter Lake has recently described as 'secret history', that is, 'a way of narrating and analysing the course of recent history in terms of the manoeuvres of various political agents, all driven, despite their frequent assertions to the contrary, by the will to power, to money, and status, rather than by any commitment to the (always already linked) causes of true religion and the commonweal'.[165]

The first meeting between Cromwell and Colonel Hutchinson mentioned in the *Memoirs* occurred in June 1643 after the rendezvous of Parliament's forces at Nottingham. By then, the regiments of 'Colonell Cromwell, Colonell Hubbard, my Lord Grey and Sir John Gell' (S80/K107) were joined by the troops of 'the younger Hotham', who, in Lucy Hutchinson's words, was 'rude' (S80/K107) and 'had a great deale of wicked witt' (S81/K108). His ill-behaviour was all the more treacherous as '[y]oung Hotham all that time carried on a private treaty with the Queene, and every day receiv'd and sent trumpetts, of which he would give no account' (S81/K108). At first, Cromwell and the Colonel agreed on the necessity of acting against Hotham and his soldiers—the 'scumme of mankind' (S81/K108). Being 'equally zealous for the publick service, [they] advis'd together to seeke a remedie, and dispatcht away a post to London [. . .] to informe the Parliament of Hotham's carriages, and the strong presumptions they had of his treachery and his ill-management of their forces' (S81/K108). According to Lucy Hutchinson's retrospective interpretation, this apparent concord was deceptive, as Cromwell started to regard John Hutchinson's moral integrity as an obstacle to his own future attempts to manipulate him. By depicting Cromwell's distrust of the Colonel and contrasting his hypocrisy with her husband's outspokenness, she levels slanderous accusations at Cromwell while setting the tone for their next meetings:

---

[164] On this type of characterization, see Chapter 6, 3 ('Politico-moral digressions'). On the use of portraits in memoir-writing, see Lesne, *La Poétique des Mémoires* 115–60. What Lesne writes about the portrait of Mazarin in French memoirs (140–51) is applicable to Lucy Hutchinson's portrait of Cromwell.

[165] See Peter Lake, *Bad Queen Bess? Libels, Secret Histories, and the Politics of Publicity in the Reign of Queen Elizabeth I* (Oxford: Oxford UP, 2016) 5. French memorialists of the latter part of the seventeenth century were particularly prone to using testimonial anecdotes and secret history, as has been shown by Karine Abiven, *L'Anecdote ou la fabrique du petit fait vrai. De Tallemant des Réaux à Voltaire (1650–1750)* (Paris: Classiques Garnier, 2015) 198–205. Significantly enough, the subtitle of Julius Hutchinson's edition of the *Memoirs* mentions 'original anecdotes of many of the most distinguished of his contemporaries'.

Those who knew the opinion Cromwell after had of Mr. Hutchinson believ'd he register'd this businesse in his mind as long as he liv'd, and made it his care to prevent him from being in any power or capacity to persue him to the same punishment when he deserv'd it; but from that time, growing into more intimate acquaintance with him, he allwayes us'd to professe the most hearty affections to him, and the greatest delight in his plainnesse and open-heartedness that is imaginable. (S82/K109)

Strikingly enough, the next private encounter, which took place at Nottingham in 1648, follows the same pattern, with an even more conspicuous rivalry between an outspoken Colonel and a deceitful Cromwell (S180/K223), as John Hutchinson seizes the opportunity to plead for the Lieutenant General to change his heart and support the cause of Parliament again. The use of reported speech here gives the impression that the episode is recounted *as it really happened*, Lucy Hutchinson turning the reader into a virtual witness to the scene—a method she uses in several other places in the *Memoirs*.[166] The idea here is that, as a behind-the-scenes memorialist, Lucy Hutchinson has a knowledge of Cromwell's passions and character that the reader wants:

The Colonell, who was the freest man in the world from concealing truth from his friend, especially when it was requir'd of him in love and plainnesse, not only told him what others thought of him, but what he himselfe conceiv'd; and how much it would darken all his glories, if he should become a slave to his owne ambition, and be guilty of what he gave the world just cause to suspect, and therefore beg'd of him to weare his heart in his face, and to scorne to delude his enemies, but to make use of his noble courage in daring to maintain what he believ'd just against all greate oposers.
(S180/K223)

From the reaction of Cromwell who made 'mighty professions of a sincere heart to [the Colonel]', Lucy Hutchinson infers again his hypocrisy and maintains that 'for this and such like plaine dealing with him, he dreaded the Collonell, and made it his particular businesse to keepe him out of the Armie' (S180/K223). The first illustration of her theory about Cromwell as a great dissembler comes with the Colonel not being given the commandment of the regiment of his late friend, Colonel Thornhagh. According to her husband,

---

[166] On this notion of virtual witnessing, see Shapin, 'Pump and Circumstance', 491. For a similar technique, see Lucy Hutchinson's account of the meeting between Ireton and the King (S172/K214).

Cromwell's 'particular carriage' towards him was 'a proofe of other things suspected of him, so destructive to the whole cause and party, as it afterwards fell out' (S183/K227). In other words, his disloyalty towards the Colonel manifested his betrayal of the national cause of Parliament.

In the pages devoted to the 1650s, Lucy Hutchinson continues to gather evidence against Cromwell, denouncing his repudiation of Christian and republican values. She mentions a third encounter in the early days of the Commonwealth when the Governorship of Hull was coveted by two opposing factions—John Hutchinson sided with the Governor of Hull against Cromwell. Her shift from reported speech to direct speech vividly dramatizes the rivalry between Cromwell and the Colonel—the ambition of Cromwell, who was not yet Protector, being manifested by his use of the royal 'we' to express his will:

> The Colonell told [Cromwell], because he saw nothing proov'd against him worthy of being ejected. "But," sayd Cromwell, "wee like him not." "Then," sayd the Colonell, "doe it upon that account, and blemish not a man that is innocent upon false accusations, because you like him not." "But," sayd Cromwell, "wee would have him out, because the Government is design'd for you, and except you putt him out you cannot have [it]." (S193/K238)

According to Lucy Hutchinson, this conflict over the governorship of Hull constitutes new evidence of Cromwell's hostility towards Colonel Hutchinson. Indeed, when the Governor of Hull, Robert Overton, was 'confirm'd in his place', Cromwell was so 'displeas'd' that he 'secretly labour'd to frustrate the attempts of all others who, for the same reason that Cromwell labour'd to keepe him [John Hutchinson] out, labour'd as much to bring him in' (S193/K239). In the 1650s, the Colonel and Cromwell were brought together again as both sat on the Council of State. By then, Colonel Hutchinson had become fully aware of Cromwell's 'lying professions' (S194/K240), which he considered to be no less than a betrayal of the godly cause. The unbridgeable gap between the two men is reflected by the sharp distinction between 'us' ('all our triumphs') and Lucy Hutchinson's mention of Cromwell's destruction of the cause:

> All this while he carried to Mr. Hutchinson the most open face, and made the most obliegeing professions of friendship imaginable, but the Colonell saw through him, and forbore not often to tell him plainely what was suspected of his ambition, what dissimulations of his were remarked, and how dishonorable to the name of God and the profession of religion, and destructive to

the most glorious cause, and dangerous to overthrow all our triumphs, these things which were suspected of him would be, if true. (S194/K240)

The final encounter, which is mentioned in the *Memoirs*, took place shortly before the Cromwell's death (3 September 1658). It starts with Colonel Hutchinson hearing that the 'Lambertonians' had designed a plot to assassinate Cromwell—a conspiracy of which the historian C. H. Firth could not find any trace.[167] 'Judging that Lambert would be the worser Tirant of the two' (S210/K258), the Colonel decided to report the plot to the Protector, but he nevertheless remained circumspect and impassive as he was aware of Cromwell's ill-intentions towards him. The conversation between the two men started 'in one of the galleries' at Whitehall and continued in 'a private place', where Cromwell was 'using all his *art* to gett out of the Collonell the knowledge of the persons engag'd in the conspiracy against him' (S211/K259, my emphasis). Each man played the role he had been ascribed from the beginning with Cromwell as the arch-hypocrite and Colonel Hutchinson as the truth-teller. In the highly theatrical discussion which followed, Cromwell expressed among other things, 'an earnest desire to restore the people's liberties' and promised to 'employ such men of honor and interest as the people should rejoice', implying he wanted the Colonel to return to public life (S211–2/K260). But as could be expected from this ironic account, he eventually proved false to Colonel Hutchinson who was soon told that, 'notwithstanding all these faire shewes, the Protector finding him too constant to be wrought upon to serve his tirannie, had resolv'd to secure his person least he should head the people, who now grew very weary of his bondage' (S212/K261). The Colonel was not arrested, however, as death stopped Cromwell from fulfilling his plan. Lucy Hutchinson describes his demise as a form of divine retribution—all his ambitions and tyranny being reduced to naught. In her view, he was not the agent of providence he took himself for: 'before his guards apprehended the Collonell, Death imprison'd himselfe, and confin'd all his vast ambition and all his cruell designes into the narrow compass of a grave' (S212/K261).[168]

It can be argued that Lucy Hutchinson's systematic record of Cromwell's ill-conduct towards Colonel Hutchinson serves as the basis for her acerbic and

---

[167] *Memoirs*, ed. Firth, 300, note 2.
[168] Lucy Hutchinson's description of Cromwell's death resonates with her account of the sudden death of another traitor, the Earl of Kingston. See Notebook, Add. MS 25901, 10^v.

polemical account of his tyranny. Her contention is that Cromwell was not intent on serving the public good when he took the title of Lord Protector, but that he was merely driven by his thirst for monarchical power, with no concern for the institution of Parliament nor for its representatives.[169] When Cromwell broke the Rump in 1653, Lucy Hutchinson claims, he was blind to the fact that 'the hand of God was mightily seene in prospering and preserving the Parliament' (S191/K236); on the contrary, he and his supporters 'endeavour'd to bring all good men into dislike of the Parliament [...] and had no care to bring in those glorious things for which they had so many yeares contended in blood and toyle' (S205/K252). Hence, her retrospective contention that 'Oliver's mutable reigne' (S207/K255)—that is, the military regimes which followed the dissolution of the Rump—'had destroyed what had been a genuine republican work-in-progress'.[170] To her, the Protector, by relying far too much on the army, had betrayed the republic, in the same way as the Presbyterians had betrayed the cause of Parliament during the Second Civil War; to her, he was not God's instrument, but a Machiavel, and his regime was a mere mockery of monarchy.

The *Memoirs*' condemnation of Cromwell's tyrannical politics is finally encapsulated in a satirical attack on the monarchical aspects of the Protectorate. Despite his refusal of the crown in March 1657, Lucy Hutchinson suspected him of aspiring to kingship.[171] The royal ambitions of Cromwell's wife and children are ridiculed just as they were in some royalist and radical playlets of the late 1640s, which targeted the grandees' wives—and especially Mrs Cromwell—in order to discredit their husbands:[172] 'His wife and children were setting up for principallity, which suited no better with any of them than scarlett on the Ape; only, to speak the truth of himselfe, he had

---

[169] On the monarchical aspects of the Protectorate, see Joad Raymond, 'An Eye-Witness to King Cromwell', *History Today* 47,7 (1997) 35–41. See also Knoppers, *Constructing Cromwell* 1–9.

[170] Jonathan Scott, *Commonwealth Principles. Republican Writing of the English Revolution* (Cambridge: Cambridge UP, 2004) 13.

[171] On the perception of the Protectorate as a monarchy without a king, see Benjamin Woodford, *Perception of a Monarchy without a King: Reactions to Oliver Cromwell's Power* (Montreal: McGill-Queen's UP, 2013) 3–19.

[172] See for instance, Man in the Moon, *A Tragi-comedy, Called New-Market-Fayre; or, A Parliament Out-Cry* ([London, 1649]) and Mercurius Melancholicus, *The Cuckoo's Nest at Westminster; or, The Parliament between Two Lady-Birds: Queen Fairfax, and Lady Cromwell* ([London], 1648). One of the first satires against Cromwell is John Cleveland, *The Character of a London Diurnall* (London, 1645). On anti-Cromwellian satires, see Knoppers, *Constructing Cromwell* 1–5, 10–30; Morrill, 'Cromwell and his Contemporaries', Wiseman, *Drama and Politics* 48–49, 67–9; Gheeraert-Graffeuille, *La Cuisine et le forum* 270–3. On Lucy Hutchinson's art of satire, see Chapter 6, 3, b ('A gallery of portraits').

much naturall greatnesse in him, and well became the place he usurp'd' (S208/K256). Lucy Hutchinson also implies that Cromwell's parody of kingship desacralized the institution of monarchy:[173] '[a]tt last he tooke upon him to make Lords and Knights, and wanted not many fooles, both of the Armie and gentry, to accept of and strut in his mock titles' (S209/K257). Cromwell's own officers are scathingly represented as 'slaves' or as the 'tirant's minions' (S210/K259) whom he manipulated: he 'overaw'd them all, and told them, it was not they who upheld him, but he them, and rated them, and made them understand what pittifull fellows they were; whereupon they all like rated dogs, clapt their tayles betweene their leggs, and beg'd his pardon' (S210/K258). Assuming a Puritan preacher's voice, Lucy Hutchinson sees Cromwell's court as 'full of sinne and vanity, and the more abominable because they had not yett quite cast away the name of God, but prophan'd it by taking it in vaine upon them. [...] Hipocrisie became an epidemicall disease, to the sad griefe of Colonell Hutchinson and all true-hearted Christians and Englishmen' (S209/K257). In these pages, Lucy Hutchinson takes on the role of polemicist, with no care about recording facts that would be validated by experience.

As a matter of fact, she offers an even more scathing portrait of the Lord Protector in her answer to Edmund Waller's *A Panegyrick to My Lord Protector* (1655).[174] According to David Norbrook, this discrepancy may come from the fact that each text was written in a specific context. When Lucy Hutchinson was writing the *Memoirs* some time between 1664 and 1667, the stakes had changed and she was less polemical. There was no longer any 'overlap between republican and royalist activities', and her aim was chiefly 'to show [Cromwell's] part in the overall history of the Good Old Cause'.[175] Another difference originates in the fact that Lucy Hutchinson's portrait of Cromwell in the *Memoirs* is retrospective, and based, as has been shown above, on her husband's experience of the General's hypocrisy. In these episodes, which are perfectly integrated into the main narrative of the *Memoirs*, Cromwell is depicted as the Colonel's companion-in-arms, until he betrayed him as well as all the values he stood for. But particular history and

---

[173] In the 'Life of Mrs. Hutchinson', Lucy Hutchinson celebrates the English monarchy: 'Better lawes and a happier constitution of government no nation ever enjoy'd, it being mixture of monarchy, aristocratie, and democracy, with sufficient fences against the pest of every one of those forms, tiranny, faction, and confusion' (S280/K5). Her view of the institution of monarchy is less positive in the *Memoirs*, in which monarchy degenerates into tyranny (S40/K60).
[174] Norbrook, 'Lucy Hutchinson versus Edmund Waller'. See also Wiseman, *Conspiracy and Virtue* 211–12.
[175] See Norbrook, 'Lucy Hutchinson versus Edmund Waller', 68.

general history do not always meet as smoothly as they do as in the chronicle of Cromwell's political career. Hence Lucy Hutchinson's choice, in order to overcome the limitations of a linear narrative, to base her relation of the English Civil War on a sophisticated system of digressions which combines the local with the national, the better to highlight the story of Colonel Hutchinson.

Chapter 6
The historian's craft (2)
Lucy Hutchinson's art of digression

Digressions were originally used in judicial oratory. Quintilian describes digressing as 'the handling of some theme, which must however have some bearing on the case, in a passage that involves digression from the logical order of our speech'.[1] He objects to an indiscriminate use of digressing and deplores that many orators are 'in the habit [...] of digressing to some pleasant and attractive topic with a view of securing the utmost amount of favour from their audience'. However, Quintilian admits, a digression can be 'advantageous', provided that it 'fits in well with the rest of the speech and follows naturally on what has preceded'. Above all, a digression should be 'brief' because 'the judge is in a hurry to get to the proof', while 'care must be taken not to nullify the effect of the *statement* by diverting the minds of the court to some other theme and wearying them by useless delay.' As recent scholarship on Renaissance digressions has shown, Quintilian's discourse on digressing was widely debated among humanists.[2] Erasmus, for example, takes up Quintilian's definition, and considers that, after *enargeia*, digressing is yet another method to enrich 'what one has to say on any subject':[3]

> Very like the methods of enrichment which I have just been discussing is the sixth method, which the Greeks call παρεκβάσις variously translated as diversion, digression, or excursus, or, as Quintilian defines it, the handling of a topic which does have a contribution to make to the successful outcome of the case, in a manner which digresses from the strict arrangement of the material.[4]

---

[1] See Quintilian, *Institutio Oratoria*, Book IV, Chapter 3: 'παρεκβάσις est, ut mea quidem fert opinio, alicuius rei, sed ad utilitatem causae pertinentis, extra ordinem excurrens tractatio.' All the following quotes by Quintilian are taken from http://penelope.uchicago.edu/Thayer/E/Roman/Texts/Quintilian/Institutio_Oratoria/4C*.html (accessed 15/04/2020).

[2] See, for instance, Gérard Milhe Poutingon, *Poétique du digressif. La digression dans la littérature de la Renaissance* (Paris: Classiques Garnier, 2012). See pages 13–42 for a summary of humanist conceptions of digressing.

[3] Erasmus, *Copia: Foundations of the Abundant Style*, in *The Collected Works of Erasmus*, vol. 24, 572.

[4] Erasmus, *Copia* 589. See Nathalie Dauvois, 'Éloge lyrique et digression: modèle rhétorique / pratique poétique', *Exercices de rhétorique* 11 (2018), https://doi.org/10.4000/rhetorique.698.

In *Of the Art Both of Writing & Judging of History*, the French Jesuit, Pierre Le Moyne, advises historians to make a very moderate use of digressions: '[l]et the *Historian* then remember, not to make unnecessary Digressions, which serve not to dress, clear, or sustain his Matter; and that those he does make, are very rare and short.'[5] For Le Moyne, as for most seventeenth-century commentators, irrelevant digressions were detrimental to a work's coherence and persuasiveness. In particular, it was argued, the introduction of a moral or interpretative discourse into a sequence of historical events impaired the effectiveness of the narrative.[6] It is in this sense that one should understand Hobbes's celebration of Thucydides. The Athenian historian did not need excursuses because his moral commentaries were secretly conveyed by his narration:

> Digressions, for instructions cause, and other such open conueyances of Precepts (which is the Philosphers part) he neuer useth, as hauing so cleerly set before mens eyes, the wayes and euents, of good and euill counsels, that the Narration it selfe doth secretly instruct the Reader, and more effectually then possibly can be done by Precept.[7]

As a matter of fact, Thucydides employs digressions far more often than Hobbes claims, in order to shed light on the motivations of historical actors, as well as on the causes of events. But he does so sparingly and with discrimination, in a way which was markedly different from Herodotus, whose digressions were mostly aimed at entertaining the reader.[8]

In the *Memoirs*' many meta-historical comments, Lucy Hutchinson testifies to her awareness of the humanist debate around the use of digressions. She recurrently apologizes for interrupting the narrative flow, but she also reminds the reader that her digressions are neither anecdotal nor decorative, but absolutely necessary from an ethical and narrative point of view. For example, after her story of the Hutchinson family settling 'in their house at Owthorpe',

---

[5] Pierre Le Moyne, *Of the Art Both of Writing & Judging of History* (London, 1695) 186. It was published in French in 1670.
[6] See Brownley, *Clarendon and the Rhetoric of Historical Form* 8–12.
[7] Hobbes, 'On the Life and History of Thucydides', *Eight Bookes of the Peloponnesian Warre*, np. On the use of digression in Bacon and Hobbes, see Levy, '*The Advancement of Learning* and Historical Thought', 220–2 and Timothy Raylor, *Philosophy, Rhetoric, and Thomas Hobbes* (Oxford: Oxford UP, 2018) 83–5.
[8] Timothy Burns, 'Hobbes et Denys d'Halicarnasse: la politique et la rhétorique chez Thucydide', *Rhétorique démocratique en temps de crise*, Actes du colloque, Nice 20–21 January 2011, http://revel.unice.fr/symposia/rhetoriquedemocratique/index.html?id=847 (accessed 15/04/2020).

in October 1641, she describes the condition of the country on the eve of the Civil War: 'But here I must make a short digression from our *particular actions* to summe up the state of the kingdome at that time [...] I shall only mention what is necessary to be remember'd for the better carrying of my purpose' (S37/K57, my emphasis). In these observations, she makes it clear that the Colonel's story cannot be understood outside the context of the Civil War. Unlike traditional chroniclers who tend to write history by 'agglomeration',[9] she therefore seeks to weave together her husband's story with the tumultuous history of the times, her aim being ultimately to explain his fate, and, beyond that, the 'Tragedie of the civill warre' (S78/K104). To do so, she combines, like Clarendon, and in Peter Burke's words, a 'traditional, "hand of God" explanation with the newer, more secular interest in secondary or "natural" causes'.[10] Thus, although she steadfastly holds on to the belief that God is the 'the principall author' (S167/K208) and that historical occurrences should not be taken as 'the common accidents of humane life', but as the 'admirable bookes of providence' (S278/K3), she chiefly focuses, in the digressions, on the political, military and moral causes of this 'greate Tragedy' (S53/K75), that is, the human dimension of the conflict. In this respect, Lucy Hutchinson stands as an heir to humanist and empirically-oriented practices.[11]

The present chapter seeks to articulate Lucy Hutchinson's use of digressions with her apologetic purpose, namely the rehabilitation of the Colonel's actions during the Civil Wars and Protectorate. For the sake of clarity, three sorts of digressions will be distinguished.[12] First the historical digressions which explore the long- and short-term causes of the Civil Wars; second, the narrative digressions which connect local and national events during the First Civil War; third, the politico-moral digressions which focus on the causes of the Colonel's persecution and foreshadow his 'martyrdom'.

---

[9] Suzuki, 'Anne Clifford and the Gendering of History', 212.

[10] Burke, *The Renaissance Sense of the Past* 93. On Clarendon and providence, see Norbrook, 'The English Revolution and English Historiography', 245, and Michael Finlayson, 'Clarendon, Providence and the Puritan Revolution', *Albion* 22 (1990): 607–32.

[11] See Kelley, 'Philosophy and Humanistic Disciplines', 752; Dubos, *Thomas Hobbes et l'histoire* 49. See also Vickers, 'Introduction', *The History of the Reign of King Henry VII*, xv–xx.

[12] The present typology is loosely based on Le Moyne's: 'But since it so pleases the Masters, let us suffer Digressions in History, and say, for Instruction to those that desire them, they are either *Geographical, Historical, Political* or *Moral*' (*Of the Art Both of Writing & Judging of History* 184–5).

1. Historical flashbacks: 'the long-conceived flame of civill warre' (S37/K57)

Lucy Hutchinson's narrative of the Civil War in Nottingham opens with a long digressive passage about 'the state of England in those dayes wherein he, whose actions I am tracing, began to enter into his part in this greate Tragedy' (S53/K75). This eighteen-page section, which, she argues, has been 'too long for that [she] intended, a bare summary, and too short to give a cleare understanding of the righteousnesse of the Parliament's cause' (S53/K75), reads as a full inquiry into the historical causes of the Civil War from the Reformation onwards.[13] It is based on Thomas May's *History of the Parliament*, but Lucy Hutchinson's advice to consult other histories suggests that she was well informed on the subject (S37/K57). Besides, such an investigation of the Civil War causes was not an isolated venture:[14] most Restoration historians, whatever their ideological inclinations, delved into this controversial issue.[15] This was notably the case of Rushworth, Hobbes, Baxter, Ludlow, Peyton, Heath, Dugdale, and Clarendon, whose various analyses reflect a wide range of interpretations of the origins of the war.[16] Clarendon, for instance, saw the Civil Wars as an 'accident' and essentially sought short-term causes for the conflict in the reign of Charles I. He took issue with Thomas May, who looked back to the reign of Elizabeth to account for the outbreak of the Civil War:

---

[13] On Lucy Hutchinson's account of the causes of the war, see Norbrook, 'The English Revolution and English Historiography', 239–40.

[14] The issue of the causes of the conflict was indeed raised even before the military conflict broke out in January 1642, as a committee was set up in Parliament 'to consider the causes of the now distempers, and the remedies' quoted by Cressy, 'Remembrancers of the Revolution', 264. On the seventeenth-century debate about the causes of the English Revolution, see Richardson, *The Debate on the English Revolution* 11–39. On today's historiographical debate, see Richardson 100–251 and Ann Hughes, *The Causes of the English Civil War* [1991] (Basingstoke: Macmillan, 1998), as well as Peter Lake, 'Post-Reformation Politics, or on Not Looking for the Long-Term Causes of the English Civil War', *The Oxford Handbook of the English Revolution*, ed. Michael J. Braddick (Oxford: Oxford UP, 2015) 20–39.

[15] MacGillivray, *Restoration Historians* 207–10; 228–9.

[16] See Rushworth, 'The Preface', *Historical Collections* [sig. a]: 'Yet certainly of some use it may be to us, and of concernment also to those that may come after us [...] to consider indifferently how we came to fall among ourselves, and so learn the true causes, the rises and growths of our late Miseries, the strange Alterations and Revolutions.' Hobbes's *Behemoth, or, An Epitome of the Civil Wars of England* (London, 1679) is mostly an investigation of the causes of the Civil Wars. In *Reliquiæ Baxterianæ*, Baxter dwells on the short-term causes of the conflict (Part I, 16–29; ed. Keeble et al., vol. 1, 242–74). On Baxter, see MacGillivray, *Restoration Historians* 159 and William Lamont, 'Richard Baxter, "Popery" and the Origins of the English Civil War', *History* 87.287 (2002): 336–52. See also Edmund Ludlow, *Memoirs of Edmund Ludlow* (Vevey, 1698) 1–18 and *A Voyce from the Tower*, ed. Worden, 7–8; Edward Peyton, *The Divine Catastrophe of the Kingly Family of the Stuarts: Or, a Short History of the Rise, Reign, and Ruine Thereof* (London, 1652) 1–70; James Heath, *A Brief Chronicle of the Late Intestine War* 1–5; William Dugdale, *A Short View of the Late Troubles in England* (London, 1644) 1–9; Hyde, *The History of the Rebellion*, vol. 1, 5–191 and passim.

I shall not then lead any man farther back in this journey, for the discovery of the entrance into those dark ways, than the beginning of this king's reign. For I am not so sharp-sighted as those, who have discerned this rebellion contriving from, if not before, the death of Queen Elizabeth, and fomented by several princes and great ministers of state in Christendom to the time that it brake out.[17]

In her eighteen-page flashback, Lucy Hutchinson looks for even more distant causes than May does, as she traces the origins of the Civil War back to Reformation times, explaining that 'the Tragedy' of the Civil War was the result of the 'greate contest betweene the Papist and Protestant' (S41/K61).[18] '[F]or the better carrying of her purpose' (S37/K57), she shows how Henry VIII's imperfect Protestant Reformation and the Popish policies of the first Stuarts left the door open for the return of Roman Catholicism and caused the outbreak of the Civil War. In this section I would like to argue that Lucy Hutchinson's anti-Catholicism in her digression is not an outlet for irrational fears, but a constructed ideology and a forceful rhetoric used both to criticize the monarchy of the first Stuarts and to explain the outbreak of the Civil War.[19]

Lucy Hutchinson first seeks long-term roots of the Civil War in Henry VIII's Protestant Reformation, by exposing how incomplete and unsatisfactory it was from a political and religious perspective.[20] She deeply regrets that it did not result in a separation of Church and State: 'When the dawne of the Gospell began to breake upon this Isle after the darke midnight of Papacy, the morning was more clowdy here than in other places by reason of the state interest, which was mixing and working it selfe into the interest of religion,

---

[17] Hyde, *The History of the Rebellion*, vol. 1, 5. See MacGillivray, *Restoration Historians* 200–10 and Norbrook, 'The English Revolution and English Historiography', 241–6.

[18] This section draws on the first section of my chapter, '"The Great Contest between the Papist and Protestant": Anti-Catholicism in Lucy Hutchinson's Memoirs of the Life of Colonel Hutchinson', *Anti-Catholicism in Britain and Ireland, 1600–2000: Practices, Representations and Ideas*, ed. Claire Gheeraert-Graffeuille and Géraldine Vaughan (Basingstoke: Palgrave Macmillan, 2020) 75–91.

[19] See Peter Lake, 'Anti-Popery: The Structure of a Prejudice', *Conflict in Early Stuart England: Studies in Religion and Politics, 1603–1642*, ed. Richard Cust and Ann Hughes (London: Longman, 1989) 72–6; Arthur F. Marotti, *Religious Ideology and Cultural Fantasy: Catholic and Anti-Catholic Discourses in Early Modern England* (Notre Dame, IN: U of Notre Dame P, 2005) 3; Clément Fatovic, 'The Anti-Catholic Roots of Liberal and Republican Conceptions of Freedom in English Political Thought', *Journal of the History of Ideas* 66.1 (2005): 38.

[20] See Alec Ryrie, 'The Slow Death of a Tyrant: Learning to Live without Henry VIII, 1547–1563', *Henry VIII and his Afterlives. Literature, Politics, and Art*, ed. Mark Rankin, Christopher Highley, and John N. King (Cambridge: Cambridge UP, 2009) 75–93. On the memory of the English Reformation, see Walsham, 'History, Memory, and the English Reformation' and Alexandra Walsham, Bronwyn Wallace, Ceri Law, and Brian Cummings, eds., *Memory and the English Reformation* (Cambridge: Cambridge UP, 2020).

and which in the end quite wrought it out' (S38/K57). Pleading for a clear distinction between spiritual and secular powers, she warns that 'spirituall weapons' are given 'for spirituall combates, and those who go about to conquer subjects for Christ with swords of steele shall find the false mettall breake to shivers when it is used, and hurtfully flie in their owne faces' (S38/K58). Lucy Hutchinson considers Henry VIII's split with Rome had positive consequences, but she categorically rejects the way in which royal supremacy combined political and spiritual authority, arguing that the concentration of political and religious authority has led to tyranny (S41/K61). In her own eyes, the Henrician Reformation was a mere transfer of the vices from the Catholic Church to the Church of England, and a continuation of episcopacy meant the resurgence of a 'tirannicall Clergie' (S39/K58). In accusatory lines, which are crossed out in the manuscript but kept by Julius Hutchinson in his editions of the *Memoirs*, she denies Henry VIII the title of Protestant reformer, his religious scheme being but 'a little rout':

> King Henry the eighth who by his regall authority cast out the Pope did not intend the people of the land should haue any ease of oppression but onely change their forreigne yoke for homebred fetters devicing the popes spoyles between himselfe & his Bishops who card not for their father at Rome so long as they enioyd their patrimony and their honors here under another head soe that I cannot subscribe to those who entitle that king to the honor of beginning a reformation all that he made was a little rout.[21]

Lucy Hutchinson's denunciation of Henry VIII's royal supremacy and, more generally, of clericalism echoes contemporary criticisms voiced by some Protestants who pleaded for a neat separation between the spiritual and political realms. Unlike those who considered the English king's ecclesiastical sovereignty as a means of resisting the advances of Popery, the Protestant reformer Martin Bucer, among others, rejected Caesaropapism and accused Henry VIII of corrupting the English Church.[22] In unpublished pages of his *Memoirs*, Ludlow similarly called Henry VIII 'that monster of mankynde' and

---

[21] *Memoirs*, DD/HU4, 63. The autobiographical fragment offers a far more positive version of the Henrician Reformation. See Hutchinson, 'The Life of Mrs Lucy Hutchinson', S281/K6-7. On current debates on Reformation historiography, see Peter Marshall, '(Re)defining the English Reformation', *Journal of British Studies* 48.3 (2009): 564-86.

[22] See Francis Oakley, 'Christian Obedience and Authority, 1520-1550', *The Cambridge History of Political Thought*, ed. Burns, 181.

called for a complete separation of Church and State.²³ The originality of Lucy Hutchinson's narrative, however, lies in her linking Henry VIII's 'Popish' reformation to the outbreak of the Civil War. Such a correlation was made neither by Ludlow nor by May in their analyses of the origins of the War.²⁴ May, in *The History of the Parliament of England*—Lucy Hutchinson's main source for her digression—does not criticize the Henrician Reformation. From the first chapter of his *History*, he approves of the settlement that was reached and praises Henry VIII's successor, 'Queene Elizabeth of glorious memory', as the sovereign who brought the English nation 'Religion reformed from Popish superstition'.²⁵ Like May, Lucy Hutchinson falls short of criticizing the Queen directly; she also calls her 'glorious' and celebrates her Protestant policy abroad. Yet, she thinks she was too lenient towards Mary Stuart (S41/K61-2), a Catholic and a descendant of the 'bloody house of Guize' (S39/K59).²⁶ Likewise, when dealing with the reign of Elizabeth's successors, she finds fault with her religious settlement—inherited from Henry VIII—which she deems far too Popish.

Lucy Hutchinson's critical treatment of the reigns of James I and Charles I is influenced by May, but she follows a more radical line than he does, blaming both kings for their Romanization of the Church.²⁷ Focusing first on the reign of James I, she begins by deconstructing the myth of the Protestant prince, who was 'educated after the strictest way of the protestant religion according to Calvin's forme' (S40/K60). She maintains that after the execution of his mother Mary Stuart, on the decision of the 'true-hearted Protestants' of Elizabeth's council (S41/K62), James VI as King of Scotland started to work towards facilitating the return of Catholicism in England: he 'manag'd a faction in the Court of the declining Queene' (S41/K62) and 'harbour'd a secrett designe of revenge upon the godly in both nations' (S43/K64). When he became King of England, despite 'that hellish pouder plott', his indulgent

---

[23] Ludlow, *A Voyce from the Watch Tower*, ed. Worden, 7–8: the quotes are drawn from unpublished sections of the Bodleian manuscript quoted by Worden in his introduction.

[24] Lucy Hutchinson thinks 'Mr. Maye's history' shows 'more indulgence to the King's guilt than can justly be allow'd' (S53/K75). On May and Hutchinson, see Norbrook, 'The English Revolution and English Historiography', 239–40.

[25] May, *The History of the Parliament* 1.

[26] See Anne McLaren, 'Gender, Religion, and Early Modern Nationalism: Elizabeth I, Mary Queen of Scots, and the Genesis of English Anti-Catholicism', *American Historical Review* 107.3 (2002): 739–67.

[27] May, *The History of the Parliament* 5–15. On Jacobean anti-Catholicism, see Carol Z. Wiener, 'The Beleaguered Isle. A Study of Elizabethan and Early Jacobean Anti-Catholicism', *Past and Present* 51 (1971): 27–62. See also Anthony Milton, 'The immortal fewde: Anti-Popery, "Negative Popery" and the Changing Climate of Religious Controversy', *Catholic and Reformed. The Roman and Protestant Churches in English Protestant Thought 1600-1640* (Cambridge: Cambridge UP, 1995) 31–92. On anti-Catholicism in seventeenth-century England, see Scott, *England's Troubles* 29–30.

treatment of Catholics continued unabated, she argues: 'the Nonconformists were cast out of doores [...], the penalties against Papists relax'd, many of them taken into favour' (S42/K62), while '[s]ecret treaties were entertain'd with the Court of Rome' (S42/K62).

With respect to James I's religious policy, Lucy Hutchinson points out that moral standards within the Church of England were lowered during his reign, ceremonialism returned, and Protestant doctrines were dangerously affected by Arminianism, which she insistently conflates with Catholicism.[28] She also signals the dangerous moves of the Anglican bishops and rejects their search for accommodation with the Catholics as a form of collusion: 'The prelates in the meane time, finding they lost ground, meditated reunion with the popish faction [...]; and now there was no more endeavour in their publick sermons to confute the errors of that Church, but to reduce our doctrines and theirs to an accommodation' (S45/S66). In addition, in a style reminiscent of Weldon's *The Court and Character of James I* (1650), she depicts the King's own court as 'a nursery of lust and intemperance', a court as depraved and decadent as the court of Rome, where swarming Papists 'found it the most ready way to destroy the doctrine of the Gospell to debosh the professors' (S42/K62). With regard to James's foreign policy, Lucy Hutchinson is of the opinion that he 'deserted and betrey'd' 'the Protestant interest abroad' (S42/K62). She reproaches him with his role in the Spanish Match—the proposed marriage between the Prince of Wales with the Infanta of Spain, a prominent topic in anti-Catholic propaganda (S45/K66). In fact, James I is portrayed here as the perfect opposite of Elizabeth whom Lucy Hutchinson, despite some reservations, celebrates as a true defender of this 'Protestant interest', 'renown'd at home and abroad for successes against her rebellious subjects in England and Ireland', and abhorred by the Pope who had 'shott all his arrowes at her head, and sett on many desperate assassinations against her' (S41/K61).

Finally, Lucy Hutchinson elaborates on the fatal influence of Catholicism in James I's England with the practice of mixed marriages between Catholics and Protestants. Her idea of a Papist conspiracy to restore Catholicism in England sounds less rational than her other arguments, but her demonization of Roman Catholics is once again much in keeping with contemporary anti-Catholic propaganda:

---

[28] See Nicholas Tyacke, *Anti-Calvinists: The Rise of English Arminianism c.1590–1640* (Oxford: Clarendon, 1987) 181–255.

next to which, a greate cause of these abominations was the mix'd marriages of Papist and protestant famelies, which, no question, was a designe of the popish party to compasse and procure them, and so successefull that I have observ'd there was not one house of ten where such a marriage was made but the better party was corrupted, the children's soules were sacrific'd to devills, the worship of God was layd aside in that famely for feare of distasting the idolater. (S42–3/K63)

What Lucy Hutchinson writes about mixed marriages in private families also applies to the monarchy, and most specifically to the reign of Charles I, who married Princess Henrietta Maria, the daughter of Henry IV and sister of Louis XIII. Although Charles was first believed to be a less depraved monarch than his father, he proved to be worse than him because he let himself be corrupted by his Catholic wife, 'a papist, a French lady of a haughty spiritt, and a greate witt and beauty, to whom he became a most uxorious husband' (S46/K67). Under her influence, Lucy Hutchinson continues, he grew into a tyrant, very much like Nero, another famous traitor and persecutor of Christians: 'as in the primitive times it is observed that the best emperors were some of them stirr'd up by Sathan to be the bitterest persecutors of the Church, so this King was a worse encroacher upon the civill and spirituall liberties of his people by farre than his father' (S46/K67). During his reign, many Protestants were obsessed with the idea of a 'Popish Plot'—allegedly the work of the Queen and of 'the Jesuits and other engineers and factors for Rome'.[29] Lucy Hutchinson herself was persuaded that the Queen, joined by the 'Archbishop [Laud] and his prelaticall crew' had 'the cruell designe of rooting out the godly out of the land' (S49/K70). To her the danger of a return of England to Catholicism was real:

The foolish Protestants were meditating reconcilliations with the Church of Rome, who embrac'd them as farre as they would goe, carrying them in hand as if there had bene a possibillity of bringing such a thing to passe; meane while they carried on their designe by them, and had so ripened it that nothing but the mercy of God prevented the utter subversion of Protestantisme in the three kingdomes. (S49/K70)

---

[29] 'The Grand Remonstrance, with the Petition accompanying it, Presented to the King, December I, 1641', *The Constitutional Documents of the Puritan Revolution 1625–1660*, ed. Samuel Rawson Gardiner, 3rd edition (Oxford: Clarendon, 1906), 206. On the Popish plot, see Potter, *Secret Rites* 45–9; Caroline M. Hibbard, *Charles I and the Popish Plot* (Chapel Hill: U of North California P, 1983).

Finally, Lucy Hutchinson retrospectively associates Henrietta Maria with Mary Stuart;[30] for her, the two French Catholic queens are responsible for England's fall: 'it hath bene observed that a French Queene never brought any happinesse to England. Some kind of fatality, too, the English imagin'd to be in her name of Marie' (S48–9/K70).

In spite of what she sees as a context of collusion between the Stuarts and the Roman Catholics, Lucy Hutchinson was confident that true Protestants would eventually win the contest against the Catholic Church 'in which all Christendom seemed to be engaged' (S41/K61). Admittedly, much blood had already been shed in this combat against Rome, in the 'Provinces of the Netherlands [...] in a resistance against the King of Spaine', as well as in France, with the King 'persecuting his protestant subjects with much inhumane violence, forc'd them to defend themselves against his unsanctified league' (S40/K60). Lucy Hutchinson, however, trusted God's providence and like many of her Puritan contemporaries, she thought that the Reformation had not gone far enough.[31] At this stage of the narrative, she thus adds her voice to the Puritan activists who wanted to lead a crusade against Papists and their allies among Anglicans in order to fight royal and clerical tyranny.[32] This anti-Catholic diatribe directed at the Stuart monarchy was perfectly audible at the Restoration when Charles II in his turn was suspected of collusion with Roman Catholics. In her subsequent account of the war and Interregnum, Lucy Hutchinson's anti-Catholicism becomes even more implicit and less obtrusive, but Popery continues to excite her fears.[33] As divisions among Puritans were exacerbated, anti-Catholicism gave way to virulent anti-Puritanism: the responsibility for the military conflict, originally ascribed to Papists, was shifted on to the Puritans, 'the more religious zelotts' (S38/K58), whose conduct eventually appears as reprehensible as that of Catholics and debauched Cavaliers.[34]

Lucy Hutchinson's analysis of the causes of the Revolution compares well with her contemporaries' investigations. So why, then, does she downplay the significance of this historical flashback and other similar analyses in the

---

[30] See McLaren, 'Gender, Religion, and Early Modern Nationalism' and Frances Dolan, *Whores of Babylon: Catholicism, Gender and Seventeenth-Century Print Culture* (Ithaca: Cornell UP, 1999).
[31] Robin Clifton, 'The Popular Fear of Catholics during the English Revolution', *Past and Present* 52 (1971): 37.
[32] See Scott, *Commonwealth Principles* 49–50; John Coffey, *Persecution and Toleration in Protestant England, 1558–1689* (London: Longman, 2000) 135–43.
[33] On the 'explanatory power' of anti-Popery, see Lake, 'Anti-Popery', 80.
[34] See Peter Lake, 'Anti-Puritanism: The Structure of a Prejudice', *Religious Politics in Post-Reformation England: Essays in Honour of Nicholas Tyacke*, ed. Kenneth Fincham and Lake (Woodbridge: Boydell, 2006) 86.

Memoirs? Why does she maintain a strong hierarchy between her 'main story', that is, the life of John Hutchinson, and her forays into general history? The first reason, which I have earlier discussed, has to do with her claim to be writing the 'life' of her husband, and not as a general history of the period.[35] A second reason is epistemological: like many of her contemporaries, Lucy Hutchinson considered that national history—of which she gives a very polemical version—was not as trustworthy as an experienced-based narrative. A third reason is more speculative. It lies in the assumption that the private genres of lives and memoirs were generally deemed more suitable for women writers than national chronicles which were a male preserve.[36] In this sense, Lucy Hutchinson's constant emphasis on the particular can be construed as another strategy of 'camouflage', allowing her to write the history of her time, without challenging the patriarchal values of her age.[37] When she writes about the origins of the war, in the margins of the *Memoirs*, Lucy Hutchinson thus emerges as a fully-fledged historian, ever so paradoxically.[38] As shall be seen, this is largely confirmed by her use of narrative digressions which offer an equally polemical view of the Civil War period.

2. Narrative digressions: a polemical history of the English Civil Wars

So as to make intelligible the exceptional role of Colonel Hutchinson during the Civil War in Nottinghamshire, Lucy Hutchinson thinks it necessary to provide a general view of the war in England. We cannot construe his life, she points out, if we do not have the 'Parliament story' in mind: 'It will not be amisse in this place to carry on the Parliament story, that wee may the better judge of things at home when we know the condition of affaires abroad' (S125/K160).[39] Especially for the period covering the years 1641–1648, she repeatedly connects her husband's military experience in Nottingham with the progress of the Parliament's cause in the other English counties.

---

[35] On life-writing, see Chapter 1.
[36] See Woolf, 'A Feminine Past', 647–50 and Briot, *Usage du monde, usage de soi* 30–1.
[37] Mayer, *History and the Early English Novel* 79: 'Hutchinson, like Clarendon and Baxter, uses lifewriting as a means of writing the history of her time.'
[38] MacGillivray, *Restoration Historians* 182.
[39] The French translation highlights connections between 'general events' and 'particular details': 'Ici je crois devoir reprendre l'histoire des affaires du parlement, afin que la connaissance des *événements généraux* facilite l'intelligence des *détails particuliers* de ce récit' (*Mémoires*, ed. Guizot, vol. 1, 429–30, my emphasis).

The best-known attempt at this kind of composition was Bacon's *History of the Reign of King Henry VII*, which combines the 'life' of Henry VII with the history of his 'times', two branches of history defined in his *Advancement of Learning*.[40] It is possible (although there is no definite evidence for this) that Lucy Hutchinson had this model in mind when she wrote her husband's life. Additionally, by the time she was writing the *Memoirs*, such a combination of a 'life' with 'its times' had become a rather current pattern in Restoration lives and memoirs.

a) Lucy Hutchinson's art of disposition

Martine Watson Brownley, in *Clarendon and the Rhetoric of Historical Form*, argues that many Civil War historians failed 'to fuse story and discourse into literary wholes', and that Clarendon was the exception in that he managed to impose a 'literary order' on the events of the 1640s and 1650s.[41] May's *History of the Parliament*, despite its historiographical ambition, was not satisfactory on this point, as he 'haphazardly assembled dates, treated events in vague summaries, and slighted the particulars of war'.[42] I wish here to follow on Brownley and show, after Royce MacGillivray, that Lucy Hutchinson's 'brilliant and perceptive' *Memoirs* also offer a coherent and comprehensive history.[43] This is easily evidenced by a quick comparison with Richard Baxter's *Reliquiæ Baxterianæ* or Margaret Cavendish's *Life of William Cavendish*.[44] Like Lucy Hutchinson, Baxter resorts to digressions to move from '[his] own matters' in Kederminster in Worcestershire to national history—parliamentary debates, observations on Cromwell, and so on[45]—but the result is, according to his editor, Matthew Sylvester, another Nonconformist

---

[40] On Bacon's conception of lives and chronicles of times, see Chapter 1, 1 ('The art of exemplarity'). Bacon's *History of the Reign of King Henry VII* was published in 1622, 1628, 1629, 1637, 1641, 1676. About the success of *Henry VII*, see Levy, '*The Advancement of Learning* and Historical Thought', 218: *Henry VII* was 'an enduring classic, and one that perfectly fulfilled the requirements for history laid down in *The Advancement*'. Bacon, in *Henry VII*, criticizes general chronicles—here the treatment of the battle of Stoke Field (16 June 1487): 'Concerning which battle the relations that are left unto us are so naked and negligent (though it be an action of so recent memory) as they rather declare the success of the day than the manner of the fight' (*Henry VII*, ed. Vickers, 35).
[41] Brownley, *Clarendon and the Rhetoric of Historical Form* 11. On Clarendon's 'comprehensive' vision of the war, see MacGillivray 199–200.
[42] Brownley, *Clarendon and the Rhetoric of Historical Form* 12.
[43] MacGillivray, *Restoration Historians* 175: 'Her opinions throughout the *Memoirs* are impressed on the reader by a style of exceptional clarity, expressiveness, and rhetorical force.'
[44] See MacGillivray, *Restoration Historians* 10, 170–85.
[45] Baxter, *Reliquiæ Baxterianæ*, Part I, §29, 19; ed. Keeble et al., vol. 1, 253. For a comparison of Baxter and Clarendon's use of digressions, see Brownley, *Clarendon and the Rhetoric of Historical Form* 31.

cleric, 'a Rhapsody rather than one continued Work'.[46] Similarly, Margaret Cavendish seeks to combine the particular with the general, but with little success, as she has little regard for national history and gives priority to her husband's life: 'Concerning the affairs and intrigues that pass'd in Scotland, and England, during the time of His Majesties [Charles II's] stay there, I am ignorant of them; neither doth it belong to me now to write, or give an account of anything else but what concerns the History of my Noble Lord and Husbands Life, and his own Actions.'[47] The result is a loose narrative construction which is on a par with the fragmentation of much of Margaret Cavendish's works.[48]

By contrast, Lucy Hutchinson's *Memoirs*, despite their relative hybridity, are not fragmented. What holds the narrative together is God's providence, which acts on both a local and a national level, as well as in the Colonel's life.[49] In the Dedication, Lucy Hutchinson was confident that the 'hand of God [was] in all things' (S6/K22), and that he 'turn'd the greate wheele in this nation' (S6/K22). In her relation of the wars, she took for granted that God stood on the side of Parliament. In November 1642, 700 Nottingham men enrolled themselves to defend their city: 'it pleas'd God here, as in other places, to carry on his worke by weake and unworthy instruments' (S70/K95).[50] During the siege of Newark, God was again with the Colonel and Nottingham's people as 'by providence of an extraordinary stormie season, they [...] were preserv'd from that danger, which no doubt was treacherously contriv'd' (S77/K103). God is also invoked to explain the 1646 victory of the New Model Army 'by whom God had perfected their victory over their enemies' (S167/K208). But God, in the *Memoirs*, is also said to exercise his special providence at individual level, especially towards the Colonel. Even before the outbreak of the Civil War, the removal of his family from London to Owthorpe is understood as being part of God's plan:

---

[46] Sylvester, 'The Preface to the Reader', Baxter, *Reliquiæ Baxterianæ*, §5, sig. b2ᵛ; ed. Keeble et al., vol. 4, 415.

[47] Cavendish, *The Life of William Cavendish* 70. See also 67–8.

[48] See, in particular, *The Worlds Olio* (London, 1655). On this aesthetic of fragmentation, see James Fitzmaurice, 'Margaret Cavendish's *Life of William*, Plutarch, and Mixed Genre', *Authorial Conquests: Essays on Genre in the Writings of William Cavendish*, ed. Line Cottegnies and Nancy Weitz (Madison, NJ: Farleigh Dickinson UP, 2003) 80–2. On the aesthetic of variety typical of the memoir genre, see Lesne, *La Poétique des Mémoires* 62.

[49] Providence is central to Lucy Hutchinson's later works. See *Religious Commonplace Book*, DD/HU3, 68–9 and *Selections from the Theological Notebook*, in *The Works of Lucy Hutchinson*, vol. 2, 103–4. On providence, see Blair Worden, 'Providence and Politics in Cromwellian England', *Past and Present* 109 (1985): 55–99.

[50] See 1 Corinthians 1:27: 'But God hath chosen the foolish things of the world to confound the wise; and God hath chosen the weak things of the world to confound the things which are mighty.'

Mr. Hutchinson was very sensible of a peculiar providence to him herein, and resolv'd to adventure no more such hazards, but to retire to that place whither God seem'd to have call'd him by giving him so good an interest there [...]. His wife, convinc'd by this kind check which God had given to her desires, that she ought to follow her husband where the Lord seem'd to call him, went allong with him, and about October 1641 they came to their house at Owthorpe.   (S37/K57)

These 'peculiar' providences are all the more significant in John Hutchinson's case, as they correspond to God calling him to play a historical role. In a three-page digression (S35–6/K54–6), which was cut in Julius Hutchinson's edition, Lucy Hutchinson draws a typological parallel between Moses and the Colonel: 'whosoe considers the following history shall find that Mr. Hutchinson againe might often take up the paralell of the greate Hebrew Prince' (S36/K55). In other words, the Colonel stands both an instrument of God's providence, and a great man, endowed with a special mission to free the people of England, here represented as a new Israel, from the Stuart tyranny. The comparison with Moses, here, is very significant: in the Renaissance, Moses, like Romulus or Theseus, was often hailed as a great man, notably by Machiavelli.[51]

There are some key moments in the narration of the First Civil War when the Colonel's life, meeting the national chronicle, takes on a national dimension. For instance, in November 1643, he received a commission for the government of the town and castle of Nottingham, from the parliamentary general, the Earl of Essex, and from Sir Thomas Fairfax's father, then 'Generall of all the North' (S105–6/K136–7). At decisive moments, he met Fairfax himself (S104/K134–5), and Cromwell (S81–2/K108–9). The role of the Colonel is also amplified when Nottingham and its surroundings become the stage of events of national significance, for example with the passage of royals or parliamentary officials. This was the case for instance in August 1642, when the King raised his standard in Nottingham (S65/K89), or in June 1643 when 'the Queene's forces came and faced the Towne' (S82/K109), or in March 1644, when Prince Rupert raised the siege of Newark, which was kept by, among others, the Colonel's soldiers (S122–5/K156–9). During the winter of 1645–1646, Nottingham's soldiers also took part in the third decisive siege of Newark which marked the end of the First Civil War (S164–6/K204–6). But more often than not, the Colonel's life, between 1641 and 1646, takes on a

---

[51] See Machiavelli, *The Prince*, ed. Skinner and Price, Chapter 6, §979–94 (Kindle edition).

national meaning thanks to Lucy Hutchinson's consummate art of digression, which connects his military role in Nottinghamshire with the war in the other English counties: 'And now were all the countryes in England noe longer idle spectators, but severall stages whereon the Tragedy of the civill warre war was acted' (S78/K104-5). As we shall see, this ingenious recourse to digressions is meant to recreate the national tragedy, thereby providing the reader with a comprehensive view of the First Civil War with, at its very centre, Nottingham and the Colonel.[52]

Lucy Hutchinson sums up her sophisticated art of literary composition with the metaphor of the armillary spheres, dear to Renaissance astronomers. With this emblem she means that one cannot understand the movement of the small spheres—the events in Nottinghamshire and the life of the Colonel—without inscribing them within the greater context of national history: 'It being necessary to carrie on the maine story for the better understanding of the motion of those lesser wheeles that moov'd within the greate Orbe, I shall but name in what posture things were abroad in the Kingdome while these affaires I relate were transacted at Nottingham' (S78/K104). This metaphor gives much weight to local events and entails that the movements of the greater orb are conditioned by the movements of the lesser wheels. It is interesting to find a similar conceit in Bacon's *History of the Reign of Henry VII* (as well as in his *Advancement of Learning*), where 'small wires', pulled by God, the equivalents of Lucy Hutchinson's 'lesser wheels', are also given a crucial role: '[i]n his fourteenth year also, by God's wonderful providence, that boweth things unto his will, and hangeth great weights upon small wires, there fell out a trifling and untoward accident that drew on great and happy effects.'[53] In both cases, it is suggested that small causes (the smaller wheels or the wires) are likely to produce great effects in history. Hence, in order to connect the 'lesser wheels' with 'the great orb', Lucy Hutchinson's idea of providing a synoptic vision of the war with, at its centre, the destiny of Colonel Hutchinson.[54]

---

[52] On the art of *disposition* in the memoir genre, see Charbonneau, *Les Silences de l'histoire* 216.

[53] Bacon, *History of the Reign of King Henry VII* 157. The same imagery was used by Bacon in his *Advancement of Learning*: 'For HISTORY of TIMES representeth the magnitude of Actions, & the publique faces and deportmēts of persons, & passeth ouer in silence the smaller passages and Motions of men and Matters. But such beeing the workemanship of God, as he doth hang the greatest waight vpon the smallest Wyars, *Maxima è Minimis suspēdēs*, it comes therefore to passe, that such Histories doe rather set forth the pompe of busines, then the true and inward resorts thereof' (*The Two Bookes* 12).

[54] Cook, 'The Story I most particularly intend', 276.

b) A synoptic view of the war

Lucy Hutchinson's most impressive use of digressions consists in connecting events in Nottinghamshire with what occurred in London and everywhere in England in order to bring out the uniqueness of the Colonel's destiny. These digressions, which match Erasmus's typology, deal with the 'exposition of actions, the descriptions of places and regions'.[55] Largely based on May's *History*, they contain essential elements to understand the military operations of the war. They are carefully introduced by various connectors (adverbs, adverbial phrases of time or place),[56] or self-reflexive comments,[57] and, in the manuscript, they are often signalled by line breaks (see Figure 6.1—Civil War Digressions—An Overview).[58] Additionally, through authorial interventions, Lucy Hutchinson highlights the relevance of her excursuses, either when she concludes the digression, or when she takes up the thread of her husband's life again. Sometimes, the transition is slightly less obtrusive, as it is only thematic. For example, after referring to the movement of the Queen's army in the second digression ('and now the Queene was preparing to march up with the assistance she had gotten to the King' [S79/K106]), she reports how the Queen went through Nottinghamshire: 'Those counties through which she was to passe could not be but sensible of their danger, especially the gentlemen at Nottingham' (S79/K106).

Ten digressions punctuate Lucy Hutchinson's narrative of the Civil Wars, from April 1642 to the autumn of 1649.[59] When put together, it becomes apparent that they follow one another and offer a consistent narrative of the Civil War. At the end of the first digression [1], Lucy Hutchinson points out the connections between them when she announces that the Parliament story shall be continued in the next digression—'the Parliament's Generall was sent out againe with their Armie; whose proceedings I shall take up againe in their due places' (S60/K84).[60] The second digression [2] logically covers the first

---

[55] Erasmus, *Copia* 589.
[56] [1]'In the meane time, at York' (S56/K79); [4] 'This summer' (S160/K199); [6] 'Assoone as the country' (S166/K207); [7] 'In the meane time' (S171/K212); [9] 'At London' (S197/K222); [10] 'This summer' (S180/K223). A similar method is used in Bacon, *Henry VII* 30: 'Meanwhile the rebels in Ireland had sent privy messengers both into Ireland and Flanders.'
[57] [2] '[I]t being necessary to carrie on the maine story for the better understanding of the motion of those lesser wheeles' (S78/K104); [3] 'It will not be amisse in this place to carry on the Parliament story' (S125/K160).
[58] As a general rule, there are fewer breaks of lines in the manuscript than in Keeble's editions. Except for one, all the ten digressions listed in Figure 6.1 correspond to a new paragraph in the manuscript.
[59] The digressions are numbered from one to ten, and the numbers are indicated between brackets.
[60] See May, *The History of the Parliament* 29–31 (Book III, Chapter II).

Digression 1: The beginnings of the Civil War (April–June 1642)
Memoirs, ed. Sutherland: 56–61; ed. Keeble: 79–84/'The Life of John Hutchinson', DD/HU4, 94–99. *['In the meane time, at Yorke, the King had sent the Parliament a message that he intended to goe in person to Ireland'* → *'of this sort was Nottinghamshire.']*

Digression 2: Royal victories (November 1642–November 1643)
Memoirs, ed. Sutherland: 78–9; ed. Keeble: 104–6/'The Life of John Hutchinson', DD/HU4, 126–8 *['It being necessary to carrie on the maine story for the better understanding of the motion of those lesser wheeles'* → *'now the Queene was preparing to march up with the assistance she had gotten to the King.']*

Digression 3: Parliament's first victories (Spring 1643–April 1645)
Memoirs, ed. Sutherland: 125–8; ed. Keeble: 160–2/'The Life of John Hutchinson', DD/HU4, 195–7 [8] *['It will not be amisse in this place to carry on Parliament story'* → *'and accordingly it succeeded in their hands.']*

Digression 4: The New Model Army's victories (June 1645–November 1645)
Memoirs, ed. Sutherland: 160–4; ed. Keeble: 199–204/'The Life of John Hutchinson', DD/HU4, 241–8. *['This summer there was another kind of progresse made in the warre than had bene before'* → *'The Scotts alsoe came and quarter'd on the other side of the Towne towards the North.']*

Digression 5: The King's flight and defeat (May–June 1646)
Memoirs, ed. Sutherland: 165–6; ed. Keeble: 206–7/'The Life of John Hutchinson', DD/HU4, 250–1. *['But the great perill wherein all of the English side were was the treachery of the Scotts'* → *'where they again sold him for a summe of monie to the Parliament.']*

Digression 6: After the First Civil War (July 1646–February 1647)
Memoirs, ed. Sutherland: 166–8; Keeble: 207–9/'The Life of John Hutchinson', DD/HU4, 251–4. *['Assoon as the country was now clear'd of all the enemies Garrisons'* → *'who conducted him honorably to his owne Mannour of Holmeby, in Northamptonshire.']*

Digression 7: The growing power of the army (June–November 1647)
Memoirs, ed. Sutherland: 171–3; ed. Keeble: 212–15/'The Life of John Hutchinson', DD/HU4, 258–62. *['In the meane time jealousies were sowne betweene the Parliament, the Citie of London, and the Armie'* → *'But I shall respite that, to return to his affaires whom I principally trace.']*

Digression 8: The King's flight and the Second Civil War (November 1647–August 1648)
Memoirs, ed. Sutherland: 174–8; ed. Keeble: 216–20/'The Life of John Hutchinson', DD/HU4, 263–9. *['While he was thus distemper'd att home' → 'voting all the English Traytors that should joyne with the Scotts, which yett at the last they did.']*

Digression 9: The rise of Cromwell (Summer 1648)
Memoirs, ed. Sutherland: 179; ed. Keeble: 222–3/'The Life of John Hutchinson', DD/HU4, 270–2. *['At London things were in a very sad posture' → 'by so doing lost his creditt with both.']*

Digression 10: The rise of Cromwell 2 (Summer and Autumn 1648)
Memoirs, ed. Sutherland: 180–4; ed. Keeble: 223–8/'The Life of John Hutchinson', DD/HU4, 272–9. *['This summer the revolt was not greater at Land than at Sea' → 'presented him with a case or two of very fine pistolls, which he accepted.']*

Figure 6.1 Civil War Digressions—An Overview

year of the Civil War, when the King's forces were everywhere stronger than those of Parliament, except in the East, where Oliver Cromwell was doing better.[61] In the West and in the North of the country, the advantage was decidedly in favour of the King, all the more so as the Queen 'landed neere Sunderland, comming out of Holland with large provisions of Arms, Ammunition, and Commanders of note' (S79/K106). The next digression [3], spanning the period that went from the defeats of Parliament, in the spring of 1643, to the Self-Denying Ordinances (3 April 1645), also covers the conflict geographically and politically. It starts by presenting the Parliament's 'low condition' (S126/K160): 'The Earl of Essex his Armie lay sick about London for recruits'; in the West, Sir William Waller 'was at length totally routed' (S126/K160), while in the North, the royalists 'were advanced into Nottingham and Lincolnshire and the adjacent Countries' (S126/K160). However, after listing Parliament's defeats, Lucy Hutchinson moves on to show that by the time of the siege of Gloucester (10 August–5 September 1643) and the battle of Newbury (20 September 1643), 'God had begun to turne

---

[61] See May, *The History of the Parliament* 35–48 (Book III, Chapter II).

the scale' (S126/K160).[62] This was a change she had anticipated in the previous digression [2]: despite a few successes on the Parliament's side, 'it was not God's time then to deliver the country of that pernitious enemie' (S121/K154).[63] The reference to God—the only one in this digression—does not entail any change in method, as Lucy Hutchinson continues to explain parliamentary victories and royalist losses as military errors and missed opportunities, not as the direct consequence of God's anger. When dealing with warfare, Lucy Hutchinson consistently writes in the humanist tradition, concentrating on human affairs, even though the general framework of the *Memoirs* is eschatological. In that her position is close to Bolton, who stresses the necessity for historians to take into account secondary causation: 'Christian Authors, while for their ease they shuffled up the reasons of events, in briefly referring all causes immediately to the Will of God, have generally neglected to inform their Readers in the ordinary means of Carriage in human Affairs, and thereby singularly maimed their Narrations.'[64] Lucy Hutchinson's description of the defeat of the Earl of Newcastle—whom she probably knew as a neighbour[65]—is a case in point, as she attributes his losses to faults of strategy without the least mention of God's providence:

> the Earle of Essex and his recruited Armie [...] persued the King's Armie to an engagement at Newberry, where the Parliament obtein'd a greate and bloody victory, and the King for ever lost that opertunity he lately had of marching up to London, and in probability subduing the Parliament. My Lord Newcastle, by a like error about the same time, sitting downe before Hull, mist the opertunity of wholly gaining all those neighbouring counties, and much wasted his greate and victorious Army, being forc'd to rise with losse and dishonor from the unyeilding Towne. (S126/K160–1)

The climax of this digression [3] is her account of the battle of Marston Moor (2 July 1644), a 'bloody encounter', in which, in Lucy Hutchinson's words, 'Cromwell, with 5000 men which he commanded, routed Prince Rupert and restor'd the other routed parliamentarians, and gain'd the most compleate

---

[62] May's *History of the Parliament of England* stops with the siege of Gloucester.
[63] In this digression [2], she deplores that the cause of Parliament was too often deserted, as many original adherents to the cause were traitors, giving the examples of Cholmley, the Hothams, and the Scot Monrose (S79/K106).
[64] Bolton, *Hypercritica: Or, A Rule of Judgment, for Writing or Reading our History* 224–5. On Bolton, see Chapter 2, 94.
[65] See Norbrook, 'Margaret Cavendish and Lucy Hutchinson', 182.

victory that had bene obtein'd in the whole warre' (S127/K161).[66] This decisive parliamentary victory is presented as a watershed both in the Civil War and in Cromwell's career. Cromwell, who was then Lieutenant General in the Earl of Manchester's army, is described as the saviour of the parliamentary cause—a role which Lucy Hutchinson emphasizes more than Thomas May in his *Breviary*, which is her main source for this passage.[67] Her exceptionally positive treatment of Cromwell here can be accounted for by the major role played by his disciplined regiments in defeating the royalist forces. It contrasts with her post-1649 pages, in which she is far more critical of the General and goes as far as portraying him as a tyrant.[68] Lucy Hutchinson's subsequent reflections in this digression deal with the royalist losses and the Queen's failure to receive help for her husband on the continent (S127/K162). They also strategically highlight the 'king's false dealing and disingenuity' in finding an agreement with Parliament (S127/K162). But Lucy Hutchinson was also concerned about the emergence of 'two apparent factions of Presbyterians and Independants' (S127/K162)—a division which she ultimately held responsible for the defeat of the Good Old Cause. Although she was very close to the Independents in Parliament and in the army, she could be, at times, very critical of these men's arrogance.[69] At this stage, however, she was still intent on opposing the strong New Model Army to Essex's far weaker army. To do so, she exposes, in an effective summary, the relentless sequence of events that went from the victory of Cromwell's Ironsides at Marston Moor to the formation of the New Model Army and its victory in the First Civil War.[70]

The next digressions [4 and 5] cover the June 1645–May 1646 period. They first tackle the successes of the New Model Army commanded by Fairfax, especially in the northern counties, including Nottinghamshire. The national chronicle and the local narrative intermingle, as we are told how, on the parliamentary side, the Colonel's troops took part in the siege of Shelford and Newark, and, on the royalist side, the 'little Garrisons in the Vale at Shelford and Wiverton' (S161/K201) were attacked by Parliament's army. A case in point is the local siege of Newark, which, on 6 May 1646, was eventually raised by the King, then a prisoner of the Scots, the last siege of the

---

[66] See Braddick, 'Marston Moor', *God's Fury* 323–55.
[67] Thomas May, *A Breviary of the History of England* [1650] (London, 1655) 106–7.
[68] For Lucy Hutchinson's overall negative view of Cromwell, see Chapter 5, 3, c.
[69] See *Memoirs* S167/K208: 'But at that time, and long after, [the Presbyterian faction] prevail'd not, till that pious people too began to admire themselves for what God had done by them, and to sett up themselves above their brethren.'
[70] The fourth digression opens on a severe comparison between the army of Essex and the New Model Army, which Lucy Hutchinson holds responsible for key military victories (S160/K199).

First Civil War before the surrender of Oxford (20 June 1646).[71] For Lucy Hutchinson the fact that the King raised his standard in Nottingham in 1642 and that he should have capitulated at Newark was obviously no coincidence: it placed Nottinghamshire—and her husband—at the very centre of national history.

The two digressions [6 and 7], which cover the period between the two Civil Wars (June 1646–August 1648), do not so much focus on the opposition between the centre—Colonel Hutchinson's Nottingham garrison—and the margins (the other English counties), as on the political duties of the Colonel who was elected MP for Nottinghamshire on 6 March 1646. At first, John Hutchinson still had links with Nottinghamshire, but he spent more and time in London: 'After the Surrender of Newark, Nottingham Towne and Castle was continued a Garrison for some time: betweene this and his greater employment att London the Governor devided himselfe' (S168/K209). By June 1647, however, he was replaced in his post of Governor of Nottingham by his kinsman, Captain Poulton. He was no longer a direct witness of military operations and local politics, but, because he attended most debates in Parliament, he became an essential source of information for Lucy Hutchinson's post-1646 narrative. Under these new circumstances, her digressions tend to bear less on military operations than on the King's conduct and the growing antagonisms between the 'Parliament, the Citie of London, and the Armie' (S171–3/K212–15). Another consequence is that her account of national history is no longer exclusively based on external sources such as May's *History* or *Breviary* or on Parliament's 'printed papers' (S53/K75), but also on the Colonel's testimony to which she directly refers. When he first attended Parliament, he thus '*found* a very bitter spiritt of discord and envie raging among them, and the Presbyterian faction [...] endeavouring a bitter persecution, upon the account of conscience' (S166/K207, my emphasis).

The digressions [8, 9, 10] interspersing the account of the Second Civil War, from Charles I's escape from Hampton Court (11–14 November 1647) to the surrender of Colchester (27 August 1648), differ from those of the First Civil War. First, John Hutchinson, as an MP for Nottingham, did not play any military role in this new conflict. Second, contrary to what happened between 1642 and 1646, there was no Civil War affecting the three kingdoms, but 'severall insurrections and revolts' (S176/K219) that took place in English counties from November 1647 to November 1648. Still, despite these

---

[71] Oxford capitulated on 24 June 1645. Harlech Castle in Wales held out until 13 March 1647. See https://en.wikipedia.org/wiki/First_English_Civil_War#1646:_conclusion (accessed 20/07/2022).

differences, Lucy Hutchinson opts again for a pattern of digressions, but her method is less systematic than in her narration of the First Civil War: the personal and the national overlap more often, as is for instance the case in her description of the Colonel's encounter with Cromwell, which had national and personal implications (S180/K223).[72] Besides, Lucy Hutchinson's account of the Second Civil War is less comprehensive, as she chooses to go through only a selection of the most salient moments, copiously drawing on May's *Breviary* again.[73] She thus offers a review of the 'tumults [...] in London' (S175/K218), the insurrections in Kent (S176/K218–19) and in Wales (S177/219),[74] Fairfax's victory in Maidstone (S176/K218), the siege of Colchester (S176/K219), the invasion of the Scottish soldiers of the Duke of Hamilton (S177, 181/K220, 225), Cromwell's victory at Preston (S181/K224), and even the revolt of the fleet, when the Vice-Admiral, Sir William Batten (who had served Parliament during the First Civil War) joined the Prince of Wales (S180/K223). After the Second Civil War, the narrative becomes less obtrusively digressive, as it is almost entirely based on the point of view of John Hutchinson, who, 'in the capacity of a Senator as he had before in that of a souldier' (S166/K207), was a direct witness of the debates and votes leading up to the climactic event in the *Memoirs*, namely the King's trial. This digression—like the previous ones— eventually sheds light on the momentous national event of the regicide, revealing a memorialist that is concerned not only with the biography of her husband but with history at large.

c) A defence of tyrannicide

Lucy Hutchinson thus uses digressions to articulate her understanding of the Civil Wars and their fatal dénouement. Unlike Hyde or May, she does not seek to write a balanced history of the wars, but, from the outset, she opts for a pro-Parliament stance and has no qualms about defending tyrannicide.[75] Her

---

[72] On this encounter between Cromwell and Colonel Hutchinson, see Chapter 5, 3, c ('Oliver Cromwell as the great dissembler').
[73] See May, *Breviary*, Book III, 'A short mention of the Originall and Progress of the Second War', 173–211.
[74] Lucy Hutchinson's account of the revolt in Wales reproduces verbatim some elements of May's relation in his *Breviary* (194–5).
[75] See Hyde, *The History of the Great Rebellion* xviii: 'it is a difficult province to write the history of the civil wars of a great and powerful nation, where the king was engaged with one part of his subjects against the other.' May stresses the bravery of both parties: 'How much valour the English Nation on both sides have been guilty of in this unnatural Warre, the World must needs know in the general fame' (*History of the Parliament* sig. B2^v).

account of the King's tyranny is meant to show that the Colonel had no choice in the end but to sign the King's death warrant. It begins in the long flashback about the causes of the Civil Wars, in which the demise of the Stuart monarchy is proleptically announced: 'severall of the kings, not satisfied with their bounded Monarchie, made attempts to convert it into an absolute soveraignety, attempts fatall both to themselves and their people, and ever unsuccessefull' (S40/K60).[76] She thus reports that James I, 'secretly grudging that his people should dare to gainesay his pleasure, and correct his misgovernment in his favourites, broke up Parliaments, violated their privilledges, imprison'd their members for things spoken in the house, and grew disaffected to them' (S45/K66). As for Charles I, he not only proved a tyrant in matters of politics and religion, but he was also 'the most obstinate person in his selfewill that ever was, and so bent upon being an absolute, uncontrowlable Soveraigne that he was resolv'd either to be such a King or none' (47/K68). This first indictment of tyranny sets the tone for all the ensuing digressions about national history, in which Lucy Hutchinson substantiates the 'charge drawne up against [Charles Stuart] for leavying warre against the Parliament and people of England, for betreying their publick trust reposed in him, and for being an implacable enemie to the Commonwealth' (S189/K234).[77] In her eyes, by raising a war against his people, Charles I betrayed the oath he had taken before his own people at his coronation to keep 'the Lawes and Customes' of England,[78] and was therefore to be held fully responsible for the tragedy that had torn England apart.[79] In her digressions about the Civil War, the core of her argument consists in showing that the King never had the intention of accepting a compromise, and that all attempts to negotiate with him were doomed and that the cause was already lost.[80] In May 1642 [1], two months before the actual outbreak of the war, both King and Parliament were ready for a military confrontation, because no agreement could be reached:

---

[76] On the issue of tyranny in Lucy Hutchinson's *Memoirs*, see Gheeraert-Graffeuille, 'Formes et figures de la tyrannie'.

[77] See Patricia Crawford, 'Charles Stuart, That Man of Blood', *Journal of British Studies* 16.2 (1977) 41–61; Robert Zaller, 'The Figure of the Tyrant in English Revolutionary Thought', *Journal of the History of Ideas* 54.4 (1993): 585–610.

[78] See Christopher Wordsworth, ed., *The Manner of Coronation of King Charles I* (London: Henry Bradshaw Liturgical Text Society, 1892) 19.

[79] See John Cook, *King Charls, his Case, or An Appeal to all rational men concerning his tryal at the High Court of Justice* (London, 1649) 39.

[80] The opinion that no agreement with the King could be reached was not rare in pamphlets and sermons. See Crawford, 'Charles Stuart, That Man of Blood', 47–8 and Como, *Radical Parliamentarians and the English Civil War* 152–5. Both historians give the example of Edward Bowles, *Plaine English: Or, A Discourse Concerning Accommodation* ([London],1643) 18–20.

Towards the end of May, the Parliament sent the King word that if he would not disband his forces, and rely upon the lawes and affections of his people for his security, as all good princes before him had done, they held themselves bound in duty to God and the people's trust reposed in them, and by the fundamentall lawes, to employ their utmost care and power for securing the Parliament and preserving the kingdome's peace. (S57–8/K80–1)

Lucy Hutchinson's digressions offer a full history of the failed negotiations between King and Parliament. In the first digression, she thus recounts how, on 10 November 1642, the King was 'presented with a Petition from the Parliament for Accommodation', and accepted 'to receive their propositions and to treate with them' (S60/K83). Two days later, however, he betrayed his word, when, by his own order, Prince Rupert's forces attacked Denzil Holles and Lord Brooke's regiments at Brentford (S60/K83–4).[81] Similarly, we learn in the next digression [2] that 'a treaty [the Oxford treaty] was ineffectually carried on betweene the King and Parliament from the 31st of January, 1642[/3] till the 17th of April, 1643' (S78/K104).[82] The third digression [3] relates how the negotiations at Uxbridge (29 January 1645–22 February 1645)[83] 'effected nothing', while the 'King's falsehood and favour of the Irish rebells' (S127/K162) were discovered. Already at this early stage, Lucy Hutchinson contends that the supporters of peace, whether on the royalist or parliamentarian side, were deluded into believing that an agreement could still be negotiated with the monarch. This divorce between the King and the Parliament was confirmed by the next round of negotiations [6] which were carried out on the basis of the Newcastle propositions (July 1646–March 1647), as the King 'wove out delayes, and would not assent to them' (S168/K209).

The balance of power between King and Parliament changed on 4 June 1647, when Charles I was made prisoner of the army by the troops of Cornet Joyce who removed him from Holmby House, where he had been kept by Parliament since January 1647 ([7], S171/K212). The King, as a captive, was in no position to negotiate. However, as soon as he arrived in Hampton Court, his situation improved and he 'liv'd rather in the condition of a guarded and attended prince than as a conquer'd and purchas'd captive' (S172/K214).

---

[81] http://bcw-project.org/timelines/1642 (accessed 21/06/2020) and *Memoirs*, ed. Keeble, 356, note 156.
[82] http://bcw-project.org/timelines/the-english-civil-war (accessed 22/06/2020).
[83] http://bcw-project.org/church-and-state/first-civil-war/uxbridge-treaty (accessed 22/06/2020). See also *Memoirs*, ed. Keeble, 364: some propositions had been presented to the King in November 1644.

According to Lucy Hutchinson's condemnatory narrative, he went as far as reconstituting a court around him: 'all his old servants had free recourse to him, all sorts of people were admitted to come to kisse his hands and doe him the obeysance as a Soveraigne. [...] the Lords formerly of his privie Councell at Oxford alsoe repair'd to him to be as a Councell attending him' (S172-3/K214-15). It is under these circumstances and during his stay at Hampton Court, she scathingly adds, that 'he drew that nation into the designe of the second warre, which furiously brake out the next summer, and was one of the highest provocations which, after the second victory, brought him to the scaffold' (S173/K215). By provoking the Second Civil War, Lucy Hutchinson contends, Charles I accelerated his tragedy, and made the search for accommodation impossible.

Lucy Hutchinson carefully justifies her accusations against the monarch in the digressions. The King, she argues, had strong allies to carry out his design against the English nation. He could rely on the loyal Cavaliers who had served him during the First Civil War, but also on the Scots and on the English Presbyterians whom he had managed to instrumentalize and use for his own ends [8]. He had, she claims, 'layd the designe of the second warre with the Scotts, and employ'd all his [art] to bring the English Presbiters to a revolt' (S174-5/K217). In her view, the alliance with the Scots, which became official in 1647, had earlier roots in the King's surrender to the Scottish army, at the end of the First Civil War; it was a major betrayal of the English people: by 'putting himselfe into the hands of their mercenary Scotch armie rather than the Parliament of England', the King, Lucy Hutchinson argues, 'shew'd such an embitter'd hate to the English nation that it turn'd many hearts against him' (S166/K206-7). Although the Presbyterians had been 'the zealousest promoters of the cause' ([6], S167/K208), there were among them some black sheep, even before the Civil War broke out (S44/K65). In the context of the London tumults of July 1647 [7], she accuses them of '[renewing] a league with the Popish interest to destroy that godly interest which they had at first so gloriously asserted' (S172/K213).

The betrayals of the Scots and the English Presbyterians were no excuse for the conduct of the King, who remained, in Lucy Hutchinson's view, an archmanipulator, with the evident intention 'to regaine by art what he had lost in fight' (S172/K214).[84] One of his strategies, as early as 1643 [3], consisted in

---

[84] See David Loewenstein, 'The King among the Radicals: Godly Republicans, Levellers, Diggers and Fifth Monarchists', *The Royal Image: Representations of Charles I* (Cambridge: Cambridge UP, 1999) 96-121, here 96-7 and 101-2 (on Lucy Hutchinson's representation of Charles I as a tyrant).

exploiting the strife between 'the two apparent factions of Presbiterians and Independents', as he 'had had hope, by their devisions to prevaile for the accomplishment of his owne ends' (S127/K162).[85] Likewise, during the Newcastle negotiations in 1646 [6], the King hoped 'a greater advantage by the difference betweene the two nations and the factions in the Citie and Parliament', as 'both he and all his party employ'd their utmost industry to cherish and augment' these factions (S168/209). When kept a prisoner by the army in 1647 [7], the King 'by reason of his dayly converse with the Officers, began to be trinkling[86] with [them], [...] and had drawne in some of them to engage to corrupt others to fall in with him' (S172/K214). By systematically exposing the King's manoeuvres, Lucy Hutchinson seeks to demonstrate that '[settling] the Kingdomse without him' (S168/K209) was inevitable. This idea, she contends, was accepted by both in the two Houses, sometime between July 1646 and March 1647, as well as among the army officers whose best efforts to negotiate with Charles I had come to naught. Besides, the King, who was still prisoner of the army, revealed to their commander, Henry Ireton, his intention of 'play[ing] [his] game as well as [he could]', to which Ireton replied: 'If your Majestie have a *game* to play, you must give us alsoe the liberty to play ours' (S172/K214). In the *Memoirs*, this most eloquent exchange is taken as definite proof that the King would never 'complie with the publick good of his people' (S172/K214). It is followed by a comment on the part of Lucy Hutchinson that Parliament was far too conciliatory with the monarch. For her, it was already too late to seek '[the King's] restitution so farre as it might be without the ruine of the good people of the land' (S172/K214). The next digression [8] demonstrates how well the King played his game and manipulated his new allies, the Presbyterians and the Scots, to reach his own ends. In a long, convoluted sentence, he is portrayed as a condescending Machiavellian schemer. Lucy Hutchinson's demystification of the King's sacred person is now complete:

> In the meane time, some months before, when the King had layd the designe of the second warre with the Scotts and employ'd all his [art] to bring the English Presbiters to a revolt, and was now full of hopes to bring about *his game*, and conquer those who had conquer'd him – after all the designe was lay'd, while he amused the Parliament with expectations of a Treaty, he privily stole away from Hampton Court by the assistance of Ashburnham and Berkley, no man for a while knew whither. (S174–5/K217, my emphasis)

---

[85] On these factions in 1645, see *Memoirs*, ed. Keeble, note 243.
[86] *OED*: 'transitive. To treat secretly or in an underhand way, intrigue (with).'

Once on the Isle of Wight, four Propositions were put to the monarch by Parliament, but, Lucy Hutchinson insists, he 'absolutely refus'd to signe them' (S175/K217). The King's rejection of the Propositions alerted the Members of Parliament who eventually came to understand that there was no use negotiating with the King and accordingly passed the 'Four Bills' on 17 January.[87]

> Wherefore the Houses debating upon the King's deniall, at length these votes were passed by both Houses on the 17th day of January: – That they would make no more addresses nor applications to the King. That no person whatsoever should make addresse or application to him. That whoever should breake this Order should incurre the penalty of high Treason. That they would receive no more messages from the King, and that no person should presume to bring [any] to either House or any other person.
>
> (S175/K217)

At this stage, and from Lucy Hutchinson's point of view at least, some kind of agreement was secured: the army approved of the Parliament's decision to break all communication with the King and 'put forth a declaration promising to stand by the Houses in them, which was sign'd by the Generall and all his Officers, at Windsor, January the 19th, 1647[/8]' (S175/K217).

From September 1648 until the execution of Charles Stuart, Lucy Hutchinson's use of digression changes, as the Colonel, in his capacity as an MP for Nottinghamshire, is directly involved in the national events leading up to the King's trial. From this moment on, the *Memoirs* chiefly adopt the Colonel's point of view, even if Lucy Hutchinson's authorial presence can be felt. This is the case in this passage where John Hutchinson is angry at the Presbyterians who decided, despite the earlier Vote of No Address, to seek accommodation with the King:

> [Colonel Hutchinson] found the Presbyterian party so prevalent there [the House] that the victories obtein'd by the Army displeas'd them, and so hot they grew in the zeale of their faction that they from thenceforth resolv'd and endeavour'd to close with the common enemie, that they might thereby compasse the destruction of their Independent Antagonists. For which end, to strengthen their faction they gott in again the late suspended members.
>
> (S186/K230)

---

[87] http://bcw-project.org/church-and-state/second-civil-war/four-bills (accessed 22/06/2020).

For Lucy Hutchinson, who is voicing her husband's republican view, accepting a 'new personal treaty' with the King amounts to a betrayal of the cause for which he and the Independents have been fighting. Through the Colonel's anti-tyrannical rhetoric, which here chiefly targets the Presbyterians, a republican outlook is taking shape:

> Collonell Hutchinson was that night among them, and being convinc'd in his conscience that both the cause, and all those who with an upright honest heart asserted and maintain'd it, were betrey'd and sold for nothing, he [...] told them that the King, after having bene exasperated and vanquisht and captiv'd, would be restor'd to that power which was inconsistent with the liberty of the people, who for all their blood and treasure and misery would reape no fruite but a confirmation of bondage, and that it had bene a thousand times better never to have struck one stroke in the quarrell than, after victory, to yeild up a righteous cause. (S187/K231)

In the rest of the digression, the Presbyterians are paradoxically held responsible for the final execution of the King and the defeat of the Cavaliers: 'they finish the destruction of him in whose restitution they were now so fiercely engag'd, for this gave heart to the vanquisht Cavaliers, and such courage to the captive King that it harden'd him and them to their ruin' (S187–8/K232). The Presbyterians are also accused of radicalizing the debate, as their violent conduct 'so frighted all the honest people that it made them as violent in their zeale to pull downe as the others were in their madnesse to restore this kingly Idoll' (S188/K232). This indictment of the Presbyterians does not mean Lucy Hutchinson approves of the role of the army. Here, she more specifically denounces the action of Colonel Thomas Pride and his men, who, on the morning following the vote, that is, on 6 December 1648, 'came and seiz'd about [forty-one] of the members as they were going to the House, and carried them to a house hard by, where they were for the present kept prisoners' (S188/K232). At this point, she takes a clear stand against the tyrannical power of the army, which was to become problematic in the 1650s when, under the impulse of Cromwell, the military Protectorate imposed itself against the parliamentary regime of the Commonwealth. In 1649, however, there remained a few men 'above factions', who, like Colonel Hutchinson, emerged above the fray and were entrusted with a high civic mission for their country:

> most of the presbyterian faction, distasted at this insolence, would no more come to their seates in the House; but the gentlemen who either were of the

other faction, *or of none att all,* but look'd upon themselves as call'd out to manage a publick trust for their country, forsooke not their seates while they were permitted to sitt in the House.   (S188/K232, my emphasis)

The public duty to which Lucy Hutchinson is here referring is the trial of the King. To make her narrative of this dramatic moment more persuasive, she chooses to take the judges' point of view and to reconstruct, from the inside, the logic that drove her husband and his fellow commissioners to vote the King's death. At this stage, individual and national histories are brought together again in a reasoned apology of regicide, which combines a republican discourse with the biblical rhetoric of the 'man of blood', a leitmotiv in contemporary justifications of regicide, especially among the godly.[88] The judges, Lucy Hutchinson argues, would be called to account if they let the King escape again, for if this ever happened, he would inevitably continue to shed innocent blood, a crime which would not only destroy the sacredness of kings but also pollute the whole nation.[89] Seen from this angle, taking part in the trial of 'Charles Stuart, that man of blood' is a moral duty and a patriotic responsibility:

> [t]he Gentlemen that were appoynted his judges, and divers others, saw in him a disposition so bent to the ruine of all that had oppos'd him, and of all the righteous and just things they had contended for, that it was upon the consciences of many of them, that if they did not execute justice upon him, God would require at their hands all the blood and desolation which should ensue by their suffering him to escape when God had brought him into their hands, and that although the mallice of the malignant party and their Apostate brethren [= the Presbyterians] seem'd to threaten them, yett they ought to cast themselves upon God while they acted with a good conscience for him and their country.   (S189–90/K234)

By thus envisaging the King's trial from the point of view of both secular and divine justice, Lucy Hutchinson forcefully asserts the legitimacy of her husband's own decision to vote in favour of the King's death at the cost of his own life. This final stage in her apology for tyrannicide makes it possible to read her digressive chronicle of the monarch's actions up until his execution—later

---

[88] See Crawford, 'Charles Stuart, That Man of Blood', 47–8 and Loewenstein, 'The King among Radicals', 105–7. See also Ludlow, *Memoirs* [1699], 150, 172–4, 265–9.
[89] Crawford, 'Charles Stuart, That Man of Blood', 42–3. See Genesis 9:6 and Numbers 35:33.

described by his supporters as Charles I's tragedy—as an ironical counterpoint to John Hutchinson's own tragedy. Lucy Hutchinson's defence of tyrannicide in these digressions is crucial as it unambiguously qualifies her as a republican historian of the Civil Wars.[90]

3. Politico-moral digressions: a defence of Colonel Hutchinson

In her narrative of the Civil War, Lucy Hutchinson also uses moral digressions which, in Erasmus's words, consist in 'the presentation of persons, and also in the handling of stories and fables' and serve to '[inveigh] against glory, luxury, lust, avarice, base affection, tyranny, wrath, and other vices, and (as if forgetting our case for a time) dwell on these subjects'.[91] These excursuses, which ultimately serve as a defence of Colonel Hutchinson, shed an alternative light on his tragedy by suggesting that it was anticipated in the persecution he suffered in Nottingham in the 1640s. They fall into two categories. The first kind of digressions focuses on Puritans as a faction whose character and conduct were, in essence, persecutory. The second kind consists in vitriolic portraits of individual men (mostly Puritans) who fought on the side of Parliament, but whose conduct towards the Colonel was ambivalent, and often cruel.

a) Lucy Hutchinson's anti-Puritanism

The first digressive passage about Puritans is included in the long historical flashback, in which Lucy Hutchinson retraces the reign of James I. She explains how the men who sought the King's favour were systematically branded with the name of 'Puritan': 'when they had once given [the people of God] a name, whatever was odious or dreadfull to the king, [they] fixt that upon the Puritane, which, according to their character, was nothing but a factious hipocrite' (S43/K64).[92] She shows, in a parody of anti-Puritan satire,

---

[90] On the *Memoirs* as a republican text, see Norbrook, 'Words more than civil'.
[91] Erasmus, *Copia* 589. On the ethical function of digressions, see Milhe Poutingon, 'Une éthique de la digression', *Poétique du digressif* 10.
[92] In the *Basilikon Doron* (1603), James I makes a harsh criticism of the Puritans of his time. See the extract in Lawrence Sasek, ed., *Images of English Puritanism: A Collection of Contemporary Sources 1589–1646* (Baton Rouge: Louisiana State UP, 1989) 215–23.

that the reproaches which were commonly levelled against the most zealous Protestants (with whom she identifies here) actually reflected the courage and justice of their cause. Contrary to the 'court account', she claims that Puritans were pious people who abided by the law, placed the public interest over their private concerns, and advocated a thorough reformation of manners.[93] In a passage that partly rewrites a speech by Sir Benjamin Rudyer to the Long Parliament, she thus denounces the relentless and unfair persecution that was endured by the godly who rejected the corrupt and unjust power of James I:[94]

> If any gentleman in his country maintain'd the good lawes of the land, or stood up for any publick interest of his country, for good order or government, he was a Puritane; and in short, all that crost the interest of the needie Courtiers, the proud encroaching priests, the theevish projectors, the lewd nobillity and gentrie, whoever was zealous for God's glory or worship, could not endure blasphemous oaths, ribald conversation, prophane scoffs, sabbath breach, derision of the word of God, and the like, whoever could endure a sermon, modest habitt or conversation, or aniething that was good, all these were Puritanes; and if Puritanes, then enemies to the king and his government, seditious, factious hipocrites, ambitious disturbers of the publick peace, and finally, the pest of [the] Kingdome, enemies of God and good men, according to the Court account. (S44/K64–5)

It is thus for the wrong reasons—defending the poor, purifying the liturgy, reforming manners, and defending the law—that the true godly were covered with opprobrium by their detractors. The memorialist-turned-satirist takes this opportunity to condemn the depraved rhetoric of anti-Puritan libels and plays:[95]

> Such false logick did the children of darknesse use to argue with against the hated children of light, whom they branded besides as an illiterate, morose,

---

[93] On anti-Puritan satire, see William P. Holden, *Anti-Puritan Satire 1572–1642* (New Haven: Yale UP, 1954), Sasek, ed., *Images of English Puritanism*, and Lake, 'Anti-Puritanism: The Structure of a Prejudice', 80–97. See also Patrick Collinson, 'Antipuritanism', *Cambridge Companion to Puritanism*, ed. John Coffey and Paul C. H. Lim (Cambridge: Cambridge UP, 2008) 19–33.

[94] See Benjamin Rudyer, *The Speeches of Sr. Benjamin Rudyer in the High Court of Parliament* (London, 1641) 3. Lucy Hutchinson's criticism is directed at the régime of James I, while Rudyer focuses on the 1630s and early 1640s.

[95] Lucy Hutchinson was not the only one to condemn an indiscriminate use of the word 'Puritan'. See Henry Parker, *A Discourse Concerning Puritans* (London, 1641) and Sasek, *Images of English Puritanism* 129–71. See also John Geree, *The Character of an Old English Puritane, or Non-conformist* (London, 1646). Geree was responding to both contemporary and old attacks against Puritans.

melancholly, discontented, craz'd sort of men, not fitt for humane conversation; and as such they made them not only the sport of the pulpitt, which was become but a more solemne stage, but every stage and every table and every puppett-play belcht forth prophane scoffes upon them.   (S44/K65)

In this passage, Lucy Hutchinson ironically conjures up the same irreverent images and methods as her adversaries. She replicates the inflexible dichotomy between 'the children of light' and 'the children of darknesse', and turns the criticism of the Puritans against her opponents.

However, although Lucy Hutchinson clearly stood on the side of the 'children of light' (i.e. Puritans), she was aware that the label 'Puritan' was no guarantee of true godliness. In her view, Puritans—and especially when they were Presbyterians—were potentially as factious as Catholics. Hence her warning against the danger of exacerbating oppositions—when writing this passage, she must have had in mind the subsequent events of the Civil War, and what a short step it was from the war of words to the war of swords: 'the two factions in those dayes grew up to greate heigths and enmities, one against the other, while the Papist wanted not industry and subtlety to blow the coales between them' (S44/K65). Besides, by pointing to the 'black sheep' among the godly, she also points out the limits of too Manichean an opposition between Puritans and their enemies: 'But to deale impartially, wee must, with sadnesse enough, confesse that the wolfe came into the fold in a sheepe's clothing [...]; for it is true that many of witt and parts, discontented when they could not obteine the preferments their ambition gap'd at, would declare themselves of the puritane party' (S44/K65).

This sombre view of the Puritans hiding their worldly ambitions behind appearances of zeal and morality suffuses Lucy Hutchinson's entire Civil War narrative, from its premises up until the trial of the King. In a two-page digression about 'Roundheads'—'the scornfull terme given to the whole Parliament party' (S63/K87)—the memorialist shows the other side of the picture, revealing that Puritans, here equated with Roundheads, were not necessarily as pure as their external conduct seemed to indicate.[96] Many Puritans, she argues, were corrupted to the point of betraying the godly cause to which they claimed such zealous dedication:

---

[96] In a 1642 pamphlet, *A Puritane Set Forth in his Lively Colours*, based on James I's own description of a Puritan in the *Basilikon Doron*, the terms 'Presbyterian' and 'Puritan' are connected together, as the author of the pamphlet starts with a warning against Puritans as 'turbulent spirits' who 'introduce a Presbyterian in the Church' (2). In the section entitled 'the round-heads character', he concludes that 'a *Puritane* or a *Round-head* (they are termini aequivalentes)' (5).

This name of Roundhead comming so opertunely in, I shall make a little digression to tell how it came up. When Puritanisme grew into a faction, the zealotts distinguisht themselves, both men and weomen, by severall affectations of habit, lookes and words, which, had it bene a reall declension of vanity, and embracing of sobriety in all those things, had bene most commendable in them; but their quick forsaking of those things when they were where they would be shew'd that they either never tooke them up for conscience, or were corrupted by their prosperity to take up those vaine things they durst not practise under persecution. (S63/K86)

In order to ridicule these Puritans, Lucy Hutchinson draws on royalist anti-Puritan satire, quoting, with approbation, the first line of Cleveland's *Hue and Cry after Sir John Presbyter*, a royalist verse satire which starts by mocking the Roundheads' short hair and long ears: 'With hayre in Characters and Luggs in Text, etc'.[97] The fact that Lucy Hutchinson should quote Cleveland's royalist anti-Presbyterian satire does not mean that she shared his political and religious ideas, but shows that there was, in the middle of the seventeenth century, a common satirical idiom, especially against Presbyterians (equated with Puritans in most places of the *Memoirs*). This shared language was not royalist, but found its roots in the Marprelate controversy, a pamphlet war which opposed Episcopalians and Puritans in 1588 and 1589 in England and Wales. This controversy owed its name to a mysterious Martin Marprelate, a Puritan who was accused by his co-religionists of using an indecorous style (satire, jest, wit, and irony) in religious disputes.[98] Their stern Puritan attitude—which was also that of the Presbyterians in the 1640s—is well summed up by Martin Marprelate: 'The Puritans are angry with me; I meane the puritane preachers. And why? Because I am too open; because I jest.'[99] In the 1640s, many pamphlets, written in the indecorous Marprelate

---

[97] John Cleveland, *The Hue and Cry after Sir John Presbyter* (London, 1649): 'With Hair in Characters, and Lugs in text: / With a splay mouth, & a nose circumflext: / With a set Ruff of Musket bore, that wears / Like Cartrages or linen Bandileers, / Exhausted of their sulpherous Contents / In Pulpit fire-works, which that Bomball vents: / The *Negative* and *Covenanting* Oath, / Like two Mustachoes, issuing from his mouth.' This poem is quoted in Lucy Hutchinson's *Literary Commonplace Book*, DD/HU1, 247-9.
[98] On the Marprelate controversy, see Patrick Collinson, 'Literature and the Church', *The Cambridge History of Early Modern Literature*, ed. David Loewenstein and Janel Mueller (Cambridge: Cambridge UP, 2002) 390-1; Ritchie D. Kendall, 'Martin Marprelate Syllogistic Laughter', *The Drama of Dissent: The Radical Poetics of Nonconformity 1380-1590* (Chapel Hill: U of North Carolina P, 1986) 173-211; Nigel Smith, 'Marprelate Revived', *Literature and Revolution in England, 1640-1660* (Yale: New Haven UP, 1994) 297-304.
[99] Martin Marprelate (pseud), *Oh Read Over D. John Bridges. Epitome* (np, 1588). An edict against satires was passed in 1599 in the wake of the Marprelate Controversy. See Cyndia Susan Clegg, *Press Censorship in Elizabethan England* (Cambridge: Cambridge UP, 1997) 216-17.

style, came off the presses, while the controversy itself was revived.[100] For example, Sir John Presbyter's character, the protagonist of Cleveland's satire,[101] was created by Richard Overton, a General Baptist and future Leveller, the author of seven Marpriest pamphlets, which recycled the polemic devices of the first controversy.[102] In this context, the fact that Lucy Hutchinson should quote Cleveland's anti-Presbyterian satire does not mean that she shared his political and religious views, but that she assumed irreverent satire to be the best means to attack the growing power of Presbyterians, and more generally, as Nigel Smith puts it, 'to strike at the orthodoxy'.[103] The comparison between Lucy Hutchinson's *Memoirs* and the Marprelate controversy cannot be pursued too far, of course, but it seems that for Lucy Hutchinson, as for Milton, true religion was not necessarily the enemy of satire, which could be a powerful instrument to confute one's enemies.[104]

What Lucy Hutchinson may have found inspiring in Cleveland's *Hue and Cry after Sir John Presbyter*—besides religious mockery—is the satirist's use of the character genre to mock Roundheads and Puritans.[105] Like the royalist satirist, she maintains that the Roundheads' habit of wearing short hair was ridiculous and deceptive: instead of being a sign of piety, it often denoted a lack of true godliness and vain formality. This is exemplified, she argues, in the Roundheads' foolish treatment of the Colonel, who had 'a very fine thicksett head of haire' (S63/K87): 'The godly of those dayes, when [Mr. Hutchinson] embrac'd their party, would not allow him to be religious because his hayre was not in their cut, nor his words in their phrase, nor such little formallities

---

[100] Smith, *Literature and Revolution* 297-9. See, for instance, Richard Overton, *New Lambeth Fayre newly Consecrated and Presented by the Pope Himselfe, cardinals, bishops, Iesuits &c* (London, 1642) or his *A New Play Called Canterburie his Change of Diet* (London, 1645).

[101] See Richard Overton, *The Nativity of Sir John Presbyter* (London, 1645) and Smith, *Literature and Revolution* 300-1 and 306-7.

[102] Smith, 'Richard Overton's Marpriest Tracts: Towards a History of Leveller Style', *The Literature of Controversy*, ed. Corns, 39-40.

[103] Smith, *Literature and Revolution* 296. Behind these satires, there were also memories of Homer, Lucian and of the Menippean satire (Smith 305-6).

[104] See John Milton, *An Apology against a Pamphlet Called A Modest Confutation of the Animadversions upon the Remonstrant against Smectymnus* (London, 1642), in *Complete Prose Works* 1: 901 ('there may be a sanctified bitterness against the enemies of truth'). See Claire Gheeraert-Graffeuille, 'Satire et diffusion des idées dans la littérature pamphlétaire à l'aube de la guerre civile anglaise, 1640-1642', *Dix-septième siècle* 195 (1997): 284-7 and Norbrook, 'Words more than civil', 73-4.

[105] See, for instance, the anonymous pamphlet, *The Character of a Cavaliere, with His Brother Separatist* (London, 1647), and, by John Cleveland, *The Character of a London-Diurnall* (London, 1644) and *The Character of a Committee-man, with the eare-marke of a sequestrator* (London, 1647). See also Smith, *Literature and Revolution* 304-5; Benjamin Boyce, *The Polemic Character 1640-1661. A Chapter in English Literary History* (New York: Octagon Books, 1969), Claire Labarbe, '"Mises en abyme" and Satirical Descriptions: "Characters" of Writing and Writers in Seventeenth-Century England', *Études Épistémè* 21 (2012), https://doi.org/10.4000/episteme.407.

altogether fitted to their humor' (S63/K87). For Lucy Hutchinson, these men, who were only pious in appearance, looked like the Gospel's 'whited sepulchres'—they 'appear beautiful outward, but are within full of dead men's bones, and all uncleanness' (Matthew 23:27):

> But as Mr. Hutchinson chose not them [the Puritans], but the God they serv'd and the truth and righteousnesse they defended, so did not their weaknesses, censures, ingratitudes and discouraging behaviour, with which he was abundantly exercis'd all his life, make him forsake them in any thing wherein they adher'd to just and honorable principles or practizes, but when they apostatized from these, none cast them off with greater indignation, how shining soever the profession were that guilt, not a temple of living grace, but a Tomb, which only held the carkase of religion. (S63/K87)

These virulent anticlerical observations come as a conclusion to Lucy Hutchinson's digression about Puritans. They are not speculative or abstract, but very much connected to the sad memories of her husband's persecution in the 1640s: 'Instead of digressing, I shall ramble into an inextricable wildernesse if I pursue this sad remembrance. To returne therefore to his actions at that time' (S63/K87). In fact, presumably because of her husband's experience of oppression, she tends to see all Presbyterians as persecutors, and her moral criticism here ties up with her very dark political view of Puritans.[106] Moreover, when it comes to recounting the Civil War in Nottinghamshire, Lucy Hutchinson's polemical pen shifts from types to individuals, and she does not hesitate to directly attack the local potentates who persecuted her husband. These critical portraits are not, strictly speaking, character sketches, but still owe much to the genre and, more generally, to the satirical tradition.

b) A gallery of portraits

Before her digression about Roundheads, Lucy Hutchinson deviates from her story to specify the allegiances (predominantly royalist) of the local gentry and aristocracy 'because [she] shall often have occasion to mention them' (S61/K84). She gives a few indications about everyone's estates and reputations, but she does not enter into the detail of their 'character', except for the Earl of Newcastle. '[No] man,' she writes, 'was a greater prince than he in all that

---

[106] See Chapter 3, 2, b, 'The Committee of Nottingham: a civil war in miniature', 151.

Northerne quarter, till a foolish ambition of glorious slavery carried him to Court, where he ran himselfe much in to debt, to purchase neglects of the King and Queene and scornes of the proud Courtiers' (S61/K84). By contrast, in another series of digressions,[107] Lucy Hutchinson offers individual portraits of the men 'whom Mr. Hutchinson was first mated with, whose *characters* it was necessary thus farre to hint at for the better carrying on of his story' (S73/K99, my emphasis). The insertion of portraits into the narration is typical of the memoir genre,[108] as well as of many Renaissance and early modern histories: Polydor Vergil, Edward Hall, John Speed, William Camden, and Edward Hyde all incorporated into their works portraits which took the form of short lives or character sketches.[109] Their models were Suetonius, Plutarch, and Tacitus. For Bacon, character sketches were particularly valuable to introduce a historical actor:

> for the character so worked into the narrative gives a better idea of the man than any formal criticism and review can; such is that of Africanus and Cato the Elder in Livy, of Tiberius, and Claudius, and Nero in Tacitus, of Septimus Severus in Herodian, of Louis XI, King of France in Philip de Comines, of Ferdinand of Spain, the Caesar Maximilian, and the Popes Leo and Clement in Francesco Guicciardini.[110]

Lucy Hutchinson's portraits undoubtedly belong to these historiographical and literary traditions. Like the other digressions punctuating the *Memoirs*, they contribute to the intelligibility of the Colonel's destiny and highlight his 'republican civility'.[111]

The portraits of the Colonel's assistants fall into two distinct categories. The first one includes the sketches of four of his enemies, namely John Gell, Charles White, James Chadwick, and Huntingdon Plumtre. With the exception of John Gell, they were all deceitful members of the Nottingham Committee.[112] Their characterization resonates with Lucy Hutchinson's

---

[107] See *Memoirs*, ed. Sutherland, 67–8; 70–2; 72–3, and ed. Keeble, 92–3; 96–9.
[108] See Lesne, *Poétique des mémoires* 123: 'whether celebratory or satirical, ample or confined within the space of an epigram, portraits are everywhere present in memoirs and are an essential feature of their poetics.' See also Charbonnier, *Les Silences de l'histoire* 110; Marc Hersant and Catherine Ramond, eds., *Les Portraits dans les récits factuels et fictionnels de l'époque classique* (Leiden: Brill, 2019) 181–284.
[109] Brownley, *Clarendon and the Rhetoric of Historical Form* 147; 152.
[110] Francis Bacon, *De Augmentis Scientiarum*, in *The Works of Francis Bacon*, ed. James S. Spedding, R. L. Ellis, and D. D. Heath, 14 vols. (London, 1857–74), vol. 5, 21.
[111] On characters and portraits in historiography, see Norbrook, 'The English Revolution and English Historiography', 242–5. On republican civility, see his 'Words more than civil', 68–84.
[112] See Chapter 3, 2, b ('The Committee of Nottingham: The Civil War in miniature').

satirical depiction of Puritans, as well as with traditional 'characters', notably the Hypocrite, the Covetous, the Envious, the Ambitious.[113] The second category includes the portraits of the six trustworthy allies of the Colonel, namely Francis Pierrepont, Francis Thornhagh, Gervase Pigott, Joseph Widmerpoole, Gervase Lomax, and Thomas Salisbury.[114] I will not expatiate on these shorter sketches, for they are less important in the *Memoirs*' apologetic scheme than the portraits of the Colonel's antagonists who serve as counterpoints to his exemplarity.

We are first given a two-page portrait of Sir John Gell, whom Lucy Hutchinson calls a 'very bad man' (S68/K92), 'violent' and 'unjust', a foul 'adulterer', having no 'piety or holiness'.[115] She also brings to the fore the negative passions—'envie, hate and ill will'—that he nourished against the Colonel, 'under the name of a friend and assistant' (S68/K93). The result is a polemical portrait of Gell, which, according to Martyn Bennett '[does] match widely held and expressed views of him held by a spectrum of other commentators'.[116] In her sketch, Lucy Hutchinson inextricably mixes character with particular historical circumstances: she emphasizes Gell's violence and cruelty as a collector of Ship Money (the tax levied by Charles in the 1630s), while denouncing his vicious attitude towards Sir John Stanhope, whom she warmly defends, probably because of family links:[117]

> About this time Sir John Gell, a gentleman in Derbyshire, who had bene Sheriffe of the County at that time when the illegall tax of Shipmony was exacted, and so violent in the prosecution of it that he sterv'd Sir John Stanhope's cattle in the pound and would not suffer any person to relieve them there, because that worthy gentleman stood out against that unjust payment. (S67/K92)[118]

---

[113] See these characters in Joseph Hall, *Characters of Vertues and Vices, In Two Bookes* (London, 1608). On the development of 'individuality' in character-writing, see Jacques Bos, 'Individuality and Inwardness in the Literary Character Sketches of the Seventeenth Century', *Journal of the Warburg and Courtauld Institutes* 61 (1998): 142–57.

[114] See Keeble's corresponding notes in his edition of the *Memoirs* and Wood, *Nottinghamshire in the Civil War*.

[115] Trevor Brighton, 'Gell, Sir John, first baronet (bap. 1593, d. 1671), parliamentarian army officer' (2004), *Oxford Dictionary of National Biography*, DOI: 10.1093/ref:odnb/10508.

[116] Bennett, 'Every County', 196–8. In an appendix to the 1906 edition, Firth demonstrates that much of Lucy Hutchinson's account is confirmed by other sources (Appendix VI, 395–7).

[117] Keeble notes that Lucy Hutchinson's sympathy for the Stanhope family may come from the fact that Sir John's youngest daughter, Katherine, was Sir Thomas Hutchinson's second wife, i.e. Lucy Hutchinson's stepmother (357, note 171).

[118] On Gell, as collector of Ship Money, see Bennett, 'Every County', 197.

After the death of Sir John Stanhope, Gell was more than ever animated by a spirit of revenge. Like Shakespeare's Richard III seducing Lady Anne, he wooed and eventually married the widow of his arch-enemy 'for nothing else but to destroy the glory of her husband and his house' (92).[119] This story elicits sharp moral condemnation on the part of Lucy Hutchinson, who characterizes Sir John's widow as a paragon of womankind and a victim of an impious, barbarous seducer:

> [he was] so revengefull that he persued his mallice to Sir John Stanhope [. . .] with such barbarisme after his death that he, pretending to search for Arms and plate, came into the Church and defac'd his monument that cost 600, breaking off the nose and other parts of it, and digg'd up a garden of flowers, the only delight of his widow, upon the same pretence; and thus woo'd that widdow, who was by all the world believ'd to be the most prudent and affectionate of womankind, but deluded by his hypocrisies, consented to marry him. (S67/K92)

In the rest of her portrait, Lucy Hutchinson continues to dwell on Gell's incivility and depravity, contrasting it with the Colonel's virtue and referring to the opposition between them as 'that naturall antipathie which is betweene good and evill' (S68/K93). She draws at least three antitheses between the two men. First, between the Colonel's disciplined troops and Gell's 'most licentious, ungovernable wretches' (S67/K92), no better than ungodly and debauched Cavaliers. Second, between the Colonel's wise use of 'Scouts and spies' and Gell's inability to manage them, which was 'another cause of envy' (S68/K93).[120] Third, between the Governor's moral integrity and Gell's vanity, falsehood, and cowardice—vices which are illustrated by his keeping 'the diurnall makers in pension' and building, through the press, his own glory (S68/K93). The aim of these three marked oppositions—very much part of Lucy Hutchinson's overall apologetic strategy—is to show that Gell, unlike the Colonel, was not morally up to the cause of Parliament.

The digression about Charles White directly follows from the previous one about Gell, with no line-break in the manuscript, but a terse comment serving as a justification to this second excursus:[121] '[b]ut to turne out of this digression into another, not altogether impertinent to the story which I would carrie

---

[119] Gell married Mary Stanhope in December 1647, but the couple separated in 1648. See Brighton, 'Gell, Sir John, first baronet'.
[120] On Gell and the press, see Bennett, 'Every County', 197–8.
[121] Nottinghamshire Archives, DD/HU4, 112.

on' (S68–9/K93). Lucy Hutchinson does not reveal the identity of the man she portrays until the very end of the digression, but she very efficiently tells his story: '[i]n Nottinghamshire, upon the edge of Derbieshire, there dwelt a man who was of meane birth and low fortunes, yet had kept company with the underling gentry of his neighbourhood' (S69/K93). Her portrait reveals all the vices that she discovers beneath White's 'vizard of godliness and humility', namely religious hypocrisy, lust, ambition, envy, malice, vainglory, and lechery, all the sins that were generally attributed to Puritans in anti-Puritan satire:

> This man had the most factious, ambitious, vaineglorious, envious, and mallitious nature that is imaginable; but he was the greatest dissembler, flatterer, traitor and hipocrite that ever was, and herein had a kind of wicked pollicy: knowing himselfe to be inferiour to all gentlemen, he put on a vizard of godlinesse and humillity, and courted the common people with all the plausibillity and flattery that could be practiz'd. All this while he was addicted to many lusts, especially to that of woemen, but practiz'd them so secretly, that they were not vulgarly taken notice of, though God, to shame him, gave him up to marrie a wench out of one of the Ale-houses he frequented; but to keepe up a fame of godlinesse, he gave large contributions to puritane preachers who had the art to stop the people's mouths from speaking ill of their benefactors. (S69/K93–4)

White's Presbyterianism and his role in the Nottingham Committee is at the core of Lucy Hutchinson's acerbic description.[122] When she calls him a 'Presbyterian persecutor', she does not speak impartially, but with her husband's—and the whole nation's—sufferings in mind.[123] His participation in Sir George Booth's royalist rising in 1659 comes as a confirmation of his political unreliability. However, by turning his political trajectory into an edifying story of rise and fall, Lucy Hutchinson shows immanent justice at work:

> By a thousand arts this fellow became popular, and insinuated himselfe so into all the gentlemen that own'd the Parliament's party, that till he was

---

[122] On Captain White, see 'The Turncoat: Charles White of Newthorpe, Nottinghamshire (d. 1661)', https://www.civilwarpetitions.ac.uk/blog/the-war-hero-the-eccentric-and-the-turncoat-the-men-behind-three-signatures/ (accessed 16/07/2020).

[123] The Presbyterian persecutor was a stock character in the pamphlets of the times. See, for example, Overton, *The Arraignment of Mr Persecution* (London, 1645), and *The Picture of an English Persecutor* (London, 1647).

discover'd some yeares after, they believ'd him a most truehearted, faithfull, vigilant, active man for the godly interest; but he could never climb higher than a Presbiterian persecutor, and there in the end fell quite off to a declar'd Cavalier in Sir George Booth's businesse. Thinking he could sway the scales of a country, he rays'd a troope brought them into Derby, and publisht a declaration of his owne for the King, then ranne away to Nottingham, and lost all his troope in the route there, and hid himselfe till the king came in, when he was rewarded for his revolt with an office, which he enjoy'd not many months, his wife and he and some of his children dying alltogether in a few dayes of a feaver little lesse than the plague.   (S69/K94)

The conclusion of the portrait closes the loop as it returns to White's early commitment for Parliament in October 1642, when he was given a commission as Captain. With such an edifying story, Lucy Hutchinson warns us against this man's cruelty towards the Colonel.[124]

In the second diptych, Lucy Hutchinson offers even darker portraits of Chadwick and Plumtre, both members of the Nottingham Committee and amongst the Colonel's 'greatest enemies', even if, at first, they 'put themselves most forward in the businesse' (S70/K96), that is, the service of Parliament. Plumtre's portrait is anticipated in an earlier passage, where he is characterized as a gifted 'young practitioner' (S22/K40), who was successful, before the Civil War, in curing George Hutchinson's epilepsy, but who was also, already, a 'profest athiest' (S26/K43). In her longer description of Plumtre, Lucy Hutchinson graphically explains how, despite his undeniable qualities, he lost his reputation as a physician 'by his most abusive tongue and other ill carriages' (S71/K96). She tells the anecdote of a 'lovely young Lady', who 'asking a medicine for wormes in her nose, he sent her an oyntment that poison'd it, which was the beauty of her beauty, and eate worse scarres into it than if she had had the smallpox' (S71/K96). She insists on Plumtre's 'intollerable pride' (S71/K96) and calls him again a 'horrible Atheist' (S70–1/K96),[125] a term which connects him with the 'atheist' type, as it is for instance delineated in Nicholas Breton's book of character sketches. The 'Atheist,' he writes, is a 'figure of desperation, who dare do any thing euen to his soules damnation [...] Hee makes Sinne a iest, Grace an

---

[124] See, for example, how, after the affair of the Cannoniers, Captain White, Salisbury, Plumtre, and Mason 'entered into close confederacy' (167–8).
[125] The term 'atheist' here designates '[o]ne who practically denies the existence of a God by disregard of moral obligation to Him; a godless man' (*OED*).

humour, Truth a fable, and Peace a Cowardice.'[126] In Plumtre's case, Lucy Hutchinson's repetition of the derogatory term 'atheist' makes it clear that any further collaboration with him was inconceivable: 'Mr. Hutchinson and his brother, in pitty to him, and remembrance of what God had done by him, still own'd him, and protected him a little against the bitter zealotts, though it was impossible for his darknesse and their light long to continue mix'd' (S71/K96). The portrait ends rather abruptly, and Lucy Hutchinson does not cover, as in the case of Gell or White, the rest of Plumtre's life. In fact, she keeps the details in store for a later digression in which she dramatizes a quarrel that occurred in the summer of 1643, when Plumtre 'was raging' (S85/K113) at the Governor's decision of drawing up the ordnance up to the Castle because, like the royalists in Nottingham, he feared for his own private goods. In this digression, she vividly contrasts her husband's dedication to 'the more public interest of the cause'—that is, his civility[127]—with Plumtre's utter contempt for it. From verbal violence they inexorably move to physical violence:

> While this was boyling upon his spiritt, he mett the Governor with some other gentlemen in the streete, and began to rayle at him for countenancing the godly townsmen, whom he call'd a company of Puritanicall prickear'd rascalls [...], and that in spight of his teeth he would have three of the most eminent of them turn'd out of the Castle. The Governor telling [him] that he would maintain [them] as the most faithfull friends to the Cause, Plumtre replied he was as honest to the Cause as the Governor. "No," sayd the Governor (who was not ignorant of his Atheisme), "that you cannot be, for you goe not upon the same Principles." The Doctor told him it was false, with such uncivill insolence that the Governor struck him, at which he departed quietly home. (S85/K113)

The conclusion of this passage confirms the hatred between the two men. After the Governor has struck him, Plumtre sends to the Governor 'a ridiculous challenge [...] which the Governor at that present only answered with contempt'. The whole story may sound trivial, but Lucy Hutchinson retrospectively reads it as a providential foreshadowing of the Colonel's sufferings

---

[126] Nicholas Breton, *The Good and the Badde, or Descriptions of the Worthies, and Vnworthies of this Age* (London, 1616). It was republished in 1643.
[127] On this key notion, see Norbrook, 'Words more than civil', 68–71.

in 1663–1664. This digression, far from distracting the readers' attention, refocuses it on the tragic destiny of the Colonel:[128]

> Though these passages may seeme too impertinent here, yet they having bene grounds and beginnings of injurious prosecutions wherewith the Governor was afterwards much exercis'd, it was not altogether unnecessary to insert them, since even these little things were linkes in the chaine of providences which measur'd out his life. (S86/K113–14)

The portrait of Chadwick follows that of Plumtre, with no comment or adverbial connection between them. In Lucy Hutchinson's eyes, the two men had many vices in common: Chadwick was, like Plumtre, a personal enemy of the Colonel's. Her summary of his rise from 'a boy that scrap'd trenchers in the house of one of the poorest justices in the County' (S71/K97) to his position as 'Deputy Recorder of Nottingham' (S72/K97) reveals his scheming nature and his 'insinuating wit and tongue'. This first glimpse at his social climbing is soon completed by a moral portrait of him as an arch-hypocrite, both in politics and religion. To crown it all, Chadwick's allegiances were not clear-cut at first, as he sought to please both the King and the Puritans. From Lucy Hutchinson's retrospective point of view, this was logical as both factions, Presbyterians and royalists, were, in her view, responsible for the persecution of the Colonel and the ultimate defeat of the Good Old Cause:

> When the King was in Towne [...], this man so insinuated into the Court that, comming to kisse the King's hand, the King told him he was a very honest man; yet by flatteries and dissimulations he kept up his credit with the godly, cutting his haire, and taking up a forme of godlinesse, the better to deceive. (S72/K97)

From this perspective, Chadwick is also seen as a living embodiment of the stereotype of the Puritan commonly mocked in anti-Puritan satire.[129] His whole life is described as a fraud: he reached a position of power, 'because he had a voluble tongue, and was crafty' (S72/K97); he 'got abundance of mony by a thousand cheates and other base wayes' (S72/K97); despite his

---

[128] Other digressions repeat Plumtre's story and confirm his ambiguous allegiances, and his insolence, and his detestation of Colonel Hutchinson. See, for instance, *Memoirs* 127–8 and 166–70.

[129] Norbrook, 'Words more than Civil', 77. According to Norbrook, Chadwick 'the base-born upstart hypocritically using religion for self-advancement, might have stepped out of the pages of Ben Jonson and the later Cavalier poets.'

affectation of godliness, he was 'a libidinous goate, for which his wife, they say, pay'd him with making him a cuckold' (S72/K97). The attack reaches its climax with the identification of Chadwick to Judas Iscariot—'[n]ever was a truer Judas since Iscariott's time than he, for he would kisse the man he had in his heart to kill' (S72/K97)—and the oxymoronic description of pleasure in villainy: 'he naturally delighted in mischief and treachery, and was so exquisite a villaine that he destroy'd those designes he might have thriven by, with overlaying them with fresh knaveries' (S72/K97–8).

As shown in this digressive gallery of local portraits, which is continued and completed in the rest of the *Memoirs*,[130] Lucy Hutchinson takes up the types of contemporary satire: the atheist, the hypocrite, the Puritan persecutor, the Committee-man, the diurnal-maker, and so on.[131] Her main goal in these digressions is evidently to settle her accounts with the Colonel's 'assistants'. But her moral excursuses do not only serve a judicial function; they also give the reader some clues to understand Lucy Hutchinson's dark moral outlook and her pessimism regarding history. In her view, many supporters of Parliament, being driven by their low passions, were not up to the godly cause they were supposed to defend. Their persecution of the Colonel anticipated in many ways his arrest and imprisonment in 1663–1664. However, the digressive construction of the *Memoirs* does not only bring out the moral depravity and Machiavellian politics of John Hutchinson's contemporaries. If perspectives are inverted, Lucy Hutchinson's clever composition highlights, by contrast, the Colonel's ideal of a godly republic. The 'true' saints were very few indeed, but the situation was not completely hopeless and there remained a strong millenarian belief that defeat against the Cavaliers was only temporary:

> when many ill usages of himselfe by godly people have bene urg'd to him, he would say that if they were truly the people of God, all their failings were to be borne; and that if God had a people in the land, as he was confident he had, it was among them and not among the Cavaliers, and therefore though he should ever be severe against their miscarriages in any person in whomsoever he found it, yett he would adhere to them that own'd God, how unkindly soever they dealt with him. (S265/K322)

---

[130] See, in the *Memoirs* (123), the acerbic portrait of Captain Palmer very much in the style of the four portraits examined here.

[131] These characters are not static like traditional Theophrastan characters, but dynamic, 'temporally structured' (Bos, 'Individuality and Inwardness', 153).

All in all, Lucy Hutchinson's systematic digressions hold together two apparently competing perspectives on history: on the one hand, a disenchanted and pessimistic view of the English Revolution, in which the Christian republic is annihilated by the Stuart monarchy, and, on the other hand, a millenarian outlook—embodied by Colonel Hutchinson—in which the republic of the saints remains the ultimate horizon. In the latter version of history, suffering has its place and importance—it is even an essential step before the final victory of the saints. From this angle, the digressions, far from being anecdotal and ornamental, give the key to understanding the complex project of the *Memoirs* and, beyond, the 'admirable bookes of providence' (S278/K3). In this light, Lucy Hutchinson's art of digression serves a fundamentally epistemological and apologetic function, closely related to her own deeply religious mindset. Her approach is reminiscent of what Pascal says about *l'ordre du cœur* ('the rule of the heart') and the art of digressing: 'Jesus Christ and Saint Paul employ the rule of love, not of intellect; for they would warm, not instruct. It is the same with Saint Augustine. This order consists chiefly in digressions on each point to indicate the end, and keep it always in sight.'[132]

---

[132] Blaise Pascal. *Thoughts, The Harvard Classics*, ed. Charles W. Eliot, trans. W. F. Trotter (New York: Collier and Son, 1910), Kindle edition, §1498. See Pascal, *Pensées*, ed. Philippe Sellier (Paris: Bordas, 1991), fragment 329, 295: 'Jésus-Christ, saint Paul ont l'ordre de la charité, non de l'esprit, car ils voulaient échauffer, non instruire. // Saint Augustin de même. Cet ordre consiste principalement à la digression sur chaque point qui a rapport à la fin, pour la montrer toujours.'

Conclusion

This book has sought to cast new light on the ways in which Lucy Hutchinson builds up her authority as a historian in the *Memoirs of the Life of Colonel Hutchinson*. It challenges the widely-held assumption that early modern women did not—and could not—write war history, a field that was supposedly gendered as masculine. This study has also evidenced how Lucy Hutchinson's successful use of several genres and traditions of history writing put her on a par with other historians and memorialists of the English Restoration, in particular Richard Baxter, Edmund Ludlow, or Edward Hyde. Like them, Lucy Hutchinson used her first-hand experience of the Civil Wars to authorize her narrative at a time of deep epistemological crisis. However, her approach to history in the *Memoirs* presents two sets of limitations. First, as it is based on the author's personal experience, it is limited in time and space, a difficulty which Lucy Hutchinson partly resolves thanks to an ingenious system of digressions which allows her to go back in time, and to combine a local account of the English Civil War with a national one. Second, her treatment of history is apologetic, and what she writes is clearly meant as a defence of Colonel Hutchinson's conduct during the Civil War Interregnum, not a factual account of these years as such. The necessity of vindicating her husband leads her to tinker with history and memory, which she thought was fully justified because she was serving a higher truth that manifested itself in the Colonel's martyrdom. From this angle, the *Memoirs* convey the promise of a godly republic and better times to come for the saints. Hence the superimposition, in the *Memoirs*, of two views of history to which I now return: first, a disenchanted, tragic vision of the English Revolution, associated with the defeat of the Good Old Cause and the death of Colonel Hutchinson; second, a millenarian perspective epitomized throughout the *Memoirs* by the latter's heroic martyrdom.

1. A tragic vision of the English Revolution

Early modern historians often described history as a spectacle. In the preface to his *Historical Collections*, John Rushworth states for example that he 'has been upon the stage continually, an Eye and Ear-witness of the greatest transactions'.[1] For most of these historians the spectacle of the Civil Wars was not an ordinary spectacle but a true 'tragedy'.[2] Dugdale saw the downfall of Charles I as the 'last Act of this afflicted King's life',[3] that is, as the dénouement of 'a lamentable tragedy',[4] a horrid act, a sacrilege. On the other hand, those who supported the King's execution preferred to regard it as the dénouement of a revenge tragedy. The Parliamentarian writer Edward Peyton refers to the 'divine catastrophe' of the regicide as the work of God, 'who, when he determined to bring this family to destruction, accomplisheth it not only by poor and weak means, but by his mightiest thunderbolts of vengeance'.[5] Lucy Hutchinson's representation of the English Civil War as a tragedy is not as Manichean as under the pens of Peyton and Dugdale, for instance. As shall be shown here, she skilfully uses the genre of tragedy in order to articulate a more complex vision of the English Revolution.

When Lucy Hutchinson mentions 'the prologue to the ensuing Tragedie' (S52/K74), she is explicitly referring to the Civil War, which was 'acted' in England (S78–79/K104–105) and which ended up with the trial of the King in 1649. In this tragedy, King Charles I, as a typical Aristotelian hero, is depicted neither as an utter villain, nor as a saint, but as 'a character between these two extremes', whose death on the scaffold was caused by a so-called 'tragic flaw', or *hamartia*, which Lucy Hutchinson locates in his obstinacy.[6] Because he refused to negotiate with Parliament, Charles I is understood to have gone against the English Constitution of King-in-Parliament, and to have betrayed the public trust. By giving the King the role of a traitor, Lucy Hutchinson, like his judges, reverses the royalist claim that the King was betrayed by his Parliament—in her version of Charles I's tragedy, the distribution of roles is not the same as in most royalist histories, in which the King is portrayed as a saint and a martyr.[7]

---

[1] John Rushworth, *Historical Collections* (London, 1659) sig. b^v.

[2] See Claire Gheeraert-Graffeuille, 'The Tragedy of Regicide in Interregnum and Restoration Histories of the English Civil Wars', *Études Épistémè* 20 (2011), https://doi.org/10.4000/episteme.430.

[3] William Dugdale, *A Short View of the Late Troubles in England* (London, 1681) 361.

[4] Hyde, *The History of the Rebellion*, vol. 4, 488.

[5] See Edward Peyton, *The Divine Catastrophe of the Kingly Family of the House of Stuarts, or, a short History of the Rise, Reign, and Ruine Thereof* (London, 1652) 71–2.

[6] See Aristotle, *The Poetics*, trans. S. H. Henry (London: Macmillan, 1922): 'There remains, then, the character between these two extremes, – that of a man who is not eminently good and just, – yet whose misfortune is brought about not by vice or depravity, but by some error or frailty.' On the King's obstinacy in the *Memoirs*, see Chapter 6, 2, c ('A defence of tyrannicide').

[7] 'My Lord, I did at the first exhibit a Charge against him, containing the highest practices of Treason, that were ever wrought on the Theater of England. That a King of England' (Bradshaw's words in *The Full Proceedings of the High Court of Justice against King Charles in Westminster Hall* [London, 1654]) 35.

Even though Lucy Hutchinson holds the King responsible for the tragedy that occurred in England, there is no sense of triumph in her account of the Interregnum. Admittedly, her assessment of the early years of the Commonwealth (1649–1653) is rather positive, '[t]he Parliament [...] having now, by the blessing of God, restor'd the Commonwealth to such a happie, rich and plentifull condition, as it was not so flourishing before the warre' (S205/K252). But she considers nonetheless that Cromwell, by dissolving the Rump Parliament in April 1653, proved disloyal to the cause of Parliament and betrayed all the political and religious values he had fought for. Even if her hopes were briefly rekindled with the Restoration of the Rump Parliament in May 1659, we, readers, are made to understand that the revival of the cause was a mere illusion.[8] In Lucy Hutchinson's view, by leaving 'a doore open'd' (S209/K257) for the Restoration, Cromwell had his share of responsibility for the failure of the Revolution. Referring to his 'triumvirs' (Harrison and Lambert), she significantly connects him with Caesar, who, like him, had been the target of several conspiracies, and had been accused of planning to restore the monarchy: 'He quitted himselfe soone of his Triumvirs, and first thrust out Harrison, then tooke away Lambert's Commission, and would have bene King but for feare of quitting his Generallship' (S208/K256).[9]

Lucy Hutchinson, however, does not see Cromwell as entirely responsible for the 'sins of the nation' (S222/K273). She attributes to the Colonel the bitter thought that 'the period of [their] prosperity was come, and hasten'd on [...] cheifely by the generall streame of the people, who were as eager for their owne destruction as the Izraelites of old for their Quailes' (S223/K273). According to John Hutchinson, the general conduct of the English people, including those of his own party, typologically repeated the sins of the people of Israel, who yearned for the 'quails' they had received when they were under the Egyptian yoke (Numbers 11: 20). Similarly, Lucy Hutchinson does not depict the return of the King as a moment of rejoicing; on the contrary, the enthusiasm of the English people on this occasion reveals the 'mutabillity of some, and the hipocrisie of others, and the servile flattery of all' (S227/K278). In other words, for Lucy Hutchinson, the national tragedy, which started with the English Civil War, neither ended with the execution of the King, nor did it end with Cromwell's rule or with the Restoration:[10] the 'sunne of liberty then sett, and all their [the three nations] glorie gave place to the fowlest mists that

---

[8] See *Memoirs*, ed. Sutherland, 214–15, and ed. Keeble, 263–4.
[9] See Scott, *Commonwealth Principles* 271.
[10] See Staves, *A Literary History of Women's Writing* 37; Clare, 'Introduction', *From Republic to Restoration* 9, and, in this same volume, Worden, '1660: Restoration and Revolution', 23–51.

ever overspread a miserable people' (S224/K274). All the achievements of those who supported the Parliament and the republic are said to have disappeared under the 'mists' of the restored monarchy, in which the Colonel only sees the 'restitution of all former tiranny and bondage' (S211/K260).[11] From this disillusioned view, which is characteristic of Nonconformist literature,[12] emerges a severe moral assessment of the Restoration world, which has 'weake eies' and 'but few people so vertuous in it as can believe, because they find themselves so short, any other could make so large a progresse in the race of piety, honor, and vertue' (S1/K16). By contrasting the Colonel's exceptional virtue with the lowly passions of her contemporaries, the memorialist implies that, as a nation, the English people were not morally ready for a truly godly republic, and suggests, very much like Milton, Sidney, and Ludlow, that the defeat of the Good Old Cause was first and foremost a moral failure.[13]

This dark moral outlook is not limited to the Restoration section or to the preface of the *Memoirs*, but it fuels Lucy Hutchinson's complex vision of history, which never consists in a Manichean opposition between the depraved supporters of monarchy and the virtuous champions of Parliament. The Civil War in Nottingham is rather described as an unnatural war of the country against itself; it is represented as a form of stasis affecting the body politic, namely a disease resulting from disorderly passions—greed, ambition, and envy—which breed factionalism, both at local and national level. Neither is Lucy Hutchinson's description of the military aspects of the Civil War Manichean. For example, when she relates the second attack on Nottingham by the Newark troops in January 1644 and the horrors that ensued, she successively adopts the perspectives of the Cavaliers and the Parliamentarians, highlighting the 'strange ebbe and flow of courage and cowardize there was in both parties that day' (S114/K147). Her account of the Protectorate is even morally bleaker, as 'now men began so to flatter with this Tirant, so to apostatize from all faith, honesty, religion and English liberty, and there was such devillish practice of trapanning growne in fashion, that it was not safe to speake to any man in those treacherous dayes' (S211/K259). According to her, the action of the army could lead to chaos as 'those

---

[11] On Lucy Hutchinson's rejection of the Restoration settlement, see Keeble, 'The Colonel's Shadow', 240.

[12] See Keeble, 'The Colonel's Shadow', 229: 'Her work takes its place beside *Samson Agonistes*, Baxter's *Reliquiæ Baxterianæ*, and the body of Nonconformist writing, as an attempt to perceive and accept God's purpose in and after the Restoration.'

[13] On the moral failure of the English Revolution, see Scott, *Commonwealth Principles* 141–2, 316–24; Norbrook, 'Words more than Civil', 78; Norbrook, 'The English Revolution and English Historiography', 236–8; Woolf, 'Narrative Historical Writing', 216.

Traytors [...] had brought the Commonwealth into such a sad confusion' (S214/K263). In these circumstances, the Colonel could not but question his own political and military commitment during the Civil War; he was, according to his wife, 'much perplexed, for now he thought his conscience, life and fortunes againe engaged with men of mixed and different interests and principles' (S214/K263). When the Convention Parliament asked the regicides to justify their former conduct, the Colonel sternly reviewed his past commitment by declaring that 'the vaine expence of his age and the greate debts his publick employments had runne him into [...] yeilded him just cause to repent that ever he forsooke his own blessed quiett to embarque in such a troubled sea, where he had made a shipwrack of all things but a good conscience' (S228/K279–80).[14] But, as a whole, the *Memoirs* tell a different story and offer a way out of this tragic perplexity at the time of Puritan defeat. Instead of casting doubt on the Colonel's commitment, they serve as a commemoration of the Colonel's martyrdom and death, and may be construed as a counter-history of the English Revolution.[15]

2. From persecution to martyrdom

As early as the dedication, Lucy Hutchinson invites the reader to look at the life of John Hutchinson in the light of his martyrdom: 'The more God chasten'd him, the more he lov'd him, kissing the rod and rejoycing in the scourge that drove him neerer to God. When God turn'd the greate wheele in this nation, he re-examin'd all his former wayes and actions, and the Lord gave him comfort, confirmation and greate advancement in his love' (S6/K22). This characterization of Colonel Hutchinson as a martyr, that is, etymologically, as a witness suffering for his faith, is neither limited to the dedication, nor to the years 1663–1664, but starts in the *Memoirs* as early as June 1643 when he was already prepared for martyrdom: 'yett was he so well perswaded in his conscience of the cause, and of God's calling him to undertake the defence of [Nottingham], that he cast by all other considerations, and cheerefully resign'd up his life and all other particular interests to God's dispose, though in all humane probability he was more likely to loose than save them' (S76/K102). Lucy Hutchinson's depiction of the Colonel's state of mind in 1643

---

[14] On this passage and the Colonel's epicureanism in the 1650s, see Norbrook, 'Introduction', *The Works of Lucy Hutchinson*, vol. 1, xxvii–xxviii. See also Adrian, *Local Negotiations* 150–2.
[15] On the notion of 'counter history', see Marc Fumaroli, 'Les Mémoires, ou l'historiographie royale en procès', *La Diplomatie de l'esprit: De Montaigne à la Fontaine* (Paris: Hermann, 1994) 217–46.

foreshadows his attitude during his final imprisonment, but also his persecution by the Nottingham Committee, for example by 'Mr. Millington', who 'encourag'd all those little men in their wicked prosecution of him' (S145/K183). In the same way, 'while the grand quarrel slept' (S208/K256), that is, during the Colonel's retirement at Owthorpe after the dissolution of the Rump Parliament in 1653, Lucy Hutchinson describes him both as a gentleman 'reduc'd into an absolute private condition' (S208/K256), and as a godly man awaiting martyrdom, who thought that his duty was 'to suffer patiently that yoake which God submitts him to till the Lord shall take it off' (S216/K265). Thus, when the Colonel is required to account for his past as a regicide, the reader is not surprised to hear that he wished to be 'a publick sacrifice' (S229/K280). This, however, was an aspiration which 'Mrs. Hutchinson' at first refused; it was only three years later, after the Colonel was arrested for his alleged involvement in the Northern Plot, that she became more compassionate towards his response to God's calling and 'submitted now to suffer with him according to his owne will' (S256/K311). In the remaining pages of her narrative, she shifts her focus to his transformation into a martyr, and recounts how, in a Christlike fashion, he gradually detached himself from all earthly attachments, dedicating himself to reading the Bible, and collecting cockle shells rather than works of art.[16] The Colonel's victory is first and foremost spiritual, and recalls that of Samson in Milton's *Samson Agonistes*: 'But patience is more oft the exercise / Of Saints, the trial of their fortitude, / Making them each his own deliverer, / And victor over all / That tyranny or fortune can inflict.'[17]

Lucy Hutchinson's vivid dramatization of the Colonel's heroic martyrdom also evokes Foxe's *Book of Martyrs*. Her aim in staging his patience is indeed to show that he belongs to the community of Protestant martyrs who preceded him.[18] She thus describes bodily signs as evidence of the wonderful nature of the Colonel's death and faithfully records his words, dying speeches being always listened to with the utmost attention and respect, especially when they came from martyrs:[19]

---

[16] On the Colonel's 'transformation', see Longfellow, *Women and Religious Writing* 193–4.
[17] Milton, *Samson Agonistes* in *The Major Works*, ed. Orgel and Goldberg, 715. See John R. Knott, *Discourses of Martyrdom in English Literature, 1563–1694* (Cambridge: Cambridge UP, 1993) 168–78; Keeble, *The Literature of Nonconformity* 187–91; Keeble, *The Restoration* 132–58.
[18] Knott, 'Introduction', 1–10; Robert W. Daniel, '"To make a second Book of Martyrs": Re-Appropriating Foxe in Nonconformist Prison Writings in Seventeenth-Century Britain', *Bunyan Studies* 23 (2019): 45–61.
[19] On last dying words, Richard Wunderli and Gerald Broce, 'The Final Moment before Death in Early Modern England', *Sixteenth Century Journal* 20.2 (1989) 259–75. See also Ralph Houlbrooke, 'The Puritan Death-Bed, c.1560–c.1660', *The Culture of English Puritanism, 1560–1700*, ed. Christopher Durston (Houndmills: Macmillan, 1996) 122–44, and Robert W. Daniel, '"My sick-bed covenants": Scriptural Patterns and Model Piety in the Early Modern Sickchamber', *People and Piety. Protestant Devotional Identities in Early Modern England*, ed. Elizabeth Clarke and Daniel (Manchester:

While he was thus speaking to them, his spiritts decay'd exceedingly fast, and his pulse grew very low, and his head allready was earth in the upper part; yett he rays'd himselfe in his bed. "And now," sayd he to the Doctor, "I would faine know your reason why you thinke me dying; I feele nothing in myself; my head is well, my heart is well, and I have no payne nor sicknesse any where." (S272/K330)

Lucy Hutchinson did not attend her husband's death, as she was then back at Owthorpe to look after family business. Drawing upon the testimonies of her brother-in-law and children, she nevertheless stages the scene as it must have happened, with a special emphasis on the reactions of the witnesses—the doctors and George Hutchinson—and making the readers, in their turn, virtual witnesses of this moving event:

The doctor, seeing this, was amazed; "Sir," sayd he, "I would be glad to be deceiv'd"; and being att a stand, he told Mr. George Hutchinson that he was surpriz'd, and knew not what to thinke, to see him so cheerefull and undisturb'd when his pulse was gone; which if it were not death, might be some strange working of the spleene. (S272/K330)

The 'miracle of grace' which Lucy Hutchinson seeks to demonstrate is confirmed by the autopsy of the Colonel's body: 'When he was embowell'd all his inwards were found exceeding sound, and no taint in any part, only two or three purple spots on his lungs: his gall, the Doctor sayd, was the largest that ever he saw in any man, and observ'd it to be a miracle of grace that he had bene so patient as he had seene him' (S273/K331). To the memorialist, these physical manifestations prove 'that the Lord not only bore up [the Colonel's] spiritts to part with all things without regret, but fill'd him full of joy and thankfullnesse, and curb'd the power of his disease, and chained up Sathan that he could not torture him in mind or body' (S275-6/K334-5). She also interprets the doctors' reactions as further evidence of authenticity of the Colonel's martyrdom: 'I am apt to thinke that it was not alone tendernesse of nature, but conviction of their owne disturbed peace, which drew those teares from the Doctors, when they saw in him that blessed peace and joy which crownes the Lord's constant martirs' (S273/K331). For Lucy Hutchinson, who plays the role of the martyrologist here, the Colonel's

---

Manchester UP, 2020) 241–58. In the same volume, see also Charles Green, "'Now the Lord hath made me a spectacle": Deathbed Narratives and Devotional Identities in the Early Seventeenth Century', 259–74.

spectacular martyrdom is a source of consolation; it was, she said, 'an admirable and unspeakeable flood of mercy which may helpe to comfort us in the losse of him' (S276/K335). Hence her solemn advice to her readers in the 'Final Meditation' to follow in the steps of the martyr-Colonel: 'I am to warn you yet before I go that you must follow him and I pray that the same consolation that made his heart invincible may bear up yours and make you cheerfully resign your soul for the testimony of Jesus.'[20]

But the Colonel's martyrdom was not only a spiritual experience; it also had a political edge to it as, after 1660, John Hutchinson was still engaged to 'defend or relieve [his country] from invading tirants' (S216/K265) and claimed that 'he would never, either in one kind or other, have any commerce at all with them [the Stuart monarchy]; [...] he was convinc'd there was a serpentine seed in them' (S265/K322).[21] Furthermore, as a martyr of God, he felt entitled to voice his confidence that 'God would bring them [the Cavaliers] downe' (S269/K327). However, despite his hostility to the monarchy, he no longer advocated armed resistance, because he had not received any 'lawfull call and meanes' (S216/K265) to do so, and because he found his own party too divided.[22] When he talked to his son just before dying, he warned him against raising arms against Charles II, as he feared that 'the rash, hot headed spiritts of many of [their] party' (S265/K323) would cause confusion if they returned to power. Accordingly, he advised him to wait for the right moment to act, and 'to behave himselfe piously and prudently and keepe free of all faction, making the publique interest only his' (S269/K327). In these conditions, the Colonel's only weapons to oppose tyranny were patience and fortitude, as well as the assurance that that there would be a way out of the wilderness for the godly.[23] In the *Memoirs*, he twice promises his son that 'a sober party must settle things' (S265/K323), and that the 'cause would revive, because the interest of God was so much involv'd in it' (S264/K321).

---

[20] Lucy Hutchinson, 'Final Meditation', *Memoirs*, ed. Keeble, 337; see *Memoirs*, DD/HU4, [421].

[21] Norbrook, 'Words more than Civil', 78. On the combination of consolation and politics, see Longfellow, *Women and Religious Writing* 192–3.

[22] The Colonel's interest in the Epistle to the Romans is mentioned twice in the *Memoirs* (S243/K297; S270/K328). In the *Theological Notebook* (in *The Works*, vol. 2, part 1, 126), Lucy Hutchinson also favours suffering over armed resistance: 'As for Magistrates I owne Magistracy to be an Ordinance of God and obedience to be due to them who abuse not his & the peoples trust declining into tirants and comanding things contrary to the Lords commands who is still to be obeyd before men and although many remedies may be lawfull in such cases for those who are lawfully calld to it yet I hold suffering the safest way.'

[23] See Keeble, 'The wilderness of this world', *Literary Culture of Nonconformity* 277–82, and Milton, *Paradise Regained*, Book III, in *The Major Works*, ed. Orgel and Goldberg, 645: 'But if there be in glory aught of good, / It may by means far different be attained / Without ambition, war, or violence; / By deeds of peace, by wisdom eminent, / By patience, temperance.'

In thus sketching a political horizon for his son, the Colonel manages to instil hope in his family and Nonconformist friends who were also enduring persecution. In the *Memoirs*' account of these final exchanges between the Colonel, his children and his brother, Lucy Hutchinson's presence as a narrator is purposefully unobtrusive. Of course, this does not mean that she takes the Restoration settlement for granted or that she dissociates herself from the Colonel's views, but by directly making the readers virtual witnesses of a Christian martyr's speeches of hope, she manages to mitigate the deep sense of defeat and despair which permeates the Restoration section as well as some of her 'Elegies', in which, in Susan Wiseman's words, she builds 'a poetics of desolation'.[24]

3. Commemoration and resistance

The Colonel's last words to his children are presented as a source of consolation and hope for the godly. Similarly, Lucy Hutchinson's account of her husband's funeral in the *Memoirs*, as well as the monument she had built to his memory in Owthorpe church, can be viewed as a form of republican resistance against the Stuart tyranny.[25]

There is no description of the Colonel's funeral as such in the *Memoirs*, but only a detailed account of the transportation of his body from Sandown Castle in Kent to his estate at Owthorpe in Nottinghamshire in September 1664. This was the Colonel's decision not to be buried according to the restored rites of the Church of England, but rather in the family church at Owthorpe:[26] 'What moov'd him to it he declar'd not; but I am apt to believe one thing was because he would not have any of those superstitions exercis'd about him being dead for the opposing of which he lost his liberty and life' (S275/K334). Lucy Hutchinson's account of the stately transportation of the Colonel's embalmed body in an emblazoned hearse invites us to look upon him as a highly respectable gentleman attached to the honour of his family, not as a republican plotter: 'As soone as the newes came to Owthorpe, the Collonell's two eldest sonnes and all his household servants went up to London with his horses, and made ready a herse, trickt with scutcheons, and six horses in mourning, with a

---

[24] Wiseman, *Conspiracy and Virtue* 223. See also Achinstein, 'Lucy Hutchinson and the Poetics of Darkness', *Literature and Dissent* 69–72.
[25] The following analysis draws on Wiseman, 'No Publick Funerall', 213–25.
[26] Wiseman, 'No Public Funerall', 218, and Norbrook, Introduction to *Selections from the Theological Notebook*, in *The Works of Lucy Hutchinson*, vol. 2, 4–5.

mourning coach and six horses to waite on it' (S273/K332).²⁷ In 1664, the public transportation of a regicide's body had a political meaning, especially when one considers that the remains of Cromwell, Ireton, Bradshaw and Pride were exhumed and hanged in January 1661, and that, more generally, dissidents and republicans had to go underground at the Restoration, as plots and rumours of a new Civil War were then widespread.²⁸ As Lucy Hutchinson points out, it was quite remarkable that, as the Colonel's hearse passed through London, there was 'not one reviling word or any indignity offer'd them all the way, but severall people were very much moov'd att that sad witnesse of the murderous cruelty of the men then in power' (S274/K333). On the contrary, the Colonel's 'worth' was recognized for its own sake: as the hearse went through Nottinghamshire, he was 'seriously bewailed [...] by all those who had bene better acquainted with his worth than the strangers among whom he died' (S274/K333). Lucy Hutchinson saw in this popular support a political gesture against the tyranny of the Stuart monarchy: '[he] was brought home with honor to his grave through the dominions of his murtherers, who were asham'd of his glories, which all their Tirannies could not extinguish with his life' (S274/K333). In her eyes, such absence of hostility, and even some sympathy and admiration, was a sign that a 'hand of God [...] over-rul'd [the Colonel's enemies'] barbarous nature' (S275/K334). It also testified to the support of part of the population for the values he embodied, notably for his dedication to the public cause. In other words, the journey of the Colonel's body from Kent to Nottinghamshire came very near to a 'publick funerall';²⁹ as such it momentarily transmuted Lucy Hutchinson's own private experience of grief into a political statement of resistance which accorded well with her original determination to build a monument to her husband's memory rather than let 'a flood of sorrow' 'carry away the deare memory of what [she has] lost' (S1/K16).³⁰

---

[27] See Nigel Llewellyn, *Art of Death: Visual Culture in the English Death Ritual, c.1500–c.1800* (London: Reaktion Books, 1991) 66–72 and Stéphane Jettot, 'Mauvais sang? L'argument généalogique dans la délégitimation des régicides anglais (1660–1798)', *Le Sang des Princes. Cultes et mémoires des souverains suppliciés (XVIe–XIXe siècles)*, ed. Paul Chopelin and Sylvène Édouard (Rennes: Presses universitaires de Rennes, 2014) 79–91.

[28] Marshall, '"Plots and Dissent": The Abortive Northern Rebellion of 1663', 113–15. On Ireton's monument and funeral, see Wiseman, 'No Publick Funerall', 215–16.

[29] See Elegy 2, 'To the Sun Shining into her Cham:l', in 'Lucy Hutchinson's Elegies', ed. Norbrook, 489.

[30] See Wiseman, 'No Publick Funerall', 216: 'There are records of an "uninscribed" coffin, "secured to the wall" in the south of the vault (if this is the Colonel's remains, someone seems to have been mindful of the fate of the regicides). If, as seems likely, Lucy Hutchinson perhaps interred her husband herself, or with a sympathetic minister, we can guess that she might well have done so by night in a practice associated with religio-political dissent and cognate with the elegies' nightworld – but this remains speculation.'

For Lucy Hutchinson, who did not want 'oblivion's curtaine' to be drawn over the Colonel's 'dead face', the 'preservation of his memory' was the reason why she decided to write his 'life'. John Hutchinson, she warns her children in the dedication, was indeed '[t]his excellent person whom I desire to commemorate to you' (S1-2-2/K16-17). In order to do so, she subtly interweaves a reformed outlook with a humanist ethos, celebrating Colonel Hutchinson both as a Civil War hero and as a Protestant martyr: 'There scarcely can such another example be given of a man attaining so greate a degree of humane excellency to cast away so wholly his crowne at the foote-stoole of gods throne and to embrace the crosse of Christ before all the glories.'[31] From the outset of her narrative, however, Lucy Hutchinson is aware of embarking on a dangerous venture, as she fears 'to injure that memory which [she] would honor, and to disgrace his name with a poore monument' (S1/K16-17). She is far less hesitant when she declares in the 'Final Meditation' that 'virtue and grace' made him immortal in the 'book of honour and virtue'.[32] This time, she appears to be fully convinced of the value of her commemorative narrative: 'His memory will never perish while there are any good men surviving who desire to preserve one of the *fairest* copies in the exemplary book of honour and virtue.'[33] The good men whom she entrusts with keeping the Colonel's memory alive were presumably his children, as well as all his friends, whether dissidents or republicans, who continued to support the Good Old Cause clandestinely under the Stuarts.

It is tempting to connect the above-mentioned passage from the 'Final Meditation' with the funerary monument in Renaissance style which Lucy Hutchinson had commissioned for the Church at Owthorpe.[34] Once again it is both the Christian martyr and the Civil War hero that this stone monument commemorates.[35] On the one hand, the armour, helmet, crest and arms of the Hutchinson family are carved on the left-hand side of the monument, to celebrate the gentleman of honour who defended the stronghold of Nottingham. On the other hand, the epitaph, which is inscribed on a plaque

---

[31] *Memoirs*, DD/HU4, 22.   [32] *Memoirs*, ed. Keeble, 337 and DD/HU4, 421.
[33] *Memoirs*, ed. Keeble, 337 and DD/HU4, 421.
[34] See Wiseman, 'No Publick Funerall', 220: 'there are strong evidentiary suggestions that the monument, *Memoirs* and elegies are to be understood together.' See Andrew Gordon and Thomas Rist, 'Introduction: The Arts of Remembrance', *The Arts of Remembrance in Early Modern England. Memorial Culture of the Post Reformation* (Abingdon: Routledge, 2013) 1-15 and Peter Sherlock, *Monuments and Memory in Early Modern England* (Aldershot: Ashgate, 2008) 231-48. See also his 'Monuments and the Reformation' (*Memory of the English Reformation*, ed. Walsham et al., 168-84) where he argues 'that commemoration of the Reformation has always been contentious, transgressing thresholds between church and state, religion and politics, victor and vanquished' (170).
[35] A photograph of the monument is to be found in Sutherland's edition of the *Memoirs*, facing page 227.

at the centre of the monument, is more concerned with the martyr. It is a copy of one of Lucy Hutchinson's 'Elegies', written around the same time as the *Memoirs*,[36] which claims that the Colonel was resurrected even before receiving the martyr's crown of victory: 'Full of this joy he mounted, he lay downe, / Threw off his ashes, and tooke up his crowne.'[37] But before this paradoxical triumph, we are reminded, not without irony, that the titles, rank and birth honoured by the stone monument are in fact only 'vaine ayrie glories':

> This monument doth not commemorate
> Vaine ayrie glorious titles, birth, and state;
> But sacred is to free, illustrious grace,
> Conducting happily a mortal's race;
> To end in triumph over death and hell.
>
> (S293)

The stone monument recapitulates and replicates Lucy Hutchinson's twofold project of memorialization in the *Memoirs*; namely it preserves the memory of a republican man of honour and of a Protestant saint, but it also conveys a more urgent political message. Indeed, both commemorative works are not turned towards the past but show instead how the Colonel's life epitomized hope for a community that would never accept the Restoration settlement, whether it be in its religious or political aspects.[38] For this reason it is important to consider the *Memoirs* as a polemical attempt to resist the Stuart monarchy's plan to cast into oblivion the memory of the 'great rebellion' and of its Puritan heroes.[39] From this perspective, the *Memoirs* are not to be taken as a personal testimony in which Lucy Hutchinson tried to make sense of her traumatic memories, but also, and significantly so, as a counter-history of the English Revolution capable of challenging official historiography in the Restoration age.

---

[36] This inscription is a copy of Elegy 21, reproduced in 'Lucy Hutchinson's Elegies', ed. Norbrook, 519. See Wiseman's analysis in 'No Publick Funerall', 221.
[37] The epitaph is reproduced in Appendix II, *Memoirs*, ed. Sutherland, 293.
[38] According to Wiseman, Lucy Hutchinson also sought 'to build a political identity in the wreckage of political and personal hopes' in her elegies ('No Publick Funerall', 230).
[39] Chedgzoy, *Women's Writing* 164–5; Scott, *Commonwealth Principles* 13–14; Scott, 'Time: Restoration Memory', *England's Troubles* 162–6.

Bibliography

Manuscripts

—Nottinghamshire Archives
Religious Commonplace Book, DD/HU3.
Literary Commonplace Book, DD/HU1.
Elegies, DD/HU2.
Memoirs, DD/HU4.
—British Library
The Notebook, Add. MS 25901.
The Notebook, Add. MS. 39779.
The Notebook, Add. MS 46172.

Primary sources

Agrippa von Nettesheim, Heinrich Cornelius. *The Vanity of Arts and Sciences* [1531]. London, 1676.
Allen, Joseph Antisell. *The True and Romantic Love-Story of Colonel and Mrs Hutchinson: A Drama in Verse*. London, 1882.
Ames, William. *The Marrow of Christian Divinity*. London, 1642.
Anderson, James. *Memorable Women of the Puritan Times*. London, 1862.
Annesley, Arthur, Earl of Anglesey. *A Letter from a Person of Honour in the Countrey Written to the Earl of Castlehaven*. London, 1681.
Annesley, Arthur. *A letter from the Right Honourable Arthur Earl of Anglesey Lord Privy - Seal*. London, 1682.
Aristotle. *The Nichomachean Ethics of Aristotle*. Trans. F. H. Peters. 5th edition. London: Kegan Paul, Trench, Truebner & Co., 1893.
Aristotle. *The Poetics*. Trans. S. H. Henry. London: Macmillan, 1922.
Bacon, Francis. *The Two Bookes of Francis Bacon. Of the Proficience and Advancement of Learning, Divine and Humane. The Second Book.* London, 1605.
Bacon, Francis. *The Essayes or Counsels, Civill and Morall*. London, 1625.
Bacon, Francis. *Sylva Sylvarum: Or A natural historie*. London, 1628.
Bacon, Francis. *The Works of Francis Bacon*, ed. James S. Spedding, R. L. Ellis, and D. D. Heath, 14 vols. London, 1857–74.
Bacon, Francis. *The Major Works*. Ed. Brian Vickers. Oxford: Oxford UP, 1996.
Bacon, Francis. *The History of the Reign of King Henry VII*. Ed. Brian Vickers. Cambridge: Cambridge UP, 1998.
Bailey, Nathan, *The Universal Etymological English Dictionary*. Vol. 2 [1727]. London, 1731.
Baron, William. *A Just Defence of the Royal Martyr King Charles I from [...] Ludlow's Memoirs*. London, 1699.

Baron, William. *Regicides, No Saints Nor Martyrs*. London, 1700.
Baxter, Richard. *Reliquiæ Baxterianæ, Or Mr Richard Baxter's Narrative of the Most Memorable Passages of his Life and Times*. Ed. Matthew Sylvester. London, 1696.
Baxter, Richard. *Reliquiæ Baxterianæ: Or, Mr. Richard Baxter's Narrative of the Most Memorable Passages of his Life and Times*. 4 vols. Ed. N. H. Keeble, John Coffey, Tim Cooper, and Tom Charlton. Oxford: Oxford UP, 2020.
Bayly, Lewis. *The Practise of Piety*. London, 1613.
Berkeley, Sir John. *Memoirs of Sir John Berkeley*. London, 1699.
Biondi, Giovanni Francesco. *History of the Civill Wares of England*. London, 1641.
Bodin, Jean. 'Of the choice of History, by way of Preface'. In Sallust, *The Two Most Worthy and Notable Histories*. Trans. Thomas Heywood. London, 1608.
Bolton, Edmund. *Hypercritica: Or, A Rule of Judgment, for Writing or Reading our History's* in *Ancient Critical Essays upon English Poets and Poësy*. Vol. 2. Ed. Joseph Haslewood. London: Robert Triphook, 1815. 221–54.
Borlase, Edmund. *The History of the Execrable Irish Rebellion*. London, 1680.
Borlase, Edmund. *Brief Reflections on the Earl of Castlehaven's Memoirs of his engagements and carriage in the wars of Ireland*. London, 1682.
Boyle, Robert. *The Sceptical Chymist: or Chymico-Physical Doubts & Paradoxes*. London, 1661.
Boyle, Robert. *Experimenta & Observationes Physicæ: Wherein are briefly treated of several subjects relating to natural philosophy in an experimental way*. London, 1691.
Boyle, Roger. *Parthenissa. A Romance in Four Parts*. London, 1655.
Brathwaite, Richard. *A Survey of History: Or, A Nursery for Gentry*. London, 1638.
Breton, Nicholas. *The Good and the Badde, or Descriptions of the Worthies, and Vnworthies of this Age*. London, 1616.
Bruce, Charles, ed. *The Book of Noble English Women: Lives Made Illustrious by Heroism*. Edinburgh: William P. Nimmo, 1875.
Bulstrode, Richard. *Memoirs and Reflections upon the Reign and Government of King Charles the Ist and K. Charles the II^d*. London, 1721.
Burder, Samuel, Thomas Gibbons and George Jerment, eds. *Memoirs of Eminently Pious Women*. Revised edition. 2 vols. London, 1827.
Burnet, Gilbert. *The Memoires of the Lives and Actions of James and William Dukes of Hamilton and Castleherald*. London, 1677.
Burnet, Gilbert. *Bishop Burnet's History of His Own Times*. Vol. 1. London, 1724–1734.
Butler, James. Duke of Ormond. *A Letter from His Grace James Duke of Ormond, Lord Lieutenant of Ireland, in answer to the Right Honourable Arthur Earl of Anglesey Lord Privy-Seal*. London, 1682.
Caesar, Julius. *Iulius Cesars Commentaryes, newly translatyd owte of laten in to englysshe*. London, 1530.
Castiglione, Baldassare. *The Courtyer of Count Baldessar Castilio Diuided Into Foure Bookes*. Trans. Thomas Hoby. London, 1561.
Caussin, Nicolas. *The Holy Court in Three Tomes*. [Rouen], 1634.
Caussin, Nicolas. *The Holy Court. The Command of Reason over the Passions [Fourth Tome]*. Trans. T. H. [Rouen], 1638.
Cavendish, Margaret. *Philosophical Fancies*. London, 1653.
Cavendish, Margaret. *Poems and Fancies*. London, 1653.
Cavendish, Margaret. *The Worlds Olio*. London, 1655.
Cavendish, Margaret. *Natures Pictures Drawn by Fancies Pencil to the Life*. London, 1656.
Cavendish, Margaret. *The Life of the Thrice Noble, High, Puissant Prince William Cavendishe*. London, 1667.

Cavendish, Margaret. *Memoirs of the Duke and Duchess of Newcastle; the Life of William Cavendish, Duke of Newcastle.* Ed. C. H. Firth. London, 1886.

Chaworth-Musters, Lina. *A Cavalier Stronghold: A Romance of the Vale of Belvoir.* London, 1890.

Chidley, Katherine. *The Justification of the Independent Churches of Christ Being an Answer to Mr Edwards His Booke.* London, 1641.

Child, Lydia Maria Francis. *Good Wives.* Vol. 3. New York: C. S. Francis & Co, 1855.

Cholmley, Hugh. *The Memoirs of Sir Hugh Cholmley [. . .] Taken from an Original Manuscript, in his own Hand-writing* [1787]. Np., 1870.

Cicero, Marcus Tullius. *De Officiis.* Trans. Andrew P. Peabody. Boston: Little, Brown, and Co., 1887.

Clarke, Samuel. *The Marrow of Ecclesiastical Historie, Conteined in the Lives of the Fathers, and Other Learned Men, and Famous Divines.* London, 1650.

Cleveland, John. *The Character of a London Diurnall.* London, 1645.

Cleveland, John. *The Character of a Committee-man, with the eare-marke of a sequestrator.* London, 1647.

Cleveland, John. *The Hue and Cry after Sir John Presbyter.* London, 1649

Cockayne, Aston. *Small Poems of Divers sort.* London, 1658.

Cook, John. *King Charls, his Case, or An Appeal to all rational men concerning his tryal at the High Court of Justice.* London, 1649.

Crosland, Camilla Newton. *Memorable Women: The Story of Their Lives.* Boston, 1854.

Davila, Enrico. *Historie of the Civill Warres of France.* London, 1647.

A Discovery of the Treacherous Attempts of the Cavaliers, to have Procured the Betraying of Nottingham Castle into their Hands. London, 1643.

de Commynes, Philippe. *Les mémoires de messire Philippe de Commines.* Paris, 1552.

de Retz, Cardinal. (Jean-François Paul de Gondi, cardinal de) *Mémoires de monsieur le Cardinal de Retz.* Amsterdam, 1717.

Donne, John. *The Complete English Poems,* ed. A. J. Smith [1971]. London: Penguin, 1996.

Dugdale, William. *A Short View of the Late Troubles in England.* London, 1644.

Duplessis-Mornay, Charlotte. *Les Mémoires de Madame de Mornay.* Ed. Nadine Kuperty-Tsur. Paris: Honoré Champion, 2010.

Edgar, Thomas. *The Lawes Resolutions of Womens Rights: Or, The Lawes Provision for Woemen.* London, 1632.

Eliza's Babes; or, The Virgins-Offering. Being Divine Poems, and Meditations. London, 1652.

Elyot, Thomas. *The Boke Named the Governour.* London, 1531.

Erasmus. *Copia: Foundations of the Abundant Style/De duplici copia verborum ac rerum commentarii duo.* Trans. Betty I. Knott. *The Collected Works of Erasmus.* Vol. 24. Ed. Craig R. Thompson. Toronto: Toronto UP, 1979.

Fairfax, Thomas. *Short Memorials of Thomas Lord Fairfax Written by Himself.* London, 1699.

Fanshawe, Ann. *The Memoirs of Lady Fanshawe.* Ed. Nicholas Harris Nicolas. London, 1829.

Fanshawe, Ann. *The Memoirs of Anne, Lady Halkett and Ann, Lady Fanshawe.* Ed. John Loftis. Oxford: Clarendon, 1979.

Finch, Heneage. *An Exact and Most Impartial Account of the Indictment [. . .] of Twenty-Nine Regicides.* London, 1660.

Flower, Benjamin. Rev. of *Memoirs of the Life of Colonel Hutchinson. Political Review and Monthly Register* 3 (1808) 241–3.

Fuller, Thomas. *Abel Redivivus; Or, the Dead yet Speaking. The Lives and Deaths of Modern Divines*. London, 1651.
Fuller, Thomas. *The Church History of Britain*. London, 1656.
Fuller, Thomas. *The Appeal of Iniured Innocence*. London, 1659.
Furetière, Antoine, ed. *Dictionnaire universel*. Paris, 1690.
Gardiner, Samuel Rawson, ed. *The Constitutional Documents of the Puritan Revolution 1625–1660*. 3rd edition. Oxford: Clarendon, 1906.
Geree, John. *The Character of an Old English Puritane, or Non-conformist*. London, 1646.
Guizot, François. *Collection des Mémoires relatifs à la Révolution d'Angleterre, accompagnés de notices et d'éclaircissements historiques*. 25 vols. Paris: Béchet, 1823–1825.
Guizot, François. *Histoire de la Révolution d'Angleterre depuis l'avènement de Charles Ier jusqu'à la restauration de Charles II. 1re partie*. Paris, 1826–1827. Trans. William Hazlitt as *The History of the English Revolution of 1640, Commonly Called the Great Rebellion*. London: D. Bogue, 1846.
Guizot, François. 'Mistriss Hutchinson'. *Études biographiques sur la révolution d'Angleterre*. Paris: Didier, 1851. 217–56. 'Mistriss Hutchinson'. *Monk's Contemporaries. Biographic Studies on the English Revolution*. Trans. Andrew R. Scoble. London: Henry Bohn, 1851. 120–40.
Guizot, François. 'Preliminary Essay on the English Revolution'. *History of Charles the First and the English Revolution*. Trans. Andrew R. Scoble. London, 1854. *Pourquoi la révolution d'Angleterre a-t-elle réussi? Discours sur l'histoire de la révolution d'Angleterre*. Paris: V. Masson, 1850.
Guizot de Witt, Henriette. *Les femmes dans l'histoire*. 2nd edition. Paris, 1889.
Halkett, Anne. *The Autobiography of Anne Lady Halkett*. Ed. John Gough Nichols. London: Camden Society, 1875.
Hall, Joseph. *Characters of Vertues and Vices, In Two Bookes*. London, 1608.
Handley, George Mansell. *Notes on the Memoirs of Colonel Hutchinson [by Mrs. L. Hutchinson]*. London: The Normal Press, [1905].
Harley, Brilliana. *Letters of the Lady Brilliana Harley*. Ed. Thomas Taylor Lewis. London: Camden Society, 1854.
Heath, James. *A Brief Chronicle of All the chief Actions so fatally falling out in these three kingdoms*. London, 1662.
Herbert, Thomas. *Memoirs of the Two Last Years of the Reign of that Unparall'd Prince, of Ever Blessed Memory, King Charles I*. London, 1702.
Heylin, Peter. *Examen Historicum: Or, A Discovery and Examination of the Mistakes, Falsities, and Defects in some Modern Histories*. London, 1659.
Hobbes, Thomas. *Behemoth, or, An Epitome of the Civil Wars of England*. London, 1679.
Holles, Denzil, *Memoirs of Denzil Lord Holles, Baron of Ifield in Sussex, from the year 1641 to 1648*. London, 1699.
Hutchinson, John. *A Narrative of the Imprisonment and Usage of Colonel John Hutchinson* [1664]. *Harleian Miscellany*. Vol. 3. London, 1745. 284–90.
Hutchinson, Lucy. *Memoirs of the Life of Colonel Hutchinson*. Ed. Julius Hutchinson. London, 1806.
Hutchinson, Lucy. *On the Principles of The Christian Religion, Addressed to her Daughter; and on Theology*. Ed. Julius Hutchinson. London, 1817.
Hutchinson, Lucy. *Mémoires de Mistriss Hutchinson*. In *Collection des Mémoires relatifs à la Révolution d'Angleterre*. Vol. 10 and 11. Ed. François Guizot. Paris, 1823–1825.
Hutchinson, Lucy. *Memoirs of the Life of Colonel Hutchinson [...] to which are added the letters of Colonel Hutchinson and other papers* [1885]. Ed. C. H. Firth. London: Routledge, 1906.

Hutchinson, Lucy. *Memoirs of the Life of Colonel Hutchinson Written by his Widow Lucy*. London: Dent, 1908.
Hutchinson, Lucy. *Memoirs of the Life of Colonel Hutchinson*. Ed. James Sutherland. London: Oxford UP, 1973.
Hutchinson, Lucy. *Memoirs of the Life of Colonel Hutchinson*. Ed. N. H. Keeble. London: Phoenix Press, 1995.
Hutchinson, Lucy. *Order and Disorder*. Ed. David Norbrook. Oxford: Blackwell, 2001.
Hutchinson, Lucy. *The Works of Lucy Hutchinson. Vol. 1. The Translation of Lucretius*. Ed. Ashley Reid Barbour, David Norbrook, and Maria Cristina Zerbino. Oxford: Oxford UP, 2012.
Hutchinson, Lucy. *The Works of Lucy Hutchinson. Vol. 2. Theological Writings and Translations*. Ed. Elizabeth Clarke, David Norbrook, and Jane Stevenson. Oxford: Oxford UP, 2018.
Hyde, Edward, Earl of Clarendon. *The Life of Edward Earl of Clarendon*. Oxford, 1759.
Hyde, Edward, Earl of Clarendon. *The History of the Rebellion and Civil Wars in England [1702-1704]* [1888]. Ed. W. Dunn Macray. 6 vols. Oxford: Clarendon, 1969.
Innes, Arthur D. *A Source-Book of English History for the Use of Schools*. Vol. 2. Cambridge: Cambridge UP, 1914.
Jeffrey, Francis. Rev. of *Memoirs of the Life of Colonel Hutchinson*, by Lucy Hutchinson. *Edinburgh Review* 13.25 (1808): 1–25.
The Kings Cabinet Opened; or, Certain Packets of Secret Letters and Papers Written with the Kings Own Hand and Taken in His Cabinet at Nasby-Field. London, 1645.
Knight, Charles. 'Shadows. The Shadow of Lucy Hutchinson'. *Household Words* 3.70 (1851): 430–2.
Laws and Ordinances of Warre, Established for the Better Conduct of the Army, by His Excellency the Earl of Essex. London, 1643.
L'Estrange, Hamon. *The Reign of King Charles: An History Faithfully and Impartially Delivered and Disposed into Annals*. London, 1655.
La Calprenède, Seigneur de Gauthier de Coste. *Cassandra the Fam'd Romance*. Trans. Charles Cotterell. London, 1661.
Le Moyne, Pierre. *De l'histoire*. Paris, 1670.
Le Moyne, Pierre. *Of the Art Both of Writing & Judging of History*. London, 1695.
Lloyd, David. *Memoires of the Lives, Actions, Sufferings & Deaths of those Noble, Reverend, and Excellent Personages, that Suffered by Death, Sequestration, Decimation*. London, 1668.
Lucan. *Lucans Pharsalia [...] Translated into English by T. M.* London, 1626.
Lucian. *How to Write History*. Trans. K. Kilburn. Loeb Classical Library 430. Cambridge, MA: Harvard UP, 1959.
Lucinge, René. *La manière de lire l'histoire* [1614]. Ed. Michael J. Heath. Geneva: Droz, 1993.
Ludlow, Edmund. *Memoirs of Edmund Ludlow Esq*. 2 vols. Vevey, 1698.
Ludlow, Edmund. *Memoirs of Lieutenant General Ludlow. With a collection of original papers serving to confirm and illustrate many important passages of this and the preceding volumes*. Vevey, 1699.
Ludlow, Edmund. *Les Mémoires d'Edmond Ludlow*. 2 vols. Amsterdam, 1699.
Ludlow, Edmund. *A Voyce from the Watch Tower*. Ed. Blair Worden. Camden Fourth Series 21. London, 1978.
Macaulay, Catherine. *The History of England, from the Accession of James I. to that of the Brunswick Line [1763-1783]*. Vol. 4. London, 1770.
Machiavelli, Niccolò. *The Prince*. Ed. Quentin Skinner and Russel Price. Cambridge: Cambridge UP, 1988.

Man in the Moon. *A Tragi-comedy, Called New-Market-Fayre; or, A Parliament Out-Cry.* [London], 1649.
May, Thomas. *The History of the Parliament of England.* London, 1647.
May, Thomas. *A Breviary of the History of the Parliament of England.* London, 1650.
Mercurius Melancholicus. *The Cuckoo's Nest at Westminster; or, The Parliament between Two Lady-Birds: Quean Fairfax, and Lady Cromwell.* [London], 1648.
Meynell, Alice. *Essays.* London: Burns & Oates, 1914.
Milton, John. *An Apology against a Pamphlet Called A Modest Confutation of the Animadversions upon the Remonstrant against Smectymnus* [1642]. In *Complete Prose Works.* Vol. 1. Ed. Don M. Wolfe. New Haven: Yale UP, 1953.
Milton, John. *Eikonoklastes* [1649]. In *Complete Prose Works.* Vol. 3. Ed. Merritt Y. Hughes. New Haven: Yale UP, 1962.
Milton, John. *Paradise Lost.* Ed. Alastair Fowler. London: Longman, 1971.
Milton, John. *Areopagitica.* In *The Major Works.* Ed. Stephen Orgel and Jonathan Goldberg. Oxford: Oxford UP, 1991.
Monro, Robert. *Monro His Expedition with the Worthy Scots Regiment.* London, 1637.
Montaigne, Michel de. *Essays.* Trans. John Florio. London, 1613.
Montaigne, Michel de. *Complete Essays.* Trans. M. A. Screech. London: Penguin, 2004.
More, Thomas. *History of Richard III.* In *The Works of Sir Thomas More.* London, 1557.
Motteville, Françoise de. *Mémoires pour servir à l'histoire d'Anne d'Autriche.* 6 vols. Amsterdam, 1750.
Noble, Mark. *The Lives of the English Regicides and other Commissioners of the Pretended High Court of Justice.* London, 1798.
Oliphant, Margaret. 'Autobiographies. N° VI. In the Time of the Commonwealth: Lucy Hutchinson, Alice Thornton'. *Blackwood's Edinburgh Magazine* 132 (1882): 90–1.
Overton, Richard. *New Lambeth Fayre.* London, 1642.
Overton, Richard. *A New Play Called Canterburie his Change of Diet.* London, 1645.
Overton, Richard. *The Nativity of Sir John Presbyter.* London, 1645.
Owen, Emily. *The Heroines of Domestic Life.* London, 1861.
Parker, Henry. *A Discourse Concerning Puritans.* London, 1641.
Patrizi, Francesco. *Della Historia Diece Dialoghi.* Venice, 1560.
Perkins, William. *The Whole Treatise of Cases of Conscience.* Cambridge, 1606.
Peyton, Edward. *The Divine Catastrophe of the Kingly Family of the Stuarts: Or, a Short History of the Rise, Reign, and Ruine Thereof.* London, 1652.
Plutarch. *The Lives of the Noble Grecians and Romanes.* Trans. Thomas North. London, 1579.
Plutarch. *Plutarch's Morals. Translated from the Greek by Several Hands. Corrected and Revised by William W. Goodwin.* Boston: Little, Brown, and Co., 1878.
Polybius. *The History of Polybius the Megalopolitan.* Trans. Edward Grimeston. London, 1633.
Prideaux, Mathias. *An Easy and Compendious Introduction for Reading all Sorts of Histories.* London, 1648.
Prynne, William. *Histro-Mastix: The Players Scourge.* London, 1633.
A Puritane Set Forth in his Lively Colours: or, K. James his description of a Puritan. London, 1642.
Puttenham, George. *The Arte of English Poesie.* London, 1589.
Raleigh, Walter. *History of the World.* London, 1614.

Rapin, René. *Instructions pour l'Histoire.* Paris, 1677.
Rapin, René. *Instructions for History.* London, 1685.
Rev. of *Memoirs of the Life of Colonel Hutchinson*, by Lucy Hutchinson. *The Monthly Review* 53 (1807): 259–73.
Rev. of *Memoirs of the Life of Colonel Hutchinson*, by Lucy Hutchinson. *Critical Review* 3 (1807): 66–89.
Rev. of *Memoirs of the Life of Colonel Hutchinson*, by Lucy Hutchinson, *Eclectic Review* 3.1 (1807): 16–25.
Rev. of *Memoirs of the Life of Colonel Hutchinson*, by Lucy Hutchinson. *The Oxford Review; or, Literary Censor* 1 (1807): 43–54.
Rev. of *Memoirs of the Life of Colonel Hutchinson*, by Lucy Hutchinson. *The Christian Examiner and Religious Miscellany*. Vol. 44. Fourth Series 9 (1847): 205–23
Reyner, Edward. *Considerations Concerning Marriage: The Honours, Duties, Benefits, Troubles, of It.* London, 1657.
Reynolds, Edward. *A Treatise of the Passions and Faculties of the Soule of Man.* London, 1640.
Rogers, Daniel. *Matrimoniall Honour, or, The Mutuall Crowne and Comfort of Godly, Loyall, and Chaste Marriage.* London, 1642.
Rudyer, Benjamin. *The Speeches of Sr. Benjamin Rudyer in the High Court of Parliament.* London, 1641.
Rushworth, John. *Historical Collections.* London, 1659.
Russell, William. *Extraordinary Women: Their Girlhood and Early Life.* London, 1857.
Sarpi, Paolo. *The Historie of the Councel of Trent.* London, 1620.
Scudéry, Madeleine de. *Artamenes, or The Grand Cyrus.* London, 1653.
Sidney, Philip. *An Apologie for Poetry.* London, 1595.
Sprigge, Joshua. *Anglia Rediviva. Englands recovery being the history of the motions, actions, and successes of the army under the immediate conduct of His Excellency Sr. Thomas Fairfax.* London, 1647.
Stendhal. *De l'amour* [1822]. Paris: Garnier Frères, 1906.
Stendhal. *Memoirs of an Egotist.* Trans. David Ellis. New York: Horizon Press, 1975.
Sutcliffe, Matthew. *Practice, Proceedings, and Lawes of Armes.* London, 1593.
The Character of a Cavaliere, with His Brother Separatist. London, 1647.
Thucydides. *Eight Bookes of the Peloponnesian Warre.* Trans. Thomas Hobbes. London, 1629.
Touchet, James. *The Memoirs of James, Lord Audley, Earl of Castlehaven, his Engagement and Carriage in the Wars of Ireland.* London, 1680.
Touchet, James. *The Memoirs of James, Lord Audley, Earl of Castlehaven [...] with an Appendix, Relating Wars abroad that he hath either seen or known.* London, 1681.
Touchet, James. *The Earl of Castlehavens Review: Or his Memoirs of his Engagement and Carriage in the Irish Wars. Enlarged and Corrected.* London, 1684.
Turner, James. *The Memoirs of His Life and Times.* Edinburgh, 1829.
Vicars, John. *Gods Arke Overtopping the Worlds Waves, or The Third Part of the Parliamentary Chronicle.* London, 1645.
Walker, Clement. *The Mystery of the two Iuntos Presbyterian and Independent.* London, 1647.
Walker, Clement. *The Compleat History of Independency.* London, 1661.
Warburton, Eliot. *Reginald Hastings: Or, A Tale of the Troubles in 164-.* London, 1850.
Warwick, Philip. *Memoirs of the Reign of King Charles I.* London, 1701.

Wheare, Degory. *De ratione et methodo legendi historias dissertatio.* London, 1623.
Whitelocke, Bulstrode. *Memorials of the English Affairs, or An historical Account of what passed from the beginning of the reign of Charles the First, to King Charles the Second his happy restauration.* London, 1682.

Secondary sources

Abiven, Karen. *L'Anecdote ou la fabrique du petit fait vrai. De Tallemant des Réaux à Voltaire (1650–1750).* Paris: Classiques Garnier, 2015.
Achinstein, Sharon. *Literature and Dissent in Milton's England.* Cambridge: Cambridge UP, 2003.
Achinstein, Sharon. 'Saints or Citizens? Ideas of Marriage in Seventeenth-Century English Republicanism'. *The Seventeenth Century* 25.2 (2010): 240–64.
Adair, John Eric. *By the Sword Divided. Eyewitness Accounts of the English Civil War* [1983, 1998]. Barton-under-Needwood: Wrens Park, 2001.
Adrian, John. 'Izaak Walton, Lucy Hutchinson, and the Experience of Civil War'. *Local Negotiations of English Nationhood, 1570–1680.* Basingstoke: Palgrave Macmillan, 2011. 120–53.
Akkerman, Nadine. *Invisible Agents: Women and Espionage in Seventeenth-Century Britain.* Oxford: Oxford UP, 2018.
Anderson, Judith H. *Biographical Truth: The Representation of Historical Persons in Tudor-Stuart Writing.* New Haven: Yale UP, 1984.
Anderson, Penelope. *Friendship's Shadows: Women's Friendship and the Politics of Betrayal in England 1640–1705.* Edinburgh: Edinburgh UP, 2012.
Armitage, David. *Civil Wars: A History in Ideas.* New York: Penguin/Alfred A. Knopf, 2017.
Barbour, Reid. *English Epicures and Stoics: Ancient Legacie in Early Stuart Culture.* Amherst: U of Massachusetts P, 1998.
Bardet, Jean-Pierre, Élisabeth Arnoul, and François-Joseph Ruggiu. *Les écrits du for privé en Europe (du Moyen Age à l'époque contemporaine).* Bordeaux : Presses universitaires de Bordeaux, 2010.
Bassnet, Madeleine. '"All the ceremonyes and civilityes": The Authorship of Diplomacy in the *Memoirs* of Ann, Lady Fanshawe'. *The Seventeenth Century* 26.1 (2011): 94–118.
Bedford, Ronald, Lloyd Davis, and Philippa Kelly. *Early Modern Autobiography: Theories, Genres, Practices.* Ann Arbor: U of Michigan P, 2006.
Bedford, Ronald, Lloyd Davis, and Philippa Kelly. *Early Modern English Lives: Autobiography and Self-Representation 1500–1660.* Aldershot: Ashgate, 2007.
Begley, Justin. 'Arthur Annesley, Margaret Cavendish, and Neo-Latin History'. *Review of English Studies* 69 (2018): 855–87.
Bennett, Martyn. *The Civil Wars Experienced. Britain and Ireland, 1638–61.* London: Routledge, 2000.
Bennett, Martyn. '"Every county had the civill warre, more or lesse within itselfe": The Realities of War in Lucy Hutchinson's Midland Shires'. *The Seventeenth Century* 30.2 (2015): 191–206.
Bennett, Martyn. 'Holding the Centre Ground: The Strategic Importance of the North idlands 1642–1646'. *East Midlands History and Heritage* 1 (2015): 4–8.
Bergamasco, Lucia. 'Hagiographie et sainteté en Angleterre aux XVIe–XVIIIe siècles'. *Annales, Économies, Sociétés, Civilisations* 5 (1993): 1053–85.

Blackburn, Thomas H. 'The Date and Evolution of Edmund Bolton's *Hypercritica*'. *Studies in Philology* 63.2 (1966): 196–202.
Bolster, Richard. 'Stendhal et les Mémoires de Lucy Hutchinson'. *Proceedings of the London Colloquium*. French Institute, 13–16 September 1983. Ed. K. G. McWatters and C. W. Thompson. Liverpool: Liverpool UP, 1987. 149–57.
Bos, Jacques. 'Individuality and Inwardness in the Literary Character Sketches of the Seventeenth Century'. *Journal of the Warburg and Courtauld Institutes* 61 (1998): 142–57.
Boyce, Benjamin. *The Polemic Character 1640–1661. A Chapter in English Literary History*. New York: Octagon Books, 1969.
Braddick, Michael J. *God's Fury, England's Fire: A New History of the English Civil Wars*. [2008]. London: Penguin, 2009.
Bradshaw, Brendan. 'Transalpine Humanism'. *The Cambridge History of Political Thought*. Ed. J. H. Burns. Cambridge: Cambridge UP, 1991. 95–131.
Breisach, Ernst. 'Two Turning-points: The Renaissance and the Reformation'. *Historiography: Ancient, Medieval & Modern [1987]*. Chicago: U of Chicago P, 2007. 171–98.
Briot, Frédéric. *Usage du monde, usage de soi. Enquête sur les mémorialistes d'Ancien Régime*. Paris: Le Seuil, 1994.
Britland, Karen. '"Kings are but Men": Elizabeth Cary's Histories of Edward II'. *Études Épistémè* 17 (2010). https://doi.org/10.4000/episteme.660.
Broomhall, Susan and Colette H. Winn, 'Femmes, écriture, foi: les Mémoires de Madame Duplessis-Mornay'. *Albineana. Cahiers d'Aubigné* 18 (2006): 587–604.
Brownley, Martine Watson. *Clarendon and the Rhetoric of Historical Form*. Philadelphia: U of Pennsylvania P, 1985.
Buford, Albert. 'History and Biography'. *A Tribute to George Coffin Taylor. Studies and Essays*. Ed. Arnold Williams. Richmond: U of North California P, 1952. 100–12.
Burden, Mark. 'Lucy Hutchinson and Puritan Education'. *The Seventeenth Century* 30.2 (2015): 163–78.
Burden, Mark. 'Editing Shadows: The Changing Text of Lucy Hutchinson's *Memoirs of the Life of Colonel Hutchinson*'. *Textual Transformations: Purposing and Repurposing Books from Richard Baxter to Samuel Taylor Coleridge*. Ed. Tessa Whitehouse and N. H. Keeble. Oxford: Oxford UP, 2019. 173–91.
Burke, Peter. 'A Survey of the Popularity of Ancient Historians, 1450–1700'. *History and Theory* 5.2 (1966): 135–52.
Burke, Peter. *The Renaissance Sense of the Past*. London: Edward Arnold, 1969.
Burke, Peter. 'Tacitism, Scepticism, and Reason of State'. *The Cambridge History of Political Thought*. Ed. J. H. Burns. Cambridge: Cambridge UP, 1991. 477–98.
Burke, Peter. *The Fortunes of the Courtier*. Cambridge: Polity Press, 1995.
Burns, Timothy. 'Hobbes et Denys d'Halicarnasse: la politique et la rhétorique chez Thucydide'. *Rhétorique démocratique en temps de crise*. Actes du colloque, Nice 20–21 January 2011. http://revel.unice.fr/symposia/rhetoriquedemocratique/index.html?id=847.
Capp, Bernard. *England's Culture Wars. Puritan Reformation and its Enemies in the Interregnum 1649–1660*. Oxford: Oxford UP, 2012.
Carlton, Charles. *Going to the Wars. The Experience of the British Civil Wars 1638–1651*. London and New York: Routledge, 1992.
Charbonneau, Frédéric. *Les Silences de l'histoire. Les Mémoires français du XVIIe siècle*. Sainte-Foy: Presses de l'Université de Laval, 2000.

Chartier, Roger. *The Order of Books: Readers, Authors, and Libraries in Europe between the Fourteenth and Eighteenth Centuries*. Trans. Lydia G. Cochrane. Stanford: Stanford UP, 1994.
Chartier, Roger. *On the Edge of the Cliff: History, Language, and Practices*. Trans. Lydia G. Cochrane. Baltimore: Johns Hopkins UP, 1997.
Chedgzoy, Kate. *Women's Writing in the British Atlantic World. Memory, Place and History, 1550–1700*. Cambridge: Cambridge UP, 2007.
Chedgzoy, Kate, Elspeth Graham, Katharine Hodgkin, and Ramona Wray, 'Researching Memory in Early Modern Studies'. *Memory Studies* 11.1 (2018): 5–20.
Christie, Edwina Louise. 'Dissimulating Romance. The Ethics of Deception in Seventeenth-Century Prose Romance'. DPhil thesis. University of Oxford, 2016.
Clare, Janet. *From Republic to Restoration: Legacies and Departures*. Manchester: Manchester UP, 2018.
Clarke, Elizabeth. 'Contextualizing the Woman Writer: Editing Lucy Hutchinson's Religious Prose'. *Editing Early Modern Women*. Ed. Sarah C. E. Ross and Paul Salzman. Cambridge: Cambridge UP, 2016. 77–95.
Clarke, Elizabeth and Robert W. Daniel. *People and Piety. Protestant Devotional Identities in Early Modern England*. Manchester: Manchester UP, 2020.
Clegg, Cyndia Susan. *Press Censorship in Elizabethan England*. Cambridge: Cambridge UP, 1997.
Clifton, Robin. 'The Popular Fear of Catholics during the English Revolution'. *Past and Present* 52 (1971): 23–55.
Cockcroft, Robert. *Rhetorical Affect in Early Modern Writing. Renaissance Passions Reconsidered*. Basingstoke: Palgrave Macmillan, 2003.
Coffey, John. *Persecution and Toleration in Protestant England, 1558–1689*. London: Longman, 2000.
Collins, John M. *Martial Law and English Laws, 1500–c.1700*. Cambridge: Cambridge UP, 2016.
Collinson, Patrick. '"A Magazine of Religious Patterns": An Erasmian Topic Transposed in English Protestantism'. *Godly People: Essays on English Protestantism and Puritanism*. London: The Hambledon Press, 1983. 498–527.
Collinson, Patrick. 'Truth, Lies, and Fiction in Sixteenth-Century Protestant Historiography'. *The Historical Imagination in Early Modern Britain. History, Rhetoric, and Fiction, 1500–1800*. Ed. Donald R. Kelley and David Harris Sacks. Cambridge: Cambridge UP, 1997. 37–68.
Collinson, Patrick. 'The Protestant Family'. *The Birthpangs of Protestant England: Religious and Cultural Change in the Sixteenth and Seventeenth Centuries*. London: Macmillan, 1998. 60–93.
Collinson, Patrick. 'Literature and the Church'. *The Cambridge History of Early Modern Literature*. Ed. David Loewenstein and Janel Mueller. Cambridge: Cambridge UP, 2002. 374–98.
Collinson, Patrick. 'Antipuritanism'. *Cambridge Companion to Puritanism*. Ed. John Coffey and Paul C. H. Lim. Cambridge: Cambridge UP, 2008. 19–33.
Como, David R. *Radical Parliamentarians and the English Civil War*. Oxford: Oxford UP, 2018.
Cook, Susan. '"The story I most particularly intend": The Narrative Style of Lucy Hutchinson'. *Critical Survey* 5.3 (1993): 271–7.
Cottegnies, Line. *L'Éclipse du regard. La poésie anglaise du baroque au classicisme (1525–1660)*. Geneva: Droz, 1997.

Cottegnies, Line. 'The Garden and the Tower: Pastoral Retreat and Configuration of the Self in Auto/Biography'. *Mapping the Self: Space, Identity, Discourse in British Auto/Biography*. Ed. Frédéric Regard and Geoffrey Wall. Saint-Étienne: Publications de l'Université de Saint-Étienne, 2003. 125–44.
Crawford, Patricia. 'Charles Stuart, That Man of Blood'. *Journal of British Studies* 16.2 (1977): 41–61.
Cressy, David. 'Gender Trouble and Cross-Dressing in Early Modern England'. *Journal of British Studies* 35.4 (1996): 438–65.
Cressy, David. *Bonfires and Bells. National Memory and the Protestant Calendar in Elizabethan and Stuart England*. Phoenix Mill: Sutton Publishing, 2004.
Cressy, David. 'Remembrancers of the Revolution: Histories and Historiographies of the 1640s'. *Huntington Library Quarterly* 68.1–2 (2005): 257–68.
Crivello, Maryline and Jean-Noël Pelen, ed. *Individu, récit, histoire*. Aix-en-Provence : Presses universitaires de Provence, 2008.
Cubitt, Geoffrey. *History and Memory*. Manchester: Manchester UP, 2007.
Cubitt, Geoffrey. 'The Political Uses of Seventeenth-Century English History in Bourbon Restoration France'. *The Historical Journal* 50.1 (2007): 73–95.
Daniel, Robert W. '"To make a second Book of Martyrs": Re-Appropriating Foxe in Nonconformist Prison Writings in Seventeenth-Century Britain.' *Bunyan Studies* 23 (2019): 45–61.
Darcy, Eamon. 'Writing the Past in Early Modern Ireland: Anglesey, Borlase and the Craft of History'. *Irish Historical Studies* 40.158 (2016): 171–91.
Dauvois, Nathalie. 'Éloge lyrique et digression: modèle rhétorique / pratique poétique'. *Exercices de rhétorique* 11 (2018). https://doi.org/10.4000/rhetorique.698.
Davies, Stephen. *Empiricism and History*. Basingstoke: Palgrave Macmillan, 2003.
Davis, Natalie Zemon. 'Gender and Genre: Women as Historical Writers, 1400–1820'. *Beyond their Sex: Learned Women of the European Past*. Ed. Patricia H. Labalme. New York: New York UP, 1980. 153–82.
Daybell, James. *The Material Letter in Early Modern England. Manuscript Letters and the Culture and Practices of Letter Writing*. Basingstoke: Palgrave Macmillan, 2012.
Daybell, James. 'Gendered Archival Practices and the Future Lives of Letters'. *Cultures of Correspondence in Early Modern Britain*. Ed. James Daybell and Andrew Gordon. Philadelphia: U of Pennsylvania P, 2016. 210–37.
Dean, Leonard P. 'Bodin's *Methodus* in England before 1625'. *Studies in Philology* 39.2 (1942): 160–6.
De Groot, Jerome. 'John Denham and Lucy Hutchinson's Commonplace Book'. *Studies in English Literature* 48.1 (2008): 147–63.
Dick, Hugh G. 'Thomas Blundeville's *The True Order and Methode of Wryting and Reading Hystories*'. *Huntington Library Quarterly* 3 (1940): 149–70.
Dolan, Frances. *Whores of Babylon: Catholicism, Gender and Seventeenth-Century Print Culture*. Ithaca: Cornell UP, 1999.
Donagan, Barbara. *War in England 1642–1649*. Oxford: Oxford UP, 2008.
Donaldson, Ian. 'National Biography and the Arts of Memory'. *Mapping Lives: The Uses of Biography*. Ed. Peter France and William St Clair. Oxford: Oxford UP, 2002. 66–82.
Dubois-Nayt, Armel. 'Anne Dowriche et l'histoire de France ou d'Angleterre?' *Études Épistémè* 17 (2010). https://doi.org/10.4000/episteme.659.
Dubos, Nicolas. ed., *Le Mal extrême: La guerre civile vue par les philosophes*. Paris: CNRS, 2010.

Dubos, Nicolas. *Thomas Hobbes et l'histoire: Système et récits à l'âge classique.* Paris: Publication de la Sorbonne, 2014.

Dunan-Page, Anne. *L'expérience puritaine. Vies et récits de dissidents (XVIIe–XVIIIe siècles).* Paris: Éditions du Cerf, 2017.

Eales, Jacqueline and Andrew Hopper. *The County Community.* Hatfield: University of Hertfordshire Press, 2012.

Ebner, Dean. *Autobiography in Seventeenth-Century England, Theology, and the Self.* The Hague: Mouton, 1971.

Everitt, Alan. *The Community of Kent and the Great Rebellion.* Leicester: Leicester UP, 1966.

Ezell, Margaret J. M. *Writing Women's Literary History.* Baltimore and London: Johns Hopkins UP, 1996.

Ezell, Margaret J. M. 'Women and Writing'. *A Companion to Early Modern Women's Writing.* Ed. Anita Pacheco. Oxford: Blackwell, 2009. 77–94.

Fatovic, Clément. 'The Anti-Catholic Roots of Liberal and Republican Conceptions of Freedom in English Political Thought'. *Journal of the History of Ideas* 66.1 (2005): 37–58.

Finlayson, Michael. 'Clarendon, Providence and the Puritan Revolution'. *Albion* 22 (1990): 607–32.

Firth, C. H. 'The "Memoirs" of Sir Richard Bulstrode'. *English Historical Review* 10 (1895): 266–335.

Firth, C. H. 'The Development of the Study of Seventeenth-Century History'. *Transactions of the Royal Historical Society. Third Series* 7 (1913): 25–48.

Fitzmaurice, James. 'Margaret Cavendish's *Life of William*, Plutarch, and Mixed Genre'. *Authorial Conquests: Essays on Genre in the Writings of William Cavendish.* Ed. Line Cottegnies and Nancy Weitz. Madison, NJ: Farleigh Dickinson UP, 2003. 80–102.

Fitzsimmons, Matthew A., Alfred G. Pundt, and Charles E. Nowell. *The Development of Historiography.* Harrisburg, PA: Stackpole Company, 1954.

Fletcher, Anthony. *Gender, Sex and Subordination in England 1500–1800.* New Haven: Yale UP, 1995.

Fraser, Antonia. *The Weaker Vessel. Woman's Lot in Seventeenth-Century England* [1984]. London: Mandarin, 1989.

Frisch, Andrea. *The Invention of the Eyewitness: Witnessing and Testimony in Early Modern France.* Chapel Hill: U of North California P, 2004.

Fumaroli, Marc. 'Mémoires et histoire: le dilemme de l'historiographie humaniste au XVIe siècle'. *Les Valeurs chez les mémorialistes français du XVIIe siècle avant la Fronde.* Ed. Noemi Hepp and Jacques Hennequin. Actes et Colloques 22. Paris: Klincksieck, 1979. 21–45.

Fumaroli, Marc. 'Les Mémoires au carrefour des genres en prose'. *La Diplomatie de l'esprit: De Montaigne à la Fontaine.* Paris: Hermann, 1994. 183–215.

Fumaroli, Marc. 'Les Mémoires, ou l'historiographie royale en procès'. *La Diplomatie de l'esprit: De Montaigne à la Fontaine.* Paris: Hermann, 1994. 217–46.

Fumaroli, Marc. 'La Confidente de la reine: Madame de Motteville et Anne d'Autriche'. *Exercices de lecture: De Rabelais à Paul Valery.* Paris: Gallimard, 2006.

Fussner, F. Smith. *The Historical Revolution. English Historical Writing and Thought 1580–1640.* London: Routledge and Kegan Paul, 1962.

Gheeraert, Tony. 'Les nuées du fantasme. Vapeurs et nuages d'Augustin à Port-Royal'. *Le Parcours du comparant. Pour une histoire littéraire des métaphores.* Ed. Xavier Bonnier. Paris: Classiques Garnier, 2014. 361–88.

Gheeraert-Graffeuille, Claire. 'Satire et diffusion des idées dans la littérature pamphlétaire à l'aube de la guerre civile anglaise, 1640–1642'. *Dix-septième siècle* 195 (1997): 281–96.
Gheeraert-Graffeuille, Claire. *La Cuisine et le forum. L'émergence des femmes sur la scène publique pendant la Révolution anglaise.* Coll. 'Des idées et des femmes'. Paris: L'Harmattan, 2005.
Gheeraert-Graffeuille, Claire. 'Lucy Hutchinson: Bonne épouse ou femme rebelle?' *Les Femmes et leurs représentations en Angleterre de la Renaissance aux Lumières.* Ed. Marlène Bernos, Sandrine Parageau, and Laetitia Sansonetti. Paris: Nouveau Monde Éditions, 2009. 81–94.
Gheeraert-Graffeuille, Claire. 'L'Atelier de l'historienne: "The Life of John Hutchinson" de Lucy Hutchinson'. *Études Épistémè* 17 (2010). https://doi.org/10.4000/episteme.663.
Gheeraert-Graffeuille, Claire. 'The Tragedy of Regicide in Interregnum and Restoration Histories of the English Civil Wars'. *Études Épistémè* 20 (2011). https://doi.org/10.4000/episteme.430.
Gheeraert-Graffeuille, Claire. 'Entre polémique et histoire: comment écrire les guerres civiles anglaises'. *La Guerre civile: représentations, idéalisations, identifications.* Ed. Emmanuel Dupraz and Claire Gheeraert-Graffeuille. Mont-Saint-Aignan: Presses universitaires de Rouen et du Havre, 2014. 51–69.
Gheeraert-Graffeuille, Claire. 'Formes et figures de la tyrannie dans les *Memoirs of the Life of Colonel Hutchinson* de Lucy Hutchinson'. *Le Prince, le despote, le tyran: figures du souverain en Europe de la Renaissance aux Lumières.* Ed. Myriam-Isabelle Ducrocq and Laïla Ghermani. Paris: Honoré Champion, 2019. 211–26.
Gheeraert-Graffeuille, Claire. '"The Great Contest between the Papist and Protestant": Anti-Catholicism in Lucy Hutchinson's Memoirs of the Life of Colonel Hutchinson'. *Anti-Catholicism in Britain and Ireland, 1600–2000: Practices, Representations and Ideas.* Ed. Claire Gheeraert-Graffeuille and Géraldine Vaughan. Basingstoke: Palgrave Macmillan, 2020. 75–91.
Guion, Béatrice. '"Une narration continue des choses vraies, grandes, et publiques": l'histoire selon le Père Le Moyne'. *Œuvres et Critiques* 35.2 (2010): 91–102.
Gill, Harry. *A Short History of Nottingham Castle.* Nottingham: Henry B. Saxton, 1904.
Gillespie, Katharine. 'Lucy Hutchinson, Hermeticism, and Republicanism in the Restoration'. *Women Writing the English Republic, 1625–1681.* Cambridge: Cambridge UP, 2017. 282–333.
Gordon, Andrew and Thomas Rist, ed. *The Arts of Remembrance in Early Modern England. Memorial Culture of the Post Reformation.* Abingdon: Routledge, 2013.
Grafton, Anthony. *What was History? The Art of History in Early Modern Europe.* Cambridge: Cambridge UP, 2007.
Greenfeld, Liah. *Nationalism: Five Roads to Modernity.* Cambridge, MA: Harvard UP, 1992.
Greengrass, Mark. 'The Experiential World of Jean Bodin'. *The Reception of Bodin.* Ed. Howell A. Lloyd. Leiden: Brill, 2013. 67–96.
Guerrier, Olivier. 'Affirmation de vérité, revendication de véracité: formes et enjeux d'une coexistence dans les récits historiques de la seconde moitié du XVIe siècle en France'. *Littératures classiques* 94.3 (2017): 85–94.
Hackett, Helen. *Women and Romance Fiction in the English Renaissance.* Cambridge: Cambridge UP, 2000.
Haldane, Angus. 'The Face of Civil War: Robert Walker (1599): His Life and Portraits'. *The British Art Journal* 17.2 (2016): 20–9.

Hammons, Pamela S. 'Lucy Hutchinson's Polluted Palaces and Ekphrastic Empire'. *Gender, Sexuality and Material Objects in English Renaissance Verse.* Farnham: Ashgate, 2010. 165–84.

Hampton, Timothy. *Writing from History. The Rhetoric of Exemplarity in Renaissance Literature.* Ithaca and London: Cornell UP, 1990.

Harris, Tim. *Restoration: Charles II and his Kingdoms 1660–1685* [2005]. London: Penguin, 2006.

Hartog, François. *Évidence de l'histoire. Ce que voient les historiens.* Paris: Édition de l'EHESS, 2005.

Hartog, François. *Anciens, modernes, sauvages.* Paris: Galaade, 2005.

Hartog, François. *Regimes of Historicity: Presentism and Experiences of Time* [2003]. Trans. Saskia Brown. New York: Columbia UP, 2015.

Hastings, Adrian. *The Construction of Nationhood: Ethnicity, Religion and Nationalism.* Cambridge: Cambridge UP, 1997.

Hersant, Marc and Éric Tourrette, eds. *La Fronde des Mémoires (1648–1750).* Paris: Classiques Garnier, 2019.

Hersant, Marc and Catherine Ramond, eds. *Les Portraits dans les récits factuels et fictionnels de l'époque classique.* Leiden: Brill, 2019.

Hibbard, Caroline M. *Charles I and the Popish Plot.* Chapel Hill: U of North California P, 1983.

Hicklin, John. *History of Nottingham Castle.* London, 1831.

Hill, Bridget and Christopher Hill. 'Catharine Macaulay's *History* and her Catalogue of Tracts'. *The Seventeenth Century* 8.2 (1993): 269–85.

Hipp, Marie-Thérèse. *Mythes et réalités; Enquêtes sur le roman et les mémoires.* Paris: Klincksieck, 1976.

Hirst, Derek. 'Remembering a Hero: Lucy Hutchinson's Memoirs of her Husband'. *The English Historical Review* 119.482 (2004): 682–91.

Hobby, Elaine. *Virtue of Necessity: English Women's Writing, 1646–1688.* London: Virago Press, 1988; Ann Arbor: U of Michigan P, 1989.

Holden, William P. *Anti-Puritan Satire 1572–1642.* New Haven: Yale UP, 1954.

Holmes, Clive. *The Eastern Association in the English Civil War.* Cambridge: Cambridge UP, 1974.

Holmes, Clive. 'The County Community in Stuart Historiography'. *Journal of British Studies* 19.2 (1980): 54–73.

Hopper, Andrew. *Turncoats and Renegadoes. Changing Sides during the English Civil Wars.* Oxford: Oxford UP, 2012.

Hopper, Andrew. 'Treachery and Conspiracy in Nottinghamshire during the English Civil War'. *East Midlands History and Heritage* 1 (2015) 19–23.

Houlbrooke, Ralph. 'The Puritan Death-Bed, *c.*1560–*c.*1660'. *The Culture of English Puritanism, 1560–1700.* Ed. Christopher Durston. Houndmills: Macmillan, 1996. 122–44.

Howell, Jr., Roger. '"Who needs another Cromwell?" The Nineteenth-century Image of Oliver Cromwell'. *Images of Oliver Cromwell.* Ed. R. C. Richardson. Manchester: Manchester UP, 1993. 96–107.

Hudson, Roger. *The Grand Quarrel: From the Civil War Memoirs of Mrs Lucy Hutchinson; Mrs Alice Thornton; Ann, Lady Fanshawe; Margaret Duchess of Newcastle; Anne, Lady Halkett, & the Letters of Brilliana, Lady Harley.* London: The Folio Society, 1993.

Hughes, Ann. 'The King, the Parliament, and the Localities during the English Civil War'. *Journal of British Studies* 24.2 (1985): 236–63.

Hughes, Ann. *Politics, Society and Civil War in Warwickshire 1620–1660*. Cambridge: Cambridge UP, 1987.
Hughes, Ann. 'Gender and Politics in Leveller Literature'. *Political Culture and Cultural Politics in Early Modern England*. Ed. Susan Dwyer Amussen and Mark A. Kishlansky. Manchester: Manchester UP, 1995. 162–89.
Hughes, Ann. *The Causes of the English Civil War* [1991]. Basingstoke: Macmillan, 1998.
Hunt, Alice. 'Les mémoires républicaines des guerres civiles anglaises dans les années 1650'. *Dix-septième siècle* 275.2 (2017): 253–8.
Hutton, Ronald. 'The Royalist War Effort'. *Reaction to the English Civil War, 1642–1649*. Ed. John Morrill. London: Macmillan, 1982. 51–66.
Hutton, Ronald. *The Restoration*. Oxford: Oxford UP, 1986.
Italiano, Gloria. 'Two Parallel Biographers of the Seventeenth Century: Margaret Cavendish and Lucy Hutchinson'. *Critical Dimensions: English, German and Comparative Literature Essays in Honour of Aurelio Zanco*, ed. Mario Curreli and Alberto Martino. Cuneo: Saste, 1978. 241–51.
Janssen, Lydia. 'Antiquarianism and National History. The Emergence of a New Scholarly Paradigm in Early Modern Historical Studies'. *History of European Ideas* 43.8 (2017): 843–56.
Jettot, Stéphane. 'Mauvais sang? L'argument généalogique dans la délégitimation des régicides anglais (1660–1798)'. *Le Sang des Princes. Cultes et mémoires des souverains suppliciés (XVIe–XIXe siècles)*. Ed. Paul Chopelin and Sylvène Édouard. Rennes: Presses universitaires de Rennes, 2014. 79–91.
Jones, Emily Griffiths. '"My Victorious Triumphs Are All Thine": Romance and Elect Community in Lucy Hutchinson's *Order and Disorder*'. *Studies in Philology* 112.1 (2015): 162–93.
Kahn, Victoria. *Wayward Contracts: The Crisis of Political Obligation in England 1640–1674*. Princeton, NJ: Princeton UP, 2004.
Keeble, N. H. *Richard Baxter: Puritan Man of Letters*. Oxford: Oxford UP, 1982.
Keeble, N. H. *The Literature of Nonconformity in Later Seventeenth-Century England*. Leicester: Leicester UP, 1987.
Keeble, N. H. 'The Autobiographer as Apologist: *Reliquiæ Baxterianæ* (1696)'. *The Literature of Controversy*. Ed. Thomas N. Corns. London: Frank Cass, 1987. 105–19.
Keeble, N. H. '"The Colonel's Shadow": Lucy Hutchinson, Women's Writing and the Civil War'. *Literature and the English Civil War*. Ed. Thomas Healey and Jonathan Sawday. Cambridge: Cambridge UP, 1990. 227–47.
Keeble, N. H. *The Restoration: England in the 1660s*. Oxford: Blackwell, 2002.
Keeble, N. H. '*Reliquiæ Baxterianæ* and the Shaping of the Seventeenth Century'. *A Concise Companion to the Study of Manuscripts, Printed Books, and the Production of Early Modern Texts*. Ed. Edward Jones. Chichester: Wiley, 2015. 229–48.
Keeble, N. H. 'Lucy Hutchinson and the Business of Memoirs'. *The Review of English Studies* 2022, https://doi.org/10.1093/res/hgac007.
Kelley, Donald R. 'Philosophy and Humanistic Disciplines: The Theory of History'. *Cambridge History of Renaissance Philosophy*. Ed. C. B. Schmitt, Jill Kraye, Eckhard Kessler, and Quentin Skinner. Cambridge: Cambridge UP, 1988. 746–62.
Kelley, Donald R. 'The Development and Context of Bodin's Method'. *Jean Bodin* [1973, 2006]. Ed. Julian H. Franklin. London: Routledge, 2016. 123–51.
Kendall, Ritchie D. *The Drama of Dissent: The Radical Poetics of Nonconformity 1380–1590*. Chapel Hill: U of North Carolina P, 1986.

Kewes, Paulina. 'History and Its Uses: Introduction'. *Huntington Library Quarterly* 68.1–2 (2005): 1–31.
Kewes, Paulina. 'Acts of Remembrance, Acts of Oblivion: Rhetoric, Law and National Memory in Early Restoration England'. *Ritual, Routine, and Regime*. Ed. Lorna Clymer. Toronto: Toronto UP, 2006. 103–31.
Kishlansky, Mark. 'Mission Impossible: Charles I, Oliver Cromwell and the Regicide'. *The English Historical Review* 125.515 (2010): 844–74.
Knoppers, Laura Lunger. *Constructing Cromwell: Ceremony, Portrait, and Print 1645–1661*. Cambridge: Cambridge UP, 2000. 107–31.
Knott, John R. *Discourses of Martyrdom in English Literature, 1563–1694*. Cambridge: Cambridge UP, 1993.
Kuperty-Tsur, Nadine. *Se dire à la Renaissance. Les Mémoires au XVIe siècle*. Paris: Vrin, 1997.
Kuperty-Tsur, Nadine. 'Le portrait de Philippe Duplessis-Mornay dans les mémoires de son épouse: entre hagiographie et apologie'. *Albineana. Cahiers d'Aubigné* 18 (2006): 565–85.
Labarbe, Claire. '"Mises en abyme" and Satirical Descriptions: "Characters" of Writing and Writers in Seventeenth-Century England'. *Études Épistémè* 21 (2012). https://doi.org/10.4000/episteme.407.
Lake, Peter. 'Anti-Popery: The Structure of a Prejudice'. *Conflict in Early Stuart England: Studies in Religion and Politics, 1603–1642*. Ed. Richard Cust and Ann Hughes. London: Longman, 1989.
Lake, Peter. 'Anti-Puritanism: The Structure of a Prejudice'. *Religious Politics in Post-Reformation England: Essays in Honour of Nicholas Tyacke*. Ed. Kenneth Fincham and Peter Lake. Woodbridge: Boydell, 2006. 80–97.
Lake, Peter. 'Post-Reformation Politics, or on Not Looking for the Long-Term Causes of the English Civil War'. *The Oxford Handbook of the English Revolution*. Ed. Michael J. Braddick. Oxford: Oxford UP, 2015. 20–39.
Lake, Peter. *Bad Queen Bess? Libels, Secret Histories, and the Politics of Publicity in the Reign of Queen Elizabeth I*. Oxford: Oxford UP, 2016.
Lamb, Mary Ellen and Mihoko Suzuki, eds. *Ashgate Critical Essays on Women Writers in England, 1550–1700: Anne Clifford and Lucy Hutchinson*. Farnham: Ashgate, 2009.
Lamont, William. 'Richard Baxter, "Popery" and the Origins of the English Civil War'. *History* 87.287 (2002): 336–52.
Langbein, John H. *Torture and the Law of Proof* [1976]. Chicago: U of Chicago P, 2006.
Lee, Christine S. 'The Meanings of Romance: Rethinking Early Modern Fiction'. *Modern Philology* 112.2 (2014): 287–311.
Legon, Edward. *Revolution Remembered. Seditious Memories after the British Civil Wars*. Manchester: Manchester UP, 2019.
Lejeune, Philippe. *On Autobiography [Le Pacte autobiographique, 1971]*. Trans. Katherine Leary. Minneapolis: U of Mineapolis P, 1989.
Lesne, Emmanuèle. *La Poétique des mémoires (1650–1685)*. Paris: Honoré Champion, 1996.
Levin, Carole. *The Heart and Stomach of a King: Elizabeth and the Politics of Sex and Power*. 2nd edition. Philadelphia: U of Pennsylvania P, 1993.
Levy, F. J. *Tudor Historical Thought*. San Marino: The Huntington Library, 1967.
Levy, Fritz. '*The Advancement of Learning* and Historical Thought'. *Francis Bacon and the Refiguring of Early Modern Thought: Essays to Commemorate the Advancement of Learning (1605–2005)*. Ed. Julie Robin Solomon and Catherine Gimelli Martin. Aldershot: Ashgate, 2005. 203–21.

Llewellyn, Nigel. *Art of Death: Visual Culture in the English Death Ritual, c.1500–c.1800*. London: Reaktion Books, 1991.
Lobo, Giuseppina Iacono. 'Lucy Hutchinson's Revisions of Conscience'. *English Literary Renaissance* 42.2 (2012): 317–41.
Loewenstein, David. 'The King among the Radicals: Godly Republicans, Levellers, Diggers and Fifth Monarchists'. *The Royal Image: Representations of Charles I*. Ed. Thomas N. Corns. Cambridge: Cambridge UP, 1999. 96–121.
Loewenstein, David. 'Milton's Nationalism and the English Revolution'. *Early Modern Nationalism*. Ed. Loewenstein and Paul Stevens. Toronto: U of Toronto P, 2008. 2–22.
Lomax, Scott. *Nottingham: The Buried Past of a Historic City Revealed [2013]*. Havertown, PA: Pen & Sword, 2019.
Longfellow, Erica. *Women and Religious Writing in England*. Cambridge: Cambridge UP, 2004.
Looser, Devoney. *British Women Writers and the Writing of History 1670–1820*. Baltimore and London: Johns Hopkins UP, 2000.
Loraux, Nicole. *La Cité divisée*. Paris: Payot, 1997.
Love, Harold and Arthur F. Marotti. 'Manuscript Transmission and Circulation'. *The Cambridge History of Early Modern English Literature*. Ed. David Loewenstein and Janel Mueller. Cambridge: Cambridge UP, 2002. 55–80.
Lurbe, Pierre. 'Du temps vécu au temps de l'histoire: les mémoires de Denzil, Lord Holles'. *Le Char ailé du temps. Temps, mémoire, histoire en Grande-Bretagne au XVIIe siècle*. Ed. Louis Roux. Saint-Étienne: Publications de l'Université de Saint-Étienne, 2003. 111–28.
Lynch, Kathleen. *Protestant Autobiography in the Seventeenth-Century Anglophone World*. Oxford: Oxford UP, 2012.
Lynch, Kathleen. 'Inscribing the Early Modern Self. The Materiality of Autobiography'. *A History of English Biography*. Ed. Adam Smyth. Cambridge: Cambridge UP, 2016. 56–69.
Lyons, John D. *Exemplum: The Rhetoric of Example in Early Modern France and Italy*. Princeton: Princeton UP, 1989.
MacGillivray, Royce. 'The Upham Thesis and the Literary Debts of Mrs. Lucy Hutchinson'. *Revue de l'université d'Ottawa* 40 (1970): 618–30.
MacGillivray, Royce. *Restoration Historians and the English Civil War*. The Hague: Martinus Nijhoff, 1974.
Mahlberg, Gaby. *The English Republican Exiles in Europe during the Restoration*. Cambridge: Cambridge UP, 2020.
Major, Philip. '"A Credible Omen of a More Glorious Event": Sir Charles Cotterell's Cassandra'. *The Review of English Studies* 60.245 (2009): 406–30.
Manning, Roger B. *Swordsmen: The Martial Ethos in the Three Kingdoms*. Oxford: Oxford UP, 2003.
Manning, Roger B. 'Styles of Command in Seventeenth-Century English Armies'. *The Journal of Military History* 71.3 (2007): 671–99.
Marotti, Arthur F. *Manuscript, Print, and the English Renaissance Lyric*. Ithaca, NY: Cornell UP, 1995.
Marotti, Arthur F., ed. *Catholicism and Anti-Catholicism in Early Modern Texts*. Basingstoke: Palgrave Macmillan, 1999.
Marotti, Arthur F. *Religious Ideology and Cultural Fantasy: Catholic and Anti-Catholic Discourses in Early Modern England*. Notre Dame, IN: U of Notre Dame P, 2005.
Marshall, Alan. '" Plots and Dissent": The Abortive Northern Rebellion of 1663'. *From Republic to Restoration. Legacies and Departure*. Ed. Janet Clare. Manchester: Manchester UP, 2018. 85–101.

Marshall, Peter. '(Re)defining the English Reformation'. *Journal of British Studies* 48.3 (2009): 564–86.
Martin, Craig. 'Religious Reform and the Reform of Aristotelianism'. *Subverting Aristotle: Religion, History and Philosophy in Early Modern Science.* Baltimore: John Hopkins UP, 2014. 86–101.
Matchinske, Megan. *Women Writing History in Early Modern Europe.* Cambridge: Cambridge UP, 2009.
Matchinske, Megan. 'History's "Silent Whispers": Representing the Past through Feeling and Form'. *Attending to Early Modern Women: Conflict and Concord.* Ed. Karen Nelson. Newark: U of Delaware P, 2013.
Mayer, Robert. *History and the Early English Novel. Matters of Fact from Bacon to Defoe.* Cambridge: Cambridge UP, 1992.
Mayer, Robert. 'Lucy Hutchinson: A Life of Writing'. *The Seventeenth Century* 22.2 (2007): 305–35.
Mayer, Thomas F. and Daniel R. Woolf. *The Rhetorics of Life-Writing in Early Modern England. Forms of Biography from Cassandra Fedele to Louis XIV.* Ann Arbor: U of Michigan P, 1995.
McKeon, Michael. *The Origins of the English Novel 1600–1740.* Baltimore: Johns Hopkins UP, 1987.
McLaren, Anne. 'Gender, Religion, and Early Modern Nationalism: Elizabeth I, Mary Queen of Scots, and the Genesis of English Anti-Catholicism'. *American Historical Review* 107.3 (2002): 739–67.
Mendelson, Sara and Patricia Crawford. *Women in Early Modern England 1550–1720.* Oxford: Clarendon, 1998.
Michel, Johann. 'Narrativité, narration, narratologie: du concept ricœurien d'identité narrative aux sciences sociales'. *Revue européenne des sciences sociales* 41.125 (2003): 125–42.
Milhe Poutingon, Gérard. *Poétique du digressif. La digression dans la littérature de la Renaissance.* Paris: Classiques Garnier, 2012.
Miller, Shannon. 'Family and Commonwealth in the Writings of Lucy Hutchinson'. *The Oxford Handbook of Literature and the English Revolution.* Ed. Laura Lunger Knoppers. Oxford: Oxford UP, 1992. 669–85.
Miller, Shannon. *Engendering the Fall: John Milton and Seventeenth-Century Women Writers.* Philadelphia: U of Pennsylvania P, 2008.
Miller, Shannon. 'Women Writers and the Narrative of the Fall'. *The History of British Women's Writing.* Vol. 3. Ed. Mihoko Suzuki. Basingstoke: Palgrave Macmillan, 2011. 64–79.
Millstone, Noah. *Manuscript Circulation and the Invention of Politics in Early Stuart England.* Cambridge: Cambridge UP, 2016.
Milton, Anthony. *Catholic and Reformed. The Roman and Protestant Churches in English Protestant Thought 1600–1640.* Cambridge: Cambridge UP, 1995.
Mitchell, Rosemary. *Picturing the Past: English History in Text and Image, 1830–1870.* Oxford: Clarendon, 2000.
Morrill, John. *The Revolt in the Provinces: Conservatives and Radicals in the English Civil War, 1630–1650.* London: Allen and Unwin, 1976. Longman, 1999.
Morrill, John, ed. *Oliver Cromwell and the English Revolution.* London: Longman, 1990.
Morrill, John. *The Nature of the English Revolution.* Harlow: Longman, 1993.
Moss, Ann. *Printed Commonplace Books and the Structuring of Renaissance Thought.* Oxford: Oxford UP, 1996.

Murphy, Erin. *Familial Forms: Politics and Genealogy in Seventeenth-Century English Literature*. Newark: University of Delaware Press, 2011.

Murphy, Erin. '"I remain, an airy phantasm": Lucy Hutchinson's Civil War Ghost Writing'. *English Literary History* 82.1 (2015): 87–113.

Murphy, Kathryn and Anita Traninger, eds. *The Emergence of Impartiality*. Leiden: Brill, 2014.

Narveson, Kate. 'The Source for Lucy Hutchinson's *On Theology*'. *Notes and Queries* 36 (1989): 40–1.

Narveson, Kate. *Bible Readers and Lay Writers in Early Modern England. Gender and Self-Definition in an Emergent Writing Culture*. Farnham: Ashgate, 2012.

Nesvet, Rebecca. 'Missing persons: Lucy Hutchinson, Feminist Biography and the Digital Archive'. *The Invention of Female Biography*. Ed. Gina Luria Walker. Abingdon: Routledge, 2018. 74–82.

Neufeld, Matthew. *The Civil Wars after 1660. Public Remembering in Late Stuart England*. Woodbridge: Boydell Press, 2013.

Newcomb, Lori Humphrey. 'Prose Fiction'. *The Cambridge Companion to Early Modern Women's Writing*. Ed. Kaura Lunger Knoppers. Cambridge: Cambridge UP, 2009. 272–86.

Noille-Clauzade, Christine. 'La figure de la description dans la théorie rhétorique classique'. *Pratiques* 109.110 (2001): 5–14

Nora, Pierre. *Rethinking France. Les Lieux de mémoire. Volume 1: The State* [1984]. Ed. David P. Jordan, trans. Mary Trouille. Chicago: U of Chicago P, 2001.

Norbrook, David. 'Lucy Hutchinson versus Edmund Waller: An Unpublished Reply to Waller's A Panegyrick to My Lord Protector'. *The Seventeenth Century* 11.1 (1996): 61–3.

Norbrook, David. 'Lucy Hutchinson's "Elegies" and the Situation of the Republican Woman Writer [with Text]'. *English Literary Renaissance* 27.3 (1997): 468–521.

Norbrook, David. *Writing the English Republic: Poetry, Rhetoric and Politics*. Cambridge: Cambridge UP, 1999.

Norbrook, David. 'Margaret Cavendish and Lucy Hutchinson: Identity, Ideology and Politics'. *In-Between* 9.1–2 (2000): 179–203.

Norbrook, David. 'The English Revolution and English Historiography'. *The Cambridge Companion to Writing of the English Revolution*. Ed. N. H. Keeble. Cambridge: Cambridge UP, 2001. 233–50.

Norbrook, David. 'Lucy Hutchinson, *Memoirs*'. *A Companion to Literature from Milton to Blake*. Ed. David Womersley. Oxford: Blackwell, 2001. 182–8.

Norbrook, David. '"Words more than civil": Republican Civility in Lucy Hutchinson's "The Life of Colonel Hutchinson"'. *Early Modern Discourses*. Ed. Jennifer Richards. Houndmills: Palgrave Macmillan, 2003. 68–84.

Norbrook, David. '"But a Copie": Textual Authority and Gender in Editions of "The Life of John Hutchinson"'. *New Ways of Looking at Old Texts III*. Ed. W. Speed Hill. Tempe, AZ: Center for Medieval and Renaissance Studies, 2004. 109–30.

Norbrook, David. 'Women, the Republic of Letters, and the Public Sphere in the Mid-Seventeenth Century'. *Criticism* 46.2 (2004): 223–40.

Norbrook, David. 'Memoirs and Oblivion: Lucy Hutchinson and the Restoration'. *Huntington Library Quarterly* 75.2 (2012): 233–83.

Norbrook, David. 'Lucy Hutchinson: Theology, Gender and Translation'. *The Seventeenth Century* 30.3 (2015): 139–62.

Ó Siochrú, Micheál. 'Atrocity, Codes of Conduct and the Irish in the British Civil Wars 1641–1653'. *Past and Present* 195.1 (2007): 55–86.

Palmer, Michael. 'Stasis in the War Narrative'. *The Oxford Handbook of Thucydides*. Ed. Ryan Balot, Sarah Forsdyke, and Edith Foster. Oxford: Oxford UP, 2017.

Parageau, Sandrine. 'Catching "the Genius of the Age": Margaret Cavendish, Historian and Witness'. *Études Épistémè* 17 (2010). https://doi.org/10.4000/episteme.662.

Parageau, Sandrine. 'Bacon, Boyle et l'écriture de l'histoire naturelle'. *Archives de philosophie* 84.1 (2021): 73–91.

Parry, Graham. *The Trophies of Time: English Antiquarians of the Seventeenth Century*. Oxford: Oxford UP, 1995.

Patrick, Patricia. '"All that appears most casuall to us": Fortune, Compassion, and reason in Lucy Hutchinson's Providentialism'. *Studies in Philology* 112.2 (2015): 327–52.

Patterson, Annabel. *Censorship and Interpretation. The Conditions of Writing and Reading in Early Modern England*. Madison: U of Wisconsin P, 1984.

Patterson, W. B. *Thomas Fuller: Discovering England's Religious Past*. Oxford: Oxford UP, 2018.

Peacey, Jason. *Print and Public Politics in the English Revolution*. Cambridge: Cambridge UP, 2013.

Peck, Linda Levy. *Consuming Splendor: Society and Culture in Seventeenth-Century England*. Cambridge: Cambridge UP, 2005.

Pert, Thomas. 'Colonel Hutchinson (1615–1664) and Nottingham in the English Civil War, 1643–1646'. *East Midlands History and Heritage* 1 (2015): 24–6.

Peters, Edward. *Torture*. Expanded edition. Philadelphia: U of Pennsylvania P, 1996.

Peters, Erin. 'Trauma Narratives of the English Civil War'. *Journal for Early Modern Cultural Studies* 16.1 (2016): 79–94.

Peters, Erin. '"L'objet de moquerie le plus colossal et le plus honteux du monde": récits de la honte nationale en 1660'. *Dix-septième siècle* 275.2 (2017): 269–84.

Philo, John-Mark. 'Elizabeth I's Translation of Tacitus: Lambeth Palace Library, MS 683.' *Review of English Studies* 71 (2020): 44–73.

Pitcher, L. V. 'Classical War Literature'. *The Cambridge Companion to War-Writing*. Ed. Kate McMcLoughlin. Cambridge: Cambridge UP, 2010. 71–80.

Plazenet, Laurence. *L'Ébahissement et la délectation. Réception comparée et poétiques du roman grec en France et en Angleterre aux XVIe et XVIIe siècles*. Paris: Champion, 1997.

Plett, Heinrich F. *Enargeia in Classical Antiquity and the Early Modern Age. The Aesthetics of Evidence*. Leiden: Brill, 2012.

Plowden, Alison. *Women All on Fire: The Women of the English Civil War*. Stroud: Sutton Publishing, 1998.

Pocock, J. G. A. *The Ancient Constitution. A Study of English Historical Thought* [1957]. Cambridge: Cambridge UP, 1987.

Pocock, J. G. A. 'Thomas May and the Narrative of the Civil War'. *Writing and Political Engagement in Seventeenth-Century England*. Ed. Derek Hirst and Richard Strier. Cambridge: Cambridge UP, 2009.

Pollmann, Judith. *Memory in Early Modern Europe 1500–1800*. Oxford: Oxford UP, 2017.

Potter, Lois. *Secret Rites and Secret Writing: Royalist Literature*. Cambridge: Cambridge UP, 1989.

Preston, Joseph H. 'Was There an Historical Revolution?' *Journal of the History of Ideas* 38.2 (1977): 353–64.

Pritchard, Allan. *English Biography in the Seventeenth Century*. Toronto: Toronto UP, 2009.

Purkiss, Diane. *Literature, Gender and Politics during the English Civil War*. Cambridge: Cambridge UP, 2005.

Race, Sidney. 'The British Museum MS. of the Life of Colonel Hutchinson and its Relation to the Published Memoirs'. *Transactions of the Thoroton Society* 18 (1914): 35–66.

Race, Sidney. 'Notes on Mrs. Hutchinson's Manuscripts'. *Notes and Queries* 145 (1923): 3-4, 26-8, 165-6.
Race, Sidney. 'Colonel Hutchinson, the Regicide'. *Notes and Queries* 197 (1952): 32-3 and *Notes and Queries* 199 (1954): 166.
Race, Sidney. 'Colonel Hutchinson: Manuscript and Printed Memoirs'. *Notes and Queries* 199 (1954): 160-3, 202-4.
Raylor, Timothy. 'Newcastle's Ghosts: Robert Payne, Ben Jonson, and the "Cavendish Circle"'. *Literary Circles and Cultural Communities in Renaissance England.* Ed. C. J. Summers and T. L. Pebworth. Columbia: U of Missouri P, 2000. 92-114.
Raylor, Timothy. *Philosophy, Rhetoric, and Thomas Hobbes.* Oxford: Oxford UP, 2018.
Raymond, Joad. 'John Hall's *A Method of History*: A Book Lost and Found (with transcription)'. *English Literary Renaissance* 28.2 (1988): 267-98.
Raymond, Joad. 'An Eye-Witness to King Cromwell'. *History Today* 47.7 (1997): 35-41.
Raymond, Joad. *Pamphlets and Pamphleteering in Early Modern Britain.* Cambridge: Cambridge UP, 2003.
Raymond, Joad. 'Irrational, Impractical and Unprofitable: Reading the News in Seventeenth-Century Britain'. *Reading, Society and Politics in Early Modern England.* Cambridge: Cambridge UP, 2003. 185-212.
Richardson, R. C. *The Debate on the English Revolution.* 3rd edition. Manchester: Manchester UP, 1998.
Ricœur, Paul. *Time and Narrative.* Vol. 3. Trans. Kathleen Blamey and David Pallauer. Chicago: U of Chicago P, 1988.
Ricœur, Paul. *Memory, History, Forgetting.* Trans. Kathleen Blamey and David Pellauer. Chicago: U of Chicago P, 2004.
Rippl, Gabriele. '"Merit, Justice, Gratitude, Duty, Fidelity": Images of Masculinity in Autobiographies of Early Modern English Gentlewomen and Aristocrats'. *Constructions of Masculinity in British Literature from the Middle Ages to the Present.* Ed. S. Horlacher. Basingstoke: Palgrave Macmillan, 2012. 69-87.
Rivers, Isabel. *Reason, Grace, and Sentiment. A Study of the Language of Religion and Ethics in England 1660-1780.* Cambridge: Cambridge UP, 1991.
Roberts, Sasha. 'Feminist Criticism and the New Formalism: Early Modern Women and Literary Engagement'. *The Impact of Feminism in English Renaissance Studies*, ed. Dympna Callaghan. Basingstoke: Palgrave, 2007. 67-92.
Rose, Mary Beth. 'Gender, Genre, and History: Seventeenth-Century English Women and the Art of Autobiography'. *Women in the Middle Ages and the Renaissance.* Ed. Mary Beth Rose. Syracuse: Syracuse UP, 1986. 245-78.
Ross, Sarah C. E. *Women, Poetry, and Politics in Seventeenth-Century Britain.* Oxford: Oxford UP, 2015.
Rousset, Jean. *Leurs yeux se rencontrèrent. La scène de première vue dans le roman.* Paris: José Corti, 1981.
Ryrie, Alec. 'The Slow Death of a Tyrant: Learning to Live without Henry VIII, 1547-1563'. *Henry VIII and his Afterlives. Literature, Politics, and Art.* Ed. Mark Rankin, Christopher Highley, and John N. King. Cambridge: Cambridge UP, 2009. 75-93.
Ryrie, Alec. *Being Protestant in Reformation Britain.* Oxford: Oxford University Press, 2013.
Salmon, J. H. M. 'Precept, Example, and Truth: Degory Wheare and the *ars historica*'. *The Historical Imagination in Early Modern Britain. History, Rhetoric, and Fiction, 1500-1800.* Ed. Donald R. Kelley and David Harris Sacks. Cambridge: Cambridge UP, 1997. 11-36.
Salzman, Paul. *An Anthology of Seventeenth-Century Fiction.* Oxford: Oxford UP, 1991.

Salzman, Paul. 'Royalist Epic and Romance'. *The Cambridge Companion to Writing of the English Revolution*. Ed. N. H. Keeble. Cambridge: Cambridge UP, 2001. 215–30.

Sasek, Lawrence, ed. *Images of English Puritanism: A Collection of Contemporary Sources 1589-1646.* Baton Rouge: Louisiana State UP, 1989.

Sawday, Jonathan. 'Re-Writing a Revolution: History, Symbol and Text in the Restoration'. *The Seventeenth Century* 7.2 (1992): 185–8.

Scott, George Ryley. *History of Torture Throughout the Ages* [1940]. London: Luxor Press, 1959.

Scott, Jonathan. 'The Peace of Silence: Thucydides and the English Civil War'. *The Certainty of Doubt: Tributes to Peter Munz*. Ed. Miles Fairburn and William Hosking Oliver. Wellington: Victoria UP, 1997.

Scott, Jonathan. *England's Troubles. Seventeenth-Century English Political Instability in European Context*. Cambridge: Cambridge UP, 2000.

Scott, Jonathan. *Commonwealth Principles. Republican Writing of the English Revolution*. Cambridge: Cambridge UP, 2004.

Scott-Baumann, Elizabeth. *Forms of Engagement. Women, Poetry and Culture 1640–1680.* Oxford: Oxford UP, 2013.

Seaward, Paul. 'Clarendon, Tacitism, and the Civil Wars of Europe'. *Huntington Library Quarterly* 68.1–2 (2005): 289–311.

Seddon, P. R. 'Colonel Hutchinson and the Disputes between the Nottinghamshire Parliamentarians, 1643–45'. *Transactions of the Thoroton Society* 98 (1994): 71–81.

Seddon, P. R. 'The Dating of the Completion of the Composition of the *Memoirs of Colonel John Hutchinson:* The Evidence of the Imprisonments of Captain John Wright and Lieutenant Richard Franck'. *Transactions of the Thoroton Society* 120 (2016): 113–21.

Seelig, Sharon Cadman. 'Pygmalion's Image: The Lives of Lucy Hutchinson'. *Autobiography and Gender in Early Modern Literature*. Cambridge: Cambridge UP, 2006. 73–89.

Sellier, Philippe. 'Pour une poétique de la légende: "La vie de Monsieur Pascal"'. *Port-Royal et la littérature*. Vol. 1. Paris: Honoré Champion, 1999. 29–48.

Serjeantson, Richard W. 'Proof and Persuasion'. *The Cambridge History of Science*. Vol. 3, *Early Modern Science*. Ed. Katharine Park and Lorraine Daston. Cambridge: Cambridge UP, 2006. 132–75.

Shagan, Ethan Howard. 'Constructing Discord: Ideology, Propaganda, and English Responses to the Irish Rebellion of 1641'. *Journal of British Studies* 36.1 (1977): 4–34.

Shapin, Steven. 'Pump and Circumstance: Robert Boyle's Literary Technology'. *Social Studies of Science* 14.4 (1984): 481–520.

Shapin, Steven. *A Social History of Truth: Civility and Science in Seventeenth-Century England*. Chicago: Chicago UP, 1994.

Shapin, Stephen and Simon Schaffer, *Leviathan and the Air-Pump. Hobbes, Boyle, and the Experimental Life*. Princeton: Princeton UP, 1985.

Shapiro, Barbara J. *Probability and Certainty in Seventeenth-Century England*. Princeton: Princeton UP, 1983.

Shapiro, Barbara J. *A Culture of Fact. England, 1550–1720*. Ithaca and London: Cornell UP, 2000.

Sharpe, Kevin and Steven N. Zwicker, eds. *Writing Lives: Biography and Textuality, Identity and Representation in Early Modern England*. Oxford: Oxford UP, 2008.

Sherlock, Peter. *Monuments and Memory in Early Modern England*. Aldershot: Ashgate, 2008.

Shuger, Debora. 'Life-Writing in Seventeenth-Century England'. *Representations of the Self from the Renaissance to Romanticism*. Ed. Patrick Coleman, Jayne Lewis, and Jill Kowalik. Cambridge: Cambridge UP, 2000. 63–78.

Smith, Hilda L. and Susan Cardinale. *Women and the Literature of the Seventeenth-Century: An Annotated Bibliography Based on Wing's Short-Title-Catalogue*. New York: Greenwood Press, 1990.

Smith, Nigel. 'Richard Overton's Marpriest Tracts: Towards a History of Leveller Style'. *The Literature of Controversy*. Ed. Thomas N. Corns. London: Frank Cass, 1987. 39–65.

Smith, Nigel. *Literature and Revolution in England, 1640–1660*. New Haven: New Haven UP, 1994.

Southcombe, George and Grand Tapsell. *Restoration Politics, Religion and Culture*. Basingstoke: Palgrave Macmillan, 2010.

Starobinski, Jean. 'Le style de l'autobiographie'. *L'Œil vivant II. La Relation critique*. Paris: Gallimard, 2001.

Staves, Susan. *A Literary History of Women's Writing in Britain, 1660–1789*. Cambridge: Cambridge UP, 2006.

Stone, W. F. 'Aristotelianism and Scholasticism in Early Modern Philosophy'. *A Companion to Early Modern Philosophy*, ed. Steven Nadler. Oxford: Blackwell, 2002. 7–24.

Stoyle, Mark. 'Remembering the English Civil War'. *The Memory of Catastrophe*. Ed. Peter Gray and Kendrick Oliver. Manchester: Manchester UP, 2004. 19–30.

Suzuki, Mihoko. 'Anne Clifford and the Gendering of History'. *Clio* 30.2 (2001): 195–219.

Suzuki, Mihoko. 'Women's Literary History in Late Eighteenth- and Nineteenth-Century France: Louise de Kéralio and Henriette Guizot de Witt: Within and Beyond the Academy'. *Generations of Women Historians Within and Beyond the Academy*. Ed. Hilda L. Smith and Melinda S. Zook. Cham: Springer International Publishing, 2018.

Todd, Margo. *Christian Humanism and the Puritan Social Order*. Cambridge: Cambridge UP, 1987.

Trill, Suzanne. 'Beyond Romance? Re-Reading the "Lives" of Anne Lady Halkett (1621/2?–1699)'. *Literature Compass* 6.2 (2009): 446–59.

Tsimbidy, Myriam. *La Mémoire des lettres. La lettre dans les Mémoires*. Paris: Classiques Garnier, 2013.

Tucker, Shawn R. *The Virtues and Vices in the Arts: A Sourcebook*. Eugene, OR: Cascade Books, 2015.

Tumbleson, Raymond. *Catholicism in the English Protestant Imagination. Nationalism, Religion, and Literature, 1660–1745*. Cambridge: Cambridge UP, 1998.

Tyacke, Nicholas. *Anti-Calvinists: The Rise of English Arminianism c.1590–1640*. Oxford: Clarendon, 1987.

Underdown, David. 'Presbyterians and Independents'. *Pride's Purge. Politics in the Puritan Revolution*. Oxford: Clarendon, 1971.

Upham, A. H. 'Lucy Hutchinson and the Duchess of Newcastle'. *Anglia* 36 (1912): 200–20.

Van Der Poel, Marc. 'The Battle of *De incertitudine*: Agrippa in the World of Humanism'. *The Humanist Theologian and his Declamations*. Leiden: Brill, 1997.

Vergnes, Sophie. 'Des discours de la discorde: Les femmes, la Fronde et l'écriture de l'histoire'. *Études Épistémè* 19 (2011). https://doi.org/10.4000/episteme.627.

Vergnes, Sophie. *Les Frondeuses. Une révolte au féminin*. Seyssel: Champ Vallon, 2013.

Vickers, Brian. *In Defence of Rhetoric*. Oxford: Clarendon, 1998.

Vine, Angus. *In Defiance of Time: Antiquarian Writing in Early Modern England*. Oxford: Oxford UP, 2010.

Wall, Anna. '"Not so much open professed enemies as close hypocritical false-hearted people": Lucy Hutchinson's Manuscript Account of the Services of John Hutchinson and Mid-Seventeenth-Century Factionalism'. *The Seventeenth Century* 36.4 (2021): 623–51.
Walsham, Alexandra. *Providence in Early Modern England*. Oxford: Oxford UP, 1999.
Walsham, Alexandra. *Charitable Hatred: Tolerance and Intolerance in England 1500–1700*. Manchester: Manchester UP, 2005.
Walsham, Alexandra. 'History, Memory and the English Reformation'. *The Historical Journal* 55.4 (2012): 899–938.
Walsham, Alexandra, Bronwyn Wallace, Ceri Law, and Brian Cummings, eds. *Memory and the English Reformation*. Cambridge: Cambridge UP, 2020.
Wanklyn, Malcolm. *Decisive Battles of the English Civil Wars: Myth and Reality*. Barnsley: Pen & Sword, 2006.
Watkins, Owen C. *The Puritan Experience: Studies in Spiritual Autobiography*. London: Routledge, 1972.
Weil, Rachel. 'Thinking about Allegiances in the English Civil War'. *History Workshop Journal* 61 (2006): 183–91.
West, Philip. 'Early Modern War Writing and the British Civil Wars'. *Cambridge Companion to War-Writing*. Ed. Kate McMcLoughlin. Cambridge: Cambridge UP, 2010. 98–111.
Wiener, Carol Z. 'The Beleaguered Isle. A Study of Elizabethan and Early Jacobean Anti-Catholicism'. *Past and Present* 51 (1971): 27–62.
Wilcher, Robert. 'Lucy Hutchinson and *Genesis*: Paraphrase, Epic, Romance'. *English: Journal of the English Association* 59.224 (2010): 25–42.
Wiseman, Susan. '"The most considerable of my troubles", Anne Halkett and the Writing of Civil War Conspiracy'. *Women Writing, 1550–1750*. Ed. J. Wallwork and P. Salzman. Bundoora, Australia: Meridian 2001. 25–45.
Wiseman, Susan. *Conspiracy and Virtue: Women, Writing, and Politics in Seventeenth-Century England*. Oxford: Oxford UP, 2006.
Wiseman, Susan. 'No "Publick funerall"? Lucy Hutchinson's Elegy, Epitaph, Monument'. *The Seventeenth Century* 30.2 (2015): 207–28.
Wolffe, John. *God and Greater Britain. Religion and National Life in Britain and Ireland 1843–1945*. London and New York: Routledge, 1994.
Wood, Alfred. *Nottinghamshire in the Civil War* [1937]. Wakefield: S. R. Publishers Limited, 1971.
Woodford, Benjamin. *Perception of a Monarchy without a King: Reactions to Oliver Cromwell's Power*. Montreal: McGill-Queen's UP, 2013.
Woolf, Daniel R. *The Idea of History in Early Stuart England*. Toronto: U of Toronto P, 1990.
Woolf, Daniel R. 'Narrative Historical Writing in Restoration England: A Preliminary Survey'. *The Restoration Mind*. Ed. W. Gerald Marshall. Newark: University of Delaware Press, 1997. 207–51.
Woolf, Daniel R. 'A Feminine Past? Gender, Genre and Historical Knowledge in England, 1500–1800'. *American Historical Review* 102.3 (1997): 645–79.
Woolf, Daniel R. *Reading History in Early Modern England*. Cambridge: Cambridge UP, 2000.
Woolf, Daniel R. 'From Hystories to the Historical: Five Transitions in Thinking about the Past, 1500–1700'. *Huntington Library Quarterly* 69.1–2 (2005): 33–70.
Worden, Blair. 'Providence and Politics in Cromwellian England'. *Past and Present* 109 (1985): 55–99.

Worden, Blair. *Roundhead Reputations. The English Civil Wars and the Passions of Posterity.* London: Penguin, 2001.
Worden, Blair. 'Historians and Poets'. *Huntington Library Quarterly* 68.1–2 (2005): 71–93.
Wordsworth, Christopher, ed. *The Manner of Coronation of King Charles I.* London: Henry Bradshaw Liturgical Text Society, 1892.
Wright, Joanne H. 'Not Just Dutiful Wives and Besotted Ladies: Epistemic Agency in the War Writing of Brilliana Harley and Margaret Cavendish'. *Early Modern Women: An Interdisciplinary Journal* 4 (2009): 1–25.
Wright, Joanne H. 'Questioning Gender, War, and the "Old Lie": The Military Expertise of Margaret Cavendish'. *The History of British Women's Writing.* Vol. 3. Ed. Mihoko Suzuki. Basingstoke: Palgrave Macmillan, 2011. 254–69.
Wunderli, Richard and Gerald Broce, 'The Final Moment before Death in Early Modern England', *Sixteenth Century Journal* 20.2 (1989): 259–75.
Wylie, William Howie. *Old and New Nottingham.* London: Longman, 1853.
Young, Peter and Norman Tuker, eds. *Military Memoirs of the Civil War: Richard Atkyns, John Gwyn.* London: Longman, 1967.
Zaller, Robert. 'The Figure of the Tyrant in English Revolutionary Thought'. *Journal of the History of Ideas* 54.4 (1993): 585–610.
Zangara, Adriana. *Voir l'histoire. Théories anciennes du récit historique IIe siècle avant J.-C.– IIe siècle après J.-C.* Paris: Vrin, 2007.
Zangara, Adriana. 'Voir l'histoire. Théories anciennes du récit historique. Présentation'. *Anabases* 7 (2008). https://doi.org/10.4000/anabases.2540.
Zimmermann, Jens, ed. *Re-Envisioning Christian Humanism: Education and the Restoration of Humanity.* Oxford: Oxford UP, 2017.
Zurcher, Amelia. *Seventeenth-Century English Romance. Allegory, Ethics and Politics.* New York: Palgrave Macmillan, 2007.
Zurcher, Amelia. 'The Political Ideologies of Revolutionary Prose Romance'. *The Oxford Handbook of Literature and the English Revolution.* Ed. Laura Lunger Knoppers. Oxford: Oxford UP, 2012. 551–65.
Zurcher, Andrew. 'Allegory and Epistolarity: Cipher and Faction in Sidney and Spenser'. *Cultures of Correspondence in Early Modern Britain.* Ed. James Daybell and Andrew Gordon. Philadelphia: U of Pennsylvania P, 2016. 210–37.

Index

For the benefit of digital users, indexed terms that span two pages (e.g., 52–53) may, on occasion, appear on only one of those pages.

Act of Indemnity and Oblivion 1–2, 19, 174, 177n.45, 178–9, 184–5, 195–6
Agrippa von Nettesheim, Heinrich Cornelius 86–7
Allen, Joseph Antisell 212–14
ambition, *see* passions
Ames, William 30n.164
Amyot, Jacques 17n.96, 40–4
Anderson, James 212–14
anecdotes 34–5, 46, 208, 245–6
anger, *see* passions
Annesley, Arthur (Earl of Anglesey) 4–6, 68–9, 103–4, 126–7
anti-Catholicism 78–82, 106–7, 150–1, 256–63, 277, 284
anti-Puritanism 20–1, 262, 282–7, 290–1, 294–5
antiquarianism and antiquarians 1–2, 41–2, 46, 85–6, 91–4, 197–8
Apsley, Sir Allen (brother of Lucy Hutchinson) 4–6, 59, 126–7, 178–9, 197–8
Aquinas, Thomas 53–6, 53n.64, 58, 60, 62, 65–8
aristocratic ethos 51–2
Aristotle 50–3, 92, 298
Arminianism 52n.59, 260
artes historicae 32, 39–44, 89–94
atheism and atheists 150–1, 292–3, 295
Augustine 15–16, 67–8, 77n.148, 82–3, 296
autobiography 4–6, 15–16, 37, 171–90, 202, 208–9, 217–18, 223–4
  spiritual autobiography 66, 66n.118, 164–5, 190
autopsy 18–19, 96, 139, 142–3

Babel 17
Bacon, Francis 42n.24, 56n.80, 84–7, 93n.57, 107–10, 121n.25, 146–7, 287–8, 288n.110
  The Advancement of Learning 11–13, 41–2, 93–4, 101–2, 107–8, 205–6
  Essays or Counsels 41–2, 162n.160, 215, 244–5
  History of the Reign of King Henry VII 45, 86n.4, 93n.57, 263–4, 267–8
Bailey, Nathan 12n.72, 99n.86, 166n.3
Ballard, Thomas 205–6, 229–30
Baptism 106–7
Baron, William 105–6
Battles 96, 100, 130–2, 138–9, 145
  Battle of Dunbar (1650) 169
  Battle of Edgehill (1642) 143n.97, 149–50, 188–9, 204–5
  Battle of Marston Moor (1644) 150–1, 271–2
  Battle of Naseby (1645) 175, 233n.117
  Battle of Newbury (1643) 268–71
Baxter, Richard 79n.156, 142–3, 243–4, 256, 297
  Reliquiæ Baxterianæ 11–13, 28n.153, 100, 120, 138, 143n.97, 161n.156, 243–4, 245n.158, 256, 264–5, 300n.12
Bennet, Henry (1st Earl of Arlington) 184–5, 191, 197–8, 200, 232–3
Berkeley, Sir John 105, 126n.45, 278
biography 11–13, 138, 180n.50, 273–4
Biondi, Giovanni Francesco 30n.160
Biron, Sir John (cousin of John Hutchinson) 45–7
Biron, Sir Richard (cousin of John Hutchinson) 46–7, 129, 151–2, 164, 197–8, 227, 240

336 INDEX

Blundeville, Thomas 41–2, 44–7, 89–90, 94n.60
Bodin, Jean 88–92, 109–10, 129n.54, 202
Bolton, Edmund 27n.149, 90–4, 268–71
Booth, Sir George 291–2
Borlase, Edmund 102–4
Boyle, Robert 120–2, 124–5, 129–30, 146–7
Boyle, Roger 207–8, 214
Bradshaw, John 20, 59, 305–6
Brathwaite, Richard 17n.96, 25–6, 40n.8, 41–2, 119, 206n.20
Breton, Nicholas 292–3
Brodrick, Sir Allen 178–9, 197–8
Bruce, Charles 181n.54
Bucer, Martin 63–4, 258–9
Buchanan, George 92, 243
Bulstrode, Richard 96
Burder, Samuel 181n.54
Burnet, Gilbert 2–3, 14–16, 98–100, 112, 202

Caesar 15–16, 29, 87–9, 99–100, 117, 145, 202, 206n.20, 299
Caesaropapism 258–9
Calamy, Edmund 63–4
Calvin 8–10, 29–31, 54–6, 63–6, 259–60
Calvinism and Calvinists 8–10, 29–31, 35–6, 53–6, 65–6, 164–5, 211, 227–8
Camden, William 25–6, 27n.147, 39–40, 85, 90n.32, 91–2, 93n.51, 130–2, 287–8
Cary, Elizabeth 22–3
Castiglione, Baldassare 47–50
causes of the English Civil War 37–8, 108, 163–4, 254–63, 267, 274–5
Caussin, Nicolas 54–6, 58n.85, 60n.90, 61, 66n.119, 68n.124, 77n.148
Cavendish, Margaret (duchess of Newcastle) 7–8, 12n.67, 13–14, 17–18, 24–8, 32–4, 46n.37, 98–9, 107–10, 180–1, 202, 206–7, 264–5
Cavendish, William (duke of Newcastle) 107–8, 111, 129, 136, 150–3, 164, 227, 232–4, 268–71, 287–8
Chadwick, Col. Sir James 155–7, 288–9, 292–5
character-writing, book of characters 284–9, 292–3
charity, *see* virtues
Charles I, King 22, 83–4, 124–5, 174, 203, 211, 256, 259–61, 274–82

execution and trial 1–2, 8–10, 125, 162–3, 192–3, 199–202, 273–4, 280–1, 297–300
King's death warrant 1–2, 57–8, 104, 114, 125, 200–1, 274–5
Charles II, King 4–6, 11–13, 20–1, 102–3, 262, 304
Chaworth, John (2nd Viscount) 129, 148n.115, 150
Chaworth-Musters, Lina 133, 223–4, 223n.80, 240–2, 300–1
Chidley, Katherine 73
Child, Lydia Maria Francis 181n.54
Cholmley, Sir Hugh 100, 102n.100, 271n.63
Cicero 31, 41–2, 52, 86–7
civility 216–17, 280, 288, 292–3
Clarke, Samuel 63–4
Cleveland, John 250n.171, 285–7
Clifford, Anne 25–6
commemoration 6–7, 22, 72–3, 300–1, 305–8
commentaries (historical genre) 15–16, 87, 93–4, 99–100, 117, 202, 206n.20
Committee of Both Kingdoms 59, 137–8, 157, 160, 231n.111
Commonwealth (the regime of the) 58–60, 67–8, 108–9, 229, 244–5, 248, 280, 299–301
Commynes, Philippe de 15–16, 26, 87–9, 94–5, 100, 113, 117, 288
companionship in marriage 119, 123–4, 170–1, 211–12, 301–2
compassion 67–8, 142, 176
Concio, Giacomo 89–90
conscience 1–2, 56–9, 125–6, 161, 177–8, 185, 193–4, 199, 201–2, 216–17, 242–3, 273, 280–1, 300–2
  liberty of conscience 157–9, 185–6
confidant (Lucy Hutchinson's role as a) 36–7, 119–28, 147–8, 170–1, 176, 180–1, 186–90
Cotterell, Charles 206–8
Cotton, Sir Robert 91–2
Cromwell, Oliver 3–4, 20, 22, 56–7, 108–9, 193–4, 200–1, 243–52, 264–74, 280, 299–300, 305–6
Cromwell, Richard 199–200
Crosland, Camila Newton 181n.54

courage, *see* virtues
courts-martial (and martial law) 235–40, 242–3

Dacre (Col. Richard) 111, 153
Daniel, Samuel 25–6
Davila, Enrico Caterino 29, 94, 100
death (Colonel Hutchinson's) 8–10, 21, 62, 69, 77–8, 170–1, 186–8, 301–8
  last dying words 70, 302–5
Denham, Sir John 31
Digby, Sir John 149–51, 164, 204–5
disguise 227–8, 236, 241–2
Dowriche, Anne 22–3
Dugdale, Sir William 85, 102n.99, 256, 297–8
Dunbar, *see* Battles
Duplessis-Mornay, Charlotte (née Charlotte Arbaleste de la Borde) 122n.30, 180–1

ear-witnessing 18–19, 119, 122
Edgehill, *see* Battles
education 22–3, 28–31, 41–2, 44, 47–50, 170–1
ekphrasis 74–8
Eliza 73
Elizabeth I 25–6, 46, 175, 256–60
Elyot, Sir Thomas 47–50
empiricism 85, 93–4, 120, 146–7, 254–5
enargeia 74–6, 93–4, 129–30, 140–1, 253
envy, *see* passions
Erasmus 63–4, 75, 129n.56, 253, 268, 282
Essex, 3rd Earl of (Robert Devereux) 237, 238n.133, 266–72
Eve 174–5, 183–4
Epicureanism 62
Exclusion Crisis 7–8
exemplarity 36, 169–70, 289, 307
experimentalism and experiments 120–2, 124–5, 146–7
experience (first-hand) 14–15, 17–18, 36, 85–7, 138, 146–7, 164–5, 297
eye-witnessing 43–4, 47–8, 88, 94–5, 99, 119–20, 138–47

factions and factionalism 156, 159–64, 248, 271–3, 277–8, 280–1, 284, 294, 300–1
Fairfax, Sir Thomas 28n.153, 105, 109–10, 151, 175, 266–7, 272–4

Fairfax, Lady Anne (née Anne Vere) 183, 250n.171
faith, *see* virtues
family history 45–7, 122n.27, 208
Fanshawe, Lady Ann 26, 28n.150, 166–8, 180–1, 224
Ficino, Marsilio 77n.148, 82n.167
fiction 90, 92, 97–9, 103–6, 112, 194–7, 207–8, 211–14, 223–5
Flower, Benjamin 212n.45
fortifications (Nottingham) 129–30, 136–8, 140–1
fortitude, *see* virtues
Foxe, John 63–4, 302
French wars of religion 22–3, 29, 97n.75, 106n.120
friendship 68–9, 123–4, 126–7, 153, 178, 209, 245–6, 248–9
Fronde (the) 27, 78n.152, 97n.74, 106, 165n.172, 166–8
Fuller, Thomas 17, 63–4, 96n.72, 99, 114

Gell, Sir John 148, 156–7, 235, 246, 288–91
genealogy 41–2, 44–7
godly lives 36, 62–72, 81–2
godly republic 247–8, 295–7
greed, *see* passions
Good Old Cause 20–1, 157–9, 201, 243–4, 248, 251–2, 271–2, 294, 297, 307
Guicciardine, Francesco 88–9, 94–5, 100
Guizot, François 3–4, 13, 162–3
Guizot de Witt, Henriette 180–1

hagiography 40, 63–5, 80–2
Halkett, Lady Anne 26, 166–9, 214n.57, 224
Hall, Edward 287–8
Hall, John 39–40, 94–5, 101
Hall, Joseph 289n.113
Harley, Lady Brilliana 26, 169
Harrington, James 85
Haselrig, Sir Arthur 126–7
Heath, James 102n.99, 108, 256
Henrietta-Maria, Queen 54–6, 122n.31, 174–5, 183, 211, 261
Henry VIII, King 257–9
Herbert, Sir Thomas 105
Herbert, Sir Percy 214
Herodotus 27, 91, 129n.54, 254

heroism 50, 62, 73, 112, 135–6, 140–1, 143, 164, 214, 297, 302, 307–8
women's heroism 168–70, 224
Heylin, Peter 97–8, 106–7
Hobbes, Thomas 29, 33, 107–8, 145–6, 245n.160, 254, 256
Holles, Sir Denzil 28n.153, 101–2, 105, 108n.125, 276
hope, see virtues
hospitality 45, 51–2
Hotham, John (1st Baronet) 234–5
Hotham, John (the younger) 234–5, 246
Howell, James 20
humanism 18–19, 29, 34–6, 43–4, 47–50, 53, 63–4, 79, 83, 85–95, 99, 109–10, 243, 253–5, 268–71, 307
Hutchinson, Charles (John Hutchinson's half-brother) 1–2, 115n.149, 182n.60
Hutchinson, Charles (the son of Julius Hutchinson, John Hutchinson's nephew) 205–6
Hutchinson, George 122, 151, 153, 155, 292–3, 303
Hutchinson, John
  A Narrative of the Imprisonment 7n.36, 111n.138, 198n.133
Hutchinson, Julius (John Hutchinson's nephew) 115n.149, 183–4, 205–6
Hutchinson, Julius (the editor) 1–3, 8–10, 13–14, 28, 73n.139, 78–80, 115, 156, 191, 205, 212–14, 219, 258, 266
Hutchinson, Lucy, Works (except Memoirs and Notebook)
  'Elegies' 10–11, 76, 79–82, 112, 182–5, 187–8, 305, 307–8
  Literary Commonplace Book 6–7, 31, 43, 49n.47, 54–6, 61, 66n.119, 68n.124, 82n.166, 285n.97
  'Lucretius' 6–7, 29, 53n.64, 62, 169–72
  On the Principles of the Christian Religion 28–31, 54–6, 170n.12
  Order and Disorder 7–8, 112–13, 183–5
  Religious Commonplace Book 29–31, 54–6, 65–6, 69, 265n.49
hybridity (generic) 34–5, 206–7, 265
hypocrites and hypocrisy 153, 246–52, 288–91, 294–5

Ingoldsby, Col. Sir Richard 192–3, 200–1
idolatry 36, 40, 72, 78–84
impartiality 17, 85, 93–4, 97, 108–9, 121–2, 127–8, 291
Independents and Independency 29–31, 156–64, 271–2, 277–80
intelligence 148–54, 231–2, 235–6
Ireton, Henry 20, 124–5, 127, 155, 201, 278, 305–6
Irish Confederate Wars 102–4
Irish Rebellion 102–4, 276

James I, King 259–60, 274–5, 282–3, 284n.96
James, Duke of York (later James II) 126–7
jealousy, see passions
Jeffrey, Francis 156, 191n.95, 212–14
Jesuits 47, 54–6, 61, 106, 261
justice, *virtues* 52, 242–3

Kingston (Countess of), see Pierrepont, Gertrude
Kingston (Earl of), see Pierrepont, Henry
Knight, Charles 133

La Calprenède (Gautier de Costes, sieur de La Calprenède) 206–7
Lambert, Maj.-Gen. John 109, 195, 243–4, 249, 299
Lambert, Lady Frances 175
Laud, William (Archbishop of Canterbury) 261
Le Moyne, Pierre 15–16, 106, 254, 255n.12
Levellers 176n.41, 184–5, 243–4, 285–6
Liberty, see conscience
Lipsius, Justus 89–90
Lives, see godly lives
Livy 29, 288
love, see virtues
Lucan 56
Lucas, Sir Charles 140–1, 154
Lucian 88, 90–1, 119, 129n.54, 286n.103
Lucretius 6–7, 29, 53n.64, 62, 169–72, 173n.29
Ludlow, Edmund 1–4, 7–8, 13–14, 28n.153, 32, 104–6, 126n.45, 147, 194–6, 243–4, 256, 258–9, 281n.88, 297, 299–300
Luther, Martin 76

Macaulay, Catharine 2-3, 16, 22-5, 197-8
Machiavelli, Niccolò 42n.24, 266
Machiavellianism 178, 243-4, 249-50, 277-8, 295
magnanimity, *see* courage
Marprelate, Martin 285-6
martial law, *see* courts-martial
Mary Stuart, Queen of Scots 175, 258-60, 262
memorialization 308
'man of blood' (the) 274-5, 281
manuscript circulation 1-8
Marprelate controversy 285-6
Marston Moor, *see* Battles
martial law, *see* courts-martial
martyrdom (John Hutchinson's martyrdom) 8-10, 50, 62, 64, 69, 179, 182, 186-7, 190, 201-3, 220-1, 242-3, 255, 297, 301-5, 307-8
martyrs (Protestant) 16, 63-4, 302-4
May, Thomas 4-8, 13-14, 17-18, 20, 29, 31-2, 95-8, 101, 108-9, 121-2, 147-8, 256-60, 264-5, 268-75
melancholy 29-31, 187-8, 209, 283-4
memory of the Civil Wars 19-22, 147, 171-2, 308
mercy 59, 67-8, 187, 226-7, 238-9, 242-3, 261, 303-4
millenarianism 70, 295-7
Milton, John 106-7, 123n35, 176, 211, 285-6, 299-302
Monck, George, 1st Duke of Albemarle 109
Monmouth, Geoffrey 91-2
Montaigne, Michel de 39, 78, 87-9, 100-1, 107-10, 145, 202
More, Sir Thomas 45, 85-6, 91-2, 243
Mortimer, Roger 130-2, 136
Moseley, Humphrey 66
Moses 70, 206-7, 245-6, 266
Motteville, Françoise de 122-3, 175n.38, 180-1

Naseby, *see* Battles
Neoplatonism 49, 77, 82, 123n.33, 187-8
Nero 261, 288
Newark (Lord), *see* Pierrepont, Henry
newsbooks (and pamphlets) 7-8, 31-2, 97-8, 110-11, 118-19, 164, 230, 243-4, 285-6, 290
Newbury, *see* Battles

Noble, Mark 1-3, 197-8
Nonconformists 29-31, 260, 264-5, 299-302, 305
Northern Plot 186-7, 301-2, 307-8
nurse (Lucy Hutchinson as a) 18-19, 66n.119, 166-9

Owthorpe 29-32, 29n.157, 54-6, 62, 66, 73n.139, 107-8, 118-19, 134-5, 169-70, 172-3, 182n.60, 265-6, 301-3, 305, 307-8

Palmer, Capt. Laurence 66-7, 150, 156-7, 204, 237n.130
pamphlets, *see* newsbooks
passions 22-4, 56, 60-2, 74, 88-9, 112, 140-3, 162-3, 247, 289, 295, 299-301
  ambition 22, 68-9, 113, 157-9, 162, 193-4, 244-5, 247-51, 283-4, 288-91, 300-1
  anger 49, 60-1, 76, 82, 108-9, 140-1, 151, 183, 279, 285-6
  dissimulation 244-5, 248-9, 294
  envy (jealousy) 59, 136-8, 156, 159-62, 273, 288-91, 300-1
  greed 59, 139-40, 156, 162, 300-1
  hate 58, 66-7, 116, 136-7, 157-61, 277, 289, 293-4
  revenge 60-1, 68, 114, 173, 189-90, 259-60, 290, 297-8
  shame 140-1, 173, 183, 291
paedobaptism 56-7
partisanship 17-18, 95-6, 102, 127-8, 141
patience 62, 64n.109, 69, 187, 301-4
patriotism 10, 82, 192-3, 281
Patrizzi, Francesco 44, 89-90
Payne, Robert 107-8
Perkins, William 30n.164, 63-4
persecution 37-8, 51-2, 112, 157-61, 255, 261-2, 273, 282-3, 285, 287, 291-2, 294-5, 301-5
petitions 118n.9, 157, 159-60, 176n.41, 177n.43, 184-5, 192, 198, 276
Peyton, Edward 256, 297-8
Philips, Katherine 33-4, 176n.41
Pierrepont, Francis (Col. Pierrepont) 137-8, 149-50, 154-5, 159-60, 199, 230-3

Pierrepont, Gertrude (Countess of Kingston) 232
Pierrepont, Henry (Lord Newark) 218–20
Pierrepont, Robert (Earl of Kingston) 230–1, 233–5
Plumtre, Huntingdon 203–4, 292–4
Plutarch 15–16, 25–6, 29–31, 36, 40–4, 46–7, 52, 63–4, 76, 83–4, 145, 287–8
Polybius 18–19, 29, 88, 90–1, 119, 129n.54
Poulton, Capt. Thomas 107, 153, 273
Popish Plot
    Popish Plot (under Charles I) 261
    Popish Plot (1678) 102–3
Presbyterians and Presbyterianism 66–7, 115, 156–61, 164, 175, 249–50, 272n.69, 277–82, 284, 287, 291, 294
Pride, Colonel Thomas 20, 159, 280–1, 305–6
Prideaux, Matthias 94–5
prisoners 66–7, 142, 144–5, 184–5, 227–8, 233–4, 236–8, 240–1
    Charles I as a prisoner 124–5, 272–3, 276–8
    John Hutchinson as a prisoner 7–8, 27, 70, 78, 112, 122, 130–2, 170–1, 176, 179, 183–4, 200, 295, 301–2, 304
Protectorate (the) 49–50, 56–7, 195–200, 229, 249–52, 280, 300–1
Providence 37–8, 56–7, 112, 143–4, 181–3, 211–12, 226–7, 254–5, 262, 265–71, 293–6
prudence, *see* virtues
Prynne, William 211n.41
Puttenham, George 43, 145

Quintilian 74–5, 253

Raleigh, Sir Walter 114
regicides 1–2, 7–8, 20, 114, 125–6, 173–4, 192–6, 198, 300–2, 305–6
republicanism 1–2, 6–10, 13–14, 21–2, 51–2, 109, 151–2, 190, 193–8, 200–2, 242–4, 248–50, 281–2, 288, 305–8
Restoration settlement (1662) 48–9, 305, 308
Retz (Cardinal, Jean-François Paul de Gondi) 14–16, 119n.14
revenge, *see* passions
Reyner, Edward 123–4

Rogers, Daniel 185–6
romance 25–6, 37–8, 98–9, 112–13, 130–4, 195–7, 206–29
Rump Parliament 56–7, 109, 125–6, 172–3, 195, 249–50, 299, 301–2
Rupert, Prince 154, 222–3, 232–3, 266–7, 271–2, 276
Rushworth, John 2–4, 97, 102n.99, 108, 256, 297–8
Russell, William 181n.54, 212–14

Sallust 25–6, 29, 88–9
Sanderson, Robert 54–6
Sarpi, Paolo 94n.60
satire 34–5, 250–1, 282–3, 285–91, 294–5
scepticism 87, 88n.21, 145n.101
scholasticism (school divinity) 29–31, 53–6
Scudéry, Madeleine 206–7
secretary (Lucy Hutchinson as the Colonel's secretary) 122–3, 127–8
secret history 245–6
Selden, John 85
Seneca 29–31, 52
Shakespeare, William
    Hamlet 189–90
    Richard II 70
    Richard III 84, 130–2, 290
shame, *see* passions
side-changing 229–35
Sidney, Algernon 194–5, 299–300
Sidney, Sir Philip 92, 208–9, 214
Slater, Matthew 227–8, 236, 238
Sleidan, Johannes 87–9, 100
sources (historical) 25–6, 85, 106, 118–22, 124–7, 241–2, 273
spies 148, 214, 235–43, 290
Sprigge, Joshua 109–10
Staël, Germaine de 15–16, 212–14
stasis 161–2, 217–18, 300–1
Stendhal 210
stories and story-telling 45, 130–2, 147, 149–50, 208, 214, 232–3, 282
Sutcliffe, Matthew 236n.126, 239–40, 242–3
Sylvester, Matthew 11–13, 120, 264–5

Tacitus 29, 56–7, 229, 287–8
temperance, *see* virtues

Thornhagh, Sir Francis 56-7, 154-7, 204, 233-4, 247-8
Thuanus (Jacques Auguste de Thou) 100
Thucydides 18-19, 27, 29-33, 88-9, 95, 99, 120, 145, 229, 254
Toland, John 101-2, 105, 107
Touchet, James (Lord Audley, Earl of Castlehaven) 102-4, 138
torture 239-43, 303-4
tragedy 22, 27-8, 46-7, 141-4, 216-18, 254-7, 266-7, 274-7, 281-2, 293-4, 297-301
Trismegistus, Hermes 77n.148, 82n.167
truth (historical) 36, 83, 88-92, 94-107, 190-202, 207-8
turncoats, *see* side-changing
Turner, Sir James 138
tyrants, tyranny and tyrannicide 22, 37-8, 130-2, 170-1, 245-6, 249-51, 257-8, 262, 266, 271-2, 274-82, 301-2, 304-6

uxoriousness 171-2, 174-5, 261

Vane, Sir Henry 159-60, 194-5, 199
veracity 70, 146-7, 195-7, 201-2
Vergil, Polydore 88-9, 92n.47, 287-8
verisimilitude 124-5, 145
Vicars, John 234, 308 241-2
Virgil 120, 215
virtual witnessing 124-5, 127-8, 247, 303, 305
virtues (theological)
  faith 29-31, 62, 64-7, 69-70, 78-9, 81-4, 130-2, 152-3, 187, 216-17, 301-2
  love (charity) 65-9, 76, 80, 242-3
  hope 65, 69-70, 170-1, 305, 308
virtues (cardinal)
  prudence (and wisdom) 52-3, 56-8, 61, 76, 91, 170-2, 211-14, 216
  justice 52-3, 58-60, 83-4, 159-60, 242-3
  temperance 52-3, 60-2, 82, 304n.23
  fortitude (and courage, magnanimity) 62, 75-6, 101, 112, 140-1, 143-4, 247, 282-3, 300-2, 304
Vives, Juan Luis 87, 92
Vossius, Gerrard 89-90

Walker, Clement 108, 156n.143
Walker, Robert 71, 74, 76, 167
Waller, Edmund 6-7, 251-2
Waller, Sir William 268-71
Warburton, Eliot 212-14
Warner, Walter 107-8
Warwick, Sir Philip 105
Wheare, Degory 33n.176, 39n.1, 89-90, 94n.64
White, Capt. Charles 156-7, 288-91, 291n.122
Whitelocke, Sir Bulstrode 102n.99, 147, 153, 244n.153
William III, King 105
Wilmot, Anne (Countess of Rochester) 4-6, 184n.70
wisdom, *see* virtues
Wycliffe, John 63-4